THE CHIEF OF STAFF

Recent Titles in
Contributions in Military Studies

THE CHIEF OF STAFF

The Military Career of General Walter Bedell Smith

D.K.R. CROSSWELL

Contributions in Military Studies, Number 110

GREENWOOD PRESS
New York • Westport, Connecticut • London

Library of Congress Cataloging-in-Publication Data

Crosswell, D.K.R. (Daniel K. R.)
   The chief of staff : the military career of General Walter Bedell
Smith / D.K.R. Crosswell.
      p.   cm.—(Contributions in military studies, ISSN 0883-6884
   ; no. 110)
   Includes bibliographical references and index.
   ISBN 0-313-27480-0 (alk. paper)
   1. Smith, Walter Bedell, 1895-1961. 2. Generals—United States—
Biography. 3. United States. Army—Biography. 4. United States—
History, Military—20th century. 5. World War, 1939-1945—
Campaigns.   I. Title.   II. Series.
E745.S57C76   1991
335'.0082—dc20   90-45328

British Library Cataloguing in Publication Data is available.

Library of Congress Catalog Card Number: 90-45328
ISBN: 0-313-27480-0
ISSN: 0883-6884

First published in 1991

Greenwood Press, 88 Post Road West, Westport, CT 06881
An imprint of Greenwood Publishing Group, Inc.

Printed in the United States of America

The paper used in this book complies with the
Permanent Paper Standard issued by the National
Information Standards Organization (Z39.48-1984).

10 9 8 7 6 5 4 3 2 1

Copyright Acknowledgments

The author and publisher are grateful to Viscount Montgomery of Alamein
CBE and the Trustees of the Imperial War Museum for granting permission to
quote from the Montgomery Collections held in the Museum.

Every reasonable effort has been made to trace the owners of copyright
materials in this book, but in some instances this has proven impossible. The
author and publisher will be glad to receive information leading to more
complete acknowledgments in subsequent printings of the book and in the
meantime extend their apologies for any omissions.

. . . to Karen

Contents

Maps and Charts

Preface

This study of the military career of General Walter Bedell Smith had its genesis in 1982 when the late Merle Miller employed me as a researcher for his last book, *Ike: As They Knew Him*. Living in Manhattan, Kansas, I had ready access to the rich holdings of the Dwight D. Eisenhower Presidential Library in Abilene. One of Miller's motives for writing the book centered on his desire to find some substance for rumors Eisenhower had an affair with his Irish driver, Kay Summersby. Former president Harry S Truman told Miller he participated in a cover-up of the Eisenhower-Summersby romance. A product of an old man's active imagination and too much bourbon, this revelation in Miller's book, *Plain Speaking: An Oral History of Harry S Truman*, produced a sensation. The popularity and financial success of the book did not blot out the sting of charges challenging Miller's ethics. Determined his book on Eisenhower would be meticulously documented, Miller engaged the services of the late Jim Peterson, Dr. John Reese, now of the United States Air Force Academy, and myself. I never found any evidence of Eisenhower's infidelity but did discover Bedell Smith.

Surprised no book on Smith existed, I decided to take on the challenge. Supported by Miller's generosity and encouragement, the research went forward. Being in Kansas was an advantage. In addition to the treasure chest of primary materials in the Eisenhower Library—the center of gravity for this project—the underutilized resources of the Combat Studies Library, Command and General Staff College lay available in Leavenworth.

My two years at James Madison University provided opportunities for expanding the research. Located in Harrisonburg, Virginia, the university is equidistant from the federal research facilities in Washington, the United States Army Military History Institute holdings in Carlisle Barracks, Pennsylvania, and the George C. Marshall Library in Lexington, Virginia. Time has robbed us of all but a few of the World War II generation of officers. While in Virginia I was fortunate to have interviewed two men who knew and served under Bedell Smith: Lieutenant General Russell Vittrup of Alexandria and Colonel Carter Burgess of Roanoke. The insights they graciously provided were important in rounding out an otherwise one-dimensional view of Smith.

I recently returned from Europe, where I reexamined my British sources. A number of years ago, Dr. William Feyerharm, a senior administrator at Kansas State University, channeled a grant in my direction to fund research in Great Britain. At long last I took the opportunity to journey to London. I trust the money was well spent.

Writing a history of Bedell Smith proved a challenging and frustrating endeavor. It could not have been completed without the aid and support of a great many people. Special thanks go out to professors Robin Higham and Donald J. Mrozek of Kansas State University and Dr. Jacob Kipp of the Soviet Army Studies Office, Fort Leavenworth, Kansas, whose always-perceptive criticisms of the original text proved invaluable. The following also read and commented on the manuscript at various stages: professors David Kromm and Loren Alexander, Kansas State University; Professor Albert Castel, Western Michigan University; and Matt M. Matthews, Matthew Raney, and Richard Hanes, officers in the United States Army. After I gave up on finding any of Smith's relatives, one contacted me. Unfortunately, Stephen Bedell Smith, a nephew, had suffered a tragic loss only days before—a house fire destroyed the remaining personal effects of the general. Nevertheless, he offered valuable information on his uncle's early life in Indianapolis.

On a personal level, I received a large measure of moral support during this long process. My parents—Earl Edward and Kathleen Crosswell—and my siblings and their spouses—sister Suzanne and her husband Fred Grigoroff and brother Frank and his wife Marilyn Crosswell—rendered much needed aid and comfort. Dr. Tom Groshens and his wife Dorolyn Childs of Manhattan and Dr. Stan McCool and Loretta Lauinger of Lawrence, Kansas, offered their hospitality and good cheer. A debt of gratitude is extended to professors Michael Galgano and David Owusu-Ansah of James Madison University.

The chief bulwark came from my long-suffering wife, Karen Kaylor. She has sacrificed a great deal during this long ordeal. Karen and Marilyn proofread the final manuscript, advancing suggestions and improving the readability of the work, while Frank lent his expertise on the personal computer. Dr. Paul Kratoska of the National University of Singapore also provided critical computer assistance. Their contributions materially enhanced the final product; any mistakes that remain are solely mine. Finally I would like to express my thanks to the people at Greenwood—Mildred Vasan, Maureen Melino, Mark Kane, and Martin McHugh—for their good offices and patience.

Introduction

The military life of Walter Bedell Smith began in 1911 when he joined the Indiana National Guard as a sixteen-year old private and ended thirty-nine years later with his retirement as a four-star general in the U.S. Army. Smith's career pattern typified the "long generation" of officers who rose to command the armies and staff the higher headquarters in the Second World War: as a member of the interwar officer corps, he held a series of training and staff positions that climaxed in his attendance at the Leavenworth Command and General Staff Schools and the Army War College; a Marshall-man, he emerged as a central figure in the innercircle of General George C. Marshall's Washington establishment, eventually heading the secretariats of the War Department General Staff, the Joint Chiefs of Staff, and the Combined Chiefs of Staff; reluctantly sacrificed by Marshall, he went on to serve as General Dwight D. Eisenhower's chief of staff in the Mediterranean and European theaters of war. Smith's "road to the top" provides a valuable vehicle for assessing the fundamental changes in the professional outlooks and institutional structures that attended the emergence of the modern military in the United States.

Military historians point to the differences between the martial and managerial styles of leadership. The traditional martial leader is viewed as a man of action, not of reflection; of common sense, not of erudition. He values personal honor and glory. The military manager, on the other hand, reflects the corporate values and bureaucratic mind of modern military organizations.

Paradoxically, U.S. military heroes—those who traditionally have received the highest honors—are cast in the double mold of citizen-soldier and martial warrior. Historically, the hero has been the embodiment of republican civil virtue, a gifted individual who believes in himself, the righteousness of his cause, and in his own intuition and native genius. This citizen-soldier ethos fundamentally challenges the very institutional and attitudinal foundations of modern military professionalism. The military manager's mentality represents the very antithesis of an entire constellation of American values. The general staff officer, the highest expression of the professional soldier ethic, is a type of officer furthest removed from the classical citizen-soldier tradition and, therefore, the least venerated.[1]

Every schoolboy knows the names of the great field commanders in U.S. history, but the nation affords little recognition to its senior staff officers. The case of Marshall best illustrates this point. In 1943, President Roosevelt explained to Eisenhower why Marshall should receive the big command for the cross-channel invasion of Europe: "Ike, you and I know who was Chief of Staff during the last years of the Civil War...but practically no one else knows. I hate to think that fifty years from now practically nobody will know who George Marshall was."[2] Marshall remained in Washington as army chief of staff, and all the honors for leading the western Allies to victory in Europe, including two terms in the White House, fell to his subordinate, Eisenhower. Just as Roosevelt had predicted, half a century after the end of the Second World War, Marshall's name is all but forgotten in the popular American mind.[3]

Reflecting popular interests, military historians have largely ignored the roles played by the leading staff officers of World War II, instead concentrating upon the more charismatic martial heroes. Smith is perhaps the best example of the "military manager" to emerge from the Second World War, yet his part has been relegated to relative obscurity. He lacked the fire of George Patton or the citizen-soldier appeal of Omar Bradley, but his contributions within the sphere of the Allied headquarters proved no less fundamental to eventual battlefield success. Staff work is indeed less glamorous than winning battles, but if the chief of staff falters in his tasks the Bradleys and Pattons could not win their battlefield laurels. This work represents the first full-length study of Bedell Smith, who emerges in these pages as a central figure in the history of U.S. participation in Europe in the Second World War.

Within two years of the war's completion, a number of inflammatory books appeared. Some were written by senior Allied officers; others were based, in whole or part, on their wartime papers. Heading the list were: Omar Bradley, *Soldier's Story*, George Patton, *War as I Knew It*, Alan Moorehead, *Montgomery*, and Harry Butcher, *My Three Years with Eisenhower*. Angered by the damage these "so-called histories" inflicted upon his reputation and the legacy of the Allied headquarters he commanded, Eisenhower enlisted the aid of his wartime chief of staff. He thought Smith should take up the gauntlet and write a history of the war in Europe for the period 1942-1945. A book by the plain-speaking Smith would set the record straight and prove "beneficial to a future historian."[4]

Others shared Eisenhower's opinion. The noted military historian, Edward Meade Earle, offered Smith a fellowship to the prestigious Advanced School at Princeton University to facilitate the writing of a history. Smith declined. Instead, he thought Eisenhower should undertake the challenge in his own book, which appeared in 1948 under the title, *Crusade in Europe*.

Smith correctly speculated that Eisenhower entertained no intention of telling "the simple unvarnished truth" about his war experiences. Bedell recommended Eisenhower not "gloss over too much" or permit himself "to do what you have done so often in the past...expose yourself to criticism by assuming responsibility for the controversial matters which come through the personal feelings, weaknesses, and idiosyncrasies of your major subordinates." "State frankly and fully," he advised, "your own estimate of the tools with which you were working. By that I mean your commanders like Patton, Montgomery, and Bradley." He exhorted his old boss not to "pull a single punch." Eisenhower owed it to himself, his associates, and history, Smith bluntly informed him, to write a critical assessment of the higher direction of the war in Europe.[5]

This exchange of letters reveals a great deal about how the Eisenhower-Smith relationship functioned. Eisenhower intended to write a sanitized account, designed to calm the waters of personal and nationalistic discord. *Crusade in Europe* perfectly reflected Eisenhower's personality and technique of leadership. Part sedative and part self-promotion, the book was meant to play the same role in peace the supreme commander performed in war—peacemaker and champion of Anglo-American collaboration. Just as he had done in the Mediterranean and Europe, Eisenhower expected Smith to do the dirty work: to write an analysis of the divisive issues and antagonistic personalities that animated the Allied headquarters. Eisenhower's whitewashing account would spread good feelings while Smith's book could only engender criticism and controversy.

Still harboring ambitions in the Army, Smith balanced the values of historical truths against the personal costs of the endeavor. Any book would provoke the enmity of scores of highly placed and powerful officers. Smith declined to undertake the mission. After he left the military, Smith finally authored a book, *Eisenhower's Six Great Decisions: Europe 1944-1945*. Extolling the virtues of Eisenhower as decisive commander, this thin volume, disappointing from a critical standpoint, produced little comment when it appeared in 1956. Despite feeling betrayed and resentful his wartime service had not translated into postwar promotions—he wanted a fifth star and the army chief of staff's chair—Bedell Smith never indulged in any form of public self-promotion. Nor did he lighten the task of future historians.

Writing a history of Smith's military career presents many problems. On several levels Smith represents a biographer's nightmare. No personal papers exist for the period before 1942, not even his army personnel (201) file. Of necessity, reliance has been placed upon memoirs and interviews of his contemporaries, secondary sources, and articles that appeared in various popular and service publications. Smith's personality is not the stuff of exciting biography. Neither colorful nor terribly interesting, Smith often remains a rather shadowy figure. He emerges as a man of conservative instincts who viewed his military responsibilities in narrow and unimaginative terms. Petulant, ascetic, strong tempered and widely disliked, Smith offers the perfect example of the authoritarian personality type.

His enigmatic personality simultaneously provides both the key and obstacle to understanding him. The hallmark of Smith's personality rested in his absolute loyalty to his two masters, Marshall and Eisenhower. Although his name is associated with Eisenhower, Smith was fanatically devoted to the army chief of staff. The senior U.S. officers were all Marshall-men; but in Smith's case, the linkage took on a psychological dimension. Not only did Smith idolize Marshall—in this he was not alone—he sought to assume the personality of his hero. "I wish that I could be like you," he confided to Marshall in a unique display of emotion, "I never can, of course...but I have tried very hard to be, and will continue to do so as long as I live."[6] A psycho-historian might well offer some perceptive hypotheses here—it is beyond the author's competence to do so—but suffice it to say Smith's fealty to Marshall transcends the normal bond of allegiance felt by a subordinate for a superior officer.

Another salient aspect of Smith's makeup was his secretiveness and hypersensitivity to criticism, bred by his obsession to please his superiors, and a marked tendency toward self-abnegation. The primary building blocks for instilling life into a historical figure—personal letters—are not available. Smith took pains to deprive historians of insights into the personal aspects of his life. He withdrew his private letters from his papers—an act that itself is suggestive. In his official correspondence, of which there is no shortage, Smith wrote to inform, but kept his feelings out of what he wrote. In his book, *Eisenhower's Six Great Decisions: Europe 1944-1945*, as the title indicates, Smith carried his reticence to the point of self-effacement. Except for fragmentary evidence, such as that provided in the letter to Marshall cited above, the biographer is left to construct a picture of Smith from his formal correspondence and the views of his contemporaries.

In the final analysis, possession of his personal letters is not as vital as it may first appear. Smith's personality tended to merge into his institutional surroundings. He took on the personality of Marshall and intentionally acted both as the chief of staff's surrogate and Eisenhower's alterego. This, combined with his enormous capacity for work, left little time or scope for the development of a private life. A product of an institution, the U.S. Army, and his relationship with Marshall, Smith dominated any headquarters he directed. In many respects Smith became the quintessential institutional man. He resisted external intrusions into his carefully constructed domain, be it from outside agencies into his headquarters or historians into his private affairs. Although he endeavored to fabricate an impenetrable mask to cover himself from the prying eye of the historian, he is best understood in relation to his institutional environment.

There are three essential objectives for this study: to examine critically the professionalization process within the officer corps in the interwar years, to analyze the evolution of the U.S. and Allied command and staff structures in the Second World War, and to survey the distillation and execution of Allied strategy in the Mediterranean and European theaters of war.

When one discusses the emergence of the modern military in the United States, one speaks of the period 1917-1945. The senior officers in World War II were not the products of some proximate "golden age" of American military professionalism as often portrayed, but rather are reflections of a long and evolutionary process. This study assumes the significant influences that informed the nature of U.S. leadership in Europe to be the outgrowth of a unique social institution, the U.S. Army of the interwar period. By studying Smith's socialization into the officer corps, those habits of mind, strategic predispositions, and values that sustained the U.S. conduct of war come into clearer focus. By explaining the intricacies of Smith's actions in the formulation and execution of strategy and in the creation of the command apparatus, a different perspective emerges.

Bedell Smith's contributions to Allied victory in Europe are inexorably bound up with those of Eisenhower. Smith, as chief of staff, was indispensable to Eisenhower as commander. Opposites in temperament, the two perfectly complemented one another in their respective roles. Eisenhower purposefully delegated authority to Smith, in part to disguise his own use of power, not to mention his own self-promotion. As is any good chief of staff, Smith was more than he appeared. Without Smith, Eisenhower would not have been free to assume an active role as supreme commander or act as defender of inter-Allied cooperation. On the other hand, without Eisenhower's unconditional support, Smith could not have exerted as much influence as he did in defining the size, organization, character, and composition of the Allied staffs. Moreover, the inertia within the headquarters enabled Smith to wield significant decision-making powers. Because of loyalty to Marshall and Eisenhower, Smith labored largely unnoticed as the headquarter's "general manager," sacrificing opportunities for high field command and incurring health problems in the process. It is impossible to comprehend fully the nature of the Allied command structures without examining the role of Bedell Smith just as it is difficult to gauge the quality and character of Eisenhower's leadership without an evaluation of the pivotal part played by his chief of staff.

Not only did Smith shape the large, vertically integrated Allied general staff structure that continues to serve as the model for NATO, he also set a high standard for future U.S. chiefs of staff. While Eisenhower may have stretched the point when he described Smith as the "best chief of staff ever," it is no exaggeration to conclude that Bedell Smith has no equal in U.S. military experience. This work is written in the belief that an account of Smith's career will prove of value in itself.

Part I

Bedell Smith and Officership in the United States Army, 1917–1939

"Born to Be a Soldier," 1895–1917

Most boys growing up in the American Midwest at the turn of the century dreamt of becoming big-league ballplayers or engineers on the railroad or something of the sort. Despite being in the age of unabashed chauvinism, most Americans did not trouble themselves with thoughts of things military. In this period one could easily live a lifetime never having laid eyes upon a soldier of the regular army. Although every U.S. city and town had its Civil War monuments, the memory of that great struggle began to fade as the century drew to a close. The explosion of martial enthusiasm that accompanied the "splendid little war" with Spain soon evaporated. Walter Bedell Smith, born and raised in this *belle époque*, was not like other boys. He wanted nothing else in life but to become a soldier.

GROWING UP IN INDIANAPOLIS

Smith was born into a middle class family on the verdant north side of Indianapolis on October 5, 1895. His father's family traced their American ancestry to Samuel Stanhope Smith, a resident of New Jersey during the American war for independence. A propertied family, the eighteenth century Smiths numbered Major General Thomas Mufflin, aide-de-camp to George Washington, signer of the Constitution, and governor of Pennsylvania, among their kinsmen. The Indiana branch of the family was not particularly noteworthy. Walter's father, William Long Smith, earned a modest but comfortable income as a silk buyer for the Pettis Dry Goods Company of Indianapolis. Smith's maternal grandparents were recent immigrants who came to Indianapolis by way of Cincinnati from the German Rhineland. In one of his rare reflections on his boyhood, Smith described his family as "normal, substantial—middle class."[1]

He was a sickly infant; the family feared for Smith's life. His health created much anxiety for his mother, Ida Francis, who carried him about, bundled in a thick blanket, on a pillow. Under the watchful ministrations of his protective mother he soon developed into a vigorous boy. From childhood called Bedell—his mother's maiden name—his stout build, the product of a heavy German diet, soon prompted the nickname "Boodle."

An uncle, Paul Bedell, remembered him as being quite a scrapper as a tyke. In summer 1902, Bedell spent a couple weeks with his uncle, and, as new kid on the block, immediately faced the challenge of the neighborhood bully, three years his senior. Having received the first blow, Bedell waded into his assailant with both fists flailing, and soon his hector beat a retreat into his own yard, there to remain for the duration of Smith's stay.[2] Boys in this period matched their pugilistic skills, one against the other, in ritualized combat to secure membership within their peer group. For young Bedell Smith, the price he paid for a leadership role was a frequent nick or scrape.

Other than the chores he performed around the house, Bedell spent his childhood in all manner of outdoor activities. In the summer he and his cohorts went fishing, played sandlot baseball, rollerskated, and one year, constructed a bicycle racetrack in a nearby vacant field; in winter, they played shinny, a variant of ice hockey.[3] Although athletic, as he grew older Bedell never demonstrated any desire to participate in organized sports, primarily because his interests developed in different directions.

As he remarked later in life, "I always wanted to be an army officer. I never thought of anything else."[4] Paul Bedell confirmed this view. "[Bedell] had been a soldier from the time he was big enough to walk," he remembered.[5] A member of the Smith clan had fought in every U.S. war since the Revolution. This must have been a source of pride to Bedell, especially being a descendant of General Mufflin. On the other hand there was his maternal grandfather, a combat veteran of the Franco-Prussian War. A spiked helmet and a Prussian needle-gun gave material substance to his grandfather's tales of Prussian cavalry riding down the French.[6] As further proof of his childhood preoccupation with military things, young Smith's favorite playthings were his toy soldiers—wax, metal, and wooden—which he diligently deployed all throughout the house.[7] Wherever the family went, Bedell brought along a box of his most prized pieces and quietly sat by himself conducting a make-believe battle.[8]

His love for the military was not confined to collecting miniatures. In his flower-filled backyard, Smith's father placed a ramshackle streetcar bought from the city. Bedell quickly transformed it into the headquarters of the Ashland Avenue Irregulars. Something of a martinet even then, "Boodle" Smith commanded the neighborhood "troops" who, under the watchful gaze of their captain, drilled to Potsdam perfection. When he faced a periodic mutiny and the neighborhood boys refused to muster, Bedell dragooned his younger brother George into performing the drill with broomsticks substituting for muskets and riding horses for cavalry. A boyhood friend, Humphrey Harrington, remembered Smith would occasionally surrender the commander's baton, but never for very long. Harrington also recalled Bedell would march everywhere he went, "sometimes with a broomstick."[9] "Boodle," no longer a fitting nickname, soon gave way to a more fitting sobriquet, "Brigadier."

Other than fishing, military matters preoccupied his young mind.[10] When it came to his attention a regular army officer was home on leave in the neighborhood, determined to see this wonder with his own eyes, Bedell stationed himself on his newfound hero's doorstep. In fact, Smith spent much of the time the young lieutenant was on leave on the porch, worshipping his *beau idéal*. Family members felt this episode gave Smith the inspiration to join the army at his first opportunity.[11] Interestingly, his hero turned out to be Hugh Drum, a future lieutenant general whose career very much paralleled Smith's.

Although blessed with a keen mind, Smith never exhibited much interest in formal studies. His grade school teacher recalled Bedell was a very intelligent child. He showed superior reading skills, the product of nightly reading sessions with his mother. However, his performance in class did not merit his promotion to the Catholic high school.[12] After attending a parochial school, Smith went on to Emmerich Manual Training High School where he received a vocational education.

At Emmerich he trained as a machinist. Indianapolis, emerging as a major transportation hub and manufacturing center, offered many employment possibilities for a young man with Smith's skills. While still in high school Bedell began working for the National Motor Car Company, one of many automobile manufacturers that sprang up in Indiana after the turn of the century.[13] Working part-time as an unskilled laborer, Bedell supplemented his income by being a soda jerk in a neighborhood drug store. Later he took a job as a mechanic with one of the many firms in Indianapolis that supplied equipment to the railroads.[14]

While many young men of his age might have been happy with his prospects, a career as a skilled tradesman did not excite the imagination of fifteen-year-old Bedell. He fully understood his parents possessed neither the financial resources or the influence to secure him an appointment to West Point, yet he still entertained dreams of a career as an officer.[15] If the regular army lay beyond his immediate reach, only his age stood between him and the second-best thing, the Indiana National Guard.

SERGEANT SMITH OF THE INDIANA NATIONAL GUARD

The day he turned sixteen, Smith joined Company D of the Second Indiana Infantry—a unit that dated its traditions back to the Indianapolis Light Infantry, a fashionable and gentlemanly volunteer regiment that existed, side by side, with the old militia. Volunteer units generally boasted better organization than other militia formations, and aside from granting social status to those in such a regiment, their chief function consisted of preserving civil order. Militant and patriotic enough on parade, like the rest of the National Guard, the Second Indiana Infantry suffered from apathy and poor organization.[16]

One can easily imagine the pride of the private as he donned his uniform for the first time. The Second Indiana Infantry was hardly a *corps d'élite*, but membership in a military unit of any type represented a fulfillment of a lifelong dream for the adolescent Smith. He still entertained notions of someday joining the regular army, but service in the Indiana National Guard at least provided him with a more mature means of playing soldier. His military career nearly ended before it began when his mother raised an objection, disquieted at the idea of "her hopeful" becoming a soldier.[17] Bedell, stretching the truth, but only slightly, told Ida Smith the company he had joined was nothing more than a social organization. Appeased, she offered no further resistance.

As a young man, Smith was torn between his longings to lead the romantic life of a career officer and the reality of his life in Indianapolis. Relatives and acquaintances remembered his lively sense of humor, but as he matured he began to display a certain sullenness, a desire to be by himself with his thoughts.[18] Bedell withdrew from his neighborhood crowd whose "pranks of the Halloween variety" no longer amused him. As a boy he developed an enduring passion for the outdoors and, as a teen, he took every opportunity to get out of the city into the countryside. A solitary person, he was happiest while fishing on the banks of the White River or hunting in the fields and forests in the immediate environs of Indianapolis. Always dexterous with his hands, he would spend countless hours in the basement of his home fashioning fishing rods he cut himself and designing and crafting trout and bass flies from simple household items.

Between his many avocations, two jobs, school, and his National Guard duties, Smith led a very active life. When he turned seventeen, Smith added yet another priority to his list—a steady girlfriend. Until then, Bedell had never shown much interest in the opposite sex.[19] That changed after he met Mary Eleanor (Nory) Cline in 1913. The Clines lived three blocks from the Smiths. Her family was, as Smith later noted, "kind of rich";[20] Mary attended a private

Catholic girls' academy. Undaunted by the obstacles in his way, Bedell began to court Nory Cline.

Smith left Emmerich without his diploma. Already employed full-time as a mechanic in the locomotive shop, Smith saw little value in remaining in school.[21] Whether from dissatisfaction with his job or merely the desire to better his prospects, Smith attempted to enrol in Butler University in Indianapolis. Unfortunately, his father developed serious health problems and lapsed into infirmity, putting an untimely end to the experiment.[22] With the added burden of supporting his mother and brother, Bedell returned to the factory.

The monthly mustering of his National Guard unit provided a welcome relief from his hectic civilian life. He could forget about the din of the factory and play the role of soldier. Even if few others did, Smith took his Guard drills seriously, eager to win promotion. The National Guard provided the police function during times of civil strife and national disaster. Smith's company mustered twice in 1913: once during serious flooding in the spring and again to restore order in the midst of a streetcar strike in the summer.[23] Detailed to secure a bridge and prevent passage over the swollen river during the flood, Bedell took up his position. This particular bridge stood a couple of blocks from his uncle, Paul Bedell's, home. Informed that National Guard troops patrolled the span, Paul Bedell decided to investigate to see if his nephew was among them. In the gathering darkness of the evening, he recognized his nephew and entered the approach to the bridge. Instead of the greeting he expected, he met with a stern warning. If he took another step, he would be under arrest. Not amused, the uncle retreated. Good soldier Smith, despite his youth and kind feelings toward his uncle, executed his duty.[24]

Smith's service during the flood gained the attention of his company commander, James Hurt. He made Bedell a corporal, then, shortly thereafter, the company sergeant. The zealous eighteen-year-old sergeant worked hard to gain the confidence of Captain Hurt. Despite the angry protests of his Guardsmen, Smith labored to make his unit the best drilled in the Indiana service. Roundly cursed by his men, Smith later attributed "some of the less attractive characteristics of [his] personality" to this difficult phase of his career.[25]

As the troops of Company D of the Indiana Infantry grudgingly took on the aspects of real soldiers, the same could not be said of the bulk of the National Guard. The outbreak of general war in Europe in August 1914 did little to invigorate the Guard. The event that did breath new life into the somnolent institution took place not in Europe but along the Mexican border. Embroiled in the amorphous political situation in Mexico, President Woodrow Wilson committed a series of blunders that exacerbated an already chaotic situation. Political conditions deteriorated in Mexico, and U.S. involvement in Europe seemed more likely by the day. Members of the Wilson cabinet, most notably Secretary of War Lidley Garrison, pushed for the creation of a Continental Army under federal control. Faced by adamant pro-Guard members of the House who opposed federalization the administration made little headway, and Wilson withdrew his support from Garrison. With no middle ground for a compromise, the conflicting factions deadlocked. Only Pancho Villa's raid on Columbus, New Mexico, in March 1916 forced a settlement.

The National Defense Act of 1916, the most comprehensive military legislation up to then enacted in U.S. history, called for a fourfold increase in the size of the National Guard. Bolstered by federal funds and subject to federal standards of training, the Guard emerged as a bulwark of the national defense. Passed in May, the law went into effect in June as Wilson federalized the National Guard for duty on the U.S.-Mexican border.

The disorders and gross inefficiencies that attended the mobilization underscored the need for far-reaching reform. Nevertheless, the salutary effects of the intensive training it received along the border did much to rectify the most pressing problem facing the National Guard. The Mexican dress rehearsal also proved invaluable for officers and the state staffs who soon faced mobilization on a grand scale for war in Europe.

The primary supporter of his family, Smith did not go to the Mexican border. Instead he served in the Indiana National Guard headquarters where as a twenty-year-old first sergeant he worked on the staff. Doubtlessly disappointed at having to remain behind, Smith could not have envisioned it would be through staff work that he would rise to the top of his profession.

SUMMONS TO WAR

The year 1917 proved eventful both for the nation and Walter Bedell Smith. Relations between the United States and Germany worsened, and on the second day of April, 1917, Wilson asked Congress for a declaration of war. This struggle took on the pattern of previous U.S. wars as large numbers of citizens augmented the small regular army. The size of the army stood at 127,151 men; the officer corps numbered only 5,959.[26] The prewar officer cadre, composed largely of West Pointers, was earmarked for high-echelon leadership and training duties. Platoon and company-grade officers were drawn from National Guard cadre and among suitable young men from the general population. By virtue of his "fine work during the flood" of 1913 and his proven leadership qualities as a noncommissioned officer, Smith's company commander recommended him for a posting to one of the newly formed officer training schools. For the twenty-one-year-old Smith, the prospect of becoming an officer represented the fulfillment of his childhood dream.

Perhaps prompted by the romance occasioned by the summons to war, Nory Cline consented to be Bedell's wife. On July 1, 1917, the couple married in a traditional Catholic ceremony. The honeymoon was short. Less than eight weeks after his marriage, Smith took the short tram ride out to Fort Benjamin Harrison where he began his officer training course.

Nearly one-half of the 200,000 men who composed the wartime officer corps received their basic training in one of the sixteen camps hurriedly established by the War Department in spring and summer 1917.[27] In the nineteen months of U.S. participation in the war, the War Department trained 182,000 officers at a rate of 30,000 each three-week period. Bedell was in the second series of reserve officer candidates processed through the system.

The youth of America responded to the call. Fort Harrison came alive with each succeeding wave of enthusiastic officer candidates. Based on the Plattsburg model—former chief of staff Leonard Wood's privately sponsored summer camp where students volunteered for military training—the atmosphere of the training camps resembled a college campus the night before a big game. The greater portion of the officer candidates were upperclassmen or recent graduates of the nation's colleges and universities. Here many old friends renewed acquaintances in a genuine spirit of collegiate camaraderie. While not a "college boy," Bedell's anxiety eased with the knowledge that he had a service background and his childhood friend, Harrington, occupied the next bunk.[28]

The college atmosphere soon gave way to the rigors of army life. The urgent need to get on with the job animated the training camps. Soldiers not billeted in the hastily constructed wooden barracks lived in sprouting tent cities. As the fair weather gave way to the autumnal rains, life in the camp became difficult.[29] Selected regular officers carried out training with a captain assigned to each student company. Smith's commanding officer, a hard-boiled regular named Captain B. C. Lockwood, scared the young cadet "to death."[30] Beneath the captain served a regular first lieutenant or one or more of the graduates of the preceding course. Lieutenant Charles Bolté, a "ninety-day wonder" from the first section, remembered he kept ahead of his students only with extreme difficulty. "When it came to teaching the .45 automatic pistol," he recalled, "I had to sit up all night long with a manual just learning how you took it apart and put it together again so the next day I could sit down as if I knew all about it and try to teach this company how to do this very complicated task. It was a case of the blind leading the blind."[31]

With time at a premium, little was wasted. Reveille sounded at 5:15 A.M., and the hectic pace of physical training, bayonet fighting, and field service maneuvers continued until 10 P.M. The training was elementary in nature, including close-order drill, weapons and marksmanship, and instruction in the conduct of scouting and patrolling. Its purpose was threefold: to instill the barest essentials of military drill, to harden the future officers physically, and to exorcise the civilian in them.[32] Perhaps too rudimentary, officer training more closely resembled recruit training, devoid of sufficient grounding in troop-leading qualities and tactical skills.

To enhance competition, the army divided the camp into two parts: one-half devoted to billeting men from Indiana, the other allotted to men from Kentucky. With no love lost between the two states, competition was stiff. The regular scene of cadets drummed out of the corps heightened the sense of competition and inspired the others to even greater efforts. In the evening, although fatigued by the day's activities, cadets studied basic tactics. As the weeks rolled by, pressure mounted. One officer candidate recalled "every minute we [are] able to read and are not studying drill regulations or something of the kind, we have that vague fear that someone else [is] getting ahead of us.[33]

As the three months wound down, camp organization changed. New companies formed based upon branch. With five years of service in the Second Indiana, Smith choose the infantry. His company, in the last week of the training schedule, went into the field for extended training. In the middle of November Smith sloshed through the mud, dug trenches, shivered in the cold temperatures, and slept on the ground—all in all, a proper initiation into the infantry.[34]

On November 27 Smith earned his gold bars. After two weeks furlough Lieutenant Smith made preparations for his first assignment as an officer in the U.S. Army. In what had to be an unhappy scene, only two weeks before Christmas, he bid good-bye to his family and wife at Union Station in Indianapolis.

Smith received orders for Camp Greene, North Carolina, one of the newly established cantonments built to house the new army. Set in the beautiful rolling, pine-covered Piedmont area of North Carolina, Camp Greene at first sight appeared the ideal site for a base. After the horrors of that last week in the field in the teeth of a premature winter, Bedell livened at the prospect of pleasant weather in the south. Fort Harrison proved to be a resort compared to what befell him in North Carolina.

His posting to the 4th Division, a regular army unit, must have pleased Smith. Unfortunately, the 4th Division existed only on paper—a set of skeleton formations. The few regular units attached to the Ivy Division served only as nucleus for a division built of volunteers and draftees. Under a scheme worked out by the War Department, regular regiments divided into three sections: one designated as the parent regiment while the remaining two served as cadre for new regiments. Regular regiments drawn from West Coast stations provided the bedrock of the division. When Smith arrived, the average company numbered thirty-five men with many having no officers at all. Despite the presence of a considerable number of regular officers, the majority of Smith's peers were, like himself, "Sears and Roebuck" officers from the second batch out of the officer training camps.[35]

The first intakes of volunteer enlisted personnel did not arrive until after the new year. There remained little for the officers to do except play cards, curse the army, and long for home. Nearby Charlotte opened its doors to the young officers with sporting events and holiday celebrations that took the edge off the boredom and homesickness. Everyone looked forward to the serious work of putting the division together.

Most of January 1918 involved processing incoming men and attending special classes directed by veteran British and French officers. Many of the volunteers proved deficient in mental aptitude or physical condition and received noncombat assignments. Ever so slowly, the companies began to take shape. Meanwhile, the officers and noncommissioned officers, having graduated from the special schools, returned to their units as instructors to impart their newly acquired expertise to their charges.[36]

The cool, crisp days of December gave way to the worst winter in memory. The War Department made no provisions for the construction of permanent barracks in the training camps that dotted the south. To make matters worse, tents were in short supply. Ten to twelve men crowded into pyramidal tents designed for eight. It frequently snowed during the night, and the blowing wind formed large drifts; then, in the afternoon, as the sun came out, the snow melted, turning the camp "into a vast sea of reddish-yellow mud."[37] Improved roads were few, and the incessant rain and intermittent snowstorms turned them into quagmires. Pack mules brought in food and drinking water. Huddled in their miserable tent cities, the troops cut green pine trees in an attempt to heat their overcrowded tents. Given the wintry conditions and the sight of men hauling timber, the base more closely resembled a northern lumber camp than a military training installation. Due to the weather the troops received only sixteen days of training in the first eleven weeks of the division's existence—little beyond the barest elements of military drill.

Smith was assigned to Company A, 1st Battalion of the 39th Infantry Regiment. The 39th, with the 47th Infantry and the 11th Machine-Gun Battalion, composed the 7th Brigade; its sister unit, the 8th Brigade, consisted of the 58th and 59th Infantry and its attached machine-gun battalion, the 12th. The inclement weather, the overly ambitious training schedule, and the slow influx of volunteers created serious problems. The 3d Division of Major General Joseph Dickman, who commanded the camp, also trained at Camp Greene. Dickman granted his division priority over training sites and expropriated much of the equipment and arms that filtered into camp. To make matters worse, many experienced officers left the 4th Division to flesh out Dickman's formations. This turnover in personnel made it difficult to build unit cohesion.

February brought no relief from the weather. An outbreak of spinal meningitis in Charlotte further restricted movement to and from the base.[38] For better than two weeks the weather permitted no training at all. The battle against the mud finally ended in the mud's favor—the entire training trench system dissolved. Finally, the weather improved during the second week of March, and with it the spirits of the veterans of Camp Greene soared. Along with better weather came relief from the tyranny of the 3d Division. When the four infantry regiments of Dickman's division marched out on March 7, 1918, the real formation of the 4th Division commenced.

The first three weeks of March brought 10,000 draftees to Greene. Units gradually approached full strength. March also saw the renewal of serious training in intensive drill and field maneuvers. Three of the four regiments completed the basic rifle course. For most of the troops this represented their first exposure to firing weapons. The only regiment that did not take part in the course was the 39th.[39]

The mobilization plan envisioned the orderly progression from individual to small-unit and finally to divisional training. Several circumstances forced the War Department to revise its training scheme, chief among them the successes of the German spring offensives. The German offensives of 1918 necessitated the dispatch of U.S. divisions to France nearly a year before originally planned. Although woefully unprepared—without even its small-unit sequence of training complete—the 4th Division received orders to begin preparation for its movement to Europe.

On April 21, 1918, advance elements began their movement to the New York City area, the port of embarkation. At Camp Mills, Long Island, the men of the division endured a strenuous week of training designed to pound the finishing touches into each company. On April 28 the first units entrained for Camp Merritt, in northern New Jersey, for their embarkation. Before the troops boarded their ships, they received a twenty-four hour leave.

Smith's family and his wife made the long train trip from Indianapolis to see Bedell before he left for France. The day he embarked he had one final chance to visit with his family. His grandfather made the trip and at the last possible moment stepped forward on the quay to give his grandson some sage soldierly advice. Perhaps some lingering anti-French sentiments inspired the veteran's parting remark. "Just remember," the old man warned, "the French Army has never been able to withstand the onslaught of the Prussian cavalry." Amidst the good-natured laughs of his fellow officers, Smith climbed the gangplank.[40]

On May 9 the 7th Brigade sailed from East Hoboken, New Jersey. In all, 35,000 men crowded on the sixteen-ship convoy for the twelve-day Atlantic crossing. To get the 39th Regiment to Europe required a true Allied effort. The bulk of the regiment sailed in an Italian ship manned by an international crew, chartered by the British government to carry U.S. troops to France. On May 23, the brigade disembarked at Brest, in Brittany.[41]

The various elements of the 4th Division landed in Europe at three widely dispersed points. Most of the 8th Brigade and the divisional headquarters entered the war zone at Liverpool in England. The bulk of the 7th Brigade landed at Brest; the remainder and the divisional artillery entered the continent at Bordeaux, in southwest France. After a week in rest camps, the 4th Division—less its artillery brigade, signal battalion, and elements of the 58th Regiment—reassembled at the Samer Training Area in Picardy, near the channel coast.[42]

General John Pershing, commander of the American Expeditionary Force (AEF), anticipated the phased arrival of complete divisions to France. According to the plan, each infantry division would undergo three one-month cycles of training under French and British supervision. The first month included preliminary small-unit training; the second phase would see U.S. battalions integrated into quiet Allied defensive sectors "to harden and accustom them to all sorts of fire"; and finally, regiments, brigades, and divisions would engage in field manuevers.[43]

At Samur, the 4th Division began its first phase of training under the guidance of the veteran British 16th [Irish] Division. The German offensive obliged Pershing, now considering the early commitment of U.S. units, to abandon the original training scheme. Instead of a full four-week training phase, the 4th Division remained at Samur for only eight days. First, the American infantrymen dug a trench system. Once it was complete, the British instructors began to demonstrate the use of weapons and the essential tactics of trench warfare. The Americans received instruction on Vickers machine guns, Lewis guns, and Stokes mortars; the British brought out flame throwers and trained the men in methods of defense against gas attacks. Eight hours a day, the pea-green U.S. troops suffered through a schedule of rigorous training that included an unbroken stretch of forty-eight hours in the trenches. In the final days the battalions practiced tactical exercises under simulated trench-warfare conditions.

This represented the first realistic training in modern warfare that any of the men, including the regulars, had experienced.[44]

On June 9 the division marched out of the Samer Training Area towards predetermined marshaling points along the Hesdin-Montreuil Railway. Two days later the troops detrained at Meaux, on the Marne, in the sector of the French 6th Army. For the next five days the American troops received yet another truncated course in military technique. The second phase of the training sequence concentrated on the problems of troop leading on the modern battlefield. Glaring differences in U.S. and French tactical doctrine and organization soon appeared. American infantry doctrine stressed the rifle and the bayonet as the principal weapons in the assault. The field manuevers displayed American reliance upon tightly packed infantry attacks and the absence of any real appreciation for the power of defensive weaponry, especially the machine gun and field artillery. Impressed by the ardor of the U.S. troops, the French officers discovered, to their dismay, American tactical doctrine bore striking similarities to the French infantry tactics of 1914-1915. Having absorbed the bitter lessons of the Frontiers, Champagne, and Verdun, the French Army now emphasized mobile infantry tactics combined with coordinated artillery support. After observing the performance of the American infantry, the French command renewed its push to amalgamate American battalions and regiments into French and British divisions.

THE AISNE-MARNE OFFENSIVE

Emerging from its century of repose during the era of "free security," the United States fielded an enormous army in France that, by November 1918, included some twenty-nine divisions. The size and speed of the American intervention contributed, in no small measure, to the disintegration of German will to continue the unequal struggle. On the other hand the collapse of the German Army in the late summer and autumn of 1918 masked the generally poor tactical performance of American units in France. Writing after the war, George Marshall pointed out the successes won by U.S. arms had been achieved against a crippled giant on the verge of exhaustion.[45] The rapid expansion of the army and its early commitment to France curtailed training and eventually contributed to battlefield failures—factors beyond American control. However, other factors, within the American purview, also adversely affected AEF effectiveness. Pershing believed the stalemate in France to be the product of a defensive attitude bred by three years of indecisive trench warfare. Instead of adjusting American organization, equipment, and tactical doctrine to the realities of the Western Front, the American commander remained wedded to his faith in the "special genius" of U.S. soldiers for "open warfare." This, combined with the American offensive spirit, would, in Pershing's view, end the deadlock and restore a war of movement.[46]

Between March 21 and the middle of July the Germans launched a series of five powerful offensives in the West in an effort to force a negotiated end to the war. The Champs des Dames offensive (May 27-June 5) succeeded in carving a deep salient in the French line, bounded roughly by Rheims, Château-Thierry, and Soissons. The Allied generalissimo, Maréchal Ferdinand Foch, requested the 4th and 28th U.S. divisions remain in the vicinity of Paris to, as Pershing later remarked, shield the French capital in the event of a German breakthrough and "ultimately for possible use in the offensive."[47]

The 4th Division was placed under the operational control of the French 6th Army, despite having completed only two weeks of the training cycle. On June 13, the 7th Brigade was attached to the French 4th Division. Two and a half weeks later, the brigade took up a position in the secondary line of trenches in the French II Corps area. Here the men of Smith's brigade had their first taste of trench warfare. In the distance the flashes and reports of the heavy artillery could be seen and heard as the German attacks spent themselves against the French prepared defenses.

Foch suspected the German offensives had passed their "point of culmination," offering the opportunity for a massive Allied counterstroke. Preparations for the counteroffensive continued even as the last German gambits to regain the strategic initiative wound down. The German command issued its halt orders on July 17; early the next morning the French counteroffensive opened up. The American divisions were to cut their teeth in offensive warfare in this, the Aisne-Marne offensive.[48]

On July 16, the 39th Regiment had left its positions in the rear to attach itself to the 33d French Division. The officers and men thought they were destined for a quiet tour of the French trenches. Instead they faced their baptism of fire without ever having so much as shot a rifle in training, much less in anger.[49]

Placed on the extreme left wing of the 6th Army, the 39th Regiment occupied a zone between the Ourcq River and the boundaries of 10th Army. The march from the secondary line of trenches was made difficult by the sustained rain and the fact that it took place in the dead of night over unknown and congested forest roads. Smith's 1st Battalion, the trailer element, was the last unit to take up its position. Fatigued by the march, disoriented by the dark and confusion, and under artillery fire for the first time, the men had hardly entered the trenches when the seventy-battery French barrage opened fire.[50]

Originally the plan called for the Americans to leap off an hour after the initial assault—the French command wanted to minimize American casualties—but orders changed when the French attacks triggered a violent

German counterbarrage on the U.S. lines. The foul weather and Foch's bold strategy achieved surprise, and the German defenders, badly disordered, fell back. Finally, at 8 A.M., after a two-and-a-half-hour delay, the regiment began its advance.

The 39th was instructed to take the Bois de Cresnes, a large thicket on a hill that dominated the terrain between the Ourcq and its tributary, the Saviéres. General Operations Order #200 underscored the "importance of the nest of batteries and Center of Resistance of Noroy [sur-Ourcq]." Continued German control of these positions threatened to block the advance of the 33d Division and complicate communications along the boundaries of the French armies. The German-occupied village of Noroy lay immediately in front of the 39th's objective, the wood. The French corps commander wanted to envelop the German position and ordered the Americans to "occupy" the woods only at "the most favorable moment"—when Noroy had fallen.[51]

The advance of the 39th illuminated the inadequacies of training, the ambiguity of the tactical doctrine, and the poor quality of American leadership. Colonel Frank Bolles, charged with securing the wood, deployed his three battalions in textbook fashion with the 1st on the right. Typical of American infantry assaults in the Great War, the 7th Brigade, in accordance to its rigid plan of attack, moved forward in dense lines over open fields. The 1st Battalion staff hastily examined maps, and seeing that the stream at their front did not present an obstacle, ordered no reconnaissance. Smith's company served as the vanguard with a machine-gun company in support. The rains had swollen the usually sluggish Saviéres over its banks, filling the river flanked by deep and difficult marshes. The Germans assumed no commander would assault across swampy ground and a flooded stream in daylight. Accordingly, the Germans faced south toward the Ourcq.

Companies A and B crossed a long field that sloped down toward the stream. The swarming French attacks occupied the Germans, who offered no artillery counterfire. Forward elements broke through the windbreak that flanked the field and scrambled down the small bluff to the river. As the units intermingled only two hundred yards from the supposed German position, the thrust bogged down in confusion. As Smith later wrote, "The floundering, the splashing, and the shouting made enough noise to alarm every German in the Marne salient." Fortunately, there were no Germans to take advantage of the precarious state of the U.S. battalion. Finally, a few American patrols succeeded in gaining the other side and entering the fringe of wood that bordered the river. A German machine gun team came up, but too late.[52]

The 2d and 3d battalions faced stiffer opposition, but the success of the 1st Battalion and the progress of the French assaults compelled the Germans to withdraw from the rise. Marching forward into the eerily defoliated woods against scattered opposition, the battalions stumbled toward their objectives. Smith's battalion collected some two hundred Germans skulking in the woods. The French commander, in view of the German withdrawal, ordered the 1st and 2d battalions to prepare for a movement into Noroy with Smith's unit designated to take the village. Plagued by poor liaison, the 3d, rather than acting as the reserve, responded to the request of the neighboring French units and moved forward. Once again, had German defenders been present, the unsupported actions of a single battalion might have ended in disaster, but such was not the case; the Americans took the town.[53] German machine guns and a battery of field guns deployed in a gully southeast of the town blocked any further advance. Veterans of a half day's combat, the 39th deployed facing the German guns to spend the night in shallow foxholes.[54]

Orders remained unchanged for the next day—a general attack was scheduled for 4 A.M. The first aim of the regiment was the removal of the German gunners who had checked the advance the preceding evening. Differences in language, doctrine, organization, and staff methods made it difficult for American formations to operate under French command. Disregarding the fact that the promised French barrage did not materialize, the Americans went over the top. Then, with the movement started, Colonel Bolles received a halt order. The poor command and control of the American regiment now bore disastrous fruit. Runners were dispatched to the rear but too late; similarly, the battalions could not be recalled. Raked by machine-gun fire in the front, the American ranks were then hit by French artillery shells as well. Unable to retreat into the creeping curtain of artillery fire, the Americans assailed the German position. The attack dislodged the Germans from the ravine but at a frightful cost to the Americans: 2 officers and 93 men killed, 11 officers and 436 men wounded, and 1 officer and 60 men reported missing.[55] One of those 11 officers wounded was Second Lieutenant Walter Bedell Smith—his career as combat platoon leader lasted something short of twenty-four hours.

Baptism into the General Staff, 1917-1920

The First World War acted as a catalyst in the evolution of the U.S. general staff system. Although a truncated and idiosyncratic general staff structure emerged out of the Root reforms (1900-1905), it made little headway against the retrenchment and institutional inertia of the "old army." Never questioning the war-winning potential of the United States or the fighting qualities of U.S. soldiers, the French and British general staffs doubted whether the Washington military establishment could mobilize sufficient manpower and matériel quickly enough to influence the course of operations on the Western Front before 1919. Several senior American officers, including Pershing and the future chief of staff, Peyton March, agreed the War Department General Staff (WDGS) appeared inadequate to meet the demands that lay ahead.[1] The experience of both the Allied and Central powers convinced certain influential Americans to push the process of change within the U.S. Army beyond its prewar limits, taking guidance from European models and finding urgency in the state of the war in spring 1917.

Pershing had never been content with the halfway Root reforms. "The adherence of the army to the bureau system," he wrote after the war, "made its general staff nominal only."[2] The French and British recommended the integration of American troops into existing Allied military formations. The AEF commander vehemently opposed these various Allied "amalgamation" schemes. As one of the forty-one officers selected to compose the original General Staff, Pershing knew only too well the many deficiencies in the American command and staff system. To prove the American officer corps could effectively plan and manage large-scale operations, he placed the organization of a general staff along European lines as an overriding priority.[3] The independence of the U.S.

Army and the professional reputation of the American officer corps stood at stake.[4]

Pointing out "a general staff broadly organized and trained for war had not hitherto existed in our army," Pershing fashioned a Prussian-style staff at his headquarters at Chaumont.[5] It consisted of four divisions: Personnel (G-1), Intelligence (G-2), Operations (G-3), and Supply (G-4). Members of the prewar General Staff and the best graduates of the staff school at Leavenworth manned the headquarters (AEFHQ).[6] Faced by serious shortages of trained staff officers, the AEF commander created a staff college at Langres. In addition to the 537 graduates of Langres, line officers were detached for staff duties to the AEFHQ, the various other headquarters in France, and the WDGS.[7] A new class of American officer received training in the procedures and the ethos of the general staff in the school of experience. Bedell Smith was one such officer.

While the AEFHQ took shape in France, the WDGS remained mired in petty details and prewar procedures in Washington. On March 4, 1918, March returned to Washington to assume the responsibilities of chief of staff. Unwilling to accept the collateral role of his predecessors, March reorganized the General Staff, investing in it new functions and power, including authority over the bureau chiefs. The new chief of staff insisted on the subordination of all field commands to the WDGS. Pershing resisted these efforts, maintaining that the War Department General Staff existed only to serve the logistical needs of the AEF.

By the end of the war, two separate general staffs existed. The division between the WDGS and AEFHQ required a highly organized, unified command structure. Ideally, command and staff relationships demand the centralization of decision-making power with a chief of staff integrated into the highest councils of state to act as the link between the vertical command structure and the horizontal line organization. The bifurcated system that emerged lent itself to efficiency—the 2 million troops organized, trained, and landed in France attest to that—but not to hierarchical subordination. The resolution of this fundamental problem would await General George Marshall and the next war.

ATTACHED TO THE GENERAL STAFF

Wounded by shell fragments, his career as combat leader both short and inglorious, Lieutenant Smith's world appeared far removed from that of the "Chaumont Circle." Evacuated to an advance first-aid station, he had his wounds cleaned and dressed. Since his condition was not life threatening, Smith remained at the first-aid station, waiting the evacuation of the seriously wounded. From the aid station Smith moved to a hastily constructed field hospital, a collection of tents concealed in a grove of trees behind the front.

The first order of business for field hospital staff involved the administration of a tetanus shot. For the lightly wounded such as Smith, the treatment may have been more traumatic than the wounding itself. As he lay in the hospital tent jammed with the casualties of the first two days of the Aisne-Marne offensive, Smith watched as the medical staff advanced from soldier to soldier injecting the serum directly into the unfortunate's stomach with a hypodermic needle "the size a railway spike."[8]

The American Medical Service received little advance warning of the counteroffensive. Suffering from shortages, chief among them trained medical staff and ambulances, the ill-prepared Medical Service nearly broke down. Finally, trucks were employed to remove the remaining casualties.[9]

The shell fragments removed, Smith moved to a base hospital. Established in permanent buildings, frequently schools, base hospitals handled the most serious cases or, as in Smith's case, provided convalescent care. Patients customarily remained at the base hospital for a week. Since his case offered no complications, Bedell Smith's stay was brief. After a short furlough he awaited orders, fully expecting to report back to his unit.

Staff officers could not graduate from the Langres school quickly enough to fill the growing demand. The War Department General Staff, the AEFHQ, and the rapidly expanding tactical headquarter staffs all required more officers. Pershing's ideas for the organization of his staff in France emerged earlier in the Baker Board Report. Headed by Colonel Chauncy Baker, a delegation of American officers traveled to Great Britain and France in May-June 1917 to evaluate the military organization and practices of the western Allies. Concluding "the nature of this war is such that we cannot safely depend upon the previous training of our officers to meet the requirements [of general staff work]," the Baker Board strongly recommended the adoption of the French—actually Prussian—system. The report discouraged the detachment of valuable regular officers to the specialized bureaus. Instead the board recommended selected officers learn the essentials of staff work while attached to a functioning headquarters. Further, the Baker Board suggested "bright young men...could be tried out for this work" among line officers and men in the officer training camps in the United States.[10]

Pershing instructed his General Headquarters G-1 Division to review the records of junior officers serving in the theater for men with "previous preparation for general staff work." Instead of channeling these selected officers through the three-month course, they were placed on immediate staff duty to perform routine staff functions, releasing experienced officers for more-essential tasks.[11] Determined to keep the general staff a small elite, Pershing and his first chief of staff, James Harbord, admitted few officers into the "Chaumont Circle."

In keeping with the policy, LeRoy Eltinge, the deputy chief of staff at Chaumont, directed the tactical commands to detach officers "who have satisfactorily performed general staff duty for at least two months" for temporary assignment to the staff. The directive included a caveat. In keeping with Pershing's desire to limit the size and prestige of the general staff, Eltinge asked "special care be exercised in the selection of officers not of the regular establishment."[12]

Smith was among those seconded to the War Department General Staff. In August, a reorganization of the WDGS required an expansion of the staff in Washington. Although not holding a regular army commission, Smith's service with the 4th Division and duty on the staff of the Indiana National Guard Headquarters during the Mexican border crisis satisfied the minimum requirements. Instead of returning to his unit for the "big push" in the Argonne, Lieutenant Smith set off for Brest and transshipment to the United States. The appointment did not allow him to exchange his crossed rifles for the coveted "G.S." designation of the General Staff. It did mean a promotion and, more importantly, the opportunity to further his prospects in the army. Commissioned first lieutenant, Smith arrived in Washington with orders to join the newly formed Bureau of Military Intelligence.

THE WAR DEPARTMENT GENERAL STAFF (1917-1918)

The first three chiefs of the War Department General Staff—Hugh Scott, Tasker Bliss, and John Biddle—willingly played the role of Pershing's rubber stamp in Washington.[13] None of them possessed a complete understanding of general staff functions, military hierarchy, or the need for coordinate control; each acquiesced to the bureaus. Wilson refused to exercise his command authority leaving his secretary of war, Newton Baker, to supervise the executive apparatus. Secretary Baker had a limited understanding of military affairs, derived primarily from reading Civil War histories. For Baker, the questions of general staff organization and principles were "purely technical" and "unimportant" as he did nothing to stop the army from coalescing into two hostile camps—Pershing's AEF and the War Department—with the secretary of war acting as the controlling link.[14]

The fundamental weakness of the military structure that emerged from the Root reforms rested in the lack of any clearly defined hierarchy of command. Pershing understood the prewar staff organization was entirely inadequate, and he abandoned it when he organized his headquarters in France. The first U.S. General Staff worthy of the name soon emerged. At the same time he knew the anachronistic War Department was unequal to the tasks it faced and in need of wholesale reorganization. Convinced of the paramount importance of his command and the need to preserve his autonomy, Pershing refused to accept the imposition of any person or agency between himself and his civilian chiefs. "Please let us not make the mistake of handicapping our army," he wrote Baker, "by attempting to control...from Washington, or by introducing any coordinate authority."[15]

Baker brought March, a member of the first General Staff, from France to put the War Department in order. When the United States entered the war, nineteen staff officers resided in the capital, twelve of whom lodged at the War College, many blocks distant from the chief of staff and the bureaus. Efficiency was hampered and staff procedures complicated as the General Staff neither supervised nor coordinated the bureaus. As George Soulé critically noted in an article in the *New Republic*, "the remoteness of the General Staff from the conduct of the war naturally inclines the army to regard it as an aloof and secret body...[which] is not to be consulted about large, immediate problems."[16] Legislation in May 1917 increased the size of the General Staff in Washington. Nevertheless, as late as July 1 the General Staff consisted of sixty-four officers, most of whom spent their time clamoring for command assignments in France.[17]

Baker believed the role of the General Staff to be managerial, and he admitted the inadequacy of the existing War Department organization. Congress also demanded action. In December 1917, the chairman of the Senate Military Affairs Committee, George Chamberlain, pronounced "the military establishment of America has fallen down."[18] To remedy the situation, Baker announced the creation of a War Council, an advisory group not unlike the War Board of the Civil War, to facilitate the flow of supplies and manpower to France. A reorganization of the General Staff followed in February 1918. General Order #14 created five main divisions: Executive, War Plans, Supply, Operation and Purchase, Storage and Traffic. On March 4, March assumed duties as acting chief of staff.[19]

General March refused to accept the passive role of his predecessors. Described by Baker as "arrogant, harsh, dictatorial, and opinionated,"[20] March quickly whipped the War Department General Staff into shape but won enemies in the process. He expanded the size and power of his Washington establishment. The February reorganization of the command structure made the chief of staff Pershing's equal and gave the chief a firm institutional base. Baker would not allow March or his staff to issue directives to Pershing. The difficulty rested in their adversarial relationship, the result of the flawed and confused command arrangements and the unwillingness of the Wilson administration to decide whether the chief of staff or Pershing would command the army.

To some degree their differences were the product of a clash of personalities. Both officers were complex, intelligent, and ambitious men who demanded absolute loyalty from their subordinates and considered their judgment nearly infallible. Ignoring the claims of the other, March and Pershing carried on business as if each exercised exclusive control over the military establishment. Relations between Washington and Chaumont deteriorated throughout 1918 as disagreements arose over everything from training programs in the United States, shipping schedules, assignment and promotion of officers, and the management of the AEF's Service of Supply to the Sam Browne belt.[21] The officer corps divided into March and Pershing factions as another fissure augmented the old staff versus line and regular versus citizen soldier schisms.

In many ways the struggle was an uneven one. Pershing held his command for nearly a year before March came to Washington. As a national hero Pershing enjoyed the full confidence of the president and the secretary of war and could rely upon powerful allies in Congress. Attentive to public opinion, Pershing cultivated his image as perfect product of the American military tradition. March, on the other hand, claimed tact did not win wars. His heavy-handed approach to Congress, grudgingly tolerated during the wartime crisis, produced opposition in the immediate postwar period.[22]

The chief of staff possessed powers to restructure "his" staff. Reorganization of the supply services loomed most exigent. March's goal centered on a thorough reordering of the general staff along Prussian lines. He sought to bring the War Department out of its nineteenth century lethargy and give institutional expression to the General Staff concept. Before March could undertake his crusade he first had to break the power of the bureaus.

March removed the recalcitrant chief of Ordnance and transferred most of the functions of the Quartermaster Corps to the newly created Purchase, Storage, and Traffic Division.[23] These reforms created a centralized system of supply, the first one in U.S. military history. Recognizing the responsibilities of the General Staff transcended logistical matters, March bypassed the War Council, abolished the Executive Division, increased the powers of the War Plans and Operations divisions, and created the Military Intelligence Division.[24] By November 1918 he had fashioned a functioning general staff. Forced to operate within the restrictions imposed by Baker and faced with Pershing's intransigence, March was unable to achieve his desired end of bringing the complete supervision of the Washington military establishment under the control of the general staff.

Believing the chief of staff and the General Staff were the cornerstones of the modern army, March attempted to define the location of power within the military structure. In late August 1918, he issued General Order #80 which held that the chief of staff "is the immediate adviser of the Secretary of War

...and is charged...with the planning, development, and execution of the Army program [and as such] takes rank and precedence over all officers of the Army."[25]

Pershing ignored March's claims of supremacy. Harbord spoke for his commander when he called March's attempt to place the AEFHQ under the War Department General Staff a "hallucination." "All you wish from America," Harbord wrote Pershing, "is such Staff Service there as will insure you a steady flow of troops and supplies. You do not want there a Staff dealing with any phase of your business here."[26] Pershing and Harbord saw nothing wrong with maintaining the system of dual command. Although the army regulations stated the chief executive commanded through the secretary of war and the chief of staff, Wilson and Baker refused to exercise effective control. As long as the sole American war aim consisted of a military victory bereft of concrete political context, Pershing easily defended the inviolability of his command. This assured the postwar military structure, as in the case after the wars of the nineteenth-century, remained imbalanced and bifurcated.

REGULAR ARMY COMMISSION

On September 1, 1918, Bedell Smith reported for duty to the Military Intelligence Division of the War Department General Staff. Less than a week old, the division emerged out of March's August reorganization. Like the other divisions of the General Staff, Military Intelligence experienced growth and alterations in function during the war years. Initially a subsection of the War College Division, the Military Intelligence staff consisted of two officers and two civilian clerks in April 1917. First expanded in size and responsibility on May 3, 1917, the Military Intelligence Section served two masters, the Executive and War Plans (War College) divisions—the only divided section. Aware of the need for improved intelligence, March reorganized the structure again in May 1918 creating a separate Military Intelligence branch. This reform was a central part of the chief of staff's incremental reformation of the General Staff. The final reorganization saw the creation of an autonomous and enlarged Military Intelligence Division.[27]

By the time March took over the War Department General Staff, Pershing had already secured the services of nearly every regular officer with prewar general staff experience or Leavenworth training. Within days of assuming his duties as chief of staff, March requested staff officers rotate between Washington and France. He asked Pershing to send thirty general staff officers back to the United States.[28] Harbord viewed this as a conspiratorial attempt by March to "undermine [Pershing's] well-laid foundation" and rob AEFHQ of nearly half its sixty-four General Staff officers.[29] March wanted to infuse his nascent staff with the AEF viewpoint, never intending the thirty officers come exclusively from Harbord's handpicked staff. Under pressure, Harbord finally relented and dispatched March thirty officers, three of whom proved suitable for general staff work. This ended the rotation scheme. In August, March's plans to reorganize and expand the General Staff in Washington prompted him to renew his request for officers from France. Smith was one of the 296 officers attached for temporary service with the General Staff.[30]

Brigadier General Marlborough Churchill, one of the thirty officers exchanged by Harbord in March, assumed duties as director of the Military Intelligence Division. In August 1918 it numbered 173 officers, 23 noncommissioned officers, and 589 civilian employees. In addition to handling conventional military intelligence functions—preparation of strategic estimates and the collection, evaluation, and dissemination of military information—the division dealt with censorship and sabotage and subversive activities inside the army and in war plants. In the eleven weeks between the August reorganization and the armistice, 109 officers, 6 NCOs, and 359 civilian employees (ranging from clerks to university professors) joined the Military Intelligence Division swelling it to 1,259 officers and men—far from the four men who staffed the Military Intelligence Section in March 1917.[31]

Without formal staff training, Smith was thrown into the breach. He was not alone. In November 1918 General March's Washington establishment of 1,073 officers, only four—all of them general officers including the chief of staff—had seen prewar general staff service.[32] During the hectic days of summer and autumn 1918, the staff strained to keep pace with the deluge of administrative details that attended the organization, dispatch, and maintenance of the American armies. Any staff expedites decision making and channels communications upward toward responsible agencies and individuals within the hierarchy of command. At the lowest level a staff acts as a clearinghouse for the mass of paperwork and facilitates the flow of documents through the system. Junior officers like Smith received incoming communications, examined their contents to determine proper disposition, and made entries on tally cards outlining subject material, source, date of receipt, and distribution. Routine matters flowed through the division for remark and concurrence and, when necessary, were forwarded to other divisions. Important correspondence was placed in a special file and brought to the attention of the secretary of the General Staff who determined disposition. Matters of an urgent nature demanded immediate action. These bypassed the routing system as special messengers relayed the documents to the proper agency.[33]

Bedell Smith's apprenticeship as a general staff officer was short lived. No sooner had he gained an understanding of the systematized framework of staff procedures and familiarized himself with the labyrinthine State War and Navy Building than he received his assignment as adjutant and intelligence officer to the then-forming 379th Infantry Brigade at Camp Sherman, near Chillicothe, Ohio. The brief exposure to the War Department General Staff provided Smith with invaluable experience. First, he had his initial exposure to official Washington. Second, service in the General Staff improved his prospects of gaining the regular army commission he had long coveted. Third, Smith's assignment to the War Department expanded his appreciation of the necessity for and functioning of high-level military organizations. Officers who spent time in the General Staff came away with an enhanced awareness of the complexity of modern warfare and the essential role of staff organization. The no-nonsense approach of March demanded a high degree of decentralization. Officers at all levels exercised their own initiative. Finally, the business methods of the war-time War Department General Staff set the standard for staff procedures for decades to come. Smith's education received during his brief appointment to General March's staff laid the solid foundation for his development as a staff officer.

During summer and autumn 1918, the War Department prepared for the expected "open warfare" campaign of 1919 and directed the formation of twenty-one new infantry divisions. The 95th Division began organization on September 5 at Camp Sherman. Established in June 1917 to serve as an officer training school and as training camp for the 83d and 84th Divisions, Camp Sherman became headquarters for the 95th. In an attempt to rectify the critical shortages of trained staff officers, the War Department established a one-month staff course at the Army War College.[34] Owing to Smith's experience in the WDGS, he proceeded directly to his assignment at Camp Sherman.

The 190th Infantry Brigade, which included the 379th Regiment, began organizing in September and by the end of October reached a strength of 6,400 officers and men.[35] Because of insufficient numbers of staff personnel, regimental and brigade staffs were amalgamated in the divisional headquarters. Smith's tasks were administrative. Attached to the adjutant's office, his section handled the flow of paperwork that attended the creation of a division. As coordinating authority between the War Department and the division, the adjutant staff dealt with the routine work of issuing assignment, transfer, and discharge papers as well as overseeing the compilation of the headquarters's files.

An influenza epidemic, which raged from September to November 1918, curtailed the training program and the end of the fighting in France removed the need for more troops. Twelve hundred recruits filtered into the division during November, and on the last day of the month orders arrived initiating demobilization. On December 3 Camp Sherman became one of thirty regional demobilization centers.[36]

By November 1918 the War Department had over 3.7 million mobilized officers and men, 1.5 million in units in the United States. The first order of business involved the discharge of men in units in the Zones of the Interior to clear the way for the reception and disposition of men and equipment from France. General March rejected a complex British model for the phased demobilization of the army in tune with the demands of the economy. March favored wholesale demobilization by military unit. By January 4, 1919, 732,766 men separated from the army; by February 1 the number rose to 1,026,766; and by May 1 nearly 2 million men had been demobilized.[37]

In December the skeleton staff of the 95th Division, absorbed into the adjutant staff of the demobilization center, helped discharge 30,527 officers and men who passed through Camp Sherman in addition to developing plans for the phased demobilization of the 84th Division. February brought orders for Smith to report to Camp Dodge, Iowa, and the 163d Depot Brigade. As a demobilization center Camp Dodge's responsibilities involved the marshaling and disposal of surplus stocks of supplies. Smith remained in this assignment for less than a month. He received orders in March to transfer to the staff of the 2d Infantry Regiment.[38]

The American entry into the European war found the 2d Regiment, a regular unit, garrisoning Fort Shafter in the Hawaiian Islands. The regiment, transferred first to Camp Fremont, California, in July 1918, arrived at Camp Dodge in September. Along with another regular regiment, the 14th, the 2d Infantry provided the foundation for the 19th Division, one of the mobile divisions created by the War Department in summer 1918.[39] On January 19, 1919, directives received from Washington ordered the immediate demobilization of all units at Camp Dodge except the two regular regiments. Smith's transfer to the 2d Regiment represented a stroke of good fortune as it guaranteed he would end his wartime service as he began it, with a regular army formation.

Smith remained in Camp Dodge with the 2d Regiment until November 1919, when the unit transferred to Camp Sherman. No longer having to perform the hectic administration duties connected with the demobilization, the young lieutenant could indulge his passion for fishing and hunting. Located a dozen miles north of Des Moines, Camp Dodge, situated in the center of a vast undulating prairie, afforded plenty of opportunities for the outdoorsman. In the spring and fall ducks abounded; the fall was deer and wild turkey season. The many streams provided the fisherman with pickerel, pike, catfish, and bass.[40]

As part of the demobilization process, National Guard and Reserve officers who expressed an interest in remaining in the army wrote an examination to determine their fitness for a commission. Despite not having shone as a student in high school, Bedell had always been an avid reader, especially of military subjects. The competition was intense. Two hundred thousand men held temporary commissions during the war, and 14,565 wrote the qualifying examination. With the passage of the National Defense Act of 1920, Congress sanctioned a peacetime officer corps of 17,717.[41] Smith, by virtue of his combat service, proven staff ability, and high scores on the examination, numbered among the officers retained on the active lists. Bedell Smith finally received his regular army commission.

The Rite of Passage: Smith's Practical Education in the "Army of the Long Generation," 1920–1929

The disappearance of the frontier deprived the army of its traditional *raison d'être*, but participation in the First World War and the extracontinental thrust of American interests produced powerful new imperatives for the reorganization of the military establishment. General staffs, empowered with the formulation of planning, the coordination of logistics, and the oversight of training, evolved in Washington and at Chaumont as exigencies of war. However, with the end of hostilities, military policies reverted to their settled nineteenth-century pattern as the army failed to escape the limits imposed by its Indian-fighting past.[1]

The National Defense Act of 1920, a sort of Magna Carta for the professional military, established a permanent structure anchored upon the regular army. In the immediate aftermath of the war, it seemed a golden age for the army was about to dawn. This vision proved short-lived. As the deep-seated antimilitary sentiment again manifested itself, the professional army withdrew into an isolationism of its own. Without popular support and denied the manpower and money the NDA of 1920 intended it to have, the interwar army stagnated. The parochialism and interpersonal rivalries that slowed the professionalization process in the "old" army reemerged. Inherently conservative and organized as a hierarchy of obedience, the officer corps reverted to its old institutional patterns. The victory of Pershing and his "Old Guard" allowed the senior officers of the 1920s through their control of the military bureaucracy to shape the character of the army according to their ideals.[2]

In many ways the interwar officer corps more closely resembled a religious order than a professional organization. The creation of a vertical organization in the War Department and General Staff improved upon the prewar system. The bedrock of the professionalization process in the 1920s and 1930s remained the progressive branch, service, and advanced command and staff schools.

Before the neophyte lieutenants and captains could gain admission into the army's school system, the initiates first completed a long catechumenical education. Conditioned by a decade of obedience to their superiors and having proven their dedication in the performance of routine administrative tasks, junior officers learned to repress everything except the traditional and habitual. The junior officers attuned to their profession understood to challenge dogma was to commit professional suicide.[3] Many officers, including some of the most promising, succumbed to "the modern devil of sordid commercialism" and left the service. Lodged in a post-World War I "hump" of officers that composed a third of the officer corps, the majority, as did Bedell Smith, remained in the service with hopes their faith and good works would result in their rise in the army. The young officers fresh from their experiences in the First World War faced a future filled with uncertainty as the U.S. military establishment was redefined once again.

THE NEW MODEL ARMY

The influential nineteenth-century American military critic Emory Upton observed American martial successes "so blinded the popular mind as to induce the belief" the United States was invincible."No error is more common," he warned, "than to mistake military resources for military strength."[4] No war better illustrated the truth of Upton's words than the First World War. Bathed in the afterglow of victory and accustomed to thinking themselves morally superior to Europeans, the American public remained ill-disposed to expand the standing army in peacetime and desired only a return to normalcy and isolationism.[5]

General March continued the tradition of John Calhoun, Upton, and Wood, working to construct a sound military policy.[6] March warned that American free security no longer existed in a world profoundly altered by the First World War. He believed the defense problems posed by an unpredictable future required the maintenance of an efficiently organized military establishment with a standing army of a half-million men as its nucleus. "Undoubtedly the country has incurred much expense," he said, "and has lost many lives on account of the improvisations which were inevitable on account of [the nation's] lack of preparedness for war."[7] March cautioned his civilian superiors unless the United States adopted a military posture consistent with its position in the world, the nation was at serious risk.

Determined to profit from the lessons of the war, March proposed measures to reorganize the defense establishment and define the degree and methods for professional control. Among the issues were the size and function of the regular army, the place of the National Guard, the advisability of a program of universal military training, and the power of the General Staff. To a large degree March succeeded in overhauling the War Department. Institutional resistance, however, made his reorganization during the war incremental and nonprogrammatic. The forces of resistance proved to be powerful and many. Traditional anti-standing army sentiment viewed unpreparedness as a virtue. Associated with this antimilitarism was the popular belief the war had been a victory over Prussianism and the diabolical German General Staff. The National Guard opposed the March Plan and propagated tales of supposed War Department conspiracies to dismantle the organized militia. The army's role in strikebreaking during the "Red Summer" of 1919 produced widespread working-class agitation against the War Department. Congress balked at the expense of maintaining a large army while influential factions assaulted Wilson's internationalism by attacking the army. Finally, the army itself, torn by internecine struggles, was far from unanimous in its support of the reorganization.[8]

Pointing out the prewar army was nothing but a relic of the Indian wars, March maintained the isolated battalion and company garrisons must give way to a system permitting entire divisions to be trained together. Inadequate numbers of trained officers compelled American divisions to go into battle unprepared, suffering heavy casualties. The chief of staff believed only through large-scale consolidated maneuvers, with improved officer education, could commanding, staff, and line officers be trained to conduct the combined arms operations inherent in modern technological war.[9]

The centerpiece of March's plan lay in his advocacy of an expanded and fully empowered general staff. The chief of staff found it ironic the Treaty of Versailles deprived the Germans of their general staff while Congress heaped such restrictions upon the American general staff as to render it superfluous.[10] The chief of staff saw no threat to the nation's security in the existence of a general staff. On the contrary, he believed the war proved that military efficiency existed in direct proportion to the degree of supervision exercised by a general staff. "Anything else," he concluded, "means failure and disaster."[11]

March's aim was to "put into legal form" the 1918 structure. Had the chief of staff been less forthright in his indictment of the military system and more conciliatory in his language and demeanor, he might have garnered congressional support. Secretary Baker, although uncompromising in his support of Pershing's independence during the war, threw himself behind March and his program. These two men knew the deplorable state of affairs that existed in the War Department upon March's assumption of the office of chief of staff. Despite their concerted public relations effort to popularize the program, the forces of retrenchment rapidly gained momentum.[12]

The Baker-March bill, first proposed on January 16, 1919, might have passed had Wilson and Pershing given it their support.[13] Congress became increasingly vitriolic, referring to March as the American Ludendorff and his legislative package as "militarism run mad."[14] Pershing made no effort to bring unity to the officer corps. His AEF staff waged war against the War Department General Staff for control of the postwar army. The AEFHQ G-5 (Training) Section developed a reorganization scheme that included a regular army of 252,400 officers and men, universal military training, the expansion of the General Staff (complete with permanently detailed officers), the abolition of the bureaus and the militia, and the absorption of the Marine Corps into the regular army.[15] Pershing refused to endorse either plan, not wishing to arouse opposition, and instead dispatched one of his top staff officers, Colonel John McAuley Palmer, to Washington.

The son of a Civil War general of volunteers, Palmer emerged as the leading proponent of the traditional American military establishment based upon a small cadre regular army and a citizen army. The professorial Palmer dismissed the Baker-March scheme before the Armed Services Committee, claiming it out of "harmony with the genius of American institutions."[16] Calling upon episodes from history to buttress his argument, Palmer, as one senator later remarked, "in an hour...had torn Peyton C. March's bill into scraps."[17]

Pershing chose to oppose the Baker-March program. He advocated a compromise plan to expand the regular army to 300,000, federalize the National Guard, reconstruct the bureaus, and implement a six-month universal military training period in an organized reserve. The General of the Armies took pains publicly to disassociate himself and his AEFHQ from the War Department General Staff, suggesting he alone was qualified to speak for the entire army.[18]

With the army divided into Pershing and March factions and as staff and line conflicts simmered, the bureau chiefs and supporters of the National Guard stepped up their agitation against the Baker-March bill. Running out of patience, Congress pressed to resolve the impasse. The issue hinged on the interrelationship of the regular army and citizen-soldier components of the defense establishment. The 1916 decision to adopt a "dual oath" to strengthen the National Guard as a viable reserve force was followed, in 1917, by the decision to scrap the volunteer system for conscription. This suggested the Uptonians had finally won the defense debate; but their triumph proved transitory. The evolving wartime reorganizations did not substantially alter the old tripartite structure of the defense establishment, nor did they settle the old problem of command. With the defeat of the March Plan, the resultant National Defense Act of 1920 ushered in a return to the traditional policies.

The NDA of 1920 was Uptonian to the degree it maintained a small nuclear army in peacetime against the possibility of a long war. The act provided for a regular army of 297,000 men in nine divisions backed by eighteen National Guard divisions (430,000 men) and a National Army. The chief component of the National Army was a proposed Officer Reserve Corps of 120,000—enough officers to command the first twenty-seven divisions (546,000 men) to be put into the field within one year of an outbreak of hostilities. The "Army of the United States" would be divided into nine corps areas. Each consisted of one regular, two National Guard, and three National Army divisions.[19]

During the 1919 defense debate, the General Staff increasingly came to be viewed negatively by the anti-War Department partisans. The war demonstrated the necessity for a general staff, yet the institution, so tainted with Prussianism in the popular mind, found few supporters. The NDA of 1920 granted the General Staff statutory expression but assigned it the narrowest military aspects of mobilization and planning. Congress not only limited the size of the General Staff to ninety-three officers, it also created a watchdog agency, the War Council, to oversee its activities.[20]

The NDA of 1920 represented the first serious attempt by Congress to formulate a modern American military structure. The act provided a framework to repeat, albeit more effectively and quickly, the mobilization of a mass army. Policymakers did not question if a 1918 type army would be relevant in a postwar period marked by international instability, nor did they consider the airplane, tank, submarine, telephonic and radio communications, or motorized field transport and the revolution in warfare these innovations foreshadowed. The legislation blithely presupposed the United States would not be an aggressor or be exposed to invasion by a hostile mass army. The act further presumed the nation enjoyed the luxury of time to complete its preparation for war before it would throw its vast material power into any war effort. The lines of the prewar command remained confused as three separate and distinct structures existed—the president with the secretary of war; the chief of staff with the bureau chiefs in the War Department; and the chief of staff with the commanders of the line.

The defeat of the War Department reorganization plan and Warren Harding's election transformed March into a lame-duck chief of staff. Pershing had the satisfaction of replacing March as chief of staff in 1921. There were those who believed—Pershing first among them—the office of chief of staff was beneath the dignity of the general of the army, and in an unprecedented step Congress resurrected the defunct office of Commanding General.[21] The general's supporters hoped the prestige and influence of Pershing would overcome the endemic feuding between staff and line, War Department and the AEF, and the bureaus and the General Staff.

Purging March's men from the War Department, Pershing ordered the War Department General Staff reorganized on the model of his headquarters at Chaumont. This model included five divisions: Personnel, Intelligence, Operations and Training, Supply, and the newly created War Plans divisions. In Pershing's view, the chief of staff possessed no command function. The duties of the chief of staff, defined by Pershing and outlined in the *Army Regulations* of 1921, were limited to advising the secretary of war and coordinating the "planning, development, and execution of the military program" by the WDGS. In addition, the War Plans Division was expected to furnish staff personnel for a commanding general-designate in the field during war. Pershing's reorganization of the command and staff structure perpetuated the system of dual control and the separation of command and staff functions that marked the higher direction of the American war effort.[22]

Sensing a growing mood of national conservativism, Pershing halted the reform movement. For the sake of internal peace and to protect the army from any further damaging public scrutiny, the War Department lapsed into the safe routine of bureaucracy and institutional inertia. As commanding general, Pershing maintained a private headquarters to which he entrusted many of the responsibilities normally the preserve of the General Staff. Isolated as a narrow planning agency, the General Staff once again suffered an eclipse at the hands of the resurgent bureaus.[23]

Under Pershing, the military establishment withdrew into the comfortable ways of the "Old Army." The chief of staff existed in name more than function, and the powers exercised by the General Staff declined in the face of the rejuvenated bureaus. The National Defense Act of 1920 and Pershing's 1921 *Regulations* established the mold of the military establishment for the next two decades. Except for the clarification of the responsibilities of the staff divisions, the existence of a General Staff for planning, and a more authoritative commanding general, the army of the interwar years willingly retreated into the self-conscious isolation of the pre-Root era. As Baker and March feared, the army failed to profit from the lessons of the world war.[24]

SERVICE IN THE PEACETIME ARMY

For Bedell Smith, the most important aspects of the 1920 act were the provisions for the expansion of the postwar officer corps. The nineteenth-century pattern of wars brought large numbers of citizens into the army. While the majority of these amateur soldiers left the army after each war, the regulars were maintained in strength larger than before the war. The First World War mirrored this experience. The National Defense Act of 1920 approximately doubled the size of the regular army while the authorized paper strength of the postwar officer corps was roughly three times that of April 1917. Under the terms of the act, 5,229 officers holding wartime temporary commissions were brought into the postwar establishment, a figure nearly equal to the strength of the prewar officer corps.[25] Having already earned a solid reputation as a staff officer, Smith was among those selected to be commissioned in this large infusion of civilians, reservists, and prior-enlisted men into the regular army. Unlike the majority of his peers, Smith kept his first lieutenancy.

March argued during the 1919 defense debate that if the nation relied on trained civilians and not on the regular army, unless expanded, the officer corps would be overwhelmed with the responsibilities of administering and training the citizen components of the defense establishment. This would, in his opinion, severely retard the professional development of the army.[26] Ignoring the warnings of the chief of staff, Congress ensured that the undermanned postwar officer corps would perform a broad array of noninstrumental functions. The growing antimilitary mood of the public and Congress's commitment to retrenchment and financial stringency led it regularly to reduce army estimates and in 1922 cut the number of officers.[27] With better than 70 percent of the regular army stationed in overseas garrisons, policing the Mexican border, or detailed to educational and training assignments, the size of the regular divisions scattered throughout the three hundred posts and stations in the continental United States dwindled to brigade strength. Realistic training proved impossible under these conditions, and, just as March predicted, the professional development of the officer corps stagnated.

With the limited number of command positions dominated by the First World War generation of field-grade officers, junior officers learned their craft in long periods of duty at isolated and uncomfortable garrison posts. Smith served in the adjutant section of the staff at Camp Sherman for two years. In November 1921, the 2d Regiment staff was consolidated at Fort Sheridan. A permanent installation established in 1872 on the shores of Lake Michigan, Fort Sheridan deserved its reputation as being among the most desirable posts in the army. Housed in well-built brick quarters only twenty-five miles from Chicago, Sheridan represented an improvement over Camp Sherman. Adjacent to the lake and within easy driving distance of the trout streams and woods of Wisconsin, Smith had plenty of opportunity to indulge his passion for the outdoors.[28]

Immersed in the drudgery of routine paperwork, his duties, never intellectually taxing, usually could be completed by noon. Most officers spent their free time improving their golf or tennis games or socializing in the officers' club. Aware of the limitations imposed upon him by his lack of formal education, Bedell embarked upon an ambitious program of self-education. With eclectic interests, Smith devoured everything from pulp detective novels to Joseph Conrad and Ford Maddox Ford. He reserved the majority of his reading time for military subjects ranging from army training and weapons manuals to the classics of military history and thought.[29] It was no accident some of the officers who spent their off-duty hours in careful study and reflection, forsaking the convivial social circle and the fashionable antiintellectualism of the period, rose to occupy positions of responsibility during the next war. While always in a distinct minority, Smith was such an officer.

Officers nurtured in this period, despite the wide range of social backgrounds and career patterns, could not escape the formative impact of that unique, strangely atavistic institution, the U.S. Army. As the institutions and relations of command reverted to their nineteenth-century form, so too did the collective *menalité* of the officer corps. In an antimilitary society with an ensconced set of attitudes anathematic to those held by the officer corps, professional officers withdrew into a self-conscious isolation from the rest of American society. With almost no influence in government or even upon the formulation of the broad aspects of military policy, the interwar army, like the army of the nineteenth-century, led an impotent, isolated life, divorced from politics and the society it served. In the American service, the interwar officer corps developed a self-image as a specialized elite, seeing themselves as devoted to the nation and above partisan politics, enjoying a code of ethics and sense of duty superior to the rest of society.[30]

The officers' sense of alienation was heightened by the institutions of the military itself. The division of the officer corps into technical and combat branches created officers of specialized expertise but undermined professionalization by constructing walls between the segments of the officer corps. If hostility existed between the specialist corps and the combat branches, relations between staff and line and between March and Pershing factions frequently bordered on belligerency. Line officers held chairborne officers in contempt as the *beau sabreur* remained the ideal.

Forced outside the state's power structure yet jealous of the political power they could not possess, the interwar officers contented themselves with the affectations of the military tradition. European manners and uniforms were adopted. Fighting spirit and traditional military qualities were valued over intellectual standards and managerial skills. Arising out of the nineteenth-century heritage of formal "old fashioned" styles and pretensions of an aristocratic lifestyle, the officers' milieu was characterized by a ceremonialism already *passé* in society at large.[31]

The glacial pace of promotions and the officer's lack of status led them to be inordinately conscious of rank and status. Officers rigidly enforced their ascriptive authority over the enlisted personnel. Fixed in language, ritual, and social intercourse, the distance between officers and enlisted men was self-sustaining. The noncommissioned officer, who enjoyed a certain degree of autonomy and considerable prestige in European armies, held a status scarcely better than the enlisted ranks.[32]

While the attitudes and institutions of the interwar army contained many centrifugal elements, the one sentiment shared by all officers was the desire for a system that guaranteed more-rapid promotion. As one critic of the interwar army noted, to reach the top, one need only avoid "syphilis, reckless taxi drivers" and refrain from "murder, rape, and peculation."[33] He overlooked the most crucial ingredient, patience. To accelerate promotions, end branch preferences, and remove incompetent officers, the 1920 act introduced two basic alterations to the 1890 guidelines. Previously, officers below the rank of major wrote qualification examinations. The postwar act established a single armywide promotion list and a system of classification. Although seniority still prevailed through the rank of colonel, promotion for the first time in American military history became tied to professional performance, not branch and political favoritism. Each year superior officers evaluated subordinates, placing them in Class A or Class B. Officers placed in the latter group lost their commissions, subject to appeal to the president. The liberality of senior officer assessments and the lengthy appeal process produced only 350 dismissals in the seventeen years following the inauguration of the program. While the system contained many flaws, it did provide a mechanism whereby promising men enjoyed improved prospects for promotion based upon professional criteria.[34]

Disillusioned by poor promotion prospects, low pay, and unattractive assignments, many officers resigned their commissions in the early and mid-1920s. The majority came from the company-grade ranks, especially those who had held wartime temporary commissions. Major budgetary cuts and the unwillingness of Congress to support the army compelled the War Department, in 1922, to cut many junior officers from the rolls while others suffered reduction in rank.[35] Unlike many other first lieutenants, West Pointers with outstanding war records among them, Smith was unaffected by the 1922 cutbacks. Now safely standing on the forward side of the large World War I "hump," Smith could look forward to steady, if excruciatingly slow, advancement.[36]

On October 16, 1922, Smith reported for duty to the VI Corps headquarters in Chicago. He soon was assigned as aide-de-camp to Brigadier General George Van Horn Moseley, commander of the 12th Infantry Brigade, headquartered at

Fort Sheridan. Aside from commanding the brigade, Moseley and his staff orchestrated and officiated at the biennial field maneuvers held in rural western Michigan. As regimental adjutant and then as member of Moseley's staff, Smith spent time in detached service at Camp Custer, Michigan. Located six miles from Battle Creek and still very much a temporary post in terms of officers' quarters and amenities, Custer served as staging area for the field exercises.

Among the rising stars of the army in the 1920s and early 1930s, Moseley, who had served as Pershing's G-4 (Supply) section chief at Chaumont, was an officer both well connected and highly regarded. Smith admired Moseley, a man referred to as possessing "the most brilliant mind in the army."[37] As deputy chief of staff in 1932, Moseley played a major role in the suppression of the Bonus March and might have moved to the top position in the army had it not been for his embrace of fascism during the New Deal period.[38] The military had long eschewed political involvement, in return it was allowed to regulate itself internally and define its code of ethics. Moseley broke this contract and resigned.

To what degree Moseley influenced Smith is difficult to discern. During his military career Smith never voted, but like most of his fellow officers he was politically conservative. In his decrying of congressional parsimony and the policy of disarmament, he mirrored the values and outlooks of the entire officer corps, not just those of General Moseley.[39] In any case, Moseley thought highly of his aide and made him head of the 12th Brigade's adjutant section, a position of considerable responsibility for an officer of Smith's rank.

Except those few weeks at Custer, Smith's two-and-a-half years on Moseley's staff were passed happily at Fort Sheridan. Having spent the first four and three-quarter years of his career as a regular officer in the VI Corps district, Smith received his first assignment outside his native midwest. Detailed to Washington, Smith reported for duty, on April 16, 1925, to the Bureau of the Budget.

In 1921, the Budget and Accounting Act created the Bureau of the Budget, a central clearinghouse through which all executive budget requests, including the War Department's, were funnelled. By law, the War Department appointed its own budget staff. Under its direction the army's appropriations and supplemental estimates were prepared and forwarded to the Bureau of the Budget. Assigned as assistant to the chief coordinator of the War Department's budget staff, Smith's duties involved helping in the preparation of the annual budget and serving as liaison between the War Department and the Bureau of the Budget.

The federal government hoped to maintain a detailed accounting of every appropriation, giving Congress maximum authority over the fiscal process.

Emphasizing this control function, expenditures approved by Congress could not be changed without authorization. Much of the work was routine, seeking to balance the needs of the army with the appropriations granted by the legislative branch. The strict line-item accounting approach left military administrators with no discretion or flexibility in the management of allocated resources. Congress appropriated a fixed sum of money for a particular program or piece of equipment, and even if conditions changed, the entire sum had to be spent. If the army failed to spend all of its appropriations, the War Department could expect to be penalized by a budget reduction in the next fiscal period. The line-item method allowed for exact cost accounting, but it contained no mechanism to evaluate the efficiency of government spending.[40]

Smith spent four years attached to the Bureau of the Budget. He gained valuable experience in high-level military administration and was introduced to the folkways of official Washington. Smith familiarized himself with the workings of the major civilian agencies. In his liaison capacity he dealt with senior politicians and public administrators. Given the army's political position on Capitol Hill in this period of fiscal retrenchment, Smith had to develop the skills of subtle diplomacy.[41]

Smith's tenure in Washington provided him with essential career experience. The changing requirements of modern military establishments produced a managerial revolution—a gradual shift in the officer's role from "heroic fighter" to technical or administrative expert, which in turn narrowed skill differentials between military and civilian elites.[42] Conditioned by the detailed business of preparing the line-item budgets, Smith became accustomed to thinking in orderly and concrete terms. Loyal to the army and committed to rational planning, Smith developed habits of mind common to any manager of a civilian organization or business enterprise—the search for more-efficient means to control an unpredictable external environment. Better preparation for the military manager could scarcely be imagined.

The War Department next detailed Smith for duty in the Philippine Islands. With his service in Washington behind him and already having carved out a solid reputation as a staff officer, Smith hoped for troop duty. Command duty, exceedingly difficult to secure in the corps districts, might more easily be obtained in overseas stations. Of all the army garrisons outside the continental United States—Alaska, the Canal Zone, Puerto Rico, Hawaii, China, and the Philippines—the latter was the most sought after.[43] In the Philippines officers affected the aristocratic lifestyles even on the salaries of lieutenants. Only a quarter of those who requested the posting received the assignment. While Smith could be pleased with his posting, he was less enthused with being forwarded to the staff of the 45th Infantry, stationed at Fort William McKinley.

Located six miles from Manila, Fort McKinley, a permanent post built in 1902-1904, served as the primary infantry garrison in the Philippines. As headquarters of the Philippine Division, McKinley housed an infantry brigade. The 45th, a Philippine Scout regiment, composed a part of that brigade. These units were maintained at near full strength, creating a critical shortage of officers.[44] Although serving as regimental adjutant, Smith periodically filled company-level vacancies on an interim basis, gaining command time. From a strictly professional standpoint, having served as an adjutant for a brigade five years earlier, Smith's appointment to the staff of a regiment represented a step backward. His disappointment was blunted by a promotion. After better than nine years as a lieutenant, his promotion to captain came through in September 1929.

The interwar army placed a high premium upon social contact, particularly in overseas outposts like Fort McKinley. Although the cavalry was then in its twilight, the horse dominated not only the sporting scene but social life as well. The Philippines Division boasted eight polo teams, two at McKinley.[45] Never much of a social creature and totally dedicated to his branch, Smith detested the horse and tried to distance himself from the circle of the horse culture. Drawing his friends from those officers who shared his outdoor interests, Smith spent his free time constructing fishing equipment from native bamboo, practising marksmanship, hunting, fishing, and indulging in his childhood passion for collecting, this time Moro arrows and bolos.[46]

On American posts, where work and residence frequently coincided, the officer's wife played an indispensable social role. Books were published, and often updated, as manuals of army etiquette for prospective army wives. In the scheme of things the possession of a good "army wife" was a professional prerequisite, and in Nory Smith, Bedell suffered no disadvantage. She was described as "tall and tweedy" and "a looker." Mrs. Smith, the product of an Indianapolis finishing school, was perfectly at home with the patrician pretensions of interwar army society, helping to compensate for her husband's social awkwardness.[47]

His two-year stint in the Philippines brought to a close the first phase of Smith's professional development. If a professional can be defined by his sense of collegial corporateness, acquired proficiency, and responsibility to the society he serves, then Captain Bedell Smith already deserved that appellation.[48] While the self-image of the officer corps remained essentially that of the nineteenth-century army and the conservativism of the senior officers deterred wholesale institutional change, officership in the interwar years became distinguished less by class and religious affiliation than by professional performance. Smith's lack of membership in the West Point band of brothers, an exclusive club in the officer corps of the 1920s dominated by the World War I "hump," did not materially affect his advancement.[49] Although his failure to secure a command assignment injured his immediate prospects in an officer corps top-heavy with administrative positions, Smith's diligence and skill as a staff officer did not go unnoted. One of his fellow officers at Fort McKinley considered Smith "the best regimental adjutant in the army."[50] Thirty-three years old, he was young for his rank and placed well ahead of the "hump." In an army that believed in the positive virtues of learning by doing, Smith acquired a high level of specialization. His practical education now complete, Smith's formal education was about to begin.

4

"Aides, Adjutants, and Asses": The Advanced Army Schools, 1930–1937

The period 1920-1940 is sometimes nostalgically seen as the "golden age" of American military professionalism. According to this view, World War I represented the watershed between the old army, with its idleness and dissipation bred by the post psychology of the Indian-fighting days, its heroic self-image and gifted amateur ethic, and its opposition to bureaucratic order, and the army of World War II, whose officers, nurtured in the interwar years, closely approximated the professional ideal. While there can be little doubt the process of professionalization had been accelerated by American participation in the First World War, the break with the past can easily be exaggerated.

Many senior American officers knew the line between the successful prosecution of the First World War and the breakdown of the military structure proved exceedingly thin. Inasmuch as the army succeeded, it did so owing to the presence of exceptional men like March and Pershing and a coterie of young Leavenworth-trained officers whose availability in the crisis lay more in the realm of accidental occurrence than systematic preparation. Determined the army would never again suffer from the lack of trained troop leaders and staff officers, March and Pershing sought to integrate an improved system of military education into the mainstream of the professionalization process.

Subsumed within a generally hostile external environment, popular demands for normalcy, disarmament, and isolationism prompted a return to the traditional nonprogrammatic approach to military affairs. The army's stagnation may be attributed to three essential factors. First, the War Department lacked affirmative policies that commanded public interest. Second, an indifferent Congress deprived the military establishment of funds. Last, the army was headed by senior officers whose group identity and normative standards, the products of pre-1917 and wartime experience, ill-disposed them to the altered military values of the postwar period of transition. The military educational system carried the torch of professionalism in the interwar years. In the opinion of many senior officers of the Second World War, the schools saved the army.[1] However, two fundamental questions remained: First, to what degree did the army's Advanced Schools—particularly the Command and General Staff School—further the professionalization process in the interwar years? Second, how did the system of education condition the thinking of the generation of officers who would command the U.S. Army in the Second World War?

THE INFANTRY SCHOOL

Returning to the United States in March 1931, Captain Smith reported to the Infantry School at Fort Benning, Georgia. Founded in 1918 as an amalgamation of the Small Arms, Machine Gun, and the old Fort Sill Infantry School, the Benning Infantry School served as a model post for the army. The largest of the twelve branch and special service schools and one of the few posts with a regiment maintained at "war strength," Fort Benning boasted a garrison of nearly 6,000 troops. Officers returning from overseas stations received special considerations, and Smith was assigned to the Advanced Officers' Course, bypassing the Company Officers' Course.[2]

Its short-lived participation as a mass army in the World War could not make over the U.S. army. The war demonstrated the inadequacies of the prewar educational system. As Upton had warned, the United States traditionally "prosecuted [its] wars with raw troops whose officers have had to be educated in the expensive school of war."[3] This remained the case in France in 1918. The organizational differentiation and subdivisions of the mass army required officers be expert in a broad array of specialized functions and be able to plan, coordinate, and supervise the highly complex operational and logistical business of modern warfare. The countless tactical failures and complications attending the coordination of the St.-Mihiel and Meuse-Argonne offensives pointed to the imperative need for a systematic program of officer education.[4]

Attempts to create a military education system in the post-Civil War period met with limited success.[5] Faced with a unique set of national characteristics and cultural values inimical to the requirements of the professional military and systematization in general, the internalized values, outlooks, and behavior of the officer corps reflected those of the parent society. Hostile to theoretical generalization and teleological definitions of purpose, viewing cosmopolitanism and erudition as contrary to the spirit of egalitarianism, the historic American mind confuses thought and action. Accustomed to thinking experience and action form individual character, the empiricist tradition held American genius rested upon the intuitive ability to overcome any obstacle by common sense and pragmatic problem-solving.[6]

In a sense the army came to represent a monument to the persistence of this consensual American empiricist attitude. Rejecting abstract theory, ideal standards of performance, and systematic formulations of action, the empiricist tradition encouraged a practical approach to military affairs. American military professionalism before the First World War was equated with the purposeful task performance of individuals. For the bulk of the officer corps, the notion of a highly organized and progressively educated set of officers seemed foreign to American methods, as European pretentiousness. For most, the ideal remained the inspired amateur, an officer of few specialties who learned his craft not through books and scientific speculations but in the only true school for a soldier, the school of learning by doing. In such an environment efforts to create a system of theoretically based training to augment skill-oriented experience made little headway.[7]

During the war several senior American officers recognized that the introduction of modern weaponry, improved communications and transport, and the extraordinary growth of the logistical functions demanded intensive professional training for all officers. In addition to the schools of instruction established by Pershing in France, March reorganized the Infantry School in 1918 followed the next year by the Signal School and the year after by the Chemical, Tank, Medical Field Service, Quartermaster, Army Finance, and Chaplain schools. With the existing Artillery, Engineer, and General Ground schools, these constituted the first level of the refurbished school system.[8]

As the system was envisioned in the National Defense Act of 1920, West Point and the nation's colleges and universities represented the basic undergraduate institutions for the army and the reserve officer corps. West Point graduates proceeded directly to their branch or service school to learn standardized troop-leading and tactical and training techniques before reporting for duty with their companies. After serving time at the company level, regular army officers returned to their branch schools to attend an Advanced Course where they studied command and staff techniques for the regiment and brigade. Having completed extended service in both command and staff assignments, those officers—senior captains and majors—who demonstrated superior capacity moved on to the Army School of the Line and General Staff School at Fort Leavenworth to prepare for service at the divisional and corps level. Those deemed qualified to discharge future command and high staff functions were selected for the Advanced Course. At the highest rung of the sequential system of education stood the War College in Washington where the cream of the officer corps spent a year dealing with strategic matters.[9]

On paper the plan seemed like a triumph for the Uptonians since it provided rotation between staff and line, promotion by merit, and a progressive program of officer education closely connected with the General Staff and the hierarchy of command. In practice, as Smith's career in the 1920s illustrated, the system was debilitated by the conditions imposed upon the army by external factors and the 1920 act. The peacetime establishment relied on the civilian components of an expansible army. As such, the army's primary concern was managerial. The sheer size and relative youth of the postwar hump and the persistent belief education was wasted on junior lieutenants ensured those who held temporary commissions during the war would not progress into the educational system until their attitudes had been forged by more than a decade of service, chiefly in administrative and training assignments. Consistent with the empiricist tradition, officers like Smith acquired their professional skills through experience without the benefit of formal education.[10]

With little inclination or incentive to pursue private study of military theory, many West Pointers boasted of never having cracked a book after leaving the Military Academy.[11] The lack of command positions at the company level precluded wholesale staff and line rotation. Officers holding lengthy nonline postings lost touch with the troops and developments within their individual branches. The inexacting judgment of officer fitness reports guaranteed preferments would be based not on merit but upon seniority. In 1927, for example, of the 3,599 officers classified, none were classed "inferior," only 47 received a "below average" rating, with the remainder placed in a category that would warrant consideration for promotion and attendance at one of the branch or service schools.[12] With no entrance examination, selection at each level of the educational ladder depended upon longevity in service, the patronage of senior officers, social connections, and efficiency ratings of at least "average." Rather than serving to educate exceptional officers, the system came to represent a routine stop on the officers' career path.[13]

Among the chief priorities of the branch schools was the indoctrination of officers into the prescribed methodologies of their individual arms. Each of the traditional combat arms—infantry, cavalry, and artillery—developed its own doctrine. The aim of doctrine is to inculcate, through education and experience, a uniform set of procedures to enable collective and coordinated task performance on the battlefield. It requires the systematic introduction of rational criteria and encourages behavior and structure aimed at reducing the fog and frictions of battle.[14] Pre-World War I field manuals, extravagantly borrowed from European precepts, existed, but no formal American doctrine emerged until after 1918.[15] Seeking to understand the revealed truths of experience in the world war, Pershing appointed two separate AEF officer boards in April

1919.[16] Their findings established the doctrines of tactics and training for the interwar army.

Bearing striking similarities to the 1914 French doctrine of the *offensive à outrance*, the conclusions of the AEF Lewis Board held "decisive results can only be accomplished by the offensive. The requisite chiefly essential to success is the possession of an infantry embedded with the desire to close with the enemy."[17] In 1922, the War Department issued the first formal doctrinal statement in American military history. Reflecting the findings of the AEF Boards, this document viewed battle as a moral contest in which the will to combat transcended firepower and technique in importance. Training remained based upon experience derived from the static warfare of World War I. Stressing the advantages of the bayonet—a highly questionable conclusion as only a fraction of 1 percent of all casualties on the Western Front were inflicted by edged weapons—the doctrine discounted the need for manuever, fire superiority, and the employment of supporting arms. With faith firmly affixed in the offensive spirit, the infantry gained acceptance as "the queen of the battlefield," the main fighting arm.[18]

To preserve its independence as the dominant arm, the infantry branch developed a doctrine in the 1920s emphasizing a rigid and mechanistic tactical approach. Although faith in open warfare persisted, at no time during the First World War did the U.S. Army wage such a campaign.[19] Had the army critically analyzed the practical experience of the AEF in France, it would have discovered the absence of effective cooperation between the infantry and its supporting arms. Extolling the virtues of ground troops in the attack, the infantry discounted the roles of the supporting arms and services, especially armor, aircraft, and logistics.

Upon the advice of the AEF boards and following his own predilections, Pershing protected the vested interests of the infantry and cavalry by dismantling the Tank Corps, making armor an adjunct to the infantry.[20] A tank battalion was attached to the Infantry School; but contact with armor was limited to watching carefully rehearsed, static demonstrations by obsolete tanks. The infantry hierarchy remained unconvinced of the battlefield utility of the tank in anything other than an ancillary tactical role. The efforts of the Air Corps to sever itself from the army bred something approaching a blanket rejection of the claims of air-power advocates.[21] Although only one hundred miles from one of the Air Corps' major installations at Maxwell Field, Alabama, an officer could complete his nine-month tour at Benning never having seen a combat aircraft. Even in the classroom little attempt was made to integrate armor and air into infantry problems.[22] At Benning, the cult of the bayonet remained in place. Rather than forge innovative approaches to the problems posed by the new technology and its impact upon infantry tactics, the techniques and practices that evolved at Benning, in the opinion of George Marshall, "would practically halt the development of an open warfare situation."[23]

Despite having no command experience in thirteen years, Smith entered the Advanced Course at Benning fully imbued with the infantry viewpoint. Reflecting the general complacency of the army and the infantry's emphasis upon the development of an open-warfare doctrine, the Benning curriculum was neither innovative nor academically rigorous. About 30 percent of the work consisted of classroom lectures and map problems; the remainder of the time was spent outdoors at the outer ranges and maneuver areas dotting the 97,000-acre reserve. In the overcrowded and poorly ventilated assembly halls, officer-students heard canned lectures cleared in advance by the editorial section to guarantee conformity with the fixed doctrine. Barracks-room discipline was maintained; conversations were prohibited as students could not question the official solutions. The aim of the course was to provide officers with guidance and experience in decision-making skills, troop leading, and uniformity in order writing. Few of the students possessed line experience, so much of the time was given over to remedial work at the platoon and company level instead of developing command and staff techniques for the regiment and brigade.[24]

In an army that remained essentially a border constabulary, the branch and service schools discharged a therapeutic function in addition to a pedagogic one. At Benning, despite being at the height of the depression, officers still lived according to the old aristocratic ethic. Known for its elaborate pageants and military parades, Benning offered a welcome relief from the drudgery of life in remote posts. Equitation continued as a required part of the curriculum, and in addition to polo, twice a week from October to April officers rode to the hounds in formal fox hunts winning for Benning the reputation as "the horsiest post" in the army. During Smith's tenure officers' wives were expected to ride, and Nory Smith developed into a good horsewomen. Not even Bedell could escape the horse culture as he enroled in a horseshoing course while at Benning, something he found amusing later in his career.[25]

The Smiths lived comfortably in a rented house, perched atop a bluff overlooking the Chattahoochie River, in nearby Columbus. In 1931, Smith's widowed mother came to live with them. With plenty of free time, Bedell took advantage of the excellent hunting afforded by the thousands of acres of yellow pine that dominated the Benning reserve. While at the Infantry School, he purchased and trained a purebred English setter; and together they ranged across the rolling terrain hunting the quail and pheasant that abounded in southwestern Georgia and neighboring Alabama.[26] At the citadel of the infantry, Bedell was not alone in his loathing of the horse. The director of the Weapons Section,

Major Omar Bradley, organized a trapshooting range for those officers who preferred to hunt on foot. Having an active interest in firearms since boyhood, Smith regularly participated in shooting competitions as he and Bradley became friends.[27]

Bradley remembered Smith as being "a bit of a Prussian," outwardly cold and retiring, with a penchant for speaking his mind. Once he broke through Smith's icy exterior, Bradley found him to be a modest and retiring man with a humorous and kind disposition. In professional terms Bradley became impressed with Smith's thorough knowledge of infantry small arms and found him in possession of an "absolutely brilliant and analytical mind."[28] As frequently the case in the interwar army, Smith's skill with the shotgun and his friendship with Bradley proved more helpful for career advancement than his performance in the classroom.[29] Near the end of the course Bradley recommended Smith for retention as an instructor.

Luck and personal connections play as important a role in an officer's rise as performance. Bradley's request for Smith's retention coincided with a chance classroom visit by George Marshall, in his final year as director of the Academic Department. Smith happened to be giving a presentation on World War I infantry battalion tactics. Impressed by the content of the material and Smith's skill in presenting it, Marshall returned to his office and remarked to Bradley "there is a man who would make a wonderful instructor." Bradley could only smile because he knew his request for Smith already lay on the director's desk.[30] Several years later, Bradley remembered Smith when a vacancy opened in the secretariat of the War Department General Staff. Reminding Marshall, now chief of staff, of the incident, Bradley suggested that Smith would be the ideal man to fill the position. This appointment proved to be the springboard for Smith's rapid rise in the Second World War.

Having graduated on June 1, 1932, Smith remained at Benning where he joined the Academic Department as an instructor in the Weapons Section. The term opened with a meeting of the section chiefs and their staffs to review the goals for the upcoming year. For the Weapons Section, the big event of the year involved a four-hour demonstration of the weapons of the infantry for incoming staff and students. For many of the men it represented their first exposure to weapons like the Browning automatic rifle, mortars, and the 37mm field gun. Smith's assigned specialty being the machine gun, he was charged with giving that demonstration.

The curriculum varied little from year to year and the work load in the Weapons Section proved undemanding, so Smith had plenty of time to devote to professional development. He read extensively and published his first two articles, "Operations of the 1st Battalion, 39th Infantry (4th Division) in the

Aisne-Marne Offensive, July 18-20, 1918"[31] and "The caliber 0.22 machine-gun,"[32] both appearing in *The Mailing List*, an Infantry School publication that enjoyed armywide circulation.

Smith completed his duties as instructor in May 1933. He then joined the Academic Department Staff as secretary to the assistant commandant, Marshall's replacement, Colonel C. W. Weeks. Eager to further his career, Smith requested transfer to the Command and General Staff School at Fort Leavenworth, Kansas. Enjoying the patronage of Weeks and with priority given to instructors from the branch schools, Smith's application gained ready approval.[33] With a solid reputation carved out for himself at Fort Benning, Smith considered himself an officer on the rise.

THE COMMAND AND GENERAL STAFF SCHOOL

During the first week of September 1933 Smith, with the other 120 members of the 1934-1935 class, assembled at Fort Leavenworth to begin the First Year Course at the Command and General Staff School. Except for the war years of 1898-1901 and 1917-1919, an advanced school had existed at Leavenworth for slightly over half a century. In 1881, without congressional sanction or the concurrence of the bureau chiefs, Commanding General William Sherman mandated the creation of the School of Application for Infantry and Cavalry at Fort Leavenworth. Sherman desired a school to teach the Civil War "hump" not only tactics but basic reading, writing, and arithmetic skills that many officers lacked. Since commanding officers remained unconvinced of the need for anything as nebulous as education, they forwarded the officers of the worst sort to Leavenworth, and the schools soon became widely known as the "kindergarten." Five years after their founding, the Leavenworth schools experienced the first in a long series of reorganizations. "It is the fault of a grossly deficient system of officering the army," wrote Arthur Wagner, the man charged with the task of reorganization, "that it should be necessary to teach arithmetic and 'correct reading aloud' to officers who are employed in a profession which is daily becoming more scientific."[34] Appreciating the fact that European superiority in technique could only be approximated by borrowing from it, under the influence of Wagner, the latter 1880s and the 1890s witnessed improvements at Leavenworth. The grammar school curriculum, narrow drill evolutions, and recitations on company-level duties gave way to a replica of the German *Kriegsakademie*'s applicatory method of instruction based upon map problems, war games, and tactical rides.

The Spanish-American War and the Philippines Insurrection caused a four-year cessation in the activities of the Leavenworth schools and created another "hump" of amateur officers. Compelled to educate this group of officers, which composed 91 percent of the postwar officer corps, Leavenworth, of necessity, became a remedial school, effectively undoing the work of Wagner in the decade before the war. The Root reforms required the renamed General Service and Staff School to train junior officers in troop leadership and staff functions. An incongruity existed in Leavenworth's mandate. The schools processed large numbers of officers, few of whom had any formal military training, through a single-year course. Yet the school's leadership was charged with creating a staff college worthy of the name. Torn between two poles, Leavenworth again emphasized company-level organization and tactics at the expense of staff procedures.

In the decade between the Root reforms and the beginning of the war in Europe, the Leavenworth program gradually cast off its remedial curriculum and, led by Major John Morrison, was again modeled on the German system. In 1907, an officer accurately stated with pride, "our *Field Service Regulations* unmistakeably show the impress of German thought. Von Moltke teaches us our strategy, Griepenkerl writes our orders, while von der Goltz tells us how they should be executed."[35] Truncated and misapplied though it may have been, the imported German system brought method where previously none existed and advanced measurably the level of American military professionalism.[36]

The familiar cycle repeated itself after the American entry into the world war and in the immediate postwar period. The war forced the suspension of the school's activities from 1917 to 1919 and produced yet another hump of experienced but uneducated officers. Unlike the Spanish American War, the world war carved out for Leavenworth a central position in the army's structure.[37] With the support of both March and Pershing, Leavenworth emerged from the war as the focal point of the army's educational system and the font of the developing doctrine.

In September 1919 March ordered the reopening and reorganization of the Leavenworth school.[38] Placing the schools directly under the chief of staff, March mandated a return to the prewar two-year program. The first year required the study of tactics and organization of the army through the division; the second year involved training in command and staff duties at corps and army level.[39] The wartime chief of staff believed the newly organized and soon-to-be-expanded system of branch and service schools would suffice to train junior officers. Leavenworth and the War College constituted graduate schools devoted to the development of commanders and staff officers. He sought to ensure the army schools would not deteriorate as they had after the Spanish-American War.

By 1923, budget cuts, the size of the officer hump, and the need to supervise the indoctrination of National Guard and Reserve officers by

Leavenworth-oriented correspondence courses resulted in the suspension of the staff portion of the curriculum and the discontinuance of the second year of instruction.[40] Mirroring the resurgent conservativism of the War Department under Pershing, Leavenworth emerged as something of a military monastery after its reorganization. Standing on a picturesque bluff overlooking the Missouri River, Leavenworth seemed untroubled by the looming revolution in arms transforming the military profession.

Leavenworth's essential task involved the dissemination of the mandated doctrine. For those charged with student development, the perceived doctrinal lessons of the world war confirmed the attachment to the offensive.[41] The authors of American military doctrine ignored the carnage wrought on the Western Front by blind adherence to the prewar tactical principles. William Naylor, senior Leavenworth instructor and influential military theorist of the interwar period, maintained that the correct application of firepower and the frontal infantry assault could breach any defense.[42] The authors of the doctrine demonstrated little interest in critically studying the operations of the U.S. Army in the First World War. Abhorring the stabilizing warfare of the trenches, American theorists scorned the paramount lessons of the war. They placed their faith in offensive action, rigid adherence to the operational doctrine, and the will to victory. In phrases best described as Fochian, postwar statements of doctrine contained in the *Field Service Regulations* and in articles in the official journals maintained victory could only be obtained through resolute, direct action. The only end in war being the total destruction of the enemy, all other actions "are means for accomplishing [the] ultimate object."[43] Once the inevitable infantry breakout occurred, either by envelopment (the preferred means) or penetration, it fell to the horse cavalry to pursue the beaten foe.[44]

The U.S. Army lacked any real operational analysis mechanism to systematically distil a method of learning by experience. It composed doctrine expecting it could rely upon the enormous manpower and matériel resources of the nation to crush any adversary. The problem revolved around the best means of employing the overwhelming warmaking potential of the United States. Viewing the AEF as the model military instrument, the authors of American doctrine derived their underpinning ideology not from Karl von Clausewitz but rather Frederick Winslow Taylor.[45] Striving to fashion doctrine along rational business lines suggested by the simplistic syllogisms of scientific management, American military theorists concluded the secret to military success lay in the efficient accumulation and direct application of superior power to achieve decision. Little appreciation for the subtleties of maneuver or the need for concentration of forces to achieve strategic advantage can be found in doctrinal statements of the period. These elements were anathema to American strategists.

Instead, military science rested upon the single-minded determination to feed irresistible power into frontal assaults all along the line until the opportunity arose for exploiting the enemy's weakness and destroying him.[46]

Tactically precise, the doctrine lacked strategic content. Hastily formulated in the first years of Pershing's tenure as chief of staff, American doctrine developed in almost total isolation, without consideration of the political, economic, or scientific-technical factors of war.[47] One of the central components of the doctrine was to preserve what Liddell Hart called the "Napoleonic fallacy," the cult of the offensive. The objective lessons that might have been derived from the study of the First World War, if not ignored, were handled superficially and irresponsibly. Because political criteria interfered with strictly instrumental military logic, interwar doctrine ignored the political aspects of grand strategy. Failing to integrate strategy with military doctrine and rejecting the potentials of mechanized warfare and airpower, the doyens of Pershing's Chaumont Clique constructed a system consistent with the role of the nineteenth-century border constabulary, not of a modern army as an appropriate instrument of American power.

Formulated in the years 1921-1923, the "Uniform Tactical Doctrine," once proclaimed, became dogma, unchanged for better than a decade and a half.[48] Military doctrine develops in officers the qualities of coordinate leadership. Leavenworth's function was to enforce orthodoxy and assure minimum standards of performance, not to encourage unusual or innovative content. At Leavenworth the commitment to doctrine shaped the curriculum. Incoming attendees were told that doctrine represented "the cumulated wisdom of many minds [that was] bound to be better than those of an individual....In other words, don't fight what the school teaches."[49] In the opinion of one Leavenworth commandant, junior officers had "no business interesting [themselves] in foreign military doctrine or in anything in American...doctrine beyond the platoon." [50]

Although the content of the curriculum remained static, the Leavenworth program experienced some changes. The one-year program provided sufficient time only for a cursory handling of the subjects covered. Since successful completion of the Leavenworth course became a *sine qua non* for promotion, some officers pushed themselves relentlessly to earn an honor diploma. The need to complete the course in a single nine-month period created high demands on students' time. Officers stayed up until the small hours trying to complete individual problems. Among the goals of the course was the development of the powers of decision making and to simulate the stresses involved in problem solving in the field. Instructors added artificial pressures lest the "course degenerate into a series of lectures, lifeless, academic and ineffectual."[51] As pressure mounted, family life deteriorated and the mid-1920s saw a rash of suicides among officers and their wives.[52] To reduce these stresses the course expanded to two years beginning with the 1928-1929 class. Other changes followed. The branch schools announced Leavenworth alone did not constitute the decisive consideration in officers' ratings. After 1927 the school ceased to publish grades and suspended designations of honor standing. All officers were attached for the duration of the two-year course and routinely graduated at its conclusion.[53]

As the curriculum remained unchanged from year to year, most officers arrived in Kansas in full possession of the notes and solutions of previous attendees. The graduates of the Infantry School enjoyed an advantage in the first-year command course because most of the map problems were identical to those used at Benning. From the beginning of October until the Christmas break, the map problems centered upon "Tactics and Technique of the Infantry" and organization and tactics for the reinforced infantry brigade, all of which had been dealt with in the Advanced Course at the Infantry School.[54]

Most officers quickly caught on to the system. Although some of the problems required several days' work, model solutions were provided in lectures and conferences, and if solutions had not been memorized in advance, they could easily be predicted.[55] Instructors, drawn from the previous year's graduates, feverishly worked to keep one step ahead of the students. As appointments lasted but a year, the primary objective of the teaching staff centered on simplifying the grading procedure, not the improvement of the quality of instruction.[56]

Armed with the knowledge that only medical casualties failed to graduate, few officers took their grades very seriously, instead spending their time out of the classroom enjoying the amenities offered by Fort Leavenworth.[57] Once the students discerned the prescribed school method and learned not to question the unassailable truths of the doctrine, success was guaranteed. The problems demanded conformity; more as an act of faith than the product of objective evidence. Those who departed from the system were penalized. Rather than encouraging initiative, the course rewarded officers who played it safe.[58] More theological than scientific, the students, like ancient priests, could chant the principles of war as a holy writ, but the Leavenworth system failed to train officers to think critically.

The First Year Course sought to produce competent tacticians. Classes, divided by branch, were conducted in the Academic Building, an architectural evolution in the center of the post. Lectures and conferences were held in the mornings while map problems dominated the afternoons. In October and again in May and June, tactical rides, command-post exercises, and terrain studies conducted on horseback dominated the coursework. Initially officers learned how to read maps and intelligence reports, formulate logistical plans, and write the five-paragraph order. Progressing to map problems, either as individuals or later in groups of ten, officers discharged simulated command and staff duties. They led theoretical attacks, conducted pursuits, formed for counterattacks, performed reconnaissances, and moved troops and equipment by rail for units ranging from the reinforced brigade to, in the closing weeks, a corps.[59]

Tactics and combat command training loomed largest in the program of study. Staff procedures were only introduced in the last weeks of the course. The thread that tied all the map problems and lectures together consisted of the ratiocinated dedication to the offensive. In problem after problem three lessons constantly were driven home: (1) American troops never retreat against anything but overwhelmingly superior forces and then only to consolidate in preparation for a counterattack; (2) the attack must be maintained along a broad front with gaps filled before the advance could continue; (3) frontal attacks had to be pressed until the enemy's flank could be turned. Leavenworth carried the wide envelopment doctrine to an extreme, and here the German offensive of 1914 provided the model.[60]

American doctrine, as evidenced by the map problems, conceded the offensive use of armor and aircraft to the "enemy." The army persisted in viewing armor as a supporting weapon for the infantry. "The primary mission of the tank," declared official doctrine, "is to facilitate the uninterrupted advance of the riflemen in attack."[61] Essentially mobile machine-gun platforms and armored only against machine guns, tanks played a subordinate tactical role: to lend fire support for the infantry, to suppress enemy machine-gun fire, and to provide a screen for the advance. Once the opponent's line had been breached, armor was expected to rally and form the reserve. Therefore, instead of spreading confusion among the enemy's command and logistical elements and demoralizing his combat units in the retreat, American armor was supposed to sit passively, awaiting armored counterattacks. With no grand tactical role, tanks assumed a static posture during the pursuit phase of operations. It fell to horse cavalry to exploit the strategic advantages.[62]

The employment of aircraft was even more primitive. Aside from its strategic bombing mission, the overriding task of the Air Corps involved the seizure of air superiority over the front. The army did not develop a close-air-support doctrine. Instead, artillery provided direct fire support while the role of interdiction devolved upon heavy railroad artillery. The primary province of aircraft in ground operations remained aerial reconnaissance or gunnery sighting; precisely those duties assigned the Air Corps in the First World War.[63]

June brought a temporary end to the hectic pace of study. All 120 officers graduated, their standing known only by their superiors and the War

Department. Smith's completion of the Infantry Advanced Course, his year as an instructor at Benning, and the hours spent in personal study all paid dividends as he graduated in the top third of his class. By the end of the school year, Smith had learned to work consistently under constant pressure and scrutiny both individually and as a member of a team. Although possessing an independent turn of mind, which explains his less-than-outstanding performance, Smith came to accept the homogeneous pattern of the Leavenworth system. Drilled in the "school solution," Smith had proven himself an officer capable of undertaking greater responsibilities.

Personal connections forged at Leavenworth loomed as important as performance on the map and maneuver problems. In the daily intercourse with faculty, staff members, and classmates, subjective judgments were also important in determining future fitness for higher command. The ability to get along with others, to cooperate, and to display leadership qualities all were significant elements of a successful professional officer's makeup. Among the instructors and students were men destined to hold important command and staff positions in the Second World War, officers like Mark Clark, Matthew Ridgway, Maxwell Taylor, George Stratemeyer, Manton Eddy, George Brett, Robert Grow, Wade Haislip, Clarence Adcock, and Edwin Sibert.[64]

After a three-month vacation, the Smiths returned to their housekeeping apartment on Kearney Street to begin their second year at Fort Leavenworth. Now fully imbued with the Leavenworth method and having made new friendships and renewed old ones, Smith looked forward to the Second Year Course.[65] Essentially the second year was designed to reinforce the doctrinal precepts laid down during the preceding year. Year two emphasized classroom instruction and map/terrain problems dealing with the handling of large units, corps, and armies. Subdivided into four sections—command, military intelligence, operations, and logistics and administration—the curriculum still concentrated on the command function but with substantial time allotted to the examination of staff duties (the ratio being 65/35). Themes such as "Tactical and Strategic Principles" and "Command, Staff, and Logistics" occupied nearly 40 percent of time devoted to formal lectures and conference. Instruction and practical exercises dealing with the tactics and techniques of the separate arms and technical staffs were interspersed throughout the year.[66]

American doctrine held the command and staff relationship must be dominated by "the captain of the team," the commander. By supervising his staff and exercising tactical command through personal contact with all his subordinates in the field, the commander's chief function centered on his ability to inspire the troops by example. Ideally a man of action, he had to know the mental and physical state of his troops, but ultimately success in battle depended upon the commander's will to win. According to the *Field Manual*, "the morale of the unit is that of its leader; it is not defeated until he is defeated."[67]

The staff's primary function was to execute the "will of the commander." With no independent command function, the chief of staff's duty lay in freeing the commander from administrative concerns and maintaining cooperation among the subdivisions of the staff. Unable to act on his own initiative, the chief of staff served merely as a conduit for the policies, decisions, and plans of the commander.[68]

The program of study mirrored the First Year Course with expanded coverage of staff procedures and an examination of the functions of the technical branches. Lectures, conferences, and an October tactical ride dominated the first half of the course. Emphasizing cooperative teamwork, the class divided into groups of eight. Each group simulated a command post. Responsibility for assembling the material, organizing the work, and managing the preparation of study schedules rotated among the members. Instructors closely observed each group's progress. As the static map problems, staff exercises, and logistical estimates gave way to more-difficult scenarios after the Christmas holiday, the performance of individuals could be more-effectively evaluated. By the end of January, after the students had been thoroughly grounded in the correct Leavenworth way, emphasis shifted toward uncontrolled map problems and command-post exercises. These exercises culminated in a seven-and-a-half-day command post exercise in June.[69]

The approach in the Second Year Course differed from the first year in one other important respect. Since the days of Wagner and Morrison, military history played a significant role in officer education at the Leavenworth schools. Before the reintroduction of the Second Year Course, Leavenworth encouraged the study of military history not to extract principles of strategy or derive practical tactical lessons but to impart the methodologies of historical research. It was presumed Leavenworth graduates would carry on their autodidactic studies. Few did because the persistent antiintellectual bias of the senior officers colored the attitudes of the entire officer corps.[70]

During the first year, like a generation of officers before him, Smith was required to write a paper dealing with the Fort Henry and Donelson campaign of the American Civil War. Officers proceeded on the basis of a prescribed "Outline of Method."[71] Building upon this foundation, second-year students wrote a major paper dealing with a historically important military operation. Officers used American doctrine as the standard for evaluating these historical case studies.

The student monographs accurately reveal military doctrine and the direction of army thinking in the 1930s. Aside from the pedestrian quality of most of the writing and the unqualified acceptance of American doctrine, the most striking characteristic of these manuscripts is the influence exerted by the lone required text book, Matthew Steele's *American Campaigns.*[72] Written in 1909, Steele's book remained the official military history text for both West Point and the Command and General Staff School until the Second World War. Not surprising, it was considered the most valuable professional book by some 128 generals and General Staff officers polled by the National Library Bureau in 1927.[73] Filling his book with axioms derived from the works of the leading nineteenth-century theorists, Steele never precisely defined the legitimate object of strategy. To reinforce a particular point, the destruction of the enemy's field army for example, Steele simply combed through his contemporary von der Goltz for a suitable quotation. In succeeding pages he claimed "it is as much the province of strategy to dishearten the hostile people as it is to defeat and destroy their army." On the one hand he accepted Clausewitz, whose principles von der Goltz maintained, while the next instant he pronounced the wisdom of Jomini, never for a moment discerning the two were contradictory.[74] The student monographs reflected the same ambiguity. As revealing, of the 785 officers who wrote Leavenworth Papers in the seven-year history of the two-year course, not a single one selected option #388: "Clausewitz—His influence on principles and doctrines of modern warfare." In the two-year curriculum Clausewitz was cited only once. The notation stated his classic work, *On War*, was "not required to be studied."[75] There is little evidence to suggest many rejected this advice.

Smith did not write a Leavenworth Paper. He was a member of a fifteen-man special group that prepared a dramatized recreation of the 1914 Battle of Tannenberg. The group studied the operations of the 8th German and 1st and 2d Russian armies from the end of the Battle of Gumbinnen through the Battle of Tannenberg. The historical narrative was combined with dialogue involving the leading personalities of both the Russian and German staffs. In the four-hour, four-act play, aided by lantern-slides and phonographic records, the drive and determination of General Paul von Hindenburg, the German commander, was sharply contrasted against the indecisiveness and lethargy of the Russian commanders. Consistent with American doctrine, the overriding lesson centered on the decisive role played by aggressive commanders, Hindenburg at army level and General Hermann von Francois at the corps level. The professionalism of the German staff officers was emphasized, but they served only in a supporting role. General Erich von Ludendorff, Hindenburg's chief of staff, was portrayed as ineffectual and at one point paralysed "by a case of nerves." Smith played the role of Colonel Max Hoffman, the chief of staff of the German Army in East Prussia. Although Hoffman masterminded the German strategy of the central position and exercised the command function during the crisis of the campaign, Smith's character remained in a supporting role. He discharged the narrow responsibilities of a chief of staff as prescribed in American practice. By ignoring details not in accordance with American doctrine, such as the central role played by Ludendorff and Hoffman in the German victory, the most valuable lessons of Tannenberg were missed.[76]

Earlier, February largely had been given over to the study of military history with the Schlieffen offensive receiving extensive attention. The failure of the German August 1914 offensive was examined to buttress the established system. During a three-week-long series of lectures and problems, the students received another healthy dose of official doctrine in the guise of military history. In the opinion of Leavenworth the German offensive miscarried because the commanders lacked the will to win, did not maintain the broad front, and relied upon a staff system that possessed too much flexibility and independent authority. The mandated interpretation held the German commanders, lacking aggressiveness, failed to achieve the breakthrough and, with their refusal to employ cavalry at the decisive moment, became prisoner of logistical constraints.[77] According to the tenets of American doctrine, aggressive leadership could overcome any obstacle, material or metaphysical. Using the maxims of their own doctrine as the basis for making historical judgments, misinterpretations were inevitable. Yet, as one of Smith's classmates later pointed out, these very misapprehensions exerted a normative influence upon the thinking of the generation of officers who led the U.S. Army in the Second World War.[78]

THE ARMY WAR COLLEGE

On June 21, 1935, Smith graduated along with the rest of his 1934-1935 "class of aides, adjutants, and asses."[79] Like most of his peers, he had not exerted himself, performing sufficiently well to graduate thirty-ninth in the class of 120.[80] With the Command and General Staff School behind him, Captain Bedell Smith, at thirty-nine, was five years younger than the average age for his grade. He confidently looked toward further advancement in the army.

During his tenure as chief of staff (1931-1935), Douglas MacArthur attempted to breathe new life into the army. By 1933 the army had shrunk to 14,000 officers and 118,750 men, about 40 percent of its authorized strength.[81] Rather than maintain nine skeleton divisions, MacArthur divided the continental United States into four army districts, each with a division attached. In addition, five under-strength brigades were formed providing at least a discernible Regular Army presence in each of the nine corps districts. To flesh out these units Congress authorized the expansion of the army to 165,000. MacArthur embarked upon the purge of older officers whose continued service, in the opinion of MacArthur's predecessor, Charles Summerall, constituted "a grave embarrassment" to the army.[82] A reduced retirement age and inducements for early retirement were proposed. To improve the quality of junior officers, MacArthur called for a system of promotion by merit and competitive examinations to determine entry into the army's advanced schools.[83]

MacArthur's consolidation scheme improved army readiness, but his efforts to improve the officer corps met with predictable obstruction within the ranks of the senior officers. Failing to get new promotion legislation through Congress owing to the lobbying efforts of high-placed senior officers, MacArthur enjoyed even less success in reorganizing the school system. Claiming entrance exams smacked of elitism, the army protested MacArthur was attempting to Prussianize Leavenworth and the War College as he had early tried to do with the Military Academy.[84]

The creation of more officer billets in line units was one of the aims of MacArthur's reorganization. The reforms had an opposite impact. By consolidating units, entire formations ceased to exist, with a corresponding reduction in command postings. By 1935 the hump had been reduced to 4,322, 3,450 of them captains. The depression slowed the number of officers leaving the army; as West Point represented virtually the only means of entry during the 1930s, company commands increasingly became the preserve of graduates of the Military Academy, especially in the infantry.[85] Finally moved to action on July 31, 1935, Congress passed a package of officer promotion bills along lines earlier suggested by MacArthur, but this had little immediate effect.

Despite his creditable performance at Leavenworth, Smith did not receive a line assignment. Resigned he might never command troops, Bedell was ordered to Fort Benning to resume instructional duties. In his two-year absence the Infantry School had continued to grow physically but changed little otherwise. As with most educational appointments, Smith thought he would remain at Benning for only one year. Well-grounded in the school approach, the year promised to be a leisurely one. Detailed to teach a class in the indirect laying of machine-gun fire, Smith published an article dealing with that subject in a 1936 edition of the *Mailing List*.[86]

While at the Infantry School Smith carved out a reputation for being tough and uncompromising. On one occasion a student had the temerity to question the school solution. When he persisted, Smith, the instructor, flew into a rage. After a stream of profanity that left the student dumbfounded, Smith roared, "When I say No; I mean NO!" Thereafter, students refrained from asking questions.[87] He did not reserve his petulance for students. Junior officers who served under Smith rarely escaped his wrath. Russell Vittrup, who retired a lieutenant general, remembered volunteering for an extra field assignment that inconvenienced Smith. The task complete, they rode back to the Academic Building together with Smith violently berating the lanky Texan lieutenant the entire way. By the time they arrived, Smith had returned to normal. Although he frequently lost his temper, he rarely kept a grudge. The young officers in the Weapons Section respected Smith and accepted his stubborn and irritable personality.[88]

Social life at Fort Benning centered around the officers' club and the polo and hunt clubs. A member of the officers' club, Smith and his wife never attended the Saturday night parties highlighting the week's social calender. The Smiths always returned social obligations but remained to themselves most of the time. While at Benning he also developed an ardent interest in gardening, particularly raising roses. Outdoor sports occupied most of Smith's leisure time. He devoted many hours training his prized hunting dog, Sport, and tying fishing flies. Several of the junior officers in the Weapons Section joined Smith in evening opossum and racoon hunts. Meanwhile, their wives gathered at the Smith house. When the men returned, their boots caked with red Georgia mud, the young officers hovered at the doorstep, afraid to walk on Nory Smith's spotless floor. Always the good host, Smith marched in, waving to the others to follow.

Except for formal affairs, Smith rarely socialized with his superiors or men of his own rank. As did many officers of the day, he played poker and bridge, but chess was his specialty. He won a reputation for being among the most accomplished players in the army. From time to time the Smiths would join other members of the Weapons Section and drive out to a nearby restaurant specializing in freshwater fish dishes. On one occasion the meal did not agree with Smith's stomach. He fled the restaurant, barely making it out the door before he threw up. This was the first indication that he suffered from a serious ulcer condition, a disorder that would plague him for the rest of his life. Aside from his health problems and the death of his mother, his tenure at Fort Benning was pleasant.[89]

Acknowledged as one of the best instructors at the Infantry School, Smith asked for and received an appointment to the War College in Washington, D.C. Theoretically, the War College stood at the summit of the sequential educational pyramid. Only superior graduates of Leavenworth were entitled to attend. In practice the War College never developed into an institution comparable to its German namesake, the *Kriegsakademie*. From its inception in 1900 as part of the Root reforms, the War College suffered from the lack of a clearly defined mission. This confusion persisted throughout the interwar years.[90] Before 1917, the War College served as a narrow planning adjunct to the general staff and not as an educational institution. With the emergence of the reformed general staff under March, the restructured War College offered a curriculum focused upon the preparation of selected officers for general staff service. As with the Command and General Staff School, the Pershing counterreformation reversed this trend. Although one of the missions of the War College centered on the development of staff officers for the division and corps, only a truncated version of the Leavenworth command course replaced the short-lived emphasis on general staff training. As a result, neither Leavenworth or the War College undertook to prepare officers for service in the staffs of operational commands or higher headquarters.

As at Leavenworth, the bulk of the War College course stressed the importance of the command function. Essentially unchanged from 1923 to 1940, the curriculum was designed to prepare officers for higher command by developing the skills of decision making. Reflecting the "old" army's intolerance for "book soldiers," the pedagogic method employed was consistent with the empiricist learning-by-doing tradition. After a cursory review of the organization, functions, and methods of the divisions of the general staff, the attendees divided into groups of six. They attended lectures and conferences, conducted map problems and command-post simulations, and prepared written estimates and oral presentations as at Leavenworth; the difference being that no grades were assigned.[91]

An examination of the curriculum and its intellectual content indicates the War College attempted to reinforce the army point of view, diverting attention away from subject matter and analytical skills. The political, grand strategic, and economic aspects of modern war were only superficially examined, chiefly through frequent lectures given by invited speakers from government, industry, and academe. In the second half of the course the class divided into five area study groups, conforming to the potential theaters of war. Each group prepared a presentation in military geography: an evaluation of the relative economic, political, and strategic positions of the countries located within the study area. This segment of the course climaxed in the preparation of a strategic war plan. Since the War College no longer was privy to the actual war plans, the hypothetical case studies, in the opinion of Bradley, proved not very realistic nor were they taken very seriously.[92]

Military history played an important role in the curriculum. Each participant wrote a biographical study of an American general. They also toured the Gettysburg and Antietam battlefields and retraced on horseback the route of Grant's 1864 campaign in Virginia. These writing assignments and staff rides employed history to extol the virtues of aggressive leadership and to reiterate the principles of war.

The year spent in Washington largely was a sinecure. Since the War College, located across the Potomac at Fort Humphreys, provided no billets, officers and their families lived in affordable apartments adjacent to the installation. With few social connections in Washington, these tight knots of officer families created their own social circle. By order of the War Department, officers attached to the War College wore mufti to avoid raising suspicions in official Washington. This added to the informal atmosphere. After attending morning lectures, afternoons were free for rounds of golf and tennis with evenings devoted to drinking, card playing, and conversation. Neither examined nor ranked, free from the pressures of Leavenworth, few worked hard, as was reflected by the quality of the presentations.[93]

The completion of the War College course on June 23, 1937, marked the end of Smith's formal education. Distinguished as a graduate of the Command and General Staff School and having attended the War College, Smith was qualified to hold a middle- and high-level command or staff assignment. Realistically he knew that the most he could expect was to retire as a lieutenant colonel.[94] Nevertheless, Smith looked upon his prospects with a large measure of satisfaction. Given his poor social and educational background before joining the army with a temporary reserve commission in 1917, he had accomplished much in his twenty-year career. However, nothing in his wildest dreams prepared him for what lay in store for him.

THE HALFWAY COVENANT: MILITARY PROFESSIONALISM AND THE INTERWAR ARMY

If Leavenworth and the War College sought to inculcate in the "long generation" of officers a uniform level of minimum competence as the foundation for military professionalism, then the Advanced Schools must be viewed as having succeeded. When the U.S. Army and Air Corps expanded from nine skeleton divisions to eighty-nine divisions and sixteen air forces, the captains and majors of 1937 held the key field commands, staffed the headquarters, and manned the War Department. Age played a large role as a discriminating factor in the selection of general officers as did graduation from the Command and General Staff School.[95] Drilled in the identical doctrine to follow the same procedures, conditioned to think alike and solve problems according to the Leavenworth formula, all speaking a standardized language, the products of the Command and General Staff School and the War College guaranteed competent officers would be available to assume the command and staff positions in the expanded army of the Second World War.

The informal linkages forged at Leavenworth and the War College provided invaluable intrinsic connections. Thirty-seven percent of the two-year graduates earned their stars, one in five of those from Smith's 1934-1935 class. Of the 120 graduates of the class, 62 became generals, 4 of them eventually gaining four stars.[96] During the war, whenever Smith dealt with a senior headquarters or operational command, he could depend upon finding a Leavenworth classmate in an important position. The connections made at Leavenworth developed within the diminutive interwar officer corps a cooperative informal network of communications that proved to be an important complement to the traditional line of command.

Leavenworth emerged as the focal point for U.S. military professionalism in the period between the wars. As with the lower branch and service schools, the mission of the Command and General Staff School centered on implanting in the collective mind of the officer corps the American way of war. The most remarkable aspect of the military educational system lay in its inability to break from the attitudinal confines of the "old" army. Paradoxically, the ideals and institutions of the American officer corps largely emerged in the years between the Civil War and the First World War, in a period lacking any immediate need for such a body. Defining its self-image as the nation's obedient servant, the officer corps vigorously defended its rights as a subculture to regulate its own organization and define its codes of ethics. The officer corps came to hold values and outlooks fundamentally different from those held by the bulk of the population. Eschewing power and political influence, withdrawn from the society it served, virtually an alien army, the ethics of the American professional military remained generally impervious to change.

Atavistic attitudes and institutional inertia combined to stifle professional developments in the post-World War I years. The heroic ideal continued to produce a group identity and a set of normative standards that sanctioned the traditional approach to military professionalism. Using themselves as models, the senior officers of the interwar army believed success rested not in intellectual curiosity or the careful study of military thought and history but in common sense and the noble art of getting things done. While Leavenworth succeeded in strengthening the bonds of common education and corporate practice, mid-career professional training could not overcome the all-pervasive spirit of the "old" army.

Conditioned in the image of their predecessors, the products of Leavenworth learned to subordinate their collective intelligence to the will of their superiors. The American system of command and control presupposed the existence of a fixed hierarchy in which the commander directed everything, leaving no freedom of action for officers holding subordinate responsibilities. The authors of the American doctrine rejected the view the natural condition of warfare is chaos; nor did they appreciate that the key to overcoming the "fogs" and "frictions" of battle lay in flexibility, the ability to seize the initiative, and the mental agility of officers at every level. Instead, Leavenworth preached a slavish obedience to superiors, a faith in the transcendental qualities of the offensive, and a perfunctory approach to military operations.

The Advanced Schools forged a consistency of outlook and a uniform technique of command; but in failing to comprehend the general staff principle and logistics at anything but a superficial level, a deprecatory attitude towards the functions of the staff and support services was sustained. Presupposing the duties of the staff consisted only of the management of manpower and matériel, as facilitator of the will of the commander, it was assumed practical experience gained in the performance of routine administrative duties by a generation of officers prepared them for service on a high staff. In a real sense, the Advanced Schools produced staff officers untrained in military operations and military intelligence—the proper domain of strategy—but skilled in the performance of administrative tasks. The lowering of the average rank of Leavenworth students after 1935 and the realization relatively few subsequent graduates would hold high command positions in the event of a war forced the War Department to restructure the curriculum at the Command and General Staff School. Returning to the one-year course in 1936-1937, emphasis belatedly shifted back to general staff duties. This reform proved to be too little-too late. With its rapid expansion after 1939, the army experienced a critical shortage of trained staff officers for both operational and higher headquarters, a situation that would hamper the American war effort in the early stages of the Second World War.

The mission of the Advanced Schools was not to emphasize creativity nor to foster the free exchange of ideas, but rather to complete the officers' socialization process. It would be facile to lay all faults to American values and traditions, for in the end individuals are responsible. At the same time it would be wrong to underestimate the limitations imposed upon the development of the officer corps by the normative influences of their institutional environment. The army's pedagogic philosophy was consistent with the American empiricist tradition as the courses of the Advanced Schools provided pragmatic justifications for those values implicit in the worship of established facts and sanctioned technique. Until the tank and airplane proved themselves in combat, the army ignored the lessons of 1918 and many of the technological innovations of the 1920s and 1930s, thinking only in terms of what was possible based upon the marching capacity of nineteenth-century infantry. Rather than harnessing the potential of mechanization and motorization, the fixed Leavenworth doctrine deterred the evolution of bold and innovative techniques. There was no analysis of the implications of Cambrai and Amiens, when the British began to wed the firepower and mobility of armor as a means of restoring decisiveness to ground operations, nor evaluation of the fundamental theories of contemporaries such as J.F.C. Fuller, Liddell Hart, Percy Hobart, and G. V. Martel. To the degree it relied upon First World War examples, Leavenworth concentrated on study of the Schlieffen offensive, a campaign that failed precisely because of its operational rigidity and its reliance upon horses and marching columns.[97]

The German army of the same period also examined the failures of the August 1914 offensive but with a fundamentally different objective. Never content to don the penitential robes of Versailles, the defeat forced the Reichswehr to rethink its methodologies, rediscovering those basic tenets of Clausewitz that had been perverted in a doctrine turned dogma. For the German theorists of the period, the solution to operational stalemate lay in fusing their own penetration infantry tactics of 1917-1918 with a combined arms integration of artillery, armor, and air, and in a system of decentralized command and control that thrived on the confusion and frenzy of a fluid war of movement. While the Americans believed in open warfare as a matter of faith, the Germans created a doctrine consistent with the demands of the new warfare.[98]

As Bedell Smith and the rest of his class spent summer 1937 vacationing, their opposite numbers in the revitalized *Kriegsakademie* already were engaged in sophisticated combined arms field maneuvers, complete with armor and close air support.[99] It is certainly true the German army did not have to wrestle with a historically rooted web of values and institutions hostile to the development of military professionalism. Similarly, the convulsions experienced in Weimar and Nazi Germany have no parallel in the United States. Yet, in its dread of innovation, rigidity of approach, empiricism, and intellectual mediocrity, the American military proved content to fight the next war according to the chimerical truths of the last.

Part II

The Towering Figure:
George C. Marshall

The Chief's Apprentice: Smith and the War Department General Staff of General Marshall, 1937–1941

The thrust of military professionalization in the interwar years emphasized the production of officers capable of performing a variety of roles: trainer of troops, student of warfare, and expert in weapons and the management of supply. A new concept of officership—one based upon specialized skills acquired through education and experience, and the commitment to collective effort—began to replace the "inspired amateur" ethic as a standard of performance. No officer could move up the military hierarchy unless he embraced the norms of the army and advanced through the educational system. Only then could he lay claim to membership in the collegial group, the officer corps. In all cases the primary, overriding obligation was to the collective whole, the U.S. Army.

There was little to distinguish Bedell Smith from his peer group. Future general officers in the Second World War typically were native-born Anglo-Americans, of middle age, who had grown up in the South or Midwest, probably on a farm or in a small town. Mostly Protestants, their fathers were likely to be farmers, small businessmen, professional men, or public officials (including military officers). Normally they were veterans of the First World War (almost a third had enlisted service), well educated (West Point or a civilian college), and had attended one or more of the army's Advanced Schools.[1] Although his social origins differed from the norm—he was Catholic, the product of an urban middle-class family, and without college education—Smith's career progression was typical. Like the majority of officers in the "long generation," Smith spent his interwar years holding staff and educational assignments. In this period of transition from the "heroic" to "managerial" leadership style—even if the former remained the ideal—there was nothing exceptional in Smith's career pattern.[2]

Bedell Smith was more than a creation of a social process. A man of considerable intellect, even if indifferent to formal study, Smith sought to master his profession through serious reading of European military literature. Thanks to long service in various staff and training jobs and his attendance of Leavenworth and the War College, Smith had all the requisite career experiences and education of a good staff officer. This does not explain his rapid rise during the Second World War. What separated Smith from other equally qualified officers were two fortuitous assignments that provided him with opportunities to demonstrate his adaptability and professional acumen. The first turning point was his 1930-1931 tour of duty at the Infantry School; the second, an outgrowth of the first, his appointment in 1939 to the secretariat of the War Department General Staff. In both cases, the crucial factor was his connection with George Marshall.

In General Marshall, Smith found his professional ideal. Long before Pearl Harbor, Marshall recognized that the chief of staff could not handle the details of administration. As executive of the War Department, Marshall, in the months following the American entry into the war, restructured the organization to create fixed lines of authority. Setting up an efficient headquarters, Marshall insisted he possess the time and power to execute the most critical decisions pertaining to grand strategy and the allotment of resources. Crucial to this equation was the agency that channeled the information necessary to make these decisions, the WDGS secretariat.

Brought into the chief of staff's headquarters as an assistant secretary a month after the outbreak of war in Europe, Smith worked closely with Marshall. During the two stress-filled years preceding Pearl Harbor, the War Department labored under the limitations of peacetime procedures. Smith came to be charged with a broad variety of important and demanding duties. Linked to Marshall by the bonds of professional training, staff experience, and similarities in personality, Smith displayed a growing confidence as he entered Marshall's inner circle. Smith's performance earned for him the chief's trust and eventual promotion to chief of the secretariat.

As secretary, Smith established a reputation as Marshall's intimate and as a genius at running the headquarters. A master of detail as well as of large issues, combining toughness with absolute loyalty to Marshall, Smith emerged as the general manager of Marshall's reorganized War Department General Staff.

MARSHALL REFORMS THE WAR DEPARTMENT

One of the most far-reaching decisions Franklin Roosevelt made as president was his choice of Marshall, then a little-known brigadier general, for army chief of staff. Marshall had been among the few persistent advocates of military reform in the interwar years. While stationed in Tienstin, China, in 1924, Marshall was appalled by the inability of graduates of the Infantry School and Leavenworth to perform the most rudimentary troop-leading tasks. He dedicated himself to reform the army's Advanced Schools. It was his firm conviction unless the professional standards of the educational system were modified, the nation could not avoid a repetition of the "chaotic state of affairs" that nearly paralyzed the army in the first few months of the First World War.[3]

When appointed assistant commandant of the Infantry School in 1927, Marshall set out to break infantry officers of their slavish imitation of prescribed technique.[4] Aware the glacial pace of promotions threatened to stagnate the professional development of the officer corps, Marshall pushed for a revision in the army's policies for admission to the advanced branch schools and Leavenworth.[5] Fearing the reintroduction of "the old Leavenworth competition," Marshall's superiors rejected his efforts as too "radical a departure from existing policies."[6] He came to understand that influential forces dedicated to preserving the imperious military-bureaucratic structure blocked the most important elements of any reform.

Discovering his advocacy of reform left him "open to all kinds of trouble," Marshall, not wanting to damage his own prospects, relied upon informal connections to encourage reform—but to little effect.[7] He lamented the interwar army's policies that rewarded mediocrity, damning talented young officers to obscurity or forcing them from the service. Marshall vowed should he ever be placed in a position of sufficient power, he would reverse the trend.[8]

With his appointment as acting chief of staff in June 1939 Marshall could initiate his reorganization. In deference to the wishes of the outgoing chief, Malin Craig, he suppressed all rumors of the impending shakeup.[9] Even after assuming the office of chief of staff (ironically the very day Germany unleashed the blitzkrieg in Poland), Marshall exercised caution, fearing his actions might antagonize Congress. Marshall remained an unknown quantity on Capitol Hill. In view of the president's refusal to build up the army, instead favoring naval construction and the expansion of the Air Corps, the chief of staff worked tirelessly to reequip the authorized forces and lay the foundations for further expansion of the ground forces. The army's cause was further injured by a feud between the secretary of war, Harry Woodring, and the assistant, Louis Johnson. Forced to move slowly, working under enormous strain, Marshall's position improved when the shock of the fall of France in June 1940 compelled Congress to triple defense spending.[10]

The chief of staff found little time to attend to purely military affairs as he felt weighed down by the responsibilities of conducting the political battles for increased appropriations. The poor performance of army and National Guard formations in the Louisiana maneuvers in summer 1940 convinced Marshall of the pressing need for the acquisition of armored, antitank, and mechanized artillery units. The inadequacies of tactical air support and command and control functions added to his worries. Having served on Pershing's AEF staff, Marshall understood the importance of staff work. The Louisiana maneuvers and the deficiencies of his own WDGS reaffirmed his long-held view the army's school system failed to prepare officers for a modern war of movement. He feared operational commands and the higher staffs would break down under the stress of an active campaign.[11] "It is a crime the way the higher staffs submerge the staffs and units below them with detailed instructions, endless paper reports, and other indications of unfamiliarities with troop doings," he wrote. "I have come almost to feel that my principal duty as a commander is to be out with the troops protecting them against my own staff."[12] The chief of staff felt buried beneath the flow of paper. Sixty-one officers had direct access to his office while some 30 major and 350 smaller commands fell under his immediate control. Although convinced "the time was long past when matters could be debated...and carried on *ad infinitum*,"[13] Marshall moved slowly for fear of sparking a palace revolt. For the time being, he retained Pershing's WDGS structure with its General Headquarters, staff divisions, special sections, and the chiefs of the arms and administrative services.

Marshall admitted his own headquarters was the "worst command post in the Army," but the hallowed branch and service loyalties and vested interests prevented his overhaul of the War Department. Pearl Harbor provided him with the opportunity to inaugurate the reorganization. Having long ago concluded the next war could not be waged with "Civil War institutions," Marshall moved quickly.[14] Recalling Colonel Joseph McNarney, a hard-driving airman, from England to spearhead the reorganization, the chief of staff worked out the details of the new setup during a single week in late January 1942. Planning his moves carefully and seeking to minimize publicity by presenting the War Department chieftains with a *fait accompli*, Marshall convened a special meeting of those about to be purged on February 5. Executed brilliantly, as even Roosevelt was kept in the dark, Marshall's coup stunned the entire Washington establishment.

According to the new table of organization, four new superadministrative agencies were created, superseding the old Pershing structure. Brought from Leavenworth in July 1940 to serve as chief of the General Headquarters, Major General Lesley McNair became head of Army Ground Forces (AGF) in charge of raising, training, and equipping the combat divisions. McNair's organization absorbed the staff of the General Headquarters, as well as the headquarters of the Chiefs of the Arms, now subordinated to AGF.[15] Major General Henry

"Hap" Arnold, designated as head of Army Air Forces, was granted increased autonomy in the hope of postponing the question of an independent air force for the duration of the war.[16] The general staff divisions (G-divisions) were subsumed within the newly created Operations Division (OPD). Taking the place of the War Plans Division, OPD consisted of scaled-down versions of the general staff sections. The administrative (G-1 and G-4) and Intelligence (G-2) divisions, reduced to a dozen officers each, became narrow planning agencies within the new OPD organization, while the Operations Division (G-2) became the keystone of the Washington "command post" and evolved as the executor of War Department strategic policy.[17] The Chiefs of Supply likewise were subordinated to the newly formed Army Service Forces. This omnibus agency oversaw procurement and logistics in addition to handling personnel, communications, hospitals, the Service of Supply commands, and the supervision of military justice. Under the command of the highly efficient and frequently abrasive Lieutenant General Brehon Somervell, the Army Service Forces emerged as the most powerful element of the revised Washington command structure.[18]

The most serious historical shortcoming of the American military hierarchy rested in the ambiguous command structure. General March tried to establish the authority of the chief of staff over the operational commands, but failed. In 1932, MacArthur, then chief of staff, remarked "the War Department has never been linked to fighting elements by that network of command and staff necessary to permit the unified functioning of the American Army."[19] This confusion was not materially changed four years later in the revised *Army Field Regulations* which identified the chief of staff as "commanding general of the Field Force" in peacetime, but mandated the president to designate a commanding general in periods of war.[20] In the immediate aftermath of Pearl Harbor, Marshall suddenly found himself in command of one active theater of war and several potential others. Pearl Harbor and the Philippines, military disasters unequaled in American military history, bestowed upon Marshall unchallenged control of the U.S. Army, even if this position violated American traditions and practices.

Like March before him, Marshall assumed direction of the War Department and reorganized it in his own fashion. McNarney held a mandate to reorganize the War Department within sixty days, and he delivered. On February 28, by executive order, Roosevelt sanctioned the work of McNarney's "soviet committee"; and, nine days later, the reorganized staff began operations. As Marshall remarked at the time, the reformed General Staff mirrored exactly the scheme he had mentally prepared when he became acting chief of staff.[21] Marshall demanded freedom from administrative detail through an "organization that would give the Chief of Staff time to devote to strategic policy and the strategic aspects and directions of the war."[22] To a large degree this had been achieved. Viewing the American command structure as "age old in custom but inappropriate to the war office of a great power," Marshall, in the space of two months, dismantled it, putting in its place the first centralized command machinery in American military history.[23]

MAJOR SMITH GOES TO WASHINGTON

Smith had a while to wait before emerging from obscurity. After completing the War College program, he returned to Fort Benning in late summer 1937 to resume duties in the Weapons Section of the Infantry School. The gathering war clouds did little to disturb the comfortable routine at Fort Benning. Settling into their third tour of duty at the Infantry School, the Smiths felt at home at Fort Benning. Surrounded by his beloved infantry and with his hunting dogs at hand, Smith did not hesitate to remain on in his capacity as weapons instructor for a second year.

The year 1939 dawned on a bright note as Smith's long awaited promotion to major became effective on New Years Day. Although spending nearly a decade as a captain, his promotion to major at age forty-three succeeded in distancing him from the bulk of the officer hump. Aside from the promotion and his contribution of another article to the *Mailing List*, the two years spent at the Infantry School proved uneventful.[24]

The infantry branch took pleasure in the news of Marshall's appointment as acting chief of staff. Craig, a cavalryman, was regarded as hostile to the infantry and the removal of the "pernicious influence" of the cavalry promised a more favorable environment for infantry officer promotions.[25] Many members of the Infantry School faculty expected their careers to receive a boost. Not immune to these hopes, Smith remembered he impressed the newly appointed chief with his presentation in 1931 and had served, albeit briefly, as secretary of the Infantry School during Marshall's last weeks at Fort Benning.

A man of enormous ambition and integrity, Marshall never doubted he would eventually hold senior rank in the army. He counseled promising young officers, impatient with their slow advancement in the interwar years, a time would come when he would be able to promote men of merit.[26] Within a matter of months after his appointment as chief of staff, Marshall began to remove older officers. Eventually he dismissed 600 colonels, many of whom he knew personally. One of the promising officers Marshall brought into his circle was Bradley, his subordinate at the Infantry School. Already serving in the War Department on deputy chief of staff Lorenzo Gasser's staff, Bradley received the important post of assistant secretary to Marshall.

No section of the WDGS was in closer contact with the chief of staff than the secretariat. The duties of the secretariat, part of Marshall's inner office, involved managing the enormous volume of correspondence that, at times, threatened to overwhelm the War Department Message Center. Bradley, along with the other assistant, Lieutenant Colonel Stanley Mickelsen, received incoming communications, judging them according to their importance. They distributed those that required action to the respective general staff divisions, reviewed staff papers referred to the chief of staff, and briefed the secretary, Colonel Orlando Ward, in advance of his morning presentation to Marshall. In addition, the three officers monitored the flow of correspondence by maintaining an official record to keep Marshall informed of the actions of the staff divisions. At the end of each week the secretariat reviewed the activities of the General Staff and submitted statements outlining why certain actions had not been completed.[27]

Critical of the procedures of the General Staff as early as 1921, Marshall had written the AEF staff had not recognized "that speed was more important than technique" and had spent all its time preparing long and complicated plans.[28] Experience in the interwar years strengthened this view. The chief insisted all communication be condensed to a single page, direct and simply worded. In the difficult years before Pearl Harbor, Marshall delegated the bulk of the routine administration to Gasser and the secretariat while he concentrated on mobilization and rearmament. Overburdened by responsibilities, Marshall's assistant secretaries drafted nearly two-thirds of all outgoing correspondence.[29] Neither Bradley nor Mickelsen proved effective in this labor as Marshall frequently felt compelled to redraft their letters. All three men agreed this wasted time and concluded they needed another officer for the job. Bradley, remembering how he "found" Bedell Smith at the Infantry School, suggested him for the letter-writing post.[30] Marshall, who had difficulty with names, did not remember Smith. Tactfully, Bradley reminded Marshall of the episode at Benning. Knowing the chief demanded his staff to have all the facts at their fingertips, Bradley had already checked into Smith's availability. As luck would have it, Smith was nearing completion of his stint at the Infantry School. Taking his assistant's advice, Marshall forwarded the necessary request to Benning.[31] Smith made no objection to the transfer. He knew that with war in Europe service in the WDGS might serve as a springboard for promotion and perhaps a senior command.

Thoroughly grounded in staff procedures, the fruit of his decade-long service as general staff acolyte, and familiar with the duties of the secretariat from his brief stay in the War Department in the First World War, Smith quickly won a place in Marshall's headquarters. Soon after arriving in the capital in October

1939, Bedell Smith was charged with a far more important duty than letter writing. In the quiet days of the interwar period, the secretariat served as liaison with the White House and the executive branch. In the hectic days following the German invasion of Poland, Marshall needed a bright young officer to cultivate the good graces of Roosevelt and his advisors. Impressed by Smith's bearing and aware of his experience in dealing with the executive branch during his posting to the Bureau of the Budget, Marshall entrusted his newly appointed assistant secretary with this sensitive responsibility.

Until the mid-nineteenth century there existed little distinction between political and military competence. As the military function became professionalized, the old linear political-military hierarchy, running from the president through the secretary of war to the uniformed commanders, began to break down. The chief executive no longer could exercise effective command without ignoring his political responsibilities. Roosevelt, however, saw no such incompatibility between the political functions of the presidency and his role as commander-in-chief. His catholic interests and political instincts compelled Roosevelt to retain authority in the hands of the president. Having served as assistant secretary of the navy and an avid yachtsman, Roosevelt possessed knowledge of naval affairs but understood little of the army. Taking his lead from domestic politics, the president tended to throw himself into problems. After giving a matter cursory consideration, he established policy guidelines, then as quickly moved on. For the first two years of Marshall's tenure as chief of staff, Roosevelt's constant meddling into purely administrative matters threatened to throw the shaky War Department structure into chaos.[32]

The Woodring-Johnson dispute continued to draw unfavorable attention to the War Department, depriving Marshall of a civilian buffer between his office and the White House. With Marshall obliged to deal with Roosevelt personally, it fell to Smith to handle the president's military aide, Major General Edwin "Pa" Watson. Major Smith courted Watson, ever mindful of the difference in rank. He could not allow their relationship to become adversarial. When Watson pulled rank as a last resort, Smith would tactfully point out he worked for General Marshall. In dealing with Watson, Smith learned the subtle art of diplomacy and the language of evasion; but, when pressed, he also knew how to be tough. While Watson disliked being outmaneuvered by an officer of junior rank, he grew to respect Smith for his integrity, loyalty to Marshall, and his knowledge of War Department business. In what could have been a potentially dangerous assignment, Smith succeeded in minimizing political interference in the War Department while winning the esteem, even friendship, of a man close to the president.

Not only did Smith's liaison position involve keeping Watson and the White House at arm's length, he also acted as Marshall's contact with Bernard Baruch. As chairman of the War Industries Board in World War I, Baruch advised successive administrations and possessed invaluable connections in the worlds of commerce and industry, politics, and academe. Marshall had known Baruch since his days as Pershing's aide in the early 1920s and sought his support for the War Department's rearmament programs. Having high contacts in the administration and Congress, Baruch could be difficult unless his ego was stroked. At government expense the financier flew to Washington or attended field maneuvers. Charged with keeping Baruch happy, Smith, day or night, had to be ready to fly to New York for consultations or to drop everything to ferry him around Washington.[33]

Smith's liaison duties did not exempt him from discharging his regular responsibilities on the secretariat. As the army expanded during 1940, so too did the size of the secretariat. By December 7, 1941, it contained six assistants and the secretary. Every day the assistants reviewed staff studies that required a decision from Marshall or Gasser. Ward daily allocated from five to ten studies to his assistants with no special assignment by subject. The assistants then boiled down the contents of these often lengthy studies into a one- or two-page position paper. Staff officers conformed to Marshall's strict format: first, a statement of the problem; second, a review of the contents; and finally, recommended action.[34] Working his staff mercilessly, Marshall took for granted perfection in the performance of routine tasks. The ability to make decisions and the self-assuredness to criticize Marshall, scarce commodities in the War Department, distinguished officers on the rise. As the chief once explained, "the Department is filled with able men who analyze well but feel compelled always to bring [problems] to me for a final solution. I must have assistants who will solve their own problems and tell me what they have done."[35]

The chief of staff made it a point to educate his inner staff. In addition to the routine job of writing staff papers, each assistant reviewed the accumulated correspondence for the preceding twenty-four-hour period. Marshall frequently used this as a pretext to initiate newly appointed officers. The veterans ushered the unfortunate into Marshall's office and collected within earshot to listen to the proceedings. The educant took his seat opposite the chief's desk and nervously awaited the general to finish whatever he was reading. The staff officer would suddenly be faced by Marshall's eyes, peering over his glasses. If not totally unnerved, he would proceed to outline the correspondence. If satisfied with the presentation, Marshall might then ask for an assessment, frequently calling for suggestions as to how the matter at hand should be disposed. The question might deal with a routine matter, or it could be of major significance. Marshall, least impressed by officers who tried to please him, insisted his underlings make decisions even if they conflicted with his own views.[36] At the end of the interview, which might only have lasted a matter of minutes, Marshall would decide whether the officer passed his trial by ordeal and deserved greater responsibilities. Many a promising career came to an end as even highly competent officers froze in the presence of Marshall. Once the chief made up his mind about someone, he rarely changed it.

The highlight of the day was the secretary's morning briefing of the chief of staff. Marshall arrived at his office in the Munitions Building promptly at 7:30, and all the assistants had to be present at least two hours earlier. Many times they spent the entire night preparing solutions for particularly nettlesome problems. After examining his logbook and reviewing the important messages that had come through the Message Center during the night, Marshall would call for Gasser and Ward. The deputy and the secretary, with one or more assistants in tow, entered the chief of staff's office and began the presentations, calling upon their subordinates when a point needed clarification. Marshall decided what actions had to be taken, all the while attentive to the suggestions of his staff whose judgment he respected. When further action was required, such as additional research or refinements in the text, Gasser or Ward made sure the task was performed.[37]

Early in Marshall's career, overwork nearly resulted in his physical collapse. To safeguard his health he made a point to leave the Munitions Building no later than 5 P.M. He left instructions not be disturbed unless something critical surfaced, requiring one of the assistants cover the Message Center during the night. As all officers had to be on duty during the day, unless, like Smith, they had special duty, the assistants learned to do without sleep, twelve and eighteen-hour days being the rule.[38]

Smith suffered the disadvantage of lacking close association with Marshall before 1939, but his performance quickly gained the chief's attention. While Marshall did not possess a penetrating intellect, he sought to surround himself with bright young officers and insisted the atmosphere at headquarters encourage independent thinking. Without a strong academic background or distinguished performance at Leavenworth, Smith could not boast of achievements similar to other members of the secretariat. Nevertheless, he won a reputation for mental acuteness. He was well liked by his immediate colleagues, especially his Leavenworth acquaintances Taylor and Ridgway. His greatest strength lay in his willingness to make decisions, a trait that elevated Smith in Marshall's estimate.

One event in particular demonstrates Smith's talent for decision making. Early in 1940 an automobile salesman approached the army with "a small, low silhouette truck" recently developed by his firm, the Bantam Motor Company.

The Quartermaster Corps and the G-4 Division rejected the model because the army had recently standardized the ton-and-a-half truck for its light transportation needs. The man took his case directly to Woodring. Too busy to see him, the secretary of war referred the salesman to Smith. Having learned never to approach Marshall without knowing all the particulars, Smith gave the matter careful consideration. Convinced of the vehicles's potential usefulness, Smith entered Marshall's office, interrupting a staff conference. Already known as the most independent figure in the secretariat, Smith alone had nerve to go into the chief of staff's presence whenever he felt the need. Smith took three minutes to lay out the case. Asked what he thought of the vehicle, Smith replied: "I think it is good." After outlining the costs and recommending the army purchase forty—Marshall suggested fifteen but deferred—the chief approved the expenditure. A few minutes later Smith reappeared. When asked what the problem was, the major replied: "I should have said it before and I say it now. That's the first damn time we have been able to get anything for this [salesman] in this whole War Department, and I think it is worthy of special comment." Of all the technical developments undertaken during his tenure as chief of staff, Marshall spoke most frequently about how this vehicle, eventually known as the "jeep," gained acceptance.[39] This and other events like it serve to illustrate both Smith's growing self-confidence and Marshall's trust in his aide.

Throughout the hectic years of 1940 and 1941, Smith enhanced his position as first among equals in the secretariat. In the entire War Department only Smith and generals Somervell and Joseph Stilwell possessed the self-assurance to enter Marshall's office without trepidation.[40] Considering Smith's rank, this not only underlines Marshall's high regard for his assistant secretary but also indicates Smith's force of character. In June 1940, Brigadier General William Bryden replaced Gasser as deputy chief of staff but quickly fell from grace because of his reluctance to take charge. Losing patience with anyone who said "show it to the Chief," Marshall placed more reliance upon the officers of his secretariat, especially Smith. While Smith's responsibilities increased, he was relieved of some of his duties as White House liaison after Henry Stimson's appointment as secretary of war in July 1940. An old supporter of the General Staff from his days as secretary of war in the Taft administration, Stimson appreciated Marshall's difficult position and strove to protect the War Department from the worst of Roosevelt's interventions.[41]

By summer 1941 Smith clearly emerged as Ward's principal assistant.[42] The post of Secretary/General Staff (SGS) customarily went to a senior colonel and was seen as a stepping stone to higher office. Ward held the assignment for two years, having been in the post when Marshall took over the War Department.

Marshall felt his own career had been handicapped by too many staff appointments. He also remembered the criticisms leveled against Pershing for allowing his staff to garner rapid promotions. The chief of staff determined promotions would go to the field commanders, "not the staff officers who clutter up the War Department."[43] That being the case, Marshall handpicked officers for command positions. In August 1941, Ward received his reward, the command of the 1st Armored Division. Considering Smith's position in the secretariat, he loomed as the obvious choice to fill the vacancy. Mindful the post promised an immediate promotion and held out the possibility of a future field command, Smith accepted the appointment.

SECRETARY OF THE GENERAL STAFF

Smith spent eighteen years in the ranks of lieutenant and captain. Made a major on January 1, 1939, he remained at that rank for less than eighteen months, promoted to lieutenant colonel on May 4, 1941, then colonel (temporary) on August 30. He also received an appointment to the General Staff Corps in 1940. Two days after getting his silver eagles he officially assumed the duties of secretary.

The primary task of the SGS was to act as the executive to the chief of staff. He held the responsibility of maintaining the headquarters at peak efficiency and responsiveness, coordinating staff activities among the various staff divisions and sections while monitoring the flow of information and instructions throughout the War Department. Smith's day routinely began before 6 A.M. Arriving at the Munitions Building, he reviewed all messages received by the Message Center overnight to determine their routing. After arranging information that required the chief's attention, Smith met with the other secretaries to organize the "morning show." Marshall, Bryden, the deputy chief of operations, the chief of intelligence, and other principal officers from the general and special staff sections regularly attended the daily staff conferences. As master of the terse report, Smith started by outlining the various problems that demanded special attention. By adding recommendations, Smith used the morning staff meetings to showcase his intimate knowledge of War Department affairs. Smith was charged with tracking staff activities and redrafting papers to conform to the chief's wishes. As such, no officer possessed a better understanding of the inner workings of the WDGS or better knew Marshall's mind than Smith. Calling on his assistants to buttress his arguments when necessary, the meetings usually took the form of a Smith lecture. Smith always carefully minimized Marshall's exposure to purely administrative problems. Through his control of the daily agenda Smith emphasized actions already completed, leaving Marshall to decide those questions beyond the competence of the General Staff.

After the presentation, with Marshall's directives in hand, Smith initiated actions consistent with his interpretation of the chief's wishes. He delegated responsibility to his assistants to draft letters and memos or to oversee research on issues raised during the morning meetings. Marshall's quiet leadership induced the members of his staff to extraordinary efforts. If things did not run according to the chief's exacting requirements, it fell to Smith to see that required actions had been executed. Although senior to Marshall's secretary, the division and section heads suffered Smith's frequent intrusions into their departmental affairs because they knew he enjoyed the chief of staff's full confidence.[44]

Smith knew how to smooth over superior officers in the WDGS. He also could extract efficient work from his subordinates. Among the cardinal roles of the secretary was to oversee the progress of staff actions and serve as the office of record for the headquarters. Experience taught Smith that Marshall insisted information be accurate and readily available. From time to time during the day, Marshall would demand to see all relevant materials concerning a question at hand. Applying the Marshall "doctrine of no surprises" to the secretariat, Smith insisted any prepared staff paper be produced from the files within a single minute. Knowing careers were ruined by incurring the wrath of the chief of staff, Smith determined never to be caught off guard by any development. In the first months after assuming the duties of SGS, Smith reorganized the filing system to facilitate the retrieval process. Periodically he would take out his watch to have staff members perform the dreaded one-minute drill. If the subordinate officer or clerk could not find the required file in the allotted time, he could expect to be vigorously reprimanded in front of the entire section. A subsequent failure resulted in the offender's summary transfer from the staff.[45]

Discharging routine administrative duties occupied the bulk of the SGS's time. The secretariat performed tasks other staff sections could not handle—making arrangements for the visits of distinguished individuals to Washington, setting up special conferences involving Marshall and representatives of the White House staff, and redrafting papers to conform to last-minute policy changes or the wishes of the chief of staff. Additionally, Smith reviewed all letters and memos originating in his office, making changes, then returning them to their author for revision. Once the paper met his specifications, Smith redirected it to the division head or Marshall for action. Many of these chores could easily have been carried out by his subordinates, but Smith demanded his desk serve as the nerve center for the entire WDGS.

Like the other General Staff sections, the responsibilities of the secretariat were poorly defined, the product of the settled practices of the interwar years. As the WDGS grew, the functions of the secretariat expanded. Fueled by ambition, Smith took advantage of the amorphous situation, emerging with a deserved reputation as an empire builder. As guardian to Marshall's office he used his position to inject himself into high-level discussions involving the senior department, branch, service, and section chiefs of the War Department. Seeking to improve his standing in the eyes of Marshall, Smith drove himself relentlessly. Working eighteen-hour days, he diligently strove to master all the details of ongoing WDGS activities. Under enormous pressure to execute his myriad administrative responsibilities, Smith continued in his capacity as liaison to the White House. Not only did he regularly meet with Watson, he came increasingly into contact with Roosevelt's inner circle, the White House press secretary, Stephen Early, and the president's chief political advisor, Harry Hopkins. Through these contacts, Smith's stature grew both in the War Department and in the estimate of men closest to the president.

Smith's apprenticeship under Marshall taught him many important lessons. Marshall fully understood the head of a large organization could not possess the mental or physical capacities to command all the complex details involved in planning and executing national military policy. The vast scale of modern warfare required subordinates to exercise a wide degree of latitude, but the principle of unity of command also demanded the senior commander be free to execute the most crucial decisions. His first priority was to fashion a smooth-running organization built upon clear lines of authority. That done, Marshall turned to selecting the proper personnel to staff it. Among the most demanding responsibilities of a chief of staff is the recognition of achievement and failure in his subordinates. There was not enough time to obtain results through consultation. Marshall demanded results and rewarded those who delivered them.

The trials of Marshall's War Department served Smith well and drove home the same message: build a solid organization and demand results from capable subordinates. Rather than be tied to detailed procedures, the successful staff officer must choose between alternatives and make decisions. Having decided upon a line of action, detailed planning and necessary adjustments would follow. Smith had been made aware of these matters most forcefully by Marshall, and as he carried out his duties his greatest support came from the chief of staff. This and his own experiences allowed Smith to emerge from this period with a heightened sense of self-confidence and the knowledge he had mastered the requirements of his profession. By making himself virtually indispensable to Marshall, Smith hoped his performance as secretary would secure a high staff or command position. He was not disappointed.

Smith and the Combined and Joint Chiefs of Staff Organizations, January–August 1942

A period of institutional instability followed Marshall's reorganization of the War Department. With prewar staff regulations all but ignored, Smith became, in essence, the chief of staff's chief of staff. Discharging sensitive duties ranging from liaison with the president to conciliator between the divisions of the General Staff, Smith emerged as one of Marshall's most-trusted associates.

In the wake of the American entry into the war, a committee of the professional military chiefs of the United States and Great Britain was formed for coordinating, planning, and directing the grand strategy of coalition warfare. Smith was selected to head the secretariat of the new Combined Chiefs of Staff (CCS). Charged with facilitating the flow of information, Smith also had the task of selling the British on the U.S. viewpoint. During these trying days of building Allied cooperation and mutual trust, Smith came to number among the better-known and better-liked members of the CCS organization. A month after the creation of the Combined Chiefs, the American members formed the Joint Chiefs of Staff (JCS) with Smith as the chief of the joint secretariat. Like the CCS, the Joint Chiefs developed machinery for planning and working committees, whose structure Smith had an important voice in organizing.

During spring and summer 1942 Smith's salesmanship and organizing skills elevated him in the eyes of the members of the Combined Chiefs. A ruthless expediter, able to integrate masses of recommendations into effective plans of action, Smith became thoroughly acquainted with high-level staff procedures and the personalities of the members of the Joint and Combined Chiefs of Staff. The potential for debilitating infighting among the service chiefs and the Anglo-American staffs made Smith's skills as a mediator between the JCS and the CCS invaluable. He displayed considerable diplomatic talent, contributing to bringing harmony to inter-Allied relations.

THE COMBINED AND JOINT CHIEFS OF STAFF

Immediately after Pearl Harbor, Winston Churchill and his Chiefs of Staff (BCOS) traveled to Washington to discuss grand strategic issues with the Americans. The British feared that the United States, reacting to the Pearl Harbor disaster and the impending fall of the Philippines, might turn its attention to the Pacific. Their apprehensions turned out to be groundless.

Throughout these meetings (ARCADIA)—held intermittently between December 22, 1941, and January 14, 1942—it became clear to the British no integrated system of control existed in Washington.[1] Field Marshal John Dill remarked in writing to General Alan Brooke, his successor as Chief of the Imperial General Staff, the United States possessed "not the slightest conception of what the war means," and the American armed forces appeared "more unready than it is possible to imagine." The British were most disturbed by a command structure that belonged "to the days of George Washington." Roosevelt made decisions while haphazardly consulting senior military and naval chiefs.[2]

Marshall agreed with Dill. As the ARCADIA conferences drew to a conclusion, the American chief of staff became convinced of the necessity for reorganization. Anxious not to involve Roosevelt in the process, Marshall kept a low profile. He determined to tackle the question of the relationship between the president and the military chiefs only after the Allied command structure had been established and the general confusion in his own headquarters remedied. He shared the British sense of urgency and welcomed their pressure for a more effective machinery of control. Marshall consulted daily with Stimson and the secretary's assistants, Robert Patterson, Robert Lovett, and John McCloy, especially the latter. Stimson's efforts to cushion the War Department from the White House met with limited success. During February 1942 it became clear Roosevelt meant to exercise close supervision of "strategy, tactics, and operations," bypassing Stimson.[3]

Roosevelt's style of leadership caused vexation and legitimate concern for Marshall. For all of his considerable political skills, Roosevelt was a dilettante when it came to military affairs. This in itself would not have been so bad. However, the president's efforts to retain exclusive authority for coordinating the varied tasks of wartime leadership—industrial, diplomatic, and strategic—threatened to throw the agencies for the higher direction of war into disorder. Roosevelt's tendency to drift and procrastinate, coupled with his refusal either to keep an official record or promptly circulate top level cables emanating from London, underlined the need for direct lines of communication. The president was sensitive to the criticisms yet preserved the confused executive structure based upon informal connections. To make matters worse, the president relied upon his civilian advisors, especially Hopkins, who knew less about military matters than did Roosevelt. Inclined to agree with the last person with whom he spoke, Roosevelt's behavior during ARCADIA finally moved Marshall to action.[4]

The army chief of staff's problems were many. First, he busied himself putting his own command in order. Second, Marshall did not want to be subordinated to a single chief of staff. In mid-February, Roosevelt's political adversaries headed by Wendell Wilkie pressed for MacArthur's return to act as supreme commander under the president. Marshall assumed he would eventually take command in the field in Europe and, like Pershing, balked at the idea of a supreme military commanding general in Washington—particularly MacArthur. Finally, the president's susceptibility to British influence threatened to isolate Marshall on grand strategic questions. Fearing the loss of his own influence, at the end of February Marshall raised the appointment of an overall military chief of staff with the president.

Marshall admired the British organization. In contrast to Roosevelt's personal administration, the British War Cabinet arrangement, Marshall thought, was predicated upon shared authority and formal lines of responsibility. Churchill exercised enormous influence as prime minister and minister of war, yet final decisions rested with the War Cabinet. The government's ministers, including Churchill, determined the broad lines of military policy in consultation with the chiefs of the British armed services. Also subordinate to the cabinet were administrative officials—civilian and military—who directed production and logistical activities. Beneath the BCOS stood the theater commanders whose scope of authority lay confined to the military realm. The prime minister and War Cabinet handled political and diplomatic affairs; the staff and administrative chiefs logistics; and the military commander operational matters. Churchill appointed General Hastings "Pug" Ismay as his personal representative to facilitate cooperation between himself, the service chiefs, and the respective administrative staffs. While Churchill possessed no formal military function as prime minister, he had more-effective control over his military forces than did his opposite number in Washington.[5] After observing the BCOS in action during the Placentia Bay Conference of August 1941 and during the ARCADIA talks, Marshall recognized the American armed services must create an alternate body of professional knowledge and military intelligence to influence Roosevelt on questions of grand strategy.

General Marshall was not alone in his view the pre-Pearl Harbor command structure required reorganization. Stimson wanted to create a unified command organization with a single chief of staff empowered to exercise the command function. Aside from grand strategy, the president would be outside this organization.[6] Congress also demanded a revision of the War Department General Staff organization and began to pressure Roosevelt for a decision. The president interpreted these suggestions as an assault upon his prerogatives and, citing Civil War experience, flatly refused to consider the appointment of an overall military commander-in-chief.[7]

Under mounting pressure, Roosevelt defended the broadest interpretation of his powers as commander-in-chief. However, he began to show signs of reconsidering his position on appointing an overall chief of staff. Marshall, the obvious choice, refused to advance himself for the post, not wanting to tie himself inextricably to the War Department. Instead he suggested Admiral William Leahy. As former Chief of Naval Operations (CNO), current ambassador to Vichy France, and friend of the president, Leahy was viewed as a neutral choice because of the admiral's reputation for getting along with the army.[8] Marshall and Stimson had made their feelings known to Roosevelt as early as February 25, but the president delayed. Finally, on July 30, more to silence his many congressional critics than to improve the efficiency of command, Roosevelt appointed Leahy "Chief of Staff to the Commander-in-Chief." As the president made explicit, Leahy would serve as Roosevelt's eyes and ears to the service chiefs, not as the supreme commander of all American forces as suggested by Marshall and others.[9]

Before an Allied grand strategy could be forged, the deep-seated American interservice rivalries had to give way to integration. The United States had never in its history maintained an organizational arrangement capable of enforcing interservice cooperation. The demands of war and the British example compelled the Americans to improvise such a structure. Largely an *ad hoc* expedient, the Joint Board was formed in January 1942. Composed of Marshall, Admiral Harold Stark (CNO), Admiral Ernest King (commander-in-chief of the fleet), and General Arnold, the Joint Board was formulated to meet with their opposites in the BCOS. At the conclusion of ARCADIA, the Joint Board, redesignated the Joint Chiefs of Staff (JCS), gained permanent status as the primary military advisory agency to the president.[10]

The pressing need for Anglo-American cooperation demanded the creation of integrated machinery for continuous high-level Allied consultation. Marshall first raised the question of establishing a single Allied command structure in the early stages of the ARCADIA talks. On January 10 the BCOS proposed to leave permanent representatives in the American capital to consult regularly with the American chiefs. Charged with formulating and executing Allied policies and plans, this committee, the Combined Chiefs of Staff, consisted of the American and British chiefs. The BCOS would be represented in Washington by the British Joint Mission under the chairmanship of Dill.

Agreeing the term "joint" designated interservice organization and matters within each nation and the term "combined" be used for those involving Allied collaboration, the respective service chiefs approved the recommendations during the final ARCADIA meeting on January 14.[11]

By mid-1942, the joint and combined organizations were in operation and, excluding alterations in the personnel of the BCOS and their Joint Staff Mission, remained in place throughout the Second World War.[12] As for the CCS machinery, General Marshall had reason to be pleased. Instead of obstructions, he found only cooperation as the British mirrored Marshall's views for the need for unity of command. The excellent relationship between the American chief of staff and Dill provided a solid bedrock for cooperation. Dill in particular proved well suited for his role, representing the British viewpoint without raising American suspicions.

Marshall was less than satisfied with the JCS setup. While Leahy provided valuable ties to the White House, he did not live up to Marshall's expectations. Content to play the role of spokesman for the president in the JCS, Leahy never sought to become a genuine chief of staff or even chairman of the Joint Chiefs. Without a chief to enforce unanimity, the JCS organization might have devolved into debilitating interservice bickering if not for the personality of Marshall and the willingness of King to compromise.

THE COMBINED CHIEFS OF STAFF

The president's practice of leadership by obscurantism threatened to exacerbate the interservice rivalries. As it also provided fertile ground for Anglo-American conflict, Marshall sought to keep all parties well informed, thereby reducing the potential for serious infighting. During the initial ARCADIA talks, Smith, as SGS, served as coordinator of the flow of information between Marshall and the Navy Department, Stimson, the White House, and the British delegation. Admiral Dudley Pound, the First Sea Lord, in commenting on these early meetings with the American chiefs of staff, noted that the British provided the secretarial arrangements for the CCS conferences because the Americans possessed no secretariat for their overall command.[13] To remedy this shortcoming Marshall appointed Smith as secretary to the Joint Board on January 23, 1942.

As one British officer observed, the American contribution to the combined secretariat was "a sickly plant."[14] Responsibility for providing the secretarial arrangements fell on Brigadier Vivian Dykes, secretary to the British Mission. Dykes praised the spirit of genuine cooperation but complained in his diary on December 29 that results were "much hampered by the uselessness of their [American] secretariat." A month passed and little changed. Circular letters never made their circuit, creating confusion and strain. "I wish they would get their secretariat set up," Dykes lamented following a particularly frustrating January 27, 1942 CCS meeting.[15]

Marshall viewed the situation as intolerable and appointed Smith as Secretary of the Combined Chiefs. A potential obstacle loomed. "Dumbie" Dykes had come to Washington for the ARCADIA conference. Formerly the Director of Plans at the War Office, Dykes was designated as Smith's subordinate despite his superior rank and powerful patrons in Dill and Ismay. In the spirit of cooperation, the British offered no objection to Smith's appointment over their man. Among the younger officers in Marshall's inner circle, Smith had impressed the British during the January meetings. Promoted to brigadier general on February 2, Smith assumed his position as Chief Secretary of the CCS a week later.

Already buried under his many responsibilities, Smith now had the added duty of working out the details of the machinery for the CCS organization. He worked under considerable pressure during the early months of 1942 to organize and staff the secretariat of the CCS. In his capacity as secretary to the JCS, Smith became intimately involved in discussions at the highest-level. These included the situation in the Philippines, munitions shipments to Great Britain and the Soviet Union, reinforcements for the Pacific, and the first tentative planning for the buildup of American forces in England (BOLERO). No longer confined to dealing with presidential aides, General Smith frequently briefed Roosevelt, coming to know the president's views on sensitive strategic matters.[16] Smith won a reputation as an officer of discretion and intelligence with the ability to impress men in high positions. A man on the rise, Smith discharged more power than many senior officers in the War Department.

During the hectic days in the first months after Pearl Harbor, the War Department was thrown into confusion by the rapid expansion and alteration in the agencies of control. Smith's early labors to streamline the secretariat of the General Staff paid dividends. Secure in the knowledge that his finely tuned staff could function without tight supervision, Smith devoted himself to other duties. On Tuesdays, the JCS met over lunch in the Public Health Building, across from the Munitions Building. Fridays saw the regular meeting of the JCS with the British Joint Staff Mission. These meetings covered all manner of strategic and logistical matters, determining the overall "joint" and "combined" requirements for the execution of American and Allied military policy. Wearing two hats, Smith divided his time between the secretariats of the WDGS/JCS staffs and that of the CCS.

Struggling with the problems of mobilization, modernization, and strategic planning, the WDGS/JCS secretariat raced to remain relevant and current.

Forced to make numerous adjustments in organization and personnel, Smith kept the program on track through his own prodigious efforts. Smith's strenuous exactions produced results, and in both his and Marshall's minds, results were all that counted. As the chief's protégé, everyone knew he acted in Marshall's name. Smith's entrée to the president, Stimson, and the chief of staff coupled with his authoritarian manner earned him the envy and disaffection, even hatred, of several highly placed officers in the War Department.[17]

Relations with the British required a fundamentally different approach. Charged with selling the British on American policy, Smith displayed a sophistication and affability that few in the War Department thought him capable. To the senior British officers, forgetting the confusion that attended their mobilization and operations in 1939 and 1940, the American defense establishment appeared in a constant state of disarray. In "Beetle"—a corruption of Bedell—they saw a man who exuded an unruffled sense of confidence and decisiveness.

The official Smith-Dykes relationship soon blossomed into a firm friendship in many ways paralleling and strengthening the personal and professional connection that developed between their respective masters, Marshall and Dill. From their first meetings Smith struck the opinionated Dykes as "absolutely sound." Their personalities—blunt-spoken, incisively intelligent, and in possession of mordant senses of humor—melded together from the beginning. "I am fortunate in having a *first-class* American opposite number," Dykes wrote his sister a month into the Smith-Dykes partnership, "who laughs at the same things I do."[18]

Even before assuming his duties as chief secretary, Smith, acting on Dykes's suggestion, assailed the Navy Department for refusing to place its Joint Staff Planners in the Public Health Building along side the army planners and the British delegation.[19] This episode illustrates several dimensions of Smith's thinking. First, he believed staffs functioned best when united and under direct supervision. Second, reflective of the attitude of his fellow army officers, Smith harbored no love for the navy. Third, and most important, the episode gave Smith an opportunity to take charge of the situation, establish his mark on the organization, and show the British he would act forcefully and impartially in the name of Allied cooperation.

Working closely with the British, especially Dykes, in the early days of the CCS setup, Smith proved himself a willing collaborator, able to harmonize his point of view with those of the British representatives. Teamwork was the guiding principle of Marshall's staff. Although Smith often seemed unwilling to work within fixed lines of authority, he appreciated the importance of Anglo-American cooperation and contributed in no small measure in avoiding damaging differences of opinion. In many important respects Smith encountered fewer problems with the British than he did with his own people. Relations with the British remained friendly and informal, free from the jealousies that strained associations within the War Department and between the services. Smith approved how the Joint Mission carried on business. In the War Department, Marshall's personality so intimidated the staff, that instead of encouraging innovation it had the opposite result.[20] In contrast, the collegial atmosphere of the Joint Mission allowed for a free exchange of views.

Since no officer possessed a more complete picture of War Department activities, Smith's views were actively sought and carried considerable weight with the British. As 1942 drew on and new British representatives rotated into the Washington organization, Smith, owing to his pivotal role as chief of the CCS secretariat and his special relationship with Marshall, exercised increased influence in the councils of the British Joint Mission. Admiral Andrew Cunningham, member of the Joint Mission and later Allied naval commander in the Mediterranean, remembered Smith's "great flair for getting on with people...[his] profound sense of humour," and his ready "wise-crack for each and every occasion."[21] Few American officers ever saw this side of Smith, a man who prided himself upon being roundly cursed as "the toughest son-of-a-bitch in the War Department."

With mutual suspicions and national rivalries never far from the surface, personal relations took on heightened importance. To cement the Smith-Dykes partnership Marshall secured quarters for the British officer next to the Smiths at Fort Myer. Far from home and family, Dykes became less a neighbor than a member of the Smith family. He frequently ate dinner with the Smiths. Usually Nory Smith cooked, sometimes game dishes like squirrel, but occasionally Beetle played chef. Whenever a Sunday offered a chance to get out of Washington, the Smiths invited Dykes along on their outings. Once they picnicked on the battlefield at Manassas, where Smith exercised his two dogs; another time they drove into the South Mountains near Frederick, Maryland, for trout fishing. Without children of her own, Nory Smith mothered Dykes, officiating over setting up housekeeping and seeing that he was well fed and content. The British officer grew attached to her, much attracted by her unaffected personality.[22]

Smith's close friendship with Dykes opened him to accusations, then and afterward, of being too "British minded," but Smith did not concern himself with others' whispering campaigns. He recognized that his personal ties with Dykes and the British produced important results. Whether through official channels or private contacts, the first seismic waves of trouble registered in the combined secretariat. Through Dykes, Smith emerged practically as a member of Dill's staff. Through Smith, the British possessed an informal pipeline to Marshall. Together they worked to defuse potentially divisive clashes. Without entangling their chiefs, Smith and Dykes used their own oblique methods to overcome obstructions. One means involved "putting the heat" on offenders, usually the U.S. Navy, through their orchestration of the agenda for the Tuesday afternoon CCS meetings. Another lever at the disposal of the two secretaries grew out of their minute taking responsibilities. After each CCS conference they "fixed up" the final version of the minutes and "cooked" the conclusions.[23] One senior War Department official remembered observing the two in action. First Smith wrote his draft then handed it to Dykes. The British officer agreed with Smith's summary except for one point. "Hell, that isn't what he said," Smith exclaimed, reading Dykes's amendment. "I know damn well it isn't," Dykes replied, "but it's what he should have said."[24] In this way, delays were averted and decisions expedited.

The various secretariatships provided Smith with positions of informal power within the official apparatus far exceeding his rank. In Smith's opinion, the WDGS's system of circulating memoranda simply did not function. Often staff sections drafted replies to signals they never received. In addition, "the White House entourage [proved] extremely cagey," recorded Dykes, in jealously retaining important communications in their hands. To fill these voids, Smith frequently borrowed cables from Dykes. This surreptitious practice had its liabilities. On one occasion Dykes allowed Smith access to a secret British memo on the condition that he keep the information to himself. Despite his promise Smith informed Marshall of the cable's contents. When Marshall raised the point with Dill, the field marshal demanded to know the source of the leak. The chief of staff merely replied it came from the Joint Planners' level. Although acutely embarrassing, the incident did not produce any dangerous fallout.[25]

Because he enjoyed the respect and confidence of Dill, the other British representatives, and British officers attached to his staff, Smith was allowed certain liberties. More vital yet, he already had won the trust of the prime minister. In the midst of ARCADIA, Churchill took an abbreviated sojourn to Florida. Recognizing Roosevelt had "no adequate link between his will and executive action" and detecting certain congruities between his views and those of Marshall, Churchill requested the American general accompany him.[26] The chief of staff brought Smith along. As was his custom, Churchill sought to achieve his ends by employing his renowned powers of persuasion. Anxious that an Allied command structure be formed, the prime minister used this opportunity to impress his outlooks upon Marshall and fortify the American chief of staff for the upcoming showdown with Roosevelt.[27]

Realizing the alliance would prosper only if national antagonisms were controlled, Churchill was determined that there exist no secrets between London and Washington. During the vacation Churchill took Smith aside and told him he had something to show him. Producing several pre-Pearl Harbor cables, the prime minister handed them to Smith. They indicated how Churchill had endeavored to draw the United States into the war. "You won't like this," he said," but I want no secrets."[28]

Churchill had an ulterior motive in mind. He measured Smith and decided Marshall's favored aide would play a key role in any Allied command structure that might emerge from ARCADIA. The British prime minister, by showing this promising colonel such compromising documents, attempted to win the American officer over to the British point of view.

Smith proved too much the Marshall-man be to caught in Churchill's web. Nevertheless he was flattered and impressed and came to trust the British prime minister implicitly. This episode exerted a formative influence upon Smith's development as an Allied staff officer. Unlike other American officers who were predisposed to see Churchillian machinations in every British action, Smith, accustomed to the secretiveness of the White House, never doubted the prime minister's integrity nor his commitment to victory. His relationship with Churchill proved to be an invaluable asset, especially later when Smith assumed his role as chief of staff to General Dwight Eisenhower in Europe.[29]

As many in the War Department soon began to see, Smith had built a special niche for himself within the CCS structure. Along with Dykes, he had created the secretariat and turned the position to his personal advantage. Smith's detractors resented his special relationships with Marshall and the British. There is no indication he saw himself in any other light than wholeheartedly serving Marshall and the cause of Allied cooperation. In personalizing this relationship, Smith associated being a good member of the Allied team indissolubly with being faithful to Marshall and his approach. His manipulation of organizational procedures—agenda rigging and minute fixing—and his betrayal of Dykes's trust in the matter of the leaked memo must be understood in this context. While the British never questioned Smith's commitment to Anglo-American cooperation, they understood his first loyalty lay with serving Marshall.

THE JOINT CHIEFS OF STAFF

While the CCS began to function smoothly, in large part because of the effectiveness of the organizational design of Smith and Dykes, the JCS continued to be plagued by institutional instability. One problem revolved around the absence of a chairman, a situation left unresolved by Leahy's appointment. Another issue centered on the size of the Washington establishment. Marshall wanted a small organization, based on that of Foch in the First World War, to handle top-level strategic decision making.[30] The chief of staff disliked the British committee system, preferring instead to centralize authority. The realities of managing the immense war effort forced Marshall and the other service chiefs to modify their views. By the summer, five committees had been created. Aside from the Joint Deputy Chiefs of Staff organization and Smith's Joint Secretariat, there existed the Joint Staff Planning Committee, including the important Joint War Plans subcommittee; the Joint Intelligence Committee (JIC), composed of representatives of the Office of Strategic Services (OSS) and the Board of Economic Warfare; and the Joint Psychological Warfare Committee.[31]

As Marshall's troubleshooter, Smith was called upon to undertake special duties. One such task was the organization of the Joint Intelligence and Psychological Warfare committees. The War Department's failure to assess available intelligence concerning Japanese activities in the Pacific pointed out the inadequacies of the prewar military intelligence system. In a rare example of interwar cooperation, the army and navy codebreakers cracked several Japanese military and diplomatic codes.[32] Provided with daily hand-carried decryptions, the existing intelligence network lacked trained area-specific analysts who might have exploited this advantage. Smith considered himself an expert in the field of military intelligence, having served in the Intelligence Division during the First World War. He had been on duty in his capacity as SGS when the PURPLE/MAGIC intercepts arrived in Marshall's office on the fateful afternoon of December 6, 1941. Since it was a Saturday, Marshall was not in his office. Without clearance to open the locked message pouch and assured by the intelligence officer the material was incomplete and fragmentary, Smith routinely secured the documents in Marshall's safe. As a result, the chief of staff did not see the warnings of the attack until 10 A.M. the next morning, by then too late.[33] While no single officer was culpable for the disaster in Hawaii, the root of the problem rested with the hopelessly backward intelligence apparatus of the War and Navy departments.

Under pressure from the White House to reorganize the intelligence machinery, the JCS heard recommendations at its March 9 meeting from Colonel William Donovan. Charged by Roosevelt to spearhead the reorganization, "Will Bill" Donovan was a civilian, notwithstanding his rank of colonel. As a civilian he became suspect in the eyes of the War Department. The WDGS, particularly the Intelligence Division head, Major General George Strong, did not want a civilian meddling in their preserve. Smith shared Strong's views. Although he thought the G-2 Division "a collection of broken down military attaches," Smith did not want to sacrifice military intelligence to a civilian agency.[34] While meeting with Donovan to prepare recommendations for the president, Smith evidenced little faith in the undertaking.

In a memo to Marshall and King, Smith expressed concern over the "dangerous possibilities to security" presented by an independent intelligence agency. He suggested the "simplest way" to solve the problem was to make Donovan chairman of the JIC, placing his organization under JCS control.[35] To Smith's surprise, Donovan's views coincided with his own. Typical of the slightly duplicitous way transactions were carried out, a natural outgrowth of the president's methods, Smith never bothered to arrange a meeting with Roosevelt. Instead, he composed the necessary order for the White House to sign. On March 22, Smith lectured the JCS on the merits of this organization. After receiving the JCS endorsement, Smith forwarded his order, via Hopkins, to the White House, where Roosevelt signed it.[36]

Smith's hostility to covert operations and psychological warfare illustrates his professional narrowness. Disliking unconventional operations of any sort, Smith neither wanted Donovan nor his organization. Donovan's "peculiar position with respect to the President," his freewheeling style, his seemingly inexhaustible funding (Smith estimated it at $100 million), and particularly his refusal to submit to sanctioned channels all served to heighten Smith's hostility. As "a defensive measure," Smith dispatched one of his assistants to serve as OSS secretary. This did little to rein in "Wild Bill." "Smith is getting completely fed up with [Donovan]," Dykes recorded in his diary on April 4.[37] Charged with civilian (propaganda and political warfare), military (guerrilla warfare), and quasi-military tasks, the OSS never found its niche in the wartime JCS structure. Smith saw little military value in OSS operations, yet pushed hard for a clarification of Donovan's position. Despite efforts to bring the OSS under military supervision, the various service intelligence divisions never managed to control Donovan's organization. Smith's enmity for special operations, particularly psychological warfare, grew over time. This proved ironic since Bedell Smith, in the postwar period, became the director of the Central Intelligence Agency, the stepchild of the OSS organization he so reluctantly reorganized in spring and summer 1942.

Another important special assignment entrusted to Smith by Marshall involved the "education" of Admiral Leahy. Returning to Washington from his diplomatic post in Vichy France, Leahy, accustomed to interwar procedures from his days as CNO, was disoriented by the hurly-burly of the new JCS structure. In March Stark stepped down as CNO, his place taken by King. In part, Leahy's selection as chief of staff to the president was meant to balance the army and navy representatives in the JCS.[38] Marshall attached much significance to weaning the admiral away from White House influence hoping Leahy would emerge as a power broker between the JCS and Roosevelt.[39] Smith acted as Leahy's coadjutor to integrate him into the JCS. In the end the project met with little success. Displaying limited appreciation for the functions of chief of staff, Leahy lacked the initiative and breadth to become a true arbiter between the more formidable personalities of Roosevelt, Marshall, and King. In any case, Leahy's primary loyalty was to Roosevelt and not the JCS.

Smith passed Marshall's test of qualification for advancement by repeatedly demonstrating his competence in these varied and demanding roles. Ever before him loomed the towering, almost superhuman, figure of Marshall. The chief of staff, a cold and impersonal man, insisted upon old-fashioned, formal relations between superior officers and their subordinates. Smith unreservedly linked his career with his patron's. Consciously trying to think and act like the chief, Smith cultivated an image of being tough, decisive, and tireless. Always "General Marshall" and "Smith," the relationship between the two men had a father and son quality to it.

Although their relationship could never be termed intimate, Smith was among the very few who dared pull the chief's leg, if ever so lightly.[40] Although Marshall showed little sense of humor, he did enjoy recounting an occasion when he got the better of his trusted assistant. Smith brought an important communication to Marshall's home in Fort Myer, only to discover the chief of staff puttering around in his garden. A fine drizzle was falling; and, as Smith stiffly stood by, his invariably well-starched uniform began to wilt. Finally, the fastidious Smith muttered, "Do I have to stand here in the rain to make my report?" "No," Marshall replied, "just turn over that pail there and sit on it."[41] While this anecdote hardly ranks among the great stories of the war, it points to a certain bond between the two men; particularly since it seemed so out of character for Marshall.

A man who accepted responsibilities perfunctorily, Smith's temperament was not well suited for success as an organizer and administrator. The chain-smoking staff officer in his immaculate uniform and Sam Browne belt—his habitual costume—was prone to mood shifts and violent outbursts of temper. While frequently obnoxious, he could be equally charming and ingratiating with people whom he wished to impress. Despite Smith's obvious personality faults, Marshall appreciated his assistant's strengths, valued his military judgments, and never doubted his dedication. At the same time, Marshall must have realized his rough subordinate, fifteen years his junior, viewed him with the eyes of a disciple and even harbored thinly disguised feelings of tenderness toward him.

Lacking patience and the capacity to subordinate himself to the needs of the institution, Smith's difficult character traits presented obstacles in his dealing with others. Smith often assumed he knew the chief of staff's mind better than Marshall did. As an incident in summer 1940 indicated, Smith began to demonstrate Marshallesque characteristics. He telephoned Charles Bolté, an officer whose career very much resembled his own. In a testy voice that belied their long acquaintance, Smith told Bolté "the boss wants to know where you want to go." Taken aback Bolté replied, "Well, wherever he wants me to go." "No," roared Smith through the telephone, "that's no answer." Bolté ended up as G-3 to the newly organized IV Corps, not exactly the assignment he would have liked.[42]

Marshall saw much of himself in Smith and tried to guide him. Smith's most apparent weakness lay in his empire building, in part a product of his overly developed sense of duty. So complete was his mastery of War Department detail that sometimes Marshall had to go over Smith's head. "I want this done," he would say, "but don't tell Smith." In the end, Marshall tolerated Smith's imperiousness because he got things done.[43]

Smith's motivations were not selfless. Knowing that the War Department General Staff served as a proving grounds for officers earmarked for the command of soon-to-be-raised divisions, Smith's frustration mounted as he watched others receive assignments he wanted. In a sense Smith became a victim of his own ambition. Determined never to let Marshall down in any respect, Bedell Smith displayed an aggressive readiness to undertake any taxing duty. Routinely working eighteen-hour days, frequently seven days a week, the pace finally began to take a toll. Never known for his patience, Smith became ever more irascible. Under constant pressure to perform and refusing to delegate any of his duties, Smith's health suffered. Eating and sleeping irregularly, with little time for exercise or recreation, Smith began to lose weight. During summer 1942 his condition worsened, yet he refused to seek medical care for fear of losing his hard-won position as Marshall's right hand.

EISENHOWER CALLS FOR BEETLE

Senior officers in the WDGS, even his many detractors, recognized Smith's potential for high command. Everything about him—his lively and forceful personality, his ability to size up any point under discussion, in short, his general military bearing—marked Smith as a man of decision. The War Department in 1942 faced a crippling shortage of officers to command the combat divisions, the result of limitations imposed by interwar policies. Many of the army's senior officers were deemed unfit to train and command the new divisions, a situation complicated by the high proportion of National Guard and overaged officers in grade.[44] Both Marshall and McNair maintained that the most vigorous and effective officers should exercise command. According to the principle of interchangeability, talented staff officers could exercise the command function, leaving staff duties in the hands of less-qualified officers.[45] By virtue of consistently high general efficiency ratings and his outstanding record in the War Department, Smith rated at the top of the list for a divisional command.

While long coveting a field command, Smith knew his standing in the army had been built upon his staff performance. Never for a moment questioning his ability to command a division nor doubting such a command might very well catapult him into a corps command, Smith understood the importance of high-level staff work.[46] In a rare disagreement with Marshall, Smith maintained that the brightest young officers should not be assigned command positions. While fully in agreement with the doctrine of interchangeability, he thought promising staff officers should be pushed onto staffs, even if such duty was avoided by men nurtured in the American military tradition of heroic leadership.[47] Throughout summer 1942 Smith became the object of a tug of war between Marshall and Eisenhower, the newly appointed commander of the European Theater (ETO). Afraid to compromise his position with Marshall, Smith remained silent, knowing the chief would make a decision consistent with the best interests of the army.[48]

Eisenhower was one of those officers elevated by Marshall into a command position. Although having only briefly met Eisenhower three times before assuming his duties as chief of staff, Marshall knew of the Kansan's standing as a staff officer. A graduate at the top of his class at Leavenworth, Eisenhower shone during the otherwise dismal Louisiana maneuvers. Five days after Pearl Harbor he received orders to report to Washington and the War Plans Division. Eisenhower rapidly proved Marshall's decision well founded and soon took over the division, renamed Operations Division in Marshall's reorganized WDGS. Like Smith, Eisenhower's ability to make tough decisions won Marshall's support. Entrusted with drawing up the BOLERO plans and serving as Marshall's representative in an important mission to the United Kingdom, Eisenhower emerged as the logical selection for commanding general of the ETOUSA when the existing commander proved unequal to the task.[49]

From the moment he knew of his appointment, Eisenhower planned to have Smith as his chief of staff.[50] The two had first met during the Carolina maneuvers in 1941. The next time Eisenhower heard from Smith was when the SGS made the call to Fort Sam Houston, Texas, to order the newly appointed brigadier general to Washington. Taking up residence at Fort Myer, Eisenhower discovered that the Smiths were his neighbors. The demands of their respective duties precluded much social contact; their relationship remained a professional one based on mutual respect.[51]

Before leaving for London to assume command, Eisenhower formally asked for Smith as his chief of staff. Eisenhower valued Smith's abilities as a staff officer. He recognized that Smith possessed a unique set of relationships with the American service chiefs, the British Joint Mission, Stimson and his assistants, the White House, and especially Marshall. With Smith as his chief of staff, Eisenhower knew he would have an efficiently run staff beneath him and an unequaled intermediary to argue his case with his superiors in Washington and the British in London. Marshall accepted Eisenhower's request for Smith but refused to indicate when the transfer could be expected. "Smith and Eisenhower are curiously nervous about London," Dykes mused on June 20, "just like two boys off to a new school."[52]

Before leaving Washington on June 23 to take up his command, Eisenhower met with Churchill, then in the United States seeking to delay a decision on the timetable for an invasion of France. The prime minister concurred that Eisenhower could not make a better selection for his chief of staff. He too had been impressed by Smith from their first acquaintance and knew of his record for impartiality. Churchill raised the question of Smith's appointment with Marshall as did Smith himself, both pointing to the need for an immediate restructuring of the ETO staff. Two days after his arrival in London, Eisenhower wrote the chief of staff, again requesting Smith's transfer to Europe. "I do not want to appear to be pushing you in the slightest degree in the matter of General Smith," he began. "[I] believe it highly desirable for him to come as soon as you could conveniently spare him. From here, that conclusion is a correct one, but I realize that your own weighty problems may dictate a considerable delay."[53]

Marshall was reluctant to surrender his trusted assistant. As originally constituted, the ETO command was a caretaker arrangement designed to lay the foundation for the proposed twenty-seven American divisions to be employed in a 1942 invasion of France. Churchill's visit and a realistic assessment of the strategic situation began to erode the WDGS's enthusiasm for an operation in Europe in 1942 (SLEDGEHAMMER). Impatient to get American troops fighting against the European Axis, Churchill and Roosevelt increased their pressure for an alterative operation in French North Africa (GYMNAST). The British leader left Washington without any firm commitment from the JCS, but he had made his mark on the president. While SLEDGEHAMMER was viewed as an emergency operation, to be staged in the event of a Soviet collapse or an alteration in the German leadership, its threatened abandonment, nevertheless, came as a blow to Marshall. The chief of staff believed he would command the American component of the invasion of France; and, with GYMNAST daily becoming more likely, the command arrangement became cloudy.[54]

In an effort to end the stalemate, Roosevelt dispatched Marshall, King, and Hopkins to London. Smith, along with Colonel Hoyt Vandenberg and Steve Early, accompanied them. Flying via Gander, Labrador, to Prestwick, Scotland, the American delegation arrived in London on July 18 on Churchill's private train. Closeted at Claridge's Hotel, Marshall, King, Eisenhower, and Smith—joined by Stark, the ETO Deputy Commander and Smith's Leavenworth classmate, Mark Clark, the head of the Service of Supply, Major General J.C.H. Lee, and the senior American airman in the United Kingdom, Carl Spaatz—prepared the case for SLEDGEHAMMER.[55]

Dill sent Dykes to London to monitor the meetings. His conversations with Smith provide an excellent barometer of the radically shifting positions assumed by the American delegation during the week-long London conference. As Dykes recorded in his diary on July 20, "opinion is at present so unformed that it is impossible to be sure of anything at this stage." A week before, back in Washington, Smith had expressed fear that the U.S. chiefs were so partisan in their opposition to the North African variant they might insist upon a redefinition of American grand strategy in favor of the Pacific. Two days later, following a War Department conference, Smith thought "the Pacific offensive [was] beginning to drop back in the batting [order]." Following the first London meetings with Eisenhower on July 18 Smith intimated the "Pacific idea was definitely *off*" and if the British handled it properly, he predicted the U.S. chiefs might not only accept GYMNAST but acquiesce to the British proposal for landings at Algiers and Oran in addition to Casablanca. Far from accepting GYMNAST, Marshall ordered Eisenhower, Smith, Clark, Lee, and Colonel Raymond Barker, Assistant Chief of Staff for Plans (ETO), to draw up detailed SLEDGEHAMMER plans for presentation to the British. "The US COS have not yet accepted the impracticability of a SLEDGEHAMMER this year," Dykes recorded, "which all our people *have*."[56]

On July 20, while Smith collaborated on plans for an operation he never considered viable, Marshall, King, and Hopkins met with Churchill and the BCOS at 10 Downing Street. The prime minister and his service chiefs were prepared to stonewall on the question of SLEDGEHAMMER. First, they saw little prospect of materially altering the strategic situation on the Eastern Front; second, the chances of a tactical disaster seemed great; and third, they would have to supply the bulk of the forces. Pointing to "the overall scheme" agreed upon at ARCADIA, the British maintained the invasion of North Africa conformed exactly to the "closing and tightening of the ring" phase of Allied grand strategy.[57]

Marshall feared the abandonment of SLEDGEHAMMER and a commitment to operations in the Mediterranean, no matter how limited, would undermine the chances of carrying out the invasion of France in 1943 (ROUNDUP) and result in the further dispersion of forces. He also found himself "arguing against the Somme" as the British refused to expose themselves to serious casualties without a solid prospect of success.[58] The fact remained the Allies simply did not possess the necessary forces, shipping, and equipment to stage even a limited invasion of the continent. The British insisted GYMNAST offered the only realistic chance of success. Mindful of Roosevelt's earlier directive to develop plans to bring American ground forces into action in 1942, Marshall and King began to see little prospect in carrying the day.

The next day Dykes took Smith for a tour of the Cabinet War Rooms. Smith confided in his opposite number that the American side had reached no conclusions, but in their frustration threatened to fall back on their Pacific card. "Beetle says that political pressure at home may *force* some action by American forces this year," wrote Dykes, "and if it can't be Europe it will have to be in the Pacific."[59]

Marshall knew irresistible political pressures would force his hand, but not in favor of a shift to the Pacific. In the July 22 meeting with Churchill and the BCOS, Marshall and King accepted that SLEDGEHAMMER could not be executed in 1942. "Disappointment," Dykes observed when he stopped at Claridge's to pick up Smith, Eisenhower, and Clark for a dinner party put on by the British chiefs, "was intense." Eisenhower thought it "the blackest day in history."[60]

The party lightened the mood of the American officers. Smith did not share Eisenhower's dire assessment of the situation. From the onset of the closed American sessions, only Smith consistently argued for the North African offensive. With Clark, he rejected the charge that Churchill sought to strangle ROUNDUP. Talking privately with Dykes after the party, Smith expressed relief SLEDGEHAMMER had been "cleared out of the way." Together they mulled over staff and planning arrangements for GYMNAST.[61]

The following morning Smith attended a downcast meeting between Marshall, King, Eisenhower, and Clark. Later in the morning, Eisenhower, Clark, and Smith left Claridge's for ETO headquarters at Grosvenor Square to work with members of the staff on a survey of the strategic situation for Marshall. Smith forcefully advanced the case for the abandonment of SLEDGEHAMMER and the acceptance of the North African offensive. In the end, the "Survey of Strategic Situation," principally written by Smith, advocated a combined GYMNAST for fall 1942.[62]

For Marshall, the decision to launch the offensive in North Africa represented the most bitter setback of the war. It not only killed SLEDGEHAMMER but made a 1943 cross-channel operation impracticable. A cable from Roosevelt arrived reiterating his demand for American troops to be engaged against the Germans in 1942 with North Africa as the highest priority.[63] Despite the recommendations of the strategic survey and Roosevelt's order, Marshall indomitably decided on making one final gambit.

Calling in Smith early July 24, Marshall ordered his secretary to arrange a meeting with Churchill and the BCOS for noon. He then handed Smith a new directive proposing the preservation of SLEDGEHAMMER and the postponement of GYMNAST until a thorough assessment of the Eastern Front could be completed. If by September 15 SLEDGEHAMMER proved unnecessary or unworkable, a combined GYMNAST would be executed. In the meantime, planning for BOLERO and ROUNDUP would continue. Smith telephoned Dykes, asking him to set up the conference in the Cabinet Offices.

Marshall's last-ditch defense amounted to little more than a face-saving effort. Churchill readily accepted the offer, knowing full well he had won. When the CCS reconvened at 3:00 P.M. to finalize the agreement a sharp clash ensued between Ismay and Smith. Marshall had earlier objected to Ismay's minute taking and insisted Smith and Dykes produce the official record. His sensibilities injured, Ismay created some procedural difficulties during the afternoon meeting. Since the whole affair translated into a bitter personal defeat for Marshall, Smith reacted angrily to Ismay's indecorous behavior.[64]

The painful meeting completed, Smith invited Dykes and another British planner, Brigadier Ian Jacob, to dinner. Everyone expressed their relief the conference was over. During their meal Smith related the difficulties he encountered playing devil's advocate within the American circle. "I am quite sure," Dykes concluded, "that without [Smith] the party would have ended in a deadlock."[65]

Marshall and Eisenhower entertained similar views. During the course of the stressful London conference, Smith discharged his duties as Marshall's secretary, drafting correspondence with Roosevelt and taking part in discussions at the highest level. He also exerted influence upon Eisenhower's thinking. Before leaving Washington, Eisenhower had expressed doubts about the viability of SLEDGEHAMMER, but with Marshall in London he now changed his stance.[66] On July 22 a morose Eisenhower thought the rejection of SLEDGEHAMMER an unmitigated disaster. The next day he accepted GYMNAST as the only feasible alternative to inactivity against the Axis in 1942. Never impressed by the concept of a sacrificial assault on the French coasts, Smith had consistently argued for the North African operation as the best of a number of poor options.

Backed by Clark, Smith won over Eisenhower in the course of their July 23 deliberations. The "Strategic Survey" bore the unmistakable impress of Smith's thinking.[67]

Smith's advocacy of the GYMNAST plan and his furtive meetings with Dykes might have convinced many that the rumors about him being "more British than the British" were true. More lasting in the minds of the men who counted were memories of Smith's bushwacking of Ismay in the final CCS meeting and an earlier bout of "plain speaking" with Admiral Louis Mountbatten at the BCOS dinner party over American demands for the removal of a particularly objectionable British planner.[68] Whether calculated or not—coming as they did at the nadir of American fortunes and aimed at two of Churchill's favorites—Smith's outbursts were roundly applauded by every member of the American delegation. In both Marshall and Eisenhower's eyes, Smith represented the perfect intermediary, reaffirming Eisenhower's desire to secure his services as chief of staff and heightening Marshall's reluctance to part with him.[69]

Whether Smith could escape the War Department and what he would escape to remained uncertain. At the final London CCS conference on July 25, the command structure for GYMNAST, renamed TORCH at Churchill's suggestion, was reviewed but not formalized. After the meeting Marshall called Eisenhower to his suite and informed him he would probably command TORCH as Marshall's deputy supreme commander.[70] Eisenhower reiterated his position on Smith's appointment. Marshall agreed on the transfer in principle but refused to specify when it would become effective. Two days later Eisenhower cabled Marshall, now back in Washington, requesting Smith be allowed to select a qualified assistant to coordinate all TORCH planning and he (Smith) be promoted to major general, effective upon his arrival in England.[71] This was followed two days later by yet another cable from London in which the anxious Eisenhower, desperate to build his staff and proceed with planning TORCH, asked Smith immediately select "two or three men to serve on that staff."[72]

Eisenhower's mood was not improved when Marshall again temporized, casting renewed doubt on whether Smith could be spared. Marshall reassured Eisenhower on July 30 Smith indeed would be sent to London as soon as possible. Less than a week later Marshall cabled Eisenhower, informing him Smith would not be available before the end of August and perhaps not even then since the orientation of Admiral Leahy was not progressing as Marshall desired.[73] Eisenhower daily became more anxious Smith would not be released to his command. Dill returned to London for talks with the BCOS and found Eisenhower waiting for him at the airport. When asked if he would intercede on Eisenhower's behalf with Marshall, Dill remained noncommittal. He told Eisenhower it would be "a great sacrifice for [Smith] to be taken away" from the CCS organization.[74] Alarmed the skeleton TORCH planning staff would be overwhelmed, Eisenhower and Clark began to assemble the staff. However, as Eisenhower reported to Marshall, they preferred "to postpone firm arrangements until you can determine whether or not you can spare him [Smith]."[75]

Marshall noted the tentative, defensive timbre of Eisenhower's cables. Reminding the chief of staff of his special problems, Eisenhower almost daily sought reassurance from Marshall.[76] Concluding his TORCH commander needed bolstering, Marshall finally decided Smith had to be sacrificed. Marshall shared Eisenhower's opinion Smith was "exceptionally qualified for service as chief of staff for [the] supreme commander"[77] and although the chief of staff wanted to retain Bedell in Washington, the situation in London demanded Smith's special talents. Concluding Eisenhower needed "someone of exactly opposite characteristics" to fortify him in his dealings with the British and his own TORCH staff, Marshall finally relented.[78]

Operating under the assumption he would eventually command in Europe, Marshall gave up Smith because he thought he would get him back. While Smith's presence would be missed in the War Department, losses there would more than be recouped by experience gained in London. In effect, by releasing Smith to Eisenhower, Marshall saw himself investing in his own future. On September 7, much to Eisenhower's relief, Smith arrived in London.

Part III

The First Campaign:
The Mediterranean

The Creation of the "Ike-Beetle" Team, September–November 1942

The building of a command structure for planning and carrying out strategy is a basic function of higher leadership in modern war. Military organizations possess two distinct lines of authority: the internal and external. The latter is defined by strategic objections; the internal aim of organization is coordinative. Internal lines are horizontal, organized according to the differentiated functions and the relative degrees of authority and corresponding responsibilities of the commander and his immediate subordinates. In the Allied command structures in the Second World War, external lines of authority were vertical, originating with the Combined Chiefs of Staff and terminating with the theater commanders. Owing to the nature of coalition warfare, no single individual could be vested with the authority and capacity to enforce cooperation. The differences in Anglo-American grand strategy and the probable lines of future developments could only be settled through a coordinate approach.

Until World War II, no U.S. officer ever commanded combined "Combined" operations composed of armies, navies, and air forces of a coalition of nations. General Eisenhower, entrusted with this allied command, had two primary organizational preoccupations: the establishment of his command authority based upon the principle of unity of command and the formulation of an integrated staff as an effective control mechanism. In both instances he had to triumph over the centrifugal influences of national antagonisms and interservice rivalries. Unity of command demanded he possess wide discretionary powers and clear control of the forces under his command. While a theater commander could not define grand strategy, the nature and form of his organization depended upon his decisions. As the Allied commander, Eisenhower set operational goals and built an organization to secure united action. To put policy into action, adapting means to ends, the commander required an efficient staff to prepare detailed operational and logistical planning and oversee its execution. Through the formal channels of the chain of command, the authority of the commander operated at every level of the staff structure. To secure unified action, Eisenhower required the services of a strong chief of staff.

According to American doctrine, the responsibilities of a chief of staff involved advising the commander, supervising the work of the general staff divisions, and serving as link between the vertical and horizontal lines of communication. Just as no precedent existed for a supreme allied commander, no set of hard and fast prewar regulations delineated the authority of his chief of staff. American prewar doctrine called for a small, executive staff organization with the authority of the chief of staff limited. The realities of creating an Allied staff headquarters demonstrated that the more complex an organization, the greater the need for delegation of authority. Command is the function most difficult to delegate. Bedell Smith was an officer to whom the supreme commander unreservedly delegated authority similar to his own.

In terms of his headquarters staff, Smith paid constant attention to the machine in action, preserving cooperation and balance in practice as well as in design and structure. Contacts among divergent personalities could degenerate into clashes unless misunderstandings and frictions, inevitable in any organization, were minimized. Cooperation involved the day-to-day and hour-to-hour workings of the integrated staff. Eisenhower delegated the responsibility for coordination to Smith.

Formal lines of the chain of command were supplemented by a network of informal, personal contacts. The necessities of war are urgent and formal channels are slow. Personal connections expedited official procedures while achieving Allied harmony of purpose. Smith took advantage of his special relationship with the British and his intimate contacts in the War Department to anticipate and overcome difficulties. Personal relationships at all levels remained close and cordial, in large part the product of the combined efforts of Eisenhower and Smith.

From the beginning, "Ike and Beetle" composed a near perfect blend of personalities. Eisenhower's strength lay in his human qualities: his modesty, common sense, optimism, and good humor. He had the power to draw people toward him. Eisenhower's smile won the immediate trust and loyalty of others. This contrasted with Smith's calculating, detached professionalism. A high-strung man who lived on his nerves, Smith's goal-oriented devotion to duty drove the Allied staff. A taskmaster to his subordinates, Smith showed the subtle skills of a diplomat in his relations with the British. He sacrificed personal considerations and used any method to achieve his end.

Bifurcation of leadership, as represented by Eisenhower and Smith, was a natural product of the Allied command structure. It resulted from the potentially contradictory natures of the two important tasks they faced: setting external strategic goals and maintaining internal cohesion. Since the two tasks frequently competed and as Eisenhower could not perform both functions of leadership simultaneously, Eisenhower and Smith each concentrated on one role. Any group functions best when the leaders cooperate, and fortunately for the cohesiveness and growth of the Allied Force Headquarters, Eisenhower and Smith came to act almost as a single personality.

PREPARATION FOR TORCH

Marshall viewed operations in the Mediterranean at best as irrelevant and at worst as harmful to the only decisive means of fighting the war—the cross-channel invasion of the Continent. Finally reconciled the Allies would go into North Africa, Marshall wrote on August 6 "TORCH...is of necessity a substitution for ROUNDUP and not a postponement of the same." Planning for the 1943 invasion of France must continue to commit the British. Convinced strategic results could be achieved only in northwest Europe, Marshall conceded, if TORCH was on, it had to be supported.[1]

Marshall's refusal to abandon ROUNDUP created a confused set of command arrangements. Eisenhower wrestled with three problems. The most pressing involved planning the amphibious landings in North Africa now a firm decision had been made for TORCH. This demanded the creation of a staff for the Allied command. Finally, there remained the necessity of settling the ETO command structure and the "development of a proper staff to plan the over-all operation (ROUNDUP)."[2]

Following the July CCS conferences in London, Eisenhower concluded a single individual should be charged with planning ROUNDUP and TORCH "in order that there would not be two agencies competing for the resources of both missions."[3] Eisenhower suggested McNarney be named temporary supreme commander to organize and command the combined forces for ROUNDUP. Marshall's refusal to appoint a commander or forward the necessary staff officers to man the two headquarters threatened to throw the command arrangements into disarray.[4]

The final decision on TORCH had not been made until August 6. Eisenhower was officially named commander. Shortly thereafter, Clark arrived as deputy commander, charged with supervising planning.[5] Eisenhower entertained many uncertainties: he had been advanced into command ahead of hundreds of senior officers, the Allies were in disagreement, Marshall opposed TORCH, the British balked at giving him clear-cut command, and Eisenhower still saw himself essentially performing a holding operation for Marshall. Staff organization and selection of subordinates occupied much of Eisenhower's time. Admitting "the job of overall organization is a very complicated one," he concluded final arrangements would "follow no particular book." He would be guided by the overriding desire to create a staff structure "that will work effectively."[6]

With the target date for TORCH set for early November, three months away, Eisenhower and Clark tentatively began to assemble a staff "built from scratch."[7] On August 2, Brigadier General Alfred Gruenther arrived from Washington to assume duties as the chief TORCH planner, relieving Eisenhower of one urgent worry.[8]

Given his lengthy experience as a staff officer, Eisenhower attached much significance to staff organization. "As long as [I am] to be commander-in-chief," he told his naval aide, Captain Harry Butcher, "[I] will have the organization [I] want."[9] Eisenhower felt compelled to define his authority as commander before proceeding. He possessed a clear idea of the shape of the desired staff organization. While serving in the War Plans Division, Eisenhower appreciated the difficulties arising from dealing with MacArthur and the short-lived Australian-British-Dutch-American Command. This strengthened his conviction an overall commander must have absolute control over planning and execution of operations. Before leaving Washington and without knowing he would eventually command in Europe, Eisenhower drafted a directive for the European Theater commander. It was essential, he wrote, "that absolute unity of command...be exercised by the Theater Commander" and the designated commander be free to organize, train, and command the combined forces of all arms and the Services of Supply under him. The American commander had to be a "Theater Commander in every sense of the word [able to] exercise planning and operational control, under the principle of unity of command."[10] His appointment as theater commander placed Eisenhower in the extraordinary position of having authored his own directive, a document he later spoke of as "the Bible."

Suffering no illusions, Eisenhower recognized he would encounter plenty of opposition from both American and British sources. Every American officer memorized the principles of war. For Eisenhower, the principle of unity of command was more than a hallowed phrase, but few other officers embraced this doctrine. The British command system employed the committee structure, with the commander of each branch serving as a coequal, answerable to their respective chiefs in the BCOS. Since they had endured two years of actual fighting, the British saw no reason to adopt an untested organization. The American command structure was hierarchical, based upon the premise the service commands could not adequately coordinate. The Americans paid lip service to the theory of unity of command but viewed the concept as suitable for a "task force," not a permanent headquarters. During ARCADIA, Marshall argued strenuously for a single unified command at the theater level, but senior American officers indicated little enthusiasm for being commanded by officers outside their branch. Moreover, the army, navy, and air corps had long since developed their own doctrines and practices and jealously defended their prerogatives.

Organizational problems dominated Eisenhower's attention. He turned most ETO concerns over to Major General Russell Hartle, the deputy theater commander, allowing himself to concentrate on the buildup of Allied Force Headquarters (AFHQ). Lee, whom Eisenhower believed to be "one of the finest officers in the army," a view he would later change, commanded the Services of Supply troops in the United Kingdom.[11] Eisenhower readily surrendered the detailed administration connected with the maintenance of American troops in the theater to Lee.[12] Freed from administrative concerns, Eisenhower proceeded organizing and staffing his headquarters.

Eisenhower wanted an entirely new Allied command organization. Since the commanding general and his deputy were Americans, Eisenhower decided to use the American staff system. He also demanded AFHQ follow the principle of balanced personnel. When an American headed one staff section as an assistant chief of staff, his assistant would be British with the title of deputy assistant. The rest of the personnel would be drawn equally, as far as possible, from American and British sources.[13] Eisenhower noted "there was no historical precedent upon which to base" the AFHQ organization. His development of a genuinely united headquarters numbered, he later concluded, "among the most important and far-reaching [decisions]...of the campaign."[14]

The TORCH commander once speculated he had held chief of staff assignments longer than anyone else in the army—long enough to trust his ability to organize and run a staff. Eisenhower thought better results could be obtained through cooperation rather than devotion to established doctrine. He wanted his staff to leave London, with its afternoon teas and nightclubs, and live "together like a football team" outside the city. Once a talented football coach and West Point standout, Eisenhower appreciated the value of team effort.[15] When an officer proved deficient, Eisenhower wasted no time criticizing him; he simply removed him. Preferring to encourage and support, he freely delegated authority, rewarding success. He believed "no successful staff can have any personal enmities existing in it," and insisted "on having a happy family."[16] A confessed fanatic for Anglo-American solidarity, Eisenhower made it clear he would not tolerate officers who could not work with their opposite numbers. Though tough on these matter, Eisenhower's strength lay in his open and gregarious personality, especially his infectious optimism and ever-present grin. These went a long way toward building a truly Allied command.

August saw the AFHQ staff beginning to take shape. Eisenhower's most vexing issue involved the lack of agreement on the objectives for TORCH. Marshall and the War Department planners evidenced little enthusiasm for the operation. During the summer CCS battles over SLEDGEHAMMER, Marshall persisted in his argument for an invasion of France (with less than ten divisions, sometime in October) even after the high costs and probable negative results of the operation were admitted.[17] The British, meanwhile, had been accused of timidity for their refusal to stage SLEDGEHAMMER.

With TORCH now decided upon, the Americans, in Dykes opinion, developed "rather cold feet...they are beginning to realise their inexperience in the face of the difficulties." Reflecting the general unease that arose out of the unsettled status of TORCH planning, Smith opined the Americans should shift their center of strategic gravity to the Pacific once North Africa had been cleared. He gloomily, but accurately, estimated Germany would not be defeated until 1945 if the Allies spread themselves out in the Mediterranean theater. Tension and tempers warmed with receipt of the first TORCH plan on August 9-10. The plan called for landings both inside the Mediterranean and at Casablanca.[18]

Rejecting the outline, Marshall offered the classic critique of "British" planning: the front was too narrow and the scale too small.[19] Following on the heels of the plan came Eisenhower's pessimistic appraisal the chances of a successful TORCH stood at less than 50 percent. Meanwhile Marshall grimly predicted the German General Staff probably knew of the Allied invasion.[20] Fearing a Spanish intervention, OPD proposed to land at Casablanca. With the lines of communication in French Morocco secured, the American planners wanted to initiate a drive eastward toward Algiers.[21]

The British were amazed. For them, the strategic objective of TORCH involved the destruction of Axis power in North Africa. Tunisia presented the key to the campaign. They saw little value in consolidating a position over one thousand miles away from Tunis while the Germans, with interior lines, seized the initiative—and Vichy-controlled Tunisia along with it. Scoffing at the Spanish threat, Churchill and the BCOS pushed for a bold strike deep inside the Mediterranean with landings in the vicinity of Tunis.[22]

Now that Eisenhower commanded TORCH, he began to see the North African operation in a fundamentally different light. Out of loyalty to Marshall, he still talked about the necessity of ROUNDUP but increasingly came alive to the strategic possibilities offered in the Mediterranean. Concluding the British planners were correct, Eisenhower thought the Casablanca attack should be deferred. Without a movement in force inside the Mediterranean, he warned

Marshall, the campaign might be reduced to "another futile and costly defensive venture."[23] Marshall continued to see TORCH as a political rather than strategic operation, a venture to satisfy Roosevelt's condition that American troops get into action at the earliest date. Although not pleased, the army chief of staff let planning in London continue on the basis of Allied landings at Algiers, Bône, and Philippeville.

The British offered a compromise. They would give in on Casablanca if King provided the ships for the operation. Since the Royal Navy stripped their Indian Ocean forces for TORCH, they saw no reason the U.S. Navy could not match their commitment. Admiral King saw matters in a fundamentally different light. He offered a single battleship as reinforcement for the Casablanca operation but nothing more. "One strong man with a small brain has sabotaged the whole system," Dykes revealingly wrote. "Beetle and I feel very low about it all." Their sense of alienation was heightened by Smith's forecast that Roosevelt would not pressure King to produce more naval forces. "It certainly looks as if the whole thing is going to be a flop," lamented Dykes.[24]

Meanwhile, Marshall refused to accept Algiers without Casablanca. Even the American and British officers charged with carrying out the operation were at odds. At an August 24 conference, Clark announced it would take no more than seven days to advance from Bône into Tunisia; the Axis would require twenty-eight days to seize and strengthen Tunisia. Entrusted with the proposed dash to Tunisia, Major General Kenneth Anderson, a dour Scotsman, snorted only someone without any experience in war could believe the Allies would beat the Axis to Tunis, whatever plan was adopted.[25] With the Americans and British and the military and naval heads at odds, it once again fell to Roosevelt and Churchill to break the deadlock.

Churchill pulled out all the stops in pressing his case for three landings with Roosevelt. Acting upon a trade—Algiers for Casablanca—suggested by the prime minister, Roosevelt told his JCS to find a solution. A cable went out to London accepting the British proposal in principle, including a provision for finding the necessary shipping and escorts. King, after holding off Marshall and the British, finally gave in to pressure from the president. "Thank God it looks as if we are going to get somewhere at last—but it is pitifully late," Dykes recorded in his diary for September 1. "I am awfully sorry for Eisenhower—he has been buggered about."[26]

The White House received the prime minister's favorable reply, but did not distribute it to the military and naval chiefs. Marshall ordered Smith to use his connections with the British to secure a copy of Churchill's communication. Without hesitation, Dykes handed over the British Mission's copy. As Dykes remembered, Smith "went into action hard."[27]

The JCS and their planners had been laboring over a response to the British without having seen Churchill's telegram. Now, armed with the document, they speedily completed their assessment. Properly prepared when finally called to the White House, the chiefs moved quickly to a final decision on forces and shipping for TORCH. A JCS-drafted cable sent to London under the president's name proposed simultaneous landings at Algiers, Oran, and Casablanca. Churchill accepted the compromise and called Eisenhower and Clark to 10 Downing Street to hammer out the details.[28]

SMITH TAKES OVER ALLIED FORCE HEADQUARTERS

Among Eisenhower's concerns during July and August had been Marshall's refusal to release Smith. While the organization slowly took shape, it lacked an engine to drive it. Despite his commitment to delegate authority, Eisenhower's frustrations mounted because he could not personally carry out each detail required of his staff. Eisenhower knew Smith was the ideal officer for the job but began to despair Marshall might retain him in the War Department.

Smith shared Eisenhower's anxieties, heightened by his recent experience in London. The July 18-25 conference provided Smith an opportunity to see the ETO headquarters in operation. He did not like what he saw. He thought Eisenhower's staff needed "a lot of strengthening." His mood did not improve when his orders to join Eisenhower were suspended again on July 30. Unable to sleep, troubled by the uncertainties still surrounding the North African operation, Smith sought out his confidant Dykes. Convinced Eisenhower badly needed his services "to take a grip of [the] staff," Smith expressed his desire to escape the War Department. Yet out of loyalty to Marshall he could not push the issue.[29] The situation became muddied when Smith received word he would be offered a divisional command. Tempted by the offer, he preferred the European staff appointment. As an escape from the uncertainty he buried himself in books borrowed from the War College Library. The titles dealt with the duties, theoretical and historical, of chiefs of staff, a clear indication where his preference lay.[30]

Finally in London, the greeting he received left no doubt of the urgency Eisenhower attached to his presence. Initially Eisenhower requested Smith's appointment as ETO chief of staff. He wanted to employ Smith's talents for getting along with the British to advance planning for BOLERO. With TORCH set, Eisenhower expressed his desire to have Smith serve as AFHQ chief of staff but left the decision to Smith. By mutual agreement they decided Smith would learn the intricacies of the European command as ETO chief of staff. Once he had shaken the slackness out of ETO headquarters and got it running according to War Department standards, he would take over the TORCH organization at Norfolk House.

The two proceeded directly to Eisenhower's country house, Telegraph Cottage, to discuss developments in Washington. Smith took the opportunity to impress Eisenhower with his intimate knowledge of the twists and turns of the ongoing TORCH debate. A party to the discussions of the WDGS, the Joint and Combined Chiefs meetings, and the White House conferences, Smith saw American leaders had to surmount their fumbling over strategy to gain any advantage from operations in North Africa. Decrying that military decisions must conform to the currents of public opinion, Smith warned a failure to settle the direction of Allied grand strategy would surely delay the decisive thrust into the continent. Their conversation turned to the potential for political trouble with the French, of which Eisenhower had little sense. Assuring the commanding general that Roosevelt was a master at handling political affairs, Smith confidently predicted TORCH would "be a pushover."

After dinner, the two generals sat before an open fire and gossiped. They talked primarily about Marshall and the great debt both men owed their benefactor. Pointing out his amusing eccentricities, they marveled at his ability to steer a path through the troubled Washington waters. Smith mentioned he soon expected his second star, not knowing Eisenhower had been pushing his case with Marshall for weeks.[31] The night ended with a pleasant walk through the adjacent golf course, a feature of any Eisenhower headquarters.[32]

Despite having flown the Atlantic the night before virtually without sleep, Smith awakened at four in the morning to the crowing of a cock pheasant. Roaming the pines and rhododendrons that highlighted the ten-acre tract, Smith returned to the cottage at seven to find Butcher brewing coffee. The day was spent in discussions as the commanding general and his chief of staff continued to dissect the strategic situation. Adjourning only for lunch and five minutes' exercise, the conversations continued into the evening, concluding with Smith's early retirement to bed.[33]

In discussions on September 9, Smith expressed an optimistic forecast for the upcoming campaign. "Once we [have] Tunisia," he said, "Rommel won't last a month."[34] This view accorded with Clark's, but it clashed with Marshall's position. Reluctant to accept an August 27 CCS directive for "the complete annihilation of Axis forces" in North Africa, Marshall forbade Eisenhower "under any circumstances" from undertaking "a reckless advance toward the border of Libya."[35] At this stage of the war Eisenhower displayed excessive loyalty to Marshall and often acted hesitantly, frequently reversing himself. Buoyed by Clark and Smith, he showed signs of independence in matters affecting his theater prerogatives. On the question of the threatened Spanish intervention, Smith agreed with Marshall. He concluded unaccounted-for German divisions probably would be used for an advance through Vichy France and Spain.[36] This demonstrated Smith's tendency to make ill-considered, hasty assessments based upon inconclusive intelligence—a trait conditioned by life in Marshall's headquarters. This view proved unfounded.

At a September 15 conference attended by the senior American officers, Eisenhower made it clear "the time has passed for dilly-dallying."[37] With D-Day for TORCH set for November 8, seven weeks away, the commanding general demanded that unproductive officers, no matter their rank, be removed. Smith required little encouragement. Two weeks after his arrival Smith's staffs already achieved the same level of performance demonstrated by his secretariat staff in the War Department. His bulldog countenance, with a square-set jaw and heavily dimpled chin, soon dominated the ETO and AFHQ staffs. "The burden of my work has been greatly lightened since the arrival of General Smith," Eisenhower reported. "He is a natural-born Chief of Staff and really takes charge of things in a big way. I wish I had a dozen like him. If I did, I would simply buy a fishing-rod and write home every week about my wonderful accomplishments in winning the war."[38]

Relieved of many of his duties as director of the TORCH staff, Eisenhower enjoyed the freedom to visit American field units, confident things remained in good hands at headquarters.[39] The commanding general's liberation from, as he put it, "the backbreaking volume" of detail stood in direct proportion to Smith's absorption in them. Forced to work fourteen-hour days, Smith and his AFHQ staff rushed to complete the thousands of details that competed for their attention. In addition to checking loading schedules, air and naval estimates, and the countless other elements of planning, Smith performed the routine duties of chief of staff to two staffs. These responsibilities included screening incoming and outgoing communication to the CCS and Marshall; monitoring the work of the staff sections; handling constant changes in personal and organization at headquarters; and attending high-level conferences involving the senior American and British officers for TORCH, the BCOS, and Churchill.

Dinners, bridge games, and informal chit-chat shared with Eisenhower, Butcher, and other cronies of the commanding general provided relief from the grind. Wanting relations among his closest advisors kept on an intimate level, Eisenhower tried to cement his friendship with Smith through social contacts. After a few weeks the experiment was abandoned.[40] Smith's demanding schedule left him little leisure time. Another reason centered on his antipathy for Butcher. Smith did not see the wisdom in Eisenhower maintaining such a close relationship with his aide. Butcher held a reserve naval commission and had been a public relations expert before the war. Eisenhower charged him with keeping a diary, and Smith correctly concluded Butcher meant to publish it after the war. An intensely private man, Smith did not trust civilians, especially "public relation hounds," who served in the headquarters.[41] Although their relationship remained friendly, "Ike" and "Beetle" from the start, their personalities were not compatible. Smith found it difficult to leave his domineering attitude at the office. Although he never rejected Eisenhower's conviviality in any substantial way, Smith preferred to guard his privacy.

Prewar regulations and doctrine, not without value as a guideline for staff organization, suffered from many serious shortcomings. Among the most obvious was the failure of prewar doctrine and training to anticipate the scope and complexity of political and civil affairs.[42] Eisenhower, who accepted CCS oversight, had little patience with political intrusions into his headquarters. He believed command authority depended upon minimizing unwanted interference from Washington and London. Although he claimed to have studied Clausewitz while serving under General Fox Conner in the 1920s, Eisenhower showed dim appreciation for the dictum "war is the continuation of state policy by different means."[43] For Eisenhower, politics lay outside the military realm. A product of an army that prided itself in its lack of political involvement, Eisenhower, as theater commander, strove to defer tough political decisions and to bend politics in a manner most expedient to attain immediate military objectives.

On August 21 Eisenhower agreed a Civil Affairs Section, headed by a representative of the State Department, be added to the AFHQ staff. To quarantine himself from political oversight, he insisted the designated official not possess any independent avenue of communication with Washington.[44] Marshall, who earlier built a defensive wall around himself in the War Department, raised no objection.

The chief function of the proposed Civil Affairs Section involved the organization of civil administration in the liberated areas. The headquarters already contained a Political Section, headed by W.N.B. Mack of the Foreign Office. In conjunction with Mack's office, the Civil Affairs Section advised the commanding general on political and diplomatic issues in addition to supervising the restoration of law and order, public works and health, and economic life in liberated and occupied territories. The man selected to eventually take over the section was Robert Murphy.

On September 16, under a cloak of secrecy, Murphy arrived from Washington to consult with Eisenhower and his staff. Smith, who knew Murphy personally from his days in Washington, met his plane and pirated him to Telegraph Cottage. A career diplomat, Murphy held minor consular posts in Paris from 1930 until after the fall of France in 1940. His duties in the 1930s involved the performance of low-level tasks that required little diplomatic skill or deep knowledge of international affairs. A devoted Catholic and anti-Communist, Murphy associated with the French extreme right. His otherwise lackluster career received a boost with the formation of the Vichy government when he became Ambassador Leahy's chargé d'affaires.[45] Early in 1941, the United States and Vichy France concluded a pact that permitted the posting of twelve vice-consuls in North Africa, ostensibly for the purchase of American goods with French assets frozen in American banks. The men selected had wide business experience but neither diplomatic nor political training. Similar to the Donovan case, Roosevelt, rather than rely upon specialists, preferred to go outside normal channels to find gifted amateurs for special missions. This proved unfortunate since the Murphy-directed mission to North Africa involved gathering military intelligence and generating political support for the United States. By associating themselves with profascist groups, the Americans gained a distorted picture of the political situation in French North Africa.[46]

Murphy's patronizing attitude toward the French and his anti-de Gaulle sentiments mirrored Roosevelt's Francophobic prejudices. Having won the president's trust, in part because he told Roosevelt what he wanted to hear, Murphy came to exert a formative influence upon American policy making in North Africa. Smith understood Murphy's standing with the president and, like everyone else, believed him to be the greatest living expert on French political affairs, both metropolitan and North African.[47]

During the conference held at Telegraph Cottage the day of his arrival in England, Murphy described the various factions, personalities, and possible political complications likely to be encountered in North Africa. Eisenhower, who at this point in his career made no secret of his lack of political sophistication, listened with "horrified intentness."[48] Seeing his descriptions had their desired effect, Murphy, to the evident relief of the commanding general, promised conditions could be arranged to guarantee success. Not only did he claim to have local officials in his pocket, Murphy pledged his influence with Général Henri Giraud assured the French Army in North Africa would rally to the Allied cause.[49]

Never questioning Murphy's estimate and eager to lay the groundwork for French-Allied cooperation, Eisenhower decided on the dispatch a senior member of AFHQ to North Africa to meet with French officials. Since the mission required a man with intimate knowledge of the TORCH plan, someone who could impress the French and speak with full authority, Eisenhower selected Smith.[50] The venture had the potential to be as exciting as it was important. Traveling under utmost secrecy, first to Gibraltar, then by submarine to the coast of Algeria, the emissary was to land in the dead of night on an uncertain beach to be spirited away for a rendezvous with the French. Circumstances forced Eisenhower to entrust the cloak-and-dagger mission to General Clark.[51]

One reason Eisenhower withheld Smith from this mission centered upon the commanding general's lingering anxiety over AFHQ's performance. Initially it was agreed the Operations Section would be topheavy in American staff while the Intelligence Section would be dominated by British officers.[52] With Marshall's delays, top officers from the Joint Planning Committee in Washington were not ordered to London, the staff instead being built upon Barker's ETO G-3 Section. Eisenhower worried planning would adversely be affected. He also feared the British, lukewarm about serving in a unified command under an American, might prove difficult. As D-Day approached, Eisenhower, eager for planning to progress and wanting the staff fully integrated, felt that he could not spare Smith's services, even for a few days.

Another consideration was Smith's standing with the BCOS and Churchill. In his liaison capacity, Smith held regular consultative discussions with the British. This required almost daily contact with General Ismay and, through him, with the BCOS and Churchill. An exponent of close Allied cooperation, Ismay became an invaluable link between the prime minister and AFHQ. The two men charted a path of least resistance: Ismay shielded AFHQ from Churchill's interferences; Smith gave expression to the British point of view in discussions with Eisenhower and Clark.[53]

Ismay could never hope to control the prime minister entirely. A zealot on the need for personal contacts, Churchill insisted upon regular meetings with Eisenhower, Clark, and Smith. On September 20, the three American officers went to Chequers, Churchill's country retreat, for talks with the prime minister and the BCOS. As Brooke commented, the prime minister "never had the slightest doubt that he had inherited all the military genius of his great ancestor, Marlborough." Churchill lectured the senior British and American officers at length on all manner of topics, as was his fashion.[54] "It means a long night," reported Butcher, "and these country boys always say how they hate it."[55]

"Our relationships with the Prime Minister are on a most informal basis," Smith related to Marshall. "Unfortunately, this happy state of affairs carries with it the obligation for a weekly dinner at No. 10 Downing Street which is usually terminated about 2:00 A.M." Smith took amusement in watching Ismay and Brooke "brace themselves for hours in straight backed dinner room chairs" listening to the prime minister's "flights into the stratosphere."[56] Bedell paid a high price for his loyalty to the British leader. These gatherings disturbed his routine, robbing him of much-needed rest. The murderous pace of staff duties again undermined Smith's fragile health; and a meal of game pie and the prime minister's homemade onion soup, with liberal amounts of brandy, triggered a serious flare up of his stomach problems.

Eisenhower feared losing his "crackerjack" chief of staff and offered to fly a specialist from the United States. Afraid "the medicos would rule-book him out of the war," Smith finally succumbed to Eisenhower's pressure and took some rest. Despite going on a buttermilk diet, Smith's condition worsened. Fond of the man he called the "American Bulldog," Churchill was shocked to see how pale Smith looked during a September 29 meeting. Taking Eisenhower into an adjoining room, the prime minister insisted Smith receive immediate medical attention. Eisenhower replied he had ordered his chief of staff to bed and arranged for an American nurse to attend Bedell at his apartment in the Dorchester Hotel.[57] With Clark temporarily in Washington, Eisenhower knew Smith's absence from headquarters required the commanding general to resume direction of the staff. Given the option of losing his chief of staff for a week or permanently, his choice was clear.

The next day, the ETO surgeon general, acting on Eisenhower's directives, issued a verbal order to Smith, sending him to the American General Hospital at Oxford. He refused to comply until he received Eisenhower's promise allowing his return to the office as soon as his condition improved. Assured Eisenhower had no intention of sending him home, Smith consented to go to the hospital. His temper was not improved by his trip to Oxford. The ambulance carrying him had two flat tires on the way. To make matters worse, after receiving a blood transfusion, the doctors informed him his condition required several days of hospital rest.

On October 1, Eisenhower took more than four hours from his busy schedule to visit Smith. The commanding general, recognizing the value of his chief of staff, wanted to put Smith's mind to rest. Finding Smith in a state of agitation, Eisenhower reassured him he had not let anyone down; and, although he was badly missed, the most important thing was for Smith to get well so he would be "useful when the big moment comes."

He did not remain long in the hospital. Concluding he had made a full recovery, Smith, as Butcher put it, flew "the coop" on October 4. Alerted of his disappearance, Eisenhower found the fugitive fast asleep in his bed in the Dorchester. Although Smith had violated a direct order, Eisenhower could not bring himself to scold his chief of staff and left without waking him. For Smith's birthday the next day, Eisenhower threw a small party. Over a game of craps, Smith loudly announced now his batteries had been charged, he was "ready to electrify the world." Although Eisenhower thought Smith had rushed his return, he was happy to have his chief of staff back in the saddle.[58]

Although Eisenhower did his best to minimize the damage created by Smith's illness, word got back to Marshall in Washington. The chief of staff shared Eisenhower's anxiety over Smith's condition. In a rare personal letter to Smith, Marshall made his displeasure clear. After expressing his relief Smith was on his feet again, Marshall pointedly informed his former assistant unless he exercised more discretion he ran the risk of losing his favor.[59] The gravity of the warning was not lost on Smith.

There was no shortage of compelling problems to be faced. Among the most demanding continued to be the need to define the size and lines of authority for the Allied command. During September and October the AFHQ staff grew in size and function. American doctrine prescribed staffs remain small, essentially planning agencies. When Smith took over AFHQ it numbered 2,068 officers and men, but as the TORCH operation neared the personnel needs of the staff increased.[60] Faced with officers who remained wedded to prewar tables of organization, Clark and to a lesser degree Eisenhower among them, Smith grew tired of the use of Foch's World War I headquarters as the inviolable model. Digging into his library, he researched the Foch organization. As expected, he found the Allied headquarters expanded continually until numbering over 800 at the war's end. He estimated it probably would have doubled in size had the war continued into 1919.[61] Smith decided to make adjustments and expand the organization and size of AFHQ as the needs of his headquarters warranted. Fully aware of Marshall's views on the subject, he decided to wait for the establishment of the headquarters in the theater of operations before building his type of organization.

In the middle of October Smith turned his attention once again to the unresolved question of the organization of the Civil Affairs Section. Since "the book" had little of value to say on the subject, Smith ignored it. The question revolved around how best to fashion the section with its ill-defined political and military functions and subordinate it to the chain of command. Smith's view on psychological and political warfare had not changed. As much of the American manpower for the section would come from Donovan's organization, he particularly wanted to exert close personal oversight over the running of the Civil Affairs Section. Reminiscent of his handling of OSS organization in the War Department, Smith organized the Psychological, Political, and Civil Liaison sections into a new Civil Affairs Section, and placed it directly under his supervision. Although the Englishman Mack had been responsible for the earlier organization of the Political Section, Smith wanted Murphy to head the restructured Civil Affairs Section. The British official accepted the lesser role as British Civil Liaison Officer. Americans were sparsely represented within the new organization, yet Murphy's direction of the Civil Affairs Section gave the impression it was an American show. To further his control of political and civil affairs and guarantee AFHQ's independence from outside interference, Smith, a week before the Allied landings, assumed the added responsibility of acting as final censor for all news releases of AFHQ activities.[62]

Except the Civil Affairs Section, Smith exerted little influence upon the organization of AFHQ. When he arrived in London Smith found an Allied staff already organized in skeleton form. His views on staff organization and the need for unity of command accorded exactly with Eisenhower's; hardly surprising since both men were the products of General Marshall's tutelage. In the two months between his arrival in London and the launching of TORCH, the principal preoccupations of the chief of staff were twofold: the forging of an integrated staff working under unity of command and the completion of operational planning. Fine-tuning the AFHQ staff and hammering out his authority as chief of staff would come later with the formation of a proper headquarters in North Africa.

The most crucial ingredient for Allied success in North Africa according to Eisenhower and Smith rested in the principle of unity of command. That could exist, in Eisenhower's estimate, only when the commanding general exercised authority over all components—ground, naval, and air—of an Allied force.[63] As Eisenhower realized, the complexity of the situation, the variety of tactical tasks, and the limits of time precluded the immediate creation of a clear-cut command structure. No single air commander was named to head the aerial component. He did succeed in establishing a separate American command, the 12th Air Force under Brigadier General James Doolittle, and bringing it, along with the RAF's Eastern Air Command, under his direct operational control. Citing the wide geographic dispersion of the Mediterranean theater, the airmen prevented the creation of a unified command.[64] The situation was scarcely better on the naval side. At least there existed a single commander, Admiral Andrew Cunningham. The British seaman sympathized with Eisenhower's plight. Cunningham thought Eisenhower seemed unsure of himself; not surprising with the imperfect command structure and the uncertainties inherent in exercising command for the first time.[65] Even though their exact relationship remained ill-defined, the two men acted as if the lines of command were clearly delineated. "So far as Cunningham and myself are concerned," Eisenhower reported, "we are prepared to accept anything that is workable and go to it."[66]

The most serious threat to Eisenhower's concept of unity of command came from the British War Office. On October 10 the War Office issued a directive to Anderson that essentially restated one given Field Marshal Douglas Haig in 1918. Eisenhower was empowered to coordinate the actions of the various armies but without control over major tactical decisions made by the British

First Army commander. If Anderson believed his situation "imperilled," he could communicate directly with London, bypassing the formal chain of command. Recognizing the directive effectively undermined the integrity of his unified command, Eisenhower strenuously objected, demanding the wording be changed.[67] On October 21 the British complied. Writing to Marshall, Eisenhower assured him the British never actually assailed the concept of unity of command but merely fashioned the original document in "a crude way." "In many instances," he pointed out, "the British are ready to go much further than some American officers in accepting and abiding by the principle [of unity of command]."[68] Greatly relieved by the reworded directive of October 21, Eisenhower felt a solid foundation for the military alliance had been laid.[69]

Smith's function was to enforce cooperation within the Allied staff. When the respective American and British planners first came together in the early days of AFHQ, Eisenhower later recalled, they did so like dogs meeting cats. Soon the differences in accent, habits, slang, and doctrine gave way to the appreciation that an important job must be performed. Smith's presence became instrumental in achieving harmony among the soldiers, seamen, and airmen of both nations. Here too the attitude of the British proved important. After TORCH became fixed, the British government made certain the officers detailed to AFHQ entertained no reservations about serving under American officers.[70] The British did not hold much faith in the quality of the ETO staff, an assessment shared by Eisenhower,[71] and carefully assigned their most able available staff officers to Smith's organization. Smith, well aware of American deficiencies in this area, came to rely most heavily upon his British subordinates, who made up the larger portion of the AFHQ staff.[72] Bedell's relationship with the British was further enhanced by his unreserved advocacy of the North African operation. The campaign offered an opportunity for green American troops and untried commanders to gain experience in combined Allied operations. He also recognized the strategic advantages in pocketing the Axis forces fighting in the western desert, views shared by Churchill and the BCOS if not the War Department. Important also was Smith's relationship with "Pug" Ismay, who saw AFHQ suffered from no lack of British support. Many American officers, envious of Smith's intimacy with the British, began to view Smith as a Churchill toady, but he cared little for what others thought. His mandate remained clear—to create a highly integrated Allied staff. Petty jealousies and long-standing prejudices had no place in such an organization as Smith worked unceasingly to exorcise dissonance from his headquarters.

The other problem Smith faced was the finalization of plans for the North African landings. After the delays of the spring and summer, planning the attack proved exceedingly difficult. The decision, once made, involved the seizure of three major ports, all in French possession. Any military operation calling for three widely separated, simultaneous assaults would be complicated under the best circumstances. TORCH proved problematical because of the special demands of conducting amphibious operations, particularly in view of the failure of Gallipoli in World War I and the bitter experience of Dieppe. While optimists subscribed to Murphy's rosy estimates of unopposed landings, the AFHQ planners could not labor under such illusions. The challenge was heightened by the realization that all previous calculations based upon earlier versions of TORCH were now rendered useless. Forced to begin anew, AFHQ planners coordinated the convergence of two convoys, rendezvousing in the Atlantic from two directions—one carrying Lieutenant General George Patton's corps from the U.S. east coast ports; the other sailing from Great Britain—and drew up a comprehensive scheme for their deployment. The resulting plans hardly represented perfection. AFHQ staff "slaved like dogs," as Eisenhower put it, and emerged from their two month-long ordeal as a functioning Allied team.

THE NATURE OF THE EISENHOWER-SMITH TEAM

Organizations are only as good as the people who staff them. Although Eisenhower prided himself in fashioning an integrated "Combined Staff...that might well serve as a rough model" for future operations, the AFHQ organization remained largely extemporized.[73] Throughout the course of the war in Europe, the Allied staff structure remained fluid, subject to the demands of coalition grand strategy. While the structure and personnel of the Allied apparatus was dynamic, its nucleus, the principle of unity of command and the personalities of its leadership, Eisenhower and Smith, remained unaltered. In "Ike" and "Beetle" Marshall had selected a winning team.

Marshall, of course, never intended Eisenhower would ultimately command the campaigns in France and Germany. The immediate task given Eisenhower, first as commanding general of the European Theater and later as commander-in-chief for the TORCH operation, involved creating an efficient command and staff structure and laying foundations for Marshall's eventual assumption of the duties of supreme commander. Wanting the best possible organization, one that accorded to his views, the army chief of staff selected Marshall-men. It was for this reason he pushed Eisenhower and sacrificed Smith.

Those who came into close contact with Eisenhower in the early days of his command were struck, as Cunningham put it, by his "rather naive wonder at attaining the high position in which he [finds] himself."[74] Only three years before he had been an unknown lieutenant colonel and now found himself a lieutenant general commanding the likes of Cunningham. On the other hand, Eisenhower postured as the small-town Kansan, as "too simple-minded to be an intriguer or attempt to be clever."[75] In point of fact, Eisenhower, a far more complex person than he appeared, possessed a sharp intelligence and used his naivete as a screen for the more Machiavellian twist in his personality. Unquestionably loyal to Marshall and appreciative of his own role as caretaker, Eisenhower was not without ambition and a burning desire to carve out a niche for himself in the Allied command structure. Although his wonderment probably outweighed his ambition at this juncture, Eisenhower gave every indication of possessing the resourcefulness to grow into the demanding role of commander-in-chief of the Allied armies.

Marshall wanted to be sure Eisenhower was not overwhelmed by his newfound position, particularly while the headquarters remained in London. Recognizing Eisenhower needed to be propped up against the British, especially Churchill and Brooke, Marshall sent Clark to the United Kingdom. Despite his much vaunted reputation, Clark showed little talent for getting along with the British or expediting planning. Marshall then dispatched Smith to London.

Enjoying the luxury of coming to London after the decision on TORCH had been made, Smith quickly emerged as Eisenhower's strongest buttress. Charged with representing the American point of view and consolidating the Anglo-American staff, Smith's unremitting addiction to duty cultivated a synthesized framework for Allied cooperation. His dyspeptic nature together with his intractable demand for immediate results and adroit mastery of administrative detail marked Smith as the perfect counterpart to Eisenhower.

No one appreciated Smith's worth more than Eisenhower. Smith's "organizational and executive abilities are so outstanding," Eisenhower reported to Marshall, "that the beneficial effects of his presence are constantly evident."[76] With confidence both in his own abilities and those of Smith, Eisenhower advised Marshall, "if both the Chief of Staff and myself are hale and hearty" there no longer existed any need to retain Clark as his deputy.[77] If Eisenhower saw himself as coach, then Smith was captain of the Allied team.

Arising from the discord and confusion of the summer, Smith's forceful personality and attention to the essential details of command achieved the results which Marshall and Eisenhower demanded of him—the welding together of an Allied staff. While the nature of the chief of staff's position and the character of the Allied staff remained undetermined, Smith had reason to be pleased with his accomplishments. Tormented by the prospects of failure, Eisenhower drew satisfaction from the knowledge he had succeeded in formulating a solid structure for the Allied command. If the TORCH landings did not succeed, Eisenhower confided to Marshall on the eve of the landings, it would have nothing to do with the failure to achieve an integrated Allied command.[78]

Allied Force Headquarters and the Invasion of North Africa, November 1942–January 1943

The North African invasion forces landed at Casablanca, Algiers, and Oran, as planned, on November 8. A week later, Allied troops occupied a defensive line east of Bône, close to the Algerian-Tunisian frontier. As the British predicted, the presence of Axis troops in Tunisia—primarily Italians stiffened by German forces under General Jürgen von Arnim—prevented the Allies from fully exploiting the strategic advantages gained by TORCH. Though surprised by the Allied landings, the Axis High Command easily adjusted to meet the threat.[1]

Eisenhower's position was less flexible. Forced to stage the Casablanca operation, the Allied supreme commander found his forces badly dispersed. He never openly said so, but Eisenhower knew the insistence of the U.S. Chiefs of Staff on the Casablanca landings both handicapped Anderson's drive for Tunis and Bizerte and dangerously overextended his own already weak forces.[2]

The objectives of the TORCH operation—the seizure of Casablanca and Algiers—were secured almost immediately. Preoccupied with the amphibious phase of the operation, the harried planners devoted little concrete thinking to future operations. The long-term aim centered on linking with General Bernard Montgomery's British 8th Army; but those forces were 1,200 miles to the east. Eisenhower took little comfort in the fact Montgomery's army was rapidly pursuing Field Marshal Erwin Rommel's Italian-German forces westward. If Rommel's battle-hardened desert army combined with von Arnim's forces in Tunisia, they could consolidate and lash out at AFHQ's forces. Eisenhower remained optimistic about Anderson's offensive towards Bizerte, but on November 30 determined local German counterattacks forced an abandonment of the Allied push. With British 1st Army assuming the defensive, the Tunisian campaign, by the first week of December, devolved into a battle of attrition.[3]

NORTH AFRICA: MOROCCO

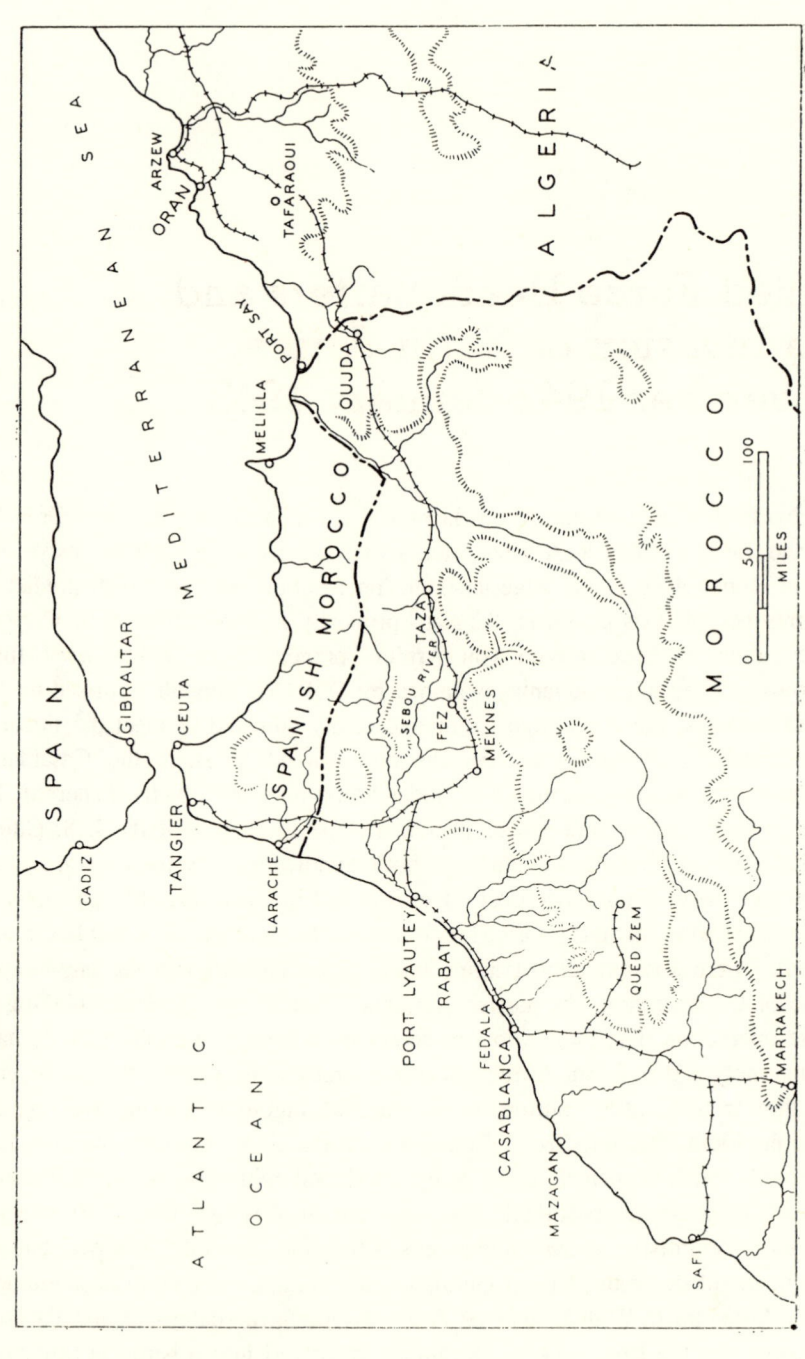

Alfred D. Chandler, ed., *The Papers of Dwight D. Eisenhower: The War Years*, vol. 5 (Baltimore: Johns Hopkins University Press, 1970), p. 52.

Many factors contributed to the failure of the forces under Eisenhower's command to take northern Tunisia. The first was the speed with which the Axis seized and reinforced Tunisia. Operating from all-weather bases only fifteen miles from the front, the Axis air forces enjoyed local air superiority and flew at will against the vital port of Bône and the exposed elements of Anderson's Blade Force. By the first week in December enemy air power alone sufficed to blunt any further Allied advance.[4] Second, Patton's corps, 700 miles distant in French Morocco, lent no support for the "race to Tunis." Third, the emphasis on getting ashore and pushing rapidly towards Tunisia threw the command arrangements into confusion.[5] Fourth, administrative and logistical necessities had been provided only for the initial landings. Without motor transport, Anderson relied upon a single rail line that forwarded only nine small trains per day—two of which hauled coal for the locomotives.[6] If the military situation were not complex enough, Eisenhower had to devote three-fourths of his time to political matters, dealing with intransigent French officials.[7] Finally, adverse weather reduced the theater to a sea of mud, seriously hampering logistics and air operations. Eisenhower typically blamed himself for the failures.[8] With the campaign in Tunisia stalemated, Eisenhower turned his attention to solving the command problems, bringing up reserves and essential supplies, and securing French military and political assistance. In each instance his chief support came from Bedell Smith.

THE POLITICAL MORASS IN ALGIERS

Initially, Smith was to move to Gibraltar five days before the TORCH landings to establish an advance headquarters. Last-minute planning and the need to maintain immediate communications between North Africa, London, and Washington required an alteration in the plan. As events unfolded, the decision to leave Smith behind in London proved to be a lucky one.

Smith wrestled with the complex business of running the Norfolk House staff and dealing with the enemy within, his ulcer. Realizing a return to the hospital meant a desk job in the War Department, Smith did his utmost to conceal the seriousness of his stomach disorder. Those in his immediate circle knew Smith's mood to be an accurate barometer of his health, and throughout his stay in London he grew increasingly vitriolic. General Frederick Morgan, a top British planner and future deputy chief of staff under Smith, comforted his American friend. The morning of the landings, Smith's stomach was "giving him very particular hell." While awaiting news from Gibraltar, Morgan tried to raise Smith's spirits, taking his mind off his pain. For over an hour the British general engaged "in merry chatter...on every subject but that of invasion in general and the invasion of Africa in particular."[9] Whether Morgan's efforts had any therapeutic effect is questionable, but the episode strengthened the bond between the two. While Smith suffered acutely, he continued to hold the fort in London for Eisenhower.

Soon after arriving in Gibraltar, Eisenhower realized the magnitude of the political problems he would face in dealing with the French. Eisenhower had no way of knowing just how poorly he had been served by Murphy. The bumbling efforts of Murphy's mission had one salutary result. American intelligence efforts were so clumsy they convinced the Germans the Allies had no serious designs in North Africa. Other than this accidental by-product there was little to recommend Murphy's actions.[10] As early as the September meeting between Murphy and the senior American officers at Telegraph Cottage, the broad lines of the French policy had been laid.[11] Roosevelt's hostility toward Général Charles de Gaulle effectively ruled out cooperation with the Free French. The only alternative rested with winning certain key Vichy figures to the Allied side. An October 17 directive, issued by Eisenhower, outlined the proposed integration of the French into the AFHQ structure. Admiral Jean Darlan, heir apparent to Marshal Henri Pétain and commander-in-chief of Vichy armed forces, was envisioned as the best choice for the role as French deputy to Eisenhower. Général Henri Giraud, meanwhile, would be named commander of French forces in the field. With this directive in mind, Clark made the preliminary "Darlan Deal" with French officials during his secret mission to Algeria.[12]

The plan started to unravel before the landings took place. Far from the pliable "noble puppet" Murphy promised, Giraud proved unaccommodating. Rather than serve as a subordinate, Giraud insisted the honor of France demanded that he command an invasion, not of North Africa, but of southern France. Giraud finally agreed to go to Algiers to broadcast an order to the French forces not to resist the landings. Unfortunately, he had no authority over the Pétainist army and was ignored. Clark hurriedly established a small advanced echelon of AFHQ in Algiers and opened negotiations for a cessation of French resistance. After four days of hectic bargaining, Darlan, who happened to be in Algiers, agreed to act as high commissioner in North Africa with Giraud placed in command of the army.[13]

Eisenhower neither understood French politics nor appreciated the psychological effect of the 1940 débâcle. He felt betrayed by any Frenchman not wholeheartedly at his service. "All of these Frogs have a single thought—ME," he complained to Smith. "It isn't this operation that's wearing me down," he lamented, "its the petty intrigue and the necessity of dealing with little, selfish, conceited worms that call themselves men."[14]

The supreme commander's mood was not improved by the general impotency he felt as he remained isolated in Gibraltar. His daily communications with Smith provided the only release. "I can not tell you how much your being in London has added to my piece of mind," he stated. "I would be completely lost without you." Reflecting his own insecurities, Eisenhower told his chief of staff he was not missing anything: "The real job is not going to start here until...the campaigning [begins] in earnest."[15]

While Eisenhower stewed in Gibraltar, a storm burst in London. On November 12, Eisenhower received a cable from Smith informing him Marshall, enthusiastic after the early successes, approved of the agreement with the French. Smith also pointed out Churchill favored the dispatch of a Free French mission to North Africa.[16] Advising caution, the prime minister hoped to sell de Gaulle on Giraud, who was unblemished by any hint of defeatism. Churchill knew no cooperation could be expected between Darlan and the Free French leader.[17] Disregarding Churchill's plea for restraint, Eisenhower flew to Algiers to press for a settlement. Before he left, the supreme commander wired Smith outlining his intentions but insisted his assistant in London blanket the agreement in total secrecy.[18]

Pleased he had finally achieved something, Eisenhower returned to Gibraltar only to be met by a communique from Smith that stunned him.[19] Hearing the political settlement, Churchill flew into one of his monumental rages. "Is this then what we are fighting for?" he railed. In the eyes of the British, Darlan was a fascist. Aside from practical political questions, there remained the serious matter of relations with the Soviet Union, the other associated states, and the European resistance movements. De Gaulle could certainly present problems, but how would Churchill explain to Marshal Stalin the spectacle of the Allies cooperating with a Nazi collaborator? For the first time Eisenhower became aware of the far-reaching implications of his expedient.[20]

It now fell to Smith to pacify the prime minister. For the next few days Eisenhower received a series of ominous-sounding letters from Smith relating the intensity of British reaction.[21] Badly stung by the criticism, Eisenhower plaintively wrote Smith, pleading with him to impress upon Churchill the weakness of the Allied position in North Africa. "It will be a long time before we can get up on our high horse and tell everyone to go to the devil," he stated.[22]

Eisenhower received support from Washington. In a November 16 press conference, Roosevelt announced his approval of the "temporary expedient," while the same day the CCS cabled Smith offering their support.[23] The War Department also defended Eisenhower, disregarding a State Department proposal for Darlan's removal.[24] Buoyed by these votes of confidence from Washington, Eisenhower felt only Smith stood behind him in London.

Smith's personal relations with the prime minister became an invaluable factor in lessening the damage created by the Darlan agreement. In daily contact with Churchill, Smith portrayed the agreement as a temporary settlement, justifiable solely from a military standpoint. The sting of the Darlan affair was diminished, to a degree, by Montgomery's victories in the western desert—Tobruk had been retaken on November 13. As Smith pointed out, Darlan's assistance, however unpalatable, had been essential in arranging an immediate cease-fire—a necessary prerequisite for Anderson's drive into Tunisia.[25] On November 20, Smith flew to Gibraltar to confer with Eisenhower. Smith outlined the difficulties of conducting the London rearguard action but assured the supreme commander the British leadership showed every sign of coming around.[26] Returning to London, Smith discovered his efforts paid off. Churchill and the War Cabinet announced their willingness to give the agreement firm support.[27] Eisenhower earlier claimed he had every reason to "thank God" Smith remained behind in London to undertake this most delicate diplomatic mission.[28]

Smith concentrated on the crisis arising from the political fray in North Africa. He also dealt with the enormous volume of correspondence that filtered through London. He received directives and questions from Eisenhower, Marshall, the CCS and the BCOS, Roosevelt, and Churchill, and attended to them all. One of his tasks involved restraining the zeal of the CCS. Soon after the successful completion of the landings, Smith received a cable from Washington broaching the idea of expanding operations in the Mediterranean. Smith warned Eisenhower on November 12 the chiefs wanted AFHQ to consider using forces intended for North Africa for an alternative invasion of Sardinia.[29] Embroiled in political matters, Eisenhower remained "unalterably opposed" to weakening the TORCH force. "I am not crying wolf nor am I growing fearful of shadows," he told Smith. Urging Smith to dispel "the apparently bland assumption that we are yet out of the woods in this proposition," Eisenhower knew he must receive reinforcements before operations in Tunisia could be pursued.[30]

In addition to briefing the supreme commander on the repercussions of the Darlan affair during the November 20-22 conferences, Smith and Eisenhower discussed the pressing manpower and matériel shortages, most importantly, the lack of adequate fighter cover. Upon his return to London on November 23 Smith took up the matter with Churchill and Air Chief Marshal Portal. By November 29 the aircraft, particularly night fighters, had been dispatched.[31]

The need to consolidate the AFHQ in the Mediterranean theater loomed large. In mid-November, the headquarters was divided between London, Gibraltar, and

Algiers. On November 15 Clark frantically called for the dispatch of staff personnel to Algiers. Smith meanwhile directed the transfer of rear-echelon functions in London to Hartle's ETO headquarters.[32] By the 25th he completed the movement of his headquarters out of London. That finished, Smith hoped for a breathing spell to master his health problems.[33]

No sooner had the Darlan affair begun to recede when another crisis developed. Churchill, concluding from some of Hartle's actions the American commitment to ROUNDUP was waning, demanded a clarification. Churchill's pointed queries prompted some heated exchanges, with Smith again called to mediate. At a November 25 meeting with Churchill and the BCOS, Smith assured the British the buildup for a 1943-1944 invasion of the continent would continue. They also discussed the military situation in North Africa. While informing them Eisenhower expected "a hard fight in Tunisia," Smith predicted it would require a stroke of luck for the Bizerte-Tunis area to be cleared by mid-December.[34]

When a general CCS conference failed to materialize in London during November, Marshall called for Smith's urgent return to Washington. On December 1 he flew to the United States but not before he reassured Eisenhower he would "avoid anything like a defensive attitude" in conversations with Roosevelt and Marshall. "I will," he pointed out, "present our viewpoint as aggressively as possible, consistent with tact."[35]

Smith remained in Washington for ten days. The first night he dined at the White House with the president, Mrs. Roosevelt, Hopkins and his wife, and Admiral Leahy. The First Lady, who monopolized the conversation over dinner, berated Eisenhower for mishandling the Darlan deal. After dinner, the men moved to the president's study to discuss the military and political situation in North Africa. Reviewing the progress of operations, Smith told his listeners he fully expected northern Tunisia would be occupied sometime in December while Tripoli would fall to Montgomery by the end of January.[36] While making the rounds in Washington he briefed Marshall and the deans of the War Department on Churchill's commitment to the cross-channel invasion and the damage caused by the political morass in Algiers. Between his many meetings, Smith found time to spend with his wife in their Fort Myer quarters. True to his word, Smith pressed Marshall on the subject of reinforcements for Eisenhower's command. Having done his best to represent the AFHQ viewpoint, Smith boarded an airplane on December 11 for Algiers.

Smith's absence from London was keenly felt. Anxious to establish his headquarters in Algiers and take charge of the battle, Eisenhower cabled Marshall the day after Smith left for Washington pleading that his chief of staff not be delayed in the United States.[37] Churchill, accustomed to having Smith at his side, worried about losing contact with AFHQ once the headquarters left London.[38] According to British method, given the formal lines of communication between London and British field commanders, Anderson issued daily situation reports directly to the War Office. Fearing erosion of unity of command, Eisenhower objected.[39] For a while Eisenhower took up the practice but soon abandoned it. The prime minister, wanting tight control over operations, complained he was being kept in the dark. Churchill approached Marshall, questioning whether Smith might not better be left in London.[40] Eager to have Smith in Algiers, Eisenhower suggested Smith spend one of every three weeks in London, and if necessary, alternate weeks, and be available for conferences as needs arose.[41] Fortunately for Smith, as communications improved, the need for such formal arrangements diminished.

In these trying days when the Grand Alliance received its first test, a pattern emerged. A constant divergence of views is inevitable in any alliance. In this first set of Allied crises, differences never approached the dangerous stage. This harmony can be attributed to two men: Churchill and Eisenhower. The prime minister proved uniquely able to manage the politicians and the service chiefs, a product of his broad experience and practical understanding of civil and military affairs. While he lacked experience, Eisenhower possessed an extraordinary ability to inspire confidence among his superiors and intense loyalty among those under him. When serious rifts loomed and the exchange of communications did not suffice, Eisenhower called upon his most trusted subordinates to deal directly with the political leadership or the respective service chiefs. Eisenhower came to entrust Smith almost exclusively with these missions, a testament to the high regard the supreme commander had for his chief of staff.

SMITH PUTS HIS STAMP ON
ALLIED FORCE HEADQUARTERS

During the first three weeks of the campaign Eisenhower commanded the theater with the aid of a handful of staff officers from his cramped headquarters in Gibraltar. Restless and eager to assume direct command, Eisenhower was sustained, as he told Smith, by the realization "we will be together in a fine headquarters one of these days," which they could "run...according to [their] own likes and dislikes."[42] On November 23, Eisenhower flew to Maison Blanche airfield, Algiers, then proceeded to the St. George Hotel where Clark had established AFHQ-Forward. Assuming direction of the headquarters, Eisenhower found the situation far from his liking. Anderson's hurried advance placed his forces beyond the headquarters' immediate control, and Clark's preoccupation with dealing with the French prevented him from properly organizing the staff.

In Eisenhower's opinion, the first order of business centered upon his asserting the command authority.[43] Although Eisenhower would have preferred more clearly defined lines of authority, his direct command of the ground and air components and his excellent working relationship with Cunningham provided a sound foundation for Anglo-American cooperation at the highest levels. Developments within the AFHQ staff, however, created concern. In London, Eisenhower asked that the BCOS assign two senior officers to AFHQ to head the intelligence and planning divisions. He also requested two administrative officers as well as a unit for political warfare and special intelligence operations. These officers joined the headquarters and, with their American colleagues, formed the nucleus of the AFHQ. Once in place, the British began to operate as if AFHQ were a British command. "The inevitable trend of the British mind towards 'committee' rather than 'single command,'" he complained, threatened to undermine his concept of unity of command.[44]

The allies did not immediately blend. Accustomed to their own procedures, the British representatives intruded, in the opinion of the Americans, into matters that did not involve them. Under normal circumstances status was determined by rank. Within the AFHQ setup, American officers frequently found themselves junior in rank to their British counterparts and equal in rank to many of their subordinates. On the other hand, the British believed, not without justification, that the Americans did not understand how a general headquarters should function. The hauteur of British officers irritated the Americans, while the ungentlemanly behavior of the Americans—their heavy drinking and indiscreet pursuit of women—shocked British sensibilities. In such an environment frictions developed.[45]

The supreme commander was disturbed by the failure to achieve staff integration, but he lacked the time to resolve the situation. According to American doctrine, the duties of the staff divisions were defined by function. Specialization within the staff would be carried as far as possible, compatible with the staff's underlying need for cooperation. Heads of divisions and sections had executive responsibilities and exercised full authority within their particular fields. The authority that bound staff levels together rested upon formal lines. Prewar doctrine ignored the personal dynamics of organizations, that coordination depended on informal relationships. American procedures encouraged segregation rather than integration as the span of authority of individual staff divisions remained fixed. Surveying the problem, Eisenhower had to discern whether the failure to achieve integration resulted from faulty organization or lack of leadership. A product of the American staff system, he naturally concluded the latter. Eisenhower anxiously anticipated Smith's arrival in Algiers and chafed at his delay in Washington. When he finally came to North Africa on December 11, Eisenhower breathed a loud sigh of relief.

The Washington mission did nothing to improve Smith's health or his foul disposition. He was accompanied on the flight from Washington by Eisenhower's brother, Milton. Their passage proved unpleasant, and shortly after his arrival, Milton advised his brother to select another chief of staff.[46] Eisenhower knew that Smith was "strong in character and abrupt by instinct" and as he put it to a British officer, "a Prussian."[47]

Nevertheless, Smith produced action and could not be spared. Eisenhower made allowances for Smith's disagreeable personality and asked others to do so as well. He appreciated his chief of staff's loyalty, even to the point of sacrificing his health. Eisenhower heard, via the rumor mill of ETO, Smith's ulcer had not improved. He knew life at headquarters would keep him from exposure to the hardships borne by front-line officers and hoped his ailment would improve.[48] In any case, Eisenhower required Smith's presence in Algiers where his conscientiousness and professionalism would stand comparison with any in the British service.

As the staff threatened to divide into personalities, Smith moved to restore formal lines of authority. From the onset, Eisenhower delegated all the details of controlling the staff to Smith. Both men assumed the basic organization to be sound. The problem involved enforcing coordination. American doctrine was particularly ambiguous on how much authority a chief of staff possessed, leaving it largely a matter of the ability and personality of the officers concerned. The "staff principle" should have reduced the commanding general's span of control and his task as coordinator. Not existing as a convention, it had to be worked out in practice. Nominally, the chief of staff reported directly to the commanding general. In fact, all official staff transactions remained the preserve of the chief of staff. The supreme commander could not deal with the details that followed from his decisions. Command and control were bound up in the personalities of the supreme commander and his chief of staff. By virtue of his position and Eisenhower's trust, Smith's functions involved an assertion of broad authority and autonomy.

Smith had to undertake an educational effort before his concept of staff structure could take form. Initiating British and American staff officers into his regime, Smith had to learn the practical lessons of organizing and running an integrated staff. In the early weeks he tried to bully his subordinates. His efforts met with little success. He, however, was not immune from the pressure around him. American officers who had worked under Bedell in London or knew his reputation were readily reined. The British, with three years of war under their belts, had confidence in their abilities to run a staff and were not easily tossed around. Smith's badgering methods produced only a decline in morale. "He's [Smith] just a neurotic with an aching ulcer," remarked Butcher.[49]

Whatever subordinates thought of Smith, Eisenhower maintained the utmost confidence in him. While subordinates were reduced to a bundle of shaking nerves in his presence, Smith used a different approach when dealing with senior British representatives in the headquarters. On one occasion he called a senior British staff officer and his American assistant into his office. Smith was unhappy a certain project had not been completed quickly enough. Although he blamed the British officer, Smith dressed down both men, then asked the American to stay behind. After apologizing for making the American a "whipping post," he explained he must appear even handed in such matters. Unsatisfied, the staff officer indignantly requested a transfer. "No, God-damn it," he shouted! "You'll stay right where you are."[50]

Smith was particularly hard on American junior officers attached to his immediate staff. It was clear the service schools had not trained captains and majors for high-level intelligence and planning. As a result he fleshed out his staff with younger officers who had proven themselves in combat units. Smith felt responsible for educating promising officers in staff duties. This also allowed Smith to put his own stamp on the headquarters. "We are putting these chaps through an all around course," he related to a senior field commander, "and by the time we are finished with them the Army will have a few thoroughly trained, high level staff officers to get us ready for the next war."[51] While he may have been a terror in his own office, he had the best interests of the army at heart. Officers who performed to his exacting standards knew they enjoyed Smith's confidence. Although he would never say so directly, they saw in his casual remarks that Smith approved of their progress.[52]

Accustomed to the querulousness of the political heads, Smith quickly mastered the warring factions within his headquarters. Recalcitrant subordinates were not tolerated. Once an officer found himself on the wrong side of Smith, as with Marshall, there was no returning to his good graces. "If you got the A treatment from Smith," an American staff officer remembered, "you took the afternoon off. If you got the B treatment, you took the rest of the week off. If you got the C treatment, you started cleaning out your desk."[53] Through these methods Smith established control over his staff. Slowly the headquarters coalesced. While his subordinates never grew to love him, Smith won their loyalty and admiration.

Having stamped his personality on the AFHQ, he proceeded with setting up his household staff and defining policies. Here again Marshall's War Department General Staff served as the model. In December, Bedell appointed Colonel Dan Gilmer as his secretary. Because he held that position in Marshall's headquarters, Smith demanded peak performance from his secretariat. Smith personally reorganized the filing system as he had done in the War Department. His reputation rested upon efficiency, and he insisted he be kept current on all matters of immediate interest to Eisenhower and the staff. He also instituted the "one-minute rule" and rigidly enforced it.[54]

Smith encountered difficulty in defining the size of AFHQ. Clark wanted to keep the staff as small as possible. Initially, AFHQ had an authorized strength of 700, a number estimated by Clark as two or three times the size necessary.[55] Smith took a more realistic stance, realizing the management of one campaign and the planning of future operations required a staff several times larger than sanctioned by the "book." By January 1943 the American contribution alone stood at 1,406. As new sections and responsibilities were added, staff size expanded. This represented a departure from American staff procedures prompting Marshall to complain that the staff threatened to expand to unmanageable proportions. On February 8, Eisenhower, seeking to mollify Marshall and protect Smith, equivocated, promising a staff reduction.[56] By May 25, the supreme commander realized it was no longer possible to keep a lid on staff size.[57] When Marshall remained unconvinced, Eisenhower, in early June, took specific issue with his chief in Washington, and by autumn 1943 AFHQ had expanded to 4,070.[58]

THE HEADQUARTERS STRUCTURE

The basic organization of AFHQ had been established in London before the campaign and conformed to the American model. Similarly, most of the principal officers had been selected before Smith's arrival. Thereafter, Eisenhower gave Smith absolute authority over staff management.

Logistics occupied a special place during the planning stage in London. Here again no historical precedent existed, and after careful theoretical study a decision was made to preserve the administrative systems of both allied powers as far as possible.[59] For coordination, the respective heads of the Logistics and Administrative divisions were responsible to their immediate superiors, the deputy chiefs of staff. General Alfred Gruenther and his British coequal, Brigadier J.F.M. Whiteley, Smith's two deputies, made sure no divided counsels existed. A similar setup existed for the Personnel Division (G-1) where the respective adjutants general managed manpower matters for the theater.

Smith found the arrangements unsatisfactory. The British organized their staffs with the G-1 and G-4 divisions supervised by a chief administrative officer (CAO). Logistical management was as complex as it was important. Transport and supply needed coordination at every level of command, both laterally in the theater and vertically back to Washington and London. Beyond that, the logistical and administrative functions were performed by many specialized services, all orchestrated by AFHQ. Initially hostile to the creation of a CAO because it appeared as a surrender to "command by committee," Smith soon altered his stance. Major General Humphrey Gale then assumed the position as chief administrative officer. Gale supervised the newly organized Movement and Transport Section, a combined staff in the G-4 Division that handled the problem of forwarding manpower and matériel to operational zones.[60]

Gale's appointment and creation of a combined section represented a minor victory for the British staff system. In part, Smith supported Gale's organization because it increased his ability to supervise administrative and logistical matters. But Smith adamantly refused to delegate authority except to Gale, preferring to centralize power in his own hands. Encouraged by their success, the British pushed for creation of combined planning and intelligence committees. These committees, composed of representatives of each service with economic and political advisers attached, planned and reviewed political and military situations under the direction of a deputy chief of staff.

During January Smith busied himself building up the planning and intelligence staffs. A disproportionate number of the officers came from the British services.[61] Since the proposed committees would be British in organization and character, Smith initially opposed their creation, citing the principle of balanced national personnel. His real motive for sabotaging the scheme centered around his conservative insistence upon a vertical organization to protect his authority. He conceded the need for enhanced coordination between intelligence and operations and agreed to Whiteley's appointment as supervisor.

Once organized, the traditional divisions of the general staff remained fixed. The duties of the staff were divided and grouped by function. Gale's organization handled the systematic control of the "accounts of war." Whiteley dealt with the preparation of estimates and plans, subject to oversight by Smith.

In addition to securing staff unification, Smith furnished Eisenhower with digested information and advice. Smith synthesized the views of the staff divisions and ironed out the bias that specialization inevitably produces. He tried to overcome the differences in outlook and to weld together the various aspects of a particular problem leading to heterogeneous action. After Eisenhower or, in his name, Smith, decided a course of action, the chief of staff coordinated policy execution in the headquarters and with the subordinate commands.

Smith knew how to run a staff conference from his days under Marshall. He initiated daily chief of staff conferences on December 24, 1942. These noon meetings were attended by Gruenther, Whiteley, Gale, the heads of the Intelligence and Operations Divisions (brigadier generals E. E.

Mockler-Ferryman and Lowell Rooks), and the assistant chiefs of staff for the attached air and naval staffs. The principal AFHQ officers exchanged views, reported on staff activities, coordinated ground-air operations, and discussed developments for operations and logistics. Frictions were avoided as participants appreciated how the actions of each service affected the others. While Smith and his key subordinates dominated the conferences, the assistant chiefs of staff for Personnel and Supply, the chief of Movements and Transportation, the adjutant general, and the chiefs of Civil Affairs, Military Government, Engineering, Public Relations, Signals, and French Rearmament sections also attended and, when necessary, made specific reports.

A short meeting between Eisenhower, Smith, and the principal AFHQ officers followed each staff conference. Eisenhower received briefings on operational matters, enemy activity and strengths, and outlines of anticipated operational planning. When Eisenhower went on inspection tours, increasingly the case after Smith stabilized the staff structure, Bedell made decisions in the supreme commander's name. The secretariat maintained a special log of all incoming and outgoing messages, which Eisenhower consulted upon his return to keep abreast of Smith's actions. When Eisenhower was in his headquarters, the two met several times a day, analyzing problems facing the command. Because the North African Theater of Operations (NATOUSA), which included the Communications Zone for logistics, remained unorganized through the middle of February, Smith acted as chief of staff to both commands.[62] On February 15, Brigadier General Everett Hughes arrived in Algiers, assuming the twin duties of deputy theater commander to Eisenhower and controller of the Com-Z headquarters. Thereafter, Smith devoted most of his energies to the AFHQ staff.[63]

Smith occasionally felt obliged to call special meetings with portions of his staff. Usually informal affairs, often held on the patio of the St. George Hotel over breakfast, these conferences addressed specific situations later raised at the Chiefs of Staff conference.[64] Smith also periodically invited senior staff members to dine at his well-appointed villa. Military and political policy matters were settled. In all cases, Smith insisted on unanimity before issues were handled formally. Whether in a staff conference or a more informal setting, Smith's methods remained the same. Always well organized, a persuasive and forceful speaker, he dominated any gathering. Although his most intimate associates might have thought him unimaginative and inflexible, Smith never wasted time making up his mind. The combination of his intellectual skills and his grim, overbearing personality made him a truly formidable force.

While the classic general staff divisions presented few organizational obstacles, forging a unified air force command and dealing with political and psychological warfare—subjects not treated in any depth at Leavenworth—bedeviled Eisenhower and Smith. On December 1 Ismay cabled Eisenhower informing him the British desired an advanced headquarters be established at Algiers to coordinate all air force activity in the Mediterranean. Under the command of Air Chief Marshal Arthur Tedder this headquarters would be subordinate to Eisenhower for TORCH operations but answerable to the BCOS for the Middle East.[65] Earlier, on November 15, Arnold suggested a similar setup for the American air forces. Under Arnold's scheme, operations of the 12th Air Force in North Africa and the 8th Air Force in the United Kingdom would be coordinated under one American commander, Major General Carl Spaatz.[66] After an exchange of communications between Algiers, London, and Washington, it was decided instead to place the British Eastern Air command and the 12th under Spaatz.

This arrangement proved short-lived. At the Casablanca conference, held January 11-25, 1943, a new command structure emerged. Tedder commanded the amalgamation of Mediterranean air forces. With Spaatz as his deputy, Tedder coordinated air power in the Mediterranean and came under Eisenhower's direct command only when operating in northwest Africa. Eisenhower would have preferred, as Tedder put it, to have "the divine right to command his own private air force," but he accepted the new organization as an improvement over the old.[67]

Tedder forwarded his senior staff officer, Air Vice Marshal Philip Wigglesworth, to Algiers to organize the headquarters and serve as connecting link between his command and AFHQ. When Tedder arrived in Algiers, Smith met him, demanding Wigglesworth be removed. Wigglesworth, Smith said, would never fit into a combined headquarters because he could not cooperate. Smith's objection really centered upon Wiggleworth's refusal to channel everything through him. Tedder refused to relieve his trusted aide or accept Smith's interference with the air commander-in-chiefs's direct access to Eisenhower.

An impasse was averted narrowly. At a second meeting the two again exchanged their views. Although Smith stated his desire for a smooth operation, he strenuously rejected the idea of an independent air force organization. Bedell's preoccupation with the air command structure dealt less with Tedder's sphere of influence than Smith's apprehension that a dangerous precedent would be set for postwar American military reorganization. Typical of most senior American officers and illustrative of his narrowness, Smith opposed the concept of an American Air Force. "So far as he [Smith] was concerned," related Tedder, "a separate air force in America 'would come over his dead body.'" After Tedder assured him he had no intention of mixing in American interservice politics, Smith backed down. Although Tedder enjoyed considerable latitude, AFHQ-air cooperation existed owing to the presence of formal lines of authority and because close bonds of friendship and mutual trust developed between the airmen and Eisenhower.[68]

On the political question the responsibilities of AFHQ remained clouded. In September 1942 the AFHQ organization was "fixed up" for Murphy better to serve Roosevelt politically and Eisenhower militarily.[69] This was followed, in mid-December, by Murphy's elevation to minister status as the president's personal representative in North Africa. He served as ambassador and chief of the Political and Civil Affairs Section.[70] On January 1, 1943, Roosevelt outlined his attitude on North Africa to Churchill. "I feel very strongly that we have a military occupation in North Africa," he wrote, "and as such our Commanding General has complete charge of all matters civil as well as military. We must not let any of our French friends forget this for a moment."[71]

Eisenhower wanted relief from the political mess and to turn his undivided attention to running the battle. When the uproar over Darlan subsided, he confided in Smith that Churchill could "kick me in the pants and put in a politician here who is as big a crook as the chief local skunk."[72] When the prime minister offered to send his "big crook" in the person of Harold Macmillan, Eisenhower took a different view. Instead, he insisted he retain full political control in the theater and that Murphy and Macmillan report directly to him.

In a secret session of Parliament on December 10, Churchill asked that a "political adviser" be sent to Algiers "to gradually assume administrative control" from AFHQ. He also approached the United States ambassador in London, John Winant, pointing out British experience in colonial administration. A transcript of the speech, leaked to the OSS, warned Roosevelt of Churchill's scheme.[73] At Casablanca an accommodation was reached. Macmillan would parallel Murphy and put the views of the Foreign Office to Eisenhower. Thus, through Smith, AFHQ received directives from the State Department and the Foreign Office, Roosevelt and Churchill.

A November 30 directive from Marshall instructed Eisenhower to turn over political affairs to Murphy.[74] Unwilling to totally divorce civil affairs from AFHQ control, Eisenhower decided to maintain a tight rein on Murphy and Macmillan through the Political and Civil Affairs Section and the creation of a Political Council. Composed of the two principal political advisers and their associates, the Political Council was presided over by Smith.[75] Both American officers knew Murphy would offer no trouble, but Macmillan was different. Suspicious of Macmillan, Eisenhower delegated Smith the responsibility of managing the British minister resident.

Smith's experience taught him the best means of dealing with the British was over an informal gin and tonic. Macmillan, as Smith's special project, was feted by the American general upon his arrival in Algiers. The conversation turned to Anglo-American political differences, and the two promised to treat each other with confidence. As their friendship matured, Macmillan thought Smith "a most charming and excellent fellow [and] a friend of Britain." Although the British diplomat communicated directly with the Foreign Office, he always appraised Smith of all British actions. For most of his stay in Algiers, Smith remained in intimate contact with Macmillan, who emerged as one of his few close friends.[76]

The supreme commander expected Smith to handle the French as adroitly as he did the British. Where Smith found the British straightforward and trustworthy, he disliked the French for their palace intrigues and their pride. Like many senior American officers, he held the French officers in contempt for their defeat in 1940. To him, the French were "the Frogs."

Smith did not, however, share Roosevelt's prejudice against de Gaulle. Influenced by Churchill and Macmillan, Smith saw de Gaulle as the only alternative to the Pétainists and Giraud.[77] Darlan's assassination on December 24, 1942, conveniently solved one nagging detail, but Giraud proved unpliable. On January 22, a "shotgun wedding" between de Gaulle and Giraud took place at Casablanca, seemingly clearing the way for the Free French leader to come to Algiers.[78] This pleased Churchill but alarmed Roosevelt, who obstructed de Gaulle's taking any role in North African affairs.

Smith had the unenviable task of upholding Roosevelt's position even if he possessed little sympathy with it. Macmillan, a Francophile, believed a stable postwar Europe depended upon a strong France. The prime minister entertained similar views, but his primary concern centered on getting de Gaulle out of London. Eisenhower and Smith, meanwhile, wanted political stability in North Africa. In Smith's estimate, if de Gaulle could calm the troubled waters in Algiers and allow the military men to fight the Germans and Italians, so much the better. Roosevelt saw matters differently.[79]

It proved exceedingly difficult to defend Roosevelt's war aims because his program for the postwar period never took concrete form. On occasions he seemed to favor a collective security arrangement, while at other times he advocated a traditional spheres of influence approach, typified in his "Four Policemen." Always influenced by the twists in American public opinion, a weak reed as the basis for foreign policy decision making, Roosevelt understood the political difficulties of maintaining American troops in Europe after the war. A revived France was necessary, yet he doubted the French could ever regain their position in Europe. The president, impressed by a State Department program to bring democracy to a defeated Germany, thought that the United States would have to do the same for the French. Fearing a social revolution once the Germans were expelled and adamant he would not be party to making de Gaulle into a "man on horseback," he proposed to occupy France as if it were a belligerent power and turn administration over to the American and British military. Once liberated, France, the nation that gave the world the first great democratic revolution, would receive the blessings of American tutelage in democracy.[80] As long as Roosevelt denied de Gaulle an active voice in Allied affairs, Smith knew he would remain in the center of a series of bitter political struggles.

Eisenhower and Smith encountered a new type of problem—dealing with public relations. Army officers, long conditioned to avoid public criticisms, were hostile to journalists. Smith disliked the presence of political advisers in Algiers, but he appreciated their value. The press, on the other hand, were a pernicious influence.[81] During the Casablanca conference and after, American and British newspapers supported de Gaulle. This compromised Roosevelt's attempt to build up Giraud. At the same time, American officers in North Africa grumbled that American papers concentrated upon Montgomery's successes at the expense of TORCH. Senior American officers, seeking to project themselves into the headlines and perhaps secure a place in history, openly cultivated connections with newsmen. Without tight controls, press reports threatened to stir up the explosive political situation, exacerbate inter-Allied rivalries, and create jealousies among American officers. They might also disclose operational secrets to Axis intelligence. Smith regarded the press as a destabilizing nuisance; Eisenhower, incensed by their handling of the Darlan affair, viewed them as a security problem.[82] Both men displayed a mania for secrecy, fundamentally mistrusting the journalists attached to their headquarters.

Despite their misgivings, Eisenhower and Smith faced the correspondents' corps. In a democracy at war, especially the United States where the public had an insatiable appetite for news, the flow of information was vital in sustaining the morale of the Home Front. The headquarters fashioned a control apparatus, balancing security needs with the demands of a free press. As in many other instances, long service in the interwar army had not prepared senior American officers for dealing with public relations. A Propaganda Operations subsection was created in the G-1 Division with Colonel Julius Holmes, from the Office of War Information (U.S.), in charge. Smith oversaw Holmes, assuming the role of censor. He also had approval of press accreditation. Since Algiers was something of an island, Smith easily regulated the coming and going of the press. Not wishing to antagonize domestic public opinion, he established only a temporary censorship policy. When newsmen reported on the poor performance of American troops in Tunisia in February, which had an adverse impact upon morale, Smith made the policy permanent. Periodic press conferences, conducted by Eisenhower or Smith, proved a more effective means of handling the press. Trying to prevent the relationship from becoming confrontational, Eisenhower brought selected journalists into his confidence.[83] Between Eisenhower's charm and Smith's straightforwardness, they won the journalists over to their point of view. The newsmen became a type of adjunct to the staff as no serious breaches of security occurred.

A final organizational concern revolved around the place of the Psychological Warfare Section within AFHQ. Smith remained sceptical of the role of psychological warfare. A Psychological Analysis and Planning subsection existed as part of the Operations Division. Composed of representatives of the OSS and the British Special Operations Executive (SOE), this body fell under Smith's direct supervision. Donovan also furnished Murphy's Political and Civil Affairs Section with specialists.[84] Always suspicious of those he could not control, Smith relied upon Murphy to keep the OSS men firmly in check and to eliminate outside interference, especially by Donovan.

IKE AND BEETLE: COMPLEMENTARY STYLES OF LEADERSHIP

Although he did not exercise much influence over the AFHQ's initial organization or the selection of personnel, Smith played an ever-increasing role after his arrival in Algiers. In most respects Smith inherited an already organized headquarters. Clark, whom Eisenhower considered the best organizer in the army, faithfully constructed AFHQ in strict conformity to American regulations.[85] Smith established additional sections as the need arose. He generally proceeded incrementally, along lines prescribed by doctrine. Having been educated in the school of practice and as the star graduate of Marshall's general staff, Smith thought there was little he did not know about staff work. Proud of his accomplishments, and viewing himself as the army's exemplary self-made man, he never suffered from self-doubt. Despite his complaints about the advance service schools' failure to prepare properly officers for high-level staff work, Smith remained conservative throughout the war. Not an original thinker, Smith's strength rested in his broad experience and forceful personality.

In the beginning of his tenure as chief of staff, Smith knew he enjoyed the full confidence of generals Marshall and Eisenhower and Churchill. He did not care if he ruffled feathers in AFHQ. With the basic soundness of the organization never questioned, what remained to be resolved was the respective authority of the supreme commander and the chief of staff.

The spirit of Marshall hovered over Eisenhower and Smith. Both constantly demonstrated their loyalty to the chief but in different ways. Eisenhower, charged with conducting operations in the Mediterranean proposed by the British over Marshall's opposition, wrote the army chief of staff often in the tense early days of the campaign, thanking him lavishly for his support. After drawing heavy criticism for the Darlan deal, losing the race for Tunis, and experiencing the practical difficulties of commanding Allied combined operations, Eisenhower needed guidance and, more importantly, reassurance from the man who selected him for the job. The supreme commander knew there existed widespread suspicion that he did not possess a tight grip on the theater. Once the tactical situation stabilized, the 8th Army closed with the TORCH force, and Smith had straightened out the staff structure, Eisenhower's uncertainties gave way to self-assuredness. Although the two never became equals, Eisenhower's growth as a commander was reflected in his maturing relationship with Marshall. Eschewing the fulsome flattery that marked his 1942 letters, Eisenhower began to urge the chief to accept expanded operations in the Mediterranean and even expressed irritation at War Department interference into his sphere of control.[86]

Smith expressed his loyalty to Marshall not in word but in deed. His actions and leadership style were influenced by his devotion to Marshall. Throughout his career as military commander, Eisenhower's single greatest weakness rested in his tendency to move with the wind, to intentionally evade making decisions, allowing events to dictate actions. This approach might have been fatal, especially since a large part of his function involved management of difficult personalities. Marshall recognized this and entrusted Smith with the responsibility of undergirding Eisenhower to extirpate contention and embolden his commander in his dealings with Churchill, de Gaulle, and the field commanders.

Although their relationship would evolve over the course of the next two and a half years as Eisenhower and Smith learned the métier of their respective offices, the basic parameters of their partnership can already be detected by January 1943. As allied supreme commander, Eisenhower had two fundamental duties—roles that, in many respects, were intrinsically contradictory. As commander-in-chief he served as a symbol of unity; as chairman of the board he exercised command. Eisenhower's need for cooperation was balanced by emphasizing the commander-in-chief role with his function as shaper of policy. At the same time he defended his authority without sacrificing his popularity.

During operations in the Mediterranean and Europe, Eisenhower fielded severe criticism for delegating too much responsibility. As he told Mountbatten, who elicited Eisenhower's advice before assuming duties as supreme commander of the China-Burma-India Theater, "no commander of an allied force can be given complete administrative and disciplinary powers over the whole command...Without a great degree of decentralization no allied command can be made to work."[87] His adherence to this policy developed from his study of leadership and his relationship with Smith in North Africa. As a leader, Eisenhower considered the people with whom he worked as tools for performing his executive function.

Eisenhower practiced three types of delegation. Where he held strong views he extended his subordinates decision-making authority but only after they provided detailed specifications. In this way he could be sure they would decide matters consistent with his stated aims. He used this method with Smith. For those technical areas where he had little or no expertise, such as intelligence and logistics, he sought the best-qualified people, simply requesting that Smith keep him informed. Eisenhower considered himself qualified to handle operational matters. Since this was the area that interested him most, where he exercised ultimate authority, he spent a proportionately greater amount of time supervising his field commanders and the representatives of the air and naval forces attached to his staff. His principal staff officers—Smith, Gruenther, Whiteley, and Gale—were men of wide experience upon whom Eisenhower relied to perform the complex duties of planning and administration, reserving the right to make final decisions for himself. He took pride in the integrated Allied staff's formation and in his ability to work with a talented group of assistants without losing control.

Smith's functions involved the maintenance of the lines of authority. Eisenhower delegated control over the headquarters staff to him. Smith possessed the authority to draft formal directives and made personal contacts and adjustments to secure coordination. By relinquishing certain authority to Smith, Eisenhower enjoyed the freedom to exercise the affective function of leadership as commander-in-chief—to go to the field and stimulate and restrain the operational commanders. As chief of staff, Smith performed functions that, theoretically, belonged to the commanding general.[88] While this did not accord to prescribed doctrine or "academic perfection," as Eisenhower freely admitted, it worked because of the complementary personalities and styles of leadership of the supreme commander and his chief of staff.[89] The surrender of considerable executive authority and the impression that he reigned more than he ruled were the prices Eisenhower paid to exercise his commander-in-chief role.

As Eisenhower expected, Smith quickly brought cohesion to AFHQ. By February 12 he felt confident enough to leave Algiers in Smith's hands to visit the operational commands. He selectively delegated more and more authority to Smith. In theory, the chief of staff's role involved the arrangement of matters for operational and logistical commands to carry out their duties, all with a maximum of unity and a minimum · of friction. In practice, Smith made interpretative decisions; while he could not lawfully exercise command over anything but his staff, he issued orders to the operational and support commands in the name of Eisenhower. This was done through the issuance of AFHQ directives. The vast majority of these were authored by Smith, often without referral to the supreme commander. Through the secretariat's log, Eisenhower knew of Smith's action but usually only after the fact. Senior officers assigned to the theater—Cunningham, Tedder, Spaatz, and Anderson—knew that strategic decisions remained Eisenhower's. As long as Smith's actions remained consistent with the agreed objectives, there was no reason to resist directives issued by the chief of staff.

Some officers opposed the practice. They thought the amiable Eisenhower had abdicated his authority to his power-grasping chief of staff. Even officers who knew Eisenhower intimately held this view. In many respects they were correct. Smith's worst flaw was his insistence upon controlling his environment. He developed a series of defense mechanisms to safeguard his authority. It was this, more than his lack of imagination, that explains his refusal to create special committees or give civil affairs and psychological warfare sections their place as independent divisions. He was not above resorting to intrigues to protect his prerogatives. He similarly used his privileges to reward loyalty and his power to undercut his supposed enemies. The British, unaffected for the most part by his conniving, exhibited a willingness to accept his idiosyncrasies. Yet the British strenuously objected to Smith's jealous defense of Eisenhower's door. Citing regulations, American officers charged that Smith exercised too much influence on operational decisions through his control of the staff and orchestration of the all-important staff conferences. No records were kept of the private conversations the two shared. Because of his mastery of the details of staff operations and Eisenhower's high regard for his strategic insights, Smith's view carried much weight in the councils of the supreme commander.

Critics failed to appreciate Eisenhower's complex, skilful, and self-conscious leadership abilities. Behind the disarming smile lay a calculated shrewdness. Eisenhower analyzed his subordinates carefully, noting their personal qualities and weaknesses. He then determined what tasks they were best suited to perform. Smith's authoritarian personality and thirst for power were well known to Eisenhower. He dealt differently with Smith, primarily because he recognized his talents and appreciated his special relationship with Marshall and the British. He also understood that his own success as a commander was inextricably bound up with Smith's ability to manage the staff and maintain the confidence of the army chief of staff and Churchill. Beneath his image as proselytizer of Allied unity existed a vast amount of indirect, carefully concealed exercise of authority. Eisenhower always sought to operate through others with his part known only to a few. After the Darlan fiasco, he appreciated the necessity of camouflaging his own activities. Not only was he quick to share credit, he sought to diffuse blame as well. Insisting on multiple advocacy and broad support for his policies, Eisenhower persuaded others to implement his plans. For this he required the goodwill of his superiors and subordinates. In Smith, Eisenhower had the ideal man to act as his chief executive officer. The two established a collegial relationship with the supreme commander very clearly acting as the senior partner. This relationship, forged in North Africa, served as the foundation for the command and staff structure that contributed to Allied success in the Mediterranean and northwestern Europe.

The North African Campaign, January–July 1943

When the Combined Chiefs of Staff agreed to the "tightening of the ring" strategy, they did so without illusion. They understood the TORCH operation would absorb manpower, shipping, and assault craft and would make the execution of ROUNDUP in 1943 improbable. At Casablanca the broad grand strategic decisions came under discussion. Marshall arrived at the SYMBOL conference prepared to close down further operations in the Mediterranean and revive the cross-channel invasion. The British, in contrast, saw the Mediterranean as key to an interdependent global strategic system. As importantly, the theater represented the only place where British forces could be employed to take advantage of military opportunities. Churchill insisted on TORCH because the Mediterranean offered the only theater where operations were feasible in 1942. The question now rotated around what to do next.

With resources already committed to the Mediterranean, the British maintained a 1943 ROUNDUP could not be carried out. The British staff wanted operations continued in the Mediterranean with the objective of making the theater a "heavy liability" for the Germans and perhaps knocking Italy out of the war in the bargain. An invasion of Sicily (or Corsica or Sardinia) and whether the Italian mainland might be attacked remained undecided. Further operations in the Mediterranean would satisfy two grand strategic requirements: (1) compel the Germans to commit reserves in the south, preventing them from reinforcing their garrisons in France, opening the door for an eventual cross-channel invasion in 1944; and (2) relieve pressure on the Soviets, fulfilling obligations to Stalin. The BCOS attempted to persuade the Americans not to write off ROUNDUP in favor of the Pacific. Instead, they encouraged them to expand operations in the only theater where results could realistically be gained in 1943—the Mediterranean.[1]

NORTH AFRICA: ALGERIA AND TUNISIA

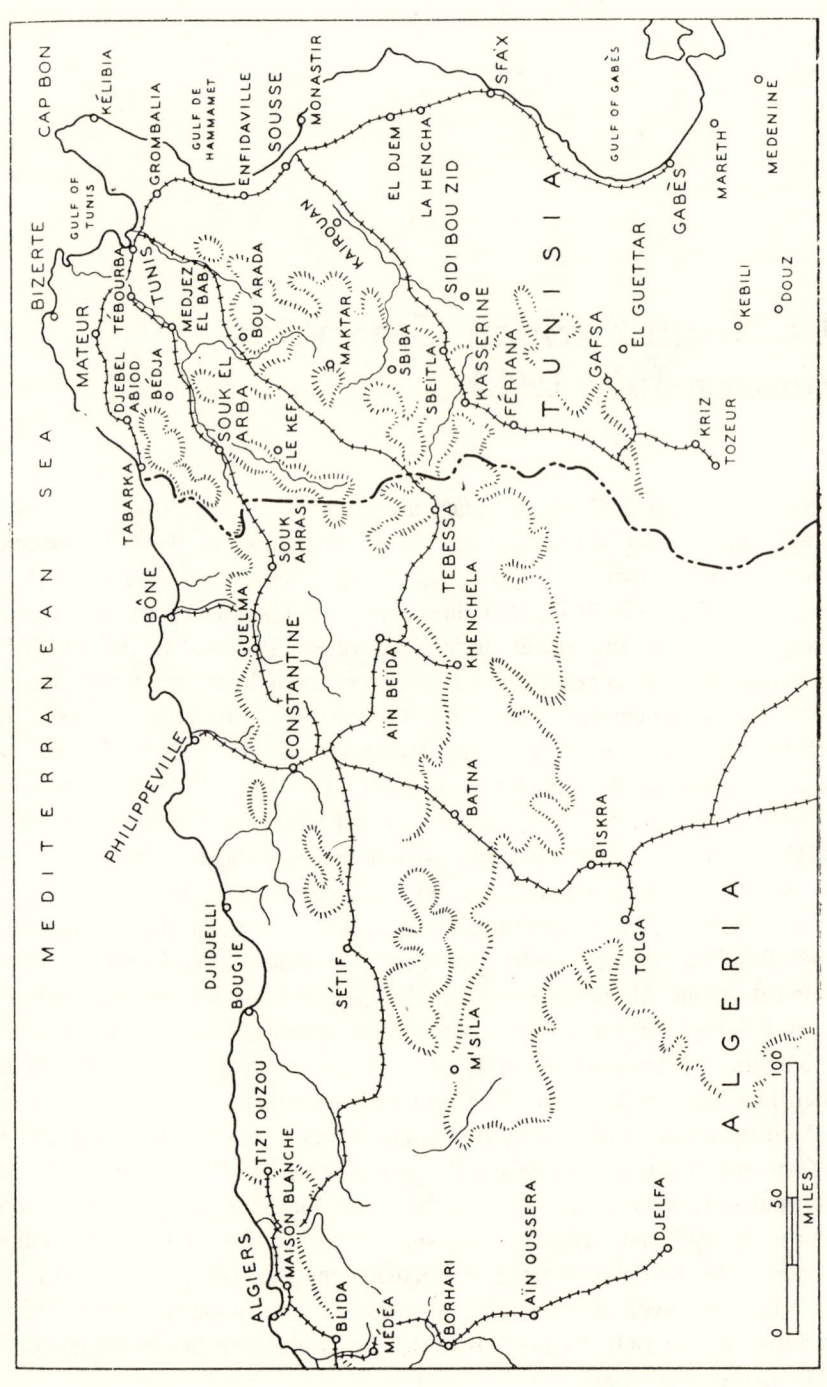

Alfred D. Chandler, ed., *The Papers of Dwight D. Eisenhower: The War Years*, vol. 5 (Baltimore: Johns Hopkins University Press, 1970), p. 53.

The American delegation arrived in Casablanca armed with little more than their suspicions. Some thought Mediterranean operations would make demands upon American resources while fulfilling British interests.[2] When the conference began, the Americans found themselves at a distinct disadvantage. The British Chiefs of Staff came prepared to state their case. They brought along a 6,000-ton ocean liner converted into a floating headquarters. When questions arose during the conversations, the British staff presented already formulated arguments supported by technical detail.[3] One British participant later remarked that the Americans, without comparable preparation,"left all their clubs at home."[4] An American opposite summed up Casablanca: "We came, we listened, and we were conquered."[5]

Marshall grudgingly accepted the British view. The defeat of the U-Boat menace received top priority. The CCS also agreed to intensify the air campaign against Germany and stage limited offensives in the Pacific. The "Europe first" principle calling for the cross-channel invasion was reaffirmed. Meanwhile, the British succeeded in gaining a commitment for the continuation of offensive operations in the Mediterranean. An invasion of Sicily was to be staged with Eisenhower named as the allied commander. While the British promised to accept the Sicilian invasion as the final act, it remained doubtful that the operations, now with their own inertia, would stop short of an assault on the Italian mainland. At Casablanca, King and Arnold indicated their approval of reinforcing successes.[6] Churchill knew he had won an important victory because Marshall could not block an open-ended decision to increase force levels in the theater.[7] The Mediterranean, at least for 1943, would remain the focal point of Allied offensive operations in Europe.

EISENHOWER STAKES OUT HIS COMMAND

For Smith and Eisenhower, the strategic decisions emerging from SYMBOL conformed to their expressed points of view. With the immense concentration of forces in the Mediterranean, it appeared ill-advised to dismantle the Allied armies now a linkup with Montgomery in Tunisia was in the offing. Eisenhower knew his old Operations Division had been stung by their rough treatment at the hands of the British at the Casablanca conference. "Frankly," he wrote General Handy, "I do not see how the 'big bosses' could have deviated far from the general course of action they adopted." He asked that the War Department not view military issues on "an American versus British basis" but seek to work together against the "real enemy." The wisest approach, in Eisenhower's estimate, was to make the best of the considerable strategic advantages offered in the theater; the alternative meant inaction in 1943.[8]

The British would have the preponderance of forces in the Mediterranean once

Montgomery moved into Tunisia. Both the War Department and Allied Force Headquarters thought the BCOS would insist on subordinating Eisenhower to General Alexander. Much to the surprise of Marshall and Eisenhower, the British made no such demand. At Casablanca a new command arrangement was devised. After the 8th Army merged with the AFHQ command, Eisenhower would function as commander-in-chief, Allied Force Headquarters with three principal subordinates. Tedder would be charged with command of a single Mediterranean airforce. Cunningham remained as naval commander.[9] Alexander, as ground commander, directed the 18th Army Group as Eisenhower's deputy commander-in-chief.[10] The same structure would also apply for planning and executing HUSKY, the invasion of Sicily.[11]

Brooke did not push for a wholesale reorganization of the new Mediterranean command for two reasons. First, Eisenhower and Smith succeeded in creating a functioning Allied headquarters. Impressed by AFHQ, Brooke saw no advantage in tampering with the existing organization. Second, the BCOS felt Alexander's direction of the battle would overcome Eisenhower's lack of tactical and strategic experience. This would free the supreme commander to mold the new command and staff structure. As Brooke saw it, "we were pushing Eisenhower up into the stratosphere and rarefied atmosphere of a Supreme Commander, where he would be free to devote his time to the political and inter-allied problems, whilst we inserted under him one of our own commanders to deal with the military situation and to restore the necessary drive and coordination which had been so seriously lacking."[12]

On January 20 Eisenhower received the first indication from Casablanca the command arrangements would be modified along lines more consistent with British practices. The position paper, "System of Air Command in Mediterranean," outlined the air force organization stating "further details will naturally be left to the Air Commander-in-Chief." Two days later another directive arrived in Algiers from the CCS concerning the command and planning arrangements for HUSKY.[13] Alexander, Tedder, and Cunningham were to cooperate as coequals with control over day-to-day operations. Alexander simultaneously "coordinated the operation of all three armies" in the Tunisian theater. Additionally, his headquarters assumed the detailed planning for HUSKY. "In regards Sicily," Alexander was charged "with the execution of the actual operation when launched."[14]

Initially, Eisenhower was pleased he would not be subordinated to a British commander. His calm acceptance of the first directive sharply contrasted with his stormy receipt of the second. He now recognized "that the Chiefs were attempting to issue directives as to how and what his subordinates were to do."[15] Brooke's criticism of Eisenhower's tactical management of the battle was not without justification, but he misread the American general's insistence upon the maintenance of unity of command. Incensed by this intrusion into his organizational setup, Eisenhower dictated a "hot message" to the CCS, complaining the new command structure created four power centers. Eisenhower took offense at the word "coordinate," which conveyed the impression the new organization would be based upon a committee system of command. Eisenhower strenuously objected to this interference with his most valued prerogatives, the ability to determine his own internal organization.[16]

Smith prevailed upon Eisenhower not to send the cable. A more moderate communication, almost an apology, was written by Smith and forwarded to Casablanca. The chief of staff knew Marshall and the JCS would soon be coming to Algiers, and the issue might better be discussed in private.[17] On January 27, the American chiefs arrived in Algiers. During deliberations Marshall agreed entirely with Eisenhower. He reassured the supreme commander the directives never intended to diminish his authority. A week later, Churchill and the British chiefs came to AFHQ. Talks with Brooke on February 5 again raised Eisenhower's anxiety.[18]

Writing to Marshall on February 8, Eisenhower bitterly reacted to what he correctly saw as Brooke's lack of confidence in him. As earlier in November and December 1942, Eisenhower demanded clear lines of internal authority. Recognizing the committee system deprived him of actual involvement in ground operations and HUSKY planning, Eisenhower resolved simply to ignore the January directives. "I will be constantly on my guard," he promised Marshall, "to prevent any important military venture depending for its control and direction upon the 'committee' system of command."[19] He proceeded to do just that.

Eisenhower's insistence upon unity of command did not originate in wounded pride alone. He did not oppose having a deputy for ground operations. Earlier he had thought Patton would fill that role but accepted Alexander with equanimity, although he was "not particularly happy about it."[20] He balked at the creation of formal headquarters that would reduce his authority and confuse coordination between the services. It also threatened to create resentment among the Allies.[21]

While, theoretically, Eisenhower had been pushed upstairs, he insisted final authority remain in his hands. Instead of exercising these powers openly, which might have produced divisiveness, he relied upon his engaging personality. Eisenhower knew his subordinates would accept his authority as final arbiter, a situation enhanced by the lack of unanimity displayed by the British commanders-in-chief. By maintaining personal relationships with Cunningham, Tedder, and Alexander and keeping AFHQ in close contact with his commanders, Eisenhower allowed his subordinates wide latitude while retaining decision making in his own hands. He limited the sphere of Alexander's independent command by insisting that he command only those forces actually in combat. The imperfect system worked; his subordinates accepted his position. Although challenges to unity of command arose in the course of the Tunisian campaign and afterwards, the arrangements functioned because his subordinates possessed confidence in the fairness of Eisenhower's judgments.

STALEMATE IN TUNISIA

Smith shared his commander's anxiety over the shape of the post-Casablanca command and staff structure. His attention also centered upon the success of the conference from a scheduling standpoint. It was his responsibility that the timetable and security measures went off as planned. Although his secretary, Carter Burgess, took care of the details, Smith garnered the credit.[22] More important, he realized if a British officer assumed command, a British staff officer would supersede him as chief of staff. With great relief, Smith learned the AFHQ organization would not be overhauled and he would remain chief of staff of an enlarged command.

Bad news also emerged from the Casablanca conference. Smith's friend and confidant Dykes died in a plane crash en route to England. The news greatly disturbed him. "Next to yourself and the children," Smith wrote Dykes's widow, "I really think no one feels his loss more deeply than I do."[23]

He had no time to dwell on personal matters. An immediate concern involved planning successive visits by the American chiefs and Churchill and the BCOS to Algiers. Security in Algiers remained slack, and Smith ordered it tightened. After spending a full day in conferences, Smith walked home to his villa where a military policeman challenged him. At gunpoint, the chief of staff laid his identification on the ground, retreated ten paces and assumed a prone position. Satisfied that he was not an assassin, the soldier let Smith pass. Smith undoubtedly took little satisfaction in the perfection of his security precautions and even less when the story made the rounds in Algiers.[24]

Marshall, King, Arnold, and other senior War Department officers arrived in Algiers on January 25. That afternoon Smith met with Somervell, the topic being the organization of the Service of Supply in the theater. Smith employed the situation to inform the Army Service Forces chief of the pressing need for trucks.[25] The meeting bore fast results as within three weeks the first of 500 trucks began off-loading in North African ports. Bedell also participated in the high-level conferences that punctuated the visit.

On February 5, Churchill and his principal staff chieftains arrived in Algiers, fresh from a tour of Anderson's command. Similar to the American visit, the two-day stay involved a series of official gatherings and informal meetings. The prime minister enjoyed being on campaign and asked his old friend Beetle to lengthen his stay by an extra day. Happy to oblige, Smith arranged a luncheon to cement an uneasy alliance between the French factions. Pleased with the arrangements, Smith went to Eisenhower's villa. Eisenhower's reaction caught Smith by surprise. The supreme commander wanted to get Churchill out of Algiers. In London, Eisenhower remarked, the prime minister was worth an army, but in Algiers he represented only a headache. As with most things, Churchill got his way and the day passed without mishap.[26]

January and February were hectic months for Smith, accommodating AFHQ to the changes produced by the SYMBOL conference. This involved organizing new subsections of the staff as well as integrating different personalities into his tight headquarters. Late in January, losing little time, Smith inaugurated the HUSKY planning section. The planning agency would remain an adjunct to the existing Operations Division until Alexander organized a new army group headquarters. Smith wanted the planners close at hand. Designated FORCE 141—from the number of the room in the St. George's Hotel where the planners first met—Smith oversaw planning despite having only the most tenuous claims for doing so.

French political affairs remained a constant irritant. Now that a stopgap solution existed for the command structure, AFHQ tackled the problem of rearming the French. At Casablanca Roosevelt presented Giraud with a signed agreement in principle pledging enough equipment for eleven divisions and a "first-line air force." Typically, Roosevelt lacked a full understanding of the difficulties this promise presented for Somervell and Allied Force HQ. Shipping, already critically short, did not exist.[27] When none of the promised matériel arrived, Giraud thought himself "hoodwinked" and threatened to resign. After a series of conferences and exchanges of communications, Smith could report to Giraud that shipping would be found. Having made this reaffirmation in late February, he stonewalled the strong-willed French officer until the first shipments docked on May 8, the day after Tunis and Bizerte fell.

Policies and agencies for the military government of Sicily, the first Axis territory to be invaded by AFHQ forces, required definition. An Allied Military Government of Occupied Territories (AMGOT) organization had been temporarily created in September 1943 while the headquarters was in London. Before Smith could adequately staff the subsection, he required direction from the political leaders. Roosevelt wanted AFHQ to exercise complete authority over the military government with American representatives dominating. The British held precisely the opposite view.[28] The situation was rendered even more uncertain with the pronouncement at Casablanca of the doctrine of unconditional surrender. Eisenhower simply wanted a settlement since he saw civil affairs only in terms of its contribution to military operations. Smith's primary concern, therefore, was to curb the autonomy of nonmilitary officials attached to his staff. Throughout the first third of 1943, the AFHQ chief of staff tried in vain to arrive at a solution satisfactory to all parties.

By mid-February, Smith succeeded in forging a functioning, integrated headquarters. So secure were Eisenhower and Smith in the smooth running of their headquarters that they both decided to make extended trips—Eisenhower to see Anderson and Major General Lloyd Fredendall, the commander of the U.S. II Corps; Smith to Tripoli. The timing proved unfortunate as the Germans unleashed a major spoiling attack in central Tunisia.

Smith flew to Tripoli on February 14 to attend a series of seminars and lectures presented by Montgomery and his commanders on the lessons of the desert campaign. That very day the Germans launched their attack towards the Kasserine Pass. The seminar was Smith's first encounter with the victor of Alamein. Patton joined Smith as the only senior American officers who made the trip, which did not escape the notice of the British general.[29] Both men went for similar reasons. Montgomery's reputation as a thorough professional was already widely accepted. Smith and Patton, avid students of military history, wanted to expand their knowledge of combined operations from the most successful Allied commander. They took advantage of this opportunity to meet Montgomery, whose monkish eccentricities also were well known. For Smith, the meeting provided an excellent vehicle to cement relations between AFHQ and the man who would play a major role in upcoming events.

Montgomery, a staff college instructor in the 1920s, conducted a week-long "staff course." He believed unless the lessons of his campaign were articulated and disseminated, the Allies would repeat costly mistakes. During his three-day stay Smith discussed future operations in Tunisia with Montgomery. The British commander thought Eisenhower's broad front in Tunisia dangerously overexposed. In a letter written to Brooke in the midst of the conference, Montgomery stated that 8th Army would "roll the whole show up from the south...If we play our cards properly we cannot fail [to have] a 1st class Dunkirk on the beaches of Tunis."[30] To Smith, he pointedly remarked his army would "come along and finish it for them [Allied Force HQ]."[31]

The AFHQ chief of staff, stung by Montgomery's hauteur, especially in view of the situation at Kasserine, asked the British general for his estimates. Montgomery boasted he would take Sfax, on the central Tunisian coast some 400 miles from Tripoli, within the next six weeks. This would require breaching the formidable Mareth Line and an advance through the defensible Gabes gap, a claim Smith regarded as preposterous. "Oh, General, come, come," was

Smith's reply.[32] Confident he would make good on his boast, Montgomery asked the American what he would be willing to wager if he succeeded. Not taking the suggestion seriously, or so he later claimed, Smith replied "anything you want." The British general did not think long and asked for a Flying Fortress "complete with an American crew." Smith agreed and the bet was finalized.[33]

Montgomery proved better than his word. On March 6 his forces sharply repulsed Rommel's attack at Medenine on the Mareth front. Two weeks later the 8th Army opened its offensive. After the initial attacks failed, Montgomery staged a flanking maneuver that nearly pocketed the Axis forces. By March 31, the enemy was in headlong retreat. A week later Montgomery linked up with U.S. II Corps (now under Patton) at El Hamma. On April 10, five days ahead of schedule, he took Sfax.

Beaming with satisfaction, Montgomery cabled Allied Forces HQ: "Have captured Sfax on 10 April. Send Fortress."[34] Smith had always treated the matter as a joke, not realizing that Montgomery expected payment. Never having told Eisenhower of the bet, Smith had to explain the embarrassing situation to the supreme commander. Eisenhower, who boiled with rage months afterward, extracted the aircraft from Arnold and informed the humorless Marshall. Worse, the successes of Montgomery contrasted sharply with the American performance at Kasserine and Patton's inability to break out of the Eastern Dorsales. Montgomery's demand coincided with press releases critical of the American forces. Always touchy about preserving his reputation, Smith, who bore responsibility for censorship, felt the Montgomery embroglio and the press leaks threatened to erode his position with Eisenhower and in his headquarters.

This celebrated affair produced emnity in Algiers but did not poison the relationship between Smith and Montgomery. Although the situation created embarrassment for Eisenhower, he understood that Montgomery's advance guaranteed a successful conclusion to Allied operations in Tunisia. A Flying Fortress represented a small price to pay. The aircraft was forwarded to Montgomery accompanied by a congratulatory letter from Eisenhower. Showing there were no hard feelings, Smith added a hand-written note at the bottom of the cable reminding Montgomery the airplane would operate "much better from landing fields in Tunis."[35] This did not end the matter. When Brooke passed through Algiers in early June, he found some smoldering resentment. Aware of Montgomery's insensibilities to the problems of Allied cooperation, the CIGS took the first opportunity to "haul him over the coals for the trouble" his nettlesome commander had created.[36]

Compared to the other aggravations faced by Allied Forces HQ, the Flying Fortress affair proved minor. The first priority centered around restoring morale in the American command after the Kasserine scare. In terms of the staff, blame for the setback was laid at Mockler-Ferryman's door. During the TORCH planning stage, Eisenhower, Smith, Clark, and Spaatz received individual indoctrination concerning the existence and use of ULTRA. Operational planning could now be based upon unimpeachable intelligence gained through possession of this device.[37] Skeptical at first, the successes of the TORCH operation whetted AFHQ's appetite for ULTRA intelligence. Relying almost exclusively upon ULTRA intercepts, ignoring conventional intelligence, Mockler-Ferryman's G-2 Division misinterpreted German strengths and intentions. On February 20 Eisenhower requested his intelligence chief's removal in a letter drafted by Smith.[38] Brigadier Kenneth Strong replaced Mockler-Ferryman on March 25, 1943.

The supreme commander knew much of the blame lay with himself and the unclear command structure. During Casablanca, criticism of Eisenhower pointed to his inexperience as a commander and that operations in Tunisia could not be managed by a headquarters in Algiers.[39] AFHQ-Advance had been established under Brigadier General Lucian Truscott on January 14 at Constantine, but this headquarters could not issue operational directives. Moreover, Giraud and Général Alphonse Juin refused to take orders from Anderson while Fredendall contented himself with directing the battle from a remote mountain bunker. Preoccupied with political wrangling in Algiers, Eisenhower failed to provide leadership as the confusion in the command continued. If not muddled enough, Alexander's 18th Army Group command was slated to assume direction of ground operations on February 18.

Montgomery's offensive stabilized the situation. Determined to finalize the command structure, Eisenhower "peremptorily ordered General Anderson to take charge of the entire battle line," including the French.[40] He also wanted to relieve Fredendall. This proved difficult because Fredendall had been Marshall's choice as field commander. On February 27 Smith went to AFHQ-Advance and Fredendall's command post and left convinced that the II Corps commander to be crazy or incompetent and probably both.[41] Returning to Algiers, Smith recommended Fredendall's immediate relief. Still Eisenhower refused to act. Only on March 5, after securing the opinion of Alexander, Anderson, Truscott, and the divisional commanders, did he follow Smith's advice and sack Fredendall.

On March 7, Eisenhower and Smith met the new II Corps commander, Patton, at the airport in Algiers for a half-hour conference. Earlier that day, Eisenhower, on Marshall's suggestion, appointed his old West Point classmate, Bradley, as Patton's deputy and the supreme commander's "eyes and ears."[42] Patton and Bradley quickly put the corps in order and renewed operations. This provided Smith with a measure of relief as his "hair stood on end" when he received ULTRA intercepts detailing the weak resistance the Germans had faced at Kasserine.[43]

The American commanders proved exceedingly prickly after Kasserine and only grudgingly accepted experienced British liaison officers at their tactical headquarters.[44] Alexander's reluctance to employ American troops added new resentment. A crisis developed when the commander of the Allied Air Support Command, Air Marshal Arthur Coningham, accused the II Corps of being unbattleworthy after Patton complained about "the total lack of air cover." The RAF made similar claims in the western desert, but now these criticisms were directed at the Americans. Convinced this episode would destroy all his work in building Allied cooperation, Eisenhower drafted a letter to Marshall saying since he no longer could control the acrimony, he should be relieved. Smith intervened, calming Eisenhower and convincing him the damage could be repaired.[45] The correspondence never left Eisenhower's office, and the bitterness passed as quickly as it brewed up. For the second time in three months Smith's sangfroid curbed Eisenhower's mercurial temper, saving him from making a potentially damaging mistake.

Less than a week after the Coningham-Patton affair, the crisis atmosphere in Algiers subsided. With the Germans holding defensive positions, attention was focused in the first three weeks of April on building strength for the climactic offensive. Reacting to his case of nerves, Eisenhower made a point of "disciplining" himself to stay away from headquarters.[46] Throughout the period Smith remained a bedrock of stability. With the military situation stabilized and Allied cooperation secured for the moment, Eisenhower allowed Smith to run the headquarters and oversee the logistical preparations for the final push. Although much fighting remained before the first strategic objective outlined at Casablanca could be attained, the result no longer remained in doubt. Everyone's energies now turned to the second aim, the invasion of Sicily.

THE DEBATE OVER HUSKY

Eisenhower played an indirect role in the planning of HUSKY. The supreme commander learned from TORCH the landings defined the contours of the rest of the campaign. Eisenhower determined the key strategic decisions would not be left to others, as had been the case with TORCH. Although he did not possess the *de jure* authority to do so, Eisenhower sought to regain control over planning for the invasion.[47] He maintained personal contacts with Cunningham and Tedder and delegated to Smith responsibility for monitoring the activities of FORCE 141.

Between February and July no less than nine HUSKY plans emerged.[48] The first plan called for three widely dispersed landings: one near Palermo on the northwestern coast of Sicily; a second on the southern coast; and the last, aimed at seizing the airfields, in southeast Sicily. Logistical considerations played a major part. The logistical planning staff, headed by Brigadier General Thomas Larkin (U.S.), was housed in the École Normale on the outskirts of Algiers. They maintained sufficient supplies could not be brought ashore over a beach and that a major port had to be captured or the attacks widened. In close cooperation with Larkin's staff, Smith favored a concentrated assault but deferred to the logisticians. Cunningham and Tedder also argued for dispersed landings based upon their desire to take the Sicilian airfields. Eisenhower and Smith could not officially intervene—Tedder maintained that they supported his view—as a final operational plan proved illusive.[49]

At a March 13 meeting between Eisenhower and his principal commanders, the landings were pushed back a month to July.[50] On April 8 Churchill pointed to the delays and a message of the previous day from Eisenhower to the CCS claiming if more than two German divisions remained in Sicily, "the operation offer[ed] scant promise of success." To the prime minister this extreme caution contrasted sharply with the presumptuous self-assurance of the Americans of the summer before. "The operations must either be entrusted to someone who believes in them or abandoned," Churchill heatedly remarked. "What Stalin would think of this when he had 185 German divisions on his front, I cannot imagine."[51]

Montgomery, Alexander's choice to lead the British forces for HUSKY, objected to any plan that called for divided landings. The British general wanted two powerful, concentrated landings in the southeastern corner of Sicily. On May 2 he flew to Algiers to present his case for the abandonment of the Palermo landings. Smith met him at Maison Blanche. Aware of the headaches he caused, Montgomery told Smith, "I expect I am a bit unpopular up here." "General," Smith retorted, "to serve under you would be a great privilege for anyone, to serve along side you wouldn't be too bad. But say, General, to serve over you is hell."[52]

Later in the afternoon Montgomery went to the St. George's Hotel to see Smith. The anticipated conference had to be delayed because weather prevented Alexander from flying to Algiers and Tedder and Cunningham refused to meet without him. Unable to find Smith in the office, Montgomery went in search of him, finding the American in the lavatory. "Then and there" the two men discussed the problem. Noticeably upset by the delays, Smith wanted a decision for political reasons and solicited Montgomery's advice. Unconcerned about the political dimensions, Montgomery saw the potential for "a 1st class disaster."[53] "To give cohesion to the whole affair," he claimed the principles of war demanded a massed landing of the U.S. 7th Army and Montgomery's 8th side by side. This would ensure the success of the endeavor and secure the vital airfields at Gela and Catania. Informed of the objections raised by the logistical planners, Montgomery simply said the specialists would have to find a way to supply the forces over the beaches.[54]

They left the lavatory and proceeded to Eisenhower's office. The supreme commander refused to have a full conference but did permit Montgomery to meet with the AFHQ staff. He prefaced the presentation by saying: "I know well that I am regarded by many people as being a troublesome person. I think this is very probably true."[55] Nobody disagreed nor was there much resistance to his plan. As Smith later pointed out, Palermo had little strategic value "so the changes desired by Monty were readily conceded despite the inherent supply problems."[56]

Montgomery did not like to be away from his headquarters, so he left Smith to argue his case. The next day Alexander arrived, and the ensuing conference produced a final agreement. The Montgomery plan provided for the seizure of the airfields, satisfying Tedder and Cunningham.[57] Montgomery proved correct about logistical complications. The DUKW amphibious vehicle allowed the supply of the landing forces over the beaches.

In the end the decision was Eisenhower's, a situation created by the inability of the British commanders to agree. The supreme commander also decided as long as Alexander remained ground commander, the two armies would retain separate supply and tactical commands. This was not in accordance with British wishes, but Eisenhower made the decision stick.[58]

Montgomery thought Allied Forces HQ "a most curious place." His criticisms are very revealing. First, he recognized that the chief objective was to reach an agreement and create a formula. Whether or not the formula proved militarily sound seemed less important than arriving at an accord. Second, he observed that none of the senior staff officers and planners looked to develop a master plan for post-HUSKY operations. He thought a headquarters like AFHQ necessary but believed priorities were confused. "The staff makes a plan and works out the details," he observed, "[but] no experienced fighting commander handles the party." Sharing Brooke's estimate of Eisenhower as an affable personality without strategic sense or practical military experience, Montgomery thought more highly of Smith.[59] "No one from Eisenhower to Alexander down really know their business," he concluded. "But the senior staff officers *thought they knew*."[60] Montgomery believed he had set AFHQ straight and left the planners to work out the details.

As he had won the debate, Montgomery wanted to "run HUSKY."[61] He thought U.S. II Corps should come under his operational command. On May 5 Montgomery wrote one of his extended letters, "Organization for Command," to Alexander. Confident Smith was his "firm ally," Montgomery told the army group commander he should "deal direct with Bedel-Smith [sic]" on the command question.[62] Montgomery flew to Algiers on May 7 to meet with Smith. The chief of staff, who made nasty remarks about Montgomery in private, agreed in principle with Montgomery on the need to achieve operational unity of command but categorically ruled out the change.[63] Citing political reasons—the blow to American morale at home—Smith said "the American contingent had to be a separate expedition" and Montgomery would have to accept the clumsy command arrangements.[64] Montgomery accepted Smith's decision as final and thereafter confined his grumbling to Alexander, with whom he knew he would have more success.

THE TRIDENT CONFERENCE

Marshall had a closed mind when it came to the Mediterranean theater. In an April 27 letter to Eisenhower Marshall suggested if HUSKY proved to be too much of a drain, it should be abandoned for a buildup for a cross-channel invasion. If HUSKY was a success (if Italy collapsed), Marshall wanted Allied Forces HQ to be prepared to seize Sardinia and/or Corsica as well as the heel of the Italian boot. He cautioned his subordinate that any large-scale invasion of the Italian mainland would cripple operations elsewhere. "You will understand that the operations outlined above," he added, "are not in keeping with my ideas of what our strategy should be....You should therefore have in mind the possible movement of a large part of your forces to the United Kingdom."[65] To reinforce his position Marshall dispatched Handy to Algiers.

The views of Eisenhower and Smith now more closely paralleled those of the BCOS than Marshall's. With one million troops in the theater, operations in the Mediterranean assumed a momentum of their own. Most of the troops were now hardened veterans, commanded by proven generals and backed by efficient and talented staffs. The prospect of knocking Italy out of the war, dim at Casablanca, now appeared bright. British intelligence observed growing partisan power in Yugoslavia and held out the hope successful operations in Italy might bring Turkey into the war. Eisenhower knew a shift of strategic priorities out of the theater would relegate him to a minor role. Anxious not to provoke Marshall, Eisenhower continued to affirm his dedication to the cross-channel invasion but tactfully advised the chief to accept a limited offensive against Italy in exchange for a definite commitment to a 1944 ROUNDUP.

A decision along those lines emerged from a major conference in Washington (TRIDENT) on May 12-25. The British requested a senior officer from AFHQ attend the conference who knew Eisenhower's mind on HUSKY and post-HUSKY planning and could speak with authority on the unresolved question of military government for Sicily. Smith was the obvious choice. Before he left, he and Eisenhower reviewed the strategic possibilities for the upcoming six to nine months. Smith assured the supreme commander that he would forcefully present a case for expanding operations against Italy. He first flew to Marrakech, Morocco, then boarded a Liberator on May 10 for Washington. The flight via the southern route set a record for its speed with Smith arriving in the American capital during the evening of May 11.[66]

Churchill, Ismay, and the BCOS were prepared to push hard for a continuation of operations in the Mediterranean for the duration of 1943. In the first meetings Brooke presented the carefully considered British position. Only by exploiting the advantages offered in the Mediterranean, he maintained, could the essential preconditions for a successful ROUNDUP be created. These included the erosion of German ground and air strength and the disruption of their ability to reinforce garrisons in France. More damning to American desires for an early ROUNDUP was the unavailability of landing craft, which seriously limited the strength of the attack. The British instead proposed an Allied invasion of the Italian mainland.

The Americans found themselves outmaneuvered again by the better-prepared British staff. Marshall raised the threat of readjusting American grand strategy by shifting priority to the Pacific. On May 18 Smith met with Brooke for an informal conference. The American pointed out Marshall's threat should not be discounted.[67] Hoping to avoid a stalemate requiring the intervention of the political heads, the British offered a compromise. In exchange for an American commitment to the Italian invasion, the British agreed to set a fixed date for the cross-channel operation (renamed OVERLORD). The Americans accepted with two provisions. The forces earmarked for the Italian invasion would be limited, and seven divisions must be withdrawn from the Mediterranean theater on November 1, 1943, for employment in the United Kingdom.[68]

Smith's presence contributed significantly to the settlement. He consistently argued for the Mediterranean strategy in his formal briefings and informal discussions with Marshall and Brooke and the other senior American and British staff officers. Many in the War Department considered Eisenhower and Smith unduly pro-British. Bedell's presentations demonstrated the soundness of the Italian variant. The conference proceeded slowly and deliberately, requiring Smith to remain in Washington ten days longer than anticipated. As early as May 14 he had written Eisenhower and assured him the ultimate decision would conform to the general lines discussed during their final conference before his departure for Washington.[69]

Smith's professionalism contributed to the beneficial outcome of the conference. At the first Washington conference and at Casablanca, higher authorities decided every detail of the TORCH operation and the campaign in North Africa. At TRIDENT, while the combined chiefs remained divided, they agreed the Mediterranean command and staff organization should be given control over decision making after the invasion had begun. This represented a vote of confidence for Eisenhower and for Smith's orchestration of the staff. His position required tact because too strong an advocacy of the British strategy would have weakened Allied Forces HQ's standing with Marshall and the War Department.

While in Washington Smith performed other tasks. First, he engaged in top-level discussions concerning civil and military administration for Sicily and Italy.[70] Second, he pushed Marshall on Bradley's retention in the Mediterranean and checked into the possibility of an award of the Legion of Merit for senior British and French commanders. From time to time Marshall pressed Smith to arrange a North African tour of the army band. The AFHQ chief of staff never accorded much importance to this, but Marshall proved adamant. To appease him, Smith finalized plans for the band's trip to Algiers.[71] He also pumped War Department officers for information regarding Marshall's intentions for Eisenhower after operations in the Mediterranean wound down. In each case Smith could rely upon a network of informal links forged during his tenure in the War Department to gain the information. Finally, the popularity of the film *Desert Victory* transformed Montgomery into an American national hero, a fact that rankled the War Department.[72] As a result a media blitz on North Africa was planned featuring Eisenhower's role. Aware of his chief's feelings concerning the press, Smith asked Eisenhower to "leave this to me." [73]

On May 27 Smith returned to Algiers. That morning he gave an extensive briefing on the TRIDENT conference to Eisenhower and the principal members of the staff. In the afternoon he and Eisenhower had a long talk. The topics of conversation included the strategic situation on the Russian front and Eisenhower's future assignment. Smith said the record of AFHQ was so highly regarded he doubted it would be broken up once the focus of Allied priorities shifted to northwestern Europe. He went so far as to predict Eisenhower would leave the Mediterranean with the seven divisions, either as American commander for OVERLORD or as allied commander-in-chief. Although doubting his chief of staff's prognostications, Eisenhower took satisfaction from the decisions coming out of the Washington conference. He owed much to Smith and his successful championing of Eisenhower's cause.[74]

Churchill decided to visit Algiers at the conclusion of TRIDENT to pressure Eisenhower to accept the Italian option. He knew the Allied Force HQ planners opposed the operation on logistical grounds, chiefly because shipping did not exist for the supply of the troops and the Italian population. Afraid he would be charged with bringing undue influence to bear on the supreme commander, Churchill asked Roosevelt for a high-ranking American officer to accompany him. Roosevelt sent Marshall to represent the contrary point of view.[75]

From the onset of the conference, which lasted from May 29 to June 3, Eisenhower made it clear he supported an invasion of the mainland if HUSKY proved successful. Churchill spoke emphatically for the invasion while Marshall, wanting to gauge German reactions to HUSKY, refused to accept any commitment beyond the invasion of Sicily and perhaps secondary landings in Sardinia or Corsica. After the Algiers conference Eisenhower maintained three options: (1) the immediate invasion of Italy if resistance in Sicily collapsed quickly, (2) the possibility of an assault on the mainland if the enemy had been overcome by mid-August, and (3) the abandonment of post-HUSKY operations if the Axis defense was prolonged. Toward these ends Eisenhower suggested the creation of two separate headquarters to plan for the alternatives—amphibious operations in Sardinia and Corsica or a crossing of the Straits of Messina.[76]

From the military standpoint the meetings were inconclusive. As Churchill remarked at the final meeting, "Post-HUSKY would be in General Eisenhower's hands." Progress was made in other areas, especially the setting of parameters for AMGOT. In territories taken from the Axis, the British wanted to exercise indirect administration while the Americans demanded AFHQ assume direct control of civil affairs. Once the fascists were removed the British thought it desirable to keep the civil bureaucratic structure in place, staffing it as far as possible with Italian civil servants. Before the conference ended a basic compromise emerged. Within each zone of occupation American and British officers would jointly exercise civil authority based on the principle of "no senior partners." This Joint Military Government fell under Lord Rennel of Rodd, the Chief Civil Affairs Officer for AMGOT, who answered ultimately to Smith.[77] These arrangements satisfied no one but conformed to existing AFHQ procedures, placing broad discretionary power in the hands of Eisenhower and Smith.

THE FRENCH AND OTHER ASSORTED HEADACHES

Between the conclusion of TRIDENT and the launching of HUSKY on July 10, Smith had plenty to occupy his attention. The French continued to present a headache. On June 4 Churchill visited the newly formed French Committee of National Liberation (FCNL) in Algiers. With the prime minister's prodding, progress was finally achieved. Roosevelt reluctantly accepted de Gaulle's expanded role in French affairs. Churchill granted Eisenhower wide latitude on matters connected to relations with de Gaulle and urged all dealings with the French be made with the committee and not individual French officials.[78]

On June 19, Smith arranged a meeting between de Gaulle and Giraud. It took place in Smith's Algiers villa. Smith chaired the meeting with the aid of an interpreter, while Macmillan and Murphy waited on the porch. The two French leaders predictably clashed. When de Gaulle staged one of his "calculated outbursts"—he stormed out of the meeting—Smith resumed negotiations with each faction.[79] He adeptly steered a middle course through the turbulence. Seeking to minimize the damage of political upheaval on the eve of HUSKY, Smith placated de Gaulle and Giraud, delaying actions until tempers cooled.[80] Finally, Macmillan worked out a formula for de Gaulle and Giraud to act as copresidents of the French Committee, a cabinet of seven French officials. De Gaulle remained outside the Allied decision-making machinery, which satisfied Roosevelt's conditions.

Throughout the torturously difficult negotiations Smith received directives from the White House, bypassing Murphy and the State Department, which compromised successive political settlements. Although Smith's actions seldom conformed to the letter of Roosevelt's demands, an effective agreement emerged. He also handled the French rearmament program through the Liaison Section and Joint Rearmament Committee of the AFHQ G-4 Division. While Eisenhower complained about his inability to escape the local political turmoil, Smith, not the supreme commander, was the officer most immediately connected with balancing political affairs in North Africa.

Faulty censorship was partly to blame; reports of the political infighting had made their way into print. This proved embarrassing to all parties, particularly Churchill, who maintained "iron censorship" in London.[81] As Eisenhower earlier admitted, AFHQ had struggled since the beginning of the campaign to find a "satisfactory answer" to the censorship question.[82] Since most leaks came from American sources, Smith tightened controls. He anguished over published accounts of the Kasserine fighting. "Jesus Christ may have walked on the waters," he complained, "but I guess we cannot do the same."[83] The American side of the staff lacked trained officers for public relations. Unable to plug leaks, Smith resorted to formal news releases and more-frequent press conferences. Although he hated public speaking and felt insecure in front of the press corps, Smith periodically met with the journalists. Not adept at disseminating misinformation, an Eisenhower specialty, Smith gave unvarnished presentations that were accepted as accurate and authoritative.

Another vexation involved psychological warfare. The formula of unconditional surrender had been given little serious study before being enunciated by Roosevelt at a Casablanca news conference.[84] Before HUSKY, the Intelligence Division interpreted the policy as one of "intimidation of the Italians by threat." AFHQ estimated that the policy was counterproductive and "strongly recommended" it be amended to present the Fascist Party as the only obstacle to an honorable peace. A cable, prepared by Strong and endorsed by Smith, was sent to Washington over the signature of the supreme commander. The communication found its way to Roosevelt's desk and the president reacted sharply. "We cannot get away from unconditional surrender," he declared, putting an end to the question.[85]

This episode illustrates that Eisenhower did not always carefully read the communications referred to Smith. The latter felt strongly that the policy needed revision, and like thousands of other communications this Intelligence Division cable was routinely channeled through headquarters. Faced with the president's reaction, Eisenhower, "exceedingly irritated" by the embarrassment created by his chief of staff, insisted that Smith exercise tighter control over his staff.[86] For Eisenhower, his duty involved only executing policies of the political heads and the Combined Chiefs. Closely connected to the operational side and more inclined to act on his own, Smith recognized the advisability of an alternative to unconditional surrender for achieving an early surrender. After the war, Smith maintained the doctrine was "very unfortunate...a constant hindrance...which cost thousands of lives in Italy and Germany."[87]

Maintaining staff integration and cohesion continued to be problematic. While managing the campaign in Tunisia and planning HUSKY, Alexander's army group headquarters remained in Tunisia. Meanwhile, Smith coordinated the activities of AFHQ-Main and Advance as well as two command posts for HUSKY—one at Amilcar on the Bay of Tunis and the other near Carthage. In addition, Tedder, Cunningham, Patton, and Montgomery had individual headquarters, which engaged in the development of tactical planning. Not only were there communications headaches; Smith also had to oversee the integration of planning for HUSKY, BRIMSTONE (Sardinia), FIREBRAND (Corsica), and BAYTOWN and MUSKET (southern Italy).

On July 17 the British chiefs declared the separation of headquarters "violates one of the most important principles of combined operation."[88] They sent their foremost communications experts to Malta to establish a central headquarters. This solved the communications problems for HUSKY but virtually cut Eisenhower off from direct contact with London and Washington.[89]

Eisenhower left Algiers on July 6 and arrived two days later in Malta to meet the commanders-in-chief.[90] On July 13 Eisenhower and Tedder returned to Amilcar, staying until their July 20th return to Algiers. In the supreme commander's extended absence, Smith controlled the theater, issuing operational orders and maintaining links with the capitals as well as coordinating the disparate threads of the several headquarters. Except for one minor mixup—when Smith ordered commandos forward from Gibraltar without

Eisenhower's knowledge—no debilitating confusion resulted from the varied complications posed by distance, limited communications, and the inevitable shakedowns of active operations.[91]

A VOTE OF CONFIDENCE

During the Tunisian campaign and the concurrent planning stage for HUSKY, Eisenhower and Smith faced the same set of issues confronted earlier in preparing and conducting TORCH. These issues included the unsettled French political situation, attempts to interpose an alien command organization, relations with the British, staff size, planning difficulties, logistical and communications complications, and providing accommodations for high-level visitors. In January 1943 some suspected Eisenhower and his staff did not possess tight control over the theater. By June the government heads and the Combined Chiefs were prepared to grant the supreme commander and AFHQ broad discretionary authority over military and political affairs. Eisenhower landed in North Africa a neophyte at invasion points determined by others. Six months later he emerged a past-master in the art of conducting coalition warfare, as effective executor of the policies of his superiors and architect of collaborative Allied efforts. His confidence grew after passing the rigorous test of commanding an active campaign. Eisenhower, no longer hesitant to defend his prerogatives, demonstrated greater willingness to assume an independent position.

Similarly, Smith broadened his education as allied chief of staff. He remained Eisenhower's loyal subordinate but did not shrink from vigorously defending his prerogatives. As chief of staff he labored in the background balancing the multitudinous mass of details that went into the conduct of modern military operations. The work was dull, painstaking, and draining. Unable to experience the exhilaration of a field commander for an objective attained, the chief of staff's rewards came from the transitory satisfaction that the work of his staff laid the foundations for victory. Unlike the field commander, who could bask in the glory of his achievements in the lull that followed the storm, the staff constantly prepared for the next operation. Like the umpire who knows he called a good game by the absence of boos when he leaves the field, Smith's rewards were vicariously enjoyed when the actions of his headquarters produced no acrimony.

In Smith's opinion, two prerequisites existed for the successful functioning of an integrated headquarters of an Allied armed force: the presence of a single supreme commander who enjoyed a broad charter of authority and possessed "a fierce determination to make the thing work," and the absence of language barriers and interpersonal rivalries. He admitted that the American staff system served as the basic organizing principle for the sake of convenience, in deference to the nationality of the supreme commander. He was amused by the prospect of future generations of officers at Leavenworth trying to place the AFHQ organization on tidy flow charts. In Smith's estimate the actual configuration of staff organization was of little consequence. The headquarters grew and developed according to no master plan but rather from a series of *ad hoc* expedients. Its efficiency was more a testament to the flexibility of Eisenhower, Smith, and the principal staff officers than to any theoretical model.

In fact, the organization of AFHQ conformed to the paradigmatic general staff to a greater extent than Smith admitted. During the North African and Tunisian campaigns the relations of a formal command-and-staff structure took shape. Eisenhower willfully retained the command function. While he remained the final arbiter, one set of commanders conducted the campaign while others planned future operations. Cunningham and Tedder, according to Smith, "naturally and rightly" considered themselves better qualified to give operational advice to Eisenhower than the AFHQ staff. Eisenhower never fully reconciled himself to the existence of parallel staffs, but Smith, insisting that intelligence and planning always be fully integrated, saw the system as eminently workable. Initially the air and naval commanders voiced concerns over the placement of senior officers from their respective services on the AFHQ staff. As Bedell noted, this fear proved groundless. Instead of diminishing their prerogatives as principal advisers to Eisenhower, the air and naval commanders-in-chief discovered interservice cooperation improved. Much of the credit belongs to Smith for his tact and goodwill in dealing with the senior British commanders.

While the organization never attained the pristine state of textbook perfection, a viable, vertically integrated command-and-staff structure emerged in North Africa. Plans, once formulated, went to the commanders-in-chief who advised Eisenhower. Differences were thrashed out at the highest level. The staff, organized to assist the commanders in the execution of operations, also orchestrated logistical arrangements. These functions involved the formal workings of the command structure. As Smith pointed out, while American officers paid lip service to the principle of unity of command, in practice, AFHQ carried out integration more completely than in commands composed exclusively of American units.

Informal connections cannot be reproduced on tables of organization; they are the product of personal interaction. In the Mediterranean Smith forged a staff that developed its own sense of corporateness. Staff officers who persisted in viewing problems strictly on national lines were ruthlessly eliminated. Through shared labors, close working relationships evolved into bonds of friendship. Once his subordinates accommodated themselves to Smith's brusqueness, the initial suspicions gave way to feelings of loyalty. Smith cast his headquarters in the image of Marshall's War Department General Staff. He placed faith in the executive organs of the staff and upon the efficiency of his system. Discovering the "canned language" taught at the respective staff colleges meant different things to British and American officers, a common language emerged. American officers came to use petrol for gasoline and their British counterparts referred to lorries as trucks. Generally, the shortest and most expressive terms gained common usage. As a corporate body, AFHQ arrived at team decisions based upon an enlightened "war council" approach.[92]

Like Eisenhower, Smith passed the probationary trials of the Mediterranean campaign. Granted considerable authority to act independently, he assumed responsibility for directing the Allied Forces Headquarters staff. Having harmonized conflicting approaches to staff work, Smith blunted intrusions that might have corrupted the elementary doctrine of unity of command. Faced with an imperfect situation, Smith straightened out the staff structure and resisted attempts to alter it. In a real sense Smith and his headquarters gained their formal stamp of approval long before Eisenhower earned the confidence of his political and military chiefs—as early as Casablanca. With the organization set and many lessons learned, Smith's obstinate determination to fashion an integrated staff was crowned with success.

The Italian Campaign, July–December 1943

On July 10 the Allied forces landed in Sicily virtually unopposed. An immediate counterattack against Patton's beachhead was beaten back. Within a few hours the airfield at Gela and the port of Licata fell to the U.S. 7th Army. Only forty-eight hours after the landings, the Allies had brought 80,000 men, 3,000 vehicles, 300 tanks, and 900 guns across the beaches. Italian units offered limited resistance; instead they surrendered *en masse* at the first opportunity. Three days after the landings Montgomery's 8th Army took Syracuse. Hard fighting lay ahead but the final outcome was scarcely in doubt.

Allied Force HQ summed up the military and political objectives for HUSKY in a July 19 letter to the Combined and British Chiefs of Staff: eliminate Italy from the war and overthrow the Fascist government. Since neither could be accomplished by operations in Sicily, AFHQ requested planning proceed on the basis of expanded operations in the southern half of the Italian peninsula, including the occupation of Rome. In the event that the Italian government did not collapse but continued resistance north of the capital, Eisenhower asked for permission to reserve forces for an advance beyond Rome. He also petitioned for authority to negotiate with any military or civilian group, or with members of the Italian royal family, who offered the prospect of an early alteration in the military and political situation.[1]

Before the CCS could reply, dramatic events in Rome gave the Allies their opportunity. On July 25 King Victor Emmanuel III and the army ordered Mussolini's arrest. Marshal Pietro Badoglio, former chief of the Italian General Staff, formed a new government. Determined to pressure the king to negotiate a separate peace, Eisenhower moved quickly. He felt if the king gained

SICILY

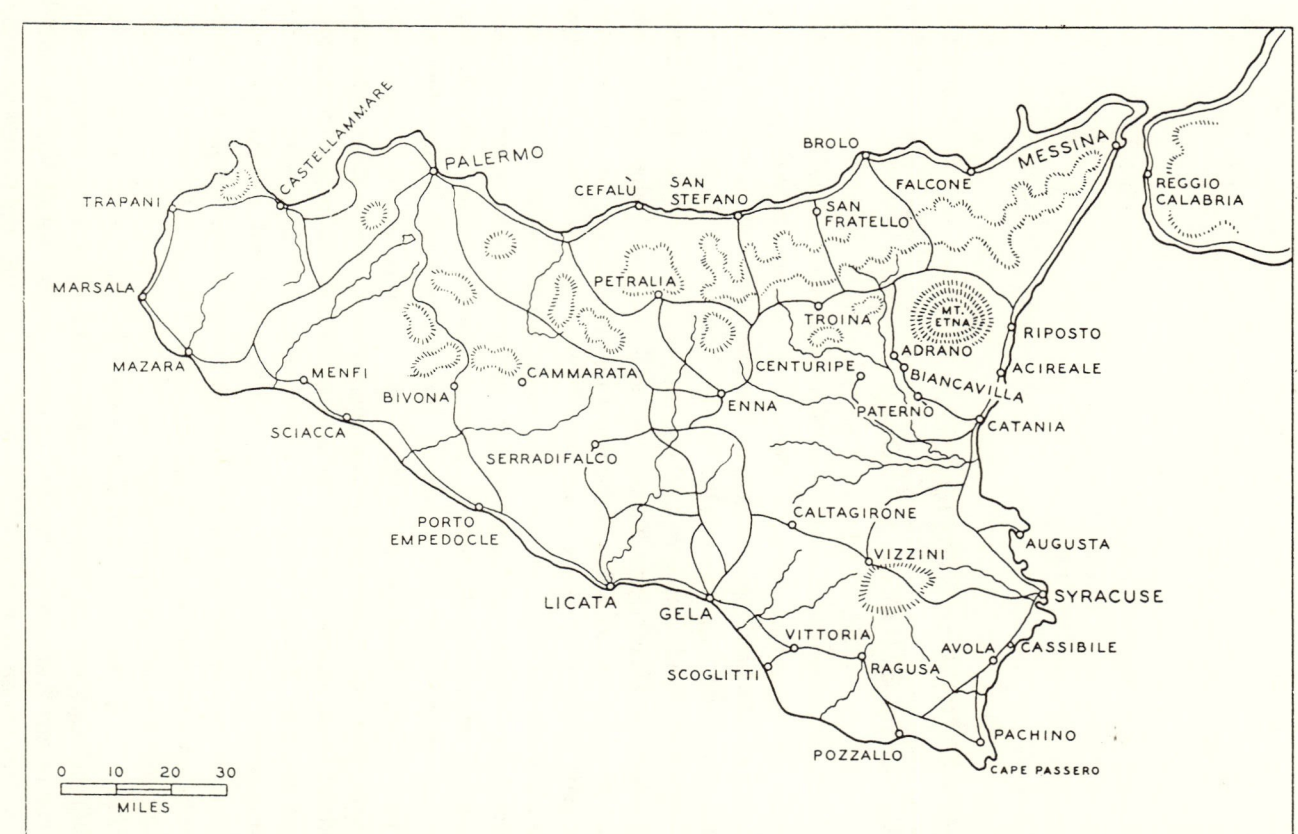

Alfred D. Chandler, ed., *The Papers of Dwight D. Eisenhower: The War Years*, vol. 5 (Baltimore: Johns Hopkins University Press, 1970), p. 54.

assurances he "would remain as a symbol of Italian unity," the Fascists might be thrown out and the Italian armed forces turned against the Germans.[2] In the negotiations that followed, Smith came to play the central role.

SICILY AND THE PLANNING FOR AVALANCHE

The overthrow of Mussolini convinced Roosevelt and Churchill an Italian capitulation would shortly follow. On July 26 Roosevelt cabled Churchill demanding "in no event should our officers in the field fix any general terms." Although he thought the Allies should treat the Italians with leniency, the president insisted the terms of an armistice be "as close as possible to unconditional surrender." Churchill, more eager to exploit the advantage, held he would deal with any non-Fascist government that could "deliver the goods."[3]

The next few days saw an exchange of communications between Washington, London, and Algiers. Roosevelt came around to Churchill's position but wanted to move slowly, mindful of the political consequences of the Darlan deal. On July 29 Marshall wrote Eisenhower, reminding him a general armistice involved political and economic questions beyond the competence of a military commander.[4] Eisenhower, weary of the debate and the close supervision of his actions, regretted 1943 was not in the age of sail. Without rapid communications, he felt he would be able to move decisively, without waiting for direction from the political heads.[5]

Macmillan emphasized the pressures on AFHQ. Describing July 29, he spent three hours rotating between his office and those of Eisenhower and Smith. Telegrams, pouring in from the CCS, Marshall, Roosevelt, Churchill, the American State Department, and the Foreign Office, were contradictory and confusing. Macmillan and Smith sorted out the incoming directives and fashioned replies. Smith and Macmillan had Eisenhower's sanction to deal directly with the political and military chiefs. They issued broad policy statements that did not conform to any of the courses proposed by authorities in London or Washington. In the oppressive heat the task proved exhausting, but together they laid the foundation for AFHQ's taking charge of negotiating with the Italians. By August 1, Churchill and Roosevelt concurred AFHQ should assume the responsibility for dealing with any Italian overtures with the proviso no binding settlement be reached without referral to the two home governments. This accorded exactly to the position taken by Smith and Macmillan on July 29.[6]

While trying to accommodate the various viewpoints on proceeding with potential Italian negotiations, Smith's attention focused upon settling a related concern, the nature of military government in Italy. In May, Smith made his "definite view" clear to Marshall: the operational commanders must be empowered with full authority over the civilian population while troops remained in the area.[7] Even after the fall of Mussolini, the CCS, afraid Eisenhower would make another Darlan-type deal, still proved reluctant to make a straightforward decision. After many twists and turns, two and a half months later, the CCS announced Alexander, as military governor of Sicily, would exercise complete control over civil administration.[8] With a decision now in hand, Smith finalized the arrangements for AMGOT policy for southern Italian territories.

In the closing days of July Smith attempted to consolidate planning for operations in Calabria. After spending several days at Amilcar and conferring with Montgomery and Patton at Syracuse, Smith worried that Sicily would not be cleared by the mid-August target date. This view conflicted with Eisenhower's optimism. He predicted Axis resistance would collapse by August 5.[9] The question centered on the most expeditious means for carrying out the CCS directive to knock Italy out of the war. Alternatives included the invasion of the toe (BUTTRESS and BAYTOWN) or the heel (MUSKET), landing further north below Naples (AVALANCHE) or in the vicinity of Naples (BARRACUDA), or moving on the islands of Sardinia and Corsica. Planning at AFHQ continued as well as in Alexander and Montgomery's headquarters. Smith's job involved orchestrating the planning at these various locations and generally keeping the projects on the rails. On July 26 the CCS in an emergency session agreed on launching AVALANCHE at the earliest date.

The CCS decision placed pressure on the AFHQ Operations Division to produce plans for an attack to be made in the Gulf of Salerno (AVALANCHE), twenty-five miles south of Naples, set for September 7. Initially, the U.S. VI Corps from Clark's 5th Army was selected for the amphibious operation. The decision to launch the assault did not relieve Smith of other planning burdens as the several options continued to be studied. By August 5 the situation in Sicily began to improve, especially since Patton's forces had seized Palermo and were making progress along the northern coastal road toward Messina.[10]

Air power was always a major consideration. Salerno was selected because it stood at the extreme range for Allied ground-based fighter cover. A need also existed for strategic bombers to interdict Axis communications and isolate the Salerno beaches. Between July 29 and August 4 AFHQ struggled with Major General Jacob Devers, commander of the ETO, for retention of heavy bombers in the Mediterranean. Eisenhower did not get his way as Devers blocked the temporary transfer of four groups of medium bombers to North Africa.[11] This angered Eisenhower, who thereafter bore ill feelings toward Devers.

AVALANCHE remained the top priority. Montgomery, again complaining AFHQ plans dangerously dissipated strength, wanted to stage a coordinated attack across the Straits of Messina and up through the toe. His arguments had merit in view of the impending withdrawal of air power from the theater. If the 8th Army commander won the debate, AVALANCHE would be impossible.[12] On August 5 Smith conferred with Alexander at his headquarters on the availability of landing craft and reinforcements for Montgomery's projected operation across the Straits of Messina (BUTTRESS).[13] The decision was made to continue planning for both projects.

Seeking to get full use of the four heavy bomber groups before their withdrawal, AFHQ wanted to bomb Naples and the railyards outside Rome. An attack on Rome, scheduled for August 3, was canceled by Smith owing to eleventh-hour efforts by the Italian government to declare their capital an open city.[14] Eisenhower had been sleeping, and Smith acted on his own initiative.[15] For the next few days Washington and London debated the question.[16] Churchill thought the bombing in Italy could be delayed. "Unless they ask for an armistice in the immediate future," he maintained, "we intend to give them all manner of hell."[17] The attack finally was carried out on August 13 as a display of Allied resolve to carry the war to the Italians.[18]

At this juncture a series of inter-allied disputes emerged from differences of opinion concerning psychological warfare and censorship policy. To capitalize on the lull in the bombing, the Psychological Warfare section issued Eisenhower-signed propaganda statements designed to weaken public support for the Italian government. Churchill wrote Hopkins complaining "politicians should do the talking and generals the fighting."[19] The prime minister opposed the issuance of any communiques pressing to explain both governments' attitudes when serious differences remained unresolved. The sensitive task of manipulating Italian public opinion, which would influence the type of government that would emerge after the war, should be left, Churchill claimed, to the political heads.[20]

Other incidents involved holes in the AFHQ censorship screen. Alexander furnished the War Office with situation reports from Sicily, and Churchill used them in a speech in Parliament. Meanwhile, Smith blacked out all news releases.[21] More embarrassing yet, a BBC broadcast reported American troops had been found eating grapes while serious fighting took place elsewhere. The Americans felt this inferred the British were doing the hard fighting. Explaining the program had been misinterpreted, the BBC editor apologized. As earlier in Tunisia, the damage, while not serious, produced the exchange of communications at the highest level before these tempests passed.[22]

One of these communications came from Eisenhower's desk. He was only too aware senior American officers caviled against him for his apparent pro-British leanings. One AFHQ official posited that the Americans "should celebrate the

4th of July as our only defeat of the British." "We haven't had too much luck since," he added.[23] When Eisenhower "wrote a scorcher to the P.M." in the aftermath of the BBC broadcast, Hughes applauded what he interpreted to be "Ike's Fourth of July."[24] Far from the declaration of independence Hughes and others hoped for, the angry cable to Churchill simply reflected Eisenhower's mounting anxiety over the state of affairs in Sicily.

Tensions created by the threat of stalemate in Sicily gave way to general optimism as the tactical situation improved. Progress, rapid on all fronts, climaxed on August 17 when Patton and Montgomery's forces entered Messina. Smith was not immune from these influences. Admitting intelligence failures contributed to the slow development of operations in Sicily, he believed Italian resistance would dissipate quickly. More sanguine about the chances of an amphibious *coup de main*, Smith advocated replacing AVALANCHE with BARRACUDA. He pushed for Montgomery's crossing of the Straits of Messina.[25]

Eisenhower's views were more optimistic yet. As his representative to the August 1943 Quebec (QUADRANT) conference related to Marshall, Eisenhower felt, even with the withdrawal of the seven divisions in November, the remaining twenty-one Allied divisions should suffice to seize and hold Rome, Sardinia, and Corsica. This would still permit a fourteen-division assault on the south of France in combination with OVERLORD.[26] As these estimates contrasted so sharply with Eisenhower's grim pronouncements of the previous weeks, Marshall wired Algiers for confirmation. Caught up in the euphoria that seized AFHQ after the successful conclusion of HUSKY, Eisenhower clearly allowed his imagination to run wild.

On August 12 Smith wired Marshall clarifying the situation. Mindful of the logistical constraints, especially the lack of shipping and landing craft, Smith's estimates proved more realistic. After visiting the commanders in the field, he gained a better appreciation of the tactical situation. The key to future operations lay in the German reaction. If the Germans fought an active defense in Italy, given the "downward curve" of Allied operations in the Mediterranean after HUSKY, they could easily hold northern Italy and perhaps force the CCS to reinforce AFHQ just to preserve the proposed line north of Rome. On the other hand, if the Germans choose not to conduct an offensive-defense, Smith felt the reduced AFHQ forces could fulfil the minimum requirements of TRIDENT. As for Sardinia and Corsica, he maintained these operations would be undertaken only under favorable circumstances. Likewise, should the Germans hold northern Italy, Smith thought a fourteen-division invasion of southern France feasible. He proposed planning for these operations continue. In any event he warned the Allies should not divert their forces from the main task in Italy until German intentions and strengths became known.[27]

This episode is illustrative of how the personalities and approaches of Eisenhower and Smith complemented one another. Behind the veneer of Eisenhower's unshakable calm, he was prone to dramatic mood swings from doleful skepticism to buoyant optimism. When his requests were denied, as when Marshall sided with Devers in the question of heavy bombers, Eisenhower could be sullen and petty. Often absent from headquarters, he frequently possessed an imperfect understanding of ongoing planning concerns and logistical requirements. Despite Smith's prodding, Eisenhower refused to assert his authority as supreme commander. "Ike says AFHQ [a] strategic headquarters," recorded Hughes in his diary, "but [he is] not going to raise [his] blood pressure to make [the] idea stick."[28] When events failed to live up to his often unrealistic estimates, Eisenhower looked for excuses. Although he never publicly reproached subordinates, he shifted the blame to others. In Sicily, he accused Montgomery of overcaution. Voiced privately, first to Butcher and then other members of his circle, his criticisms became more caustic as time passed. All this served as a warning of things to come.

In time, Smith also fell prey to this view. Nevertheless he more fully appreciated the differences between American and British national character and training. Whereas the American, less well trained in staff work, was seen as an aggressive operator, his British opposite insisted on thorough planning and meticulous execution of directives. The American, impatient with detailed planning, wanted to conduct operations believing deficiencies in organization and administration would be overcome by his native talent to improvise. For staff work Smith believed these traits combined to produce greater strength. At the operational level these differences provided the potential for serious breakdowns.[29]

Smith could be thrown into an opprobrious fury by the slightest hint of inefficiency but remained phlegmatic in the face of the worst crisis. Often called upon to play the role of Cassandra, Smith restrained Eisenhower's overzealousness. Influenced by his principal assistants, especially the British trio of Whiteley, Gale, and Strong, Smith's own extremism was bridled. Although given to making extemporaneous decisions, his generally circumspect approach to problem solving counterbalanced the supreme commander's exuberance.

THE ITALIAN SURRENDER

At the Quebec conference, the British accepted March 1, 1944, as the target date for OVERLORD and agreed the Mediterranean would be deprived of reinforcements after November 1, 1943. An invasion of southern France was sanctioned but on a scale much smaller than Eisenhower's estimate. Finally, the United States blocked any extension of Allied operations into the Balkans. At Quebec, as during the second Washington conference, the BCOS argued for a continuation of Allied activities in the Mediterranean. This deepened the War Department's suspicions as it seemed the British were incapable of keeping an agreement. However, when the British revealed they had received armistice feelers from Badoglio, the BCOS demand for expanding the scope of AFHQ operations gained added weight. Ironically, they found themselves using Eisenhower's stated views as justification. Since the Italians were not likely to move unless the Allies supported them on a considerable scale, the CCS endorsed both AVALANCHE and BAYTOWN. The subsidiary options, BARRACUDA and BUTTRESS, were canceled. The British X Corps, originally earmarked to land at Reggio (BUTTRESS), was designated for an expanded AVALANCHE.[30]

The collapse of the Mussolini regime caught AFHQ by surprise. On July 28, Badoglio and the king of Italy decided to approach the Allies. Acting through the Vatican, the Italian government contacted the British ambassador to Portugal, Ronald Campbell. Not asking for terms, the Italians informed the British that unless the Allies intervened militarily the Badoglio government could not undertake a *volte-face*.

The AFHQ staff had already drawn up a simple instrument of surrender, the "short terms," which provided for "unconditional surrender" while studiously avoiding the use of that phrase. London produced a set of detailed surrender terms defining the scope of "unconditional surrender." Eisenhower and Smith wanted to employ the "short terms" as a vehicle for negotiations should an Italian surrender appear imminent. In the meantime, Roosevelt and Churchill, about to meet at Quebec, could finalize the surrender terms.

On August 15 the assistant to the chief of the General Staff of the Armed Forces of Italy, Brigadier General Giuseppi Castellano, arrived in Madrid for secret discussions with the British ambassador, Samuel Hoare. Castellano possessed authority from Badoglio to negotiate only with representatives of the Allied command in the Mediterranean. He did not, as Foreign Secretary Anthony Eden informed Churchill, have the credentials to work out an armistice. The Italians anticipated a major Allied invasion of the mainland, and Castellano hoped to arrange unified action before the Germans could consolidate their hold on Italy. Eden thought the offer tempting but saw "all sorts of difficulties both military and political" and recommended not entering into any bargain with the Italians.[31]

On August 16 the CCS sent a cable to Algiers, the "Quebec Memorandum."[32] The CCS directed Eisenhower to send two senior staff officers—one American, one British—to meet Castellano. The emissaries were instructed to tell the Italian general the Allies would accept only an unconditional surrender. With time at a premium, Eisenhower could negotiate on the basis of the "short terms." If the Italians announced an armistice at once and sent their naval and air forces and merchant shipping to Allied territory, Eisenhower had the authority to soften the terms. The Allied response became contingent upon the degree of Italian collaboration and the level of resistance offered the Germans. Instructed not to reveal his military intentions, Eisenhower could not offer the Italians any concrete inducements to surrender. In addition, the AFHQ representatives were not to answer any questions regarding Allied operational plans for Italy. Meanwhile, Churchill and Roosevelt would hammer out the "long terms" to include economic, political, and financial conditions the Italians would eventually be required to sign.[33]

Eisenhower had no difficulty in selecting his representatives. An obvious choice, Smith then was touring Sicily. In fact, he spent August 17 watching the victorious entry of the Allied forces into Messina.[34] Initially unable to locate him, Eisenhower issued strict orders Smith be found and returned to Algiers. Arriving in Algiers around noon on August 19, Smith received a quick briefing on the maneuvering to date between Castellano and the British. Smith had not previously known about the Italian peace feelers.[35] He was, however, familiar with the "short terms" because they had been based upon a draft written by his Intelligence and Operations divisions.[36] Earlier, Eisenhower had conferred with Strong, delegated to be Smith's companion on the adventure. The supreme commander wanted a military agreement without the complications of formal negotiations. The political aspects could be settled once the Allies were ashore.[37]

In the four hours between his arrival in Algiers and the departure for Gibraltar, Smith hastily secured some civilian clothes. Smith and Strong were instructed to make the trip in the guise of businessmen. Mr. Smith arrived at Maison Blanche dressed in a new suit. His appearance prompted Macmillan to burst out in laughter. Smith, who still wore the Sam Browne belt, caste-symbol of Pershing's AEF, looked entirely out of place when not in uniform. Indeed, Smith's choice of clothing—an "appalling Norfolk jacket," ill-fitting grey flannel trousers, crowned by a hat with a feather—illustrated only too well he had rarely been out of uniform since 1917. With no time to make substitutions, Macmillan at least persuaded him to dispense with the hat, pointing out that "no British traveller of whatever class would walk about with [that] unusual decoration." On this note, the "amateur theatrical" began.[38]

At Gibraltar, Smith and Strong received further instructions. To gain an entry visa into Portugal, the two required passports. Since Smith's passport listed his next-of-kin as the adjutant-general of the U.S. Army, he was issued with British papers. Before setting off on the last leg of their journey, Smith dropped by Strong's quarters. Much to Strong's amazement, Smith showed him how he had outfitted himself for the adventure. Under each arm Smith displayed a holster; he then produced two other pistols concealed in his hip pockets. "If we were cornered," Strong remembered, "I envisaged a desperate gunfight in the best Western manner."[39]

Met at the Lisbon airport by a representative of the American Embassy, the men spent the day hiding in the apartment of the American chargé d'affaires. At 10:30 p.m. they drove to the British Embassy to met with Castellano. For the next nine hours Smith and Strong, at times joined by Campbell and the American chargé, conferred with the Italian general and a representative of the Italian Foreign Office. From the beginning Smith made it clear he was authorized by Eisenhower "to communicate terms on which he [Eisenhower] is prepared to agree to the cessation of hostilities between the Allied Forces under his command and the Italian forces." He added that Eisenhower wanted no political interference into military matters.[40]

The American general informed the Italian the Allies were prepared to accept an Italian surrender. Taken by surprise, Castellano replied the purpose of the meeting was to discuss what aid the Allies would provide Italy not to negotiate a surrender, which in any event Castellano had no authority to undertake. With the Italian representative clearly off balance by this ultimatum, Smith stated he would only discuss surrender and then read the "short terms" paragraph by paragraph. Like Castellano, Smith's hands were tied by directives from the CCS and Eisenhower. Citing the humane treatment of the Sicilian population by the Allied military government and emphasizing the Quebec memorandum provided for moderation of terms in accordance with Italian cooperation, Smith continued to press Castellano.

After an exchange of views, Smith left the Italians to study the document. Upon their return, Smith and Strong clarified their position. Castellano took the opportunity to impress upon Smith the physical presence of German forces in Italy made it practically impossible for the Italians to leave the war. Smith replied that while he might discuss certain points he could not grant any concessions. Castellano hinted the Badoglio government wanted to arrange an alliance with the Allies, but Smith bluntly retorted such matters of "high government policy" had to be decided by the political heads.

Strong produced a map and asked Castellano to indicate the German order of battle. The information confirmed Allied intelligence estimates and indicated the Italian could be trusted. Smith, like most American officers, held a low opinion of Italians—the product of ethnic stereotypes common in the country at large. He regarded Castellano as a competent enough officer but, since in his opinion, Italians "simply do not have the same attitudes as we do," Smith never entirely trusted the Italian staff officer. Sensing that the Italians feared the Germans more than they did the prospect of an Allied invasion, Smith and Strong began to bluff Castellano. As Smith later related: "In war you do not play the game with all your cards down."[41]

Castellano, in a private conversation with Strong, indicated he did not trust the Allies and wondered if they possessed the capacity and resolve to execute the daring operations the situation demanded. The Italian general stated the Italians thought the Allies ought to launch an invasion north of Rome with fifteen divisions. Clearly the Italian General Staff was entirely ignorant of Allied strengths and intentions since AFHQ stretched resources to stage limited landings with only five divisions. Guessing Castellano understood more English than he acknowledged, the two Allied officers let it slip that the invasion force would contain twenty divisions.

Aware of the limited Allied capacities for only restricted operations in the near future but eager to push his advantage, Smith suggested the king and his ministers might "temporarily" leave Rome while the battle for the capital raged. Undoubtedly impressed, Castellano told the AFHQ representatives he would take the short terms back to Badoglio. At this point Smith told Castellano that in addition to the terms under discussion the Italian government would receive a more thorough document enumerating political and economic requirements. When Castellano asked the time and place of the Allied invasion be disclosed, Smith promised only that AFHQ would announce the location of the landings five or six hours before the invasion took place. Another meeting was arranged for August 31, probably to take place in Sicily. Smith and Castellano agreed a confirmation or rejection of the short terms be sent on or about August 30. Before Castellano returned to Rome, the British furnished him with a special transmitter and the appropriate cipher.[42]

The next day Smith and Strong returned to Algiers confident they fulfilled their mission. Campbell, present during part of the interview, thought the diplomatic conversations were the most brilliantly conducted negotiations he had ever attended.[43] Without surrendering anything, Smith had secured much important intelligence. Most revealing was the knowledge the Badoglio government suffered from internal divisions and "an intense hatred and intense fear of the Germans." If, as Smith reported to the CCS, they received "reasonable assurance of protection and support," the Italian government probably would cooperate, but not before they made a renewed effort to gain cobelligerent status.[44] Although he had been instructed to demand an unconditional surrender, Smith deliberately avoided using the term. "Our aim was to get Italy out of the war," he later recalled. "But we needed a government in Italy and no government which signed 'unconditional surrender' would have lasted 48-hours."[45]

On August 27 the long terms arrived with instructions they be used in any further negotiations. The document also arrived in Lisbon, two days after a second negotiator arrived from Rome. General Giacomo Zanussi represented the other faction within the Badoglio government, one centered around General Mario Roatta, the commander-in-chief of the Italian Army. Campbell, acting on instructions, furnished Zanussi with the long terms. This compromised AFHQ's position.

Zanussi's appearance muddied the waters. Since neither Italian mission knew of the other's existence, it was not clear who held real power in Rome. Eisenhower's instructions obliged him to seek unconditional surrender, but negotiations already were underway based on the short terms. Zanussi held a copy of the contradictory long terms. Equally unclear was the degree of authority AFHQ possessed in accepting Italian terms. Finally, in order to secure meaningful Italian cooperation, AFHQ would have to seize much of southern Italy and perhaps revive planning for an assault north of Naples.[46] At the same time, the headquarters, embroiled in finalizing plans for a strengthened AVALANCHE, realized the strength of German forces they would face. Not expecting any active Italian support, Smith advised concessions be made to secure Italian passivity, particularly on the question of unconditional surrender.[47]

Since Zanussi had a copy of the long terms and represented the pro-German faction, Eisenhower requested he not be allowed to return to Rome and instead fly to Algiers. Unfortunately, he had already notified Rome of the existence of the document, the opening line of which contained the unconditional surrender clause. Castellano, in a book written after the war, claimed that Zanussi, considered a spy by AFHQ, was to be shot.[48] Smith denied this, but AFHQ resorted to arm-twisting to keep him in their custody until the confusion lessened.[49] Zanussi eventually consented to surrender the document on condition the long terms be forwarded to the Italian government. Lancia de Tracia of the Italian Foreign Office, who accompanied the Italian general, returned to Rome with a letter from Zanussi recommending acceptance of the short terms. Having received permission from the CCS to proceed with negotiations on the basis of the "military terms," Smith, Macmillan, Murphy, and Zanussi flew to Alexander's headquarters, Cassibile, Sicily, on August 31 to meet Castellano.

The Italians refused to announce the armistice, to which they agreed in principle, until the Allies landed in force in Italy. They reiterated their scheme for a fifteen-division invasion north of Rome. Castellano pointed out the military situation in Italy had taken a turn for the worse. Confirming AFHQ estimates, he reported German ground forces in Italy now numbered twenty divisions. Smith replied unless the Italians accepted the armistice by the time of the AVALANCHE landing, they would be treated as enemies. Crushed, Castellano now began to question Allied strength. What good would an armistice be if the Germans captured the government and occupied Italy unmolested?[50] Castellano pleaded for help in holding Rome. He pointed out four and a half Italian divisions held the area around the Italian capital but they possessed limited fuel and ammunition reserves. At this juncture Smith suggested an Allied airborne division might be available for an operation to seize Rome. While Castellano flew back to Rome, the AFHQ chief of staff wired Eisenhower asking if such an operation could be staged.[51]

Smith felt strongly the Rome operation was imperative. Eisenhower supported his chief of staff but left the final decision to Alexander. Anxious to get a commitment, Smith urged Alexander to sanction the plan and recommended using the U.S. 82d Airborne Division.[52] The British general readily agreed and the 15th Army Group planners set to work to improvise an outline for this operation (GIANT II). Meanwhile, Castellano encouraged Badoglio to sign the short terms. While Alexander's staff frantically labored on GIANT II, the Italians on the basis of this operation decided to accept the Allied terms.[53]

On September 2 Smith, Macmillan, and Murphy met again with Castellano in Sicily. Under an agreement with the Soviets, only Eisenhower possessed authorization to sign an armistice with the Italians. Late in the afternoon Alexander and Smith cabled Eisenhower pointing out "operational reasons" might require them to sign the armistice agreement.[54] Remembering the Darlan affair, the supreme commander delegated responsibility to Smith, in part because he wanted to distance himself because he thought the deal "crooked."[55] The way was clear for Smith to proceed when AFHQ received the go-ahead from the French Committee and the Soviets.[56] Earlier, Churchill and Roosevelt agreed the Italian settlement should be guided by military considerations. The armistice constituted, in Eisenhower's words, only a "preliminary document."[57]

The "operational reasons" alluded to by Smith involved Castellano's refusal to sign the armistice. The conference began by Smith bluntly asking whether Castellano had authority to sign the surrender. The Italian staff officer believed the purpose of the meeting was to arrange cooperation for the Allied landings and the Rome air-drop and replied he possessed no such mandate. Smith simply reiterated the Allies could not commit themselves until they had an Italian surrender in hand. When Castellano and Zanussi asked for information on the size and location of the invasion, Smith, losing his temper, curtly told them the Allies intended to drive the Germans out of Italy no matter what the German strength or the Italian attitude. Italy would become a battlefield and the civilian suffering could only be lessened by a speedy Italian acceptance of the Allied conditions.

After this heated exchange Smith decided to further intimidate Castellano. A meeting was hurriedly arranged between the Italian general and Alexander. When Castellano renewed his protests, Alexander, surrounded by his beribboned staff, staged some calculated histrionics of his own. Alexander angrily announced if the Italians continued their disgraceful procrastination, the Allies would be forced to bomb Rome. Further, Alexander explained they would not be allowed to leave until the armistice had been signed. Negotiating with a noose around their necks, the Italians were left alone in the midst of the headquarters to ponder their limited options.

Acting on Smith's suggestion, Castellano signaled Rome for instructions. The ruse had its desired result. After some confused communications with Rome, Castellano received permission to sign the short terms. Montgomery's BAYTOWN landings, which went in that morning, provided the final impetus.[58]

Late in the afternoon of September 3 Eisenhower, on Smith's request, flew in from Tunis. Not wishing to himself be party to the agreement, he stayed only long enough to witness the signing. With little ceremony, appropriately under an olive tree, Smith and Castellano affixed their signatures to the instrument. The supreme commander left immediately, leaving Bedell the unpleasant duty of presenting Castellano with the "long terms." Despite having been aware of the document, the Italian government had attached no significance to it. In all his discussions Smith deliberately avoided any use of the phrase "unconditional surrender." According to Smith, the short terms satisfied all the military requirements for the occupation of Italy, which fulfilled AFHQ's primary concern.[59]

Castellano believed the just-signed agreement prepared the way for Italian cobelligerent status. Realizing he had been duped, he angrily protested. Reminded by Smith the Quebec memorandum allowed for modification of the terms, Castellano remained unconvinced. Faced with the possibility Castellano might repudiate the agreement signed only minutes before, Smith sat down and wrote an amendment declaring "the additional clauses have only a relative value insofar as Italy collaborates in the war against the Germans."[60] Still not appeased, Castellano agreed an official announcement of the armistice would be made, subject to the approval of the Badoglio government, on September 8, a few hours before the AVALANCHE forces were to hit the beaches at Salerno.

Smith's satisfaction with his role in bluffing the Italians into an armistice was tempered by knowledge the agreement held by the narrowest of margins. He understood that the Badoglio-Castellano faction represented a small group in the Italian government and command. Not until the AVALANCHE and GIANT II operations were carried out and an official announcement of the armistice made would there be reason for celebration.

The GIANT II plan emerged from a hurried all-night planning session headed by Alexander's American chief of staff, General Lyman Lemnitzer.[61] Smith attached enormous significance to the seizure of Rome. After the war he still regretted that GIANT II had not been executed. In his estimate it held great strategic promise. Against the five divisions (four demoralized Italian divisions and an airborne force scarcely more than a regiment), Smith thought the two and a half imbalanced German divisions in Rome would be powerless. Believing Rome could be held "indefinitely" with the aid of the city's populace, Bedell concluded the Germans, who had no stomach for street fighting, would be compelled to "retire immediately to the North—to the regions of the Gothic Line."[62] This assumption rested upon the receipt of Italian support. But just days before, Smith discounted meaningful Italian assistance, claiming the most the Allies could realistically hope for was an armistice, perhaps a portion of the Italian fleet and the containment of twenty German divisions. Now, flushed by his success as a diplomat, he envisioned capturing all of southern Italy, including Rome, with the investment of six Allied divisions in three widely dispersed operations.

Although the whole fantastic scheme depended upon a miraculous transformation of Italy from enemy to associated power, Smith's view received much support. Cunningham, who earlier vetoed BARRACUDA because of the lack of Allied fighter cover, told Smith he would "land guns up at the first bridge on the Tiber."[63] Alexander and Eisenhower also lent their support as did Strong, Smith's most trusted adviser. There were dissenting voices. Tedder opposed AVALANCHE and thought little of GIANT II. The two officers charged with the mission, Smith's Leavenworth classmates and associates in Marshall's secretariat, Ridgway and Taylor of the 82d Airborne, were sceptical from the beginning. It was decided Taylor would slip clandestinely into Rome to survey the situation.[64]

Taylor guessed Smith's bullying had extracted promises of support from Castellano that could not be kept. He radioed back the Italians possessed neither the will nor the means to hold Rome. Owing to difficulties in transmitting the message, Taylor sent a two-word communication, "situation innocuous," the prearranged code to cancel the air-drop. Badoglio, disregarding the Smith-Castellano agreement, told Taylor the armistice announcement and AVALANCHE must be postponed. Several factors prompted the Italians to change their minds, chief among them their supposition no invasion would be staged before September 15 at the earliest. A communication from Badoglio, repudiating the Cassibile agreement, was encoded and transmitted.[65]

Eisenhower left Algiers for Amilcar the morning of September 8. Shortly afterwards, Badoglio's message renouncing the armistice agreement reached AFHQ. Badly shaken, Smith sent a cable to the CCS asking if AFHQ should proceed with the armistice announcement "for the tactical deception value."[66]

Arriving at the Tunisian command post, the supreme commander was handed both Badoglio's communication and Smith's cable. In disbelief, Eisenhower had a bout of nerves, irritated as much with Smith as with Badoglio. He immediately wired the Italian leader, stating his intent to broadcast the announcement as planned, and if the Italians refused to cooperate he would publish the "full record of the affair."[67] He ordered Castellano to come to Tunis hoping he could influence Badoglio in Rome. Eisenhower sent Lemnitzer to Sicily to stop GIANT II. Despite Taylor's "innocuous" cable, 62 planes were already airborne when Lemnitzer landed. A disaster was avoided only by the narrowest of margins.[68]

After the war, both Smith and Strong remained convinced the cancellation of GIANT II was a major mistake. Smith thought a person with authority should have been sent to Rome; someone who would have threatened to line the Italian leadership up against the wall and shoot them if they did not carry out the bargain.[69] Strong believed Bedell Smith was the ideal man for that job.[70] Smith thought otherwise but agreed sending Taylor had been an error. "[It] is a good example...that it is a mistake to send a specialist when what is needed is someone who can make a decision and enforce it."[71]

Eisenhower carried out the broadcast on schedule at 6:30 P.M., September 8.[72] After waiting ten minutes for Badoglio's announcement, the supreme commander authorized Radio Algiers to broadcast the Italian proclamation.[73] Meanwhile, Badoglio conferred with the king and the leaders of the military government. Their position seemed hopeless. If they refused to make an announcement, Eisenhower would publish the negotiation proceedings, leaving the Italian government at the mercy of the Germans. If they made the announcement, the Germans would seize Rome and northern Italy. Finally, the king decided Italy could not change sides again and ordered Badoglio to make the announcement. At 7:45 P.M., over Radio Rome, the Italian marshal made the proclamation. Eight and a half hours later, in the early morning of September 9, the American VI and British X Corps landed on their beachheads in Salerno Bay.[74]

While the Italian government debated remaining in Rome, the Germans merely disarmed the Italian Army and occupied the air bases. During the afternoon of September 9, Cunningham rushed elements of his fleet, plus the British 1st

Airborne Division, into the harbor at Taranto. The Italians, having agreed to surrender the fleet, passed the British ships as they entered the harbor. The next day it set sail for Malta. Elsewhere, major elements of the Italian fleet were lost to the Luftwaffe while making for prearranged Allied controlled ports. Nonetheless, the Allies succeeded in neutralizing the last powerful threat to their position in the Mediterranean, the Italian Navy. With little importance attached to securing active Italian land and air support, AFHQ was satisfied with the developments of September 8-9.

The collapse of Italy vindicated the Mediterranean strategy mapped out at Casablanca nine months before. Italy had been knocked out of the war, and the Allies secured the Italian fleet. By the end of 1943 forty German divisions would be diverted to Italy and the Balkans, filling the void left by the Italian withdrawal. As Montgomery confided in his diary, "we have done very well."[75]

THE FOUR-RING CIRCUS

AFHQ had no time to bask in their success. AVALANCHE ran into prepared German defenses. The Germans anticipated an amphibious operation somewhere within the range of Allied land-based aviation and positioned the 16th Panzer Division in a mobile defense in and around Salerno. Field Marshal Albert Kesselring, commander of German forces in southern Italy, withdrew forces facing Montgomery, feeding elements into counterattacks against the tenuous Allied beachheads. On September 12 he launched his major counterthrust. Four days later German intelligence reported the American 36th Division in "headlong flight."[76] As after Kasserine, thrown into a panic, AFHQ issued a "cry for help" to Montgomery.

The British general never saw the value of AVALANCHE. On August 30 he tried to dissuade Alexander from launching the attack. As with TORCH and HUSKY, Montgomery could discern no coherent objectives to be gained by conducting widely dispersed operations. Without any defined objective, Montgomery's skeletonized 8th Army was committed piecemeal in the boot of Italy, 300 miles from the main assault at Salerno. In his view, BAYTOWN, a pointless diversion of strength, would have been better as a threat. If it had been intended to draw German power away from Salerno, Montgomery thought the two operations should have been staged simultaneously. In fact, they had never been conceived as interrelated until Clark's forces were in danger of losing the beachheads.[77]

SOUTHERN ITALY

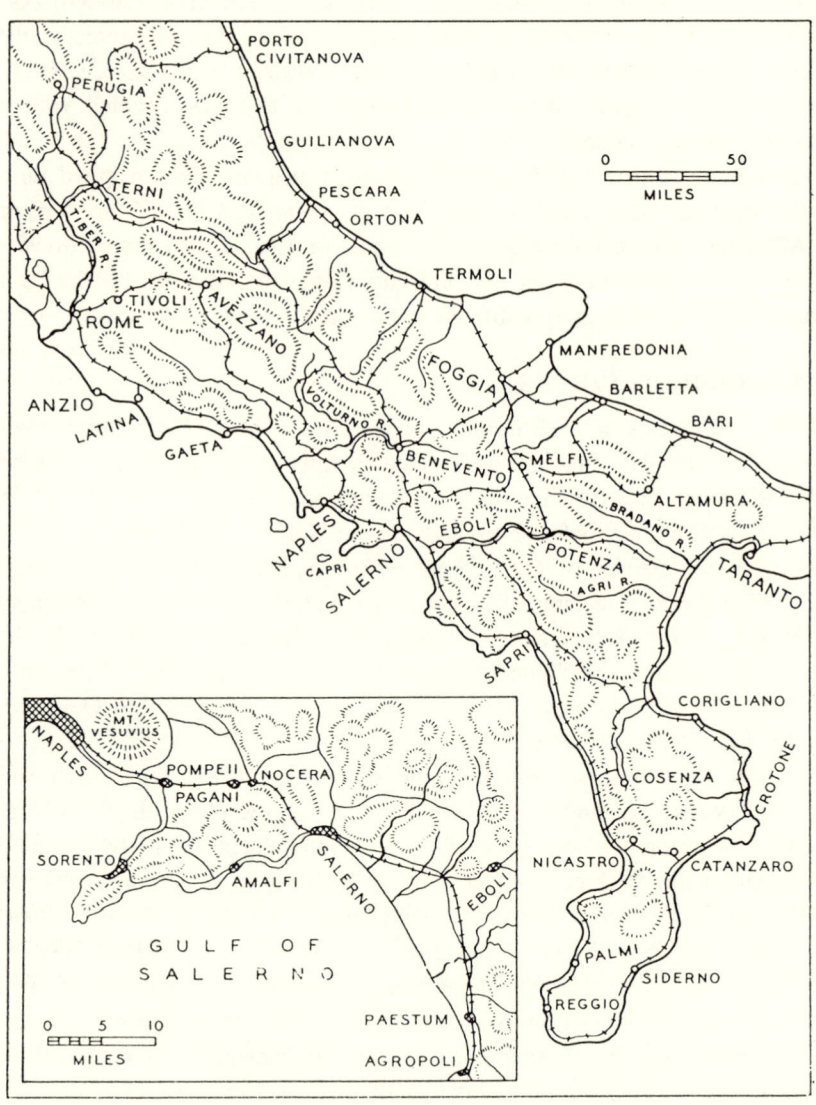

Alfred D. Chandler, ed., *The Papers of Dwight D. Eisenhower: The War Years*, vol. 5 (Baltimore: Johns Hopkins University Press, 1970), p. 56.

Montgomery's professionalism was wounded by, in his view, the opportunistic amateurism of AFHQ. "The way the whole party was stage-managed," he remarked, "is past all belief."[78] Confronted by the chance to save Clark and add lustre to his reputation, Montgomery paused. Worried Clark would have to evacuate, Montgomery feared the prospect of having to face the Germans alone.[79] Despite Clark's exposed position, 8th Army's tentative advance compelled Kesselring to break off the attacks but not before serious hostility surfaced between AFHQ and Montgomery. Undoubtedly, Montgomery's criticisms of Allied Force HQ handling of the twin operations had merit as did the charges leveled by Eisenhower and Smith concerning the British commander's caution. By September 17 the crisis had passed, but the shadows cast by the near-disaster of AVALANCHE were long ones.

Eisenhower maintained his optimism throughout the crisis, buoyed by the flexibility of the Mediterranean command. The commanders-in-chief met daily with Eisenhower at Malta and Amilcar. The supreme commander told Marshall he was astonished by "how much the staff, working at 'full tilt,' could accomplish."[80] Most of the credit belonged to Smith. As Eisenhower remarked to McNarney on September 16: "If ever I should write any memoirs...I should certainly have to devote a full chapter to the debt I owe to Smith. He is a fellow who carries a tremendous load and does it so ably as to excite my admiration every day."[81]

During the Salerno battle, Smith remained in Algiers acting as *de facto* theater commander. On September 10 Smith urged Marshall to prod Roosevelt and Churchill into acceptance of the Badoglio government to encourage "the Italians to oppose with the fiercest possible resistance every German in Italy."[82] The next day the two governments made public a letter to Badoglio, calling upon the Italian marshal to lead the Italian people against the German invader. Eisenhower conveyed the message directly to Badoglio.[83] In the meantime Smith acted as intermediary, negotiating with the CCS and BCOS. He requested retention of forces and landing craft earmarked to leave the theater and dispatch of heavy bombers from the United Kingdom. Devers and Bomber Command complied quickly.[84] Pressing their advantage, Eisenhower and Smith asked the B-24s be kept in the Mediterranean, but Marshall vetoed their proposals.[85] Remarking the only way AFHQ could get matériel from the CCS was during a crisis, Smith suggested a special section be created to keep the home front frightened.[86]

Key political decisions were left entirely to the judgment of AFHQ during the hectic weeks that surrounded the Italian surrender. To concentrate upon military operations, Eisenhower depended on Smith to see he was not distracted by what seemed like unnecessary political interruptions. Aided by Macmillan and

Murphy, Smith dealt with the French and Italians.

Noting the preoccupation of AFHQ with Italian affairs, de Gaulle on September 25 proposed a single strong executive replace the existing system of dual FCNL command. Giraud's political naivete prompted him to rely upon Jean Monnet, a man outside the French factions who enjoyed the confidence of Hopkins and Smith.[87] Anxious to settle the French leadership question, Smith, who long favored an increased role for de Gaulle, raised no objections when Giraud removed himself from the copresidency of the FCNL. Thereafter de Gaulle moved quickly to consolidate his position over the French Committee.

A credible Italian government had to be created to sign the final surrender and coalesce support. The royal family, Badoglio, a couple generals, and some courtiers escaped from Rome and established a nucleus of a government in the Adriatic city of Brindisi. The septuagenarian king and Badoglio, who wanted cobelligerent status without forces to fight, did not constitute much of a government, but it represented the only one with which the Allies had to work. Eisenhower dispatched Mason-MacFarlane, Macmillan, and Murphy to Brindisi to establish formal ties with the Italian government.

On September 17 Murphy and Macmillan returned. Smith conferred with them and drafted a long situation report to the CCS. He pointed out AFHQ intended to employ the Italian garrisons on Sardinia and Corsica for coastal defense and the Italian fleet for transport. These activities were inconsistent with the terms of the armistice, which called for the demobilization of the Italian armed forces. Requesting a new policy formulation, Smith wanted the Badoglio government granted "some form of *de facto* recognition...as a co-belligerent or military associate." Recognizing such a policy exposed the governments to "considerable opposition and criticism," he recommended "the burden be placed upon us, on the ground of military necessity, which I am convinced should be the governing factor."[88]

Not happy with Smith's telegram, Eisenhower drafted a new one. Eisenhower maintained future relations with Italy could follow two courses: accept Italy as a military associate and strengthen Badoglio, or assume the heavy liability of setting up an Allied military government. Of the two courses Eisenhower "strongly recommended the first." Smith concurred, and the communication was forwarded on September 20.[89]

On September 26 Smith flew to Brindisi, where he prepared groundwork for an Eisenhower-Badoglio conference. He returned from Italy with Badoglio's complete agreement to meet Eisenhower on Malta on September 29, there to sign the official surrender. Smith's meeting with Victor Emmanuel and Badoglio convinced him "there was something fundamentally lacking in all the top men."[90] He told reporters that "the Italian government, at the present time, consists of the king, Marshal Badoglio, two or three generals, and a couple of part-time stenographers. The day that I was there, a couple of cheap help from the Foreign Office (an Under-Secretary or two) came down from Rome on foot."[91]

The king was, in Smith's opinion, "absolutely pitiful." Badoglio "had been a good general but he was an old man—without decision—and given to crying."[92] While the marshal was at least receptive, the king refused to declare war on Germany or promise free elections after the war. He did authorize Badoglio to sign the long terms.[93] "The King-Badoglio government is a pretty weak affair," confessed Eisenhower, "yet it is the only medium through which Italians can be inspired to help us."[94]

On September 29, aboard the battleship *HMS Nelson* in Valetta Harbor, Malta, Eisenhower and Badoglio signed the "Instrument of Surrender of Italy." Cunningham, Smith, Alexander, Macmillan, Murphy, and an array of lesser officials looked on. After the signing Eisenhower handed Badoglio a letter, written by Smith, which, in essence, stated the agreement was outdated.[95] When the Italian marshal asked the phrase "unconditional surrender" be altered, Eisenhower promised to consult the political heads. After a week's exchange of cables, Churchill and Roosevelt agreed and Smith rewrote Article One, leaving out the objectionable phrase.[96]

For Smith, the Lisbon "party" and the signing of the Cassibile surrender represented "one of the most interesting experiences" of his career. For compensation he watched the review of the Italian fleet off Bizerte and the formal surrender in Malta. Throughout September and October he crossed the Mediterranean in his C-47, flying between Algiers and Sicily, Italy, and Tunisia. "I now commute...like any suburban tripper," he remarked. "I have developed a perfect drill which consists of boarding the plane, blowing up the air mattress and stretching out with a book."[97] These trips provided him with his only respite from the pressures of his position. Reading chiefly detective novels, which he exchanged with Brigadier General Theodore Roosevelt, Jr., Smith did find time to give the then newly published *Makers of Modern Strategy*, edited by Edward Mead Earle, careful study.[98]

Among his concerns was the establishment of an Italian Military Mission at AFHQ. Smith brought his "pet Wop" Castellano to Algiers on September 13 to inaugurate the mission. "So you see," he wrote Pug Ismay, "our two ring circus has developed first into three rings and now four rings, counting the French and Italians."[99]

September 12 saw the Italian king declare war on Germany, prompted by assurances received from Alexander and Eisenhower that Rome would soon fall. This estimate, like many before it, proved illusory. On October 8,

Kesselring brought three additional divisions into the line south of the city. After securing Sardinia, Corsica, and the vital airfield at Foggia, the Allies met a determined enemy, superior in numbers and occupying highly defensible terrain. Alexander's operations in Italy ground to a virtual halt. By the middle of October the Germans succeeded in stalemating the battle.

Early in September Marshall wanted Eisenhower to come to Washington for a discussion of "matters pertaining to your theater."[100] The supreme commander not only believed Rome would soon fall but envisioned an Allied advance into the Po Valley. Such an operation required substantial forces and matériel intended for withdrawal from the theater be retained. Always careful to soothe Marshall's suspicions, Eisenhower pointed out "we [he and Smith] feel that we might be drifting a bit away from your thoughts."[101] Since "nothing particularly bother[ed] us," he wrote, and with the delicate Italian political problem brought under control by Smith, Eisenhower dispatched the only officer at AFHQ who could "make sure we are on the right track"—his chief of staff.[102]

Before Smith left on October 5, his forty-eighth birthday, Eisenhower gave him a detailed memorandum outlining those points that needed clarification. One set involved organizational matters—plans for reorganizing American infantry divisions and setting up a new strategic air force (the 15th) in Italy. Anxious to share lessons learned in the Mediterranean, Eisenhower asked Smith to impress upon Marshall the need for a unified air command for OVERLORD, an operation everyone assumed the chief would lead. He also told Smith to argue Patton's case. Patton's position had been badly injured by the famous slapping incident in a Sicilian field hospital, but Eisenhower recommended the flamboyant general for an army command. On the political front, Smith was charged with making certain the French rearmament program continued and Washington appreciated the need to prevent a collapse of the Badoglio government. Most important, Eisenhower insisted that Smith push for the maintenance of Allied combat and logistical strength in the Mediterranean.[103] To make sure his chief of staff understood his mission, Eisenhower flew to Algiers for a conference. This marked the first time in a month that the supreme commander had been in his headquarters.[104] To buttress his position further, Eisenhower wrote two letters to Marshall, reviewing the points Smith would raise and emphasizing the belief "no other operation could help OVERLORD so much as the early establishment of this Allied force in the Po Valley."[105]

One of the primary objectives of the Smith mission was not mentioned in Eisenhower's letters to Marshall. Since the middle of September, AFHQ was alive with scuttlebutt concerning Eisenhower's future.[106] In the weeks after the Malta surrender, a number of important officials came through AFHQ. Secretary of the Navy Frank Knox told Eisenhower a decision had been reached at Quebec to give the OVERLORD command to Marshall. Although King and Arnold wanted Marshall to remain in Washington, Knox predicted the army chief of staff would go to London and Eisenhower would take his place in the War Department. Two days later, on October 3, Mountbatten confirmed the story. Eisenhower wanted Smith to "find the lay of the land" in Washington. Told under no circumstances to raise the question with Marshall, if the topic should arise Eisenhower wanted Smith to tell Marshall he hoped to remain in the Mediterranean or command an army group in OVERLORD. In any case, Smith should pump his War Department cronies for information.[107]

As the case any time Smith left the command, Eisenhower requested Marshall not keep Bedell for more than two or three days. "I sorely need him back as soon as possible," he complained.[108] Smith remained in the United States two weeks. On his return he brought bad news. He found little support in the War Department for Eisenhower's scheme for an advance into northern Italy. The landing-craft situation appeared equally bleak. Instead of receiving more equipment, the CCS intended to strip the Mediterranean command of most of what it possessed. More depressing yet, Smith confirmed Marshall would go to OVERLORD on January 1 and Roosevelt was "sold on" Eisenhower's assuming the duties of chief of staff. This came from the highest authority, the president himself who Smith had met at Hyde Park on October 10.[109]

Since the QUADRANT conference, AFHQ had an inkling a British officer would be named to command Allied forces in the Mediterranean. This being the case, Eisenhower began to build up Hughes's position as deputy commander to protect American interests in the Mediterranean theater.[110] Smith and Hughes had been engaged in a power struggle since the creation of the North African Theater of Operations command (NATOUSA) in March. In the early stages, the struggle was an unequal one. When Hughes tried to tighten the organization of the American Communications Zone, Smith told him to stop edging into his preserve. Accusing Hughes of "empire building," Smith resorted to a "you go or I do" tactic to put his opponent in place.[111] Thereafter, relations between the two officers worsened.

Although Hughes was among Eisenhower's oldest friends, the supreme commander invariably supported Smith. Hughes resented this and Smith's interference in matters outside the book definition of the chief of staff's position. "Murphy goes to Smith about Theater matters," Hughes wrote in his diary, "Smith gives all the answers."[112] Hughes also took issue when Smith surrounded himself with British officers. He emerged as the leader of the anti-British faction in the headquarters. Patton, another buddy of Hughes's, was also a charter member of this large and growing club. Smith and Hughes even squabbled over minor things such as Smith's paternalistic control over the WACs and his new sedan.[113]

As Smith put it to Hughes, "I like to throw my weight around and then quiet down."[114] This technique was calculated and not connected to his ulcer as Smith's defenders claimed. His control of the supreme commander's door granted Smith enormous leverage, but in the case of a close personal friend like Hughes he could not always isolate Eisenhower. While Smith attended the Washington conference in May, Hughes pushed Eisenhower for a reorganization of theater logistics. Although American and British supply organizations were separate, Gale, as headquarters CAO, actually controlled logistics. Smith confided in Hughes he would be named as Gale's American opposite number. Throughout an entire month, Smith put off Hughes with promises, announcing on June 27 the existing organization would stand. July saw HUSKY and an end to any discussion of staff reorganization.[115]

Upon his return from Washington in October, Smith was informed by Eisenhower AFHQ no longer could dictate to NATOUSA. In his absence Hughes again influenced Eisenhower. Naturally unhappy, Smith did not push the issue with the usual determination. For the next week Hughes prepared for an "explosion," but it never came, leaving the NATOUSA commander to surmise Smith's good mood was a product of knowing he would return to Washington or go to London.[116]

Smith did indeed think his days in the Mediterranean were numbered. Eisenhower concluded Smith was the only American qualified to assume command of the theater. This was out of the question as command would require Smith's promotion to full general, over more senior American officers such as Bradley and Patton.[117] As it stood, Eisenhower could not even secure Bedell's promotion to lieutenant general.[118] Smith told his superior he did not want the Mediterranean command; he would rather serve out the war under Eisenhower. His spirits boosted, relaxed after being reunited with his wife, Smith looked forward to the next couple of months, buoyed by the knowledge he enjoyed the unreserved confidence of Eisenhower and, more importantly, Marshall.[119] Whether he ended up in the War Department under Eisenhower or in OVERLORD under Marshall, Smith knew his star would continue to rise.

A WINTER OF DISCONTENT

At Churchill's insistence, the CCS and the political heads prepared to meet again, first in Cairo, then with Stalin in Teheran. The issue of the "second front" in 1944 topped their agenda. Secondary issues included the command structure for OVERLORD and the advantages of secondary operations in the Mediterranean. Smith flew to Malta on November 17 and had a long

conversation with Churchill, who remained unconvinced of the wisdom of
OVERLORD. Returning to Algiers, Smith predicted that the Cairo conference
would be the "hottest one" yet.[120]

On November 18 Eisenhower flew to Malta, conferring with Churchill and
the BCOS. During conversations, the topic of Eisenhower's leaving the theater
arose. If that happened, Churchill wanted Smith left in the Mediterranean to
help the new British commander. Pointedly refusing to give way, Eisenhower
insisted "this was one point on which I would not yield, except under directions
from the president."[121] Two days later, Eisenhower flew to Oran to greet
Roosevelt's party. For the next month, Eisenhower was away from headquarters,
leaving Smith in charge.

At Teheran, the "old Bolshevik," as Roosevelt called Stalin, forced the
president to decide on a commander for OVERLORD. As late as Teheran,
Roosevelt still had not made up his mind. As was usually the case, events
forced his hand. The British refused to accept Marshall's appointment as
commander of Anglo-American forces in the war against Germany. Roosevelt
felt anything less would be a demotion for Marshall. More to the point, the
president had reservations about Eisenhower's ability to deal with MacArthur
and Congress and dreaded the idea of Marshall leaving his post as chief
American advocate in the CCS. Sometime before the second Cairo conference
the Americans dropped their insistence for an overall command. Still shrinking
from making a decision, Roosevelt wanted Marshall to state his preference.
When he refused to do so, Roosevelt announced Eisenhower was his choice to
command OVERLORD.[122]

The big appointment made events in the Mediterranean seem anticlimactic for
Eisenhower. During the first week of October Eisenhower, believing Rome
would fall by the end of the month, instructed Smith not to move AFHQ-Main
to Naples.[123] As a result the unsettled conditions of the command made AFHQ
tentative. Not until November 13 did Smith make a firm decision to center the
theater headquarters in the Caserta Palace, north of Naples. He also selected a
sumptuous villa for himself while Butcher laid claim to the crown prince's
hunting lodge for Eisenhower.[124]

With relative calm descending on the Italian front, Smith managed to take
some time off for a couple of hunting trips, one in North Africa and another
with Eisenhower in Italy. With the autumn mornings turning snappy, Smith
yearned "to sit in a duck blind."[125] Unable to bring his shotgun from the States,
he acquired one from the French Sûreté and ammunition from Ivan Cobbold,
a fellow outdoorsman and close personal friend, from London.[126] The Tunisian
countryside was rugged, and quail was plentiful. Although he complained Arab
beaters could not match his dogs, he relished getting "out from behind [the]

desk for a change and out of doors with a gun in [his] hands."[127]

While in Tunisia Smith made a long-delayed trip to the site of ancient Carthage. He leapt from the staff car and quickly walked through the ruins, then motioned for his driver to follow him. Smith, lost in thought, intently studied the site, then he wheeled to face the sergeant. Obviously moved by the scene, Smith asked, "What do you think?" His driver, entirely indifferent, surveyed the ruins and replied, "the Germans sure bombed the Hell out of this place." At first astonished, when he realized his driver had been serious, Smith broke out in laughter. This little event furnished Smith with his favorite story, one he never tired telling.[128].

Unlike London, where Eisenhower and Smith frequently spent their evenings in the company of the supreme commander's circle, in North Africa the two rarely socialized together. Smith's days were filled with the routine tasks of running the staff and coordinating AFHQ actions with London, Washington, the headquarters of the commanders-in-chief, as well as the subordinate commands. That is not to say Smith was a total recluse. In addition to attending formal functions and informal dinners, he occasionally entertained in his Algiers villa. Described as "practically a palace," the estate featured two vast drawing rooms decorated with mosaics, art treasures, and Oriental rugs. The grounds contained extensive gardens and terraces. Those accustomed to the austere and hard-driving "official" chief of staff were surprised by the lavishness of the fare—expensive champagne and fine food—and the graciousness of their host.[129]

Like Eisenhower, Smith had a female companion, Ethel Westerman, the nurse who treated him during his confinement in the hospital in Oxford.[130] As with Eisenhower's driver and secretary, Kay Summersby, rumors made the rounds Smith was having an affair with his nurse. More likely, both Eisenhower and Smith succumbed more to peer pressure than libido. In an army that placed enormous emphasis upon an early marriage and made provisions no station would be without the salutary presence of officers' wives, American officers had little opportunity to "sow wild oats." Suddenly discovering themselves elevated in rank, with plenty of money, and far from their wives, many American officers behaved like fraternity boys. Yet despite sensational claims to the contrary, it is extremely unlikely Eisenhower or Smith engaged in any extramarital relations. Not only would it be out of character—Smith's attachment to his wife was deep and genuine—little time or opportunity presented itself for the pursuit of such activities. Both did, however, enjoy a platonic relationship with someone not in the chain of command. In Captain Westerman, Smith found a kindred spirit. A devout Catholic and well educated, Westerman provided Smith with an understanding ear. Their friendship lasted the duration of the war.[131]

While Smith ran AFHQ, Eisenhower occupied his remaining time in the theater, robbing the Mediterranean of personnel for OVERLORD. General Henry Maitland "Jumbo" Wilson received the Mediterranean command while Devers was to assume the American theater command, both effective on January 1, 1944. Eisenhower insisted that Smith accompany him to London. He also wanted Patton as an army commander, despite the uproar over the slapping incident. Shortly after the event took place, Eisenhower met with the press and asked them to sit on the story. Nevertheless, in late November, Drew Pearson, a noted radio commentator, reported the story, adding Patton had not been reprimanded.[132]

The story created a sensation, and the War Department demanded an explanation. Eisenhower, hoping to minimize his involvement, ordered Smith to reply. Not a member of the "West Point Protective Society," Smith made no effort to disguise Patton's excesses. Hearing through the headquarters' grapevine that Smith would write the communication, Hughes raced to his old friend's rescue. After reading the cable, Hughes suggested that it be modified. Bedell accepted and forwarded Hughes's sanitized revision. Hughes relayed the story to Patton who, assuming the worst, bore a grudge against Smith.[133]

Eisenhower faced a difficult dilemma. He felt compelled to shield Patton, a man Eisenhower valued both as a friend and an army commander. At the same time he wanted to avoid censure for mishandling the affair. Having learned the lesson of the Darlan mess, Eisenhower took the path of least resistance. He made himself unavailable and handed Smith responsibility for confronting the press. On November 23, Smith conducted a news conference designed to deflect charges Eisenhower had covered up the affair. After pointing out Patton's special abilities made him too valuable to send home and explaining Eisenhower's reasons for suppressing the story, Smith admitted the general had not been officially reprimanded. The result of this disclosure was electric, and instead of controlling the flames Smith's official version fanned them.

Smith merely told the truth; Patton had been only reprimanded privately. Eisenhower was not interested in presenting the facts, he wanted to divert criticism away from himself. Now Eisenhower and his command came under attack in the press and on Capitol Hill. Distressed over the adverse reaction, Eisenhower rode out the storm. Although unhappy with Smith's performance, he defended him. Smith, Eisenhower wrote, made a "bad mistake" but as his "ablest and finest officer," the supreme commander had "no intention of throwing valuable men to the wolves."[134]

Just when Eisenhower thought he had succeeded in pirating his selected staff officers from AFHQ, Churchill renewed efforts to keep Smith in the Mediterranean. When Smith got word of this, he immediately phoned

Eisenhower, desperate for the supreme commander to intervene. The prime minister insisted Smith's ability to manage the French and Italians made him indispensable.[135] For three days, December 10-12, the theater command was thrown into a turmoil. Even though Smith would have been assured his third star if he remained in the Mediterranean, he pushed for the transfer. Finally, Eisenhower said there would simply be no argument; he would say "no" and insist he exercise his prerogative to select his chief of staff. When Churchill met Eisenhower again on Malta, the supreme commander merely grinned at the prime minister and told him the subject of Smith's retention in the theater was undebatable. Seeming to acquiesce, Churchill said he hoped Smith would remain in the Mediterranean long enough to indoctrinate Wilson. Not entirely satisfied, Churchill nonetheless did not raise the issue again.[136]

Anxious to get to London and rapidly losing interest in Mediterranean problems, Eisenhower and Smith decided on a trip to Italy to establish a new headquarters in Naples and to "get muddy for a week."[137] What promised to be a triumphant tour turned into a depressing ordeal. It rained constantly and their moods were not improved by the heavy fog. After a long drive to visit the 5th Army front on December 21, Eisenhower invited Smith to dinner. Smith declined, and the supreme commander, losing his temper, told Bedell no subordinate could refuse his hospitality. Annoyed, Smith said he would quit. Eisenhower replied it would be fine with him, adding it could easily be arranged for Smith to remain behind in the Mediterranean. After this childish exchange both men became sullen. Smith apologized and Eisenhower said that all would be forgotten. One lesson was driven home. As Smith told Burgess, "never vacation with the boss."[138]

Upon returning to AFHQ-Advance in Naples, Smith received word de Gaulle had arrested three former Vichyite officials in an effort to even old scores. Appropriately, the last major question Smith handled before leaving the Mediterranean involved French political affairs. The next morning, December 22, he flew to Algiers for discussions with Macmillan.[139] After the events of the previous week, Smith was happy back at headquarters. He also conferred with Churchill, then confined to a sickbed in Tunisia. Roosevelt had reacted predictably and demanded the release of the three Frenchmen. Smith cabled Washington, informing the president de Gaulle could only see the preemptory demand as an ultimatum.[140] As Smith pointed out, the resulting crisis would reopen old wounds and materially delay French rearmament. By December 26 Roosevelt agreed and ordered AFHQ to make a mild protest. On December 30, Eisenhower had a long talk with de Gaulle. As he told Smith, "it was a love feast and we made mutual promises of great cooperation."[141] Just as the campaign in the Mediterranean had began, so too it ended, with Eisenhower and Smith surmounting yet another French crisis.[142]

A "GOOD TEAM"

In one of his epistles written after the Sicilian campaign Montgomery reflected upon command and staff relationships. "It is in the realm of teams on the highest level," he observed, "that we so often go wrong." In enumerating the qualities of a good commander, doubtless those he identified in himself, Montgomery held that the most important element of command rested in making tough decisions when confronted by difficult and complex problems. Decisions in war cannot, he believed, be the product of compromise. Without a decisive leader, no staff can function. With the ability to make decisions and control operations once they commenced, a commander, in the opinion of the British general, must remain clear of all the details. A good commander must choose able advisors, work with his staff, and possess charm and tact (which Montgomery recognized he lacked). Although a good team depends upon cooperation, a commander cannot be too accessible because the tendency to listen to too many people erodes the vital capability to make decisions and stand by them. Montgomery also believed commanding officers should look the part, have tactical experience, and possess moral courage.

As for a chief of staff, Montgomery thought his primary function lay in the realm of compensating for the inadequacies of the commander. The commander-staff relationship must be a collaborative effort based upon reciprocity. In the case of Alexander, Montgomery believed he "lost the gift of quick decision" and required a "chief of staff who is the 'cat's whiskers' and who will tell him what is wanted." Since, in Montgomery's view, this situation did not exist, "15th Army Group has been completely and utterly ineffective." When a commander lacks drive, he requires a chief of staff "who knows the whole business and will get on with it." A good chief of staff must provide the commander with advice, outline the operational repercussions of any course of action, and manage all the details of war. Ultimately, the chief of staff's main responsibility is to inform the commander in his decision making. Montgomery also thought it necessary no jealousies or personal animosities exist between the commander and his chief of staff as they should be close friends. They must work together, removing friction and smoothing over problems arising from human relationships.

Montgomery included "Ike and Beetle" among his exclusive list of "good teams" (along with Churchill and Brooke and Alexander and himself). Although he thought difficulties arose when the commanding general and the chief of staff were both staff officers without broad tactical experience, Montgomery believed Eisenhower and Smith possessed the abilities and personal qualities necessary for running an Allied command. "Eisenhower is a very 'big' man," he commented, "who takes the large view and keeps clear of all the detail. Bedell Smith implements all the big decisions and keeps the whole show on the rails." While the British general hinted Eisenhower sometimes lacked drive, this was balanced by Smith's activist role as chief of staff.[143]

Montgomery's observations on the nature of command mirrored Eisenhower's at this stage of the war. Responding to charges he bent "over backwards" to please the British, Eisenhower explained an allied command functioned "only if the Chief is truly self-effacing." A commanding general "must have a fund of patience and good humor" so when "he necessarily drags out the big stick it is more effective."[144] As evidenced here, Eisenhower held that good relations with his commanders and staff were crucial to the working of the Mediterranean command. Eisenhower's physical presence, his human qualities, and his ability to work with subordinates compensated for his lack of tactical experience. With an active mind and the unique talent to inspire tremendous loyalty and affection among his subordinates, Eisenhower rarely resorted to the "big stick." When he did, he left it to Smith to wield.

Equally vital was the way the staff worked. In January 1943 Eisenhower commented on the "fun" he had quarrelling with his staff. "Every once in a while Staff Officers get all confused in a bunch of charts and drawing lines on blank paper. I take a fiendish delight in ripping them to pieces," he said.[145] For him, the critical element involved blending personalities and approaches to achieve "a constant objectivity of viewpoint" allowing American and British officers to "unite and work together efficiently." After the shock of setbacks in Tunisia, AFHQ came to share a basic pattern of thought, imbued with the Allied approach. "In achieving this result," he reflected, "no individual was more responsible than my Chief of Staff."[146]

Eisenhower used the analogy of the team to describe his relationship with Smith. "In the long period that he has served as my Chief of Staff," he told Marshall, "we have developed a team work that I believe is effective and of which the principal ingredient is confidence in each other."[147] Smith discharged his functions as headquarters executive and supported Eisenhower in the face of the onslaught of conflicting political and military views. Eisenhower relied upon Smith to deal with Roosevelt, Churchill, Marshall, and Brooke on issues critical to AFHQ. When a crisis surfaced, the supreme commander expected his chief of staff to intervene personally. Smith built strong relationships with his principal military subordinates, with Murphy and Macmillan, and with de Gaulle and Badoglio. Forging a consensus between divergent opinions and cooperation between divisive personalities, Smith exerted a formative influence upon policy making critical to the command as a whole.

Mindful that Marshall had sent him to stiffen Eisenhower against the British, Smith pushed his boss to exercise command. He announced in a September staff conference "the duties and responsibilities of the Commander-in-Chief must be redefined." Senior American officers at AFHQ concurred but saw little prospect of Eisenhower pressing the issue. "Why should we worry," Hughes questioned, "when apparently even Ike doesn't know what he can tell the other commanders-in-chief?"[148] Despite Smith's best efforts, Eisenhower refused to rock the Allied boat. The role of supreme commander remained amorphous.

The supreme commander fully appreciated the debt he owed Smith. "He is by all odds," he remarked, "the most competent and marvellous Chief of Staff that any commander was ever lucky enough to have."[149] Fearing Churchill might insist Smith stay in the Mediterranean, Eisenhower implored Marshall "*not* to agree to any assignment for him that would break up our present intimate association." Eisenhower believed each was necessary to the other. "Whatever effectiveness I may have...and this applies to General Smith's effectiveness," he continued, "[is] increased by maintaining our existing relationship."[150]

For Eisenhower, the ideal organization was his AFHQ team. After his designation as OVERLORD commander, he brought his influence to bear, stealing away key personnel from AFHQ. But without the mainspring, Smith, the machine would not run as efficiently. "I don't know how I would carry along without him," he complained.[151] As it turned out, he need not have worried. Smith and the inner core of AFHQ went to London, composing the nucleus of the Supreme Headquarters that would guide Allied fortunes in the campaign in northwestern Europe.

Part IV

Northwest Europe

Preparing OVERLORD, January–June 1944

On December 31, 1943, Eisenhower left Algiers en route for Washington. At Marshall's insistence he came home for some much-needed rest. At first reluctant, Eisenhower appreciated his command was safe in Smith's hands. "There is scarcely anything I can tell you," he informed Smith, "that you cannot handle as well as I."[1]

Before leaving the Mediterranean, Eisenhower again insisted Smith be free to assume his new responsibilities in London. Churchill still wanted Smith to assist Wilson in Algiers, while Marshall thought Eisenhower's chief of staff should remain in the Mediterranean at least until the middle of February "purely because of American interests."[2] Eisenhower demanded Smith proceed to London to evaluate firsthand COSSAC planning and organization. Smith would return to Algiers for a week or more to clean up some outstanding details. The supreme commander then wanted him to return to London to begin organizing the new staff and overseeing planning for OVERLORD.[3] Citing the pressing necessity to finalize the command structure and planning for OVERLORD, Eisenhower won the debate.

THE COSSAC PLAN REJECTED

After Christmas, Smith flew to London. Arriving at Norfolk House, he found the old headquarters little changed from 1942. Meeting first with Morgan, Smith was informed by the COSSAC (Chief of Staff-Supreme Allied Commander) head that he had "an immense amount of work to get through in a limited time."[4] The most demanding problem involved planning.

On July 27, 1943, Morgan's staff produced the first tangible outline plan for OVERLORD. None of the COSSAC planners entertained any illusions about the perfection of the plan. They knew the forces allotted were too small, yet

COSSAC's directives mandated the assault be based upon available landing craft. Given a D-Day set for May 1, 1944, the landing-craft situation provided COSSAC with no latitude. The invasion's initial wave would consist of a maximum of three divisions. COSSAC received little guidance from the CCS, particularly in the realm of long-term political objectives. Despite its obvious shortcomings Morgan's plan offered the first concrete proposals for OVERLORD and decided that the invasion forces would land in Normandy. Morgan's most vexing problem was his staff had no commander capable of making decisions. This situation changed with Smith's arrival.[5]

Smith first saw the COSSAC plan in a November briefing conducted by Morgan in Washington. Having played a central role in planning TORCH, HUSKY, and AVALANCHE, Smith "nearly fell out of [his] seat" when Morgan mentioned OVERLORD would be staged with three divisions.[6] In late October, Eisenhower had been briefed by a COSSAC planner about OVERLORD.[7] Discussing the plan with Smith in November, having then only an academic interest in OVERLORD, Eisenhower said: "My God, if I were going to do it I would want [a beachhead large enough to accommodate] ten or twelve divisions."[8] Once named supreme commander for OVERLORD, Eisenhower summoned Montgomery to Algiers to discuss the COSSAC plan. Designated to command the ground forces in the assault but unfamiliar with the proposed invasion plan, the British general met with Eisenhower on December 27. During the conference Eisenhower called in Smith, and they decided "off the cuff" the initial assault needed broadening to five divisions.[9] As Smith pointed out in a postwar interview, "we were all unanimous...the addition of divisions was accepted by acclamation."[10]

Montgomery came to England shortly after Smith, assuming command of the 21st Army Group. His first move was to purge the existing command. He brought the nucleus of his staff from 8th Army, leading to the comment that "the Gentlemen are out and the Players are in." Montgomery began a detailed examination of the tactical plan. The British general wanted to set up his own headquarters as commander-in-chief of ground forces. Smith, adamant no separate establishment be created between Eisenhower and his commanders, blocked the effort.[11] Thereafter, Montgomery took charge of planning for an enlarged OVERLORD.

On January 5 Smith wrote a long letter to Eisenhower outlining the plan's shortcomings. "There had been much wishful thinking in connection with COSSAC," he observed. Recalling the first few days on the Salerno beachheads, Smith thought the "rates of advance after landing...entirely too optimistic." Aside from the likelihood of German counterattacks, "the principal weakness is the proposal to pass an enormous force of men, matériel and equipment in column over narrow and very restricted beaches." After discussing the COSSAC plan with Montgomery, Smith informed Eisenhower the ground commander insisted on strengthening the assault to five divisions and broadening the front from twenty-six to forty miles. As always, there remained the shortage of landing craft.

Smith thought the solution was the transfer of landing craft from the Mediterranean at the expense of SHINGLE (the landing at Anzio set for January 21) and ANVIL, the invasion of southern France. Montgomery wanted to revert to a pre-Cairo AFHQ-COSSAC agreement that abandoned the southern France operation except as a threat. "I completely agree with Monty in his belief that the assault is too weak and on too narrow a front," he stated. Furthermore he thought SHINGLE should be dropped. Smith and most of the planners thought the threat of ANVIL would accomplish as much as an assault. Careful to assure his chief nothing was being decided in his absence, Smith told Eisenhower he had instructed the COSSAC staff to develop detailed planning on the assumption additional landing craft would be found.[12]

For Eisenhower, ANVIL represented a *sine qua non* for a successful OVERLORD.[13] In response to Smith's letter, Eisenhower agreed on broadening the Normandy landings but rejected the idea ANVIL would be effective as a threat. "Only in event that OVERLORD cannot possibly be broadened without abandonment of ANVIL," he cautioned, "would I consider making such a recommendation to the Combined Chiefs."[14]

On January 8 Smith arranged a meeting between himself and the commanders-in-chief, Montgomery, Air Chief Marshal Trafford Leigh-Mallory for air, and Admiral Bertram Ramsay, the Allied naval commander (ANCXF). All four opposed ANVIL on purely military grounds. Later that day Smith cabled Washington asking Eisenhower, in light of the views of his commanders-in-chief, to discuss ANVIL with Marshall and Handy. "I do not see how we can possibly do both ANVIL and OVERLORD," he told Eisenhower. "If OVERLORD is to be the main effort, ANVIL will have to be sacrificed."[15]

Smith also warned Eisenhower difficulties threatened the nature of the command structure. As after TORCH, the key issue revolved around the structure and composition of the air command. At Eisenhower's request, Tedder was named deputy supreme commander, largely a position without portfolio. Operational command of the invasion air forces went to Leigh-Mallory. Seen in some circles as a heretic for his less-than-total faith in strategic bombing, Leigh-Mallory petitioned for authority over both tactical and strategic air forces. A man who made enemies more readily than friends, Leigh-Mallory could count on little support from the RAF. Another associated problem involved the British desire to create two tactical air forces. Portal had opposed the single air command setup in the Mediterranean and organized the air establishment for OVERLORD according to his own views.

Tedder's appointment presented a red flag to Smith, who thought little of Tedder and regarded him as lazy, "not a big man [who] wanted authority without responsibility." Smith viewed the deputy commander position as "both unnecessary and undesirable...The deputy has nothing to do except get into the hair of the chief of staff, who has enough troubles without this added encumbrance."[16] In AFHQ, Smith functioned as chief of staff and de facto deputy commander to Eisenhower. With an officer of Tedder's prestige loged between the supreme commander and chief of staff, Smith saw his position as Eisenhower's right arm threatened. This fear, and perhaps a genuine concern for the untidiness of the air command structure, prompted Smith to push for a clarification of Tedder's function as deputy and Leigh-Mallory's as air commander-in-chief. "I don't think there is a place for both of them," he advised Eisenhower. "I personally believe that Tedder should be the real Air Commander and your adviser on air matters."[17]

On January 1 Smith sought the opinion of Spaatz and Major General Ira Eaker, the leading American bomber commanders. Hoping to organize the OVERLORD air command along lines practiced in the Mediterranean, Smith wanted to streamline the setup by creating a single headquarters for the Strategic Air Forces. Smith thought the maintenance of separate tactical and strategic air forces unworkable and asked Eisenhower to raise the question with the CCS.[18]

Eisenhower, alarmed by Smith, cabled Marshall: "I most earnestly request that you throw your full weight into opposing the tendency to organize in advance the sub-echelons of the OVERLORD operation in such a way as to tie the hands of the command." Eisenhower wanted to apply the lessons learned in the Mediterranean. "I think it a tragedy to give us such rigid directives as to preclude the application of those lessons." [19] Marshall agreed, and the air organization was shelved.

Smith's attention centered on organizing his new headquarters. Here too, the Mediterranean experience served as a guide. As initially envisioned, COSSAC would have functioned as the nucleus of a Marshall-commanded staff. Marshall wanted a small headquarters for directing operations. The bulk of the administration, tactical planning, and logistical management would be handled at the army group, army, and corps levels. Smith opposed this view. Arguing a small headquarters would inevitably grow into a large one, Smith decided "we should start out with a big staff." More importantly, Smith, irritated by claims Eisenhower was a political commander, insisted the supreme commander retain management of logistics and strategic planning. As Smith knew, AFHQ's ability to dictate the flow of manpower and matériel provided the instrument for headquarter's control of the operational commanders. "I argued for a full staff," he told a postwar interviewer, "and got Eisenhower to see it my way."[20]

Since it was assumed an American, probably Marshall, would command OVERLORD, Morgan organized the COSSAC staff along American lines. Smith came to London prepared to reform COSSAC in the image of AFHQ. He felt civil affairs, press relations, and psychological warfare all would require large staffs. Since COSSAC essentially constituted a planning staff, Smith thought he could graft administrative and supply divisions and special sections onto the existing structure without serious disruption. "Although the organization is very top heavy," he reported to Eisenhower, "the present organization of COSSAC headquarters can be made to conform to the setup you want." Naturally, Smith wanted the familiar faces of those schooled in AFHQ technique brought into the new organization.[21]

Eisenhower instructed Smith to prevent higher authorities, particularly the British chiefs of staff, from "dictating details of our organization."[22] On New Year's Eve, Smith met Brooke to discuss the transfer of the backbone of AFHQ—Whiteley, Gale, and Strong—to London. Here again, Smith relied upon his special relations with the British. Brooke thought more highly of Smith than he did of Eisenhower and believed "the combination of Eisenhower and Smith had much to be said for it."[23] Agreeing Gale and Whiteley might join Smith, Brooke courteously demurred in the case of Strong. Smith continued to push the issue, pointing out Strong, who formerly headed the German section of the War Office and served as military attache in Berlin, was wasted in the Mediterranean. Brooke testily replied by saying responsibility for distributing the staff on all fronts lay with him. "You can rely on me to take their various requirements into account," he said. "I will have no string-pulling." At this point, Smith jumped up and made for the door, pausing only to inform the startled CIGS he was "not being helpful." This led to a heated exchange. "You'll get nothing this way," retorted Brooke, bringing the meeting to an end.[24]

Surprised by Smith's tactics, Brooke complained to Eisenhower shortly after the supreme commander's arrival in London on January 15. Eisenhower was astonished to hear of Smith's outburst, not because it was out of character but because it represented the first criticism ever leveled at Smith by a British officer. According to Smith, Brooke was the only superior officer who ever complained about him.[25] Eisenhower apologized for his chief of staff, explaining Smith "fights for what he wants" and intended no disrespect.[26] In the end Brooke gave way. Strong took over as head of the Intelligence Division in May 1944.

On January 4 Smith flew to Algiers. Here he took up the struggle, this time with Devers, to raid AFHQ of key command personnel. Smith went over the list of transfers with one of Devers's assistants, convincing him of the necessity of each case. Understandably irritated by Smith's intrusion, Devers obstinately refused to surrender Truscott, among others. Once again, Marshall backed Devers, not improving relations between the North African and Eisenhower's command.[27]

Smith flew on to Marrakech on January 9, conferring with Churchill and Wilson. The prime minister, recuperating from a bout with pneumonia, wanted to make a firm decision on the Anzio operation. Smith thought SHINGLE "a calculated risk" but worth the gamble.[28] The decision to launch the Anzio landings on January 22 was made. Discussing the air command situation, Smith extracted a promise from Churchill that Tedder would command the Allied Expeditionary Air Forces.[29] Satisfied, Smith returned to Algiers to organize the transfer of the headquarters to England.

On January 18, two and a half tons of baggage was loaded on two B-17s, nearly half of it personal, much of it Smith's. As Hughes recorded, "Beadle [sic] off for [the] U.K. with pomp and circumstance." Flying through heavy fog, the aircraft strayed over France and for some time was feared lost. Fighters were dispersed to locate and guide the B-17s, which eventually found their way to England.[30] Two days later Smith assumed his duties as chief of staff, Supreme Headquarters, Allied Expeditionary Force (SHAEF).

THE ANVIL DEBATE

During the preparation phase in London, the supreme commander was preoccupied with three issues: the lack of landing craft that hindered finalization of operational planning, the inability to define the air command or arrive at a "coordinate plan" for air operations before and during OVERLORD, and the need to gain acceptance of the French Committee.[31] The first two, directly involving grand strategy and theater planning, were Eisenhower's principal concerns. Acting on Marshall's advice, Eisenhower left the political headaches to Smith.[32] To his ground and naval commanders, Montgomery and Ramsay, devolved the responsibility for developing operational and tactical planning.

By the end of March, after tortuous arguments, Eisenhower won the debate over command and mission of the air forces. At one point Eisenhower threatened to resign if matters were not settled in his favor.[33] As always, he fought to preserve clear lines of authority. A tangled and intricate command structure emerged on April 14, in which the supreme commander, Tedder, and

Portal all played a role. The Combined Chiefs formally handed over control of the strategic bomber forces to SHAEF for the invasion period.[34]

The other component of the air debate involved the use of air power. Eisenhower and Leigh-Mallory wanted the heavy bombers to smash the communication and transportation network in the north of France, the Low Countries, and western Germany. The objective centered on sealing off the battle zone and interdicting the movement of German reinforcements and matériel into Normandy. Air Marshal Arthur Harris and General Spaatz, supported by Churchill, Arnold, and Portal, thought Leigh-Mallory's "Transportation Plan" a misdirection of effort. The air force men wanted to continue pounding German factories, especially those producing fighter aircraft and refined petroleum. This disagreement, which related to the old debate over the proper use of strategic bombing, was also resolved in Eisenhower's favor.[35]

The most hotly contested strategic debate concerned whether or not to stage the operation in the south of France. As Smith pointed out, the division of opinion was not American-British. Churchill, Montgomery, Brooke, and Smith opposed ANVIL, while Roosevelt, the American chiefs of staff, Eisenhower, and Cunningham, now First Sea Lord, wanted the operation.[36] The prime minister opposed ANVIL because it weakened Allied forces in Italy. This partially explained his insistence on the Anzio landings, an operation Eisenhower and Smith never supported. Roosevelt's advocacy of ANVIL was based solely upon political considerations. Since he agreed to ANVIL at Teheran and because the western Allies "had made previous promises to the Russians which [they] had not been able to meet," Roosevelt felt the Allies must go through with the operation.[37] The views of Smith and Montgomery were based upon military considerations. They held ANVIL would weaken OVERLORD, jeopardizing the ability of the Allies to conduct the landings and build up forces once they gained a foothold in Normandy. Unable to agree, the American chiefs left the decision up to Eisenhower.[38]

Under mounting pressure from Churchill, Brooke, and Montgomery, Eisenhower began exhibiting signs of weakening. Marshall and the JCS continued to back Eisenhower. They wanted ANVIL to proceed to draw forces out of Italy and to deprive Alexander and Clark of forces that might be used in operations in the Balkans toward the Ljubljana Gap. With the Germans contesting Rome and the Anzio forces contained in their beachhead, Marshall started to show signs of changing his position on ANVIL. In a White House meeting on February 21 attended by Roosevelt and the JCS, Marshall came out in opposition to ANVIL. In his view, as long as German units remained tied down in Italy, the Soviets would not object to the cancellation of ANVIL. After the Darlan affair, Marshall did not contest political issues with the White House, and when the president insisted political considerations took precedence, the army chief of staff withdrew. Commenting on the ANVIL debate, Marshall pointed out to Eisenhower "the British and American Chiefs of Staff seem to have completely reversed themselves and we have become Mediterraneanites and they heavily pro-OVERLORD." The army chief of staff wanted to be "certain that localitis [was] not developing and that the pressures [had] not warped your judgment." If Eisenhower remained wedded to ANVIL, Marshall promised to use all his influence to carry the argument in Washington.[39]

Eisenhower refused to back down on ANVIL. As entries in Butcher's Diary and his own indicate, Eisenhower was afraid he would appear lacking in "initiative" and "boldness" if he retreated on ANVIL.[40] On February 8 he proposed delaying OVERLORD a month (to June 1) to build up landing-craft reserves for both an expanded cross-channel invasion and a two-division ANVIL.[41] Trying to arbitrate between the conflicting demands of OVERLORD and ANVIL, Eisenhower also dealt tactfully with Marshall who badgered the supreme commander into considering an utterly fantastic air-drop of an Allied airborne division on Evreux, forty-five miles from Paris.[42]

By February 20 Eisenhower and Smith started to despair not only for ANVIL but also for OVERLORD. As Smith explained to Handy, Eisenhower had begun "to believe that the Italian situation...[was] very likely to make ANVIL impossible." He further conceded that ANVIL could not be launched simultaneously with OVERLORD. Both he and the supreme commander thought planning and preparation for ANVIL should continue so the invasion of southern France "might be put on a little later." In any case Smith estimated the final decision on ANVIL could be delayed another month.

Smith then raised the stakes. He explained how "the buffer of German divisions confronting us across the Channel is just now approaching the absolute maximum we can handle." If OVERLORD could not be executed, the center of gravity should shift back to the Mediterranean. Subtly and without any outward manifestations of localitis, Smith informed the War Department that unless OVERLORD received reinforcements—especially landing craft, including some from the Mediterranean—the cross-channel invasion might be postponed.[43]

After a month of "sweating," Eisenhower intimated to Smith on February 26 he would reverse his position and call off ANVIL in exchange for the release of Mediterranean landing craft for OVERLORD. Smith intervened, talking Eisenhower out of sending a cable to Marshall. Despite deep reservations as regards ANVIL, Smith feared SHAEF would lose credibility and "give the impression of changing our minds too quickly."[44] There was more to Smith's actions than simple loyalty to the Marshall technique of command. Bedell not only tried to prevent Eisenhower from acquiescing on the ANVIL question, he goaded Eisenhower to control OVERLORD from the beginning—to take command of the ground battle on the day after the landings (D +1). Smith reminded Eisenhower that after Alexander's appointment as ground commander in the Mediterranean, AFHQ found itself bypassed and overshadowed by the 15th Army Group headquarters. Faced with an ongoing British press campaign to elevate Montgomery to the station of Britain's greatest general since Wellington, Smith insisted Eisenhower combat the impression the British commanders-in-chief exerted authority over planning and the orchestration of OVERLORD.[45] "I kept arguing with him on the question and pushing him to take over," remarked Smith. "[I] wanted to handle it [OVERLORD] like a river crossing."[46]

With Smith's intervention, the issue remained unresolved throughout March and into April. Smith continued to complain SHAEF planning estimates for OVERLORD were based upon the "very lowest, skimpiest, measliest figure that we can possibly calculate on the assumption there would be a strong landing in the Mediterranean."[47] He buttressed Eisenhower because he believed as long as the debate raged, OVERLORD would not lose emphasis to Italy with the British. Bedell saw other benefits. A successful ANVIL would open up the port of Marseilles with divisions committed to the operation eventually coming under SHAEF's control. However, as he admitted to Butcher, the chief reason Smith delayed making a decision on ANVIL stemmed from his desire to retain leverage in his own hands.[48] He agreed with Handy of OPD, SHAEF must retain ANVIL as long as possible even if the difficulties and uncertainty were "enough to drive you mad."[49]

The Americans continued to stonewall despite realizing, as Marshall emphasized to Eisenhower on March 17, "the only clear cut decision would be to cancel ANVIL."[50] As with TORCH, Marshall threatened to transfer priority to the Pacific if the British did not reduce the level of their Mediterranean operations. Roosevelt resolved the impasse by forcing Admiral King to provide the necessary landing craft for a five-division OVERLORD. Roosevelt and Churchill agreed the final decision on ANVIL would wait until July. In the meantime the battle for Rome would take precedence in the Mediterranean theater. While the compromise satisfied no one, it did permit SHAEF to concentrate its energies on preparing for the big invasion.

Eisenhower held his first supreme commander's conference on January 21. The discussions centered on the OVERLORD plan. Three weeks earlier Smith and Montgomery received a briefing on the plan from the COSSAC staff.[51] Typical of Montgomery, he declared the plan militarily unsound and proceeded to outline his ideas. During the period before the January 21 conference

Montgomery frequently met with the planners and the air and naval staffs to prepare for a revised OVERLORD.[52]

This first supreme commander's conference proved crucial. Montgomery wanted to "rope off" the Normandy beachheads in sufficient strength before his old adversary, Rommel, could use his armor reserves. This involved a five-division assault and employment of airborne troops on either flank. With the beachheads seized by the infantry, armored brigades would land and quickly penetrate into the interior. Montgomery realized the battle would depend on the ability of the Anglo-Canadian forces on the eastern shoulder of the Allied position to block against German counterattacks. Once the Allied lodgments were secure, Bradley's 1st Army would make for Cherbourg. With a major port in Allied hands, Montgomery and Bradley would begin offensive operations to the south while Patton's 3d Army broke out into Brittany. The hinge upon which Montgomery would hold and pivot was the strategically important high ground southeast of Caen.[53]

Eisenhower and Smith supported Montgomery's plan. The supreme commander ordered COSSAC to prepare an alternative plan for presentation at the next commander's conference. A new plan was in Smith's hands two days later, January 23, on the eve of the conference. Morgan's staff thought Montgomery's plan did not provide sufficient concentration around Caen. The revised COSSAC plan called for a four-division assault in the vital Caen-Bayeax sector.

Montgomery and Smith discussed the new plan that night. Despite promising Morgan no decision would be reached until the whole problem could be thrashed out, Smith accepted the Montgomery plan. He proceeded to Hayes's Lodge, Eisenhower's London residence, to report a decision had been concluded between COSSAC and Montgomery.[54]

Nothing suggests Eisenhower ever saw the compromise plan, nor was COSSAC party to the agreement. Smith's reasons for making the decision without consulting Morgan are unknown. He viewed the COSSAC plan as unworkable and knew Eisenhower's preference for the expanded assault. Knowing Montgomery's mind, Smith probably thought it pointless to debate the merits of the respective plans.[55] If left to the CCS to decide, intolerable delays might result, leading to greater complications. Most likely Smith's actions were motivated by the old Marshall dictum, "better to make a decision, even if incorrect, than no decision at all."[56] The supreme commander accepted the decision without question. "An agreement has been made," reported Eisenhower's naval aide, "along lines desired by both Ike and Monty."[57]

FROM COSSAC TO SHAEF

The decision made, Smith turned his attention to building a staff whose basic structure already had been laid by Morgan. In theory, all operational, administrative, logistical, and civil-political matters moved up the chain of command to Eisenhower, Tedder, Smith, and the three SHAEF deputy chiefs of staff, Morgan, Gale, and Air Vice Marshal James Robb. In practice, Tedder, with no independent staff organization, coordinated the activities of the Allied air forces and served as Eisenhower's liaison with the BCOS. As in AFHQ, Eisenhower delegated executive control of the headquarters to Smith, including wide discretionary powers to discharge many functions properly belonging to the supreme commander. In other words, Eisenhower commanded the Allied armed forces while Smith directed SHAEF. Beneath Smith stood the principal staff sections: the secretariat, the four General Staff divisions, a number of additional sections, and five military missions (to France, the Netherlands, Belgium, Denmark, and Norway).[58]

Between January 20 and February 12 Smith transformed COSSAC into SHAEF. He retained much of the existing COSSAC staff as a planning group at Norfolk House until SHAEF could be established at Bushy Park, near Kingston (WIDEWING). Direct communications did not exist between Bushy Park and Washington, so part of the secretariat remained at Norfolk House. Otherwise, Smith wanted his headquarters out of London.[59] A second headquarters, SHAEF-Advance (SHARPENER) was set up near Portsmouth, adjacent to Ramsay's headquarters and Montgomery's proposed command post. Anxious that Eisenhower command the assault, Smith considered the creation of SHAEF-Advance a priority, staffing it with personnel brought up from AFHQ.[60]

After developing an integrated staff in Algiers, Smith built SHAEF around the nucleus of men brought from the Mediterranean. For several months the members of COSSAC worked together effectively, but they soon realized Smith intended on having his brand of headquarters. When one of Morgan's senior staff officers aired views contrary to Smith's concepts of staff structure, he was told by the chief of staff not to trouble himself because he would "not be [around] to carry [the reorganization] out." News quickly spread that while Smith accepted the existing staff, several senior officers, including division heads, would be replaced.[61] The COSSAC officers resented the newcomers' boasts of having "sand in their boots." On the other hand, the AFHQ officers in the new staff complained the COSSAC people lacked knowledge of active operations and tended to be academic in their approach to planning. Morgan's officers initially found it difficult to accommodate themselves to their new chief, but over time the antagonism subsided.[62]

Although organized along American lines, COSSAC functioned like a British staff. In British practice the Intelligence Division prepared estimates that were forwarded to the Operations Division. After developing the outline the planners presented their proposal to the next-higher echelon within the Operations Division. At each level sat representatives of the three armed services as well as one from the Foreign Office. When a plan was prepared, it presumably enjoyed the sanction of the services and the political leadership. The American system worked in an opposite fashion. Actions originated at the top of the structure and flowed down through the levels of the staff. Once the detailed planning had been completed, Smith would decide which actions to take. After referring the question to the headquarters of the commanders-in-chief, Smith would present the final plan to Eisenhower. With his stamp of approval the plan became firmly fixed as policy.[63]

General Clark observed both systems in operation and believed British staff methods superior. When the British made a policy decision, Clark told a postwar interviewer, "their whole echelon of command all the way down [knew] exactly what it [was]....When [the American staff made] a decision, nobody down the line [knew] anything."[64] A senior American officer who served under Smith in the Mediterranean and Europe noted that "the British never were used to our staff system. They never quite understood it because, of course, it's not a very logical thing."[65]

The American assertion of unity of command held true for the staff as well as the line. Whereas Morgan strove for cooperation by employing his winning personality and allowing his functionally organized staff autonomy, Smith demanded subordinates confine themselves to carrying out his directives. Like Clark, Smith thought the American staff system cumbersome but decided against fashioning SHAEF along British lines.[66] Because of the size of the headquarters, Smith's approach proved effective. Dealing with differences in staff procedures and overcoming antagonisms between the COSSAC and AFHQ personnel, Smith recognized lingering "staff vs. line" jealousies fictionalized the American component of SHAEF. It was crucial that the chief of staff possessed the decision-making power for the headquarters.[67]

Considerable rancor continued to exist within the headquarters. Satisfied with the Administrative, Operations, and Supply divisions, Smith wanted to remove the head of the Intelligence Division, Major General P. Y. Whitefoord. During Smith's first trip to London, the two disagreed over the organization and handling of G-2 matters. Whitefoord, a British officer, insisted on preserving close ties with the War Office. He also staffed his division with Oxford dons. Moreover, G-2 functioned according to the British committee method. Smith objected to the academic atmosphere of the division and characteristically resisted any effort to organize the staff along lines that would diminish his superintendence.[68]

Remembering the problems with Mockler-Ferryman, Smith told the COSSAC Intelligence head either he accept Smith's views and methods or he would have to go. Bedell already had made up his mind. Only Strong would be satisfactory as Smith's G-2. When Whitefoord declined to submit, Smith coldbloodedly removed him, replacing him first with Whiteley and finally with Strong.[69]

In addition to Whiteley, Smith brought Colonel Edward Foord, an ULTRA expert, from Algiers along with Major General Thomas Betts. Sensing his appointment might create friction, Betts approached Smith, asking if he should return to AFHQ. "Quick on the trigger," Smith thought Betts was complaining because he did not get the appointment as division head. Instead of reacting in his customary fashion, Smith gently persuaded Betts to remain. This led the American officer to surmise Bedell had purged Whitefoord as a calculated example for the rest of the headquarters.[70]

The British system also created an intermediary level of the headquarters between the chief of staff and the general staff divisions, the deputy chiefs of staff. Recognizing the demonstrated value of coordinating Administration and Logistics, Smith insisted Gale be named chief administrative officer in the Supreme Headquarters. Eisenhower shared this view. With his "irreplaceable quality of being able to handle British and American supply problems," Eisenhower told Smith "he would be unwilling to undertake another large Allied Command without Gale's administrative assistance."[71] Unlike the Mediterranean where the CAO exerted great influence over theaterwide logistics and administration, in Europe, the Americans and British would manage their own affairs. Unable to play the central role he did in AFHQ, Gale still fulfilled the important functions of coordinating the activities of the G-1 and G-4 divisions of the headquarters in addition to serving as chairman of several joint committees dealing with supply matters. Considered "a first-class manager...practically a genius," by one of his American colleagues, Gale's talents were not wasted by Smith.[72]

Since Smith named Whiteley interim head of the Intelligence Division, he could not act as SHAEF deputy chief of staff for Intelligence and Operations, the role he played in Algiers. As a result, Bedell Smith asked Morgan to stay on as his deputy. Although Morgan's contributions have been largely overlooked, without his gentle prodding of the COSSAC planners throughout summer and autumn 1943, a spring 1944 OVERLORD would have proved exceedingly difficult.

No one appreciated Morgan's contributions more than Smith. Breaking precedent, Smith once interceded on Morgan's behalf, asking the British to give him a vacant corps command. Montgomery agreed, but Brooke vetoed the proposal, making no secret of his lack of confidence in Morgan.[73] Viewed as overly friendly with the Americans, Morgan compromised his standing with the British chief of staff.[74] Anxious to take advantage of the British general's intimate knowledge of OVERLORD planning, Smith invited Morgan to remain at SHAEF. Not specifically charged with those responsibilities discharged by Whiteley in Algiers, as deputy chief of staff, Morgan became Smith's troubleshooter, coordinating the activities of the staff divisions and sections.

Among Morgan's greatest attributes was his talent for acting as a balancing wheel for Smith. In the opinion of the American G-1 Barker, Bedell Smith frequently made "Napoleonic decisions" without weighing all the options. Instead of openly dissenting with Smith, Morgan would say, "Yes, Beetle, quite right. I'm sure you're right about that." Then he tactfully presented alternative courses of action. Soon Smith realized he had "gone off half-cocked" and reversed his position. In this way, several potentially damaging errors were averted, many of which might have had serious military and political repercussions. "Nobody knows how much we owe Freddy Morgan," reflected Barker, "for his level headed handling of Bedell Smith."[75] Aware of the debt he owed the British officer, Smith said Morgan was a man he would not "willingly have dispensed with."[76]

Reflective of the importance attached to maintaining close cooperation with the air forces, Robb was added as Smith's third deputy in March 1944. Before assuming his duties in SHAEF, Robb served as adviser to Eisenhower in AFHQ. Following the formation of the Northwest African Air Forces in 1943, Robb commanded the RAF component as deputy to Spaatz. On the dissolution of Leigh-Mallory's command in October 1944, Robb was redesignated chief of the air staff (SHAEF), and he remained with Smith for the duration of the war.[77]

Shortly after assuming direction of the headquarters, Smith reorganized the Central Secretariat of COSSAC. After experimenting with a joint secretariat, unhappy with the results, Smith elevated Colonel Dan Gilmer, his secretary in Algiers, to Secretary/General Staff. Smith thought highly of Gilmer but he was practically alone in this view. Gilmer antagonized several senior officers in the headquarters until finally Whiteley threatened to resign if Smith's abrasive secretary was not transferred.[78] Lieutenant Colonel Ford Trimble succeeded Gilmer in March. So much was demanded of Smith's secretary that three of the four officers who held the post in Europe resigned, unable to abide his constant harassment. As in Algiers, the overworked secretariat bound the inner headquarters together.[79]

The heart of SHAEF was the Operations Division. Headed by a COSSAC holdover, Major General Harold "Pinky" Bull (U.S.), the G-3 Division combined planning and operations. Initially, the functions were united in a single agency, but in May, Smith created separate Planning and Operations staffs. The Planning staff prepared current estimates of the military situation, outlined plans for future operations, and drew up detailed plans for the posthostilities period. Before D-Day the Planning Section expanded upon existing COSSAC studies for speedy occupations of France, Norway, and Germany in the event of a sudden German collapse (RANKIN A, B, C). The Planning Section also developed operational plans for the post-Normandy period. The Operations Section prepared and issued directives, developed daily and weekly combined situation and intelligence reports, and served as connecting link between SHAEF and the operational headquarters, the associated and allied governments, and the French Resistance.[80]

When Strong took over the Intelligence Division (G-2) in late May, Whiteley moved from that division to become Bull's deputy. Although subordinated to Bull, Whiteley dominated the division as head of the Planning Section. In many respects Whiteley was very much like Smith. A conventional officer with a narrow mind, Whiteley possessed an enormous capacity for work.[81] Having served as deputy chief of staff in AFHQ, Whiteley possessed a thorough understanding of all aspects of intelligence and operational planning.

Since Montgomery controlled planning for the invasion and would exercise command of ground operations in Normandy, the Planning Section's principal responsibility involved the development of plans for operations after the Allied forces broke out of their lodgments. From the earliest stages of the post-OVERLORD planning SHAEF accommodated itself to Montgomery's plan. Smith directed Whiteley, then head of the Intelligence Division, to formulate broad outline plans for the campaign in northwest Europe. The result was the first concrete statement of the broad front strategy. As his chief American assistant Brigadier General Thomas Betts related, the decision was made after a fifteen minute discussion.[82]

The decision to land the Anglo-Canadian forces on the eastern flank (SWORD, GOLD, and JUNO beaches) was dictated by the existing concentration of Allied forces in the south of England, not the product of long-range planning.[83] When American divisions first landed in the United Kingdom, they garrisoned southwest England. The choice evolved based entirely upon logistical and not operational considerations.[84] In developing the COSSAC plan, Morgan appreciated the manpower deficiencies the British army would face in Europe. During SHAEF's post-OVERLORD planning, he voiced doubts whether the British would possess enough strength to spearhead the proposed drive through the north of France into the Low Countries.[85] After some discussion about switching flanks the proposal was abandoned. Such a complex movement could not be realistically executed because of the strain it would impose upon transportation in England.[86] It was agreed, at least in the headquarters, that an American army would have to be detached to Montgomery's army group until the Ruhr industrial complex had fallen.[87]

The Intelligence Division, second in importance only to the Operations Division, handled conventional intelligence gathering. Before the invasion the G-2 Division collated, evaluated, and disseminated information gained through aerial reconnaissance and covert operations on the continent. The most critical component of the division was also the most secret, the special ULTRA detachment. Leading a furtive existence, only Whiteley (later Strong), Betts, Foord, and his principal assistants knew of ULTRA's existence. The SHAEF team received decryptions from the British intelligence complex at Bletchley Park. Before D-Day, ULTRA provided invaluable information on German deployments and movements in the north of France as well as intelligence on the success of the elaborate deception plan (FORTITUDE) to cover the invasion.[88]

Of all the SHAEF divisions, none was more British in organization, character, and personnel than Intelligence. After much agitation, Smith finally succumbed to Strong in late June 1944 and allowed for the establishment of a Joint Intelligence Committee (JIC/SHAEF). Modeled faithfully on the London Joint Intelligence Committee, the SHAEF version had a complement of military, naval, and air officers in addition to American and British political and economic advisers. In close contact with its parent London organization, the JIC/SHAEF reviewed the political and military situation in the theater of operations. Never convinced of its need, Smith obstructed communications between the headquarters and London after SHAEF left the United Kingdom. Despite his grudging tolerance of the Joint Intelligence Committee/SHAEF, Smith received valuable support from this agency, particularly for handling civil and political affairs.[89]

The exact responsibilities of the Administrative and Supply divisions were never entirely understood. COSSAC planned to create a joint G-1 division with the appropriate subsections and special staffs. When Morgan reorganized the staff, separate G-1 and G-4 divisions were established to satisfy American requirements. Barker headed the Administrative Division, a staff dominated by American officers and enlisted personnel. The G-4 Division was directed by Major General Robert Crawford, also an American. Differences in logistical arrangements necessitated separate American and British logistical staffs.[90]

As in the Mediterranean, Eisenhower wore two hats: one as supreme commander and the other as commander of all American forces in the European theater. Simplifying the command structure, the supreme commander ordered consolidation of his theater headquarters (ETOUSA) and the Services of Supply command which dealt with logistical matters for the theater.[91] The enlarged headquarters, formed in mid-February 1944, fell under Smith's formal supervision as he assumed the responsibilities of chief of staff, European Theater. In practice Lee controlled logistics as deputy theater commander for Supply and Administration. With Lee handling the manpower and matériel requirements for ETOUSA, it remained uncertain how effectively SHAEF could oversee administrative or supply matters. In avoiding duplication of effort, Eisenhower's expedient created the very thing he hoped to avert. He decided to ignore the problem, postponing the reorganization of the command until after he assumed command on the continent.[92]

"UNCIVIL" CIVIL AFFAIRS AND PRESS RELATIONS

Reflecting on the problems facing the command at the end of March, Eisenhower felt satisfied with the progress made on operational planning, staff organization, and the logistical buildup. Much of the credit he gave to Smith. In areas where he depended upon the combined chiefs for direction—OVERLORD vs. ANVIL, the organization and command of the air forces, civil and political affairs—progress was slow.[93]

Smith proved very good in handling familiar organizational problems, such as handling the traditional general staff divisions. No innovator, Smith experienced difficulties navigating in areas unchartered by American staff manuals. As Morgan remembered, civil affairs produced the "most vexations" for Smith. "There are plenty of affairs," Morgan quipped, "but the difficulty was to keep them civil."[94]

In the Mediterranean, Smith observed the "smaller agencies [he listed censorship, press relations, subversive activities, and propaganda] are the real headaches for a commander and his chief of staff [and that] their placement [within the general staff] is simply a matter of convenience."[95] Nevertheless, his experiences in AFHQ demonstrated the important function of civil and political affairs. Although the War Department expressed its satisfaction with the existing organization, Smith objected to the COSSAC organization because it granted Civil Affairs status as an independent division.[96] After a cursory examination of Morgan's setup, Smith determined the dual Anglo-American structure to be too "ponderous and unwieldy."[97] His chief complaint centered on the British character and organization of the division. Smith disliked the division's close ties to the War Office. Furthermore, the COSSAC Civil Affairs handbook delegated discretionary powers to the operational commanders.[98]

Reminding the COSSAC planners he had come from an active theater, Smith informed them he intended to organize civil affairs along lines practiced in AFHQ. He did not like the idea of surrendering civil affairs to the operational commanders or subordinating political affairs to the chain of command. Nor was he in favor of creating a general staff division for Civil Affairs.[99] In AFHQ he worked through civilians like Murphy and Macmillan, handling problems at the headquarters level, largely on informal lines. If the Civil Affairs group developed in accordance to the COSSAC guidelines, Smith recognized that his ability to influence political decisions would be curtailed. Instead of orchestrating civil and political affairs as he had done in AFHQ, Smith's function would involve only the supervision of civil affairs planning.

At a February 10 conference Smith grudgingly conceded on the point of creating a Civil Affairs Division. This ended the anomalous position of Civil Affairs within the Allied staff structure. Although an advocate of large staffs, Smith insisted the new division be limited to thirty-five officers, responsible only for policy making, review, and advising the chief of staff. Detailed planning would be carried on outside the new G-5 Division, and Smith retained his superintendent powers.[100] Rather than have parallel liaison sections for each military mission, the division was subdivided into six advisory groups (legal, fiscal, supply, governmental, economic, and information).[101] This "functional" organization was a concession to the British head, Major General Roger Lumley. Not pleased with the arrangement, Smith's efforts centered on settling the matter as quickly as possible. Whatever shape the organization took, Smith knew he enjoyed a "completely free hand" and the unqualified support of the War Department.[102]

As with Whitefoord, Smith took an immediate dislike to Lumley and his assistant, Colonel Karl Bendetsen. He wasted no time purging Bendetsen and maneuvered for an American to replace Lumley. First he requested Assistant Secretary of War John McCloy be named to the post. Stimson refused to release McCloy. Under pressure from the British and the War Department to nominate a military man, Smith asked for Lucius Clay or John Hilldring, two major generals in the War Department. Pointing to Marshall's "forceable" opposition to any "breakout from the [War Department] jailhouse," Hilldring suggested Bedell look elsewhere.[103] Stymied at every turn, Smith accepted Eisenhower's intervention and named a British officer to head the division. Anxious always to dodge complications with the War Department and the British, Eisenhower did not want to leave himself open to charges of meddling in political matters. On April 22, after a three-month-long rear-guard action,

Smith accepted Lieutenant General A. E. Grassett, a Canadian, as replacement of the independent-minded Lumley.

Smith's mandated settlement of the G-5 organization satisfied no one. Although the Civil Affairs Division took up its place at Bushy Park, several issues remained unresolved. First, it seemed unclear who controlled the division. Grassett's appointment did little to end the rift between Civil Affairs and the chief of staff. Second, uncertainty remained whether SHEAF or the army groups would oversee actual civil affairs on the continent. Third, Smith obfuscated on the point when SHEAF would relinquish civil administration to the reconstituted governments in liberated Europe. Churchill and Roosevelt agreed at the Quebec conference not to form military governments in the liberated countries of western Europe to hasten the transfer of power to the national governments. Eisenhower and Smith disagreed with the policy as they continued to assert military requirements came first. These differences debilitated the actions of the new division.[104]

Citing the poor performance of Grassett's division, a direct result of his own malevolence, Smith ordered two further reorganizations. The first divided G-5 into two sections: one for the formulation of policy and the other for liaison with the "country branches." These sections, Policy and Operations, fell under Smith's direct supervision. The latter was placed under the chief of staff's protege from the AMGOT organization, Brigadier General Frank McSherry.[105] This was followed by a second restructuring of the Civil Affairs Division in May. Smith further strengthened his control by removing intermediate sections between SHAEF and the commands, a victory over the "committee" approach.[106] He did, however, agree the execution of civil and political affairs would be the province of the military commanders.[107] In effect this solution conformed to Lumley's original outline presented three months earlier.

Smith's penchant for quick decisions produced only uncertainty and confusion. Because he attached so much importance to preserving his lines of authority, Smith purposefully interfered in the workings of Lumley and Grassett's affairs. Immersed in civil affairs questions, he seemed more concerned with tidying up the loose conglomeration of G-5 functions and tightening his own executive control than in achieving results. Convinced of the workability of the AFHQ model, Smith showed little understanding that political affairs in Europe would be infinitely more complex than in the Mediterranean. On the positive side, the reorganizations removed the overlapping civil affairs command channels and prepared the way for improved integration of civil and military logistics. On balance, Smith's refusal to accept a functional organization in favor of the rigid, linear Mediterranean approach and his insistence on close supervision ensured the invasion would begin before civil affairs policies could be tailored to the military plan.[108]

The final organizational problem faced by the SHAEF chief of staff during the preinvasion period involved creating an apparatus to handle psychological warfare and press relations.[109] Morgan created a Publicity and Psychological Warfare Section for his COSSAC staff after examining the AFHQ setup. Although Smith remained unconvinced the section merited independence as a general staff division, he tentatively accepted the creation of a Publicity and Psychological Warfare Division (G-6) in February.[110]

By April, Brigadier General Robert McClure, the division head, complained the "fundamentally different organizations" needed to be separated. McClure previously headed Smith's Information and Censorship Section in AFHQ. He wanted to maintain Psychological Warfare as a G-division while creating a separate Public Relations Section. Smith had other ideas.[111]

Agreeing to the creation of the G-6 Division only to "dignify" its functions—perhaps in his own mind—Smith now moved to deactivate it. Believing psychological warfare and censorship should be directly controlled by the chief of staff, Smith thought it a mistake to pass on these duties to subordinates. After the April 13 reorganization, Smith assumed tight supervision over both psychological warfare and public relations despite admitting he was "far from adept" in managing these matters.[112]

Smith's mind remained closed to the possibilities of psychological warfare. He saw little likelihood in breaking German military morale through leaflet drops and broadcasts, particularly within Roosevelt's insistence on unconditional surrender. On one occasion, he wrote a tongue-in-cheek cable to Marshall saying he would finally concede psychological warfare had a military application after all. A German ship reportedly had been sunk off Marseilles under a deluge of propaganda leaflets. This episode demonstrates the continued close relationship between Smith and Marshall—it is difficult imagining anyone else writing Marshall in such a manner—and Smith's jaundiced view of psychological warfare.[113] In this he was not alone. Bradley and Montgomery shared Smith's scepticism and moved slowly in incorporating general staff sections in their respective headquarters to handle psychological warfare matters.

Press relations were deemed more important. Smith grappled with censorship policy throughout the campaign in the Mediterranean. While at AFHQ, Eisenhower and Smith frequently joked the only group they hated more than the fascists were the journalists.[114] There was more than a little truth revealed in these remarks. The flap over the Patton affair left lasting hard feelings. At the same time they understood the need for cultivating good press relations. Public opinion, especially American public opinion, exerted powerful influences upon policy making in Washington and London. SHAEF was not immune from these influences.

American officers stayed abreast of press coverage in the United States. They frequently asked their wives to forward newspapers and magazine articles from home. Afraid uneven press coverage might fuel interbranch jealousies as in the First World War, Marshall often asked Smith to use his influence with the newsmen to secure stories for certain officers. When Smith replied he had more compelling concerns, Marshall threatened to dispatch a "Marine lieutenant" to get the job done.[115] Outside his native Indianapolis, Smith's contributions went unnoticed in the United States, contributing to his sensitivity in this area. This did not escape the attention of Marshall who asked Eisenhower to remedy the oversight. A feature article appeared in *Life* after D-Day chronicling the career of Smith and his central role in the planning phase of the invasion.[116]

Press relations in the Second World War involved far broader issues than serving to stroke the egos of senior officers. The dilemma revolved around the necessity of maintaining strict security while at the same time providing the home front with information about their fighting men and women. As chief censor in the theater, Smith had to weigh the thorny questions involving the place of a free press in the conduct of a modern, coalition war. He tried to balance the risks inherent in a tight censorship program while considering the impact of secrecy upon the conduct of military operations.

Throughout his tenure in London Smith regularly faced these delicate problems. When deprived of hard information, journalists employed their many contacts to uncover stories. To the headquarter's alarm, articles surfaced accurately estimating the timing and scope of the invasion. Moreover, in England, Smith could not control press activities as rigidly as in Algiers. As the invasion date neared, the size of the press corps grew. Initially, Smith applied a closed system. When this failed to achieve the desired results, he gradually sped up the accreditation process.[117] In an effort to curtail speculative stories, Smith brought selected journalists and commentators into his confidence. After May 16, Eisenhower conducted irregular "off the record" news conferences. Once accredited, the newsman became a "quasi-staff officer." The correspondents received information in carefully prescribed doses without compromising security.[118] Despite their profound mistrust of journalists, Eisenhower and Smith artfully managed the fifth estate.

A MOST ACUTELY ANNOYING PROBLEM:
THE FRENCH QUESTION

On February 7 Smith thought SHAEF had taken shape, but it seemed like a "long, uphill pull."[119] Five weeks later he reported to Colonel Frank McCarthy in the War Department that "things generally are going well—very well—and we are very confident. There is less of the pre-operation 'jitters' than ever before."[120] One of his assistants considered the task complete. "It [SHAEF] is a honey," reported Brigadier General Thomas Davis. "I think it is even better than the one developed for Allied Forces." Although Bedell faced some opposition at the onset, Davis said "discontent was put down in 'typical Smith fashion.'"[121] Davis's views were shared by Eisenhower who marveled at the ability of his chief of staff to hammer out a cooperative SHAEF team.[122]

Eisenhower relied upon Smith to use his special relationships with Marshall and War Department officials to iron out inevitable differences of opinion. The War Department periodically dispatched experts to London to help solve special problems. Smith disliked these intrusions but restrained himself in the interest of pacifying Marshall. The landing-craft situation continued to bedevil the planners. The War Department sent a team of experts to London to show SHAEF how to combat load landing craft. Based on experiences in the Central Pacific, the War Department estimated SHAEF could get 30 percent more lift from the same number of vessels.[123] Viewing these officers as "desk soldiers," Smith tactfully told them to forget the theoretical capacities of the various categories of landing craft and look at the practical problems. "We had to tell them the facts of life," Smith remembered.[124] Arnold later sent a group of colonels to argue for a massive airborne operation in the vicinity of Paris. Here again, Smith patiently listened but rejected the plan as unrealistic.[125]

More important, Smith buttressed Eisenhower's position with the British. No sooner had the supreme commander gained control over the new air command on April 15 than new challenges emerged. Bombing transportation and communication targets in northern France involved strikes against population centers. Churchill and Eden feared heavy bombing of French cities so far in advance of the landings would have dire consequences for postwar Anglo-French relations.[126] The bomber barons, both American and British, seized the issue, arguing priority should be given to the bombing offensive in Germany. Never reconciling themselves to surrendering control of the heavy bombers to SHAEF, Harris and Spaatz renewed their arguments against the transportation plan. On May 5, the French Committee of National Liberation added fuel to the fire when they filed an official protest.[127]

For the first two weeks of May the issue remained unresolved. Churchill asked Roosevelt to settle the matter. The president deferred to Marshall but, aware of Eisenhower's strong sentiments, he referred the question back to SHAEF.[128] Wishing to avert another protracted political battle with the French, Eisenhower sidestepped the problem. Insisting the bombing would continue in any case, the supreme commander left Smith to deal with the political fallout.

On May 16 Eisenhower left for Northern Ireland to inspect troops, something he did with increasing regularity. Smith visited Général Pierre Koenig, the chief of the French Military Mission in London. Much to his surprise the French general took, as Smith recalled, "a much more cold-blooded view" than did SHAEF. "This is war," Koenig told Smith, "and it must be expected that people will be killed. We would take the anticipated loss to be rid of the Germans."[129] With Koenig's assurance in his pocket, Smith pushed Churchill to drop his opposition to the transportation plan. Faced by Eisenhower, Smith, Tedder, and Portal, all of whom professed their faith in the operation, Churchill succumbed.[130]

Despite the myriad of other problems confronting Smith, Eisenhower delegated the responsibility of handling the French to his chief of staff.[131] Before leaving Algiers Smith had conferred with de Gaulle and produced a draft of an agreement with the FCNL. The French leader accepted Eisenhower's command over French forces in exchange for assurances French troops would play a conspicuous role in the liberation of their homeland, including a "presence" in northwestern France. In Eisenhower's name, Smith had promised that "a token force, preferably a Division" would participate in the liberation of Paris.[132]

Once in London, Smith discovered neither Roosevelt nor the State Department had any intention of dealing with the FCNL on civil affairs matters. This threatened to invalidate the Smith-de Gaulle agreement of December 27, 1943. If SHAEF ignored de Gaulle on questions of civil affairs, the FCNL would surely refuse to cooperate on military matters. For months Smith had viewed the committee as the only realistic "vehicle" for cooperating with the French. As he had done in the Mediterranean, he proposed to continue holding informal discussions with de Gaulle's representative in London, Koenig.[133]

For better than two months Roosevelt delayed making a decision on the French question. On March 8 SHAEF received a directive from the Combined Chiefs forbidding contact with the French.[134] The president reversed his position on March 15 when he granted SHAEF authority to establish civil affairs agreements with the FCNL. This did not constitute a recognition of the committee as the government of France, but it allowed Smith to reopen contacts with Koenig.[135] On March 19, arrangements were made for formal links between SHAEF and the FCNL in London on military and civil affairs. Further, Smith promised to take Koenig into his "full confidence regarding plans for the employment of French forces in France."[136]

No sooner had Smith offered this promise when his position with the FCNL suffered a further setback. SHAEF received orders prohibiting military liaison with de Gaulle on all matters pertaining to ANVIL or OVERLORD.[137] Fearing leaks, the French were not to be advised that ANVIL might be canceled. This policy remained in effect until April 17.[138] Despite these proscriptions Smith continued appraising Koenig of the broad outlines of Allied planning; Koenig was a thoroughly professional and reliable officer in Smith's estimate. The French general won Smith's trust when he opened an April 25 discussion by saying that questions concerning French sovereignty could be decided at a later date. This was precisely what Smith wanted to hear.[139]

The climate improved after the March 19 Smith-Koenig agreement. Eisenhower increased his pressure upon Washington for full recognition of the FCNL, and early in April Roosevelt instructed Eisenhower to deal with any French group that would render military aid in support of OVERLORD. On April 14, the visiting under secretary of state, Edward Stettinius, told Eisenhower and Smith that Roosevelt's health was failing and he had become "increasingly difficult to deal with because he changed his mind so often."[140] The supreme commander then decided to enter into the political fray and requested de Gaulle be allowed to come to London. Eisenhower wanted to bring de Gaulle into his confidence, inform him of the place and date of OVERLORD, and work out a series of civil affairs agreements.[141] Under pressure from Churchill, Roosevelt agreed on the condition Eisenhower not be involved "on the political level."[142] Further, if de Gaulle was informed about OVERLORD, he would have to remain in London until after D-Day.

These stipulations placed SHAEF in an impossible position. Smith telephoned Churchill, and both agreed de Gaulle would never agree to placing himself under virtual house arrest in London. Roosevelt had acquiesced allowing SHAEF to pursue agreements on civil affairs yet refused to permit Eisenhower to enter into political discussions with de Gaulle. Moreover, the president's fiats were unilateral, threatening injury to Eisenhower's standing with Churchill. As a result nothing came of Eisenhower's initiative. Preliminary discussions were carried out between SHAEF and Koenig with considerable success in terms of coordinating military policy but, when de Gaulle was finally invited to London by Churchill on June 1, no agreement on civil and political issues had been concluded.[143]

Two other political issues occupied Smith's time. Eisenhower considered Roosevelt's position on military zones of occupation in Germany as ill advised and, with Smith, felt strongly the policy of unconditional surrender in need to modification. While in Washington in January, Eisenhower discussed the newly formed European Advisory Commission's plan to divide Germany into three

The quintessential view of Bedell Smith—working at his desk, immaculate in appearance, a spent cigarette at his side. His deeply furrowed bulldog countenance and the razor-sharp creases of his uniform reflect the tenacity and acuteness that marked his personality. Courtesy of the Dwight D. Eisenhower Library.

Allied Force Headquarters: Eisenhower, Tedder, Alexander, and Cunningham pose on the steps of the St. George Hotel, Algiers, with Macmillan and Smith in the background.

A week after the HUSKY landings, Smith flies to Sicily. Here he confers on the hood of a staff car with Alexander and 15th Army Group's two commanders, Montgomery (left) and Patton (center), at Syracuse Airfield, July 25, 1943.

The Italian Surrender: Eisenhower shakes the hand of General Castellano, the Italian signator. This photo reveals much of the Eisenhower-Smith relationship. A crisp, smiling Eisenhower whisks through to accept the Italian surrender. The strain of the negotiations is evident in Smith's appearance—the dishevelled hair and uniform wilted from perspiration.

Smith carries the conversation while Roosevelt, flanked by Eisenhower and Spaatz, intently listens. After touring the Tunisian battlefields, the presidential party dines with the 3rd Photo Reconnaissance Wing, La Marsa Airfield, Tunis. The president's son, Elliott, served in the Air Corps unit. Courtesy of the Dwight D. Eisenhower Library.

Supreme Headquarters for the Normandy Invasion. Flanking Eisenhower from left to right: Bradley, Ramsay, Tedder, Montgomery, Leigh-Mallory, and Smith, January, 1944. Courtesy of the Dwight D. Eisenhower Library.

A rare photograph of Smith away from headquarters. During the Ardennes Crisis, Smith flew to Alsace with specific instructions for 6th Army Group. He meets Devers and Patch at 7th Army's Command Post, January 5, 1945. Courtesy of the Dwight D. Eisenhower Library.

The German Surrender: A ramrod-stiff Jodl stands at attention opposite an implacable Smith. Sitting across from Jodl are, from left to right, Morgan (obscured), Sevez, Burroughs, Smith, Suslaparov, Spaatz, Robb, and Bull (on the corner). Butcher stands in the background behind Burroughs. Strong, acting as interpreter, stands behind Jodl. Courtesy of the Dwight D. Eisenhower Library.

zones of occupation. The supreme commander thought Germany should be administered jointly by the Big Three, and SHAEF would provide an excellent vehicle to act as the controlling mechanism.[144]

On May 3 Smith opened direct communications with the Soviet mission in London. Throughout the month Smith developed the SHAEF policy for dealing with the Soviets. Initially reluctant to open talks on Germany, Smith confined himself to an exchange of views on peripheral issues such as Allied intentions in Norway (RANKIN B).[145] On May 17 Smith cabled Washington suggesting SHAEF not open discussions with the Soviets on matters relating to Germany. Later that day he reversed himself, now asking permission to initiate a series of dialogues.[146] Four days later in a communication to the combined chiefs Smith enumerated a list of "common interests" to be explored in relation to the pre- and postsurrender periods.[147] However, the management of German occupation was not included in the list. Smith's about-face bore several salutary results, chief among them building trust between SHAEF and the Soviet Military Mission in London.

While Smith was establishing SHAEF policy for dealing with the Soviet Union, Eisenhower became suspicious of Stalin's intentions. On one hand he concluded the entire enterprise was academic, since Roosevelt was intent upon "an early complete post-Armistice evacuation of Europe by all American fighting forces."[148] The supreme commander thought the creation of a coalition military government would facilitate the speedy removal of all occupation forces. He also told Smith the Soviets would "undoubtedly demand the utilization of German labor in order to restore their own devastated districts" and predicted they would exert tight control over the Balkans. However, he did not see these actions as particularly threatening.[149]

The second question centered on unconditional surrender. Smith had not made his opposition to the policy secret. When Stettinius was in London, Eisenhower and Smith pushed for clarification of the policy "by announcing the principles on which the treatment of a defeated Germany would be based." SHAEF desired a tripartite statement that might contribute to Hitler's overthrow. They also proposed that after the Normandy landings succeeded, the headquarters announce guarantees of law, order, and political justice. Smith said "for all available evidence, in default of such declarations, it would be impossible to exploit the crisis in the German Army which will undoubtedly arise immediately after a successful Allied landing."[150]

In hindsight such a policy might have enjoyed some success, particularly in view of the attempted assassination of Hitler on July 20, 1944. Roosevelt did not appreciate his commanders interfering with political decision making and refused to alter his stance.[151] In fairness to the president, it was extremely unlikely that Churchill or Stalin would have agreed to an alteration along lines proposed by Eisenhower and Smith. In any event the attempt failed to change Allied policy. SHAEF never received a directive setting either pre- or postsurrender policy for the proposed zones of occupation. The situation at the end of May remained as it had been in February. Despite his oft-repeated claims of being apolitical, Eisenhower involved himself in political maneuvering. He believed the president in error and was unhappy when Roosevelt put him off.

In the weeks before D-Day, these political problems, especially difficulties with the French, proved, in Eisenhower's opinion, among the "most acutely annoying" of the war.[152] While Eisenhower was annoyed, it was Smith who dealt with the daily aggravations and frustrations of the detailed negotiations.

ACCUMULATED STRESSES

From January 20, when he assumed direction of SHAEF, to D-Day Smith suffered under constant strain. By the middle of April the command structure was set and the major operational decisions made. It now devolved upon the commanders-in-chief to prepare the detailed planning with SHAEF serving as central clearinghouse. Increasingly Eisenhower spent time visiting Allied units and watching exercises—twenty-six divisions, twenty-four airfields, five ships of war, and innumerable depots, hospitals, and other installations.[153] Smith was left to manage the command and communicate with Washington and the various headquarters. The communication tasks themselves were demanding. When the British took over AFHQ, Wilson found it necessary to create an entire staff section to handle the correspondence carried out singlehandedly by Smith.[154] The opening of the Bushy Park headquarters on March 15 did not relieve Smith of organizational headaches, as the G-5 and G-6 divisions continued to absorb much of his attention.

Smith was particularly eager to move the headquarters out of London. Plans were finalized as early as January 20 to move the headquarters to Bushy Park, thirty minutes by automobile from Norfolk House in central London. Eisenhower thought the intermingling of officers in messes and living quarters would expedite the "welding of an allied command."[155] Smith wanted to have the staff working around the clock in three shifts, and Norfolk House did not provide sufficient space.

Originally intending to begin the transfer on February 1, Smith faced a good deal of opposition as it took "weeks to pry" the staff officers out of London. When officers complained there was nothing to occupy their time at night, Smith replied: "Why not work. That's what I [do]."[156] He also wanted to place the headquarters on a field operations basis, perhaps as a reaction to charges the staff was composed of "desk soldiers."

Another preoccupation was security. Allied intelligence indicated the Germans were preparing to unleash their Vengeance weapons on London. Smith worried one such weapon might take out the entire headquarters staff. Bearing a grudge against Smith for his handling of the press after the slapping incident, Patton circulated the story of finding Smith cowering in a sheltered ridge in Sicily during a salvo of outgoing American artillery. Rumors spread that Smith's impatience to move the headquarters stemmed from personal cowardice. The destructiveness of the buzz bombs bore out Smith's worries. In fact, he narrowly escaped a brush with death. On June 18 Smith canceled at the last moment an invitation to attend a service at the Guard's Chapel at Wellington Barracks, London. His close friend, Ivan Cobbald, died, victim of a German rocket.[157]

On the surface Bushy Park looked like any military installation. Many people passed by without ever knowing the Supreme Headquarters was housed behind the high brick wall. In the center of the ever-expanding complex were two partially subterranean, heavily camouflaged buildings. At the far end of one of the buildings stood Eisenhower's office. Down the corridor were the offices of Smith, the secretary of the General Staff, the deputy chiefs of staff, and the G-division heads.[158] Smith's office, separated from Eisenhower's by Butcher's, was spartanly appointed. The first thing visitors saw upon entering his office was the dominating picture of General Marshall that hung over the desk. Its inscription served as a constant reminder that, while Smith remained virtually unknown in the United States, he enjoyed the "affectionate regards and...complete confidence" of Marshall. As a war correspondent correctly put it, the "inscription tells most of what needs to be told about Beedle Smith ...[General] Smith is a soldier's soldier who cares more for the confidence of his chief and less for publicity than probably anybody in the Army."[159]

Smith sometimes joked about being the unknown man. Late in February he related a story to Butcher involving a speech made by Churchill in the House of Commons. When the prime minister told Parliament Eisenhower would command the invasion, the announcement received cheers. He claimed great gains had been made under Eisenhower in the Mediterranean and "unprecedented unity" was achieved under his command. The House erupted into prolonged cheers. Next Churchill stated Tedder would serve as Eisenhower's deputy; the statement prompted more cheers. Finally, he added that Walter Bedell Smith was to be chief of staff. The house fell silent.[160]

Smith took comfort in the knowledge he enjoyed the high esteem and trust of the British. In some circles his military professionalism was more highly regarded than Eisenhower's. Both Brooke and Montgomery trusted his strategic sense and he continued having close relationships with Ismay, Portal, and Cunningham. As Donovan of the OSS told Smith, Churchill appreciated the "pivotal place you occupy." The prime minister spoke of his absolute trust in Smith's character and his reliance upon the American officer's abilities. "He spoke of you," related Donovan, "as he did of no other American officer."[161]

Intimations such as these bolstered Smith. While he seemed as tenacious and self-assured as ever, the unrelenting strain began to take its toll. On January 7 he received word of his promotion to lieutenant general. Although he joked about his new star "being worth $40 per month," Smith thought the promotion overdue.[162] The third star did make it easier to deal with "the rather overpowering collection of lieutenant generals" under his command.[163] Still, the rank he coveted most was permanent brigadier general. He took little comfort in the fact that he had been made Knight Commander of the Order of the Bath in January 1944, so long as he remained Lieutenant Colonel Smith on the permanent roster of the U.S. Army.[164]

Smith prospects were set back by a few ill-conceived remarks made by Patton on April 25. Addressing a women's club in Knutsford, England, Patton, forgetting the Soviets, talked about the United States and Great Britain dominating the postwar world. Overlooked in the British press, Patton's statements produced a sensation in the United States. Roosevelt had nominated Smith for promotion to permanent brigadier general in October 1943. Because Patton's name appeared on the same promotion calender, Marshall reported all the promotions were "killed."[165] Extremely aggravated, Smith telephoned Patton, angrily pointing out that his "unfortunate remarks" had cost them both their permanent promotions. In no position to alienate a man so close to Eisenhower, Patton played the sycophant to Smith, something he found distasteful. Relations, already poor between the two, grew worse.[166]

Later that same day Smith received a call that shook him to the very depths. German E-Boats ran the gauntlet of a destroyer screen and sank two landing-craft and damaged a third with much loss of life. This action reduced the landing craft reserve to zero. After weeks of wrangling with the Joint Chiefs to release additional landing craft, Smith now had to plead for more.[167]

The month of May offered no relief for Smith. Irritated by "the injunction of secrecy in dealing with the French," Smith struggled writing an announcement to be broadcast to the French people in conjunction with the landings. Presuming de Gaulle would agree to make the proclamation and mindful of the criticisms that arose during the Darlan affair, Smith "walked on eggs" to find the appropriate language.[168] To make matters worse, intelligence indicated the Germans had completed thirty launching sites for their rocket weapons. Other intelligence indicated the construction of extensive underwater obstacles on the Normandy beaches.[169] Frustrations dogged Smith at every turn.

Smith entertained no doubts the Allies could effect a landing but shared the concern the Germans could take advantage of the excellent east-west communications in Normandy and regain the tactical initiative. He worried that the aerial interdiction and deception plans might not succeed. Bedell thought it unlikely the German high command had not put together a picture of the invasion plan. While ULTRA intercepts continued to indicate the German command remained divided on the location of the invasion, Normandy or the Pas de Calais, Smith fully expected the German 15th Army in the Pas de Calais to be released against the Allied forces. Confiding in Butcher in the middle of May, he estimated the odds of holding the beachhead at 50/50 but worth the risk. Smith's realism sharply contrasted with the optimism of his commander.[170]

All these accumulated anxieties exacted a heavy price on Smith's health. Except for a short trip in April to Scotland for salmon fishing, Smith had no respite from his sixteen-hour days. Inviting Butcher to his billet on May 11 for lunch, Smith intimated that he would never be fit enough to undertake another campaign as chief of staff—a very uncharacteristic admission of weakness. "Beetle said he was damned well going to get out of the Army after the war," Butcher related in his diary. "He was fed up."[171]

If he did not have enough to occupy his mind, Smith found himself the subject of an investigation by the inspector general's office. The IQ inquired into charges Smith misused government funds and property for his own gain. Having grown accustomed to his perquisites in Algiers, Smith found the cost of high living more expensive in the British capital. His old nemesis, Hughes, came to London to serve as Eisenhower's "eyes and ears." Hughes took delight in chronicling Smith's mounting distress. On May 6 Hughes reported Smith had overspent badly on purchases of amenities. "Beadle looked at his bills," Hughes logged in his diary, "and is now scared." A week later, Hughes and Patton visited Purdey's Gun Shop. They found an expensive antique shotgun being held for Smith. The noted gunsmith, a personal friend of Bedell's, had received two American carbine rifles from Smith. They also discovered that Smith supplied Mrs. Purdey with food from American sources. "Reminds me of Beadle's saying," Hughes recorded. "The photos are expensive. I'll charge them to my entertainment allowance."

When Hughes mentioned seeing the shotgun, Smith lost his temper and accused Patton of creating trouble. Following up on the story, Hughes uncovered Smith had been issued the two weapons, reported them lost, and paid for them. Since word reached him that the IQ people were looking into the charges, Hughes decided to sit on the story. Intensely irritated by the probe,

Smith threatened to fire anybody who delved too closely into his private affairs. Nothing came of the investigation, but the episode created additional stress on the already overtaxed chief of staff.[172]

Smith also encountered problems with the deputy theater commander, Lee. A man of deep religious convictions (Eisenhower called him Cromwell), Lee took a special proprietary interest in theater logistics as chief of the Service of Supply. Eisenhower came to dislike Lee. A martinet to those beneath him and a currier of favor of his superiors, Lee enjoyed the protection of General Somervell in Washington who engineered his subordinate's elevation to lieutenant general in January 1944. This complicated relations between Smith and Lee. Moveover, Lee traveled throughout Great Britain in a sumptuously appointed train of a dozen coaches. Referred to as "Jesus Christ Himself"—a nickname based on his initials—Lee treated the Service of Supply organization as a personal fiefdom and worked to insolate himself from SHAEF. Paying little attention to Smith, Lee routinely went over his head to Eisenhower.[173] This infuriated Smith who thought Lee's command should be subordinated to his headquarters. For all his many faults Lee proved an efficient administrator. Not wanting to create difficulties that would reverberate back to the War Department, Eisenhower found it easier just to tolerate Lee.[174]

Smith had little time to undertake a thorough evaluation of the potential logistical problems to be faced on the continent. Furthermore he had no disposition for doing so. Smith did not trust logisticians. "I never believe what the supply man tells us," he professed. "He always has twenty-five per cent reserve in his hip pocket."[175] A product of Leavenworth and his experience in the Mediterranean, Smith possessed no real understanding for the enormity of the supply difficulties looming in the campaign in Europe. A prominent logistician pointed out the interwar generation of officers received their supply training in a brief "G-4 Course" at Leavenworth taught by line officers who had only a superficial grasp of logistics and the principles of organization. "[The] only result was an evident distaste for the subject [of logistics] on the part of would-be strategists and tacticians," wrote Major General Henry Aurand. "Regulars were ignorant of the logistical art," he continued, and demonstrated a "mere speaking acquaintance with basic organizational principles." Aurand numbered Smith among the worst offenders. "Bedell himself will deny any part of being a logistician," he observed. "He hates them." Smith's attitude toward airmen and special service officers leaves little reason to doubt the accuracy of Aurand's conclusions.[176]

In the Mediterranean a relatively simple command structure sufficed, allowing AFHQ to oversee supply. Smith had Gale who orchestrated theaterwide logistics. A consistent pattern emerged in London as Smith tried to build

SHAEF into an expanded version of AFHQ. This approach proved inadequate as a model for the Civil Affairs and Publicity and Psychological Warfare divisions as it would for logistics. Smith did not seem to appreciate that logistical requirements would be multiplied for operations in Europe. Overlooking the potential difficulties, Smith's interim solution involved expanding the G-4 Division at headquarters. Lee, *ex-officio* American chief administrative officer, was not integrated into the Supreme Headquarters and therefore did not discharge duties analogous to those carried out by Gale in AFHQ.[177] Nothing suggests the badly organized and internally divided European Theater command structure troubled Smith in the weeks before the invasion. As long as manpower and matériel requirements were met, the type of controlling mechanism mattered little to Smith. As with the uncomprehended G-5 and G-6 divisions, Smith accepted the disjointed command system, content to delay the reorganization until the active campaign commenced. He would later have reason to regret this decision.

SHAEF GOES ON A WAR FOOTING

Following a May 15 conference at Montgomery's London headquarters, Eisenhower announced the preliminary planning phase at an end. With the invasion set for June 5, Smith's task now focused on the completion of all preparations by June 1.[178]

SHAEF was placed on a full war footing on May 26. Eisenhower and Smith settled into the routine established in AFHQ. At 9:30 in the morning Smith convened the daily general staff meeting attended by the heads of the divisions, the deputy chiefs of staff, and those officers with presentations to make. After discussing issues raised during the conference, Smith decided what actions to take, which required further study, and which matters to place before Eisenhower. After the chief of staff conference, Smith, usually with one or more officers in tow, walked up the hall to the supreme commander's office. Reviewing those problems that demanded Eisenhower's attention, final determinations were made. If immediate action was needed Eisenhower would dictate a directive, but usually outgoing messages were written by a division chief or Smith for the commander's signature. During the course of an average day, Smith, the only officer who had the right to walk into Eisenhower's office without knocking, frequently conferred with his boss.[179]

On the surface the headquarters ran like a well-oiled clock. Despite some dissatisfaction with the inability to conclude civil and political agreements with the French—which he blamed on the politicians—Smith had ample reason to be pleased with the executive organs of his headquarters.

Never for a moment doubting the basic soundness of the American staff system, Smith's insistence upon a vertical staff structure ensured the superintendent function would be his. This system worked well in the Mediterranean and Bushy Park where the headquarters remained relatively small—4,914 on July 12, 1944—but SHAEF would eventually grow to 16,000.[180] Actions generated in SHAEF moved slowly through the chain of command with Smith acting as final arbiter. Smith demanded direction come from above, leaving division and section heads little individual authority. Except for the Intelligence Division, Smith's orthodoxy prevented him from practicing any delegation for fear the committee system might take root. During the static phase before D-Day when all energies were directed toward planning, the American linear system met the challenge. It remained unclear what would happen when operations demanded rapid decisions and improvisation. Smith's lack of confidence in functionally organized staffs and his mistrust of the committee approach colored his thinking from the beginning. Experience in the Mediterranean confirmed his preconceived ideas.

No bureaucratized structure can function strictly along formal lines. Much depends upon the willingness of individuals to work together and compromise on conflicting views. For all his faith in unity of command and his hypersensitivity over being seen only as a friendly peacemaker, Eisenhower depended upon the vagaries of personal relationships to cement cooperation. In the Mediterranean, Eisenhower and Smith relied upon their excellent personal friendships with Alexander, Tedder, and Cunningham to overcome differences of opinion. From the onset of Eisenhower's assumption of the European command, it became obvious the situation would be radically different with Montgomery, Leigh-Mallory, and Ramsay.[181] Preoccupied with the ANVIL debate and the struggle over the command and the strategic use of air power, Eisenhower expended little thought on the specific nature of the post-Normandy command structure. Unable to achieve the command system he desired, Eisenhower depended on informal linkages to coordinate actions.

Eisenhower and Smith envisioned a change in the command structure at some undetermined juncture after the completion of the Normandy fighting but delayed making a formal decision. As the SHAEF planners expected a slow advance through France, neither Eisenhower nor his chief of staff saw any danger in altering the command mechanism in the middle of an active campaign. Failing to anticipate that the tempers, prejudices, and ambitions of subordinate commanders might undermine the best organization, Eisenhower never made his intentions known. Smith pushed him to assert himself as commander. "I was tired of the concept," he told a postwar interviewer, "to the effect that Eisenhower was a political commander way up on the pedestal." Despite Smith's prodding, Eisenhower temporized.[182]

Eisenhower's brand of subtle leadership worked. Rather than exercise command as a tough operator, he chose to work through others. Since his task centered on building an Allied team, he depended upon the goodwill of the difficult personalities under him. Eisenhower tried to smooth out personal differences, but if that approach failed he left it to Smith to wield his "cat and nine tails and beat [opposition] into line."[183] Above all, the supreme commander sought to deflect criticism and to avoid the intrusion of the British and the War Department into his affairs. A restructuring of the command would have created acrimony necessitating protracted negotiations. With ANVIL and the transportation plan in mind, he shelved the question of the post-Normandy reorganization. This may have been a result of intentional evasiveness on his part or perhaps he simply lacked nerve. Whatever the motive, this inaction produced a schism between the supreme commander and Montgomery on the issue of ground command as well as a confused logistical setup that contributed to serious supply shortages in late summer and autumn 1944. Both could have been avoided had the command structure been finalized in advance of the Normandy landings.

If one holds perfection as a standard, obviously the pre-OVERLORD command and staff organization fell short of the mark. Criticism can be levelled against Eisenhower for spending a disproportionate amount of time away from headquarters, for delegating too much authority to Smith, the commanders-in-chief, and Lee, and for deferring on pressing decisions. Conversely, given the enormity of the responsibilities he faced and the limited time frame, the accomplishments of Eisenhower in directing the preparation phase of OVERLORD must rank among the more substantial of the war in the West. Smith's part in the process was pivotal. The inadequacies of Eisenhower's style of leadership must be tempered by his achievements. Despite the many frustrations, problems, and flaws in the command apparatus, the groundwork for success in the great operation to commence on June 6 was surely laid.

Normandy and the Battle of France, June–November 1944

On the evening of June 4, 1944, Eisenhower presided over one of the most important councils of war in military history. Smith, Tedder, the commanders-in-chiefs, and various other high-ranking officers from the Supreme Headquarters were in attendance. They met at Southwick House, Admiral Ramsay's headquarters north of Portsmouth, to make the fateful decision to launch the invasion of Normandy.[1] Outside, the wind blew and rain fell; inside, the officers sat in easy chairs over coffee. At 9:30, Group Captain J. M. Stagg, SHAEF meteorological officer, opened the conference by reporting a break in the weather could be expected throughout June 5 and into the morning of June 6. Ramsay then pointed out that the American Task Force would have to be told if the invasion was on within the half hour. If the operation was postponed, the ships would be recalled and remain unavailable until June 8. By then the tidal conditions would be wrong. A delay meant putting off OVERLORD until June 19.

The decision was Eisenhower's. Looking out a window at the raging tempest, he doubted if the operation could be staged. Characteristically, Eisenhower turned first to Smith and asked for his opinion. "It's a helluva gamble," Smith said, "but it's the best possible gamble." Montgomery agreed: "I would say—Go!"[2] Smith was struck by the "loneliness and isolation of a commander at a time when such a momentous decision was to be taken by him, with full knowledge that failure or success rest on his individual decision."[3] After weighing the options Eisenhower calmly said, "I am quite positive that the order must be given." Ramsay rushed from the room to give the order to the fleets.

At 4:30 in the morning the conference reconvened. There was still time to recall the more than 5,000 ships steaming toward their assembly points. Again

Staggs opened the meeting, this time with a more optimistic report. After a short discussion all eyes turned to Eisenhower. Smith, Montgomery, Ramsay, and Tedder all thought the attack should proceed. Leigh-Mallory saw the operation as "chancey" but concurred. After a moment's pause, the supreme commander said, "O.K. let's go." With that, the decisive campaign in the western European theater was set into motion.[4]

Within a half-minute Eisenhower was alone pondering his fateful decision. The rest of the assemblage hurried to their respective command posts. Each knew they faced their gravest test. Everything done to date was merely preparation for the operation in northwest Europe. For months all the senior Allied officers had been eaten up with anxiety and doubt. Forgotten were all the vexations of the preparation period. The agony of waiting was over. What mattered was the seizure of the beachhead and the initiation of the great campaign to liberate France and the Low Countries and to defeat Nazi Germany.

THE BATTLE OF NORMANDY

After months of intensive planning and preparations for D-Day, the fate of the great enterprise would be decided on the landing zones and hedgerows of Normandy. The Allies enjoyed three distinct advantages. The elaborate deception plan (FORTITUDE) convinced the German Supreme Command the Pas de Calais region would be the focus of Allied operations. Second, the intensive bombing campaign succeeded in severing all critical transportation arteries to Normandy. Finally, as ULTRA intelligence indicated, a fragmented command structure existed within OB West (Oberbefehlshaben West). Together, these advantages achieved surprise and frustrated the initial German response.

By the end of June 6 the Allied forces carved out five beachheads on the Normandy coast. The Atlantic Wall had been breached, but the slowness in linking the beachheads threw the drives inland off balance. On June 8 serious gaps remained between the sectors, particularly on either side of OMAHA beach. A massive storm hit Normandy following the landings, seriously disrupting the flow of manpower and matériel.

Alarmed by the overly optimistic news reporting of the invasion, Smith convened an impromptu press conference to brief the journalists on the many difficulties yet to be faced. He opened by outlining the serious logistical bottlenecks created by the adverse weather conditions. After explaining the tactical situation in the landing zones, Smith told them Caen had not been taken as planned. However, in view of the slow German buildup, Bedell thought "the bad break of the weather [had] not been fatal." In conclusion, he asked the

NORMANDY

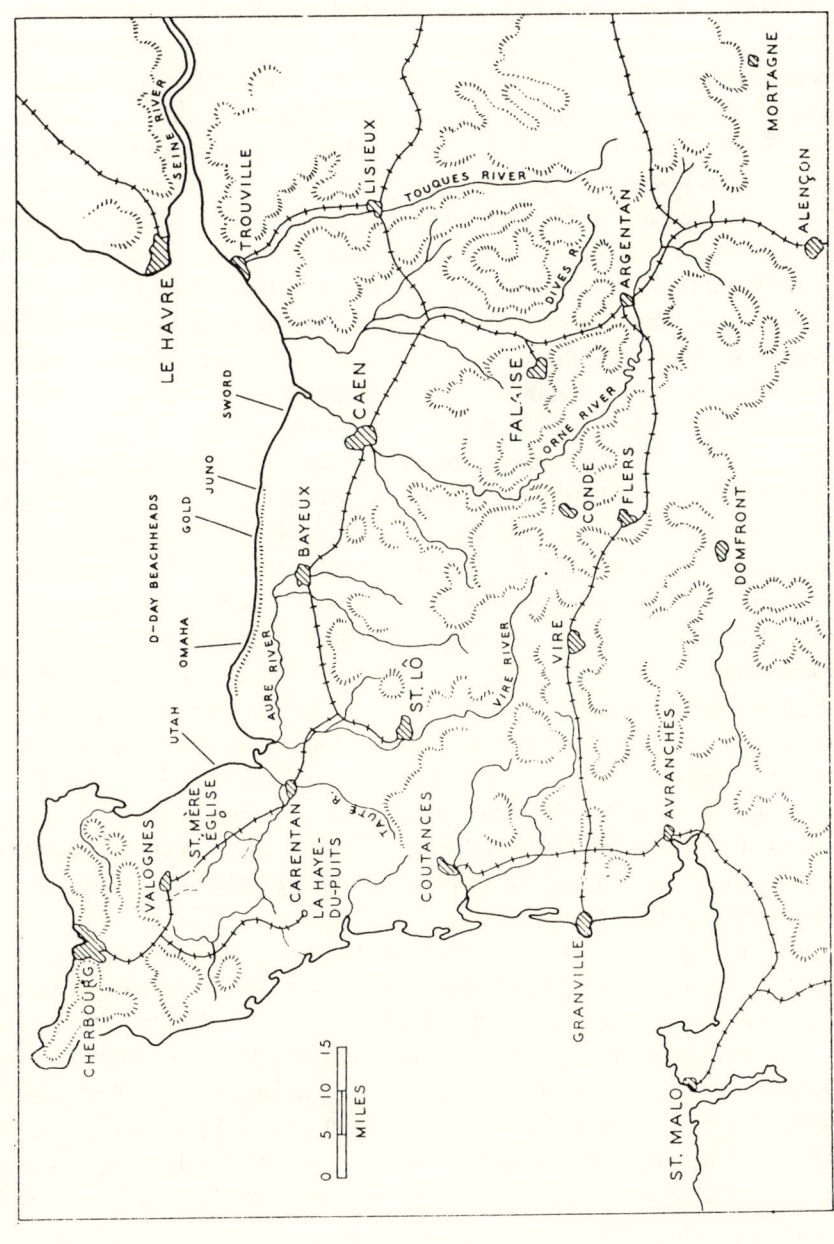

Alfred D. Chandler, ed., *The Papers of Dwight D. Eisenhower: The War Years*, vol. 5 (Baltimore: Johns Hopkins University Press, 1970), p. 58.

press to exercise restraint in their reporting so as not to build up false hopes on the respective home fronts.[5]

Impatient to survey the situation in person, Smith requested he be flown over the channel to confer with Bradley. On June 10 the DC-3 took off from Portsmouth intending to land on a hastily built airstrip in Normandy. The foul weather continued, and the aircraft flew into a dense bank of fog. After some nervous moments over France the pilot decided to return to base, but neglected to inform his passengers. Much to his surprise, Smith emerged from the plane to discover himself back in Portsmouth. "Smart major," remarked Smith, referring to the pilot's abandoning the mission. The chief of staff would have to content himself with reading the incoming situation reports.[6]

The incoming information painted a gloomy picture. Montgomery's plan called for rapid advances from the beachheads. Bradley's 1st Army had two objectives: the capture of Caumont and the closure of the Cotentin Peninsula. In the all-important eastern sector, the 2nd British Army was directed to seize Caen and "push [the] flank eastwards" in anticipation of the German armored counterattack. In neither case did the attacking forces attain their D-Day objectives. In failing to take Caen, a series of positional battles ensued. Montgomery lost much of his flexibility and initiative—the preservation of which he considered the keys to victory.[7] With his front overextended and too shallow to launch a major offensive with the full combat power available to him, Montgomery made his first alteration in the original plan. From the onset his grand design hinged upon anchoring the left, leaving Bradley free from serious German opposition to complete the capture of the Contentin and the port of Cherbourg. The British commander recognized this could not be accomplished through defensive tactics. When the anticipated German counterattack never materialized, Montgomery launched a major attack on June 18 designed to take Caen by envelopment.[8] Failing to take the city, Montgomery altered his approach a second time.

From June 18 to July 18 Montgomery fought a series of local frontal actions.[9] As the British general had foreseen, Caen acted like a magnet, drawing in German reinforcements. The German high command clung to the belief at least one other invasion attempt would be conducted, probably at the mouth of the Seine or the Pas de Calais.[10] Largely owing to aerial interdiction, German panzer divisions earmarked to join the fighting on the day of the landing took two weeks to enter the line against the British. Those units, taken from the German 15th Army in the Pas de Calais and elsewhere, were committed piecemeal around the Orne River and Caen rather than on the weakened German left flank. Fully appraised of the overall strategic picture, Montgomery opted to postpone any deep penetration attacks in the Caen sector. Despite the shrinking British manpower pool, Montgomery embarked upon a battle of attrition—an anathematic approach to the Allied ground commander.[11]

Montgomery's handling of the campaign produced mounting criticisms both at SHAEF and in the American press. The British general faced a difficult dilemma: how to fight a battle of attrition while avoiding unnecessary casualties, especially among the 2nd Army's dwindling infantry assets. As Smith pointed out, Montgomery was correct in his assessment of the strategic situation. Neither the British shield nor Bradley's advance lived up to expectations.[12] In the hope of retaining the strategic initiative and gaining room for maneuver on the right, Montgomery resorted to a blocking role around Caen. Montgomery never acknowledged there had been any change in the plan.

Throughout the Normandy fighting, Montgomery issued a number of operational directives "as lofty as the Ten Commandments."[13] In part these were designed to keep morale high. They also reflected Montgomery's refusal to admit the pristine purity of his plan had been compromised. Although he maintained the breakout would occur in the American zone, this became explicit only in his June 30 directive (M-505).[14] The confidence of Montgomery's Normandy pronouncements contrasted with the stalemate of June and the first weeks of July. At SHAEF, Eisenhower and Smith concluded the fundamental plan had failed. They erroneously thought, as Smith told his staff, Montgomery had intended a "drive across the Orne from Caen toward the south and southeast in the direction of Paris [and] had fundamentally changed his plan on June 30th."[15] The revised scheme of attack substantially altered its form, but the integrity of the original plan remained the same. Increasingly Eisenhower and Smith entertained misgivings of Montgomery's conduct of the operation. Their doubts were fueled by Tedder and Morgan who disliked and mistrusted Montgomery.[16]

While the fighting raged in Normandy, Eisenhower remained in England. Smith recalled he acted like a football coach, running up and down the sidelines exhorting his commanders to attack.[17] On June 24, Eisenhower visited Bradley in France. At this juncture, according to Smith, Eisenhower resolved "that the full weight of the U.S. strength should be used to breakout into the open on [the] right."[18] This had always been the *sine qua non* for success in Normandy—a point Montgomery made clear as early as his May 15 conference in London and from which he never substantially deviated. Eisenhower and Smith thought Montgomery's plan called for breakouts on both flanks. "Monty intended to make his main effort in this good tank country [beyond Caen]," Smith recalled, "coupled with the swing to the right by the Americans." "Monty has always planned his big battles for direct penetration—he likes direct attacks, which is why he is good for assaults and no good on envelopments—but he wins his battles by envelopments he never planned," he concluded.[19]

While Smith correctly recognized the need for "changes...in the original tactical plan," he was wrong in claiming Montgomery did not adjust his thinking until June 30. He had been intimately acquainted with the plan from its very inception, yet Smith's faulty assessment of Montgomery's orchestration of the battle can be attributed to the growing divisiveness between the British general and SHAEF. As Smith remarked after the war, it was impossible "to give a correct portrayal of Montgomery without showing him to be a S.O.B."[20]

On June 26, Cherbourg capitulated, weeks behind schedule. The chief culprit was the weather. Logistical bottlenecks prevented Bradley from simultaneously taking the strategic port and driving south out of the Cotentin. This delay allowed the Germans to improvise a line of defense in the thickly hedged bocage country between La Huye du Puits and St.Lô. The long-awaited American breakout could be launched only on July 3.[21]

Montgomery renewed his attacks against Caen and gained a large part of the ruins of the city on July 9 (CHARNWOOD). In Bradley's sector, the American attacks stalled in the face of tough German infantry. Montgomery's forces faced eight panzer divisions and an array of infantry on a twenty-mile front between Caumont and Caen. To assist Bradley he attacked toward Thury-Harcourt, but the poor tactical performance of the British allowed the Germans to halt the thrust at Viller-Bocage.[22] The British commander shifted the weight and direction of his attacks, avoiding enemy strength, with the object of pinning German armor on the eastern flank. Criticisms increased as neither advance prospered. As Smith noted, Montgomery and Bradley "kept their heads and went about their business."[23]

On July 2-5 Eisenhower made a tour of the Normandy headquarters, spending most of his time with Bradley. When he returned to SHAEF he was "smouldering over the whole business."[24] After discussing the situation with Smith and Tedder, the supreme commander drafted a letter "tactfully telling Monty to get a move on."[25] The July 7 communication, more exhortatory than demanding, called upon Montgomery to abandon his two- or three-division attacks in favor of a fully coordinated assault by his entire army.[26]

The next day Montgomery launched his corps-strength attack which finally took Caen west of the Orne. Butcher's diary indicates that throughout July Eisenhower's pique mounted over what he considered Montgomery's undue caution.[27] The growing chorus of criticism of Montgomery was directed not by Americans but British officers, particularly senior airmen. Air Marshal Coningham and Montgomery were engaged in a feud over tactical air support in Normandy. Tedder "agreed with Coningham that the Army did not seem prepared to fight its own battles." Having just returned from France, Portal informed Tedder on July 8 "the problem was Montgomery, who could be neither removed nor moved to action."[28]

It was against Eisenhower's philosophy of command to interfere with his operational commanders, but pressures mounted on him to assume control in Normandy. Smith pushed Eisenhower to take direct command from the beginning. Marshall added his voice as well. Meanwhile, the American press claimed Eisenhower was a mere figurehead; the British commanders-in-chiefs were running the campaign. Alive to the political dimensions, Eisenhower knew he could not relieve Montgomery. From a military standpoint he was not prepared to alter the command structure at this most critical juncture in the fighting. Caught in a dilemma, Eisenhower boiled inside.[29]

Venting his anger to his intimates, Eisenhower's blood pressure rose to a dangerous level. "The slowness of the battle, the desire to be more active in it himself, his inward but generally unspoken criticisms of Monty for being so cautious: all pump up his system," recorded Butcher on July 19. "His troubles are not from physical exertion, they are from the mental strain and worry." Following his naval aide's advice, Eisenhower consulted the head of the SHAEF Medical section, Major General Albert Kenner. Fearing the ETO gossipmongers would pick up the story and relay it to Washington, Kenner secretly prescribed some "slow down medicine" to bring the supreme commander's blood pressure down. After a day's rest in his caravan, Eisenhower felt better, and over dinner with Smith openly discussed the possibility of sacking Montgomery. The next day, July 21, he had Butcher telephone Smith, cautioning him not to mention the subject of Montgomery with anyone.[30]

On July 26, over dinner with Churchill at 10 Downing Street, Eisenhower and Smith decried Montgomery's "stickiness." The prime minister agreed the offensive should proceed along the entire front but was shocked by the vehemence of the American generals' arguments. After Eisenhower and Smith departed, Churchill called Brooke. The following night a dinner was arranged to allow the supreme commander and his chief of staff an opportunity to repeat their charges to Brooke. Defending his protege and Montgomery's concept of the battle, Brooke told Eisenhower it would be better for him to discuss the matter openly with the British commander rather than cavil behind his back.[31]

The meeting with Montgomery never took place. Major General Frank "Simbo" Simpson, director of Military Operations at the War Office, thought Eisenhower "knew jolly well that...Monty would run circles around him with a clear exposition of his strategy and tactics."[32] There might have been considerable truth in this view. Eisenhower characteristically avoided personal confrontations, preferring to work behind the scenes. He also showed a marked tendency to defer making decisions until events charted his course. In this case the opening of the long-awaited American offensive to break out of the bocage initiated the beginning of the third phase of the Normandy battle. Its success relieved Eisenhower of the responsibility of making a decision.

While the senior officers in England grew ever-more critical of Montgomery, the ground commander began to lay the foundations for the breakout phase of the campaign. On July 10 Montgomery met with his army commanders and informed them his "policy remain[ed] unchanged." Since in his opinion the fighting at Caen "proceeded entirely according to plan," Montgomery instructed Bradley to prepare for a wide swing on the right. The ground commander also suggested Bradley concentrate his forces rather than attack all along his front. This accorded exactly to Bradley's estimates; but before any offensive could be undertaken the Americans had to advance through the bocage.[33]

Two days later Dempsey, finding the bocage as difficult as did Bradley, asked permission to stage a breakout at Caen.[34] At this point no one talked of a breakthrough of the German defenses. The objective was to break out of the constrictive lodgment area preparatory to a general, phased advance.[35] Montgomery agreed and the attack (GOODWOOD) was staged on July 18-20 in conjunction with Bradley's two-division strong operation west of St. Lô. Again, neither attack accomplished its objective. GOODWOOD failed to achieve any breakout beyond Caen because of the spotty tactical performance of the British and Canadian divisions. The American attack also failed to make much headway. In both cases German resistance limited Allied success. GOODWOOD inaugurated a shift in Montgomery's approach from positional attacks to the development of operations aimed at a breakout into territory more suited to mobile warfare.

Independent of Montgomery but consistent with the master plan, Bradley developed plans for the breakout at St. Lô (COBRA). The British attack failed in the tactical sense but succeeded at the strategic level. Four German corps were tied up in the British sector. Generalfeldmarschal Günther von Kluge, who replaced von Rundstedt early in July, tried to release armor in front of Montgomery and replace it with infantry. With each effort a British attack forced the German commander to commit his dwindling panzers. As a result, Bradley's forces, having staked out their position and probed the German defenses, faced only a thin cordon of infantry. Only around Caen were the Germans able to build a defense-in-depth.[36]

Bradley attacked behind a massive carpet of bombing on July 26. The next day Montgomery redirected a British armored corps from Caumont toward Vire to support Bradley. The Germans collapsed before the American onslaught, their only mobile reserve virtually destroyed. Patton's 3d Army, committed to spearhead the breakout, broke through to Avranches and beyond. The plan called for Patton's army to wheel into Brittany to open the ports of Brest and L'Orient while Bradley's 1st Army swung "southward and eastward" toward Paris and the Seine.[37]

At this point Hitler made a fateful error. He ordered von Kluge's panzers to counterattack toward Mortain with the aim of restoring the German left flank. ULTRA provided Bradley with intelligence about the strength and direction of the attack. The American general immediately mastered the situation. Determined the German counterattack would not impede Patton's breakout, Bradley decided to block von Kluge's reposte with elements of Major General J. Lawton Collin's VII Corps backed by the powerful Allied airforces. By shifting the German center of gravity westward, the Mortain counteroffensive practically ensured the pocketing of German Army Group B in Normandy. As Bradley told Henry Morgenthau, the visiting secretary of the treasury: "This is an opportunity that comes to a commander not more than once in a century. We are about to destroy an entire German army."[38] A SHAEF plan (LUCKY STRIKE) envisioned such an eventuality.[39] Patton dispatched a single corps towards Brittany while continuing his lightning advance up the Loire. The German counterattack presented the Allied command with a textbook opportunity to fight a battle of annihilation in Normandy.[40]

Essentially, the LUCKY STRIKE plan was executed after the breakthrough. On August 13 SHAEF ordered Patton to make a tight swing northward toward Argentan while the British and Canadians pushed south toward Falaise. For a numbers of reasons, including determined German resistance, the pocket was not closed.[41] Although elements of the German forces in Normandy escaped to the Seine, the results of the campaign exceeded even the most ambitious estimates. For all intents and purposes the fate of the German armies in France was sealed.

No campaign in the west produced as much controversy as Normandy, but in the end Montgomery was vindicated. The battle did not develop in strict accordance to the plan as he later maintained. However, Montgomery's flexibility, his ability to adapt to the situation, and his perseverance in the face of harsh criticism and a worsening British manpower problem eventually enabled Bradley to reclaim the initiative and stage the great breakout in the west. "I am no Montgomery lover," Smith confided in Eisenhower, "but I give him his full due and believe that for certain types of operations he is without an equal." The Battle of Normandy was such an operation.[42]

BROAD FRONT VERSUS NARROW FRONT

Long before D-Day, SHAEF planned for an advance into Germany. The Operations Division's planners did not foresee a sudden German collapse in France. Gearing for an orderly, ponderous advance eastward towards the German frontier, SHAEF constructed an intricate logistical apparatus. Montgomery would retain command of the ground forces until Eisenhower assumed overall command. After the Anglo-Canadian (21st) and American (12th) Army groups were regrouped and their advance logistical bases moved forward, the offensive would continue north and east of the Seine. Eisenhower intended to employ his forces on a broad advance to eventually include the Allied forces advancing up the Rhône from the ANVIL/DRAGOON beachhead. Montgomery's armies were to force their way through Belgium toward the Ruhr industrial complex while Bradley's forces covered the right flank. The main axis of advance, posited a May 1944 planning paper, would be along the line Amiens-Mauberge-Liége-the Ruhr with a subsidiary axis on the line Verdun-Metz. The original OVERLORD plan called for an advance into Germany on either side of the Ardennes with the northern thrust having priority.[43] Eisenhower hoped the Germans would sign an armistice before the Allies penetrated into Germany, a repeat of November 1918.

Of all the controversies arising during the European campaign, none tested the alliance more than the differences over the "broad front versus narrow front" strategies. Although the plan evolved from a consensus of SHAEF planners, the "broad front" approach, more than any other factor, was the product of American doctrine. British doctrine called for a concentration of force applied at the critical point. Their philosophy of command insisted a separate commander execute each aspect of battle. American doctrine stood in direct opposition. For the Americans the end of strategy was the singleminded commitment to the destruction of the enemy's main force by direct application of overwhelming power. This can be consistently seen in every major American strategic pronouncement from the Victory Program of 1941 through Marshall's unrelenting advocacy of the head-on strategy for ROUNDUP/OVERLORD to Eisenhower's insistence on the broad front.[44]

Ingrained in the minds of senior American officers, the broad-front approach became the *leitmotif* of American warmaking. Leavenworth doctrine called for a rapid decision by smashing the enemy by sheer weight. Failing to achieve victory before the battle lines became rigid, the objective involved the seizure of territory in an effort to restrict the enemy's flexibility. Eschewing maneuver, the aim involved the maintenance of constant pressure all along the line until the material advantages permitted the resumption of a massive offensive. By concentrating upon the decisive battle and placing emphasis on the strict adherence to doctrine and planning, the American approach displayed a marked tendency to underestimate the value of surprise, maneuver, flexible logistical management, and the fighting capacity of the enemy.[45]

The fundamental disparity between British and American military doctrine did not produce serious friction in the Mediterranean because the British monopolized the key commands, enabling them to subtly engineer Eisenhower's actions. Eisenhower was content to play the role of chairman of the board in the Mediterranean command. With British officers holding all three commander-in-chief positions for OVERLORD and dominating the upper echelon of the Supreme Headquarters, the British expected to exert a formative influence over Eisenhower in the campaign in Europe as well. Believing Eisenhower to be more malleable than Marshall, the British expressed relief when Roosevelt decided in favor of the latter to command in Europe.

Montgomery's plan for Normandy conformed to American precepts. Because success in Normandy depended upon the consolidation of the lodgment and an offensive battle of attrition before a general breakout toward the Seine, Eisenhower and the senior Americans at SHAEF accepted the scheme without serious question. Differences did emerge over ANVIL, the most significant and irritating problem of the planning period. Eisenhower conceived of ANVIL not as a diversion but rather as an integral component of his broad-front approach. Even before D-Day Eisenhower intended to overrun France, bring his forces up to the Rhine, make two or three crossings, encircle the Ruhr, and spread throughout Germany. He saw the taking of the south French ports as crucial, enabling him to utilize all the American divisions allotted to his European command.[46]

In their postwar memoirs both Eisenhower and Smith declared no campaign in military history unfolded in closer accordance to the plan than OVERLORD. Throughout the developmental phase of the OVERLORD plan both men harkened back to their days at Leavenworth. "I know of no single year in my whole service," wrote Eisenhower in February, 1944, "that I go back to in my memories more than my student year at Leavenworth."[47] Smith went even further, admitting the exegesis of the advance through France lay in the Leavenworth command course, especially the study of the Schlieffen plan. Both men found it ironic the Allies intended to employ a massive broad-front advance through France as the preliminary phase for the great "sickle-cut" envelopment of the Ruhr.[48] "This general plan, carefully outlined at staff meetings before D-Day," Eisenhower maintained, "was never abandoned, even momentarily throughout the campaign."[49]

Montgomery and Brooke were aware of the SHAEF plan but did not raise questions. The British thought the plans represented only broad outlines of actions to be undertaken in the event of a phased German withdrawal through France. They did not appreciate that Eisenhower and Smith viewed the plan as final. With the broad-front strategy, Eisenhower believed his duty involved providing the inspired leadership necessary to assure the execution of the plan and to prevent any rupture in the alliance. The roots of the Eisenhower-Montgomery conflict had their origins in misunderstandings that developed during the planning phase. Based on dissimilar concepts of war, it was no coincidence the clash over strategy evolved along national lines.

The differences in strategy necessarily involved the question of command. Montgomery operated under the assumption Eisenhower should delegate command over the two army groups to a single ground commander. He had as his precedent the Mediterranean command. The supreme commander agreed "a single battlefield commander" was needed, but since the envisioned advance encompassed the area from Switzerland to the North Sea he did not see how "one man [could] keep a 'battle grasp' upon the overall situation and direct it intelligently." Eisenhower planned to grant his army group and army commanders broad authority within more or less clearly defined zones of operations while SHAEF reserved the right to adjust these boundaries, assign reinforcements and air support, and shift emphasis in logistical arrangements. A single ground commander, involved in the detailed conduct of battle, could not make such broad decisions.[50]

The breakout and encircling of the German Army Group B left no time for the luxury of a pause at the Seine. On August 1, Eisenhower activated the U.S. 12th Army Group under Bradley. Lieutenant General Courtney Hodges assumed direction of the American 1st Army. Patton's 3rd Army composed the other half of Bradley's command. Montgomery would continue to direct the battle until Eisenhower officially took command on September 1.

Serious complications arose. The British press reacted angrily to the changes, interpreting Bradley's elevation as a demotion for Montgomery. The furore in the British newspapers produced a reaction in the United States.[51] In the hope of quelling public acrimony, Marshall insisted that Eisenhower seize the reins of command as quickly as possible.[52]

SHAEF was not prepared to take advantage of the Allied success. For political reasons—to get Eisenhower into the battle zone—and his desire to have the staff operating like "rough field soldiers," Smith had unwisely moved SHAEF-Forward from Portsmouth to the seacoast resort of Granville, just north of Avranches on the Cotentin. The vast headquarters was divided between Bushy Park, Portsmouth, and Granville. To make matters worse, not only was the site of the advance headquarters remote and inaccessible, it lacked sufficient communications.[53] As critical, Eisenhower's disinclination to tackle the question of reorganizing Lee's command came back to haunt him. The rout of the Germans in Normandy compounded by a successful landing in the south of France on August 15 presented a logistician's nightmare. Finally, the Civil Affairs Division was ill prepared for a rapid advance. Smith's intransigent demand that the organization accord to his partisan view prevented the formulation of general policies for liberated Europe. As the Allied pursuit moved eastward, the ability of the headquarters to exert any form of command and control lessened.

Convinced Eisenhower and SHAEF were unequal to the task and mindful his tenure as ground commander would soon end, Montgomery attempted to build a consensus among the army commanders favoring a "full-blooded" thrust toward the Ruhr and beyond. Pivoting on Paris, this force of forty divisions would advance over the Rhine and, in conjunction with a powerful air force in Belgium, seize the industrial belt before the Germans could consolidate their defense. Believing wrongly he had Bradley's support, the British commander prepared to set his case before Eisenhower.[54]

On August 23 Eisenhower came to Montgomery's headquarters at Conde-sur-Noireau to discuss future operations. Smith flew from London to attend the conference. This marked Smith's first visit with Montgomery since D-Day. The British general once numbered Smith among his personal friends and shared Brooke's view Bedell "had brains...[and was] certainly one of the best American officers."[55] He also recognized Smith stiffened Eisenhower and "kept him on the rails." After backbiting surfaced during the Normandy fighting, Montgomery saw Smith, far from being his confederate in the headquarters, emerge as one of his most virulent critics. Reluctant to believe the worst, Montgomery felt "Bedell Smith is all right...He is intensely 'national,' but I would say he is a good member of the Allied team."[56] The 21st Army Group commander never lost sight of the fact the leading British officers at SHAEF—Tedder, Morgan, Gale, Whiteley, and Strong—were arrayed against him. The only way he could persuade Eisenhower to adopt the narrow thrust was to get him alone and win the American over by the force of his arguments. Bluntly, Montgomery demanded Smith not be permitted to enter into the discussions.

While Smith and his opposite number in 21st Army Group, Major General "Freddie" de Guingand, sat in an adjacent orchard, their chiefs met alone. With all the tact he could muster, Montgomery showcased his views. Despite his best efforts he still appeared patronizing. Montgomery wanted SHAEF to put nine divisions of Hodges's 1st Army under British command while reducing Patton to a secondary role. Believing Eisenhower must remain above the land battle to retain his objectivity, Montgomery thought either he or Bradley should control ground operations. Furthermore, he pointed out logistical resources would not support a simultaneous advance by all the Allied armies. In trying to be strong everywhere, Montgomery thought the Allies too weak to achieve decisive results at any one place.[57]

Refusing to surrender on the broad front, Eisenhower compromised. Montgomery's northern thrust would continue to receive priority until the V-Weapon launching sites, Antwerp, and the Belgian airfields were in Allied hands. To accomplish this, Eisenhower promised to order Hodges's entire army to advance into Belgium. Montgomery would possess temporary "operational control" over Hodges.[58] In the meantime, Patton would advance eastward seeking to link with the Allied forces moving up the Rhône. As Butcher recorded in his diary, Eisenhower did not oppose giving the northern thrust priority, he merely thought its execution should not be "to the exclusion of all other maneuver." While Montgomery did not get everything he wanted, the supreme commander's assurances represented more than the British general expected.[59]

It became clear neither man possessed much confidence in the other. Dating back to Italy, Eisenhower thought Montgomery overcautious and doubted his ability to lead a bold thrust.[60] Montgomery regarded Eisenhower as a staff officer without an understanding of practical war. In addition, there was constant divergence of doctrinal views. As Brooke complained, Eisenhower and Smith had "some conception of attacking on the whole front...which must be an American doctrine judging by Mark Clark with Fifth Army in Italy."[61] The styles of leadership and the personalities of Eisenhower and Montgomery conflicted. The supreme commander, modest and an unobtrusive committeeman, sought the best advice available and worked toward a consensus. As a twentieth-century general, Eisenhower commanded through others. Montgomery led by inspiration, leading a hermetic life at his headquarters where he developed his plans in isolation. Their differences in personality, professional background, and position made disagreements inevitable.

On August 29 SHAEF issued a new directive. In the six days between his meeting with Montgomery and the issuance of the directive, Eisenhower retreated from his position. He began to refer to Montgomery's narrow thrust as "pencil-like," which is difficult to reconcile with the British general's forty-division-strong plan.[62] Eisenhower spent August 26-27 with Bradley, who protested vigorously at surrendering control of 1st Army to the British.[63] In the meantime, a special meeting of the senior SHAEF staff officers took place in Smith's trailer. Smith closely questioned each man in turn. Gale, the supply expert, stated the logistical situation alone negated Montgomery's proposal. Until Antwerp became available and forward airfields constructed, Montgomery would have to draw the bulk of his supplies over lines stretching back to the beaches in Normandy. To starve Bradley of supply would have paralyzed many American divisions. Morgan, Strong, and Whiteley, British officers who always spoke their minds, stated flatly Montgomery did not possess the drive to carry off the bold offensive, even if the logistical situation had been favorable. Armed with a considered staff opinion, Smith pushed Eisenhower to alter his decision.[64] Confronted by Smith and mindful of Bradley's opposition, Eisenhower backed away from giving Montgomery operational control over Hodges.[65]

Montgomery was infuriated by what he saw as the supreme commander's bad faith. In fairness to Eisenhower, Montgomery's ideas at the time were much less clear than he suggests in his postwar memoirs. His ill conceived and exaggerated talk of a "knife-like thrust" to Berlin did much to undermine his position.[66] When Eisenhower met with Montgomery on August 23, the 21st Army Group had advanced scarcely eighty miles beyond the Seine. As Smith said, the narrow thrust was viewed as "the most fantastic bit of balderdash ever proposed by a competent general."[67] However, when Eisenhower and Montgomery met for a major conference on September 10 in Brussels, the previously slow British advance had outstripped Patton's. Dempsey's forces halted on the Meuse-Escort Canal 280 miles beyond the Siene, with Antwerp, the airfields, and the excellent Belgian rail net—all virtually intact—securely in their grasp. The 21st Army Group enjoyed a "very favorable" supply situation whereas the diminished flow of logistics created by transportation bottlenecks brought Bradley to a virtual halt by September 5.[68] A SHAEF intelligence report indicated the Germans possessed only the equivalent of two weak armored and nine disordered infantry divisions north of the Ardennes. According to a German estimate of September 27, the Allies held a superiority of ten to one in tanks, three to one in artillery, and an "almost unlimited" advantage in the air along the entire front.[69] While Berlin lay beyond the scope of Allied operations, the Ruhr, only 130 miles distant, was not. Rarely in military history had such an opportunity existed.

During the September 10 Brussels meeting, Montgomery resorted to an unusually denunciatory harangue to bring Eisenhower around to his point of view. Once again a minority of one among the senior commanders and staff officers in the theater, Montgomery was convinced the broad front, "the doughboy tactics of maintaining direct pressure all along the line" as one American officer explained it, would permit the Germans to improvise a defense before the campaigning season drew to an end. As Montgomery viewed matters, dispersal of effort typified the American approach to war since the North African landings. The "doughboy tactics" would produce, in his opinion, a stalemate, just as they had in the First World War.[70]

Eisenhower refused to "give him everything" but did agree to a less-ambitious plan involving the use of the 1st Airborne Army and elements of British 2nd Army to secure a crossing of the Rhine at Arnhem in the Netherlands, outflanking the West Wall.[71] Montgomery pushed for this operation (MARKET GARDEN) even though it deflected his advance north and reduced his resources for 1st Canadian Army's clearing of the approaches to Antwerp. These disadvantages were offset in Montgomery's mind by the opportunity of regaining the initiative for 21st Army Group while moving the SHAEF center of gravity toward the north. He hoped the airborne battle would compel Eisenhower to reinforce success and give the British field marshal command over elements of Hodges's army for a drive into Germany along the northern route.[72]

By early September the "victory disease" took hold at SHAEF. "The defeat of the German armies is complete," Eisenhower noted on September 5, "and the only thing now needed to realize the whole conception is speed"—an amazing view given the immobilization of Bradley's forces for lack of supplies.[73] Eisenhower's overconfidence prompted his assention to MARKET GARDEN and intimation to Montgomery on September 15 "Clearly, Berlin is the main prize...There is no doubt, whatsoever, in my mind, that we should concentrate all our energies and resources on a rapid thrust to Berlin."[74] The supreme commander estimated the collapse of German resistance assured the speedy seizure of the Ruhr, Saar, and Frankfurt areas. On August 24 he had informed Marshall he could not do "everything that we should like to do simultaneously," but by September 5 he proposed to do just that. Reacting predictably, Montgomery replied on September 18 Eisenhower must either drive on the Ruhr and Berlin along the northern route or develop offensive operations under Bradley through Frankfurt toward Leipzig-Dresden.[75] Montgomery knew from experience unless he received a concrete commitment from Eisenhower, the other offensives would serve only to exhaust the stretched SHAEF maintenance capacities.

The very day Montgomery sent his angry protest to SHAEF, Eisenhower told Marshall "This team is working well. Without exception all concerned have now fully accepted my conception [of future strategy]."[76] Two days later, on the 20th, he replied to Montgomery claiming there were no great differences between them. "Never at any time have I implied that I was considering an advance into Germany with all armies moving abreast," he continued. While reaffirming his preference for "the all-out offensive into Germany from the Ruhr to Berlin," he reiterated Bradley must continue moving toward Cologne and the Saar.[77] The next day Montgomery responded he did not agree his views were in accord with Eisenhower's. If Hodges was not directed to advance in conjunction with Dempsey, Montgomery predicted "you will not get the Ruhr."[78]

On September 22 the most important conference since D-Day convened at SHAEF in the Trianon Palace Hotel in Versailles to evaluate the strategic situation. Deciding he was too involved with directing the battle of Arnhem, which would continue until September 26, Montgomery sent de Guingand in his place. He knew the twenty-three generals, admirals, and air marshals at Versailles would be hostile and his chief of staff enjoyed the best of relations with Eisenhower and Smith.[79] "Simbo" Simpson, representing the War Office and a firm supporter of Montgomery, also attended the meeting.

Before the conference convened, Simpson sought out Smith in his office for a private conversation. Like Brooke and Montgomery, Simpson assumed Bedell Smith was the authoritative voice for the headquarters. Hoping to enlist the SHAEF chief of staff's support, the British general carefully presented Montgomery's case for the northern thrust. After patiently listening, Smith replied to the various points raised in the presentation. What Simpson heard both pleased and surprised him.

On the question of logistics for Montgomery's proposed movement along the northern axis, Smith assured Simpson both he and Eisenhower understood, and fully intended to give the 21st Army Group all necessary matériel support. "All that Eisenhower was concerned about," Simpson recorded, "was that Monty should go straight off to Berlin on a narrow front."

Sensing an understanding could be forged between SHAEF and Montgomery, Simpson reassured Smith while an "advance to Berlin might come later," for the moment the British field marshal had his sights exclusively on the Ruhr. "It was at once clear to me," Simpson wrote Smith two days later, "that you fully understand [Montgomery's] situation and were doing everything to help him." Significantly, the issue of Antwerp did not arise, suggestive that Smith, and by inference SHAEF, were not unduly troubled by Montgomery's relegation of the opening of the strategic port to the status of a secondary objective—after Dempsey's projected movement toward the Ruhr.

By now Smith had grown weary of Eisenhower's refusal to assert command. As he saw matters, the supreme commander's talent for dissimulation succeeded only in confusing Montgomery and confounding SHAEF's efforts to control subordinate American commanders. The threat loomed that SHAEF might sacrifice credibility. "The trouble with Ike," Smith observed wistfully, "instead of giving direct and clear orders, [he] dresses them up in polite language; and that is why our senior American commanders take advantage." Smith promised Simpson that Eisenhower had given him full authority to chastise Bradley and Patton for ignoring SHAEF directives.

On the question of command, Smith assured the British general he would argue in favor of Montgomery's movement toward the Ruhr even to the point of ignoring the "political implications" of placing Hodges under 21st Army Group. As Smith explained, Stimson recently informed SHAEF Roosevelt no longer would permit Americans to serve under British command. "Ike is quite prepared now to disobey this instruction and put Hodges...under Monty," Smith announced. "If it is the best way to get to the Ruhr, and thus win the war, the chips then fall as they will."[80]

For his part Smith had not made an about-face as Simpson concluded; he merely renewed his efforts to convince Eisenhower to seize the reins of command. Montgomery's plan offered, in Smith's opinion, the only means for maintaining the initiative before German defenses hardened. However unpalatable to senior American officers in the theater and to public opinion at home, Smith decided Montgomery's offensive deserved adequate manpower and matériel reserves, including command over 1st Army.

Smith knew Simpson enjoyed close relations with Brooke and Montgomery and the substance of their conversation would soon reach the ears of the two field marshals. Reflective of their mania for secrecy, Eisenhower and Smith never kept notes of their daily conference. Doubtlessly, the points raised by Smith in his talk with Simpson were discussed with Eisenhower. Despite his penchant for making sweeping, sometimes ill-considered statements, Smith never would have confided in Simpson had he not been convinced Eisenhower shared these same views.

Eisenhower's conversion was far from complete, as his Versailles policy statements soon illustrated. Too tidy a political axeman to allow the chips to fall anywhere, Eisenhower's instincts told him to defer making a decision. From a purely military standpoint Montgomery's plan had much to recommended it. From a political point of view and Eisenhower's desire to avoid intrusions into his sphere, Montgomery's offensive bode ill. Shifting American strength north would place a substantial portion of it under British command. Eisenhower knew this would provoke a storm of hostile public opinion, irritate his political bosses and Congress in Washington, and set off an acrimonious clash with Bradley and Patton. The one constant in Eisenhower's actions was his refusal to undertake any action that might jeopardize his popularity. Eisenhower preferred to engage in some calculated sophistry and incur the wrath of Brooke and Montgomery than to expose himself to damaging criticism.

Once again Eisenhower sought to give something to everyone. Taking pains to restate the northern thrust toward the Ruhr and Montgomery's efforts to open Antwerp continued to enjoy priority, Eisenhower nonetheless granted Bradley freedom to pursue his own designs. Eisenhower balked at placing Hodges under

Montgomery's operational command instead instructing 1st Army to communicate directly with 21st Army Group—presumably only in an emergency. While Patton would cease offensive operations until the logistical situation improved, Hodges received permission to continue operations toward Cologne and Bonn. When Bradley objected, offering an alternative plan for a full-scale offensive against the Ruhr on the 300-mile central front, Smith rejected the scheme on logistical grounds.[81] Although the supreme commander's announcements fell far short of Smith's promises to Simpson, de Guingand felt satisfied enough to wire his chief informing him the northern offensive received "100 per cent support."[82]

Given the timbre of the communication between SHAEF and Montgomery during September and Eisenhower's pronouncements at Versailles, the British commander concluded he had won the debate. By October 10 it became equally clear Eisenhower had no intention of implementing his decision. Instead of a bridgehead over the Rhine, Montgomery's MARKET GARDEN succeeded only in carving out a narrow and exposed salient. In the meantime, Antwerp remained closed while Patton actively pirated supplies intended for Hodges and continued his unauthorized advance. Montgomery correctly presumed Eisenhower, Bradley, and Smith knew of Patton's actions yet did nothing. The British Minister of Defense, James Grigg, placed the blame on SHAEF. "Ike has assured you that your thrust gets priority," he wrote Montgomery, "his staff ably supported by Gale are in practice disregarding his pledge." [83]

After Arnhem, Montgomery became more convinced than ever a ground commander was necessary. Once he decided on a particular course, Montgomery felt justified in bringing pressure to bear to win his point. His isolation at Tactical Headquarters and his frustration over Eisenhower's quiescence inevitably heightened the friction between Montgomery and SHAEF. On October 9 Smith telephoned Montgomery demanding to know when headquarters could expect the Scheldt to be cleared. Heated words followed. Montgomery reminded Smith the Ruhr and not Antwerp was the "main effort." As Montgomery pointed out, it was the Americans who needed Antwerp, not the British. "Purple with rage," Smith hurled the receiver to Morgan. "Here," Smith said, "you tell your countryman what to do." Morgan knew he was committing what amounted to professional suicide but calmly told the field marshal unless the port was opened his supplies would be cut.[84]

Instead of being grateful for Eisenhower's support, Montgomery renewed his campaign to concentrate effort for a northern offensive under a single command. Despite their clash over the phone the previous day, the field marshal persisted in thinking Smith could be won over to his point of view. Incapable of accepting blame for the failure of MARKET GARDEN and illustrating once again his obtuseness, Montgomery claimed in a letter to Smith that the Arnhem operation foundered because SHAEF refused to enforce cooperation between 21st and 12th Army groups. He included a memorandum, "Notes on Command in Western Europe," in which he outlined in unvarnished terms his critical assessment of the campaign. "Eisenhower's idea has always been for the *whole line* to go forward, to capture the Ruhr, *and* the Saar, *and* the Frankfurt area," he wrote, "line up the armies on the Rhine, and then decided what to do next...The Americans have outstripped their maintenance and as a result we have lost flexibility on the front as a whole." "We are now unlikely to get the Ruhr *or* the Saar *or* Frankfurt," he continued. "In fact," he opined, "we have 'mucked' the whole show and we have only ourselves to blame." Again raising the command question, he stated "all our troubles can be traced to the fact that there is no one commander in charge of the land battle. The supreme commander runs it himself from SHAEF by means of long telegrams. SHAEF is not an operational headquarters and never can be."[85]

Smith naturally fumed when he read Montgomery's latest homily, but he also saw an opportunity. He recognized Montgomery finally exceeded his bounds. Five days earlier Montgomery had attended a conference at Versailles where Ramsay inveighed against him for the failure to open Antwerp, a view endorsed by Brooke. Montgomery found himself isolated, even if he failed to realize it. But Smith knew Eisenhower's stock also had fallen throughout September. He had accepted the Arnhem operation, despite its many attendant risks, which delayed the opening of Antwerp. The supreme commander's precatory approach to Montgomery and Bradley allowed them to assign their own operational priorities. Marshall, touring the theater, made no effort to disguise his unhappiness with the strategic situation, particularly Antwerp. With the approaches to the Belgian port still in German hands, Marshall and Brooke considered issuing a "flat order" to open Antwerp. Spurred by the Smith-Montgomery wrangle over the phone, Eisenhower finally abandoned his coaxing and permitted Smith to dispatch a directive to 21st Army Group that clearly designated Antwerp as the top priority in the theater.[86] These contentious military disputes exacted a heavy toll on Eisenhower, who characteristically accepted his own share of the blame for Allied setbacks. Knowing Eisenhower's mood, Smith spared no time in showing him Montgomery's latest denunciatory exposition. At long last Eisenhower's severely tested patience melted away. A crisis had been reached.

Realizing Eisenhower bore little risk in forcing a showdown with Montgomery, Smith wanted to see the fractious field marshal humbled. He also appreciated the importance of moving with dispatch before Eisenhower's resolve evaporated. With Marshall slated to leave France the next day, Smith pushed hard. He calculated Eisenhower would not prevaricate with Marshall standing over his shoulder.

Finally bending to Smith's prodding, Eisenhower asked Whiteley to draft a diplomatically worded reprimand of Montgomery which the SHAEF chief of staff edited. The communication stated "in the frankest possible way," Antwerp remained "the real issue at hand," not the question of command. If Montgomery felt unhappy with the state of affairs, he could "refer the matter to higher authority for any action they may choose to take, however drastic."[87] When he saw the letter, Eisenhower thought it too strongly worded. Smith disagreed, as did Marshall, who reviewed the letter that night at Eisenhower's headquarters. Eisenhower could do nothing but concur. The letter, hand-carried to Montgomery, went out the next day, October 13.

The letter had its desired effect. Montgomery replied that "you will hear no more on the subject of command from me."[88] Although Montgomery would resuscitate the command question, Eisenhower had finally been galvanized into action. In a very real sense Eisenhower's October letters represent the beginning of his assertion of supreme command.

On November 2, satisfied his version of unity of command had been assured, Eisenhower set starting dates for 12th and 21st Army groups to open operations designed to destroy German forces west of the Rhine. Meanwhile, Devers' 6th Army Group (7th U.S. Army and 1st French Army), after having linked with Patton at Dijon on September 15, attacked toward Alsace-Lorraine. Shortly thereafter, Lieutenant General William Simpson's 9th U.S. Army advanced to occupy a position between Montgomery's army group and U.S.1st Army. The ambitious objectives indicated that despite mounting German resistance SHAEF maintained its optimism.[89]

Neither Montgomery nor Brooke was so sanguine. To them, operations drifted along without direction—a view shared by Bradley, Hodges, and Patton. The senior British officers decided to "counter the pernicious American strategy of attacking all along the line."[90] As Montgomery complained to his chief, Eisenhower "has never commanded anything before in his whole career. Now, for the first time, he has elected to take direct command of very large-scale operations and he does not know how to do it."[91] Brooke confided in his diary on November 27 "Ike is incapable of running a land battle and it is all dependent on how well Monty can handle him."[92]

On November 30 Montgomery requested a conference to reopen the question of theater strategy and command authority. He began his letter by saying, "We have...failed, and we have suffered a strategic reverse." The field marshal repeated Brooke's point the Allies had to get away from the doctrine of attacking "everywhere and concentrate on a single thrust." Fearing Eisenhower would be supported by the anti-Montgomery camarilla, he suggested "that we want no one else at the meeting, except Chiefs of Staff, who must not speak."[93]

The message provoked an angry response from SHAEF. Not only was Eisenhower irritated by Montgomery's renewed assault upon his command and strategic views, he resented the insult to Smith. For once Eisenhower did not mince words. "Bedell is my Chief of Staff because I trust him and respect his judgment," he said in his December 1 reply. "I will not by any means insult him that he should remain mute at any conference he and I both attend."[94]

On December 7 the conference took place at Maastricht. The disagreement took on the familiar form of the September debate. Montgomery's intense advocacy of a single offensive made no impact upon Eisenhower. Whereas previously Eisenhower met Montgomery alone or, as at the Brussels conference, with Tedder, the Maastrict meeting was attended by Bradley, Smith, and the deputy supreme commander. In other words, the three most-vocal opponents of the narrow front and men with the greatest influence on Eisenhower were in attendance. Montgomery, an outsider in an American headquarters, felt Eisenhower had "obviously been 'got at' by the three officers." "The result [of the conference]," he related to Grigg, "was a complete failure, and he [Eisenhower] went back on all the points he had agreed to when alone with me." "I personally regard the whole thing," he related to Brooke, "as quite dreadful."[95]

The Maastricht conference failed to clear the air between SHAEF and Montgomery, yet there could be no doubt the supreme commander meant to advance on a broad front to the Rhine, clearing the Germans west of the river barrier.[96] Incoming American reinforcements would go to the northernmost armies (Simpson's 9th and Hodges's 1st) but this provided little consolation to the British. It was clear the British had lost the strategic debate. More importantly, it became evident the British now occupied the political and military position Churchill had long feared. The preponderance of military forces in the theater were American. Of the fifty-five Allied divisions under Eisenhower, twenty-eight were American compared to eighteen British and Canadian divisions. Thereafter the British would play the role of "junior partner" in the alliance.

In the final analysis there was no chance Eisenhower would have stopped Patton, relegated Bradley to essentially an administrative role, or put Hodges under a British commander. Although he loudly and repeatedly claimed to have made decisions solely on military grounds, Eisenhower's broad-front strategy had as much to do with politics as it did with logistical considerations and military doctrine. No matter how brilliant the narrow-front strategy, Eisenhower could never have permitted the British the glory of spearheading the advance. Additionally, American divisions piled up in the theater. Eisenhower needed the broad front to deploy them. Even before the August 23 meeting, the supreme commander informed Montgomery the need to place the American divisions in line had "an importance second only to the destruction of the remaining enemy forces on our front."[97] Public opinion in the United States, Roosevelt, and Congress would not have allowed a British general to lead the final battle in Europe, nor would Marshall. Had Bradley and Patton held the northern front, Eisenhower's views might have been different. In any case there was no telling Marshall the enormous effort made to raise and train the American armies was unnecessary. All things considered, Eisenhower could not make decisions without weighing all the political ramifications—something Montgomery proved incapable of understanding.[98]

From a strictly military point of view Eisenhower's insistence on the broad front was in perfect accord with American doctrine and his own basic conservatism. To Eisenhower the greatest military quality lay in the ability "to weigh calmly the factors involved in a problem and so reach a rock-like decision."[99] The broad front clearly constituted one such decision. The German collapse in France presented SHAEF with a series of opportunities, yet Eisenhower's commitment to the single approach was so complete he adhered to it exclusively, even to the point of sacrificing strategic flexibility. Despite the emphasis on the principles of the objective and offensive in American doctrine, Eisenhower seemed less intent upon destroying the German armies than on seizing territory. Eisenhower, tied to doctrine and past attitudes, proved incapable of adjusting to new circumstances.

"WHAT HAS THE SUPREME COMMAND AMOUNTED TO?"

The command and staff structures created for OVERLORD remained essentially unaltered for the duration of the war. When Eisenhower assumed active command on September 1, he commanded two army groups of four armies, the naval units attached to the theater, and the Allied tactical and strategic air forces. Two months later he commanded seven armies (four American), the Allied airborne army, the tactical air forces and, through Tedder as coordinating link, first call on the strategic air forces.[100] In addition to his responsibilities for an active theater of operations stretching from the Netherlands to the Mediterranean, Eisenhower commanded American ground, support, and air forces in the United Kingdom. The Supreme Headquarters served as the conduit through which everything was channeled. Aside from the supreme commander, nobody handled such a broad range of problems and burdensome responsibilities as Bedell Smith.

Because Eisenhower decided to abandon his role as chairman of the board in favor of active command, Smith found himself thrust into the front rank of strategic decisionmakers. As chief of staff he exerted influence in the highest councils of command and increasingly played a direct role in the day-to-day running of operations. Critics of Eisenhower wondered if he had not surrendered the command function to his power-hungry chief of staff. While concentrating upon his leadership functions, Eisenhower delegated to Smith near-total supervision over the time-consuming and frustrating political and logistical problems. Finally, Smith oversaw the workings of the enormous headquarters.

The first order of business involved the transfer of SHAEF to the continent. Anxious to have a functioning headquarters in France, Smith hurried the establishment of SHAEF-Forward at Granville. Immediately after the headquarters became operational on September 1, it became obvious Smith made a serious blunder. On September 5 the U.S. 9th Army was activated. Ten days later Devers's army group was amalgamated into SHAEF. Meanwhile, the Allied armies advanced into the Netherlands and closed on the German frontier. Guilty of too-strict attention to the pre-D-Day plan, Smith's decision to locate the headquarters in Normandy placed SHAEF out of contact with the operational commands. During the Arnhem fighting, Leigh-Mallory frantically called Montgomery's headquarters to receive information on the progress of the battle. Not only inaccessible, Granville still lacked adequate communications.[101] "We were sort of silent," remembered Betts of SHAEF's short tenure in Normandy. Even Smith admitted the communications were "atrocious; the worst I have had so far in any of our headquarters setups."[102]

As the advance reached its climax during September, Smith was burdened with the movement of the headquarters to the Trianon Palace Hotel in Versailles. Fearing the attractions of Paris would prove too strong, Eisenhower and Smith decided not to center the headquarters in the capital. Without permission, Lee set up his Communication Zone headquarters in Paris—requisitioning 655 choice hotels and buildings.[103] At a time when the shortages of transportation were most acutely felt, two huge headquarters completed their moves to Paris and Versailles. By the time SHAEF-Main became fully operational on September 26, Eisenhower opened another headquarters at Rheims. Smith coordinated the activities of a large forward headquarters, an expanding SHAEF-Main in Versailles, and a larger rear echelon in London. The disorders in the headquarters throughout September contributed to the inability of Eisenhower to assert his authority.[104]

Eisenhower enjoyed the reputation as champion of inter-Allied cooperation and facilitator of coordinated effort. Smith handled the responsibilities of working behind the scenes, acting as hatchet-man for the supreme commander.

Because Eisenhower's relations with Ramsay, Leigh-Mallory, and Montgomery were conducted on a formal basis, Bedell handled most of the personal communications. In the Mediterranean Eisenhower and Smith had shared intimate relationships with Cunningham, Tedder, and Alexander. In Europe their relationship was impersonal with Ramsay, strained with Leigh-Mallory, and hostile with Montgomery. This made cooperation far more difficult to achieve. At the end of September the naval and air commands were reorganized, but Smith continued in his difficult capacity as intermediary between SHAEF and Montgomery.[105] Additionally, Smith's responsibilities included coordinating the activities of the American army groups, and as chief of staff for ETOUSA, he oversaw Lee's command. Finally, he acted as connecting link between SHAEF and the combined chiefs.

By far the most taxing problem involved relations with Montgomery. Smith was all too well aware of Montgomery's "intransigent attitude and behind the scenes conniving to get his way with regards to military operations, to enhance his own prestige and to obtain a major measure of command."[106] The rift widened between Montgomery and Smith. Owing to his growing personal animosity toward the ascetic Montgomery, Smith took every opportunity to discredit the narrow-front strategy. At the same time he grew increasingly impatient with Eisenhower's refusal to put Montgomery in his place. Remembering Marshall initially dispatched him to Europe to stiffen Eisenhower against the British, Smith cajoled the supreme commander into insisting upon strict adherence to the principle of unity of command and the guidelines of the strategic plan. He felt Eisenhower lacked the moral courage and "firmness of will" to handle Montgomery.[107] Throughout September, Eisenhower's refusal to stand up to Montgomery produced uncertainty. Only in a broad sense did Eisenhower direct operations. The detailed work of tactical command and the overall control of the staff and logistics Eisenhower delegated to his principal subordinates—Montgomery, Bradley, Devers, Smith, and Lee. As Bradley remarked, "what [has] the Supreme Command amounted to?"[108]

On strategic questions Eisenhower and Smith rarely disagreed. The Arnhem operation was an exception. Smith knew the Airborne Army was burning a hole in SHAEF's pocket. No less than nine airborne drops had been planned and abandoned during the advance through France. Each time armor would take the objective before the drop could be staged. This required substantial airlift capacity be withheld for a week to ten days in anticipation of each operation. This added to the critical shortage of transportation. From Washington, Marshall demanded the airborne forces be employed. Recognizing the need to maintain the airborne as SHAEF's only strategic reserve, Smith thought the Arnhem plan contained many flaws. Smith and his intelligence chief, Strong, predicted that MARKET GARDEN would fail.[109]

On September 9 Montgomery asked for a responsible staff officer to come forward "to explain things to him."[110] Three days later, Smith flew to Brussels. His immediate task involved convincing Montgomery to launch the operation on September 17 as planned. As an incentive he offered to provide an additional 1,000 tons of supplies a day.[111] Taking advantage of the situation, he laid out the argument against the Arnhem drop. Conventional intelligence, ULTRA, and Dutch resistance sources all confirmed segments of two German panzer divisions occupied the environs of the city. Smith urged Montgomery to abandon Arnhem or add another division to the initial landing. The field marshal, whose real aim involved more than securing the Rhine bridgehead at Arnhem, ridiculed the idea. As Smith recalled, he "waved my objections airily aside."[112] While failing to change Montgomery's mind, the conference reduced the tensions between the British commander and the SHAEF chief of staff. On a personal level, Montgomery appreciated Smith's efforts to provide matériel support for his effort to breach the Rhine.[113]

The disagreements over the advance against Germany and the command structure were not the only headaches confronting the headquarters. The failure of MARKET GARDEN ended the bright hopes of establishing a bridgehead across the Rhine before winter. The Allies had a preponderance of manpower, guns and armor, and airpower on the western front by October 1, but after the lightning drives through France the logistical supplies gave out. The plan held that the command structure would be altered at an undetermined time after the breakout from Normandy. According to the prelanding schedule, Lee's Communication Zone (Com Z) was to supply a twelve-division offensive over the Seine on D +120. Instead, by September 30 (D +116), the headquarters had to support fifty-four divisions 180 miles beyond the Seine. The advance multiplied the logistical problems, and despite frantic efforts to improvise there simply was no time to implement the necessary adjustments to the enormous logistical machine.[114]

The headquarter's failure to fashion an adequate command and staff structure for supply represents the gravest shortcoming of the planning phase and the preinvasion period. During the Normandy fighting SHAEF belatedly tackled the question of reorganizing the logistical side of the ETO command. Several influential officers thought the Service of Supply apparatus needed restructuring before its transfer to the continent. Hughes, the leading spokesman for the reformers, hoped Eisenhower would "straighten out" the logistics chain of command by circulating a memorandum "telling people to stick to their knitting." Four weeks later, Hughes commented that the reorganization created a "lot of fuss and no change."[115]

The interminable wrangling angered Eisenhower. When Hughes pressed him to push the reorganization on Smith, the supreme commander lost his temper. "The man is crazy," Hughes wrote of Eisenhower. "He won't issue orders that stick. He will pound on the desk and shout." Trying to avoid trouble with Somervell, Eisenhower delegated responsibility to Smith. In an effort to reassure Hughes, Eisenhower admitted "that in North Africa Beadle [sic] was young, ambitious, an empire builder. Now he is a Lt. General [and is] willing to do his job." Not convinced Smith would remain bound within the limits of his authority, Hughes, fed up with carrying the struggle for Lee, gave up on the idea of reorganizing Com Z. "All goes back to Beadle," he chronicled in his diary.[116]

Smith was no logistician, yet he came to make major supply decisions. In the Mediterranean, AFHQ's control over logistics—decisions regarding which forces would receive manpower and matériel—granted Eisenhower leverage over events. In Europe, Smith understood success would depend upon SHAEF's ability to send forward troops and equipment at a higher rate than did the Germans. In referring to the Mediterranean, where a relatively small staff managed on the whole a static environment, Smith failed to anticipate the tremendous problems inherent in conducting mobile warfare on a huge scale.

Under the existing structure, Lee possessed virtual independent control over logistics. In addition to commanding Com Z, Lee served as deputy commander of ETO. Because Smith insisted ETO possess no staff, Lee used his Com Z headquarters in a double role. These overlapping arrangements satisfied neither Eisenhower nor Smith, but neither general evidenced any willingness to hammer out a clear-cut mechanism to control supply.[117]

To remedy the situation Smith tried to exert control by redesignating the axes of command. For him, the problem rested not in the structure but in the lack of centralization. In Smith's view the Mediterranean setup offered the ideal model. Gale managed American and British supply which permitted the headquarters to influence all major actions in the theater. In Europe SHAEF merely coordinated the respective American and British supply groups. On the American side, Eisenhower commanded the theater but granted Lee virtually an autonomous role. When the system ran into trouble, Smith shifted the blame undeservedly to Lee.[118]

Smith calculatedly used logistics as a means of directing operations at the front. Recognizing Patton's "ardor for glory," and fearing he "might stick his neck out too far in the wrong direction," Smith limited 3d Army's supplies.[119] At the same time, enough gasoline found its way to Patton to enable him to reach Metz in late August. When SHAEF wanted to build a fire under Montgomery in Belgium, Smith used logistics as a lever. He never saw the problem from the logisticians' point of view nor would he admit the system itself contained flaws. "The system we had was workable," he later remarked. "No question that with a reshuffling of personnel it would have been perfect."[120]

What Smith meant by a reshuffling of personnel was the removal of Lee and his semiautonomous Base Section and Service chiefs. Perhaps the most universally disliked officer in Europe, Lee infuriated Eisenhower and Smith when he presented SHAEF with a *fait accompli* by moving his Com Z headquarters into Paris. Eisenhower restrained himself because Lee enjoyed the support of Marshall and Somervell. Running the risk of provoking War Department displeasure, on three separate occasions Smith laid the groundwork for Eisenhower to fire Lee. Each time Eisenhower backed down. "We couldn't relieve him over a bunch of little things," Smith related. "So we kept him on...One of the crosses we had to bear."[121]

In an effort to end Lee's special status, Eisenhower gradually reduced his duties as deputy theater commander. The supply problem of late August and September presented Smith with an opportunity to seize a greater measure of control over logistics. As SHAEF chief of staff, Smith utilized the American side of the headquarters as an ETO staff.[122] Eisenhower refused to create another staff level, and increasingly Smith used his staff to administer the flow of replacements and matériel. To further cement his superintendence of support functions, Smith convinced Eisenhower to appoint Major General Royal Lord as Lee's chief of staff. A Smith protégé, Lord's official title was Deputy Chief of Staff of ETOUSA. As such, he reported directly to Smith. Lord issued directives to Lee in Smith's name then carried them out in Lee's.[123] As Smith remembered, "I was chief of staff in the theater. I sometimes had to make that clear to the boys at Com Z."[124]

The shortages in ammunition and gasoline in August were followed by manpower deficiencies in December. Once again Smith blamed Lee. Since Lee controlled only those matters Smith deigned not to touch, it is difficult to hold Com Z responsible. In each case the War Department dispatched delegations to investigate these problems. Smith bitterly resented outsiders delving into his headquarters. In the first instance he made an example of Major General Henry Aurand who was sent packing when the War Department logistician made the mistake of speaking his mind.[125] In the second case Smith ushered another major general, Leroy Lutes, forward to survey the situation in the operational commands. A man of considerable weight in the War Department, Lutes received the red-carpet treatment.[126] In fact, Smith wanted to maneuver Lutes into Lee's position.[127]

The seriousness of the manpower shortage prompted Marshall to dispatch Lieutenant General Ben Lear to Europe to replace Lee as deputy commander. Marshall's rival in 1939 for the chief of staff's job, Lear was a highly respected officer. Smith used the Lear appointment to his own advantage, indoctrinating Lear into the headquarters.[128] Rather overwhelmed by Smith and the political infighting in ETO and troubled with a prostate ailment, Lear presented no real difficulties.[129] As Smith pointed out, Lear "helped to outrank Lee."[130] To guarantee Lear would not interfere with Smith's control of the headquarters, Brigadier General Charles Bonesteel was appointed head of the General Inspectorate Section, ETO.[131] As Smith's "eyes and ears" in Lear's office, Bonesteel kept the chief of staff appraised of all the inner workings in ETO. Aggressive, ambitious, and preoccupied by the desire to avoid criticism and to preserve his position of dominance, Smith successfully beat back any challenges to diminish his place in the command hierarchy he painstakingly won.

On the lighter side, Smith catered to Marshall's continued demand to get the Army Band more publicity. Throughout the war, Marshall demonstrated an obsession to elevate the Army Band over the more famous Marine Corps Band. Once again, he threatened to "send a Marine officer over" to get the job done. This gibe was calculated to get Smith's goat. Smith's rather curt reply pointed out it seemed "hard to interest the press in a band" with the Allied armies advancing on the German frontier.[132] At one point Smith called Glen Miller, the famous orchestra leader, into his office and insisted he take over direction of the Army Band. When Miller refused, Smith reacted violently and threw the musician out. The interview lasted three minutes.[133] In the end, Smith failed Marshall as the Marine Band preserved its position.

Many influential politicians also made their appearance at headquarters. Alarmed by the pro-Communist elements within the French Forces of the Interior, SHAEF wanted to "soft pedal" the contribution of the Resistance, instead emphasizing the role played by the 1st French Army in the liberation. Unsure how to implement the policy, Devers decided to dispatch Colonel Henry Cabot Lodge, late of the U.S. Senate, to Versailles. Knowing Smith would take a dim view of his using a powerful politician as an emissary, Devers needed a personal contact. He called in Vittrup from his G-3 section. "How well do you know Beetle Smith?" he asked. When the staff officer replied that he had served under Smith in the Infantry School and the JCS/CCS Chiefs of Staff Secretariat, Devers ordered Vittrup to accompany Lodge to SHAEF. Arriving at headquarters, Smith, glad to see his old subordinate, came out to greet Vittrup. At this point Lodge stepped between the two men and introduced himself. Smith glowered at Lodge and loudly berated him for his discourteousness. Entirely taken aback, the stunned senator saluted and stood aside while Smith took Vittrup into his office for a private chat.[134] Events such as this illustrate Smith had no patience with civilians who intruded into his domain, even if they were proud Boston patricians in uniform.

THE END OF JOAN OF ARC

The area that Eisenhower most willingly surrendered authority to Smith was responsibility for handling sensitive political aspects of military actions and coordinating them with Washington, London, the French, Soviets, and the lesser allies. Lacking either affirmative or consistent political guidance from Roosevelt or the State Department, Eisenhower simply avoided making political decisions. After the storm of protest produced by his management of the Darlan affair—his first critical decision as a supreme commander—the badly shaken Eisenhower determined never again to expose himself to criticisms of a political nature, especially where the French were concerned. On difficult questions that required a strong and courageous stand, Eisenhower evaded taking action. He waited upon events, telling all parties what they wanted to hear to preserve the surface tranquility. In an effort to deflect blame from himself, Eisenhower empowered Smith to undertake high-level diplomatic missions on his behalf.

The breakout from Normandy found SHAEF ill prepared for the civil administrative problems posed by the liberation of France and the occupation of Germany.[135] June produced a number of sharp clashes that threatened to poison the working relationship between Smith and de Gaulle. On the eve of the invasion de Gaulle refused to make a D-Day announcement because he objected to a paragraph in Eisenhower's "canned statement." As Smith reported, "the French thing was in a hell of a mess." Smith thought SHAEF should not beg de Gaulle.[136] If he balked at making an announcement, SHAEF should proceed with their radio transmissions. De Gaulle would merely injure himself politically. McClure wondered if SHAEF could "ruin de Gaulle so he can't get back to France." "As far as I'm concerned," Smith snapped, "[I] would be delighted." Asked if he thought de Gaulle was more intent upon "fighting the president or the Germans," Smith replied, "he is fighting anybody not for de Gaulle. I have nothing but contempt for him."[137] Passions soon cooled, and when Eisenhower threatened to follow Smith's advice, de Gaulle relented.

No sooner had this little storm subsided than another confrontation brewed over civil affairs policy for liberated France. Furious that SHAEF issued counterfeit invasion currency without his compliance, de Gaulle refused to sign any civil affairs agreements until the French Committee on National Liberation received formal recognition. Since de Gaulle never trusted Murphy, who served as American political officer at SHAEF, Smith carried out the tedious discussions. Like de Gaulle, Smith saw the problem as essentially political and blamed the State Department for the impasse. For SHAEF the immediate objective was the integration of the French into the military command structure. Because Koenig proved amenable to the SHAEF point of view, Smith pushed for his elevation to the status of an Allied commander.[138]

Working closely with Koenig, Smith won acceptance of the invasion francs. By July 4 Koenig took his position as commander-in-chief of the French Forces of the Interior. French liaison officers joined the staffs of the Anglo-American commands while others served in the SHAEF Civil Affairs Division. Koenig's support proved invaluable as the French relieved SHAEF of many civil affairs responsibilities. Hoping to divest himself of these duties, Smith charged Morgan with much of the responsibility for conducting liaison with the French.[139]

With the military question largely resolved, attention focused on achieving a high-level political settlement. Against Smith's advice, de Gaulle flew to France on August 18, intent upon forming a provisional government.[140] A crisis was reached when General Jacques LeClerc made it clear he would follow de Gaulle's directive and advance on Paris, whatever SHAEF's orders, despite Koenig's assurances French forces under Eisenhower would obey the supreme commander. LeClerc's entry into Paris on August 25 altered the situation. This forced the Allied governments to authorize SHAEF to deal with the FCNL as the de facto authority in France.[141] Moving quickly, Smith negotiated an agreement that settled jurisdictional, currency, and property questions in addition to granting to the FCNL administrative authority over liberated areas in France. Thereafter France would be divided into two areas: the forward zone under SHAEF and the zone of the interior under the FCNL.[142]

The settlement, signed on August 25, accorded nicely with Smith's intentions. His primary concern remained the speedy transfer of civil administration to French authorities in the hope Washington would finally accept de Gaulle as the legitimate leader of France. As eager to surrender political responsibilities as de Gaulle was to exercise them, Smith looked forward to a time when he could concentrate his energies on purely military matters. De Gaulle's unilateral formation of a provisional government on August 30 did not in the least distress Smith. By the middle of September it became clear to everyone, including such bitter opponents of the FCNL as Secretary of State Hull, de Gaulle commanded the support of the bulk of the French population. Nevertheless Roosevelt refused to alter his policy.[143]

Throughout August and September Smith became deeply involved with civil affairs. The French situation commanded most of his attention. Rapidly losing patience with Washington, Smith worked behind the scenes to move toward a political settlement. Not only did he want to relinquish the civil affairs burden, he hoped to shift the responsibility of feeding and supplying France during the winter to de Gaulle. Better the provisional government be blamed for the lack of food, coal, and transportation, he reasoned, than SHAEF.[144]

On October 20 Smith met with Jefferson Caffrey, the American representative to de Gaulle. After two months of negotiating they reached a final accord on the outstanding question of the respective responsibilities of SHAEF and the Zone of the Interior. Although relations with de Gaulle still could be explosive, Smith believed the French general had overcome his "Joan of Arc complex." In his opinion, the recognition of the provisional government could no longer be delayed. Smith thought the planned October 23 announcement of the creation of the Zone of the Interior offered an ideal opportunity for the Allied governments to officially recognize de Gaulle. Immediately following their meeting both men wrote letters to Washington—Caffrey to Hull and Smith to the Joint Chiefs. These communications had their desired impact. Roosevelt at long last agreed to recognize de Gaulle, and the announcement was made on October 23 as Smith requested.[145]

Smith could take a great deal of personal satisfaction from the recognition of the French provisional government. Through official channels and behind-the-scenes maneuvering, he had worked toward that end since North Africa. Never in awe of the political heads, if convinced of the correctness of his views, he defended them against Roosevelt or Churchill as doggedly as he would have against one of his subordinates. In his estimation military expediency demanded a French government. As the FCNL offered the only viable option, Smith treated de Gaulle and Koenig as the legitimate heads of the French state and army, despite Roosevelt's injunctions to the contrary. As a result, de Gaulle trusted Smith as he did no other American, civilian or military. Although their relationship never became friendly, it was based on mutual respect. In the end, Washington's acceptance of de Gaulle, though long delayed, vindicated Smith's advocacy of the policy and represented a crowning triumph in his two-year tenure as *de facto* American ambassador to the FCNL.

The recognition of the French government did not end Smith's civil affairs obligations. With the battle of Germany looming, new problems surfaced—the execution of Allied policy in occupied Germany, military liaison with the Soviets, and relief for the Dutch. SHAEF made little headway in defining policy for the occupation of Germany. The War Department gave Smith little guidance on Germany, primarily because they received mixed signals from the White House and the State Department. When his headquarters was accused by the War Department of providing "vacillating leadership" on the question of military government for Germany, Smith confessed being "non-committal." He purposely stalled, hoping Marshall would forward McCloy for the job.[146]

While German policy added new complications, the October 23 recognition of de Gaulle did remove his most troublesome burden. Thereafter he could work through formal channels. Although Smith's military roles were many, none proved more significant than his contributions as Eisenhower's "foreign minister."

THE AUTUMNAL STALEMATE

Two overriding factors contributed to the Allied inability to end the war in 1944. First, SHAEF's failure to foresee and prepare for a rapid advance beyond the French frontier assured the Allied armies they would not have the means to crush the Wehrmacht. Second, and more damning, the Allied armies suffered from cautious generalship. Senior American officers might ridicule Montgomery for his "stickiness" and obsession with "tidying his maintenance," but the field marshal understood the need for strategic boldness and tight control over logistics. While Eisenhower rejected the narrow-front strategy and MARKET GARDEN fell short of its objective, a quality of aggressiveness existed in Montgomery's thinking that was lacking in his many detractors. The inability of the Allied forces to complete the destruction of the German forces in the Falaise pocket or close the Scheldt forelands permitted them to fight another day. Around the nucleus of escaped headquarters and skeleton units, new armies resumed the defense along the frontiers, in Lorraine, and in the Netherlands with startling effect.

The slashing advances of August and September gave way to the static slugging matches of November and December. The battles along the Franco-German frontier summoned up memories of the set-piece attacks of World War I—with correspondingly high casualty figures. Manpower shortages partially explain the failure of the broad-front approach. Montgomery's delay in opening Antwerp, his cannibalization of Anglo-Canadian divisions, and the relative inactivity of 21st Army Group after Arnhem-Antwerp all testify to British manpower deficiencies. While not as hard-pressed, American divisions could not replace their losses. No reserve could be created nor exhausted divisions rested and refitted without either abandoning the broad front or risking the paper-thin Ardennes sector. Gambling the Germans would not inflict a "nasty little Kasserine" on his "fearfully stretched" forces in the Ardennes, Eisenhower allowed Bradley and Devers to fritter away their offensive power at Aachen and the Huertgen Forest, at Metz, and in Lorraine and Alsace.[147] SHAEF possessed neither the strength to win the campaign with the broad-front strategy nor the reserves to abandon it. Instead of the path to victory, Eisenhower's broad front ended in a strategic *cul-de-sac*.

A military critic must not assess a commander's decisions as if they are a sum of arithmetic. The campaign in France was brought to a successful conclusion, more than fulfilling the requirements set down in the OVERLORD plan. Nothing more could be asked of a coalition general. Similarly, it is ahistorical to ascribe the conditions of a bipolar Europe to military decisions made in 1944. At that point in the war nobody, including Churchill, possessed a prescient view of the shape of the postwar map of Europe.[148] Certainly Eisenhower can not be faulted for not being a prophet.

Logistics, the coming of winter, American public opinion, and the effects a military setback might have had on the alliance all weighed heavily on Eisenhower's mind. More alive to the risks than the possibilities afforded by the fluid advance of September, Eisenhower's actions were guided by the desire to guard against suffering a catastrophe in France. In the end, one immutable fact remains: Eisenhower's refusal to take risks sacrificed a brilliant opportunity to bring the war to a speedier conclusion on terms more favorable to the western democracies.

The Battle of the Bulge,
December 1944–January 1945

The November-December stalemate did not unduly dismay the American commanders. They remained optimistic that the battles of the frontiers would wear the enemy down. After all, Leavenworth doctrine taught stationary battles of attrition were necessary preconditions for the decisive envelopment stage to follow. In Normandy the Allies fought a set-piece positional battle of wastage until the breakthrough opened up the mobile phase of the campaign. Now, on the frontiers, American officers took heart that their aggressiveness would not be curbed by the hesitant Montgomery. Confusing mounting casualty figures for aggressive leadership, senior American commanders congratulated themselves that operations proceeded according to plan. They could not go far wrong if they followed the Leavenworth book.

Eisenhower's broad-front strategy would have been entirely appropriate had the Allies possessed the overwhelming manpower and matériel superiority his approach demanded. As the events of November demonstrated, the ninety-division gamble had gone terribly wrong. The Wehrmacht, through a "truly colossal effort" organized or reconstituted at least five panzer and five parachute divisions by the middle of November. These formations formed a new strategic reserve SHAEF G-2 predicted would be used in "a final showdown before the winter."[1] German actions mattered little since American field commanders believed that as long as they attacked all along the line, they retained the strategic initiative. The fact SHAEF possessed no real reserves and the manpower pipeline was dry alarmed only the pessimists.

The supreme commander faced a dilemma. The "badly stretched condition" of his armies caused him "constant concern," but he chose to do nothing.[2] As Eisenhower saw matters, his range of options was limited. He could not bolster

Alfred D. Chandler, ed., *The Papers of Dwight D. Eisenhower: The War Years*, vol. 5 (Baltimore: Johns Hopkins University Press, 1970), p. 59.

the weak Ardennes without sacrificing the broad front. Talk of going on the defensive was anathema to any American commander. Seeing no other way out of the stalemate, Eisenhower decided to continue pounding away. Reluctant as ever to take risks, Eisenhower gambled the Germans would not hit him where he was most vulnerable—the Ardennes.

The Germans did precisely that. Cautious generals often project their own traits upon their adversaries. Eisenhower knew his opposite number, von Rundstedt, had a reputation for operational conservatism. However, Hitler, not von Rundstedt, now acted as German supreme commander. Hitler and his field commanders and staff officers rarely agreed on operational questions, particularly after the failures in Russia. On the proposed Ardennes offensive (WACHT AM RHEIN), few generals raised dissenting opinions. The Führer relied upon his intuition; the professional officer corps drew their inspiration from German doctrine and Clausewitz. "When the disproportion of power is so great," the Prussian theorist wrote in *On War*, "that no limitation of our object can ensure us safety from catastrophe...then the tension of forces will, or should, be concentrated on one desperate blow." A general who "is hard pressed, expecting little help from things which promise none," Clausewitz posited, "will place his whole and last trust in the moral superiority which despair always gives the brave."[3] Whatever historical examples Clausewitz had in mind when he penned these lines, they apply equally well to German thinking in autumn 1944. Those officers privy to the plan saw little prospect of another sickle-cut through the Ardennes as in 1940. Better an "honorable downfall," they reasoned, than a slow, grinding constriction at the hands of the converging Allied armies.

Presented with a textbook opportunity to launch their "desperate blow" into a vulnerable front, three German armies opened their final gambit to reverse the strategic situation in the West. The Battle of the Bulge was the Mortain counteroffensive writ large, but this time SHAEF did not enjoy the luxury of advance warning by ULTRA. Having achieved both concentration and surprise, the Germans penetrated the thinly held front in their own narrow front variant.

Eisenhower and Smith maintained after the war they immediately recognized the German attack proffered an opportunity to destroy in detail the remaining offensive capacity of the German armies in the West. During the crisis Eisenhower resolutely seized the mantle of leadership. Gone was the wavering, uncertain Eisenhower of the advance through France. Confronted with hard operational and command questions—to pin the shoulders of the German penetration and canalize their attacks while holding St. Vith and Bastogne; to give Montgomery command over Hodges and Simpson's armies north of the

Bulge; and to eliminate the salient at the waist and not the base—Eisenhower did not tarry in making tough and unpopular decisions.

His many critics marveled at the supreme commander's apparent transformation. An enigma to both his contemporaries and historians, Eisenhower's behind-the-scenes style of leadership depended upon compromise and multiple advocacy for any action undertaken. To observers it looked like he was afflicted with indecision. This view contrasted sharply with the decisive commander of the Bulge.

Eisenhower did not abandon his subtle style of leadership. After making the broad operational decisions, he left Montgomery, Bradley, and Patton to fight the battle. Nor did he alter his basic strategic conservatism. Just as he had beaten the Germans in France, Eisenhower defeated them in the Ardennes through a deliberately cautious approach. There was, however, one important difference. After the elimination of the Bulge, there could no longer be any doubt of SHAEF's ability to command the Allied armies.

THE GERMAN ARDENNES OFFENSIVE

With his October 28 directive Eisenhower set into motion a general offensive along a front two hundred miles long (from Arnhem to Metz). The American 1st and 9th Armies advanced from Aachen, which had fallen to Hodges on October 21, through the Eifel towards the Rhine at Cologne and Bonn. Although this thrust enjoyed first call on supplies, Patton received permission from Bradley to renew his drive into the Saar "when logistics permit." The 3d Army commander then repeated his old tactic and became so involved in the fighting around Metz during the first weeks of November that Bradley felt compelled to support him. This deprived the primary effort north of the Ardennes of any real chance for success. When Hodges opened his offensive in mid-November after waiting two weeks for the weather to improve, he ran into fierce German opposition. Fighting in difficult terrain made worse by the appalling weather and the critical shortages of ammunition, 1st Army's attacks bogged down in the Huertgen Forest and stopped at the Roer River. Aside from taking the Metz forts, Bradley's offensives failed. As Brooke correctly noted: "This offensive could only be classified as the first strategic reverse that we had suffered since landing in France."[4]

Privately, Brooke harbored hopes a reverse might compel Eisenhower to see the folly of his broad-front approach.[5] "As regards the strategy," he confided in his diary, "the American conception of always attacking all along the front, irrespective of strength available, was sheer madness. In the present offensive we had attacked on six Army fronts without any reserves anywhere."[6] He felt strongly Eisenhower's actions needlessly prolonged the war and presented the

British with an insoluble manpower problem.[7] On November 2, Smith traveled to London to outline Eisenhower's plans for the November offensive to Churchill and Brooke. Brooke took little solace from Smith's assurances the broad front was developing according to plan. The battles of attrition along the Siegfried Line were chewing up the dwindling German reserves of manpower and matériel.[8] In the aftermath of the November offensives, Brooke considered the Allied position dangerous. Pointing to the similarity between Eisenhower's deployment in November 1944 and that of the Anglo-French armies in spring 1940, Brooke was troubled by the lack of a strategic reserve. As a result Brooke reopened the command question. He thought the only solution was the appointment of Bradley as ground commander with Tedder serving as air commander. Montgomery would be placed over all forces north of the Ardennes with Patton commanding the southern group of armies. Only then, he reasoned, could Eisenhower fulfil his true responsibilities as supreme commander.[9]

Weighed down with his many responsibilities, Smith's fragile health gave way in late November. He developed a painful case of neuritis, forcing him to spend the first three days of December in bed. Marshall wrote Smith confiding he "wished...[Smith] were the type who would turn over [his duties] to a Deputy for the time being and relax on the Riviera for a couple of weeks." However, he realized "there is no possibility of getting you from your job."[10] Smith replied on January 3, 1945, the attack of neuritis was "a blessing in disguise." Fully rested, he reported he "never felt better." This was scarcely the case, but Smith always took care to cover the severity of his health problems, especially from Marshall. "There is nothing wrong with any of us that a good breakthrough won't cure," he remarked.[11]   •

Smith may have hoped for a breakthrough but, like Brooke, the military situation troubled him.[12] His intelligence chief, Strong, pointed to reports hinting the Germans were preparing for a counteroffensive. ULTRA offered little help. With plenty of circumstantial intelligence evidence, Strong thought it likely the Germans might hit the Allies where they were weakest: in the Ardennes or east of the Vosges. Both Smith and Strong assumed the Germans would open a "spoiling attack...at the first bad break in the weather."[13] Impressed by Strong's arguments, Smith sent him forward to warn Bradley.[14]

The 12th Army Group commander did not entirely rule out the possibility of an enemy attack. However, Bradley busily prepared to reopen the offensive in the Roer sector, scheduled to begin on December 16. If the Germans attacked in the Ardennes, he concluded, they would be vulnerable elsewhere. In any event Bradley thought it unlikely the Germans could beat him to the punch. In the end he dismissed Strong by saying, "Let them come."[15]

Bradley's offensive began on schedule; so too did the German.[16] German military thought stressed victory could only be obtained through a decisive act, not through cumulative attrition. No sooner had the Germans retreated into the Siegfried Line than the High Command began to consider the possibilities of launching a major counterstroke. Their thinking paralleled Hitler's. As early as September Hitler conceived of a second blitzkrieg through the Ardennes. By the third week in November he convinced himself a repetition of 1940 could be achieved. The Allies, having reached their "point of culmination" and deployed on either side of the Ardennes for yet another double thrust, offered the Germans an exposed center where four weak divisions held a seventy-five mile front. Carefully husbanding and concentrating his armored and air forces, Hitler wanted to strike the Allies at the point of maximum confusion. His military objective involved rolling up the British in Belgium and seizing Antwerp. The political objective centered on Hitler's hope to force the Allies to sue for a negotiated end to the war.[17]

While the two German armor thrusts penetrated the American front, Eisenhower met with Bradley, Spaatz, and the senior SHAEF staff officers in Versailles. The topic of discussion ostensibly centered on the lack of a strategic reserve in the theater. Smith pushed for the conference to infuse new direction into the campaign, especially for Eisenhower to prompt Bradley into greater efforts in the Roer sector.[18] Just as the meeting commenced, Strong was called away. At the door stood Betts, Strong's assistant G-2, who informed his chief of the German attack.

Strong returned to the conference table and passed on the report. Smith immediately turned to Bradley reminding the army group commander Eisenhower and he had warned of the possibility of a "nasty little Kasserine" in the weakly defended Ardennes. "You've been wishing for a counterattack," Smith told Bradley. "Now it looks as though you've got it." Unmoved by the news, Bradley replied he had two divisions—the 7th and 10th Armored—in reserve. In his opinion these units would suffice to blunt what he assumed to be a diversionary attack.[19]

That night Eisenhower hosted a reception at his Sainte Germaine house to celebrate the marriage of his valet. Champagne flowed, in part celebrating Eisenhower's confirmation as a five-star general. During a bridge game, Eisenhower and Bradley were interrupted by Strong with news of Major General Troy Middleton's VIII Corps front having broken in five places. Seemingly unconcerned, Bradley still thought the threat minor. They returned to their game. Five rubbers of bridge and a bottle of scotch later, they retired to bed.[20]

A little hung over, the revelers slept late the next morning. Making no particular effort to return to his headquarters at Luxembourg, Bradley made the rounds through the headquarters chatting with his friends. As Hughes noted in his diary: "Brad says the Germans have started a big counterattack toward Hodges. Very calm about it. Seemed routine from his lack of emphasis."[21]

Throughout the day of the 17th, intelligence hardened. It became clear the German attack constituted a major threat. Headquarters did not think the Germans could muster sufficient strength to alter the strategic situation in the West. If the Germans launched a desperate gamble, Smith was convinced they would sustain such heavy losses so as to cripple their defenses west of the Rhine. "Any army can go through your force," Smith claimed after the war, "if they are willing to risk losses or if they are willing to weaken their own front. The Germans did both."[22]

Referring to Tunisia in 1943 and the Mortain counterattack in Normandy, Eisenhower recognized Hitler's refusal to yield territory had allowed the Allies to destroy two entire German armies. As the supreme commander immediately grasped, the Ardennes offensive offered the Allied forces with yet another opportunity.[23] As Brooke admitted, "in the hour of crisis...calamity acted on Eisenhower like a restorative and brought out all the greatness in his character."[24] Once he determined this was no spoiling attack, the supreme commander took over direction of the battle. Ordering Hodges and Patton to break off their attacks, Eisenhower, over Bradley's opposition, committed the two armored divisions (7th at the vital road junction of St. Vith; the 10th securing the southern shoulder of the bulge). The only other reserves at SHAEF's disposal were the 82d and 101st Airborne divisions.[25]

Eisenhower ordered the airborne divisions to prepare for immediate deployment but the question remained where. The supreme commander left that to Smith, Whiteley, and Strong. They met in Smith's office where a large map of the Ardennes stretched before them on the floor. The first order of business involved assessing the German intentions. Believing von Rundstedt, who once again commanded the German armies in the West, to be essentially a conservative, they concluded the Germans sought to split the 21st and 12th Army groups by advancing to the Meuse. This estimate closely approximated the German field marshal's view. The key was to hold the shoulders of the penetration, constrict the base, and canalize the two panzer armies into a narrow corridor. If these conditions could be met, the Germans could not maintain the initiative.[26] Pouring over the map and using a captured German sword as a pointer, Smith asked Strong to locate critical road junctions along the German axes of advance. The 7th Armored Division already held St. Vith in the north and pointing to Bastogne, Strong said "this place...looks all right." When Smith asked his G-2 if the reinforcements could get there by road, he replied they could.[27]

Speed was of the utmost importance. As Smith conferred with his staff, the German vanguard stood only hours from the town. Turning to Lord, the Com Z chief of staff, Smith inquired how long it would take to get the 101st Airborne Division to Bastogne. "He gave me a time," Smith remembered, "[and] he beat it by six hours."[28] When the airborne troops arrived to join a combat command of the 10th Armored Division, they already were receiving small arms-fire, so close was the margin of success.[29]

To Eisenhower and Smith, the problem revolved less on how to stop the German onslaught than how best to exploit it. In a letter of December 18 to his commanders, Eisenhower outlined what actions had been taken to block the German advance. He discussed his intention to launch an immediate counterattack from the north. On the 6th Army Group front, he wanted the Colmar Pocket reduced, but otherwise Devers was instructed to abandon his offensive and shift his center of gravity northward. In the center, Patton prepared an advance against the German southern flank.[30]

Eisenhower drove to Verdun the next day to lay the foundation for the counterattack with Bradley, Devers, and Patton. Once again, Montgomery sent de Guingand in his stead. General Strong accompanied Eisenhower and began the conference by updating the intelligence picture. There no longer could be any doubt the Germans had launched a major counteroffensive with twenty divisions already identified and more in reserve. After Strong completed his presentation, Eisenhower outlined his intentions for constricting the advance and counterattacking from the north and south. He admitted these attacks could not be conducted simultaneously and turned to Patton and asked how long it would take to develop an attack against the German left. Patton, who considered this the most sublime moment in his military career, replied without hesitation, "on December 22: with three divisions."

Possessing a strong intuitive sense for the strategic moment and well read in military history, Patton was not surprised when the news reached him of the German attack in the Ardennes. Before he had left for Verdun, Patton instructed his staff, thought to be mediocre by Bradley's staff officers, to prepare groundwork for a movement to the north. Although Eisenhower doubted he could execute the extremely difficult "oblique order" by December 22, he instructed Patton to proceed as soon as possible.[31]

By December 19, the day of the Verdun meeting, it became evident a wedge had been driven between 1st and 3d armies. Generals Whiteley and Betts went forward to Montgomery and Hodges's headquarters to survey the situation. Whiteley reported the British possessed information that Hodges had lost grip on the battle; an assessment corroborated by Betts. "As far as fighting a war was concerned," Betts observed, "the First Army was thinking in terms of a battalion here and something else there but they seemed to have no plan at all for meeting these attacks. And I couldn't see any orders going forth." Whiteley, who now headed the Operations Division in Bull's absence, and Betts confirmed Bradley, for most of the preceding forty-eight hours, had lost contact with Hodges's headquarters.

When Strong returned from Verdun, Betts reported his findings to the G-2 head. "Well, you must go and report this to Beetle Smith," replied Strong. Betts went to see Smith. "It's my recommendation that you relieve the First Army commander," he told Bedell. Although he later considered Hodges "the weakest commander we had," Smith could not bring himself to initiate actions to relieve his old Infantry School chief.[32] "He sort of grunted," recalled Betts, "and that was that."[33]

By midnight the situation became increasingly difficult. Strong, buoyed by Whiteley and Betts, concluded "that the time had come to inform Bedell Smith about my growing doubts whether the Allies were matching up to the situation." In Strong's estimate the Meuse line might be broken by the Germans at Namur within the next forty-eight hours. Smith installed an army cot in his office to rest when the opportunity arose. Finding Smith asleep, Strong and Whiteley woke him. Strong reviewed the deteriorating tactical situation, emphasizing the breakdown of communications between Bradley and Hodges. Although an outspoken critic of Montgomery, Whiteley urged the field marshall be given command of the American forces north of the salient.

"Whenever there is any real trouble, the British do not appear to trust the Americans to handle it efficiently," Smith snarled. He told them their proposal was "completely unacceptable," and since they had lost confidence in SHAEF's management of the battle, they "no longer [were] acceptable as staff officers to Eisenhower." With that, the British officers beat a retreat, fully expecting to be relieved next morning.[34]

Unable to sleep, Smith cabled Montgomery. Abandoning any hope of Hodges retrieving the situation through a counteroffensive, Smith pondered a series of unpleasant choices. He wanted to yield ground in the north, shorten the American lines, and build up reserves "for the purpose of destroying the enemy in Belgium." This approach enjoyed the added benefit of allowing the 1st Army to consolidate along its line of communications, enabling Bradley to reassert control over American forces north of the salient. Smith solicited Montgomery's views.[35]

Troubled by the idea of surrendering command of 1st Army to Montgomery, Smith toyed with the idea of Eisenhower assuming direct operational control. Glancing at a map, he traced the road system and noted the axis of the German advance. Rheims was in a worse location than Bradley's Luxembourg headquarters from a communications standpoint; nor did SHAEF possess a mobile tactical command center. Clearly, there could be no question of Eisenhower taking over the battle. Exhausting all the options, Smith faced the fact Eisenhower might now have to do what he had resisted for the last three months—place Montgomery over the 1st Army.

Needing to be absolutely convinced, Smith called Bradley. The discussion soon centered on the possible command shift. When Bedell discovered Bradley's headquarters had been out of communications with Hodges and Simpson, he quickly made up his mind. "It was an open and shut case," Smith remembered.[36] "Dividing the front would save us a great deal of trouble," he explained to Bradley. "It [the transfer] seems the logical thing to do." Smith pressed the point, asking if the change of command made sense if Montgomery were an American. "Beetle," Bradley replied, "it's hard for me to object. Certainly if Monty's were an American command, I would agree with you entirely."[37]

During the chief of staff meeting the next morning, December 20, Smith remained uncharacteristically quiet. Appearing preoccupied, he weighed the options in his head. He knew that Strong and Whiteley's views enjoyed the support of Betts, an American. Smith also recognized his British subordinates had the backing of Brooke. He worried about the repercussions of the command shift's negative impact on American civilian morale and hurt feelings on the American side. In any event, surrendering command to Montgomery, even if the situation demanded it, was a bitter pill to swallow.

When the conference broke up the senior officers walked down the hall toward Eisenhower's office. Smith joined Strong and Whiteley. Seizing Strong's arm, the chief of staff told him he intended to recommend to Eisenhower that Montgomery be given command over the 1st and 9th Armies north of the "bulge." He asked the British officers to remain silent because, in view of the situation, the proposal should come from an American.[38]

After listening to Smith's assessment, Eisenhower telephoned Bradley. Although Bradley protested loudly, it was in vain. The conversation ended when the supreme commander said, "Well Brad, those are my orders." He called Montgomery to make the shift official.[39] The Germans had unleashed their offensive in the expectation a military setback would decouple the western Allies. Eisenhower's decision proved the fallacy of Hitler's forlorn hope.

As was his custom, whenever he "flared up," Smith tried to make amends. Later that day he apologized to Strong and Whiteley. "What made me really mad," he told Strong, "was that I knew you were right. But my American feelings got the better of me."[40]

Three hours after receiving the call from SHAEF, Montgomery strode into Hodges's headquarters "like Christ come to cleanse the temple." Montgomery could be accused of many things, but indecision was not among them. Despite having heard nothing from SHAEF until Smith's cable of December 20, the field marshal had not been idle. On December 19 he established patrols along the Meuse crossings between Liége and Namur and put four British divisions into motion toward the threatened area. With his rear secure, Montgomery outlined his intentions to Hodges and Simpson: to hold the northern shoulder of the Bulge, to "sort out" the American divisions, and to organize a reserve corps from elements of 1st and 9th armies that would deliver the counterattack. Far from intending to "destroy the enemy in Belgium," Montgomery expected to fight a defensive battle with American troops. He was prepared to surrender American-held ground, stretch the German maintenance, and invite their armor to exhaust itself against prepared defenses before going over to the offensive. It would be a repeat of Alam Halfa and Medenine. Unless the Germans broke through, Montgomery planned to use his British divisions as a strategic reserve. The present American embarrassment in the Ardennes, in his opinion, should not deflect him from the more important objective, his northern thrust toward the Rhine and the Ruhr.[41]

Montgomery found 1st Army headquarters in total disarray and Hodges badly shaken. He immediately notified Smith that Hodges should be relieved. As he could not do it, Bedell should handle it. Smith told Montgomery SHAEF would not back away from making the decision but asked for twenty-four hours. The next day, de Guingand called Smith. "Hodges is not the man I would pick," said the British staff officer, "but he is much better [today]."[42]

Behind the seeming calm at headquarters, signs of alarm surfaced. Smith placed a blackout on all news that produced the impression in the United States the Allies had suffered a major defeat in Europe.[43] Second, the manpower shortage prompted Eisenhower to resort to an extraordinary expedient. General Gasser, Smith's old boss and now War Department manpower expert, arrived in Versailles to investigate charges the theater command had not made the best use of its personnel. His visit coincided with a War Department remark Washington "no longer [would] bleed [itself] much more...to meet deficiencies" in Europe.[44] Earlier, Lee had pointed out his black troops represented the only untapped reservoir of manpower in the theater. Without giving the matter much thought, Eisenhower issued an invitation to black soldiers to volunteer for the infantry offering them the opportunity to serve "without regard to color or race."[45]

When Smith saw the directive, he exploded. He warned Eisenhower in a sternly worded memo "every negro organization, pressure group and newspaper will take the attitude that, while the War Department segregates colored troops...the Army is perfectly willing to put them in front lines mixed with white soldiers, and have them do battle when an emergency arises." "Two years ago," he continued, "I would have considered the...statement the most dangerous thing that I had ever seen in regard to negro relations."

Reflecting the racial views of the officer corps of the period, Smith considered blacks incapable of combat duty. Unwilling to spark a social revolution and under pressure from Smith, Eisenhower backed down. Redrafting the circular, he stated he did not want "to run counter to regs in a time like this." In the end, black soldiers volunteered but were placed in segregated platoons under white leadership.[46]

The manpower situation grew more acute: in December, Bradley's Army Group suffered 134,400 casualties while the January schedule called for him to receive only 18,000 replacements. Fully 80 percent of the losses were sustained in rifle units where critical shortages had existed before the German offensive. Moreover, the theater was down to a twenty-one-day supply of ammunition—40 percent of authorization.[47]

Reminded the Combined Chiefs came forward with manpower and matériel in Italy when AFHQ had run into trouble, Smith determined to make the "poorest mouth" possible. "We exploited the Ardennes crisis for all it was worth," he told a postwar interviewer. "Here they [the War Department] had cut down ammunition production and it hit us just at the time of the Bulge. We were short of men, so we yelled loud...We asked for everything we could get."[48] Churchill responded by calling up an additional quarter-million men, cutting deeply into Great Britain's remaining industrial manpower. Smith told his assistants he should "go on record to our Masters in Washington that if they want us to win the war over here they must find us another ten Divisions."[49] Assuming an alarmist tone, Smith's cables to Washington during the crisis pushed the War Department into meeting his demands.

After the war, Smith gave the impression he never doubted the outcome of the battle. "[Strong] asked me three times one day if I thought we would hold at Bastogne. I thought so," he remembered. "How do you know," Strong asked? "Because the commanders there think they can hold today," he replied. He thought back to his days as a "Young Turk" at Leavenworth. "I remember that we had been taught the great opportunities offered by a counteroffensive," he remarked. "We were also taught that one division of good men, properly handled, could not be driven out of a position...no matter the force thrown against it (this not quite true, but we remembered it). We had at Bastogne our best division...I believed [they] would hold."[50]

Smith's hard shell cracked, if only momentarily, during the height of the crisis. Under severe stress, his health worsened. Intelligence reported special German forces were at large trying to assassinate Eisenhower and Smith, among others. The entire headquarters came under virtual house arrest as security tightened. Murphy, over from London, spent a night with Bedell Smith during the height of the scare. A large, wall-enclosed garden surrounded Smith's Versailles quarters. Nine guards were posted in the compound. Smith and Murphy were awoke in the middle of the night by rifle fire in the courtyard. Murphy emerged from his room to discover Smith, dressed in his pyjamas, armed with a carbine. With Smith in the lead, they rushed into the garden. The courtyard was alive with the fusillade. The next morning the body of the intruder was found—a stray cat riddled with bullets.[51]

While SHAEF overestimated the threat posed by the German commandos, it drew the correct conclusions regarding the nature of the German offensive. By December 23 the crisis had passed, ending the defensive phase of the battle. Patton attacked, as promised, on the 22d. By the 23d Montgomery deployed armor from the British XXX Corps along the Meuse between Namur and Givet. In the north, two infantry and an armored division assembled under Collins for the counterattack. In the meantime the weather broke, and SHAEF, for the first time since the attack began, got its air forces into the skies. The Germans continued their attacks until the 26th, presenting the Allies with another textbook opportunity to destroy the pocket.

A NEAR-FATAL CASE OF FIELDMARSHALITIS

At a conference on December 21, Eisenhower outlined his plans for the counterattack to his senior assistants at SHAEF.[52] Patton wanted to strike at the base of the bulge—not the waist. The 3d Army commander saw a chance to envelop the Germans and place his forces in a position to advance quickly to the Rhine. He planned to move with dispatch, ignoring the principles of mass and concentration. Smith agreed fully with Patton's views, but Eisenhower and Bradley demurred.[53] The supreme commander, whose vision always exceeded his nerve, thought Patton too weak to execute this hazardous movement. Instead he ordered Patton to drive on Bastogne and relieve pressure on the southern flank. This he accomplished on December 26.

In the north Montgomery set January 1 for the date of Collins's attack. He saw the northern counterattack as a limited holding operation against the tip of the German salient. To attack the bulge at its base, as Collins demanded, he needed to redeploy the attacking forces further east on a road system oriented north-south, with roads impassable, and in the teeth of German resistance. True to character, Montgomery informed SHAEF he would not begin the attack until all preparations had been made. Moreover, he still thought the Germans capable of one last major thrust. The Allied attack was postponed until January 3.[54]

This placed Eisenhower in a very difficult position. Thinking Montgomery would advance on New Year's Day, Bradley received orders to reopen his attacks. Eisenhower also wanted the British XXX Corps committed. To those at headquarters, it appeared like a replay of Normandy. In Smith's opinion Montgomery's "inherent overcautiousness was going to cause us to miss the opportunity of inflicting a severe defeat on the enemy."[55] On December 28 Eisenhower went forward to confer with Montgomery. The field marshal reopened the question of the command for the northern thrust over the Rhine. As Brooke correctly guessed from London, Montgomery's strong advocacy of his position aggravated Eisenhower. Montgomery, entirely lacking in the ability to see anyone else's point of view and demonstrating remarkable tactlessness, followed up the meeting by sending a letter to SHAEF raising the old questions of strategy and command. The British field marshal wanted an ironclad guarantee he would retain command of the American forces assigned to him and his northern thrust would still enjoy priority. His timing could not have been worse.[56]

Throughout the December crisis, Eisenhower's confidence grew perceptibly. On two occasions—December 29 and 30—Eisenhower drafted blistering letters to Montgomery but refrained, at Smith's insistence, from sending them for fear of provoking a conflict with the British. No longer willing to suffer Montgomery's outrages, after months of frustration, he decided to make an issue of their different approaches. Convinced he would win any showdown with Montgomery, Eisenhower prepared a cable to the Combined Chiefs in which he stated one or the other would have to be removed.

If the cable had been sent, Montgomery's head would have surely rolled. He was saved by the decisive action of his loyal subordinate, de Guingand. After having been informed by a liaison officer of the depth of ill feeling against Montgomery in Bradley's headquarters, de Guingand telephoned his old friend "Beetle" to sound him out. The reply shocked de Guingand who immediately decided to fly to Versailles, despite terrible weather conditions.

Landing at Orly airport after a hair-raising flight, de Guingand found Smith waiting for him in his Cadillac staff car. Smith told de Guingand that Eisenhower and Bradley viewed any delay in opening the counteroffensive intolerable and the operational question must go to higher authorities for a solution. "I think we had better go right over and see Ike," Smith said, "otherwise it will certainly be too late."

The two chiefs of staff found Eisenhower and Tedder in the supreme commander's office. Eisenhower looked weary and upon seeing de Guingand asked, "What are you doing here Freddie?" De Guingand replied, "Well, I've come on a very important mission." Smith took the floor and explained de

Guingand had come to shed some light on the issue. Eisenhower said he simply was fed up with Montgomery's campaign to usurp his responsibilities and dictate the direction of decision making. The supreme commander pointed out at the Maastrict conference Montgomery received control of the 9th Army for his proposed thrust north of Düsseldorf. Eisenhower was not willing to go beyond that commitment. "I think you had better read it," Eisenhower said as he handed the startled British officer the cable. "At the moment we've just agreed upon a signal we're sending to General Marshall," he continued. The blunt message made it clear a new, and potentially final rupture had surfaced in inter-Allied relations. De Guingand suffered under no illusions what would happen if the cable went out.

"I then made my little speech, and I was in deadly earnest," recalled de Guingand. He pointed out Montgomery, isolated in his headquarters, did not understand the seriousness of the situation. Finishing his earnest plea, de Guingand asked if Eisenhower might not sit on the signal for twenty-four hours to allow him a chance to put the situation right.

Tedder intervened and said, " No, we've decided on the signal, it must go." Stressing the damage already created, Eisenhower seemed intent upon following Tedder's lead. De Guingand began to despair until finally Smith entered the discussion. Perhaps remembering Montgomery had given him twenty-four hours on the question of Hodges's relief, Smith urged de Guingand be given the delay. After a further exchange of views, Smith won out.[57]

Relieved and gratified by Smith's actions, de Guingand accepted his colleague's invitation to spend the night. After tidying up some loose ends in his office, Smith led de Guingand back to his comfortable house. Despite being a general in a republican army, Smith took full advantage of his position, living the life of a conqueror in the city of Louis XIV. Visitors remarked on the magnificence of his wine cellar. He dispensed his patronage widely. The American ambassador in Paris, Jefferson Caffery, and his friends in the War Department, Marshall, Arnold, and Handy, were among the recipients of cases of champagne and cognac.[58] Suffering under a renewed assault from his ulcer, Smith drank heavily, possibly to deaden the pain. He and de Guingand discussed their many mutual problems over Old Fashioned cocktails. "I never left [one of these sessions] without feeling that we had made good use of our time," de Guingand recalled.[59]

Flying back to Montgomery's headquarters, de Guingand went immediately to the field marshal. At first incredulous, Montgomery's tough outer crust finally gave way. He broke down and asked his chief of staff for advice. De Guingand drafted an apologetic signal which Montgomery read and forwarded with only minor alterations. Chastened at long last, the sober Montgomery acknowledged

Eisenhower would hear no more from him on the subject of command.[60] Together, the eleventh-hour actions of de Guingand and Smith saved a final breach between their two chiefs.

While Smith contended with this new case of "fieldmarshalitis," serious trouble brewed up with the French. On January 1 the Germans opened an offensive in Alsace to regain Strasbourg and divert Patton from the Ardennes. Eisenhower wanted to shorten his lines, pull divisions away from Devers's 6th Army Group, and give up Strasbourg. Smith disagreed: either Devers should hold his ground, which he favored, or fall back in detail. A final decision was postponed.[61]

De Gaulle asked for a major conference to be held in Versailles on January 3.[62] The day before, Smith had a fiery session with Général Alphonse-Pierre Juin. De Gaulle's chief of staff and Smith were not on the best of terms. Earlier they clashed over rearmament policies for the French.[63] With passions aroused, Juin told Smith the French would withdraw their forces from SHAEF's control if Eisenhower ordered Devers to fall back to the Vosges. "Juin said things to me," Smith related to Eisenhower, "which, if he had been an American, I would have socked him in the jaw."[64]

Churchill and Brooke came from London to discuss the most recent Eisenhower-Montgomery flareup. They remained after lunch to observe the "memorable" conference between Eisenhower, Smith, de Gaulle, and Juin.[65] De Gaulle considered the proposed retreat a disaster. "If we were at a Kriegspiel, I should say you were right," de Gaulle remarked. "But I must consider the matter from another point of view. Retreat in Alsace would yield French territory to the enemy. In the realm of strategy this would be only a maneuver. But for France, it would be a national disaster. For Alsace is sacred ground."[66]

A political discussion ensued. In the end, Eisenhower decided Strasbourg could not be abandoned for political reasons. As he explained to Marshall, execution of the original plan would have created far-ranging political repercussion for de Gaulle's government and threatened the Allies' line of communications. "It was clearly a military necessity," he concluded, "to prevent this."[67]

Smith confided in Handy, "at best the French are a constant psychological problem." He correctly assumed de Gaulle and Juin's threat to remove the French forces from SHAEF's command had been a bluff. "But it is difficult doing business on such a basis," he told Handy, "and it [dealing with the French] requires a reservoir of tact and diplomacy exceeding my normal level of supply." To avoid any misunderstanding, Smith and Juin flew to 6th Army Group area to deliver the orders.[68]

On January 3, Collins opened his attack. The Germans, having depleted their flanks of reserves for the fighting around Bastogne, possessed little strength to resist. Nevertheless, it took thirteen days of heavy fighting for Collins and Patton to seal the pocket at Houffalize. On January 12 the Soviets opened a massive winter offensive in Poland, assuring the Germans could not reinforce their troops in the West. Although the Americans suffered a bloody nose, the Germans sustained irreplaceable losses in manpower and matériel. Still, the Germans managed to extract most of their remaining forces from the Allied pincer movement and fought a tough withdrawal. While the Allied commanders had hoped for greater results, the Battle of the Ardennes ensured that the upcoming campaign in the Rhineland would be fought against a thin, static enemy.

Even Eisenhower's critics admired his handling of the battle—except Montgomery. On January 7, at the height of the Allied counterattacks, the field marshal held a press conference. With characteristic insensitivity he boasted of "straightening out" the command crisis after the initial German penetration. Summing up the progress of the battle, Montgomery, exhibiting what de Guingand termed his "'what a good boy am I' attitude" to the fullest, explained how he had first "headed off," then "seen off" the German panzer thrusts, and now was busy "writing [them] off."[69] Intending to give recognition to the American officers and men who served under him, his ill-considered remarks produced the opposite impression—that Montgomery had saved the Americans from disaster.

Taken by themselves, Montgomery's statements were not without a certain ring of truth. As Smith admitted in a December 28 staff conference, Montgomery's prompt actions "restored the situation in the US Army area in the northern flank and got this [1st] Army straightened out by bringing order out of disorder."[70] Many American officers who served under the field marshal during the Ardennes fighting saw matters in much the same light. The quaint public-school jargon aside, his account of the fighting in the northern sector accurately outlined Montgomery's thinking and his conduct of the battle.

The issue, however, was not the veracity of Montgomery's statements but rather his astounding display of captiousness. This became more galling as it had been less than a week since Eisenhower had threatened to sack him. As obtuse on political and personal matters as he was acute on military questions, Montgomery remained blind to the importance SHAEF attached to public opinion. He endeavored to use press conferences as forums to argue his case for continuing in command of the 1st and 9th armies after the conclusion of the Ardennes fighting. Invariably his own worst enemy, Montgomery's transparent efforts backfired. Instead of winning the Americans over to his point of view, he succeeded in earning their lasting enmity.

Montgomery's claims infuriated Bradley and Patton, particularly the former. Still smarting from surrendering control over Hodges and worried he had lost Eisenhower's confidence, Bradley interpreted Montgomery's remarks as an effort to pour salt into an open wound. Bradley's hopes for pocketing the German forces in the salient evaporated and he blamed Montgomery. Determined never again to allow Montgomery to "tweak our Yankee noses," Bradley vowed to resign if Eisenhower ever placed him under British command—a threat repeated by Patton.[71] Faced by the defection of his two senior field commanders, Eisenhower would never again seriously consider the question of placing Montgomery in command of ground operations.

From beginning to end the Bulge had been an American battle and an American victory. The reconstructed German panzer divisions, gutted in the fighting around Caen, were finally written off in the Ardennes. Likewise, the Luftwaffe lost hundreds of aircraft and aircrew, all without appreciable gain. For the Germans the Ardennes offensive ended in complete failure. The Ardennes fighting set back the opening of the Rhineland campaign by six weeks, but the Allies came out of the battle in a stronger position than when the Bulge commenced. Smith's December 22 cry for help brought forward reinforcements in the form of two divisions, whose arrival produced "an immediate and complete change in heart."[72] During the fighting in the Ardennes and Alsace, against the best available German troops, the American armies demonstrated high levels of maturity and combat power. The U.S. Army came of age during the battles of December and January.

SHAEF'S FINEST MOMENT

The campaigns in France and along the frontiers reveal much about the Eisenhower-Smith partnership. On the surface Eisenhower appears to be a sum of paradoxes: the incisive commander who vacillated, frequently seeming to mirror the views of the last person out the door; outwardly, a conciliator who avoided controversy and exhibited remarkable patience, yet one who boiled inside. Although possessing an excellent command of the language, his directives were studies in tergiversation; with an athletically inspired faith in teamwork and a distaste for partisanship, he consciously practiced deception and manipulated those who served under him.

Eisenhower's strength rested not in the traditional realm of strategist or heroic leader but rather in his ability to handle people and avoid divisive problems. Had he enumerated the essential ingredients of his leadership style, the list might have sounded like the recipe for success in the military offered in a popular contemporary motion picture. In the 1943 British comedy, *The Life and Death of Colonel Blimp*, a senior man in the War Office told a young officer if he wanted to "get on in the Army," he should follow four cardinal rules. First, never trouble yourself with things you do not understand. Second, never go off half-cocked. Third, keep your mouth shut. And last, avoid politicians like the plague. Any officer who followed these principles, he promised, would go far in the military. This formula sums up nicely Eisenhower's approach to men and problems.[73]

The key to understanding Eisenhower's style of leadership lies in its covert character. One can identify five techniques by which Eisenhower concealed the direct, personal aspects of his leadership style: (1) the selective delegation of authority to subordinates, allowing them considerable freedom while simultaneously using them as foils to deflect criticism from himself; (2) the insightful evaluation of friends and antagonists and the careful calculation of the help or damage they might render in any situation; (3) the avoidance of making unilateral decisions, insisting upon multiple advocacy for any major policy shift; (4) the refusal to engage in personality clashes; and (5) the intentional use of evasiveness and ambiguity to screen his actions and unbalance his critics. Beneath the amiable "Ike" existed the hard-minded operator. In achieving his various ends, Eisenhower worked through others, and the individual most responsible for his success was Bedell Smith.

In the strictest sense, Eisenhower does not rank among history's "great captains." He did emerge, however, as an excellent choice for supreme commander. Indeed, it is difficult to imagine anyone better suited for the role. Certainly Marshall—cold, friendless, and unapproachable—possessed neither the subtlety nor the patience to keep the peace among the hostile factions. Since at one level war is the clash of independent wills, irrational forces—personal animosities, ambition, institutional inertia—play disproportionate roles. Eisenhower's virtue as a commander rested in his ability to broker competing national, personal, and strategic sensitivities and susceptibilities. His role as coordinator—more political than military—obliged him to seek compromises rather than provide decisive leadership from above. During the advance through France, Eisenhower inclined one way and then the other, refusing to seize overall command or to reconcile the various operational approaches to a single, ultimate objective. Bradley and Montgomery could leave a conference convinced Eisenhower accepted each of their discordant views. Since Eisenhower's style of leadership depended upon delegation of authority, his willful subordinates exploited the supreme commander's ambiguity to the hilt. Eisenhower accepted this as an inevitable, if exasperating, result of his method of decentralized command.

Since his basic task involved persuading others to implement his plans, Eisenhower needed their goodwill. The supreme commander's cautious strategic approach and his role as neutral power-broker produced many calumnious comments by others about Eisenhower's military abilities. Even these did not break down his solely tried patience; nor did he ever reply in kind. He sublimated his strong temper, knowing personal and national rivalries simmered not far beneath the surface calm. The one constant in Eisenhower's approach was the effort to preserve Allied harmony.

"Ike's strategical and tactical job was easy," Kenneth Strong believed. "Play of personalities was his big job."[74] Eisenhower carefully assessed his principal subordinates, calculating their strengths and weaknesses. In Smith's opinion Eisenhower considered his commanders and staff officers "the tools with which he worked." He used them "in accordance with their particular capacity."[75] Eisenhower's magnetic personality provided the raw material to perform his integrative task. By all accounts he inspired those around him not by force of character but by his simplicity, his commonsense Kansas approach to men and events, and his naturalness and genuine sense of humor. "His personality [was] such that it impressed itself immediately upon senior subordinates as completely frank, completely honest, very human and considerate," Smith remembered.[76] Despite the stress of his position he retained an unfailing optimism that infected everyone around him. Eisenhower also understood the spiritual aspect of war. He spent a substantial amount of time visiting troops, talking to them informally. There was little of the "brass hat" about him. Senior officers and privates alike responded to his enthusiasm. While critics pointed to his lack of field experience, in the position he held, that was not essential. His chief duties involved the preservation of the integrity of the Allied command and the execution of the strategic decisions of the coalition. This required a set of intimate personal skills that gave positive substance to the rhetoric of Allied cooperation and teamwork. These traits Eisenhower possessed in profusion.

As chief of staff, Smith's primary concerns were the fulfillment of the ostensible objectives of centralization, rigor, and the maintenance of unity of command. Being likeable was much less crucial than being active, intelligent, and well informed. Like any chief of staff, Smith funneled information and advice to his commander. Since Eisenhower's time and energies were expended on combatting divisiveness within the command and in building morale, he selectively delegated executive authority to Smith. As the SHAEF Supply Division head Major General Robert Crawford noted, "Bedell...tried to get everything in his hands, but that was to keep things from Ike. Bedell Smith [was] exceptionally valuable because he [knew] exactly how Ike would react on most questions and could act for him."[77]

Because Smith dealt with the details in Versailles, Eisenhower could inspect forward units or stay in his headquarters in Rheims. There were those who thought—chiefly Brooke and Montgomery—that no one was running the land battle. Others—the American operational commanders included—wondered if Smith did not command the theater. After visiting France, ambassador to the Soviet Union Averell Harriman saw "no reason in the world" for Eisenhower to be in Rheims with his little entourage, far removed from his Versailles headquarters but not appreciably closer to the front. Harriman thought Smith encouraged Eisenhower to go forward because he could accomplish more with the supreme commander out of headquarters.[78] In fact there was no real reason why Eisenhower had to be at Versailles. In war, the decisions that set operations into motion are brief in terms of the time expended and in the form of their expression. It is the detailed consequences of these decisions that are exacting and intricate. Eisenhower could discharge his integrative function better in Rheims than he could in Versailles.

In Smith's estimate Eisenhower was "an exponent of decentralization" who accorded his commanders and staff "a full measure of confidence and a very large measure of independent authority."[79] The subordinate who enjoyed the most confidence and the largest grant of independence was Bedell Smith. After the supreme commander indicated the broad outlines of his intentions, Smith worked out the details in consultation with his principal assistants in SHAEF and ETO. Smith prepared the orders, explained the thinking behind the decision to his superiors in Washington, and followed up on the instructions to satisfy himself they were being executed. If matters languished, he took steps to iron out the obstacles, whether personal or material, that prevented the fulfillment of the supreme commander's intentions. "From the standpoint of a person who could take care of the things Ike wanted done, and who would protect Ike's interests," another SHAEF officer remembered, "[Bedell] was unbeatable."[80]

The SHAEF mechanism of command deliberately operated by simultaneously employing formal and informal connections. Eisenhower preferred not to use his rank to straighten out personal conflicts. "Ike always had to have...someone who'd do the dirty work for him," Smith intimated after the war. "He always had to have someone else do the firing, or the reprimanding, or give any order which he knew people would find unpleasant." Eisenhower also depended upon his chief of staff to enforce his directives. Since Eisenhower always had "to be the nice guy," Smith played the villain.[81] If Eisenhower could not smooth out personal disagreements, he left it to Smith to wield his "cat and nine tails and beat [opposition] into line."[82] This created certain stresses for Smith. Empowered to make interpretative decisions, in accordance with the objectives, Smith's actions necessarily involved the command function. His enforcement of coordination, inevitably biased, led to friction as he exercised authority not theoretically invested in a chief of staff. Although junior to the operational and theater commanders, Smith's authority was greater than those of Bradley, Devers, or Lee because he discharged more-extensive responsibilities. The commanders had the right to remonstrate directly to the supreme commander if they disagreed with any of Smith's actions; none did because they knew criticism of the chief of staff would bring no result. As one of his Secretaries/General Staff, Colonel Ford Trimble, remembered, "Bedell kept the Indian sign on nearly everybody."[83]

Where Eisenhower exercised a vast amount of indirect, carefully concealed influence in his dealings with his senior American subordinates, this approach produced only friction with the British. The London military hierarchy never reconciled themselves to having a relatively inexperienced American soldier placed in the role of supreme commander. Another difficulty emerged over the constant divergence of views. As Montgomery pointed out, "it was always very clear...that Ike and I were poles apart when it came to the conduct of war."[84] Aside from doctrinal differences, a wide rift in personalities existed between Eisenhower and the British field marshal. Apart from the personalities of the protagonists and the strategic implications involved, there were two basic causes of this problem. First, Eisenhower and Montgomery rarely understood each other, and since they met infrequently it proved difficult to reconcile their differences. The studied ambiguity of Eisenhower's letters and directives contributed to the difficulties. Second, there did not exist a common basis for mutual respect and understanding—so prominent in Eisenhower's relationships with the senior American officers.

To assert himself as supreme commander would have resulted in a breach with Montgomery and the intervention of the combined chiefs and the political heads—something Eisenhower and Smith guarded against. At one level Montgomery, as British theater commander, was Eisenhower's equal. The supreme commander granted the field marshal the right to express his views. Eisenhower patiently listened to Montgomery's lectures and seemed to agree the Allied armies must drive into Germany along the northern axis. Throughout their exchanges Eisenhower was at times deliberately evasive, even untruthful. He dangled the northern thrust before Montgomery as the ultimate prize. In the meantime, Eisenhower told the field marshal he could not give concrete expression to the final objective until intermediate objectives had been secured. In this way he spurred Montgomery to action while keeping him in check until it proved too late to alter the sweep of the advance. While he may have lacked the moral courage to deal with Montgomery, a view endorsed by Smith, his entire leadership style depended upon the refusal to engage in personalities.[85] He sought to placate personal hostilities, to deflate the importance of nationalist disagreements and personality, and to preserve the Allied command structure. His peacemaking posture required he look uncertain, appear to vacillate, and engage in some calculated duplicity. In the end his labors prevented a schism in the alliance without compromising unity of command or surrendering overall direction of the campaign.

The relationship between Eisenhower and Smith was symbiotic: Smith's personality and style of leadership perfectly complemented those of Eisenhower. His categorical judgments, acerbic impatience, and fanatical obsession with efficiency made him indispensable to Eisenhower. Together they possessed the professional knowledge and personal qualities required for the discharge of command; each was necessary to the other. When a commander and a chief of staff have similar personalities, the result is to weaken the relationship. Eisenhower's veiled, indirect leadership demanded an activist chief of staff. The Eisenhower-Smith relationship not only survived divergences in personality and opinion, it prospered because of them. Their differences produced strength.

More than a sounding board, confidant, and drafter of communications, Smith emerged in France and Belgium as a decisionmaker who exercised considerable power. Eisenhower consciously delegated authority to Smith to camouflage his own involvement as shaper of policy. He used Smith as a lightning rod to ward off criticisms from himself. However, as the strategic debate flared around him, Eisenhower could not always escape the center of controversy. When he finally asserted his authority as supreme commander, first in October and more conclusively during the Bulge, it was largely at Smith's insistence.[86] Placed within the hierarchical SHAEF organization, Smith, out of strong personal conviction, felt compelled to drive Eisenhower into exercising his formal prerogatives as Allied commander. As a senior SHAEF officer remarked, Smith "supplied the pepper and the fire" in the relationship.[87]

Not a profound thinker, Smith preferred the systematic; his character tended toward arbitrary execution of policy instead of initiation. His views on how to manage a general staff essentially were those long-sanctioned by conventional thinking in the U.S. Army. Smith attempted to apply his concepts of staff organization reinforced by experience in the Mediterranean on a very large scale in SHAEF. Possessing intelligence, acuteness, and an enormous capacity for work, Bedell Smith felt it necessary to introduce checks and controls over the collective staff.

Tough-minded, aggressive in his personal relations, and preoccupied with dominating his environment, Smith commanded respect but lacked the warmth that elicits affection. He consequently was never popular. While the two remained friends, Smith's brusqueness made him increasingly *persona non gratia* in Eisenhower's circle. As Eisenhower's British aide put it, "Bedell [had] no value outside military business...[He was] not a man who could give Ike that sympathetic aid he needed at some critical moments."[88]

Smith's worst flaw was his reactionary insistence upon defending his authority. In part this may be explained by the fact he was a self-made general, not part of the West Point "old boy" network. He took pride in being known as a "number one square-wheeled S.O.B."[89] Dreading criticism from his superiors, he developed an elaborate set of Byzantine defense mechanisms to insulate himself. A British officer thought Smith maneuvered "to separate General Eisenhower from his headquarters and [the] rest of the staff until SHAEF was almost solely Bedell's headquarters." [90]

Throughout his tenure as Eisenhower's chief of staff, several examples of Smith's highly irascible and often vindictive nature can be found. In the opinion of Tedder's aide, Wing Commander Leslie Scarman, Smith "seemed a little afraid [for] his position." Since he perceived Tedder as a threat, Smith isolated the deputy supreme commander, especially on political and civil affairs questions. Scarman recalled several incidents when Eisenhower asked Tedder's opinion "on something he had never seen." Tedder never pushed the issue, confident he enjoyed Eisenhower's trust.[91] Smith did not reserve his machinations for British officers. When the War Department raised questions concerning the logistical setup, Smith found a scapegoat in Lee. With the press he resorted to unnecessary censorship and interfered with the activities of the war correspondents. He did not welcome external constraints of any type, even if sent by his mentor, Marshall. Scant regard was afforded successive War Department delegations. As in the case of Aurand, Smith used his position to curb or remove officers who spoke out. He refused to appoint competent outsiders to key positions for fear they might disrupt his carefully constructed machine. When Marshall insisted upon the creation of an intermediate command level for logistics, Smith busily engaged in intrigues to undermine Lear's authority. Smith's aloofness, his unpopularity, his mean-spiritedness, and his refusal to delegate authority must be ascribed to defects of personality rather than intellect.

Eisenhower made allowances for Smith's "Prussian" personality and expected others to do so as well.[92] As Eisenhower remarked after the war, Smith was like a crutch to a one-legged man. In hindsight, the supreme commander granted too much power to Smith. The headquarters came to be dominated by Smith's autocratic personality. His thinking was confined to rigid formulae and inflexible points of view. Forging SHAEF in the image of his Mediterranean staff, Smith demonstrated a marked intolerance to concepts incompatible with his preconceived ideas. During the pre-OVERLORD period when he hammered out the SHAEF organization, Smith showed himself unable to cope with ambiguous situations. Instead of reorganizing the logistical side of the theater headquarters or creating expanded, functionally organized staff divisions to handle the relatively new areas of civil affairs and public relations, he fought a series of delaying actions designed to preserve his superintendence over these aspects of the headquarters. In point of fact his system was the negation of system as his obsessive drive to control his environment prompted him inexorably to centralize every species of authority in himself. By establishing conformity, he succeeded in reducing uncertainties in small things and to that extent offset the greater uncertainties of war. In fashioning his headquarters he failed to strike a balance between centralization and decentralization, discipline and initiative, authority and individual responsibility. As a result, during the advance through France, SHAEF proved incapable of responding to rapidly changing conditions.

The Battle of the Bulge was, as Churchill later claimed, "the greatest American battle of the war." Brilliant generalship did not account for the victory. While Eisenhower and Smith claimed they anticipated a German counteroffensive, they never foresaw its magnitude nor did they plan for its contingency. In the end the determined resistance of small knots of American soldiers deprived the Germans of momentum and with it any hope of reaching the Meuse. Only after the hard-pressed American divisions wrestled the initiative from the German panzers could SHAEF execute its plan to eliminate the salient.

Opening with portents of disaster, the Battle of the Bulge turned into SHAEF's finest moment. While the ponderous movements to close the Bulge and pocket the head of the German penetration denied the Allies the all-embracing victory Eisenhower predicted, the Germans had been dealt a deadly blow. Like many of their detractors in the Allied camp, the German high command misassessed the Eisenhower-Smith team. The German General Staff thought SHAEF would not act to constrict the German attack until it received direction from London and Washington. In the meantime they expected their panzers to be crossing the Meuse.[93] In the crisis Eisenhower and Smith refused to panic. They recognized the German attack as a major offensive and acted accordingly. Bradley was overruled and the defenses concentrated at St. Vith, Bastogne, and the Meuse. Overriding national considerations and the objections of the senior American commanders, SHAEF gave Montgomery command of the forces north of the salient. When Patton called for a risky counterattack with insufficient strength, SHAEF instead shortened its lines and accumulated reserves to attain a "methodical and sure" reduction of the Bulge. It became evident once the Allied armies completed the elimination of the enemy forces west of the Rhine, a breakthrough and pursuit into Germany would be assured. It was equally clear that SHAEF would direct it.

The Campaign for Germany, January–May 1945

In a sense, Eisenhower's decision to fight a campaign of attrition on the frontiers paid dividends, albeit unintended. The German counteroffensive in the Ardennes failed because its objective exceeded the means of the German armies. By the same token the strategy of exhausting the Germans took a heavy toll upon the American forces. SHAEF possessed the forces to blunt the German attack but not the reserves to exploit their success. Just as in the four previous cases—Normandy, along the Seine, the Scheldt, and in the Rhône Valley—the advancing Allied armies fell short of pocketing or cutting off the retreat of beaten German forces. Once again the Allies failed to complete the destruction of a German Army group in a classic battle of annihilation in the Ardennes.

The outcome of the Battle of the Bulge differed in one crucial respect. Whereas the Germans recuperated from their débâcle in France, there was no recovery from their disaster in the Ardennes. In the words of the German commander, von Rundstedt, the Ardennes had "broken the backbone of the [German] Western Front."[1]

In terms of grand strategy, the Ardennes victory profoundly influenced SHAEF's authority in directing the final campaign in Germany. Eisenhower redirected Bradley's advance toward the northeast: Hodges's along the line Prüm-Bonn, and Patton's toward Frankfurt. Instead of giving Montgomery's advance priority, Eisenhower intended to cross the Rhine south of the Ruhr in tandem with the 21st Army Group. The American armies conducted what amounted to a narrow-front offensive to the exclusion of its most consistent proponents. As Smith later pointed out, the victorious thrust into Germany was right out of the Leavenworth lecture hall—a Schlieffen "sickle cut" in reverse.

GERMANY

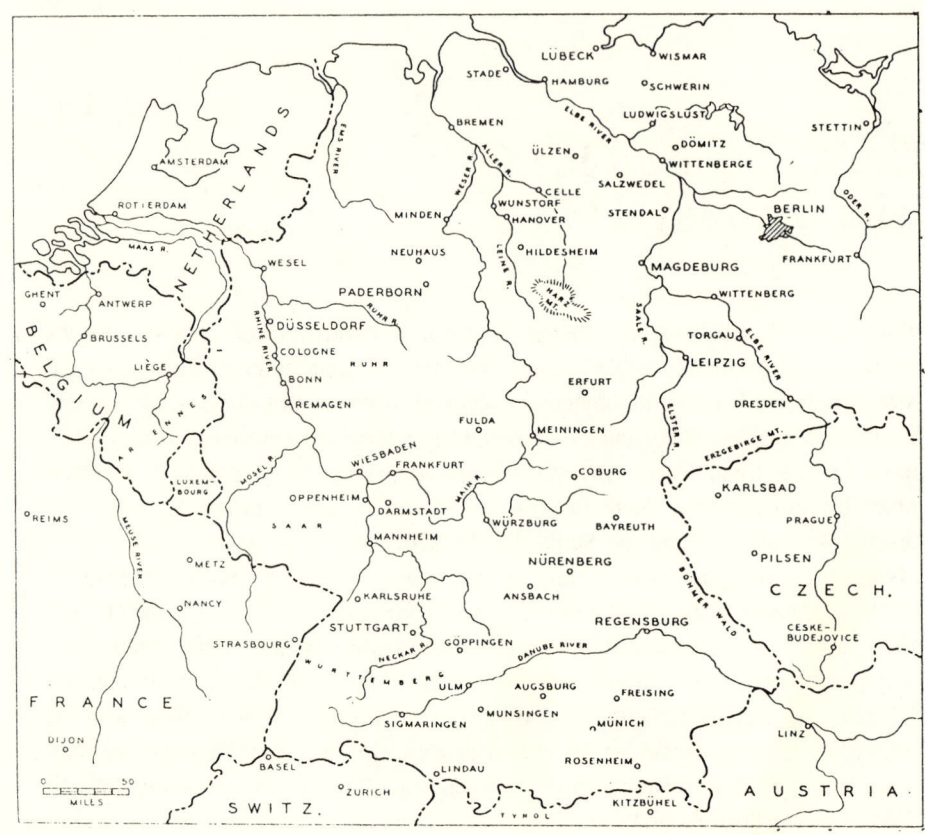

Alfred D. Chandler, ed., *The Papers of Dwight D. Eisenhower: The War Years*, vol. 5 (Baltimore: Johns Hopkins University Press, 1970), p. 60.

Despite failing health, Smith played a central part in the final acts of the war in Europe. After Eisenhower asserted his authority over ground operations, he turned increasingly to his chief of staff for operational advice. During the climatic last six months of the war—the Battle of the Bulge, the clearing of the Rhineland, and the decision not to drive on Berlin—only Bradley's voice carried as much weight in Eisenhower's mind as that of Smith. At the Malta conference in January 1945, Smith defended Eisenhower's independence by beating back the last serious attempt by the British to alter the direction of Allied strategy and interpose a ground commander into the headquarters. Finally, it fell to Smith to negotiate and sign the German surrender.

THE MALTA CONFERENCE

In the pre-D-Day OVERLORD planning, it was assumed the Germans would conduct a series of withdrawals back to the Rhine once the West Wall had been broken. In light of Normandy and the Ardennes, SHAEF concluded the German forces would never willingly surrender territory west of the Rhine. Eisenhower proposed to launch a set of interlocking offensives designed to split the German defenses, defeat them in detail, and bring the three Allied army groups up to the Rhine. If the offensives attained their objectives, the bulk of the German Army in the West would be destroyed. In the event the attacks succeeded only in dislodging the enemy from the West Wall, their divisions still would be reduced in strength and demoralized. Once the Allies closed along the entire length of the Rhine, the barrier would permit Eisenhower to mass strength for multiple crossings, leaving the German defenses overextended and vulnerable.[2]

On the basis of the staff studies, Eisenhower decided to launch coordinated offensives. In the north the Canadian Army and the British XXX Corps would attack southeast from Nijmegen, clearing the Reichwald, to seize ground west of the Rhine (VERITABLE). The American 9th Army remained under Montgomery's command—Hodges's army having reverted to Bradley on January 17—and was assigned the task of attacking northeast while linking with the Canadians (GRENADE). Once these operations cleared the west bank of the Rhine north of Düsseldorf, Montgomery could prepare for a thirty-five-division-strong crossing of the river by Dempsey's army. "Without exception all of us have agreed from the beginning," Eisenhower told Marshall on January 10, "that the main invasion into Germany...should be by the north flank. Terrain, length of our own lines of communication and location of important geographical objectives in Germany, all confirm the necessity of making the principal invasion along the northern line. Long before D-day this general concept of operations was outlined by my staff and approved by me."[3]

In the center, Hodges and Patton were ordered to penetrate the West Wall and advance to the Rhine between Cologne and Koblenz. Eisenhower saw these operations as "the principal *supporting* attack[s]." Since Montgomery could utilize only thirty-five divisions, SHAEF began construction of a strategic reserve of twenty divisions. In all, Eisenhower had eighty-five divisions at his disposal. If Bradley's offensives proved promising, Eisenhower wanted to retain enough reserves to reinforce success swiftly. "We must be able to go forward [everywhere]," he told Marshall. "Flexibility requires reserves."[4] Meanwhile, Eisenhower reinforced Devers in the south hoping to eliminate the Colmar Pocket, a thorn in SHAEF's side since the autumn.

During the Bulge fighting, SHAEF assumed detailed direction of Bradley and Devers's commands, including movements down to divisional level. Eisenhower and Smith were particularly unhappy with Devers's management of the Alsace campaign. Despite enjoying a numerical advantage of about two to one, Devers's command seemed paralyzed whenever the Germans moved a division. As Smith commented acidly to Robb, SHAEF did not have "much confidence in our friend Jakey." Indeed, Eisenhower spoke openly of replacing Devers with Patch.[5]

With the Bulge on the verge of elimination, SHAEF finalized plans for the Rhineland campaign. Frustrated by the failure to pocket the Germans in the Ardennes and the disappointing news from 6th Army Group area, Smith railed against Eisenhower's policy of reconciling competing personalities and strategies. "We never do anything bold," he complained in his morning conference on January 16. "There are always at least seventeen people to be dealt with so we must compromise, and a compromise is never bold." Exasperated, he asked, "How long is it going to take us to make up our minds to do anything."[6]

Eisenhower remained in Versailles January 14-20, prodding his staff to make a plan for the final campaign. Each morning SHAEF held its routine staff conference. Since full-blown conferences became too time-consuming and on the whole unproductive, Smith delegated the chairmanship of these sessions to Morgan or Gale. In the meantime his other principal deputies and the division chiefs attended an informal gathering in Smith's office. "Taking the 20th of January as a typical day," Robb recorded, "we find Bedell sitting at his desk, Strong and Morgan on the couch, the 'Air,' Spaatz and I, each on an arm of the big easy chair, and Bull, sword in hand, holding the floor, lamps with their talc overlays spread before him." The Colmar Pocket topped the agenda that day. Eisenhower demanded the deduction of the pocket as a precondition for Montgomery and Bradley's offensives west of the Rhine. "Hell of a gamble," Smith said, "so much depends upon the French." Smith went on to say he thought Devers should retire and consolidate but had refrained from discussing the matter with the 6th Army Group commander for fear he would mistake

Bedell's suggestion for an order. The discussion was broken momentarily when Smith's secretary, Major Ruth Briggs, entered with coffee. Reaching her boss, she asked, "General, will you have a cup today?" When he replied he would not, everyone in the room knew immediately "his gastric trouble had caught up with him again."[7]

The conferences of January 14-20 were particularly important. Although the Rhineland offensives had been planned in early autumn 1944, they took specific form during the January meetings. On January 20 Eisenhower dispatched a seven-page cable to the Combined Chiefs outlining his intentions, the fruit of the January SHAEF conferences.[8]

The conferences had been held at the request of the Combined Chiefs.[9] Dismayed by Eisenhower's pre-Ardennes estimate that he did not expect to cross the Rhine until May 1945, the British reopened the old debate over strategy and the command structure.[10] Straining after years of total mobilization, the British leadership despaired about their postwar position. For the British, victory alone no longer sufficed; all now depended upon the circumstances of that victory. Having staked everything on ending the war in Europe in 1944, Churchill faced the grim reality of the balance of forces in the theater (the ratio stood at sixty-one American divisions to fifteen under-strength Commonwealth divisions). If he was to retain an independent voice in strategic matters or the postwar settlement, Churchill knew the British must play a conspicuous role in the campaign in Germany out of all proportion to their material contributions. The war had to end as quickly as possible. Failing that, either a British officer must be named as overall ground commander or substantial American forces be kept under Montgomery's command.[11] In a last desperate gambit, the British asked for a concrete assessment of Eisenhower's intentions—his January 20 Appreciation—and pushed for Alexander's appointment as deputy supreme commander. More worrisome, evidence mounted Marshall was also growing impatient with Eisenhower's methodical strategy.[12] A major conference was scheduled for the end of January at Malta as a preliminary to the three-power Yalta meetings. At Malta, Brooke hoped to persuade Marshall of the necessity for both a reorganization of the higher direction of war and the adoption of a strengthened, British-led, northern thrust.

Proud of the War Department's efforts in assembling and supplying the American armies in northwest Europe and resentful of British attempts to infuse Alexander into SHAEF, Marshall steadfastly opposed any alteration in the command structure. Responding to calls for Alexander's transfer to SHAEF in the British press, the army chief of staff wrote Eisenhower, insisting he "*not* appoint [a] British overall ground commander." Both reinforcing and warning Eisenhower, Marshall told him in a December 30 communication: "You not only have our complete confidence but there would be a terrific resentment in this country following such action." Marshall worried that Churchill would pressure Eisenhower into making concessions.[13]

Marshall's intuition proved correct. When Churchill and Brooke were in Paris on January 3, they raised the question whether Tedder might not be replaced by Alexander as deputy supreme commander.[14] This would increase the British voice in ground operations without the necessity of adding a new echelon to the command structure. Given his close relationship with Alexander and the fact the British field marshal understood ground operations better than Tedder, Eisenhower accepted the idea a change might be desirable. "He actually accepted the notion of a ground commander," Smith recalled. When Eisenhower showed Smith a draft letter to that effect, the chief of staff opposed sending it and called for Whiteley.[15]

The Deputy G-3, whose opinion Eisenhower valued, vehemently rejected the proposal. After some discussion, the cable was altered to lay down those conditions under which Eisenhower would accept Alexander as deputy without portfolio.[16] "The organization for command is, of course, not ideal, but it is the most practicable one," the revised communication read, "considering the questions of nationality involved and the personalities available within the theater." The roles of SHAEF centered on determining priorities, developing communications, and deciding upon strategy. In Eisenhower's opinion this could best be done with the existing arrangements.[17]

All attention then turned to the Malta Conference where the basic strategy for the Rhineland campaign and the breakout into Germany would be settled. Neither Eisenhower nor Montgomery attended the meetings, willingly surrendering the debate to their respective bosses. The supreme commander did journey to Marseilles on January 28 to confer with Marshall. Marshall reassured Eisenhower he supported the broad-front advance and would resign before accepting a British ground commander interposed between Eisenhower and the army groups. Equally adamant in his views, Brooke came to Malta determined to carry the argument.[18]

Smith, accompanied by his G-3 Bull, attended the conference as a SHAEF representative. Eisenhower knew his trusted assistant could not be bullied by Churchill or Brooke, and he enjoyed excellent relations with Cunningham and Portal, the other British service chiefs. Smith had two missions: to retain the plan to eliminate the German forces west of the Rhine and guard against any breakdown in Allied cooperation.

The Malta Conference began on January 30, 1945. The first business session opened with Smith and Bull describing the SHAEF plan for a two-pronged offensive: one north of Düsseldorf, the other toward Frankfurt. Smith argued for clearing the Germans west of the Rhine. Once that was completed, the Allies armies would mass sufficient strength to "make a truly successful invasion with all forces available." He highlighted "arrangements were underway" to reinforce Montgomery's drive to thirty-six divisions. "In General Eisenhower's view the thrust in the north was absolutely essential," Smith told the service chiefs, but the southern offensive was "necessary and desirable and to be undertaken if at all possible." He went on to state SHAEF entertained no intention of halting "until the Germans were cleared west of the Rhine if an opportunity developed."

Although reluctant to assign specific timetables and objectives for the Rhine crossings and the breakthrough phase, Smith outlined the SHAEF plan for a linkup of Montgomery and Bradley at Kassel, pocketing the Ruhr. Since the northern thrust offered "the greatest strategic rewards," he promised it would be concentrated and backed by sufficient reserves to exploit any pursuit toward Berlin.

The British suspected Eisenhower's insistence on closing along the Rhine would again disperse Allied offensive strength. In response, Smith assured Brooke SHAEF proposed to "put into the northern thrust every single division which could be maintained logistically." He estimated another ten divisions could be fed into Montgomery's drive "to exploit success."

Smith elaborated further on SHAEF grand strategy. He pointed out Bradley's offensive toward Frankfurt constituted only a subsidiary effort designed to draw off German strength and provide an alternative route of advance should the main effort fail. Much to Brooke's surprise the two main stumbling blocks evaporated: Montgomery's offensive would receive full support, and Eisenhower had seemingly abandoned his insistence upon clearing the Rhineland before effecting a crossing. Although Smith's explanation differed significantly from Eisenhower's January 20 Appreciation, Brooke confided in his diary the BCOS "would probably be prepared to approve Bedell's statements," providing Eisenhower accepted the revised directive.[19]

Smith joined the American Joint Chiefs for an afternoon conference. He explained why SHAEF abandoned the drive toward Cologne-Bonn in favor of Frankfurt. Somewhat less strident in his advocacy of the northern thrust before an exclusively American audience, Smith maintained Montgomery's attack could not succeed without Bradley's offensive. He petitioned the Joint Chiefs not to allow the British to tie SHEAF's hands, underscoring the need to preserve operational flexibility. On Alexander's appointment, Smith doubted the British had come to a firm decision on the question, particularly in view of Montgomery's negative "attitude on the matter."[20]

Smith anticipated the British would not accept the vaguely worded Appreciation and cabled Eisenhower that Brooke wanted "something in writing to clinch the fact that the main effort on the north [was] to be pushed and that you are not to delay other operations until you have eliminated every German west of the Rhine." He suggested Eisenhower reword his directive prioritizing his objectives: (1) the northern offensive, (2) the removal of German resistance north of the Mosel, and (3) the elimination of other enemy forces west of the Rhine that threaten other Rhine crossings. "If you agree to the above changes," he ended, "we think this will settle the whole matter."[21]

Eisenhower responded by telling Smith he could "assure the Combined Chiefs of Staff that I will seize the Rhine crossing in the North immediately...without waiting to close the Rhine throughout its length." Then he equivocated: "I will advance across the Rhine in the North with maximum strength and complete determination as soon as the situation in the South allows me to collect the necessary forces and do this without incurring unnecessary risks."[22]

Brooke, unimpressed with Eisenhower's lukewarm response, continued to express dissatisfaction during the meetings of January 31. The British offered to reinforce Montgomery with five British and Canadian divisions from Italy in the expectation Marshall might agree to give the northern variant priority and back Alexander's appointment. Instead, they received only a vague "clarification" of Eisenhower's intentions and a tentative agreement upon Alexander's future appointment.

During the night of January 31, Smith visited Brooke in his room at Governor's House. The interview started poorly when Brooke said he doubted if Eisenhower was "strong enough" to control his headstrong subordinates. "Goddamn it," Smith flared, "Let's have it out here and now." Asking to speak off the record, he demanded to know exactly what Brooke meant. Taken aback by Smith's display of temper, Brooke said Eisenhower was "tolerant to a fault with subordinates including Montgomery." Smith analyzed Eisenhower's style of leadership, pointing out the Allied team could only be held together through a combination of flexibility and sternness. He told Brooke any alteration in the command structure would be interpreted as a vote of no confidence in Eisenhower, and if the British insisted on pressing the point, they should move for the Combined Chiefs to relieve the supreme commander. Risking little by this approach—Smith knew Brooke stood alone on this issue—the field marshal backed down. Weakly responding Eisenhower was a good "chairman of the board," Brooke said he had no intention of getting rid of him.

The two turned their attention to the strategic question. Smith confided in Brooke SHAEF had erred in France by being too often deflected from the objective. He explained reserves were being collected and SHAEF would take full advantage of any opportunity for a quick crossing of the Rhine—without waiting to close to the river all along its length. Relieved, Brooke felt the American general understood the need for concentration in the north and believed, as formulator and executor of SHAEF planning, Smith would see that Eisenhower did not stray from the essential strategy. With their views in seeming accordance, they parted.[23]

The frank exchange of views between Smith and Brooke allayed the CIGS's worst fears about the upcoming campaign. The next day, February 1, Smith raised the issue of Alexander's appointment. The American chiefs, disinclined to accept Smith's assessment, bristled at the very idea of surrendering power to the British at this stage in the war. Admiral King lost his temper as mutual suspicions, never far from the surface, threatened to open a serious rift. Marshall calmed the waters and asked Smith to step out of the room. The Combined Chiefs then thrashed out the question.[24] Given the preponderance of American forces in the theater, the attitude of the American chiefs and public opinion, and the strength of Marshall's convictions, Eisenhower continued as director of Allied operations. The question of Alexander's appointment did not die. It resurfaced from time to time until March 1945, but after Malta it lost its urgency. The following day, the British accepted Eisenhower's redrafted directive.[25] As Ismay told Churchill: "General Eisenhower's intentions are more or less exactly what you and the Chiefs of Staff would have them be."[26]

The Malta conference produced some of the most bitter confrontations of the war. Brooke's distrust of Eisenhower stemmed from his view the supreme commander lacked force of will. Brooke was convinced Smith "appreciated the dangers of Ike's strategy [of dispersion]" and would "use his influence to guide him."[27] Having long considered Smith a more able soldier than Eisenhower, Brooke was satisfied he had won Bedell over to his strategic conceptions. Brooke and Montgomery later concluded the Malta Conference had convinced Eisenhower, through Smith, concentration of effort was indispensable to Allied victory in spring 1945. In their evaluation the campaign in Germany vindicated their approach. In fact no such conversion took place. The British misunderstood the nature of the Eisenhower-Smith relationship. Like others, the British field marshals mistakenly thought Smith, not Eisenhower, was the man piloting the SHAEF ship. Although Smith made every appearance of agreeing with the British view, in fact his masterfully conducted defense of the SHAEF strategy preserved Eisenhower's independence. Once again the supreme commander owed much to his chief of staff.

BERLIN AND THE NATIONAL REDOUBT

Within a week of the closing of the Malta conference the initial phase of the Rhineland offensive was well under way. On February 2 Bradley renewed his drive against the Roer. Eight days later the dams fell into American hands. On February 8 Montgomery launched VERITABLE. The next day Devers finally reduced the Colmar Pocket. The lone setback occurred when the Germans opened the flood gates on the Roer, forcing a two-week postponement of Simpson's offensive. Overcoming several obstacles and opposed by the best remaining troops the Germans could muster in the West, the Anglo-Canadian divisions succeeded in attaining most of their objectives by February 23. That day also saw Simpson and Hodges launch successful assaults. Further to the south Patton cleared the West Wall and moved quickly up the Mosel toward Koblenz. By March 10 the Rhine was closed from the Mosel north. The first phase of the campaign came to a successful end.

Growing impatient in his subordinate role, Patton transformed his "active defense" into a series of full-blooded offensives. Throughout February and March he demanded reinforcement. Having moved to his forward headquarters at Rheims, Eisenhower left Smith in charge in Versailles. In effect Smith commanded not only the headquarters but also what Patton termed "Smith's new toy, SHAEF reserve."[28] If Patton wanted reinforcements he would have to pry them away from Bedell Smith. A curious aspect of Smith's personality was his inability to gauge other people's feelings toward him. Smith once told Patton he was his "best friend." Patton, on the other hand, never considered Smith "a special friend." Indeed, Patton came to despise Smith, blaming Bedell for his removal from command of the 3d Army following the flap over Patton's handling of the de-Nazification program in postwar Bavaria. On his deathbed Patton instructed his wife to tell the surgeon "under no circumstances," allow Smith to visit him. "It may be fatal," he said, "if I have to see that old sonuvabitch." Patton carried his empathy to the grave. Mrs. Patton ordered Smith's name be dropped from the list of honorary pallbearers, placing the general's black aide in his place. While relations worsened between the two men after the end of hostilities, at no time during the war could their relationship be characterized as anything other than strained.[29]

On February 16 Patton flew to Paris to plead his case for reinforcements with Smith. During their conference Patton steered the conversation to a discussion of his manpower requirements. "I suppose you don't know the high strategy," Smith said, "but I am convinced that *my* [italics added] northern effort cannot logistically support more than thirty-five divisions. As we have eighty-three divisions, that leaves a few I can use anywhere else, and I want you to be prepared to resume the old offensive through Saarlautern." Patton could hardly believe his ears. "How many divisions would you require?" Smith inquired. Not to push his luck, Patton asked for five. To his great amazement, Smith told him, "I think you should have twelve." "I had never known how great he really was," Patton sarcastically mused in his diary that night.[30]

Patton's attacks failed to secure Trier as ordered on February 27. He feared SHAEF would pull the plug on his offensive. Bradley, once again ignoring SHAEF directives, told Patton to "keep on going until we receive orders to stop from higher authority." "He also said," Patton recorded in his diary, "that he would not listen to the telephone." Trier fell on March 1. Pleased, Patton telephoned Smith to give him the news.[31]

Upon reaching the Rhine, Patton received orders to attack southeast, across the Mosel, in conjunction with Patch's drive up from the Saar. By this stage in the war Bradley and Patton seemed less intent upon fighting the Germans than stymieing SHAEF's efforts to grant Montgomery's northern thrust priority. Patton summed up their feelings best when he wrote in his diary it was "essential that the 1st and 3d Armies get themselves so committed down here that they [SHAEF] cannot move us north for the British instilled idea of attacking on the Ruhr Plain [sic]."[32] To continue his drive, Patton required more reinforcements and once again approached Smith on the question. This time he found Smith cool to the suggestion an armored division be detached from Patch's army to Patton's XX Corps. Sensing nothing could be gained through formal channels, Patton asked Smith to fly forward to discuss the situation in person.

The wily 3d Army commander knew that no time in his career had Smith been presented with a guard of honor. Hoping to stroke Smith's ego and thereby soften him, Patton arranged an elaborate military review. Patton's reading of Smith could not have been more accurate. Much pleased by his reception, Smith withdrew his opposition to the proposed shift. The 12th Armored Division soon was added to the 3d Army's order of battle.[33]

Reinforced, Patton's forces drove south. With Patch's 7th Army, he destroyed the remaining elements of the German 7th Army in the Palatinate. By March 21 the Anglo-American armies controlled the Rhine's left bank from Arnhem to the Swiss frontier. The Rhineland campaign fulfilled Eisenhower's basic objective—the destruction of the German armies west of the Rhine. It opened with the Germans fielding sixty understrength divisions. By the conclusion of the campaign they had no more than the equivalent of twenty-six divisions in the West.

As importantly, the Americans succeeded in staking out two bridgeheads on the east bank. On March 7 a two-battalion task force of Hodges's 9th Armored Division unexpectedly discovered the Ludendorff Bridge at Remagen intact. In an excellent display of small-unit initiative, the Americans seized the railway viaduct just as the Germans prepared its demolition. Within hours American forces secured the lodgment and attacked eastward. The Germans, their division and corps headquarters in the midst of reorganization, were caught off balance by the speed of the American advance, and desperately fed in their remaining reserves to seal off the bridgehead. In the opinion of the new German commander, Kesselring, "never was there more concentrated bad luck at one place than at Remagen." The loss of the bridge unhinged, in Reichmarschall Hermann Göring's view, the "entire defensive scheme" along the Rhine. To defend the Remagen Gap, the German command stripped the area Mainz-Mannheim.[34] Seizing the opportunity, Patton staged a crossing at Oppenheim on March 22, a day before Montgomery's long-planned operation north of the Ruhr. The dramatic and unforeseen successes of Hodges and Patton altered the course of the campaign in Germany.[35]

As planned, Dempsey's army, behind a massive artillery and aerial bombardment and supported by a two-division airborne drop, crossed the Rhine on March 23 in the last major Allied offensive in the West. The next day Simpson began his crossings. Within four days the northern bridgehead was thirty-five miles wide, twenty-five miles deep, with twenty divisions prepared to advance across Westphalia to the Elbe and Berlin. True to the original concept outlined at Malta, Eisenhower gave Montgomery the logistical support the field marshal had demanded. Once the thin crust of the German defense had been broken, Kesselring, could do nothing. For Eisenhower the only question was how to destroy the remaining enemy forces as quickly as possible.[36] Once Bradley crossed the Rhine and began his advance, he could, with justification, assert prior claim upon logistical support.

While the Allies crossed the Rhine, Eisenhower took a short vacation on the French Riviera. Throughout February, people close to the supreme commander detected changes in his personality. He became quarrelsome and argumentative, given to making long self-congratulatory speeches. Usually quick to praise others, he seemed "all too willing to accept loyal service and unwilling to say 'thank you.'"[37] When his old friend Hughes came into his office with a problem, Eisenhower first ignored him, then launched into a bitter tirade. "He acted like a crazy man," Hughes remembered.[38] Over lunch, Eisenhower talked freely about his many worries. He was afraid Marshall would agree with published reports the Allies had overextended themselves. He also fretted about Marshall's criticisms concerning soldiers' complaints. Other problems, of a personal nature, ate at him. For months his wife Mamie had heard rumors about Eisenhower's alleged affair with Kay Summersby. Demanding reassurances, she gave him "hell." "Ike [was] on the defensive," Hughes confided in his diary, "guard up, worried, self-isolated."[39] Noting these symptoms, Hughes concluded "Beetle [was] the cause of most of the trouble."[40]

Far from the cause of Eisenhower's complaints, Smith insisted his boss take a few days off. Despite his own worsening health, Smith promised to carry the ball in Eisenhower's absence. Finally giving in, Eisenhower, accompanied by Bradley, flew to Cannes on March 19, where he remained for five days.

Eisenhower was a commander who reflected, rather than created, the consensus of Allied—chiefly American—strategic opinion. Against this background he felt compelled to act. Bradley and Smith exerted the most influence on Eisenhower's decision making. There was an ebb and flow in their respective relationships with Eisenhower. During the Ardennes, Smith's voice dominated; after the elimination of the Bulge, Bradley again became the officer Eisenhower relied upon most for advice.

Sharing similar backgrounds and outlooks, Bradley numbered among Eisenhower's oldest friends. Eisenhower considered Bradley's "tactical and strategical judgments...almost unimpeachable."[41] He knew his old West Point classmate would provide moral support; an element lacking in Eisenhower's relationship with Smith. While at Cannes the two plotted the final course for the campaign in Europe.

Like Eisenhower, Bradley's military instincts were conservative. Remembering the carnage of the street fighting in Aachen, the 12th Army Group commander counseled against a drive to Berlin. He estimated casualties in excess of 100,000, "a pretty stiff price for a prestige objective."[42] Instead of an offensive against the German capital, Bradley thought more could be achieved by a push through the center. There was, of course, more involved in Bradley's rejection of the Berlin offensive than military considerations.

Beneath the veneer of the selfless, stolid "soldier's general" there existed a man who thirsted for recognition and revenge. Bradley emerged from the Battle of the Bulge with a tarnished reputation and hurt feelings. What better means to assure a place in the annals of military history than leading to victory the greatest field army ever assembled under an American officer? If not inducement enough, there remained the factor of revenge. Any offensive towards Berlin would necessarily place Montgomery in a central role. An offensive in the center meant Montgomery's forces would be reduced to guarding Bradley's flank; at the least deprive the field marshal of the extended command of the 9th Army. Without Simpson's army, Montgomery would be hard pressed to accomplish secondary objectives: the liberation of the Netherlands, seizure of the north German ports, and closure of the Baltic Corridor. Blinded by contempt for Montgomery, Bradley closed his mind to the possibilities offered by continuing operations in the north, if not against Berlin, at least toward the Baltic.

Bradley's arguments proved instrumental in forcing Eisenhower's hand. Orders went out for Smith to prepare the groundwork for a shift of emphasis to Bradley's front. Logistical timetables were redrawn and plans for the reinforcement and resupply of 12th Army Group's corps finalized.[43] On March 27 Marshall cabled Eisenhower suggesting the broad front advance continue, away from Berlin, aiming instead for Munich and Linz.[44] This communication killed any lingering doubts Eisenhower may have entertained about his proposed line of action.

German forces in the West were collapsing. On March 28, Hodges's forces held Marburg and Giessen while Patton, bypassing Frankfurt, stood at Lauterbach. The 1st Army continued its drive north through the Frankfurt Corridor toward Kassel, seeking a junction with Simpson's 9th Army and completion of the double envelopment of the Ruhr. After visits to Montgomery and Bradley, Eisenhower decided to announce his main thrust would be in the center toward Dresden. To make sure 12th Army Group possessed sufficient strength, he wired Montgomery, telling him once the Ruhr Pocket was closed the 9th Army would revert to Bradley. With the addition of the newly activated 15th Army under Major General Leonard Gerow, Bradley's forces would mop up the Ruhr and, while Montgomery protected the northern flank, 12th Army Group would deliver the *coup de main* on the line Erfurt-Leipzig-Dresden.[45] Two days later, Eisenhower sent a message to the Allied Military Mission in Moscow disclosing the plan to Stalin.[46] In effect, Eisenhower presented the British with a *fait accompli*.

Churchill and Montgomery reacted sharply to Eisenhower's decision to attack on the central front. They claimed the transfer of Simpson's army would make it impossible to take the German capital. The prime minister tried to change Eisenhower's mind. Writing on March 31 he implored Eisenhower to reconsider. "Berlin has yet lost its military and certainly not it political significance," he asserted. The British felt betrayed by Eisenhower's about-face. Since September 1944 he repeatedly talked in terms of Berlin being "the most important objective in Germany." Now, on March 31, the eve of the closing of the Ruhr Pocket, Eisenhower declared "that place has become, so far as I am concerned, nothing but a geographic location...My purpose is to destroy the enemy's forces and his power to resist." He thought this could best be accomplished by linking up with the Soviets by the shortest route possible.[47]

Eisenhower never accepted the contention he had altered his basic strategy. As he pointed out to Churchill, the strategy in Europe had unfolded exactly as envisioned in May 1944.[48] He claimed he always meant to concentrate his forces and launch, after closing the Ruhr Pocket, "one main attack calculated to accomplish, in conjunction with the Russians, the destruction of the enemy armed forces." Pointing to the old British argument for a single thrust, Eisenhower said he was "merely following the principle that Field Marshal Brooke has always shouted to me."[49]

For Churchill the military phase of the war in Europe ended with the closing and reduction of the Ruhr Pocket. Foremost in his mind was the shape of postwar Europe. Noting the ideological differences between the Western democracies and the Soviet Union and Stalin's consistent refusal to appraise the British and American governments of the Red Army's operations, the prime minister saw no reason to live up to the letter of the zonal boundaries agreed upon at Quebec in late 1944 and confirmed at Yalta. Although he and Eden had not totally abandoned the hopes of continuing tripartite cooperation into the postwar period, their overriding concern centered on Great Britain's emergence from the war in the strongest position possible. This seemed particularly important in view of Roosevelt's declaration American troops would not remain in Europe for more than two years after the conclusion of the war.[50]

Whereas the broad versus narrow front controversy had revealed the doctrinal asymmetry in the American and British approaches to war, the Berlin question demonstrated the convergence of Allied grand strategy. Churchill deemed it of great importance for Eisenhower to advance as far east as possible, remain in place, and then refer the question to the heads of government.[51] Conversely, American war aims rested on the simple thread of the quick victory over Germany, the redeployment of strength into the Pacific, and the construction of arrangements for postwar cooperation among the great powers. Throughout the war American policymakers regarded strategy as politically neutral. The conduct of operations was viewed as a purely military instrument whose lone objective centered on the destruction of the enemy's armed forces. Roosevelt delegated strategic matters to Marshall who in turn deferred to his theater commanders.[52] War, in the American view, had to be guided not by political objectives but by the narrow rules and imperatives of the professional military. In seeing war as something separate and apart from the political process, American civilian and military leaders divorced political ends from military means. The problem rested not in the failure of means but in the lack of coherence and realism in the American definition of ends.

While war possesses its own grammar, it does not have its own logic. Although he claimed to have been a scholar of Clausewitz, Eisenhower demonstrated scant appreciation for the Prussian military thinker's cardinal principle: war is nothing other than the continuation of state policy by other means. "Policy is the guiding intelligence and war only the instrument,"

Clausewitz observed. "No other possibility exists, then, than to subordinate the military point of view to the political."[53] Eisenhower never understood why the prime minister was "so determined to intermingle political and military considerations."[54] As Smith informed the press on April 21, "its [Eisenhower's] job to accomplish his mission as quickly and economically as he possibly can without regard to political factors."[55]

The British saw Eisenhower's decision not to advance on Berlin as hopelessly ingenuous and American policy devoid of sophisticated ideological or political nuances. In their opinion, as Germany lay militarily prostrate, political considerations took on heightened importance. By mid-April it became clear the alliance no longer was one of equals. Within the Combined Chiefs the British confined themselves to rubber stamping Eisenhower's actions. Churchill, of the opinion it was too late to expect the Americans suddenly to discover wars were fought for political advantage and aware of Great Britain's exhaustion, finally gave in. Eisenhower was granted complete freedom of action.

Smith did not exert much influence on the decision to bypass Berlin. After nearly three years of unbroken attention to his duties, Smith approached the end of his tether. During the week when the supreme commander reassessed the strategic situation, Smith's health finally gave way. For months he covered the extent of his health problems, but in the aftermath of the Ardennes crisis Bedell's condition worsened. At Malta the stress took its toll. Forced to absorb too much "foreign matter" during the rounds of luncheons and dinners that attended the conference, Smith suffered a recurrence of his stomach complaint. To add to his distress, he went to three functions with Marshall. "You know the poor view he takes of anybody who looks as though they even had dandruff or athlete's foot," he joked with Handy. "Consequently, I was obliged to be my bright and smiling self while going around in circles inside."[56] At the end of March he was forced to spend several days in bed. His absence from headquarters coincided with Eisenhower's decision not to drive on Berlin.[57]

Smith's views mirrored exactly those of his commander. "The line of the Elbe," Smith later remarked, "was decided upon as a purely military tactical matter." The SHAEF planners concluded the Germans would retreat into Bavaria, Austria, and Bohemia. "In any case, we needed a definite line of demarcation," he told a postwar interviewer, "and the Elbe [was] the most convenient...we wanted a point where we could yoo-hoo across to our comrades before embracing them." In his view Germany had two hearts—the political, Berlin, and the industrial, the Ruhr. "The latter has ceased to beat," he remarked, "and the former was about to stop." In his view, Berlin no longer possessed any military value.[58]

Smith changed his views after the war. In summer 1945 he told a surprised Kenneth Strong the Soviet Union was a nation of the future and Great Britain one of the past. The war had broken British power and the United States would seek a postwar alliance with the Soviet Union. Strong concluded Smith reflected official American policy.[59] Two years later, while serving as United States ambassador to Moscow, Smith's assessment took a 180 degree turn. As he sat across the conference table from the Soviets, he mused how different things would have been had the United States followed Churchill's lead. However, given American wartime public opinion, Smith thought anyone who would have proposed the seizure of Berlin would have been hung from "a lamp post." "We leaned over backward to give [the Soviets] a proper deal," he lamented, "and it was a mistake."[60]

As German resistance evaporated, Smith once again played a major role in fashioning the final twist of Allied strategy. By April 18 most of Simpson and Hodges's armies closed to the Elbe River. Simpson crossed the river as early as April 12 and asked for permission to drive the fifty miles to the German capital. In his estimate he possessed all the strength necessary and required only permission from headquarters.[61] The Soviets, still thirty-five miles from Berlin on the Oder River and facing furious resistance, were not scheduled to open their offensive until April 16. Eisenhower refused to give Simpson the green light and on April 21 informed the Soviets he intended to stop along the Elbe-Molde Line.[62] Attention shifted to destroying the remaining German forces in the north and south.

With resistance collapsing, Eisenhower and Smith saw ghosts in the form of the "National Redoubt." SHAEF intelligence had closely monitored the development of the "Alpine Defense Zone" since early December, 1944. As late as April 10 the SHAEF Joint Intelligence Committee concluded "there is no evidence to show that the strategy of the German High Command is being conducted with the view of occupying the so-called National Redoubt." [63] Nevertheless, Eisenhower, Bradley, and Smith became convinced the Germans intended to stage their *Gotterdammerung* in the mountain fastness of Bavaria and western Austria.[64] Smith estimated between 100 and 150 Germans divisions remained in the field in the south—excluding German forces in Italy—with the bulk of them falling back toward the National Redoubt. The plot might more properly have been found in the cheap spy novels Eisenhower and Smith liked to read than in the councils of the Allied high command. Without hard intelligence, Eisenhower attached the highest importance to thwarting the German plans.

In a major press conference on April 21, Smith explained the reasoning behind the realignment of the strategic priorities and the redirection of Allied strength away from Berlin. "From a purely military point of view," he said, "[Berlin] doesn't have much significance any more—not anything compared to that of the so-called National Redoubt." Concluding Hitler, the German government, and high command had ensconced themselves in vast underground Alpine installations, he believed German forces in the Netherlands, Denmark, and Norway would continue fighting until the National Redoubt had been reduced. "Our target now, if we are going to bring this war to an end and bring it to an end in a hell of a hurry, is this National Redoubt, and we are organizing our strength in that direction," he told the press. "We may find that when we have cut the head from the snake the tail won't wiggle very long."[65]

The day after the press conference reports filtered into SHAEF the "Reds [were] in Berlin" yet Smith persisted in the belief there was "no hope for [a] quick victory."[66] The same day, three Allied armies opened the offensive in the south. In the end the decision to reduce the National Redoubt—which proved to be nonexistent—offered the only possible strategic argument for abandoning the drive on Berlin and Prague. Their decision to advance into Bavaria removed all doubt the German and Czech capitals would fall to the Soviets.

In the north, Dempsey's army drove towards Lübeck while the Canadian army fought against the only organized defense in the western theater, Generaloberst Johannes Blaskowitz's Army Group H in the Netherlands. Since early in December SHAEF had known of the desperate plight of the Dutch population under German occupation.[67] On December 16 Dutch Prime Minister Pieter Gerbrandy pleaded with Eisenhower to speed operations in the north. "The Dutch government," he wrote, "cannot accept the fact that merely corpses will be liberated."[68] During the battles of the Ardennes and the Rhineland, SHAEF had other priorities. Again in February Gerbrandy appealed to the Allied command, this time directly to Bedell Smith. "To comply with...the Dutch Government's [requests]," Smith replied, "is impossible. We have no troops for it, and the war may last until autumn 1945."[69] Conditions in the Netherlands worsened and suggestions food be landed at Rotterdam in neutral shipping or airdropped by Allied aircraft were overruled for fear of supply confiscation by the Germans.[70]

By April 15 the Canadian 1st Army isolated the German forces behind the Greebe Line. Arthur Seyss-Inquart, Reichkommissar for the Netherlands, hoping, in Churchill's words, "to save face and that of the German command in western Holland," approached the Allies with a proposition. Communicating through the Dutch Underground, Seyss-Inquart offered to open Amsterdam to food and coal shipments and desist from persecuting "political prisoners" in exchange for an Allied halt along the Greebe Line. If the Allies refused, the Germans would open the dikes.[71]

The Nazi offer set off a flurry of communications between SHAEF, London, Washington, and Moscow. Churchill, loath to accept Nazi blackmail, could not bring himself to be party to the devastation of entire districts of the Netherlands. He advised Eisenhower to open negotiations. The prime minister forwarded an impassioned appeal from Gerbrandy.[72] Considering the options, Eisenhower accepted Seyss-Inquart's terms because, as he explained to Marshall, "they are to our military advantage."[73] On April 24, SHAEF received permission to proceed. The next day, Eisenhower ordered Montgomery to cease offensive actions in the Netherlands "pending [the] outcome of negotiations." After some hurried exchanges between SHAEF, 21st Army Group and the German command, a conference was arranged for April 30 at a school in Achterveld.[74]

Smith and Strong represented SHAEF, Prince Bernhard the Dutch government, and Arthur Seyss-Inquart, the Germans. Major General Ivan Suslaparov, the Soviet representative at SHAEF, de Guingand, and Brigadier General E. T. Williams for 21st Army Group, various relief experts, and representatives of the three German services also were present. Both sides drove to Achterveld, but the Germans were compelled to walk the final distance to the school. To add insult to injury, Prince Bernhard arrived in Seyss-Inquart's captured Mercedes.

The proceedings got off to an unexpected beginning. A women who accompanied Seyss-Inquart angrily demanded the return of three parcels left in the Mercedes when the Dutch Underground liberated the car. Once this dispute was settled—to the evident dissatisfaction of the accuser—the real business began.

Smith read SHAEF's proposals for food shipments. The Germans agreed in principle; timetables for the shipments were drawn by the respective staffs. The desire to relieve the Dutch civilian population constituted the most obvious reason for the conference. One of Smith's subordinates could easily have handled that task. Smith attended the meeting with Seyss-Inquart hoping he could convince the Reichkommissar to agree to a truce or an unconditional surrender. Seyss-Inquart replied he possessed no authority over military questions and as long as a government functioned in Germany, there could be no surrender in the Netherlands. Seeing he achieved little with this approach, Smith, to the disgust of at least one of the Allied observers, "wheedled." He talked about his German ancestry and the need for avoiding unnecessary bloodshed. "The solemnity [of the occasion]," remembered Williams, "had been spoiled by Bernhardt's giggling."[75]

Frustrated and a little embarrassed by his clumsy appeal to the Nazi's sensibilities, Smith, acting upon advice given him by Seyss-Inquart's doctor, requested they speak privately. Dropping all pretense of formality, Smith asked if Seyss-Inquart understood this constituted his last chance. "Yes, I realize that," the German nodded stiffly. "The consequences to you yourself will be serious," Smith continued. "You know what your acts have been here. You know the feeling of the Dutch people toward you. You know you will probably be shot." After a moment's hesitation, Seyss-Inquart grimly rejoined, "that leaves me cold." Not without a certain sense of satisfaction, Smith sardonically replied, "It usually does." With that, the interview ended.[76]

On April 30, as Soviet troops began to overrun Berlin, Hitler committed suicide. With the official announcement the next day, everyone at SHAEF knew the end of the war was near.[77] May 2 saw the surrender of German forces in Italy. The following day a delegation of high-ranking officers from the new rump government under Grossadmiral Karl Dönitz arrived at Montgomery's headquarters at Lüneburg Heath to discuss the possibility of a partial surrender in the north. Under instructions from SHAEF, Montgomery refused to accept anything but the surrender of all German forces in Denmark, the Netherlands, the Frisian Islands, Heligoland, and Schleswig-Holstein.[78] Taken together, it became obvious the German collapse was imminent.

THE GERMAN SURRENDER

While the combat commands sighed with relief, the first week of May proved to be one of the most hectic of the war for SHAEF. "This period was a single unit of time," Smith remembered. "Scarcely anyone left headquarters. We ate when we were hungry, slept when we could no longer keep awake. Twelve o'clock on the dial of a watch might mean noon or midnight. A man looked toward the window to find out."[79] There were hundreds of loose ends yet to be tied together: trying to keep current on operations that moved so quickly divisional commanders often could not locate their own units, administer the relief of the Dutch and attend to a myriad of other civil affairs problems, communicate with the Soviets to assure no confusion arose when the allies linked up, and prepare the instruments of surrender.

At Ploen, Dönitz's headquarters, the Germans did not sleep either. Their problems were of a fundamentally different sort. In a conference held on May 2, Dönitz's principal military and political advisers convinced him to seek piecemeal surrenders of the German units at the army group level and below in the West while continuing the battle in the East to save what they could from the Soviets. When Montgomery refused the German terms, Dönitz decided to surrender unconditionally on the British front.[80] He believed the only way he could buy time in the East was to negotiate partial capitulations in the West. The grand admiral instructed his naval chief, Generaladmiral Hans von Friedeburg, to contact SHAEF and arrange a meeting to discuss surrender terms. Although the Germans refused to surrender on all fronts, in a demonstration of good faith, Dönitz suspended the activities of his U-Boats and released King Leopold of Belgium.[81]

A detailed document defining the terms of surrender and the respective American, British, and Soviet zones of occupation had been drafted by the European Advisory Commission before the Normandy invasion. Smith saw the documents while at Bushy Park, but because SHAEF was preoccupied with planning the invasion and organizational differences delayed the finalization of civil affairs policy, he concluded the instruments of surrender premature. With the collapse of Germany looming, Smith forgot these documents existed and they had received the approval of the three governments. It was quite natural Smith dismissed these surrender terms as outdated because France added a fourth wheel to the alliance.[82]

The headquarters formulated other plans for the final surrender near the end of April. Because of their experience in handling the Italian surrender, Eisenhower delegated Smith and Strong responsibility for negotiating the German capitulation. On May 4 Smith informed Ambassador Winart in London SHAEF did not possess authority from the political heads or the Combined Chiefs to proceed on the basis of the existing European Advisory Commission document. Convinced the EAC instrument of surrender to be "too long," Eisenhower ordered his staff to prepare a "shorter version." The supreme commander worried the Soviets might reject a surrender under SHAEF auspices but concluded Stalin's government would accept any accord that ended the fighting as soon as possible. After a feverish day's labor the staff completed two documents. The first, the "Act of Military Surrender," provided for the unconditional surrender of the German armed forces on all fronts. In the second document, the "Undertaking Given by Certain Emissaries to the Allied High Command," the Germans would agree to send representatives of the High Command to formally ratify the military surrender at a location and place decided upon by SHAEF and the Soviet government. Eisenhower made sure the Soviets concurred with these arrangements before giving the documents his authoritative approval.[83]

On May 5 the Friedeburg group made their way to Rheims, SHAEF-Main since March 1. The Germans clung to the hope they could bring their troops facing the Soviets west to surrender to the Americans and British. Friedeburg's plane had been grounded at Brussels; he continued his trip to Rheims by automobile. In the meantime Smith received a message from Montgomery outlining the likely German strategy for delaying negotiations. Eisenhower already had told Bedell the only acceptable terms were immediate and unconditional surrender of all German forces. Furthermore, he made it clear he would not see any German until the surrender had been completed. To Smith fell the final responsibility of managing the German capitulation.

With the German arrival delayed, Smith resorted to one of his clever ruses. The War Room on the first floor of the École Professionelle et Technique de Garçon was ringed with huge situation maps. In the center a large swastika dominated the wall from which rose a graphic thermometer revealing the number of Germans (4,035,051) taken prisoner by Allied forces. Friedeburg would be ushered here to await his interview with Smith. To heighten the German admiral's sense of doom, a new situation map was prepared. It accurately showed the current positions of Allied and German forces, but two large red arrows—one from the West cutting off German forces in Bohemia and Yugoslavia, the other from the East—were added. Although imaginary, these converging attacks were meant to convey the sheer hopelessness of the German situation.[84]

When Friedeburg and his associates arrived, the map was ready and laid out on Smith's desk. After a suitable period the Germans were brought into Smith's office. Strong, the only other Allied officer present, acted as interpreter. As Montgomery warned, Friedeburg tried to discuss surrendering the German forces only on the Western Front. Smith merely said there appeared to be nothing to discuss since the Allies could only accept unconditional surrender. In a scene reminiscent of the Italian negotiations of 1943, Smith and Strong refused to discuss anything but unconditional surrender while Friedeburg protested he did not have the authority to capitulate. During the course of their discussions Smith noted Friedeburg's eyes, welling up with tears, scanned the map between them. "Obviously," Smith said, "you do not entirely realize the hopelessness of the German situation." Smith found himself sympathizing with the pathetic German's plight. It was "a terrible thing for a man to see himself as completely helpless," he remembered.[85]

After his interview with Smith, Friedeburg and his three aides were escorted into a second-floor conference room. The dispirited Germans took their seats opposite Smith, Spaatz, Morgan, Robb, and Strong. A series of detailed discussions ensued. Friedeburg continued to insist surrender to the Russians was "unthinkable." Smith replied if the Germans promptly surrendered on all fronts, they would be treated "with the normal dictates of humanity."[86] On the other hand, if they refused, the western Allies would close the front to refugees and hold the German command responsible for the needless loss of life and property. Smith told Friedeburg either he sign the surrender or request someone be sent by Dönitz with the full authority to do so. Convinced his position was untenable, Friedeburg asked permission to communicate with his headquarters.[87]

Since the German negotiators did not possess their code, the message went to Montgomery's headquarters then on to Flensburg, the seat of Dönitz's government. The German head of state wanted to stall for more time, if only for forty-eight hours, to allow as many German soldiers and civilians as possible to get into the western zones. He dispatched Generaloberst Alfred Jodl, chief of the Operations Staff of the German High Command (OKW) and strongest advocate of continuing the battle in the East, to Rheims hoping the general could convince Eisenhower of the impossibility of surrendering to the Soviets. The Germans held out the desperate wish differences would emerge between the Allied powers, buying time for German nationals to make their way into the western zone.[88]

May 6 was a day full of mounting tension at SHAEF. All afternoon Eisenhower sat in his office waiting for a Soviet reply to the surrender terms dispatched through Major General John Deane, the head of the American Military Mission in Moscow. Finally, Soviet approval came through for Susloparov to sign the instrument of surrender.[89]

Smith's day was filled with petty irritations. Eisenhower disapproved of press arrangements for the surrender ceremony. Deciding the proceedings were "not going to be a Hollywood show," Smith ordered the War Room cleared of cameras and sound equipment. This created a number of headaches for Butcher, who had been charged with handling press relations. Unhappy with Smith's arbitrary ruling, Butcher thought "Beetle's tummy was bothering him" and took the matter up with Eisenhower. With more-important worries, Eisenhower simply said the surrender "was Beetle's show" and if he did not want any publicity "that was the answer." Smith had taken the opportunity for a short afternoon nap. Returning to headquarters at 5 P.M., he found Butcher waiting for him. "The nap had improved his disposition," recorded Butcher, "he was gracious, understanding, and cooperative." A compromise was reached on press arrangements for the surrender ceremony. Heaving a sigh of relief, Butcher told Bedell what a "sweat [he] had been in." "Your sweat," Smith retorted sharply, "What do you think the rest of us are doing."[90] A few minutes later, Jodl, accompanied by de Guingand, arrived.

Just as Smith had made Castellano cool his heels before the final negotiations leading to the Italian surrender, he made Jodl and Friedeburg wait before they were brought into his office at 6:15. With Strong serving as interpreter, Smith allowed Jodl to make his presentation. The Germans would surrender to the Western Allies, Jodl told Smith, but they needed twenty-four hours to communicate instructions to isolated units. It was obvious Jodl wanted time. Acting on Eisenhower's instructions, Smith flatly refused the German request saying the Germans must capitulate on both fronts. He delivered an ultimatum:

Unless Jodl accepted the terms by midnight, the Anglo-American forces would seal the front. No Germans would be allowed to cross the line.

Leaving the Germans to contemplate their options, Smith and Strong conferred with Eisenhower. They pointed out Jodl maintained Flensburg did not possess adequate lines of communications to the German field commands—this was confirmed by Allied intercepts—and it might prove impossible to implement the surrender unless the Germans received a twenty-four-hour cease-fire. Eisenhower agreed to the delay.

On their way back to Smith's office, Strong suggested they try a "soldier-to-soldier" approach. Strong had served in Berlin before the war and knew the importance the German officer corps attached to honor. Smith agreed to give it a try. After making the concession of the cease-fire, Smith told Jodl the German officers and soldiers had done their best to preserve their military traditions and the High Command "had faced insoluble political pressures." If the German Army surrendered, it could salvage a measure of honor and prestige. He reminded the German general the officer corps would be afforded the protection of the Geneva Conventions. "It was a good, long speech made with a straight face," Strong recorded, "showing a fine understanding of the German mentality." Impressed by Smith's words, Jodl asked he and Friedeburg be allowed to discuss the matter in private.[91]

About an hour later Jodl emerged from the meeting convinced of the futility of temporizing any further. He requested permission to communicate with Dönitz. After outlining the Allied conditions, Jodl told Dönitz he saw "no alternative other than chaos or signature" and asked for "immediate radio confirmation whether authorization for signing can be put into effect. Hostilities will then cease on 9 May 0001 hours our time." Meanwhile, the German military situation deteriorated as Prague rose up in insurrection making it impossible to extricate their forces from Bohemia. A little after the midnight deadline a reply arrived from Flensburg. Dönitz authorized Jodl "full power" to conclude the surrender.[92]

At 2:30 A.M. the Allied delegation, led by Smith, entered the War Room. Five minutes later, the Germans, escorted by Strong, followed. Jodl bowed stiffly and took up his seat opposite Smith. On Jodl's left sat Friedeburg; at his right, Major Friedrich Oxenius, his aide. Opposite sat the Allied signators and witnesses: Susloparov, Spaatz, Robb, Bull, Admiral Harold Burroughs, the Chief of Staff of Allied naval forces, and Major Général François Sevez, the French representative, and Morgan. Smith formally asked Jodl if he was prepared to sign the surrender; the German general, in a steady voice, replied in the affirmative. Strong, standing behind the Germans, placed the "Act of Military Surrender" before Jodl. After he signed the document, Strong passed it to

Smith, who affixed his signature. Suslaparov and Sevez followed in turn. The second document was then signed. Jodl, through Strong, made a brief statement that ended with a plea the victors treat the German soldiers and civilians with generosity. There was no reply. The entire ceremony took less than fifteen minutes.[93]

Smith was struck both by the lack of emotion displayed by the Allied officers around the table and by the steely cold military bearing of the Germans.[94] At the completion of the signing, Smith took Jodl to see the supreme commander. Entering Eisenhower's office, Smith announced the war was over. Fixing his eyes upon Jodl, Eisenhower, flanked by Tedder, asked if the German understood completely the terms of the surrender. When Jodl replied he did, the supreme commander told him he would be held personally responsible for any breach of the agreement. After the German general said he understood, Eisenhower curtly dismissed him. The interview lasted but a couple of minutes.[95]

Eisenhower gathered his SHAEF team together while photographers captured the historic moment. A short newsreel and a radio recording were made. After the journalists left, Smith said as an appropriate final act, the staff should prepare a message for the Combined Chiefs. It was natural he would think of Marshall at this moment. Together they tried to find the correct words. "I tried one myself," Smith recalled, "and like my associates, groped for resounding phrases as fitting accolades to the Great Crusade and indicative of our dedication to the great task just completed."[96] Eisenhower watched in silence. Thanking them for their efforts, he dictated the message himself. It read: "The mission of this Allied force was fulfilled at 0241 local time, May 7, 1945."[97] With that, the war in Europe came to an end.

Epilogue

The Years of Frustration, 1945–1961

During June 1945 one victory celebration followed another. On June 15 Smith flew to Paris, the first stop on his return trip to the United States. The procession snaked through the streets of Paris, emerging at the Arc de Triomphe. Here, beneath the flag-draped monument, France honored the leaders of the Supreme Allied command, Eisenhower and his principal deputies, Bedell Smith, and Tedder. First, de Gaulle awarded Eisenhower with the Compangon de là Libération. Smith's formal decoration with the Grand-croix de la Légion de Mérite followed. After placing the ribbon around Smith's neck, de Gaulle stooped and kissed him on both cheeks. Following Tedder's presentation and a brief ceremony at the Tomb of the Unknown Soldier, the Allied officers received a march-past by French soldiers.

Leaving Orly Airport, Smith made a flight to Bermuda, where he enjoyed a twenty-four hour stopover. In the company of Marshall and Eisenhower, Smith put his time to good use—he caught a dozen fish in the crystal clear waters. On June 18 he flew to Washington for a reunion with his wife. They had not seen each other since November 1943.

On June 21 Smith took part in the victory parade in Washington. Taking Marshall's place beside Eisenhower in the lead automobile, they rode from the Pentagon to the Capitol where Eisenhower addressed Congress. From Washington, Bedell and Nory Smith went on to their native Indianapolis where he received the honors of the city.[1]

Although he had no way of knowing it at the time, this round of victory celebrations, fittingly ending in Indianapolis, the city he left twenty-eight years before as a young lieutenant, marked the climax of Smith's military career. Not yet fifty, he had every reason to be proud of his accomplishments in the U.S. Army. Without benefit of a West Point ring he had risen from humble circumstances to the rank of lieutenant general. The fact he had attained an enviable position within the Allied armies was proven by the list of his honors and decorations: four American Distinguished Service Medals; two British knighthoods; the Soviet Order of Kutuzov (First Class); and the French *Grand-croix de la Légion d'honneur*.[2] More personally satisfying, he had won and kept the confidence and respect of Roosevelt, Churchill, Marshall, Eisenhower, and de Gaulle.

The war in Europe now over, he set his sights upon further advancement in the army. His keenest desire was to follow in the footsteps of Marshall as chief of staff. He was to be disappointed. In the sixteen years between the end of the war and his death, although far from empty, Smith never received the honors he thought himself due. The dénouement of his career was filled with bitterness and personal disappointment.

AMBASSADOR TO MOSCOW

After a short stay in the United States, Smith returned to Frankfurt to resume his duties as SHAEF chief of staff. In August Eisenhower nominated Smith as his first choice to assume the command of American forces in Europe. This meant a promotion to full general and his elevation over more-senior officers, including Patton. The position also would give Smith his first command posting since 1918. Most important, the European command might provide the bridge to the chief of staff's office.[3]

Much to Smith's disappointment, the War Department named Lieutenant General Lucius Clay as Eisenhower's successor in Germany. As December neared—and his transfer from Europe—Smith began to worry about his prospects. A wholesale reduction in the long list of general officers loomed on the not-too-distant horizon. In a letter to Eisenhower on November 28, Smith pleaded with the new chief of staff for any appointment. "It doesn't make a bit of difference what [position] it is," he wrote. Preferring a field command to a Washington desk, Smith went so far as to request a reduction to his permanent rank if that would facilitate his placement.[4]

Eisenhower reassured his old associate not to worry about the future. "There are a dozen places where I would like to use you," he wrote in reply.[5] Smith never made it to the Pentagon. As relations worsened with the Soviet Union, President Truman looked for an experienced and hard-boiled man for the arduous job of ambassador to Moscow; someone who would not be bullied by Stalin. In a surprise move, Truman offered the job to Smith.

Putting aside personal preferences, he consented to stand for nomination for the post. In his recommendation to Congress, Truman requested and received special legislation permitting Smith to retain his permanent military rank of major general. Without giving up his military status but sacrificing any real prospects of advancement in the Pentagon, Smith began his career as a diplomat.

Smith's first official responsibility as Harriman's successor was to attend the Paris Peace Conference in 1946 as a member of the American delegation. Typical of his approach, in the time before taking up residency in Moscow, Smith immersed himself in reading works on Russian history.[6] Smith possessed wide military diplomatic experience as Eisenhower's ambassador, but during the war when he spoke he did so with "four million men and 15,000 heavy bombers behind [him]."[7] As U.S. ambassador to the Soviet Union in the immediate postwar years, Smith bore the brunt of worsening relations between the former allies. Smith the diplomat acted like Smith the soldier. He carried out his duties with a cold tenacity of purpose but with little flexibility. During his three-year tenure in Moscow, American-Soviet relations deteriorated, and although no one in Washington blamed this on Smith, his hard-line posture and lack of imagination did little to allay Soviet suspicions of American intentions.

While in the Russian capital Smith analyzed the Soviet leadership and adumbrated the future course of Soviet-American relations. *My Three Years in Moscow*, published in 1950, was Smith's account of his experiences. The book focused on Smith's interpretation of the historic Soviet world view. In the Soviet approach to foreign affairs, he commented, there existed no commonality of interests with the West. He saw the relationship as inherently antagonistic, based upon the internalized nature of Soviet power with its secretive totalitarian structure and its external drive for European hegemony. As a result, the struggle between the West and the Soviet Union was seen by Smith as long-term and irreconcilable.

"We [the United States] are forced into a continued struggle for a free way of life that might extend over a period of many years," he wrote. "We dare not allow ourselves any false sense of security." For Smith, the Soviets would not risk war with the West but would seek to achieve their objectives by other means.[8] He believed only a consistent long-range policy based upon the firm resolve to oppose Soviet expansionism could preserve American security. "We must anticipate that the Soviet tactic will be to attempt to wear us down, to exasperate us, to keep probing for weak spots," he concluded, "and we must cultivate firmness and patience to a degree we have never before required."[9]

DIRECTOR OF THE CENTRAL INTELLIGENCE AGENCY

In March 1949 Smith returned to the United States. Truman offered him the post of under secretary of state for European Affairs, but Smith declined the appointment. He still harbored hopes of earning his fourth star and following

Bradley into the chief of staff's office. The army had other ideas. Instead of an appointment to a meaningful post, Bradley sent him to replace Hodges in command of the 1st Army on Governor's Island, New York. It was painfully clear that Smith's military career had reached its end. Although command of the 1st Army meant a fourth star, Smith knew the posting was nothing more than a sinecure, where senior officers sat out their remaining years of active duty. Like Hodges, Smith was expected to retire after a genteel tour of duty in New York City.

Feeling betrayed by the army he loved, Smith's mounting disappointment contributed to his deteriorating health. Racked by a series of health problems, he could no longer tolerate the pain that had been his constant companion for years. Smith's attention to duty had exacted a high price. His ulcers had grown acute; unable to eat a normal diet, he suffered from malnutrition and gastritis. The only solution lay in radical surgery.[10]

Smith's confinement to the wilderness, albeit New York City, did not last long. His time was absorbed in convalescing after the operation and in writing *My Three Years in Moscow*.[11] In September 1950 Truman appointed him director of the Central Intelligence Agency. On two earlier occasions Smith had turned down the position. One reason centered on his reluctance to undertake a thorough housecleaning of the intelligence agency. Another involved his less-than-total support for the civilian intelligence organization. Both during his stint with the Joint Chiefs and as chief of staff in the Mediterranean and Europe, Smith had demonstrated little regard for OSS operations. But in the light of the failures of the CIA to anticipate the North Korean invasion of the south, Smith told Eisenhower he "could not refuse for a third time."[12] To a friend he was more candid when he wrote: "I expect the worst and I am sure I won't be disappointed."[13]

Smith's appointment to the intelligence job was considered of vital importance. His book had won him a reputation as the nation's foremost expert on Communist activities.[14] Typically, his first actions involved a reorganization of the agency that focused decision making in the director's hands. Second, he tightened security.

The record of the infant CIA had been anything but good. Under the agency's first director, Rear Admiral Roscoe Hillenkoetter, the CIA's performance failed to live up to even the most modest expectations. The intelligence organization fared little better under Smith. Less than two months after assuming direction of the CIA, Smith endorsed the view, based largely on military intelligence, that the Chinese would not intervene in the Korean War. The Joint Chiefs and the National Security Council, with the Smith-generated memorandum in mind, concluded the Chinese would not take unilateral action. When they did, the

United Nations forces suffered a major military setback.[15] Similarly, the CIA failed to appraise correctly the situation in Iran, to anticipate the revolution in Egypt, or to predict a succession of coups in Latin America. Responding to the rising chorus of criticism in Congress, Smith characteristically responded by wrapping a cloak of secrecy around the CIA. Among his actions, Smith embarked upon a program to develop a corps of career intelligence officers. He also restructured the flow of intelligence giving only the uppermost officials a comprehensive picture of the agency's actions.[16]

After having spent three years in Moscow, Smith held the Soviets in utter contempt. Not only was he a dedicated "cold warrior," Smith loathed socialism in all its forms. Like many, he feared creeping socialism in the United States. He viewed the mildest liberal utterance as subversive. For example, after Nelson Rockefeller made a lukewarm speech in favor of labor unions, Smith branded him a "Red."[17] He began to see conspiracies of "parlor pinks" everywhere in Washington. In September 1952, with the presidential campaigns at their peak, Smith set off a furore when he testified before a Senate committee that the State Department had been infiltrated by Communists as early as 1945 and that this was widely known in official circles. He also claimed Communists had insinuated themselves into the CIA. These disclosures, entirely unsupported by any hard evidence, fanned the growing flames of McCarthyism.[18]

Smith never quite understood that the requirements of holding high political office in peacetime differed from those of a senior military officer in war. "[His] sensitiveness to the nuances of politics, as opposed to how you run a war," one State Department official observed of Smith, "was limited."[19] He also experienced difficulty with the press. Always uneasy out of his ordered environment, Smith's rough style and technically correct statements frequently confused journalists. In September 1945, for instance, his replies to questions arising from Patton's "denazification" program in Bavaria indicated Smith agreed with employing former members of the Nazi party in sensitive administrative positions. Fortunately for Smith "the press was asleep at the switch." He was not as lucky in the aftermath of his congressional testimony. His ill-considered remarks thrust him and the CIA into the middle of a seething campaign issue. Headlines read: "Red Spies in U.S. Intelligence Agency." Trying to mend the damage, Smith telephoned Eisenhower and the Democratic Party's presidential nominee, Governor Adlai Stevenson, urging both candidates to refrain from making the CIA into a campaign issue. Smith did succeed in controlling the situation. The CIA was not subjected to close scrutiny either by the press or congressional investigating groups. His statements, however, gave ammunition for Republican charges that the Truman administration had been "soft on Communists."[20]

The 1950 stomach operation did not solve his health problems. Smith lost so much weight that his doctors were at the point of ordering him to step down from his post.[21] Although only fifty-seven, Smith looked much older. His "fishy eyes" were deeply sunk into his gaunt, wrinkled face. Once stocky, the CIA director now was but an emaciated, cadaverous shadow of his former self.

As his stomach problems worsened, so too did his foul temper. He made life intolerable for those in direct contact with him, and there were those who thought his temper influenced his decision making. Unhappy with the post from the beginning, Smith made no secret of his desire to leave the CIA. Despite the obstacles Smith succeeded in turning the intelligence agency around. No longer plagued by indecisiveness at the top, the CIA under Smith ceased to labor under uncertainty of its peacetime organization or its political feasibility. In his seventeen-month-long tenure as director he succeeded in reconstructing and streamlining the agency. Much of the credit for the CIA's subsequent development is due to Smith.[22]

SHORT OF EXPECTATIONS:
IKE'S ASSISTANT SECRETARY OF STATE

It was natural that Eisenhower, upon election as president, would want his wartime alter-ego to hold an important position in his administration. When the president-elect asked Smith if he desired a post in the Republican administration, he responded by saying "what I would like to do is get a fifth star and retire."[23] He was to do neither. John Foster Dulles, Eisenhower's choice as secretary of state, pushed for Smith's appointment as under secretary. The offer held few attractions for Smith. After being director of the CIA, the job of number-two man in the State Department appeared as a demotion. However, out of loyalty to Eisenhower, Smith accepted the position. In February 1952 Smith, the only man to hold a high position within both the Truman and Eisenhower administrations, took up his duties.

As he told a *New York Times* correspondent, Smith assumed he would serve as Dulles's chief of staff. As a competent executive and organizer and with his background as ambassador to the Soviet Union and intelligence chief, Smith possessed ideal qualifications for the position. Many Washington insiders thought Smith's appointment heralded a reconstitution of the old "Ike-Beetle" team and predicted the new under secretary of state would emerge as a power behind the throne.[24] As it turned out, Eisenhower and Dulles had different ideas.

Recognizing Smith's many liabilities, the president took pains to distance himself from his old partner. Dulles's motives were more calculating. The secretary of state, a suspicious man, saw Smith as a threat. He wanted Smith as his assistant because, as a close personal friend of the president, the under secretary would keep the lines of communication open between the State Department and the White House. Dulles feared Smith's loyalty would be directed toward Eisenhower and not the State Department. He worried his assistant would serve as the White House's "eyes and ears" in Dulles's preserve. Dulles also envied Smith's relationship with Eisenhower. Whereas relations between Eisenhower and Dulles were conducted on a formal level, Smith would pick up the phone and say, "God damn it Ike, I think..."[25]

There was yet another reason why Dulles wanted Smith posted to the State Department. The secretary of state wanted to control the intelligence apparatus and this would prove difficult if Smith continued on as CIA director. Knowing his brother, Allen Dulles, was Smith's likely successor as CIA head, Dulles manuevered to move Smith into the position in the State Department. As a result, tensions existed between Smith and John Foster Dulles from the onset of their partnership.[26]

Theirs was never a partnership of equals. Dulles had no intention of granting Smith any measure of control over the conduct of foreign policy. Instead, he saw Smith merely as an administrator and executor of policy. This conflicted with Smith's understanding of his functions. He saw himself as "the policy chief of staff" and the active head of "the thinking side of the State Department as distinct from the actual administrative side."[27] It quickly became evident that Dulles did not intend to employ Smith's considerable talents in any meaningful way.

There were no real policy differences between Smith and Dulles. As did his chief, Smith saw the Truman policy of containment as morally bankrupt. As he told the *Times*, "Containment invites a draw; I do not think we want a draw." He also advocated an ambitious policy of expanding the American nuclear arsenal aiming at achieving total military supremacy over the Soviets. In his estimate, the policy of "passive resistance" must give way to an activist foreign policy characterized by "determined opposition."[28]

It is not clear just what Smith's role was under Dulles. When Dulles's diplomatic missions took him out of Washington, as they frequently did, Smith served as acting secretary of state. Dulles never reversed any decisions Smith made in his absence, yet he refused to give him a voice in policy making when the secretary of state was in Washington. On September 3, 1953, Eisenhower created the Operations Coordinating Board to oversee security programs and appointed Smith as its chairman. Although the OCB was designed to bind together the planning and execution of foreign policy strategy—it reported directly to the National Security Council—in fact, owing to Dulles's intransigence, the new agency never carved out its own niche. For the disillusioned Smith, his position in Washington seemed like a dead end.[29]

During his last months in the State Department Smith found himself at the center of two major foreign policy events. The first, a high visibility role at the Geneva Conference of 1954 that ended the First Indochina War; the second, a covert operation that overthrew a freely elected government in Guatemala.

In May 1954 Smith flew to Europe in a last-ditch attempt to convince the British to join with the United States in an intervention in southeast Asia to save the beleaguered French forces at Dien Bien Phu.[30] After holding discussions in London and Paris, where he found little support for the scheme, Smith moved on to Geneva to attend the opening of the conference. While in Paris, Smith told the French that Eisenhower would recognize and give economic and military support to any anti-Communist regime emerging in South Vietnam. Seeing the newly elected French government would end the war on whatever terms, the Americans wanted to arrange matters to guarantee at least part of Indochina would remain outside the sphere of Communist control.[31]

The Soviet delegation, headed by Foreign Minister V. M. Molotov, was equally anxious to find a quick solution. To expedite matters, a confidential meeting was arranged between Smith and Molotov. Smith found Molotov's manner and style of diplomacy much changed from his days in Moscow, a product of Stalin's death the year before. Both men spoke frankly and objectively about the prospects of an early settlement. The American acknowledged that two hostile ideological camps existed in southeast Asia and that the communist and nationalist forces of Ho Chi Minh, well organized and disciplined, controlled large belts of the countryside. The solution, Smith told Molotov, lay in an immediate military armistice and a withdrawal of forces into defined areas preparatory to a final political settlement supervised by neutral authorities. The Soviet foreign minister agreed with the American's assessment.[32]

Smith flew back to Washington only to retrace his step in June. In the meantime, Molotov and Chinese foreign minister Chou En-Lai had exerted pressure on the Vietminh leadership to accept the terms of the agreement. Essentially, the final accord came remarkably close to Smith's outline to Molotov in May: the creation of the Laotian and Cambodian states, the cessation of armed struggle, and the temporary division of Vietnam along the seventeenth parallel until an internationally supervised general election could be held in 1956 to decide the issue of reunification.

Despite the fact Smith played a key part in moving the sides towards a settlement, Dulles instructed him to play only a passive role at the final Geneva meetings. When finally the Geneva Accords were to be signed, the State Department forbade Smith from becoming a "cosignatory with the Communists in any Declaration." Instead, the under secretary issued what amounted to a repudiation of the accords and a unilateral American guarantee of the sovereignty of the "government" of South Vietnam. The path to American involvement in southeast Asia began with the unsigned declaration of Geneva.[33]

At Geneva, Smith merely executed the policies of John Foster Dulles. The Guatemalan coup, on the other hand, remains Smith's lone tour de force as under secretary of state. In September 1953 the CIA planned, in league with Anastasio Somoza of Nicaragua, to overthrow the government of Jacobo Arbenz Guzman of Guatemala. In the atmosphere of the excesses of McCarthyism and the loyalty and security programs of both the Truman and Eisenhower administrations, the foreign policy machine of the United States operated under a broad definition of what constituted the "Communist threat." In the bipolar world of the 1950s, the premise the Soviet Union stood behind all subversion of American interests went unquestioned. For the State Department, Guatemala represented a Soviet attempt to build an outpost of Communism in the Western Hemisphere.[34]

Smith fully accepted this view. While at the CIA, Smith had been in contact with envoys from several Latin American nations, including those of Nicaragua. Somoza offered to "clean up Guatemala for you [the United States] in no time." All he required of the United States were guns and money. Arms were duly sent to Nicaragua in a United Fruit Company freighter in crates marked "agricultural machinery." Smith had little faith in Somoza's claims and wanted the operation postponed to tighten planning. When Secretary of State Dean Acheson brought the plan to Truman's attention, the president ordered the mission canceled.[35]

As under secretary of state, Smith devoted a good deal of attention to Latin American affairs as Dulles possessed little interest in the region. In a March 5, 1954, memorandum, Smith wrote "the most important question facing the Cabinet [is] to make up its mind that Latin America is important...timely action [is] extremely desirable to prevent Communism from spreading seriously beyond Guatemala."

The Guatemalan coup was revived in autumn 1953. A United Fruit Company lobbyist enlisted Smith's aid to pressure Allen Dulles into going ahead with the operation. Dulles needed little prompting as the CIA increased their support for the "Army of Liberation," training in Nicaragua. The plan centered upon an invasion of Guatemala while, in the meantime, CIA operatives within the Central America nation engineered internal disruptions.

The affair began when Smith ordered the American ambassador in Guatemala City, John Perrifoy, to put the CIA plan into operation.[36] Meanwhile Smith met with congressional leaders who promised to keep all knowledge of the coup quiet until after the overthrow had been completed.[37] The operations went better than expected. Arbenz's government toppled and the American involvement covered up—all in a nice, clean, low-risk operation.

Managing the Guatemalan coup proved to be Smith's final responsibility in the State Department. Throughout summer 1954 his health deteriorated. As one of Dulles's aides remembered, in "the last ten years of his life [there] never passed a comfortable minute. I mean he was a physical wreck."[38] After nearly four decades of service to his country Smith resigned his post on October 1, 1954. He did so in a spirit of alienation and rancor.

THE BITTER RETIREMENT

Since he received neither his fifth star, the appointment of chief of staff, or the honors and public recognition to which he felt entitled, Smith took advantage of his position for material gain. If he could not attain fame in public service, he decided to gain a fortune in the private sector.

With his customary assiduousness Smith turned his attention to making money. He had grown old and tired in the service of the United States, but he saw no reason why he had to remain in modest circumstances as well. As in most of his endeavors, Smith's efforts to amass a fortune met with success. Even as an officer he had never shrunk from using his influence to obtain advantages, ranging from his shady dealings with the gunmaker Purdey to his requisitioning of villas, fine wine cellars, or fishing lodges for his own purposes.

His action after leaving the State Department grazed the fine edge of malfeasance. For instance he did not even wait a decent interval before assuming a position as director and member of the executive committee of the United Fruit Company. He left the State Department on October 1 and before the month expired took up his position with the fruit company. The multinational fruit company, which stood to lose much if Arbenz nationalized Guatemalan products, cooperated fully in the overthrow. However, Smith's negotiating for the private job while the coup was being planned and executed transcended the bounds of ethical if not criminal behavior.[39] In 1958 Smith was appointed as a special advisor to the secretary of state on disarmament. At the same time Smith, an outspoken proponent of nuclear expansion, served as president and chairman of the board of AMF Atomics Incorporated and of the Associated Missile Products Company, two corporations with large Pentagon contracts. He also served as vice-chairman of the American Machine and Foundry Company and director of RCA and the Corning Glass Company.

It is indeed ironic at the time when Eisenhower warned the nation of the dangers of the developing military-industrial complex, his most trusted wartime associate emerged as among the first representatives of that connection. When

Smith died he left an estate valued at nearly $2.5 million—the vast majority of which he acquired in the six and a half years after he left government service.[40]

Smith's drive to enrich himself stemmed from his bitterness over treatment at the hands of his old comrades, particularly Eisenhower. His wealth may have given him a measure of satisfaction, but it offered slight consolation. In his retirement he reaped the bitter fruit of his cheerless approach to human relations. During the war Smith's relations with men like Eisenhower and Bradley rested on professional regard and a narrow military sense of loyalty rather than genuine personal or social intimacy. Moreover, his actions as chief of staff won him grudging respect but they also engendered strong personal enmity. Although his stomach problems contributed to his nasty disposition, those who knew him before the war thought him naturally mean-spirited. Not outwardly given to signs of self-doubt, his irascible personality was a product of his own feelings of insecurity. He resented the camaraderie of the West Pointers. The close friendships between Eisenhower, Bradley, Patton, and Hughes served to heighten his sense of alienation from their inner circle. None of his wartime relationships with senior American officers survived the war. The only friendships that endured after the war were with junior members of his staff—none of whom had professional military backgrounds—and with British officers like Strong, Morgan, and de Guingand.[41]

He explained to the British members of his inner staff in a circular letter in 1945, characteristically contained in a form letter, "I am not too articulate where my feelings are concerned."[42] Since he took pains to deprive historians of his personal letters, especially those to his wife, we are left to construct a picture of Smith only from his official actions. Perhaps some grey personalities must remain grey.

Only on two occasions did Bedell Smith reveal his pent up feelings. Once, to the historian Forrest Pogue, he lost control and wept when he reflected on the great debt he owed General Marshall.[43] The other occasion was in the company of his Washington neighbor, then-Vice President Richard Nixon. Exchanging their views over whiskies, they concurred Eisenhower had exploited them in his rise to the top. "He was very tired," Nixon recorded, "and he uncharacteristically began showing emotions. Tears began to stream down his cheeks." Summing up his heartfelt estimate of Eisenhower's manipulative personality and style of leadership, Smith tellingly remarked: "I was just Ike's prat boy. Ike always had to have a prat boy."[44] He carried these intense resentments to his grave.

NO CAISSONS OR POMP:
THE QUIET DEATH OF BEDELL SMITH

On July 20, 1961, Smith was stricken with a heart attack in his Washington home. After a night's stay in the hospital he died the next morning. His body, ravaged by health problems, could no longer sustain the fight.[45]

Before he passed away, Smith left instructions his funeral be a simple affair—no horse-drawn caisson or excessive military pomp. A requiem mass was celebrated, directed by Bishop William Arnold of New York and attended by Francis Cardinal Spellman. The list of honorary pallbearers included Eisenhower, Allen Dulles, his former Secretary/General Staff Carter Burgess, and General George Decker, army chief of staff.

After the mass, Smith's remains were placed into a motor hearse. The funeral procession made its way across the Potomac to Arlington National Cemetery. Entering the grounds, the line of vehicles drove toward the Tomb of the Unknown Soldier. Only two hundred yards from the memorial the procession came to a halt. Here, on a shady hill, General Walter Bedell Smith was laid to final rest.[46]

It was fitting that this place was selected. Just a few short paces away stood the grave of General Marshall. In a sense, Smith's passage had come full circle. In life, so too in death, he and Marshall were connected.

CHART 1: ALLIED COMBINED COMMAND STRUCTURE

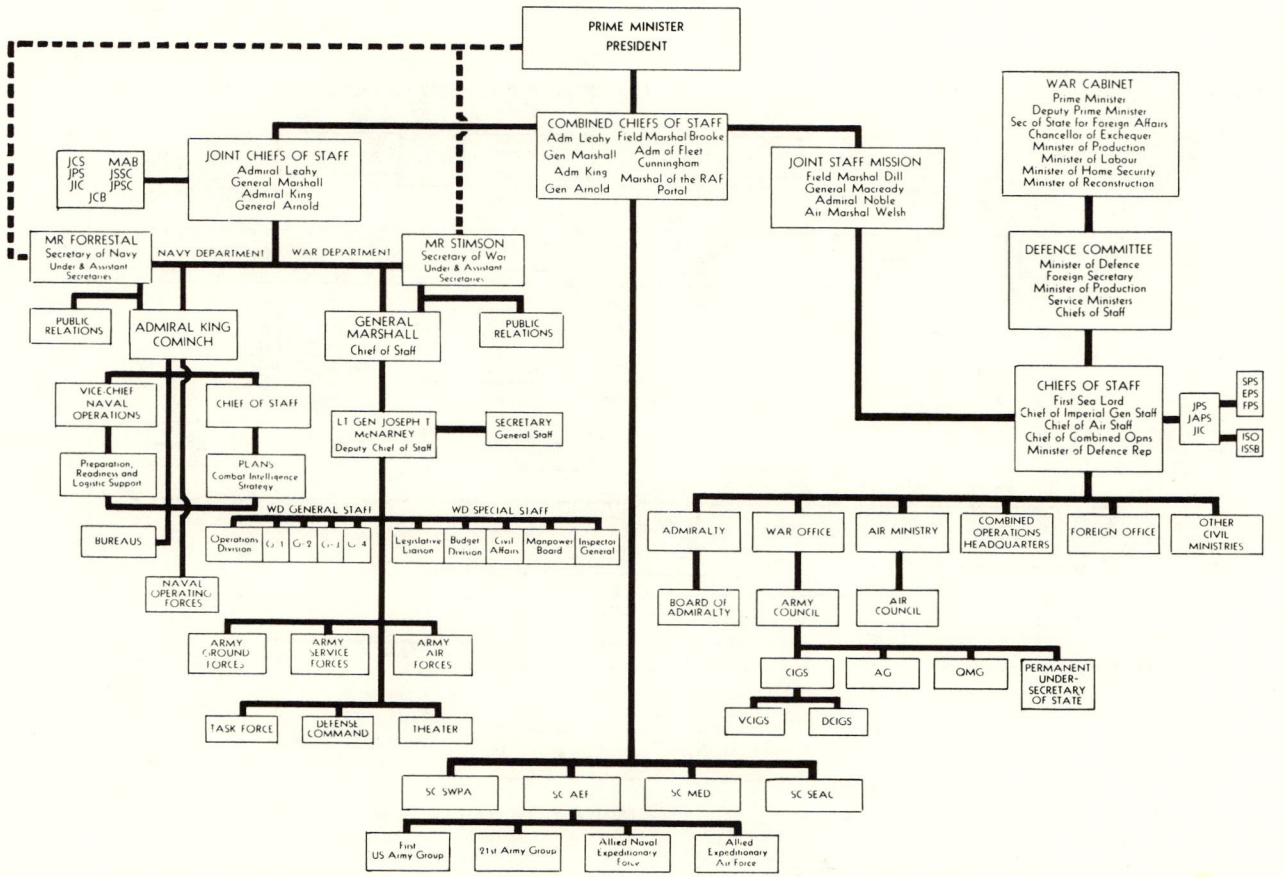

Forrest C. Pogue, *The Supreme Command*, in United States Army in World War II series (Washington, D.C.: Department of the Army, 1954), 38.

CHART 2: AFHQ COMMAND AND STAFF STRUCTURE

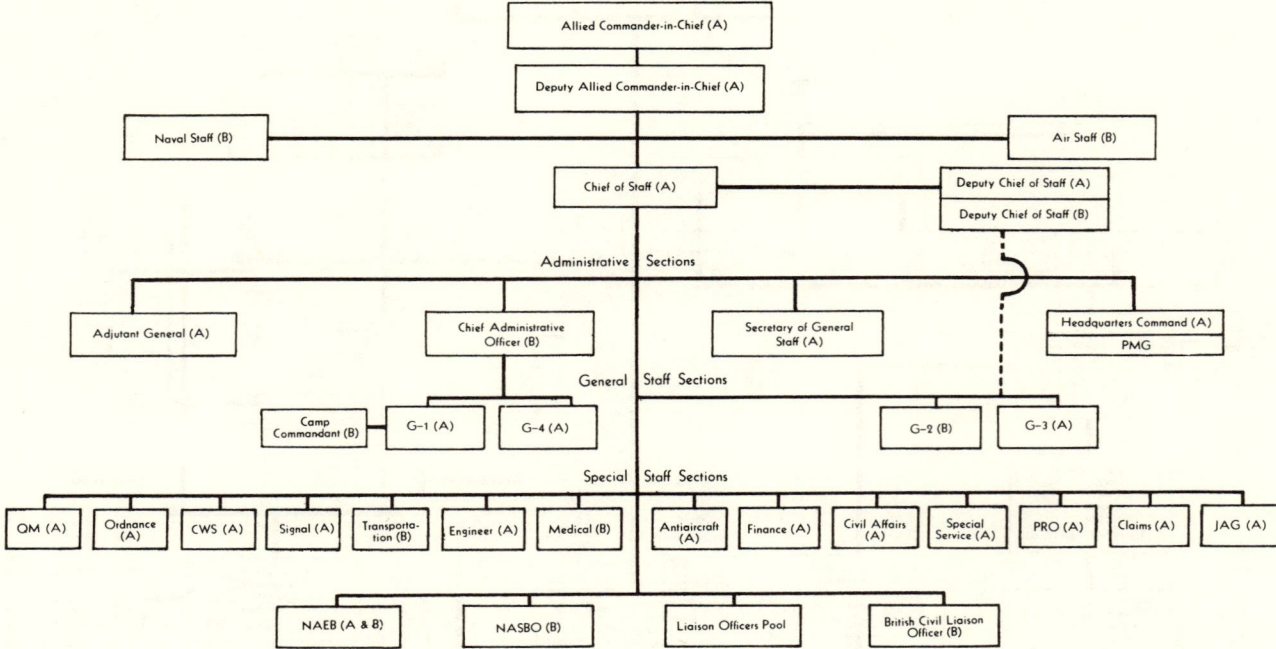

George F. Howe, *Northwest Africa: Seizing the Initiative in the West*, in United States Army in World War II series (Washington, D.C.: Department of the Army, 1957), 34.

CHART 3: SHAEF COMMAND AND STAFF STRUCTURE

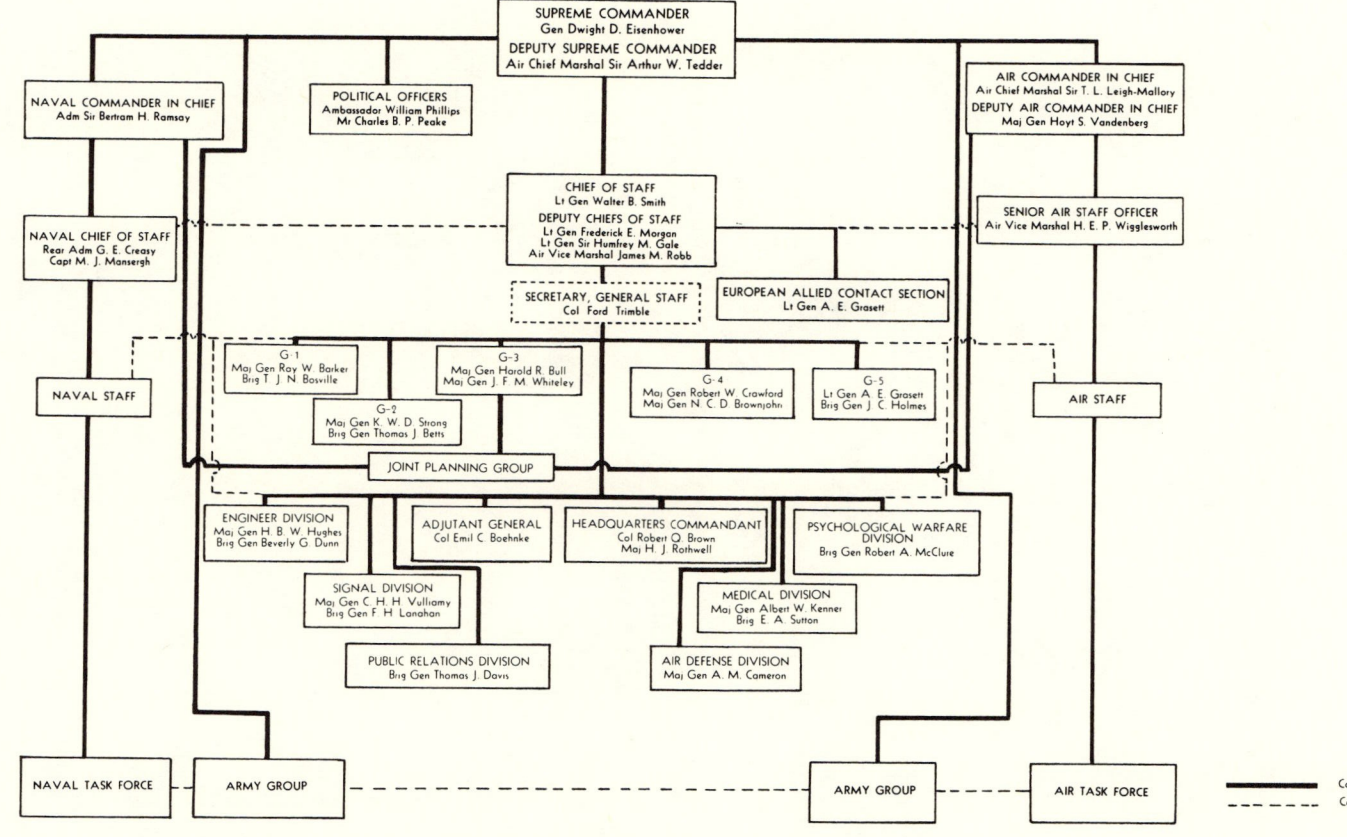

Forrest C. Pogue, *The Supreme Command*, in United States Army in World War II series (Washington, D.C.: Department of the Army, 1954), 67.

Glossary

AEAF	Allied Expeditionary Air Forces, SHAEF
AEAF	Allied Expeditionary Air Force
AEF	American Expeditionary Force, World War I
AEFHQ	American Expeditionary Force Headquarters.
AFHQ	Allied Force Headquarters
AMGOT	Allied Military Government of Occupied Territories
ANCXF	Allied Naval Commander-in-Chief, Northwest Europe
ANVIL	Allied invasion of the south of France. Later changed to DRAGOON.
ARCADIA	United States-British Combined Chiefs Meeting, Washington, December 1941 - January 1942
AVALANCHE	Amphibious landing at Salerno, Italy.
BARRACUDA	Plan for amphibious operation in the vicinity of Naples
BAYTOWN	Allied crossing of the Straits of Messina.
BCOS	British Chiefs of Staff
BODYGUARD	Allied deception plan to cover Normandy landings.
BOLERO	Buildup of United States forces in Great Britain
BRIMSTONE	Planned seizure of Sardinia
BUTTRESS	Planned operations into Italian toe.
CAO	Chief Administrative Officer
CCS	Combined Chiefs of Staff
CIGS	Chief, Imperial General Staff
COBRA	1st U.S. Army offensive in Normandy, July 25, 1944
CNO	Chief of Naval Operations
Com Z	Communications Zone - United States logistical command
COSSAC	Chief of Staff, Supreme Allied Commander

DRAGOON	Allied invasion of the south of France
DUKW	Amphibious assault vehicle
EAC	European Advisory Commission
ETO/ETOUSA	European Theater of Operation
FCNL	French Committee on National Liberation
FIREBRAND	Plan for operations in Corsica
FORCE 141	Planning Agency, AFHQ
FORTITUDE	Cover operations to conceal Normandy landing
G-1	Personnel Division of the general staff
G-2	Intelligence Division
G-3	Operations Division
G-4	Administration/Supply Division
G-5	Civil Affairs Division
G-6	Public Relations and Psychological Warfare Division
GIANT II	Plan to drop American airborne troops near Rome.
GARDEN	21st Army Group operation in the Netherlands to open a corridor over the Lower Rhine in conjunction with MARKET.
GOODWOOD	British assault east of Caen, July, 1944.
GRENADE	U.S. 9th Army offensive in the Roer sector in combination with Canadian 1st Army's VERITABLE.
GYMNAST	North African invasion plan, 1941.
HUSKY	Invasion of Sicily.
JCS	Joint Chiefs of Staff
JIC	Joint Intelligence Committee
LUFTWAFFE	German Air Force
LUCKYSTRIKE	Plan to breakout into Normandy.
MARKET	Allied airborne operation to seize bridgeheads in the Eindhoven-Nijmegen-Arnhem area of the Netherlands (September 1944) in conjunction with ground operation (GARDEN).
MULBERRY	Artificial harbors, part of Normandy operation.
MUSKET	Plan for operations into southern Italy
NATOUSA	North African Theater of Operations
NEPTUNE	Landing phase of OVERLORD PLAN, landings in Normandy, June, 1944.
OKW	Oberkommado der Wehrmacht. German High Command, oversaw operations in the West.
OPD	Operations and Planning Division, WDGS

OSS	Office of Strategic Services - U.S. intelligence service.
OVERLORD	Allied master plan for campaign in northwest Europe beginning with NEPTUNE phase.
PLUNDER	21st Army Group crossing of the Rhine north of Wesel, March, 1945.
QUADRANT	Combined Chiefs of Staff Meeting, Quebec, 1943.
RAF	Royal Air Force
RANKIN	Allied contingency plans in the advent of German collapse.
ROUNDUP	Predated OVERLORD; plan for cross-Channel invasion of France, 1943.
SGS	Secretary/General Staff
SHAEF	Supreme Headquarters, Allied Expeditionary Force
SHARPENER	Supreme Commander's Advanced Command, Portsmouth, May, 1944.
SHINGLE	Allied amphibious operation at Anzio, Italy, January, 1944.
SLEDGEHAMMER	Cross-channel invasion of Europe, autumn, 1942.
SOE	Special Operations Executive; British Intelligence Operation
SOS	Services of Supply
SYMBOL	Casablanca Conference, January, 1943.
TORCH	Allied campaign in North Africa; landings in Morocco and Algeria, November, 1942.
TRIDENT	Combined Chiefs of Staff Meeting, Washington, 1943.
ULTRA	Allied interception of German code; decrypting device.
VENGEANCE	German rocket weapons
VERITABLE	21st Army Group operation for Anglo-Canadian forces to clear the Rhineland between the Maas and the Rhine, February, 1945.
WACHT AM RHEIN	German Ardennes Offensive, December, 1944
WIDEWING	SHAEF Headquarters, Bushy Park, London.

Notes

INTRODUCTION

1. Dixon Wecter, *The Hero in America* (Ann Arbor, Mich., 1963); Christine Scriabini, "American Attitudes towards a Martial Presidency," *Military Affairs* 63 (December 1983): 165-72.

2. Dwight Eisenhower, *Crusade in Europe* (Garden City, N.Y., 1948), 197.

3. Steve Bates, "Marshall Plan Under Way In Leesburg: Group Appeals to Europe To Save General's House," *Washington Post*, July 9, 1989.

4. Eisenhower to Smith, November 28, 1947, Pre-Presidential Papers, Dwight D. Eisenhower Presidential Library, Abilene, Kansas.

5. Smith to Eisenhower, April 1, 1947, Pre-Presidential Papers.

6. Smith to Marshall, December 3, 1945, George C. Marshall Papers, George C. Marshall Library, Lexington, Virginia.

CHAPTER 1

1. During the Second World War Indianapolis suddenly discovered that one of its native sons had risen to great heights in the army. Throughout the war, particularly after Smith presided over the first Italian surrender and later the German capitulation, there appeared a number of articles in the Indianapolis newspapers dealing with General Eisenhower's chief of staff. As Smith was an unknown before the war, even in his home town, and since his rapid rise in the army shocked even his own family, most of the articles sought to explain the Bedell Smith phenomenon.

These articles, collected in the Indiana State Library in Indianapolis, provide excellent biographical material on Smith's life before he entered the military. *Indianapolis Star*, May 8, 1945, Walter Bedell Smith File, Indiana State Library [hereafter cited as Smith File, ISL]. See also *Indianapolis News*, June 19, 1945, Smith File, ISL.

2. *Indianapolis Star*, September 16, 1943, Smith File, ISL.

3. *Indianapolis Star*, May 8, 1945, Smith File, ISL.

4. "Indiana's Walter Bedell Smith," in *Indianapolis Star Magazine*, October 18, 1953, Smith File, ISL, 13.

5. *Indianapolis Times*, April 3, 1949, Smith File, ISL.

6. Charles C. Wertenbaker, "The Invasion Plan: Smith, Eisenhower's Chief of Staff, Worked Out the Secret, Closely Guarded Moves," *Life* 16 (June 12, 1944), 94.

7. *Indianapolis Star*, September 26, 1943, Smith File, ISL.

8. *Indianapolis Times*, September 16, 1943, Smith File, ISL.

9. *Indianapolis Star*, August 19, 1950, Smith File, ISL.

10. For Smith, fishing became an obsession. After the war he wrote several articles about the finer aspects of fresh-water fishing, including one in an encyclopedia. See Harold Hinton, "Soldier, Diplomat, Intelligence Chief," *New York Times Magazine*, August 27, 1950, 50.

11. *Indianapolis News*, June 6, 1944; *Indianapolis Star*, October 4, 1943, and August 19, 1950, Smith File, ISL.

12. His grade-school teacher, Mrs. Lucy Wilson Thomas, remembered Smith "as a marvellous reader and a very intelligent child; such children are a joy to any teacher." *Indianapolis Star*, May 8, 1945, Smith File, ISL.

13. Fifty different cities in Indiana boasted an assembling or manufacturing plant for automobiles with fifty different makes built in Indianapolis alone. The National Motor Car Company, where Smith was employed, existed for thirty-one years until it closed in 1934. Wallace Spencer Hamilton, "Indiana's Place in Automobile History," *Indiana Historical Bulletin* 44 (January 1967): 12, 18.

14. "Indiana's Walter Bedell Smith," 12; and *Indianapolis Star*, May 8, 1945, Smith File, ISL.

15. "Indiana's Walter Bedell Smith," 13.

16. Indiana enlisted 3.5 per 1,000 eligible men, the lowest in the nation. John K. Mahon, *History of the Militia and the National Guard* (New York, 1983), 141. For the history of the Indiana National Guard see William Watt and James Spears, *Indiana's Citizen Soldiers: The Militia and National Guard in Indiana History* (Indianapolis, 1980).

17. "Indiana's Walter Bedell Smith," 13.

18. *Indianapolis News*, June 19, 1945; and *Indianapolis Times*, April 3, 1949, Smith File, ISL.

19. This observation was made by a close friend and classmate, H. F. Weinmann, who remarked that Smith "didn't care much for girls until he was seventeen." In *Indianapolis News*, June 19, 1945, Smith File, ISL. See also an interview with Mary Cline Smith, *Indianapolis Star*, May 8, 1945, Smith File, ISL.

20. "Indiana's Walter Bedell Smith," 14.

21. Smith possessed all the necessary credits to graduate but he never bothered to attend the graduation ceremony. His diploma was sent to him afterwards, when he was director of the Central Intelligence Agency during the Eisenhower administration. See *Indianapolis Star*, May 8 1945, Smith File, ISL.

22. W. H. Lawrence, "'Beetle' Is Back on the Eisenhower Team," *New York Times Magazine*, March 1, 1953, 12.

23. *Indianapolis Star*, May 8, 1945, Smith File, ISL. Smith discussed his service in 1913 with his old company commander, Smith to James Hurt, January 27, 1944, Walter Bedell Smith Papers, Eisenhower Library.

24. *Indianapolis Star*, September 26, 1943, Smith File, ISL.

25. Lawrence, "Eisenhower Team," 12.

26. Historical Division, Department of the Army, *Order of Battle of the United States Land Forces in the World War, American Expeditionary Forces*, 3 vols (in 4 parts) (Washington, D.C., 1931-49) vol. 3: 554-55.

27. Edward M. Coffman, *The War to End All Wars: The American Military Experience in World War I* (New York, 1968), 55; Russell Weigley, *Towards an American Army: American Military Thought from Washington to Marshall* (New York, 1962), 199-222.

28. *Indianapolis Star*, August 19, 1950, Smith File, ISL.

29. Edmund Arpin was an officer candidate at Fort Benjamin Harrison while Smith was there and he too was assigned to Camp Greene, North Carolina, during winter and spring 1917-1918. See Arpin, "A Wisconsinite in World War I: Reminiscences of Edmund P. Arpin, Jr.," Ira Berlin, ed., *Wisconsin Magazine of History* 51 (Autumn, 1967): 3-25.

30. Lockwood rose to the rank of brigadier general and served under Smith when he was a lieutenant general. See "Indiana's Walter Bedell Smith," 14.

31. Cited in Coffman, *War to End All Wars*, 57.

32. Coffman quotes Frederick T. Edwards who attended, in the second section, the training course at Fort Sheridan, Illinois. Ibid., 55.

33. Arpin, "Wisconsinite in World War I," 4-5.

34. Christian A. Bach and Henry Noble Hall, *The Fourth Division* (Garden City, N.J., 1920), 18.

35. American Battle Monument Commission, *Fourth Division: Summary of Operations in the World War* (Washington, D.C., 1944), 5.

36. Bach and Hall, *Fourth Division*, 22.

37. Arpin, "Wisconsinite in World War I," 6.

38. Bach and Hall, *Fourth Division*, 23.

39. Ibid., 27.

40. Westerbaker, "Invasion," 94.

41. Bach and Hall, *Fourth Division*, 39-40.

42. Historical Section, Army War College, *Order of Battle of the United States Land Forces in the World War, American Expeditionary Forces -- Divisions* (Washington, D.C., 1931), 63-64.

43. Harold Fiske, "Report of G-5, AEF" (June 30, 1919), cited in Timothy K. Nenninger, "Tactical Dysfunction in the AEF," *Military Affairs* (October 1987): 180.

44. Bach and Hall, *Fourth Division*, 59; Laurence Stallings, *The Doughboys: The Story of the A.E.F.* (New York, 1963), 159.

45. George C. Marshall, "Profiting by War Experience," *Infantry Journal* 18 (January-June 1921): 34-37.

46. The best analysis of Pershing's views are presented in Donald Smythe, *Pershing: General of the Armies* (Bloomington, Ind., 1986); Nenninger, "American Military Effectiveness in the First World War," in *Military Effectiveness*, Allan Millett and Williamson Murray, eds., 3 vols. (Boston, 1988), vol. 1: 116-156. See also James Rainey, "Ambivalent Warfare: The Tactical Doctrine of the AEF in World War I," *Parameters* (September 1983): 35-46; Nenninger, "Tactical Dysfunction in the AEF," 177-81.

47. Pershing's report on the Bonbom Conference with Foch is contained in Historical Division, Department of the Army, *Military Operations of the American Expeditionary Forces: Champagne-Marne and Aisne-Marne* (Washington, D.C., 1938), 217-18.

48. Marshal Foch's orders for the offensive are contained in ibid., 223-56.

49. Stallings, *Doughboys*, 159; and Bach and Hall, *Fourth Division*, 59.

50. Battle Monuments Commission, *Fourth Division*, 16; Bach and Hall, *Fourth Division*, 69-70.

51. "*Ordre Général d'Opérations, No. 200, Première Partie, G- 3, No. 2563*," French II Corps, July 17, 1918, in *Military Operations of the A.E.F.*, 399-401.

52. Smith wrote a personal experience monograph while at the Infantry School at Fort Benning, Georgia, (1931-32), "Operations of the 1st Battalion, 39th Infantry (Fourth Division) in the Aisne-Marne Offensive, July 18-20, 1918," *Mailing List*, 4: 137-53. See also Infantry School, "Surprise -- Example Two," *Infantry in Battle* (Washington, D.C., 1934), 113-16.

53. Bach and Hall, *Fourth Division*, 66-73; American Battle Monument Commission, *Fourth Division*, 19-21.

54. Bach and Hall, 74.

55. "Casualties--Aisne-Marne Offensive and Visle Sector," American Battle Monument Commission, *Fourth Division*, 34; Stallings, *Doughboys*, 160.

CHAPTER 2

1. For Pershing's views, see Pershing, *My Experience in the World War*, 2 vols. (New York, 1931) vol 1: 124-29. For March's views, see March, *The Nation at War* (New York, 1932), 3, 42-43. General Bullard stated that "if we really have a great war, our War Department will quickly break down," cited in Allan Millett, *The General: Robert L. Bullard and Officership in the United States Army, 1881-1925* (Westport, Conn., 1975), 309.

2. John J. Pershing, "General Staff at General Headquarters," June 30, 1919, reprinted in Historical Division, Department of the Army, *United States Army in the World War, 1917 - 1919*. 17 vols. (Washington, 1948), vol. 12: 90. [Hereafter cited as *USA/WW, 1917-1919*]

3. Pershing, "Report of Commander-in-Chief, A.E.F., Staff Sections and Services," November 19, 1918, *USA/WW, 1917-1919*, vol. 12: 2. See also Pershing, "Final Report," Pershing to Baker, September 1, 1919, in ibid., 20.

4. Pershing suffers from no lack of biographers. Frank E. Vandiver, *Black Jack: The Life and Times of John J. Pershing* 2 vols. (College Station, Tex., 1977); Richard O'Connor, *Black Jack Pershing* (Garden City, N.Y., 1961); Donald Smythe, *Guerrilla Warrior: The Early Life of John J. Pershing* (New York, 1973) and *Pershing: General of the Armies*; Frederick Palmer, *John J. Pershing* (Westport, Conn., 1948); and, Richard Goldhurst, *Pipe Clay and Drill--John J. Pershing: The Classic American Soldier* (New York, 1977).

5. Pershing, "Reports of Commander-in-Chief," Pershing to Baker, November 19, 1918, in *USA/WW, 1917-1919*, vol. 12: 2-3.

6. In one of his first cables to the War Department, Pershing requested twenty-seven officers for general staff duties; twenty were Leavenworth-men. This reversed the pre-1917 trend when only twenty post-1900 graduates of the Leavenworth schools had served on the General Staff. In 1917 less than 10 percent of the army's career officers had attended either Leavenworth or the War College. Nenninger, *Leavenworth and the Old Army: Education, Professionalism, and the Officer Corps of the United States Army, 1881-1918*, (Westport, Conn., 1978), 135, 159.

7. Coffman, "The American Military Generation Gap in World War I," Proceedings of the Second Military History Symposium, United States Air Force Academy, 1968, *Command and Commanders in Modern Military History* (Washington, D.C., 1971), 35-43; Harbord, "Personalities and Relationships in the American Expeditionary Forces," Army War College lecture, April 29, 1933, reprinted in pamphlet form in *Congressional Record*, May 1, 1933.

8. Edmund Arpin was wounded in the Aisne Offensive and his account of the stages of his medical treatment serve as the foundation for mine of Smith's. Arpin, "Wisconsinite in World War I," 3-25.

9. "Report: Medical," December 31, 1918, cited in *USA/WW, 1917-1919*, vol. 14: 110, 118.

10. Baker Board Reports, July 26, 1917, in *United States in the World War: Organization of the American Expeditionary Force* (Washington, D.C., 1918), 78-79.

11. Pershing wanted to model the American staff in accordance with French practice and British experience. Pershing, "Report of Commander-in-Chief," *USA/WW, 1917-1919*, vol 12: 20-21, 23; Pershing, "General Staff at General Headquarters," June 30, 1919, ibid., 90-94. Harbord wrote that "it was at once evident that the peacetime organization of our General Staff must give way to one based on the actual war experience of our Allies." J. G. Harbord, "The American General Staff," in *The American Expeditionary Forces: Its Organization and Accomplishments* (Evanston, Ill., 1929), 64.

12. LeRoy Eltinge, "General Staff Officers," cited in *USA/WW, 1917-1919*, vol. 12: 18.

13. Bliss saw his role essentially to serve as "Assistant Chief of Staff of the A.E.F.," not chief of staff of the military establishment. Tasker Bliss to Pershing, March 17, 1921, as cited in Smythe, "Pershing-March Conflict in World War I," *Parameters* 11 (December 1981): 53-62. See also Coffman, *Hilt of the Sword: The Career of Peyton C. March*, (Madison, Wis., 1966), 115, 123.

14. Frederick Palmer, *Newton D. Palmer*, 2 vols. (New York, 1931) vol. 1: 14-15; Daniel D. Beaver, *Newton D. Baker and the American War Effort* (Lincoln, Neb., 1966), 1-49; and Smythe, "'Your Authority in France Will Be Supreme': The Baker-Pershing Relationship in World War I," *Parameters* 9 (September 1979): 38-45.

15. Cited in T. Harry Williams, *The History of American Wars: From 1745 to 1918* (New York, 1981), 403.

16. George Soulé, *The New Republic*, cited in Coffman, *War to End All Wars*, 52.

17. F. Q. C. Gardner to March, November 18, 1918, as cited in Coffman, *Hilt of the Sword*, 42.

18. Chamberlain was quoted in the *New York Times*, January 20, 1918.

19. "War Department General Staff," in *Order of Battle: Zone of the Interior* (Washington, D.C., 1948), 32-39; Coffman, *Hilt of the Sword*, 50.

20. Cited in Smythe, "Pershing-March Conflict," 55.

21. Pershing, soon after landing in France, ordered the Sam Browne belt worn by officers detached to Chaumont. Soon the practice spread to the entire officer corps as the British over-the-shoulder belt became a caste symbol setting the AEF officer apart from the enlisted ranks and the officers in the National Guard and the Zone of the Interior. March thought the strap a waste of leather and money, but Pershing's views prevailed.

22. For a discussion of the rift between Chaumont and the War Department and the struggle for supremacy between Pershing and March, see Smythe, "Pershing-March Conflict," and "Over There: The Pershing Story," *Army* (December 1980): 34-38; Coffman, *War to End All Wars*, 157-86, and *Hilt of the Sword*, 104-18; and Vandiver, "John J. Pershing and the Anatomy of Leadership," Harmon Lecture #6, United States Air Force Academy (Colorado Springs, Colo., 1963). After the war, both men renewed the battle with the pen. See March, *Nation at War*; Pershing, *Experiences in War*. Perhaps the best book written by any of the participants is Harbord, *The American Army in France, 1917-1919* (Boston, 1936). Although March is directly referred to only six times, Harbord's book was written in refutation of March's. See also, Smythe, "Battle of the Books: Pershing Versus March," *Army* (September 1972): 30-32.

23. The Quartermaster Bureau all but disappeared during March's reorganization. See Erna Risch, *The Quartermaster Corps: Organization, Supply and Service* (Washington, D.C., 1953).

For a discussion of the wartime eclipse of the bureaus by the War Department General Staff, see Coffman, *Hilt of the Sword*, 119-33; Beaver, *Baker*, 90-109, 156-71, and "George W. Goethals and the P.S. and T.," in Beaver, ed., *Some Pathways in Twentieth Century History* (Detroit, 1969).

24. March believed that no such Aulic Council was necessary. Aside from being extralegal, he maintained that if the chief of staff and the General Staff were not competent to discharge their proper functions, the problem rested not in the General Staff principle but in the individuals holding the offices.

The chief of staff found it "unbelievable" that no proper military intelligence apparatus existed in the War Department General Staff. He immediately set about to rectify that situation. March, *Nation at War*, 40, 48-9, 226-27.

25. War Department General Staff Order #80, August 26, 1918, cited in "War Department General Staff," Historical Division, Army War College, *Order of Battle*: *Zone of the Interior*, 42.

26. Harbord to Pershing, March 16, 1918, cited in Smythe, "Pershing-March Conflict," 59. See also James Harbord, "Personalities and Personal Relationships in the American Expeditionary Forces," 3-10.

27. For the outline of the reorganizations of the Military Intelligence Division, see "War Department General Staff," 29-49.

28. March to Pershing, March 14, 1918, as cited in Smythe, "Pershing-March Conflict," 57.

29. Harbord to Pershing, March 16, 1918, ibid.

30. Seventy-seven nonregular army officers were among the 296 selected to serve with the General Staff. Eltinge, "General Staff Officers," cited in *USA/WW, 1917-1919*, vol. 14: 95.

31. For an outline of the expansion in size and function of the Military Intelligence Division, see "War Department General Staff," 43-44; March, *Nation at War*, 226.

32. Coffman, *Hilt of the Sword*, 151.

33. Coffman, "The Battle against Red Tape: Business Methods of the War Department General Staff, 1917-1918," *Military Affairs* 26 (Spring 1962): 1-10.

34. *Zone of the Interior*, 637.

35. Ibid.

36. Ibid., 663.

37. Ibid.; and March, *Nation at War*, 310-29.

38. Unless otherwise noted, Smith's First World War and interwar service records are derived from "Walter Bedell Smith," *War Department Biographies, American Generals in European Theater*, RG-319, Records of the Army Staff, National Archives, Washington, D.C.

39. *Order of Battle*, 658-59.

40. C. C. Keney, A Prospect of Fort Dodge," *Palimpsest*, 13 (1932): 106-130.

41. *Report of the Chief of Staff, United States Army: 1920*, 12-13, 34-35; *Report of the Chief of Staff: 1921*, 54.

CHAPTER 3

1. For a discussion of the failures of postbellum experience to prepare the army for the European wars, see Robert M. Utley,"The Contribution of the Frontier to the American Military Tradition," in *American Military on the Frontier*, James P. Tate, ed., 7th Military History Symposium, United States Air Force Academy (Washington, D.C., 1978), 3-13.

2. The term Old Guard was used by Marshall's "prophets," young officers who advocated reform of the army. Charles T. Lanham to Marshall, October 25, 1935, *The*

Papers of George Catlett Marshall, Larry I. Bland and Sharon Ritenour, eds. (Baltimore, 1981), vol 1: 440. [hereafter cited as *Marshall Papers*].

The correspondence of Marshall provide unequaled insights into army life and internal politics in the interwar army.

3. The most celebrated cases are those of George Patton and Dwight Eisenhower. In separate articles that appeared in the *Infantry Journal* in 1920, both officers advocated an independent role for armor. Since this questioned the ascendant role of infantry, they were ordered by the first Chief of Infantry, Charles Farnsworth, to conform to infantry doctrine or face court-martial. Even as late as the mid-1930s, relatively senior officers corresponded secretly in order to protect themselves.

Patton, "Tank in Future Wars," *Infantry Journal* (May 1920): 958-62, [hereafter cited as *IJ*]; Eisenhower, "A Tank Discussion," *IJ* (November 1920): 453-58, and *At Ease* (Garden City, N.Y., 1967), 173; Marshall to Stuart Heintzelman, December 4 and December 18, 1933, *Marshall Papers*, vol 1: 413-14.

4. Upton, *Military Policy of the United States* (Washington, D.C. 1904), vii.

5. Stephen Ambrose, "The Military and American Society: An Overview," in Ambrose and James Berber, eds., *The Military in America* (New York, 1972), 4; Raymond G. O'Connor, *American Defense Policy in Perspective* (New York, 1965), 215.

6. John Calhoun, as secretary of war, oversaw the 1821 reorganization of the War Department and created the office of commanding general. He failed in his attempt to create an "expansible army" around the nucleus of a cadre army. The expansible army concept remained an integral part in the military policy debate and served as the foundation for Upton's advocacy of a strong professionalized army modeled on that of Prussia. Leonard Wood, as chief of staff, also attempted to augment the military establishment but, unlike Upton, saw the militia, based on universal military training, as the foundation of American defense.

7. Peyton C. March, *War Department Annual Report, 1919* (Washington, D.C., 1921), 471. Earlier, Upton and Wood voiced the same opinion.

8. For a thorough examination of March's views and the opposition he faced, see Coffman, *Hilt of the Sword*, chaps. 14-15. See also Walter Millis, *Arms and Men* (New York, 1956), 241- 42; Weigley, *History of the United States Army* (New York, 1967), 395-99.

9. March, *Annual Report, 1919*, clearly sets out his views, especially 471-76.

10. Ibid., 472.

11. March to Baker, August 2, 1918, as cited in Coffman, *Hilt of the Sword*, 123.

12. In addition to Coffman, see Beaver, *Baker*.

13. S. Hubert Dent, Jr., of Alabama, chairman of the House Military Committee, introduced the bill. See U.S. Congress, House Committee on Military Affairs, Hearings, "Army Reorganization," 66th Cong., 1st Sess. 2 vols. (Washington, D.C., 1919); U.S. Congress, Senate Committee on Military Affairs, Hearings, "Reorganization of the Army," 66th Cong., 1st and 2d Sess. 2 vols. (Washington, D.C., 1920).

14. Senator James Wadsworth of New York, chairman of the Senate Military Affairs Committee, favored preparedness but ridiculed March's attempt to Prussianize the army.

Echoing similar views, Senator Harry New believed that the March-Baker Bill "smack[ed] too much of that militarism which is righteously abhorrent to our national ideals." For the political aspects of the reorganization debate, see Bernard L. Boylan, "Army Reorganization, 1920: The Legislative Story," *Mid-America* 44 (April 1967): 115-28.

15. Although subsequently revised, the Chaumont plan was devised by Harold Fiske, chief of the Training Section. The plan was first circulated to other staff sections on December 6, 1918. Coffman, *Hilt of the Sword*, 177-78.

16. Palmer testified before the Senate committee on October 9, 1919; see Senate, *Reorganization of the Army*, 1177.

17. Wadsworth, as cited in Coffman, *Hilt of the Sword*, 199.

18. Ibid., 201-3; Senate, *Reorganization of the Army*, 1572-1651.

19. The act is printed in *Congressional Record*, 66th Cong., 1 sess. vol. 59, part 8, 7813-33.

20. The War Council of the War Department consisted of the secretary and assistant secretary of war and the chief of staff. For a discussion of the General Staff emerging out of the 1920 Act, see Otto Nelson, *National Security and the General Staff* (Washington, D.C., 1940), 274-313.

21. Some congressmen talked of making Pershing chief of staff for life, but Baker successfully blocked that scheme. Initially, Pershing's role as commanding general was largely titular--he became a member of the War Council--but when he assumed the office of Chief of Staff/Commanding General on July 1, 1921, his duties, at least on paper, involved both command of the regular army and control of the War Department.

22. The organization and procedures of the General Staff, as established in the *Army Regulations, 1921*, are contained in "Staff Principles," *Field Service Staff Manual* (Ft. Leavenworth, Kansas, 1925), 1-13.

23. Secretary of War John W. Weeks named Harbord as the executive assistant to the Chief of Staff/Commanding General. Not only did Harbord physically occupy the chief of staff's office, he discharged the functions of chief of staff. Harbord, therefore, was chief of staff in everything but name.

Pershing's General Headquarters assumed many of the duties performed by the War Department General Staff during the war. Most of the other wartime missions of the General Staff, lost under the terms of the 1920 act, reverted to the bureau chiefs. Under the new chain of command all procurement matters were handled by the various bureaus whose chiefs reported, not to the chief of staff, but to the assistant secretary of war.

See Coffman, *Hilt of the Sword*, 228-29; Nelson, *National Security and the General Staff*, 284-85.

24. Wilson considered vetoing the final bill but was dissuaded from doing so by Baker. While the legislation did not provide for "as effective [a] reorganization as the country ought to have" and despite his belief that "many things the war has taught us...we have not learned," Baker felt that the bill should be signed for the sake of the public interest. Baker to Wilson, June 3, 1920, as cited in Coffman, *Hilt of the Sword*, 209.

25. In April 1917 the army consisted of 5,959 officers and 127,151 men. The NDA of 1920 authorized an expansion of the army to 17,717 officers and 280,000 men. "Annual Report of the Chief of Staff, 1920," in *Report of Secretary of War to the President* (Washington, D.C., 1922), 12-13, 34-35 [hereafter cited as *Report C/S, (appropriate year)*].

26. *Report C/S, 1922*, 111-21.

27. Appropriations for the War Department sank from $1,008,300,000 in 1920 to a low of $246,092,000 in 1925. *Army Almanac* (Washington, D.C., 1950), 693.

28. Biographical material derived from "Walter Bedell Smith," *War Department Biographies*. Description of interwar posts taken from Charles J. Sullivan, *Army Posts and Towns* (Los Angeles, 1942).

29. Articles that appeared during the war and after speak of Smith's self-improvement efforts undertaken in the interwar years. A 1944 article in *Life* spoke of the "classics in warfare which the General has absorbed avidly over the years." Wertenbaker, "The Invasion Plan," 94. See also William Snyder, "Walter Bedell Smith: Eisenhower's Chief of Staff," *Military Affairs* (January 1984): 6.

30. The officer's socialization process and their membership within the social hierarchy of the army created what is referred to as the "military mind." Isolated from civil society, the value system of the officer corps was typified by political conservatism, emphasis on traditional values of family and religion, and the reliance upon ascriptive authority in intrapersonal relations.

Morris Janowitz, *The Professional Soldier: A Social and Political Portrait* (Glencoe, Ill., 1960), chaps. 9 and 12; Samuel Huntington, *Soldier and the State* (Cambridge, Mass., 1957), 7-18, 59-79; C. Wright Mills, *The Power Elite* (New York, 1956), 195; and Bengt Abrahamsson, *Military Professionalization and Political Power* (Beverly Hills, Calif., 1972), chap. 4, 98-100.

31. The best description of the psychological and social life in the army of the period is by Noel Parrish, an Army Air Corps officer writing after the Second World War. "Ground and air officers alike stubbornly carried out their duties among a people hoping and trying to believe that all officers were as useless as their sabre chains. It was a weird, almost furtive existence, like that of a fireman trying to guard a wooden city whose occupants believe it was fireproof. In such an atmosphere of unreality officers sometimes felt a little ghostly or bewildered, or turned to the affectations of imported uniforms or mannerisms, the imitation of the well-to-do and the horse culture." Parrish, "New Responsibilities of Air Force Officers," *Air University Review* 23 (March-April 1972): 15-16.

See also Richard C. Brown, "Social Attitudes of American Generals, 1898-1940," (Ph.D. dissertation, University of Wisconsin, 1951); C. H. Coates and R. J. Pellegrin, *Military Sociology; a Study of American Military Institutions and Military Life* (Washington, D.C., 1965); Kemble, *Image of the Army Officer in America: Background for Current Views* (Westport, Conn., 1973), chap. 16.

32. A September 1935 *Fortune* article examines the social position of enlisted men, NCOs, and officers in the interwar period. "Who's Who in the Army Now?" *Fortune*

12 (September 1935). See also Martin Van Creveld, *Fighting Power* (Westport Conn., 1982), 20-21, 23-24, 26, 124-25.

33. Unattributed article, "Who's Who in the Army Now?", 39.

34. Between 1920 and 1937, 1,428 officers were placed provisionally in Class B: 350 were dismissed; 493 left the service before their cases were finalized, and 577 won reestablishment to Class A. Cited in Coffman and Peter R. Herrly, "The American Regular Army Officer Corps Between the World Wars," *Armed Forces and Society* 4 (November 1977): 58, 71.

35. In 1921 the regular army was reduced to 150,000, prompting the resignation of 1,000 officers. In addition, in 1920-1921, the army placed 384 officers in the Class B category of whom 110 were eliminated. The next year 27 others were removed.

36. By way of illustration, D. D. Eisenhower, a graduate of the 1915 West Point class, became a lieutenant-colonel during the last year of the war, was reduced in 1920 to major and in 1922 to captain, only to be promoted to lieutenant-colonel again in 1936.

The size and relative youth of the "hump" stagnated promotions in the company grades for two decades. Take the example of products of the West Point class of 1918. The majority were reduced in rank from first to second lieutenant in 1922, and only a congressional bill secured them promotion to captain thirteen years later. Coffman and Herrly, "Between the World Wars," 57.

37. So believed Patrick J. Hurly, secretary of war in the Hoover administration. Don Lohbeck, *Patrick J. Hurly* (Chicago, 1956), 101.

38. Moseley actively supported ultrarightist and anti-Semitic causes in the mid-1930s. Writing to Smith in August 1944, Moseley pleaded with Smith not to hold his record against his two sons. Calling himself a defender of "the highest principles upon which our government was founded," Moseley claimed that accusations that he was a fascist were "wholly unfair." Eisenhower, who worked under Moseley in the War Department, saw it the same way.

C. Clayton James discusses Moseley's political views, *The Years of MacArthur*, 2 vols. (Boston, 1970), vol 1: 383. Moseley to Smith, August 11, 1944, Smith Papers; Eisenhower, *At Ease* (Garden City, N.Y., 1967), 218.

39. Although none of the prewar correspondence now exists, Moseley and Smith were in occasional contact with one another. Snyder interview of Mrs. Irene Ord, widow of Major General James G. Ord and Smith's neighbor in the 1920s. Snyder, "Walter Bedell Smith," 13.

40. For an outline of the duties of the Bureau of the Budget in regards the army, see *Army Almanac*, 11-12. For a discussion of the functions of the Bureau, see Philip E. Present, "Budget and Program Evolution: On the Road to Accountability," in *People and Public Administration*, Present, ed. (Pacific Palisades, Calif., 1979): 241-50; Allen Schick, "The Road to PPB: The Stages of Budget Reform," *Public Administration Review* XXVI (December 1966): 243-58.

41. Smith's connections with civilian agencies during this period were discussed in a CBS news program, "Newsmakers," January 8, 1950. Transcript found in Smith Papers.

42. For a discussion of the ongoing "managerial revolution," see Janowitz, *Professional Soldier*; Abrahamsson, *Military Professionalization*, 35-36.

43. Adjutant General figures indicate that 80 percent of officers requesting overseas service gave the Philippines as either their first or second choice. John Wickerling, "The Natives of Northern Luzon," *IJ* 22 (February 1926): 141.

44. Elam Stewart, "Fort William McKinley," *IJ* 33 (April 1927): 347-49.

45. The U.S. Army spent $1 million per year on polo, which, in the opinion of Major General Johnson Hagood, commander of the 3d Army, had no military value. Of the 20,000 horses maintained by the army, 10 percent were polo ponies. "Who's Who in the Army Now?", 40.

46. Wertenbaker, "The Invasion Plan," 94.

47. For thumbnail sketches of Mrs. Smith, see ibid.; *Indianapolis Star* interview, May 8, 1945, ISL.

Everett Hughes, Deputy Chief of Staff in the Mediterranean under Eisenhower, referred to her as a "looker." *Hughes Diary, 1943-44*, Papers of Everett S. Hughes, Manuscripts Division, Library of Congress. Copy in author's possession.

48. The definition of professionalism employed is adopted from Huntington, *Soldier and State*, and "Power, Expertise, and the Military Profession," in K. G. Lynn, ed., *The Professions in America* (Boston, 1965); Janowitz, *Professional Soldier*; Abrahamsson, *Military Professionalization*, chap. 3.

49. Smith did not believe that his career was hampered by his lack of a West Point ring. See Transcript, "Newsmakers."

After 1930, except for the Medical Corps and the chaplaincy, West Point provided the only means of entry into the officer corps, yet only 37 percent of interwar officers were products of the U.S.M.A. Coffman and Herrly, 63.

50. Unidentified officer, quoted in Harold Hinton, "Soldier, Diplomat, Intelligence Chief," *New York Times Magazine*, August, 27, 1950, 30.

CHAPTER 4

1. A common theme in World War II autobiographies and oral histories is that the school system, particularly Leavenworth, saved the army in the interwar period. See Omar N. Bradley and Clay Blair, *A General's Life* (New York, 1983), chaps. 6-10; Taylor *Swords and Plowshares*, 29-31; J. Lawton Collins, *Lightning Joe* (Baton Rouge, La, 1979), 56-57; and Albert Wedemeyer, *Wedemeyer Reports* (New York, 1958), 50-53. See also Barbara Tuchman, *Stilwell and the American Experience in China, 1911-1945* (New York, 1977), 90-91; Martin Blumenson, *Mark Clark* (New York, 1984), 33-34; Stephen Ambrose, *Eisenhower*, 2 vols. (New York, 1983) vol 1: 79-82, 85-86.

While generally critical of the unenlightening content of the Leavenworth school curriculum, several senior officers agreed that the army's educational system provided the foundation for American military professionalism. See the oral histories of Raymond Barker, Thomas Betts, Charles Bolté, Jacob Devers, John Leonard, Leroy Lutes, Arthur Nevin, and William Simpson, Eisenhower Library. The Arthur Nevins oral history comes from the Collection of the Columbia University Research Office.

2. A. B. Warfield, "Fort Benning: The Home of the Infantry School," *IJ* 32 (June 1928): 30-31; *History of Fort Benning*, U.S. Army official monograph, United States Army Military History Institute Research Collection, Carlisle Barracks, Pa [hereafter cited as USAMHI].

3. Upton, *Military Policy of the United States*, 321.

4. Marshall to Stuart Heintzelman, December 18, 1933, as cited in *Marshall Papers*, vol 1: 415-16.

5. For a discussion of the military educational system before the First World War, see Timothy Nenninger, *The Leavenworth Schools and the Old Army*; George Pappas, *Prudens Futuri: The U. S. Army War College* (Carlisle Barracks, Pa, 1967), chaps. 1-4.

6. For the development of American empiricism, see Daniel Boorstin, *The Americans* (New York, 1965), 191-265; George Novack, *Empiricism and its Evolution* (New York, 1966); Richard Hofstadter, *Anti-Intellectualism in American Life* (Boston, 1963), 155-56.

7. For the impact of empiricism upon the "old" army, see Huntington, *Soldier and State*; Jack C. Lane, *Armed Progressives: General Leonard Wood* (Novato, Calif., 1978); Kemble, *Image of the Officer in America*, section 4, chap. 15.

8. The branch and service schools were located as follows: Artillery, Ft. Sill; Engineer, Ft. Humphreys; General Service, Ft. Riley; Infantry, Ft. Benning; Signals, Ft. Monmouth; Chemical, Edgewood Arsenal; Tank, Ft. Meade; Chaplain, Carlisle Barracks; Army Finance, St. Louis; Adjutant-Quartermaster, Camp Lee. The Tank School lost its independent status in 1932, its functions moved to the Infantry School.

9. For a concise statement of the organization and missions of the army educational system, see John Masland and Laurence Radway, *Soldiers and Scholars: Military Education and National Policy* (Princeton, N.J., 1957). For a description of the structure of the military educational system, see *Army Almanac*, 333-401.

10. Brigadier General J. Franklin Bell, commandant of Leavenworth from 1903 to 1906, mandated that only senior captains and majors might attend the advanced school-- a policy that remained in place until 1933-34 when a sprinkling of junior captains (like Smith) and lieutenants were admitted. Since during the interwar period the mean age of majors was slightly over 45 years with an average of eighteen years of commissioned service, the educational system served chiefly to reinforce an already extant set of procedures and attitudes. The statistics are taken from Coffman and Herrly, 67.

11. Tuchman, *Stilwell*, 90; Charles Kirkpatrick, "Filling the Gaps: Reevaluating Officer Professional Education in the Inter-War Army, 1920-1940," paper presented at the American Military Institute Conference, Lexington, Va. (April 1989): 30-31.

12. "Notes of the Chief of Infantry," *IJ* 30 (February 1927): 181.

13. While director of the Academic Department at the Infantry School, Marshall, writing to the chief of infantry, General Allen, pointed out that the existing system of sending only senior captains and majors to the advanced course and Leavenworth constituted a "detriment to the efficiency of the army." He believed that unless younger officers received greater access to the educational system, based upon merit and not seniority, the army would suffer enormous handicaps in the event of a mobilization. Memo for the Commandant, Marshall to Allen, January 9, 1928, "Selection of Infantry

officers for the Advanced School, Infantry School, and the Command and General Staff School," *Marshall Papers*, vol. 1: 324-26.

14. For a thorough examination of the development of military doctrine, see Barry R. Posen, *The Sources of Military Doctrine* (Ithaca, N.Y., 1984).

15. Writing in 1915, Commodore Dudley Knox pointed out that it was "extraordinary that both American services as a whole are unfamiliar even with the meaning of the term 'doctrine' when used in its purely military sense, and fail to comprehend its importance as well as its role in bringing about timely and united actions in the midst of hostilities." Knox, "The Role of Doctrine in Naval Warfare," *United States Naval Institute Proceedings*, reprinted in *War and Doctrine*, John A. Hixson, ed. (Ft. Leavenworth, 1984): 108-22.

16. The two AEF groups were the Supreme Board, appointed to study tactical and organizational questions of the combat arms, and the Lewis (or Infantry) Board.

17. For the findings of the AEF boards, see *Report of Superior Board on Organization and Tactics, 1919* and *Proceedings of the Lewis Board, 1919*, Combined Arms Library, Ft. Leavenworth, Kansas. In addition to the previous citations, see *Field Service Regulations, 1923*, Combined Arms Library.

18. A discussion of the development of infantry doctrine is contained in George Hoffman, "The Demise of the U.S. Tank Corps and the Medium Tank Development Program," *Military Affairs* 37 (February 1973): 20-25.

Casualty statistic taken from John Keegan, *The Face of Battle* (New York, 1976), 264.

19. Marshall, "Profiting By War Experience," *IJ* 18 (January-June 1921): 34-37; Marshall to Leslie McNair, March 4, 1939, *Marshall Papers*, vol. 1: 707.

20. *Field Service Regulations, 1923*, 21-23; General Service Schools, *Tactics and Techniques of the Separate Branches* (Ft. Leavenworth, 1925), and *The Employment of Tanks in Combat* (Ft. Leavenworth, 1925); C. H. Rarey, "Lessons from the Use of Tanks by the American Army," *IJ* 23 (January-June 1928): 515; Hoffman, "Demise of the Tank Corps."

21. Eugene Emme, "Air Power and Warfare, 1903-1941: The American Dimension," in Alfred Hurley and Robert Ehrhart, eds., *Air Power and Warfare*, Proceedings of the 8th Military History Symposium, USAF Academy, 1978 (Washington, D.C., 1979), 56-82; Alfred F. Hurley, *Billy Mitchell: Crusader for Air Power* (New York, 1964), 112, 128-129.

22. Bradley and Blair, *General's Life*, 56.

23. Marshall to Heintzelman, December 4, 1933, *Marshall Papers*, vol. 1: 411.

24. The curriculum at the Infantry School is discussed in Warfield, "Fort Benning"; Bradley and Blair, 54-56, 65-73; Collins, *Lightning Joe*, 47-52; Forrest Pogue, *George C. Marshall: Education of a General* (New York, 1963), 249-61.

25. Coffman, "Social History of the Old Army," USAMHI, Audio-Visual Archives; Pogue, *Education of a General*, 261; Wertenbaker, "The Invasion Plan," 95.

26. Smith's days at Ft. Benning are discussed in Wertenbaker, "The Invasion Plan," 94; *Indianapolis Star* article, September 26, 1943, ISL.

27. Bradley and Blair, 69.

28. Ibid.

29. Officers complained that instructor appointments hinged upon social connections rather than professional competence. In any case, instructor postings were not highly sought after. Wedemeyer, *Wedemeyer Reports*, 50; Marshall, "Memo to the Commandant," January 9, 1928.

30. Bradley and Blair, 69.

31. *Mailing List* 4 (1931-32): 137-153, reprinted in abbreviated form in *Infantry Journal*, *Infantry in Battle* (Washington, D.C., 1939), 113-16.

32. *Mailing List* 12 (1932-33): 113-40.

33. Chief of Infantry, "Policy on Command and General Staff School," *IJ* 30 (January-June 1927): 63-64.

34. Arthur L. Wagner, "The Military Necessities of the United States and the Best Provisions for Meeting Them," *Journal of the Military Service Institution* 5 (September 1884): 262.

35. Gilbert A. Youngberg, "The Present Tendencies of German Tactics," *IJ* 3 (January 1907): 30-55.

36. For an examination of the Leavenworth "method of application," see Nenninger, *Leavenworth*, chaps. 4-5; Boyd Dastrup, *The U.S. Command and General Staff College* (Manhattan, Kansas, 1982), 12-59; *A Brief Outline History of the General Service Schools*, Vertical Files/History, Combined Arms Library.

37. Pershing, in a speech at Leavenworth on November 2, 1921, stated that "our successful handling of great masses of partially trained troops in operations...could not have been possible" without the contribution of Leavenworth-trained officers." Cited in Dastrup, 64.

38. *War Department, Order #112*, September 25, 1919.

39. *Annual Report of the Commandant, 1920*, 3, 4, 18-19 [hereafter cited as *AR*, corresponding year].

40. *AR*, 1928, 8.

41. Captain R. E. Beebe, a Leavenworth administrator, maintained that "the tactical principles and doctrines heretofore recognized and taught at the Leavenworth schools have been tested in the European war and have been found as sound today [1923] as heretofore." Beebe's opinion mirrored the official Leavenworth stand. Cited in Dastrup, 63.

42. William Naylor, *The Conduct of War* (Ft. Leavenworth, 1920), 5-7, and "Principles of War," Command Course, Army War College, January 5, 1922, Combined Arms Library.

43. "Instructor Memorandum for 1921," *IJ* 19 (July-December 1921): 190; *Field Service Regulations, 1923*; Oliver Robinson, *The Fundamentals of Military Strategy* (Washington, D.C., 1928), 16, 66-75, 93; *Field Service Regulations*, 1934, "Operations"; Reuben Jenkins, "Offensive Doctrine: Opening Phase of the Battle," *Military Review* 20 (June 1940): 5-16.

44. In addition to Naylor, *The Conduct of War* and "Principles of War," see George Meyers, *Strategy* (Washington, D.C., 1928).

45. Frederick Winslow Taylor, in his influential *The Principles of Scientific Management*, advocated corporate solutions to social and organizational problems, that the efficient organization of society by skilled experts would produce utilitarian good. See Samuel Haber, *Efficiency and Uplift: Scientific Management in the Progressive Era, 1890-1920* (New York, 1964). For the theory's impact on the War Department see H. G. J. Aitken, *Taylorism at Watertown Arsenal, 1908-1915* (New York, 1960). See van Creveld, *Fighting Power*, 37-41.

Root maintained that "the Government of the United States [was] the only great establishment that [had] not profited from the lessons of modern industry" and embarked upon his reforms to rectify that situation. See Walter Millis, *Arms and Men*, chap. 5; Weigley, "The Elihu Root Reforms and the Progressive Era," in *Command and Commanders in Modern Warfare*, 15-17; Philip L. Semsch, "Elihu Root and the General Staff," *Military Affairs* 27 (Spring 1963): 16-27; James Hewes, "The United States Army General Staff, 1900-1917," *Military Affairs* 38 (April 1974): 64-69.

46. Weigley, *Eisenhower's Lieutenants* (Bloomington, Ind., 1981), 1-7, and "To the Crossing of the Rhine: American Strategic Thought to World War II," *Armed Forces and Society* 5 (February 1979): 302-20; Edward Luttwack, "The American Style of Warfare and the Military Balance," *Survival* 21 (March-April 1979): 57-60; van Creveld, *Fighting Power*, 166-74.

47. Marshall to Pershing, June 22, 1923, *Marshall Papers*, vol. 1: 231.

48. An officer of the period wrote that his Leavenworth instructors "were not teaching war. They were teaching Dogma." Bradford Chynoweth, *Bellamy Park: Memoirs of Bradford Grethen Chynoweth* (Hicksville, N.Y., 1975), 121-23. Compare Naylor, Robinson, and Meyers, along with the 1923 *Field Regulations*, to the last *Field Service Regulations* (FM 100-5) before the war to see how little doctrine changed in the period between the wars.

49. Charles Bundel, *Selected Professional Papers* (Ft. Leavenworth, 1939), 98.

50. Cited in Leslie Anders, *Gentle Knight: The Life and Times of Major General Edwin Forrest Harding* (Kent, Ohio, 1985), 157-58.

51. H. H. Pfeil, "Why Leavenworth?", *IJ* 30 (January-June 1927): 31.

52. In the 1920s Leavenworth prided itself in having at least one suicide a year. Thomas Betts, Oral History. Interestingly, while the reforms instituted in 1928-29 had the desired effect of reducing suicides among officers, in the years 1930 through 1932, five wives tried to take their lives, two succeeding. Charles Bolté, Oral History.

53. *AR*, 1928-29, 8-9.

54. A Young Graduate (probably Eisenhower), "The Leavenworth Course," *IJ* 30 (June 1927): 575-600.

55. Bradley and Blair, *A General's Life*, 60-61.

56. Marshall to Heintzelman, December 4, 1933, *Marshall Papers*, vol. 1: 410-11; Wedemeyer, *Wedemeyer Reports*, 50.

57. *AR*, (1929-36 inclusive); A Young Graduate, "Leavenworth Course," 592.

58. Marshall to Heitzelman, December 4, 18, 1933, *Marshall Papers*, vol. 1: 409-416.

59. My analysis of the Leavenworth curriculum is derived from the examination of the *Annual Reports* of the respective commandants, *Faculty Board Proceedings, Schedules*, texts, and the map/maneuver problems for the years 1924-1925, 1928-1929, 1930-1938, all available in the Combined Arms Library. Valuable insights into the course can be obtained from the study of the student monographs (1930-1938) contained in the Vertical File/History. Lastly, one can consult official publications issued by the Command and General Staff School, C. A. Willoughby, "The Command and General Staff School," 1934, Vertical File; *Wartime History of the Command and General Staff School, 1939-45* (Ft. Leavenworth, 1945); Orville L. Eaton, *An Analytical Study of Methods of Instruction at the Command and General Staff School* (Ft. Leavenworth, 1946), especially 322-33.

60. While the content of the curriculum varied little from year to year, for the purposes of this study only the texts for the First and Second Year Course for 1933-34 and 1934-35 will be cited.

See *First Year Course: Command and G-2 Course Text, 1933-34*; *Problems: First Year Course, 1933-34*; *First Year Class, Schedule, 1933-34*; *Second Year Course*: *Command Course Text, 1934-35*; *Problems: Second Year Course, 1934-35*; *Problems*: *Second Year Course*; *Discussion of Problems, 1934-35*; *G-2 Course, 1934-35*; *G-3 and G-4 Course, 1934-35*; *Second Year Course, Schedule, 1934-35*. See also, *AR*, 1933-34 and *AR*, 1934-35.

As early as 1920, Marshall already detected a marked fascination on the part of senior American officers for the Schlieffen Offensive. Marshall to James MacAndrew, July 9, 1920, *Marshall Papers*, vol. 1: 197. See also J. M. Scammell, "German War Doctrine and Plans," *IJ* 30 (March 1927): 275-286.

61. *Adjutant General's Report*, 1922.

62. For doctrine as it pertains to the employment of armor see Course at the Command and General Staff School, 1933-34, *Problems*, "Infantry Brigade in Defense," Map Problem 5-I, November 16, 1933; "Tactical employment of reinforced brigade in attack in a wide envelopment," MP 7-I, December 5, 1933; "Attack of mechanized cavalry regiment against hostile mechanized force in envelopment," MP 8-I, December 10, 1933; "Division detached from corps; at a disadvantage in numbers; holding the defensive but preparing to concentrate for a counter-attack," MP 15-II, April 12, 1934; "Principles of pursuit," General Terrain Exercise 7, June 6, 1934.

General Betts commented that Leavenworth "never taught you much about the strategic use of armor." In fact armor was viewed as having no strategic role. Betts, Oral History.

63. In the entire first-year course only a single problem was devoted to the employment of the Air Corps, this dealing with the difficulties in interpreting aerial reconnaissance and gunnery spotting *Problems, 1933-34*, "Employment of division air service," MP 12-I, March 25, 1933. The use of aerial observation and gunnery sighting was also touched upon in "Division in pursuit."

Betts believed that the "teaching on the use of aircraft was very primitive." Betts, Oral History.

In terms of air doctrine, the close-air support mission of the Air Corps was first developed in 1923 and remained unaltered until 1939. See *Field Service Regulations,*

1923, 21-23; General Service Schools, *Tactics and Techniques of the Separate Arms* (Ft. Leavenworth, 1925), 117.

64. For a roster of the faculty, staff, and students, see *AR, 1934-35,* 1-6.

65. Bolté thought that the second-year course was virtually useless, "a buddy year." Bolté, Oral History.

66. By course, "Map Problems and Terrain Exercises" comprised eighty-two one-hour periods; "Tactical and Strategic Principles" (dealing with the Schlieffen plan), 42; "Command, Staff, Logistics," 34; "Military History" (chiefly the preparation and presentation of the Leavenworth Paper, a translation from a foreign source, or some special project), 25. Illustrative of the place of the horse in the army of the period, thirty-two hours were given over to "Equitation." See, Course at C & GSS, *Schedule.*

67. *FM 100-5,* 34.

68. As with the case of infantry tactics and the employment of armor and aircraft, so too were the elements and principles of command and staff relations frozen. See General Staff Study, "Staff Organization and Principles," *War Department, Document #858* (Washington, D.C., 1918); "Division Commander and his General Staff," *Mailing List* 4 (December 1924): 79-155; General Service School, *Field Service Staff Manual* (Ft. Leavenworth, 1925); C & GSS, *Command and Staff Principles* (Ft. Leavenworth, 1937); War Department, *Staff Officers' Field Manual* (Washington, D.C., 1940); E. C. Harwood, *Staff Principles and Procedures* (Army Service Command, 1945).

69. In addition to the Second Year Text cited in note #58, see Charles L. Heller, "World War I and the Interwar Years, 1916-1939," in *A Brief History of Fort Leavenworth,* John W. Partin, ed. (Ft. Leavenworth, 1983), 49-55; Michael King, "Making the Leaders of World War II," in *A Brief History of the U.S. Army Command and General Staff College, 1881-1981* (Ft. Leavenworth, 1981), 19-23.

In terms of doctrine, see Course at the C & GSS, *Command Course Text, 1934-35,* "Highlights of Tactics and Strategic Series," I-260, February 21, 1935.

The daily course work is outlined in *Second Year Class: Schedule for 1934-35,* and a general overview is provided in Commandant Heintzelman's, *AR, 1934-35.*

70. For the role played by military history in the Leavenworth curriculum, see Nenninger, *Leavenworth and the Old Army.*

71. Course at the C & GSS, 1933-34, *Problems,* "Historical Research," MP 1-IV, November 28-December 7, 1933.

To facilitate primary research during the Morrison period (1901-1912), Arthur Conger acquired the expansive *War of the Rebellion* series. Thereafter, the American Civil War loomed large in the history section of the course.

72. Matthew Steele, *American Campaigns* (Washington, D.C., 1909).

73. "Reviews and Discussions," *IJ* 30 (January 1927): 78-79.

74. For a critique of Steele, see Jay Luvaas, "Military Legacy of the American Civil War," Audio-Visual Archives, USAMHI.

75. *Problems: Second Year Course,* 150.

76. "Battle of Tannenberg," Vertical File (filed under Walter L. Weible, Class of 1935), Combined Arms Library.

The group received a "superior" rating for the project, with the recommendation that studies of the like should be a regular component of the course. Among the members of this special were three future four-star generals, Mark Clark, Matt Ridgway, and Bedell Smith.

See C. A. Willoughby, "Reviews in Research Papers," May 31, 1935, and Troup Miller, "Individual Research Studies, Class of 1935," both in Vertical Files, Combined Arms Library.

77. Course at C & GSS, *Command Course Text, 1934-35*, "Tactical and Strategic Principles," I-201-204, September 11-14, 1934; "Operations of an Interior Army," I-253, February 8, I-255, February 10, 1935; "Operations of Flank Army," I-257-58, February 15-18; "Highlights of Tactics and Strategic Series," I-260, February 21, 1935.

78. Maxwell Taylor made this point in *Swords and Plowshares*, 30, which he expanded upon in a December 10, 1984 letter to the author.

79. In the class of 1933-1935, new age provisions allowed relatively junior officers with less time in grade to attend Leavenworth including the revolutionary act of admitting six lieutenants. Since few of the officers had held anything except staff jobs, the class was seen as being composed of "aides, adjutants, and asses." Taylor letter to author, December 10, 1984.

80. *Faculty Board Proceedings*, June 16, 1935.

81. At its nadir in 1933, the size of the army ranked seventeenth, behind that of Belgium. "Who's Who in the Army?", 41.

82. Summerall, *War Department Annual Report, 1930*, 141-42.

83. Discussion of MacArthur's tenure as chief of staff is taken from Mark S. Watson, *Chief of Staff: Prewar Plans and Preparations* (Washington, D.C., 1950), 15-36.

84. MacArthur had been appointed by March as superintendent of West Point in summer 1919. Empowered to bring the Military Academy into the twentieth century, MacArthur, meeting with such powerful opposition, was compelled to step down before ending his four-year tenure. Like so many of the March reforms, this stillborn experiment fell prey to the Pershing-led conservative backlash.

85. Coffman and Herrly, 62-70; "Who's Who in the Army?", 39.

86. "Machine-gun indirect laying using aerial photography," *Mailing List* 16 (1936): 229-50.

87. Otto Nelson to Smith, March 4, 1944, Smith Papers.

88. Eight of the ten officers in the Weapons Section rose to general rank. Interview with Russell Vittrup, November 15, 1988.

89. Wertenbaker, "The Invasion Plan," 95; Hayden Twiggs to Smith, January 25, 1946, Smith Papers; Vittrup Interview.

90. For a discussion of the Army War College, see Pappas, *Prudens Futuri*; Stetson Conn, *The Army War College, 1899-1940*, bound manuscript in USAMHI.

91. "Course at War College," *Course of Instruction, 1936-37*, USAMHI; Lytle Brown, "The United States Army War College," *Military Engineer* 19 (July-August 1927): 294-97; Oswald H. Saunders, "The Army War College," *Military Engineer* 26 (March-April 1934): 101-104; Troup Miller, "Correspondence with the Commandant, War

College," June 1936, USAHMI; Collins, *Lightning Joe*, 90-94; Pappas, *Prudens Futuri*, 129-30.

92. Bradley's view conforms to the majority opinion. The one officer who defends the War College program is Collins, whose advocacy might be explained by the fact that he served two years as an instructor after his year as a student (1937-1940). Bradley and Blair, *A General's Life*, 74; Collins, *Lightning Joe*, 90-91.

93. Ambrose, *Eisenhower*, vol. 1: 85; Bradley and Blair, *A General's Life*, 74-75.

94. A 1927 study suggested that of the 5,800 officers in the hump, half the commissioned personnel, 1,259, had no prospect of retiring above the rank of major. While the 1935 legislation helped somewhat, even for officers in advance of the hump, men like Eisenhower and Bradley, entertained no realistic hope of ever gaining general officer rank. Charles Bolté and John Dahlquest, like Smith at the fore of the hump with records much like his own, estimated that they would retire in the 1950s as lieutenant colonels.

"Editorial Comment," *IJ* 30 (January 1927): 73-75; Ambrose, *Eisenhower*, vol. 1: 100-01; Bradley and Blair, 94; Coffman and Herrly, 58-59.

95. Kent Roberts Greenfield, *The Army Ground Forces: The Organization of Ground Combat Troops* (Washington, D.C., 1947), 48-51; Robert Palmer, *The Army Ground Forces: The Procurement and Training of Combat Troops* (Washington, D.C., 1948), 97-100, 103; Roger Cirillo, "Memorandum for the Deputy Commandant: Two-Year Course, 1930-36," October 4, 1983, Combat Studies Institute, Ft. Leavenworth.

96. Cirillo, "Two-Year Course."

97. General Fuller's article, "Tactics and Mechanization," appeared in a 1927 edition of the *Infantry Journal* in which he outlined his theory of armored warfare but its impact was minimized by an editorial comment by Colonel Frank Cocheu, assistant commandant of the Infantry School, who upheld the cult of the bayonet. Earlier, Fuller's "principles of war," taken from the .1920 *British Field Service Regulations*, were accepted and listed in the American *Training Regulations* of 1921. Fuller had set forth his eight principles in a 335-page book but the American regulations merely listed them without elaboration. The principles were removed from the 1928 *Training Regulations*, but they continued to be taught at Leavenworth. As for Liddell Hart, a staff reviewer for the General Service Schools pronounced his *Paris, Or the Future of War* "of negative value to the instructors of these schools." Liddell Hart's *Great Captains Unveiled* received similar treatment.

Fuller, "Tactics and Mechanization," *IJ* 30 (May 1927): 457-465, and *The Foundations of the Science of War* (London, 1925); *War Department Training Regulations*, 1921, # 10-5; *Review of Current Military Writing* 5 (October-December 1925): 20, and VII (January-March 1928): 262-263.

98. For a discussion of the wedding of the German *Aufsgetragstaktik* to armored theory, see Larry Addington, *The Blitzkrieg Era and the German General Staff, 1865-1941* (New Brunswick, N.J., 1971); see also van Creveld, *Fighting Power*, 36-37.

99. Leavenworth was not entirely unaware of German development. The 1939 *FM 100-5*, as van Creveld points out, contained several paragraphs taken directly out of the 1936 *Heeres Dienstvorschrift 300, Truppenführung*, yet in emphasizing rigid managerial control over operational flexibility, the overall effect was to suggest a fundamentally different conception of war. Patton commented that, while some officers sought to study the German doctrinal system, they found it too difficult for them to understand.

van Creveld, *Fighting Power*, 28-41; Blumenson, ed., *The Patton Papers, 1940-1945*, 2 vols. (Boston, 1974), vol. 2: 486. See also, W. R. Nichols, *German War College Problems* (Ft. Leavenworth, 1935).

CHAPTER 5

For this chapter I drew heavily upon the works of Forrest C. Pogue, particularly his *George C. Marshall: Ordeal and Hope, 1939-1942*. Especially helpful also were the "War Department" volumes of the *United States Army in World War II* series. Mark Watson's *Chief of Staff: Pre-War Plans and Preparations* is devoted to the period before American entry into the war and serves as a useful complement to Pogue. Ray Cline's *Washington Command Post* gives the most complete account of the planning and directional organizations of the Marshall War Department. The other topical editions of the "War Department" series (Kent Roberts Greenfield, Robert Palmer, *The Army Ground Forces*; Greenfield, Palmer, and Bell I. Wiley, *The Organization of Ground Combat Troops*; Maurice Matloff and Edwin Snell, *Strategic Planning for Coalition Warfare, 1941-42*; Richard Leighton and Robert Coakley, *Global Logistics and Strategy, 1940-43*) contain valuable background material. Otto Nelson's *National Security and the General Staff* is also an important source for this period. Where pagination is not indicated, the entry of *passim* should be understood.

1. A statistical analysis of the *Official Army Registers* for 1925, 1933, and 1940 reveal the composite officer of the period between the wars. Coffman and Herrly, "The American Regular Army Officer Corps Between the World Wars."

2. Morris Janowitz, *The Professional Soldier*, 40-46.

3. For a complete examination of Marshall's views regarding the need for systematic reform, see Pogue, *George C. Marshall: Education of a General, 1880-1939* (New York, 1963). See also Marshall to Heintzelman, December 4, 1933, *Marshall Papers*, vol. 1: 409-413.

4. Marshall to Heintzelman, December 4 and 13, 1933, *Marshall Papers*, vol. 1: 409-13, 415.

5. Memo for the Commandant, January 9, 1928, *Marshall Papers*, vol. 1: 324.

6. Chief of Infantry, Major General Allen's reply to Marshall's January 9 Memo, cited in *Marshall Papers*, vol. 1: 32; Major Elmer Rice to Colonel Lorenzo Gasser, August 6, 1929, cited in *Marshall Papers*, vol. 1: 326.

7. Marshall to Heintzelman, December 4 and 13, 1933.

8. Marshall to Edwin Harding, October 31, 1934, *Marshall Papers*, vol. 1: 440.

9. Marshall to Lesley McNair, February 23, 1939, *Marshall Papers*, vol. 1: 703.

10. Marshall to Mrs. Maude Adams, January 2, 1940, cited in Pogue, *Ordeal and Hope*, 11.

11. Marshall to Heintzelman, December 4, 1933.

12. Marshall to Paul Peabody, April 6, 1937, *Marshall Papers*, vol. 1: 531.

13. Marshall to Secretariat of the WDGS, cited in Pogue, *Ordeal and Hope*, 289.

14. Marshall to Hjalman Erickson, March 18, 1942, in ibid.

15. Greenfield and Robert Palmer, *The Army Ground Forces* (Washington, D.C., 1947).

16. United States Air Force Historical Division, *The Army Air Corps in World War II* series, *Plans and Early Operations* (Chicago, 1948).

17. Cline, *Washington Command Post: The Operations Division* (Washington, D.C., 1951), 70-74, 90-142.

18. Leighton and Coakley, *Global Logistics and Strategy, 1940-43* (Washington, D.C., 1955). Watson's *Chief of Staff* examines the War Department's programs in the period 1939-1941. For a discussion of Marshall's views and his role in the reorganization, see Pogue, *Ordeal and Hope*, 289-301.

19. MacArthur to Commanding Generals of the Four Armies, October 22, 1932, cited in Cline, *Washington Command Post*, 28.

20. Nelson, *General Staff*, 274-313; Watson, *Chief of Staff*, 57-84.

21. Marshall to Palmer, March 12, 1942, cited in Pogue, *Ordeal and Hope*, 298.

22. Cited in ibid., 293.

23. Marshall to Gasser, August 4, 1939, cited in ibid., 8.

24. It is difficult to pinpoint authorship of *Mailing List* articles. Individuals did not sign their contributions for fear of repercussions. The 1934 editor remarked that "if a lieutenant signed an article many an officer of field rank would never read it." Charles Lanham to Marshall, October 25, 1934, *Marshall Papers*, vol. 1: 440. Three articles dealing with weapons appeared in *Mailing List* 18 (1939): 141-204, but unlike the previous two articles, one cannot determine which one Smith wrote.

25. Henry Aurand, a member of Craig's staff at the War College, talked of the "pernicious influence" of the cavalry. His views were not unique. John Reese, *Henry Aurand*, Ph.D. dissertation, Kansas State University (1983), 21-23.

26. Pogue, "United States General Staff," and "Marshall and the Army," Audio-Visual Archives, USAMHI.

27. This, and subsequent descriptions of the workings of the secretariat of the General Staff are taken from Pogue, *Ordeal and Hope*, 8, and *Organizer of Victory*, 60-64; Bradley and Blair, *General's Story*, 83-85; Collins, *Lightning Joe*, 95-97; Taylor, *Swords and Plowshares*, 38-41; Robert Gallagher, "Memories of Peace and War: Interview with General Maxwell Taylor," *American Heritage* 32 (April/May 1981): 4-17; Cline, *Washington Command Post*, 24.

28. Marshall, "Profitting from War Experience."

29. Pogue, *Organizer of Victory*, 60.

30. Bradley and Blair, *General's Story*, 84.

31. Marshall to Commanding General of Ft. Benning, August 14, 1939, Marshall Papers.

32. For discussions of Roosevelt's methods of leadership and relations with the War Department see Richard Steele, *The First Offensive: Roosevelt, Marshall, and the Making of American Strategy* (Bloomington, Ind., 1973); Pogue. *Ordeal and Hope*, 22-33, 63-70, 78-79, and "The Conduct of the War in the United States: Problems and Practice," *Revue d'Historique de la Deuxième Guerre Mondiale* 100 (1975): 67-94; Robert Dallak, "Roosevelt," and George Kennan, "Comment," in "World War II: Thirty Years After -- Allied Leadership in the Second World War," *Survey* 21 (Winter/Spring 1975): 1-10, 29-31.

33. For a discussion of Smith's role as liaison officer to Watson and Baruch, see Pogue, "Marshall and the War Department," and "United States General Staff."

34. Collins's description of the format, *Lightning Joe*, 94.

35. Eisenhower, *Crusade in Europe* (New York, 1948), 21-22.

36. As Marshall told Bradley, "unless I hear all the arguments for or against an action I am about to take, I don't know whether or not I'm right." Officers who opposed Marshall and were prepared to back it up won his esteem. Bradley and Blair, 83-84.

Taylor discussed his first presentation to Marshall, *Swords and Plowshares*, 39. See also Eisenhower, *Crusade in Europe*, 16-18.

37. Harry Butcher, *My Three Years with Eisenhower: The Personal Diary of Captain Harry C. Butcher* (New York, 1946), 90-93.

38. Pogue, *Ordeal and Hope*, 60, 65-66.

39. Smith to Marshall, July 29, 1943, Marshall Papers; Pogue, *Organizer of Victory*, 137-38.

40. Pogue, "United States General Staff," and "Marshall and the Army."

41. The best works dealing with Stimson as secretary of war under Roosevelt are Elting Morison, *Turmoil and Tradition: A Study of the Life and Times of Henry L. Stimson* (Boston, 1960); Richard Current, *Secretary Stimson* (New Brunswick, N.J., 1954); and Stimson and McGeorge Bundy, *On Active Service in Peace and War* (New York, 1948). For relations between Stimson and Marshall, see Pogue, *Ordeal and Hope*, 42.

42. Taylor, *Swords and Plowshares*, 38.

43. Cited in Ambrose, *Supreme Commander: The War Years of General Dwight D. Eisenhower* (Garden City, N.Y., 1970), 21.

44. In addition to the sources cited above, see Pogue interview of Smith, July 25, 1958. Original file at Marshall Library.

45. Smith employed these methods, based upon experience gained in Marshall's headquarters, while chief of staff to Eisenhower. The "one-minute" drill, described as the "two-minute" rule by Pogue, is described in *Ordeal and Hope*, 408.

CHAPTER 6

1. For accounts of the ARCADIA conferences, see Robert E. Sherwood, *Roosevelt and Hopkins: An Intimate History* (New York, 1948), 456-57, 470-72; Pogue, *Ordeal and Hope*, 261-288; I. R. M. Butler and M. A. Gwyer, *Grand Strategy*, vol 3. *June 1941 - August 1942*, part 1 by Gwyer, (London, 1964), 386-87; Winston Churchill, *The Second*

World War, 6 vols. (Boston, 1948-53), vol. 5, *The Grand Alliance*, 674-76; and Arthur Bryant, *The Turn of the Tide, a History of the War Years Based on the Diaries of Field Marshal Lord Alanbrooke, Chief of the Imperial General Staff* (London, 1957), 233-38. The Lord Alanbrooke Diary and Papers are housed in the Centre for Military Archives, King's College, London. For the purposes of this book reliance will be placed on Bryant where possible.

2. Dill to Alan Brooke, January 3, 1942, in Bryant, *Turn of the Tide*, 234. For an account of Dill's period in Washington see Alex Danchev, *Very Special Relationship: Field Marshal Sir John Dill and the Anglo-American Alliance 1941-44* (London, 1986).

3. Pogue, *Organizer of Victory*, 69.

4. Alan Brooke wrote in his diary, "I do not think that his [Roosevelt's] military is on a par with his political sense." Alan Brooke Diary, June 26, 1942, Bryant, *Turn of the Tide*, 334.

Hopkins himself admitted his lack of understanding of military affairs. See Sherwood, *Roosevelt and Hopkins*, 11.

Hopkins gradually came to appreciate military and diplomatic matters but there is much truth in what Bill Bullitt said of him: that by the time he died he had begun to become an educated man, but it was the most expensive education the United States ever gave to any one person.

5. Samuel Huntington compares and contrasts American and British institutions of civilian control of the military in *The Soldier and the State*, 163-65, 178, 185-187, 191-92.

6. Stimson Diary, February 25, 1942, as cited in Pogue, *Ordeal and Hope*, 473 n.

7. At the end of January 1942 Representative John J. Cochran (Democrat, Missouri) wrote Roosevelt, sounding him out on the need for an overall military commander. For Cochran's letter of January 28 and Roosevelt's January 30 reply, see Richard Steele, *Roosevelt, Marshall, and the Making of American Strategy*, 90.

8. Stimson Diary, February 25, 1942, cited in Morison, *Turmoil and Tradition*, 542. See also, Steele, 90-91.

9. William D. Leahy, *I Was There* (New York, 1950), 94, 96-98.

10. The most thorough account of the JCS organization is Verne Davis's unpublished manuscript, "History of the Joint Chiefs of Staff in World War II," Historical Section, Joint Secretariat of the Joint Chiefs of Staff. 2 vols. Manuscript in Center of Military History Files, USAMHI. See also, Cline, 98-106; Nelson, 397-404.

11. Matloff and Snell, *Strategic Planning for Coalition Warfare*, discuss the Allied command structure, especially 140-52. See also, Pogue, *Supreme Command* (Washington, D.C., 1954), 37-41, *Ordeal and Hope*, 282-88; and Gordon Harrison, *Cross-Channel Attack* (Washington, D.C., 1951), chap. 1.

12. The original Joint Mission consisted of Lt. Gen. Sir Colville Weymss, Air Chief Marshal Sir Arthur Harris, and Admiral Sir Charles Little. Major General R. H. Dewing replaced Weymss in March 1942 who in turn was replaced by Lieutenant General G. Macready in June. For the RAF, Air Vice Marshal D. C. S. Evell took the place of

Harris in February while Admiral Sir Andrew B. Cunningham replaced Little in June as the Royal Navy representative.

13. Minutes of the British War Cabinet, January 17, 1942, as cited in Steele, *Roosevelt, Marshall, and the Making of American Strategy*, 91.

14. Jo Hollis to William Sterling, January 14, 1942, cited in Danchev, *Establishing the Anglo-American Alliance: The World War Diaries of Brigadier Vivian Dykes* (London, 1990), 90-91 [hereafter cited as Dykes Diary, with appropriate date].

15. Dykes Diary, December 29 1941, and January 27, 1942.

16. For the extent of Smith's War Department activities during 1942, see the extensive file of correspondence between the secretary and Marshall in War Department, Chief of Staff of the Army, "Notes on Conferences," WD, CSA Binders, RG-218, National Archives; Records of the Joint Chiefs of Staff, Meetings of the Joint Chiefs of Staff and the Combined Chiefs of Staff, 7 reels. (Frederick, Md.: University Publications of America Microfilm Series, 1983) [hereafter cited as JCS Meetings, with appropriate number and date].

17. As a 1950 article put it, "A large segment of the Regular Army officers has no use for him and will hear no good about him -- except in his professional capacity. Friend and foe alike describe him as a hard man." Harold Hinton, "Soldier, Diplomat, and Intelligence Chief," *New York Times Magazine*, August 27, 1950, 30.

18. Dykes to Mary Ravenshear, March 8, 1942, Dykes Papers, cited in Danchev, *The Diaries of Brigadier Vivian Dykes*, 8.

19. Dykes Diary, February 7 and 14, 1942.

20. For a view of Marshall's impact upon the officers in his inner-circle, in this case Eisenhower, see Ambrose, *Supreme Commander*, 8-9, 20-22.

21. A. B. Cunningham, *A Sailor's Odyssey* (New York, 1956), 466.

22. Dykes Diary, March 22, April 11 and 20, and September 24, 1942.

23. Dykes Diary, February 10 and 17, April 7, July 25, 1942.

24. Thomas Handy Oral History, USAMHI, cited in Danchev, *The Diaries of Brigadier Vivian Dykes*, 7.

25. On another occasion Smith thought he burnt a secret British memo by mistake. "Poor old Beetle in a hell of a stew," Dykes reported. Dykes Diary, April 3, July 2, and September 2, 1942.

26. Cited in Steele, *Roosevelt, Marshall, and the Making of American Strategy*, 91.

27. An account of the Florida trip is contained in Pogue, *Ordeal and Hope*, 287-88.

28. For the exchange between Churchill and Smith and Smith's views on the prime minister, see Pogue interview with Smith, May 9, 1947. In the files of the Office of the Chief of Military History Collection, USAMHI.

29. For Smith's views on Churchill, see ibid.

30. For Smith's views on Marshall's desire to create a "very small headquarters on the Foch order," see ibid.

31. The Joint Planning Committee met as early as February 13, 1942 but did not receive official sanction until May 1943. In addition to preparing "joint" war plans and

furnishing the War and Navy departments with strategic guidance, it represented the JCS on the Combined Staff Planning Committee.

32. For examinations of the activities of the codebreakers, see Ronald Clark, *The Man Who Broke PURPLE* (Boston, 1977); David Kahn, *The Codebreakers* (New York, 1973); and Ronald Lewin, *The American Magic* (New York, 1982).

33. Affidavit of W. B. Smith, June 15, 1945, in *Pearl Harbor Hearings*, United States Congress, Joint Committee on the Investigation of the Pearl Harbor Attack, copy in Smith Papers; Pogue interview of Smith, July 29, 1958, USAMHI.

34. Smith to Lucian Truscott, December 15, 1943, Smith Papers.

35. Smith to Marshall and King, March 12, 1942, in CCS 385, Sec 1, RG-218.

36. For a revealing set of insights into Smith's views on Donovan and his organization, see Joint Chiefs of Staff, "Minutes, JCS 5th Meeting," March 9, 1942; "Minutes, JCS 6th Meeting," March 16, 1942; "Minutes, JCS 7th Meeting," March 22, 1942, RG-218, Records of the Joint Chiefs of Staff, National Archives, Washington, D.C.; and Smith to Marshall and King, March 23, see CCS 385, Sec 1, RG-218, Records of the JCS.

37. Smith to Marshall and King, March 14, 1942, CCS 385, Section 1, RG-218, Joint Chiefs of Staff, "Minutes, JCS 21st Meeting," June 23, 1942, RG-218, Records of the JCS, Dykes Diary, March 14 and April 4, 1942.

38. Morison, *Turmoil and Tradition*, 542.

39. Marshall to Eisenhower, July 30, 1942, in Alfred D. Chandler, Jr., ed., *The Papers of Dwight David Eisenhower: The War Years*, 5 vols. (Baltimore, 1970). vol. 1., # 395, n. 3 [hereafter cited, subject to subject, date, *EP*, with appropriate number].

40. Pogue, "United States General Staff."

41. Dean Acheson, *Sketches from Life of Men I Have Known* (New York, 1961), 159.

42. Bolté, Oral History.

43. Pogue, "United States General Staff."

44. Greenfield et al., *The Army Ground Forces*, 48-51.

45. Palmer, Wiley, and William Keast, *The Procurement and Training of Ground Combat Troops* (Washington, D.C., 1946), 97-100.

46. Smith's reflections on his reputation are expressed in W. H. Lawrence, "Tough Man for a Tough Job," *New York Times Magazine*, March 17, 1946, 61.

47. "American military theories are correct. [Staff officers of proven ability] are equally good as commanders." Smith to Field Marshal Jan Smuts, November 20, 1946, Smith Correspondence, Smith Papers.

48. Illustrative of Marshall's view of the members of his staff seeking command appointments, he told Eisenhower. "Take your case. I know that you were recommended by one general for division command and by another for corps command...I'm glad they have that opinion of you, but you are going to stay here and fill your position, and that's that...While this may seem a sacrifice to you, that's the way it must be." Cited in Dwight D. Eisenhower, *At Ease: Stories I Tell to Friends* (New York, 1967), 249.

49. Ambrose discusses this phase of Eisenhower's career in Ambrose, *Supreme Commander*, chaps. 1-2.

50. Butcher, *Three Years with Eisenhower*, 61.

51. The early Smith-Eisenhower connection is examined in CBS "Newsmakers," January 8, 1950. Transcript in Smith Papers. The text of the phone conversation is in Ambrose, *Supreme Commander*, 3.

52. Dykes Diary, June 20, 1942.

53. Eisenhower to Marshall, June 26, 1942, *EP*, #353.

54. Marshall to Eisenhower, July 13, 1942, discussed in *EP*, #371, n. 1. For an examination of the military planning debate between Churchill's visit to Washington (June 21-24) and the arrival of the American team in London (July 18) see Matloff and Snell, *Strategic Planning for Coaltion Warfare*, 266-78.

55. Eisenhower to Butcher, July 20, 1942, *EP*, #384.

56. Dykes Diary, July 15, 18, and 20, 1942.

57. Matloff and Snell, *Strategic Planning for Coalition Warfare*, 278, Leo Meyer, "The Decision to Invade North Africa," in Greenfield, ed., *Command Decisions* (Washington, D.C., 1960); Leighton, "OVERLORD Revisited: An Interpretation of American Strategy in the European War 1942-44," *American Historical Review* 68 (July 1963): 926-27.

58. "General Marshall was...pouring forth the most cogent and logical arguments in favour of a prompt invasion of the Continent...Lord Cherwell [Professor Lindermann] remarked to him, 'It's no use -- you are arguing against the casualties on the Somme.'" Cited in Keegan, *The Face of Battle*, 280.

59. Dykes Diary, July 21, 1942.

60. Dykes Diary, July 22, 1942; Butcher, *Three Years with Eisenhower*, 29-30.

61. Dykes Diary, July 22, 1942.

62. To George Catlett Marshall, "Survey of Strategic Situation," July 23, 1942, *EP*, # 389; Dykes Diary, July 24, 1942; Dykes Memo, August 15, 1942, cited in Danchev, *The Diaries of Brigadier Vivian Dykes*, 189.

63. Directive reprinted in Matloff and Snell, *Strategic Planning for Coalition Warfare*, 272-81.

64. "Minutes, CCS 32d meeting," July 24, 1942, RG-218, Records of the JCS; Marshall and King to Roosevelt, July 24, 1942, Chief of Staff File, RG-319, Records of the Army Staff; Dykes Diary, July 24, 1942.

65. Dykes Diary, July 24, 1942

66. Dykes Diary, July 22, 1942.

67. Butcher, *Three Years with Eisenhower*, 29-30.

68. Dykes Diary, July 22, 1942.

69. Pogue, *Ordeal and Hope*, 408-9.

70. Butcher, *Three Years with Eisenhower*, 32; Matloff and Snell, *Strategic Planning for Coalition Warfare*, 281-83; Pogue, *Ordeal and Hope*, 348.

71. Eisenhower to Marshall, July 27, 1942, *EP*, #395.

72. Eisenhower to Marshall, July 29, 1942, *EP*, #399.

73. Marshall to Eisenhower, July 30 and August 5, 1942, Pre-Presidential Papers, Eisenhower Library.

74. Cited in Reginald MacDonald-Buchanan, "Notes on General Marshall," Macdonald-Buchanan Papers, Marshall Library.

75. Eisenhower Memo, "Staff Requirements: Future Operations," July [27] 1942, *EP*, #397; Eisenhower to Marshall, August 7, 1942, *EP*, #415; Butcher, *Three Years with Eisenhower*, 45-47, 61.

76. For an analysis and reprints of the Eisenhower correspondence with Marshall in the period before the launching of TORCH, see Joseph Hobbs, *Dear General: Eisenhower's Wartime Letters to Marshall* (Baltimore, 1971), 1-60.

77. Eisenhower to Marshall, August 7, 1942, *EP*, #415.

78. Pogue interview of Marshall, December 7, 1956, cited in *Marshall Papers*, vol. 1: 200.

CHAPTER 7

1. Marshall to Eisenhower, August 6, 1942, Pre-Presidential Papers, Eisenhower Library; Matloff and Snell, *Strategic Planning*, 282-84; George Howe, *Northwest Africa: Seizing the Initiative in the West*. U.S. Army in World War II. (Washington, D.C., 1957), 10-14.

2. Eisenhower to Marshall, July 29, 1942, *EP*, #399.

3. In several letters to Marshall, Eisenhower indicated his need to retain command of ETO during his stay in North Africa. The BCOS wanted to appoint a deputy commander in charge of SLEDGEHAMMER/ROUNDUP planning. In the end Eisenhower retained command of ETO, exercising it through his American deputy, General Hartle. Marshall to Eisenhower, August 12, 1942, Pre-Presidential Papers.

For the impact of TORCH on the ETO command, see Leighton and Coakley, *Logistics and Strategy*, vol. 1: 480-87.

4. Eisenhower, "Command Arrangements for BOLERO," June 3, 1942, *EP*, #319.

5. Eisenhower, *Crusade in Europe*, 76.

6. Eisenhower to Marshall, June 30, 1942, *EP*, #358.

7. Eisenhower, "Staff Requirements," July [27] 1942, *EP*, #397; Eisenhower to Marshall, July 29, 1942, *EP*, #399.

8. Eisenhower requested Gruenther on July 27, 1942. Eisenhower to Marshall, July 27, 1942, *EP*, #395.

9. Butcher, *Three Years with Eisenhower*, 45.

10. Eisenhower to Marshall, May 12, 1942, *EP*, #293; Eisenhower, *Crusade in Europe*, 50. Earlier, Eisenhower had drawn up a directive for the first Allied supreme commander, General Archibald Wavell. Eisenhower to Marshall, December 26, 1941, *EP*, #24.

11. Butcher, *Three Years with Eisenhower*, 7.

12. Eisenhower to Operations Division, August 16, 1942, *EP*, #433; Eisenhower, *Crusade in Europe*, 55-56.

13. E. Dwight Salmon et al., "History of Allied Forces Headquarters," in Smith Collection, Eisenhower Library; Eisenhower, *Crusade in Europe*, 74-77; Howe, *Northwest Africa*, 32-37.

14. Cited in Salmon et al., "History of Allied Forces Headquarters."

15. Butcher, *Three Years with Eisenhower*, 7.

16. Eisenhower, *Crusade in Europe*, 34-35. See also, Ambrose, *Supreme Commander*, 55-56.

17. As late as August 19 Marshall informed some of his staff "that the operations in North Africa was still subject to the vicissitudes of war." Pogue, *Ordeal and Hope*, 400.

18. Dykes Diary, July 22, August 3, 6, and 14, 1942; Matloff and Snell, *Strategic Planning for Coaltion Warfare*, 286-88.

19. Dykes Diary, August 14, 1942.

20. Eisenhower felt that the chances of seizing Tunisia before the Axis to be "considerably" less than 50 percent. Eisenhower to Marshall, August 15, 1942, *EP*, #430. Marshall told Eisenhower that he agreed with the OPD estimate--that unless the Casablanca landings were staged, the chance of success was less than 50 percent. Marshall to Eisenhower, August 14, 1942, Pre-Presidential Papers; Butcher, *Three Years with Eisenhower*, 67.

21. Eisenhower, *Crusade in Europe*, 77-80; Howe, *Northwest Africa*, 25-31; Matloff and Snell, *Strategic Planning*, 288-93, cover the debate.

22. Eisenhower laid out British objectives to the Casablanca landings in Eisenhower to Thomas Handy [Operations Division] and Marshall, August 13, 1942, *EP*, #424; Churchill, *Hinge of Fate*, 530-31; Matloff and Snell, *Strategic Planning*, 290-93.

23. Eisenhower to Handy and Marshall, August 13, 1942, *EP*, #424.

24. Dykes Diary, August 27 and 28, 1942.

25. Butcher, *Three Years with Eisenhower*, 72, 77.

26. Dykes Diary, September 1, 1942.

27. Dykes Diary, September 2, 1942.

28. Eisenhower to Marshall, September 3, 1942, *EP*, #477; Churchill, *Hinge of Fate*, 530-38; Matloff and Snell, *Strategic Planning*, 290-93.

29. Dykes Diary, July 29 and 30, 1942.

30. Smith to J. R. Deane, September 9, 1943, Smith Correspondence, Smith Papers.

31. Eisenhower recommended Smith's promotion to major general as early as July 27, 1942. Eisenhower to Marshall, July 27, 1942, *EP*, #395. He raised the question again on October 3. Eisenhower to Marshall, October 3, 1942, *EP*, #534.

32. An account of Smith's first day in London is in Butcher, *Three Years with Eisenhower*, 90-93.

33. Ibid., 93.

34. Ibid., 92.

35. Cited in Howe, *Northwest Africa*, 29.

36. Butcher, *Three Years with Eisenhower*, 97.

37. Eisenhower to Butcher, "Memo," September 15, 1942, *EP*, #502.

38. Eisenhower to Charles Gailey, September 19, 1942, *EP*, #510.

39. Eisenhower to Marshall, October 12, 1942, *EP*, #544; Butcher, *Three Years with Eisenhower*, 104.

40. During the two months between Smith's arrival in London and the launching of TORCH, Smith spent twenty evenings with Eisenhower at Telegraph Cottage. The

frequency of Smith's visits declined as D-Day approached and the practice ended once headquarters was relocated in Algiers. See, "Chronology," *EP*, vol. 5: 88-97.

41. Interview with Carter Burgess, November, 19, 1988.

42. FM 101-5 did not include a public affairs section in the table of organization for special general staff divisions. FM 101-5, 19-20, 26.

43. Under the guidance of General Conner, Eisenhower read *On War* "at least three times." Later, when president, Eisenhower, in reply to a question inquiring what books exerted the greatest effect upon him replied: "From a military side, if I had to select one book, I think it would be *On War* by Clausewitz." See William Pickett, "Eisenhower as a Student of Clausewitz," *Military Review* 65 (July 1985): 22-27.

44. Eisenhower to AGWAR, August 21, 1942, *EP*, #443; Butcher, *Three Years with Eisenhower*, 68.

45. Murphy tells his own story in *Diplomat Among Warriors* (New York, 1964).

46. Leon Blair, "Amateurs in Diplomacy: The American Vice-Consuls in North Africa, 1941-43," *Historian* 35 (August 1973): 607-20.

47. Butcher, *Three Years with Eisenhower*, 103-4.

48. Murphy, *Diplomat Among Warriors*, 104-5.

49. For an account of Murphy's diplomatic maneuvering, see Murphy, *Diplomat Among Warriors*, 124-61; Eisenhower, *Crusade in Europe*, 86-88; Howe, *Northwest Africa*, 77-83.

50. Butcher, *Three Years with Eisenhower*, 110.

51. Murphy, *Diplomat Among Warriors*, 109-23; Mark Clark, *Calculated Risk*, 67-89.

52. Eisenhower, "Staff Requirements"; Eisenhower to Marshall, August 17, 1942, *EP*, #435.

53. Hastings Ismay, *Memoirs* (New York, 1960), 262-63.

54. Alan Brooke Diary, June 26, 1942, in Byrant, *Turn of the Tide*, 334.

55. Butcher, *Three Years with Eisenhower*, 117.

56. Smith to Marshall, October 22, 1942, Smith Papers.

57. Butcher, *Three Years with Eisenhower*, 125.

58. For an account of Smith's hospitalization, his escape, and the birthday party, see ibid., 124-27, 132, 134.

59. Marshall to Smith, October 19, 1942, Smith Papers.

60. Salmon, et. al., "History of Allied Force Headquarters."

61. Pogue interview of Smith, May 8, 1947.

62. Eisenhower to Marshall, September 12, 1942, *EP*, #497; Eisenhower and Marshall, September 21, 1942, *EP*, #514; Butcher, *Three Years with Eisenhower*, 143-44.

63. Eisenhower to Marshall, October 20, 1942, *EP*, #559.

64. Eisenhower believed the failure to create a unified command for air to be among the errors of the North African campaign. See Eisenhower, "Commander-in-Chief's Dispatch, North African Campaign, 1942-43," in Smith Papers. For a discussion of the creation of the Allied air command, see Frank Craven and James Cate, eds., *Europe: TORCH to POINTBLANK, August 1942-December 1943*, The Army Air Forces in World War II, Vol. 2 (Chicago, 1949), 56-60.

65. Eisenhower ranked Cunningham as the best officer under his command and judged other officers relative to the British admiral. Eisenhower, "Memo," June 11, 1943, in *Eisenhower Diaries*, Robert Ferrel, ed., (New York, 1981), 93. For Cunningham's estimate of Eisenhower, see Oliver Warner, *Cunningham of Hyndhope: Admiral of the Fleet* (London, 1967), 185.

66. Eisenhower to Marshall, October 3, 1942, *EP*, #534.

67. Eisenhower to Ismay, October 10, 1942, *EP*, #541.

68. Eisenhower to Marshall, October 20, 1942, *EP*, #559.

69. The final directive is printed in Howe, *Northwest Africa*, 36.

70. Eisenhower to Marshall, November 7, 1942, *EP*, #585.

71. As Eisenhower later reported: "Before Beetle Smith came there was literally almost no one, except myself, in the Headquarters that had ever served intimately in the War Department." Eisenhower to Gailey, January 5, 1943, *EP*, #751.

72. Smith to Marshall, October 22, 1942, Smith Papers.

When Smith took over the staff, there were 344 British officers detailed to AFHQ; 205 Americans. Cited in Salmon et al., "History of Allied Forces Headquarters."

73. Eisenhower to Marshall, November 7, 1942, *EP*, #585.

74. Warner, *Cunningham*, 185.

75. Eisenhower to Fox Conner, August 21, 1942, Pre-Presidential Papers.

76. Eisenhower to Marshall, October 12, 1942, *EP*, #544.

77. Eisenhower to Marshall, October 3, 1942, *EP*, #534.

78. Eisenhower to Marshall, November 7, 1942, *EP*, #585.

CHAPTER 8

1. General Walter Warlimont, the deputy chief of the Wehrmachtsführungsstab, in a postwar interview acknowledged that the German High Command, preoccupied with the Russian Front, was "caught completely by surprise" in North Africa. "No one realized that there was a buildup for North Africa," he added. Copies of Warlimont's interview, conducted in summer 1945, are in the Smith Papers, Eisenhower Library. See also, Howe, *Northwest Africa*, 72-77.

2. Eisenhower, *Crusade in Europe*, 116.

3. Eisenhower to Marshall, November 30, 1942, *EP*, #673; Eisenhower to CCS, December 3, 1942, *EP*, #685; Howe, *Northwest Africa*, 312-21.

4. Allied fighter units, operating from bases 120 miles from the front, could not even protect ground troops from obsolescent Axis aircraft. For an assessment of the air situation see Eisenhower to Churchill, December 5, 1942, *EP*, #692. See also Craven and Cates, *TORCH to POINTBLANK*, 88-89.

5. Anderson pointed out that three factors were responsible for his failure to take northern Tunisia: ineffective administration; enemy air superiority; and the slow rate of reinforcement. *EP*, #685, n. 1.

6. Eisenhower to CCS, December 3, 1942, *EP*, #685; Eisenhower to Handy, December 7, 1942, *EP*, #698.

7. Eisenhower to Smith, November 18, 1942, *EP*, #641.

8. Eisenhower to Handy, December 7, 1942, *EP*, #698. See also Craven and Cates, *TORCH to POINTBLANK*, 87-91.

9. Sir Frederick Morgan, *Overture to Overlord* (Garden City, N.Y., 1950), 9; Smith to Eisenhower, November 6, 1942, Smith Papers.

10. Anthony Cave Brown, *The Last Hero: Wild Bill Donovan* (New York, 1982), 242-64.

11. Butcher, *Three Years with Eisenhower*, 143-46.

12. Eisenhower to Marshall, October 17, 1942, *EP*, #557.

13. Murphy, *Diplomat Among Warriors*, 136-38; Howe, *Northwest Africa*, 262-71.

14. Eisenhower to Smith, November 9, 1942, *EP*, #592.

15. Eisenhower to Smith, November 11, 1942, *EP*, #609.

16. Smith to Eisenhower, November 12, 1942, Smith Papers.

17. Churchill to Eisenhower, November 13, 1942, Smith Papers.

18. Eisenhower to Smith, November 13, 1942, *EP*, #621; Murphy, *Diplomat Among Warriors*, 139-40.

19. Smith considerably understated the situation when he said the deal was "coolly received." Smith to Eisenhower, November 14, 1942, Smith Papers.

20. Churchill, *Hinge of Fate*, 653-54; Herbert Feis, *Churchill-Roosevelt-Stalin: The War They Waged and the Peace They Sought* (Princeton, 1957); William Langer, *Our Vichy Gamble* (New York, 1947), 357-60.

21. Smith to Eisenhower, November 15, 1942; Smith to Eisenhower, November 16, 1942, Smith Papers.

22. Eisenhower to Smith, November 14, 1942, *EP*, #625.

23. The text of Roosevelt's public announcement is quoted in Sherwood, *Roosevelt and Hopkins*, 653-54; CCS to Smith, November 16, 1942, Smith Papers.

24. Howe, *Northwest Africa*, 268-69.

25. Churchill, *Hinge of Fate*, 632-33; Bryant, *Turn of the Tide*, 426.

26. Butcher, *Three Years with Eisenhower*, 201.

27. Smith to Marshall, November 24, 1942; Smith to Eisenhower, November 25, 1942, Smith Papers.

28. Eisenhower to Smith, November 14, 1942, *EP*, #625.

29. Smith to Eisenhower, November 12, 1942, Smith Papers.

30. Eisenhower to Smith, November 12, 1942, *EP*, #615 and 616.

31. Butcher, *Three Years with Eisenhower*, 201.

32. Smith to Eisenhower, November 15; Smith to Eisenhower, November 16, 1942, Smith Papers.

33. Smith to Eisenhower, November 25, 1942, Smith Papers.

34. Secretary/General Staff, "Minutes of Staff Conference," November 25, 1942, RG-218, Records of the JCS.

35. Smith to Eisenhower, November 25, 1942, Smith Papers.

36. Leahy, *I Was There*, 137.

37. Eisenhower to Marshall, December 2, 1942, *EP*, #681.

38. Eisenhower to Marshall, December 5, 1942, *EP*, #691.

39. Eisenhower to Alan Brooke, November 26, 1942, *EP*, #667.

40. Smith to Eisenhower, November 27, 1942, Smith Papers.

41. Eisenhower to Marshall, December 5, 1942, *EP*, #691.

42. Eisenhower to Smith, November 11, 1942, *EP*, #609 and 616.

43. Eisenhower believed that British practice involved a deterioration of the lines of authority. He resolved to "take the British by the horns." Stimson and Bundy, *On Active Service*, 551; Feis, *Churchill-Roosevelt-Stalin*, 321.

44. Pogue, *Supreme Command*, 37.

45. Ambrose, *Supreme Commander*, 146; General Sir Ian Jacob Diary, December 30, 1942, cited in Ambrose, 681, n. 20.

46. Butcher, *Three Years with Eisenhower*, 221.

47. For Eisenhower's estimate of Smith, see *Crusade in Europe*, 54-55. See also Ambrose, *Supreme Commander*, 82.

48. Eisenhower to Marshall, October 12, 1942, *EP*, #544.

49. Butcher, *Three Years with Eisenhower*, 225-26.

50. Reminiscences of Arthur Nevins, in the Collection of the Columbia University Oral History Research Office. [hereafter, Nevins, Oral History.]

51. Smith to Truscott, December 15, 1943, Smith Papers.

52. Interviews with Russel Vittrup, November 15, 1988, and Burgess. A good description of Smith's relations with his American subordinates drawn from interviews with Major Ruth Briggs and Burgess is in Snyder, "Eisenhower's Chief of Staff," 9-10.

53. Interview with Burgess; Dan Gilmer, Oral History, Eisenhower Library; Salmon et al., "History of Allied Force Headquarters."

54. Clark to Eisenhower, November 19, 1942, Pre-Presidential Papers.

55. Eisenhower to Marshall, February 8, 1943, *EP*, #811.

56. Eisenhower to Marshall, May 25, 1943, *EP*, #1020.

57. Salmon et al., "History of Allied Force Headquarters."

58. Eisenhower, "Commander-in-Chief's Dispatch, North African Campaign, 1942-43: Campaign in Retrospect," Smith Papers.

59. Salmon et al., "History of Allied Force Headquarters."

60. Ismay to Smith, January 7, 1943; Ismay to Smith, January 31, 1943; Smith to Ismay, February 20, 1943, Smith Papers.

61. The format of Smith's staff conferences is outlined in Salmon et al., "History of Allied Force Headquarters."

62. Howe, *Northwest Africa*, 495-96.

63. Smith to Noel Mason-MacFarlane, December 15, 1943, Smith Papers.

64. Ismay to Eisenhower, December 1, 1942, Pre-Presidential Papers; Eisenhower to Ismay, December 3, 1942, *EP*, #684. See also Sir Arthur Tedder, *With Prejudice: The War Memoirs of Marshal of the Royal Air Force Lord Tedder* (London, 1966), 369-74.

65. Arnold to Eisenhower, December 15, 1942, Pre-Presidential Papers. See also Craven and Cates, *TORCH to POINTBLANK*, 63-66.

66. Tedder, *With Prejudice*, 404.

67. Tedder is the best source for descriptions of the difficulties involved in achieving a workable air command structure. For the Tedder-Smith meeting, see Tedder, *With Prejudice*, 405.

68. Eisenhower to Marshall, September 21, 1942, *EP*, #514.

69. Eisenhower to Marshall, November 26, 1942, *EP*, #668; Murphy, *Diplomat Among Warriors*, 144-48.

70. United States Department of State, *Foreign Relations of the United States: Diplomatic Papers, 1943*, 6 vols. (Washington, D.C., 1963-65). Vol. 2: *Europe*, 24.

71. Eisenhower to Smith, November 18, 1942, *EP*, #642.

72. Brown, *The Last Hero*, 263.

73. Marshall to Eisenhower, November 30, 1942, Pre-Presidential Papers.

74. Harold Macmillan, *The Blast of War* (London, 1967), 273.

75. For Macmillan's views on Smith and his description of the relationship see ibid., 222-25, 273.

76. Butcher, *Three Years with Eisenhower*, 185; Macmillan, *Blast of War*, 346.

77. Murphy, *Diplomat Among Warriors*, 171-76.

78. Macmillan, *Blast of War*, 455.

79. United States Department of State, *Foreign Relations, 1943*, vol. 2: 111-13; Milton Viorst, *Hostile Allies: Roosevelt and Charles de Gaulle* (New York, 1965), 54, 167-82; Feis, *Churchill-Roosevelt-Stalin*, 138-40.

80. Eisenhower handwritten note to Marshall, November 27, 1942, Smith Papers.

81. Ambrose, *Supreme Commander*, 130, 132, 180.

82. Eisenhower, "Dispatch: Campaign in Retrospect."

83. Salmon et al., "History of Allied Force Headquarters."

84. Howe, *Northwest Africa*, 58-59.

85. Eisenhower to Marshall, August 24, 1943, *EP*, #1205.

86. For Eisenhower's correspondence with Marshall, see Hobbes, *Dear General*, 61-131.

87. This September 1943 "Memorandum for an Allied Commander" is the most revealing statement of Eisenhower's views on the question of the leadership and organization for integrated command. Eisenhower to Admiral Lord Louis Mountbatten, September 14, 1943, *EP*, #1256.

88. For Smith's views of the relationship of the Supreme Commander and his staff, see address of W. B. Smith, "Problems of an Integrated Headquarters," *Journal of the Royal United Service Institute* 90 (November 1945): 455-62. Original in Smith Papers.

89. Eisenhower, "Memorandum for an Allied Commander."

CHAPTER 9

1. Michael Howard, *The Mediterranean in British Strategy* (London, 1968).

2. Wedemeyer, *Wedemeyer Reports*, 105-06.

3. Byrant, *Turn of the Tide*, 442-43, 541.

4. General Ian Jacob, as quoted in Ambrose, *Supreme Commander*, 158.

5. Wedemeyer, 192.

6. Harrison, *Cross-Channel Invasion*, 36-46.

7. U.S. Department of State, *Foreign Relations, The Conference at Washington, 1941-1942* and *Casablanca, 1943* (Washington, D.C., 1968); Churchill, *Hinge of Fate*, 675-95; Sherwood, *Roosevelt and Hopkins*, 667-97.

8. Eisenhower to Handy, January 28, 1943, *EP*, #796.

9. For the naval command see Samuel Eliot Morison, *Operations in North African Waters, October 1942 - June 1943*, History of the United States Naval Operations in World War II, vol 2 (Boston, 1962). See also the same series, *Sicily-Salerno-Anzio*, vol. 9 (Boston, 1964).

10. For Alexander's views on the command structure and Eisenhower, see Harold Alexander, *The Alexander Memoirs, 1940-45*, John North, ed. (London, 1965), 10-11.

11. Eisenhower, *Crusade in Europe*, 138; Albert Garland and Howard Smyth, *Sicily and the Surrender of Italy*. U.S. Army in World War II Series. (Washington, D.C., 1965), 10-11.

12. Bryant, *Turn of the Tide*, 448, 452-55.

13. CCS 163, "System of Air Command in the Mediterranean," January 20, 1943, and CCS 171, "Operation HUSKY, Directive to Commander-in-Chief, Allied Expeditionary Force in North Africa," January 23, 1943, Smith Papers.

14. Eisenhower to Marshall, February 8, 1943, *EP*, #811.

15. Butcher, *Three Years with Eisenhower*, 258.

16. Eisenhower Memorandum, January 23, 1943, Butcher Diary, Eisenhower Library. The Butcher Diary, which occupies nearly four boxes, differs in places from the published version [hereafter cited as Butcher Diary with appropriate date].

17. Ibid.

18. Eisenhower to Marshall, February 8, 1943, *EP*, #811, n. 2.

19. Eisenhower to Marshall, February 8, 1943, *EP*, #811.

20. Eisenhower to Alexander, January 29, 1943, *EP*, #799; Eisenhower to Marshall, January 30, 1942, *EP*, #800.

21. Eisenhower to Marshall, January 10, 1943, *EP*, #765.

22. Interview with Burgess; Butcher, *Three Years with Eisenhower*, 249.

23. Smith to Mrs. Dykes, January 30, 1943, cited in Danchev, *Very Special Relationship*, 25.

24. For Somervell's trip to North Africa, see "Records of Headquarters, Army Service Forces," RG-160, National Archives. See also Somervell, "Matters to be Discussed with General Eisenhower," Smith Papers.

25. Churchill's visit is discussed in Butcher, *Three Years with Eisenhower* 254-58.

26. Smith pointed out as late as July 1943 that the Allies were short 300,000 tons of shipping. Butcher, *Three Years with Eisenhower*, 363.

27. Marcel Vigneras, *Rearming the French*, U.S. Army in World War II Series. (Washington, D.C., 1959), is the official account of American efforts to equip Giraud's forces.

28. The exchange between Algiers, London, and Washington concerning AMGOT policy is reprinted in Harry Coles and Albert Weinberg, *Civil Affairs: Soldiers Become Governors*. U.S. Army in World War II Series. (Washington, D.C., 1964), 160-68.

29. Montgomery to Brooke, February 15, 1943, Montgomery Papers, cited in Nigel Hamilton, *Monty: Master of the Battlefield* (London, 1983), 143 [hereafter cited Hamilton, *Monty*, vol. 2: page number]. The Montgomery Papers are now available in the Imperial War Museum, London. For the purposes of this book reliance will be placed in published sources where possible.

30. Montgomery to Brooke, February 16, 1943, in Hamilton, *Monty*, vol. 2: 145.

31. Ibid., 148.

32. Butcher Diary, April 17, 1943.

33. For this episode, see Montgomery to Brooke, April 12, 1943, cited in Montgomery, *Memoirs*, 147; Hamilton, *Monty*, vol. 2: 151; Alun Chalfont, *Montgomery of Alamein* (London, 1976), 206-07.

34. Montgomery to Eisenhower, April 10, 1943, Pre-Presidential Papers.

35. Eisenhower to Montgomery, April 12, 1943, Pre-Presidential Papers.

36. Alanbrooke Papers, cited in Ronald Lewin, *Montgomery as Military Commander* (New York, 1971), 139.

37. Lewin, *Ultra Goes to War* (New York, 1978), 317-18.

38. Eisenhower to Brooke, February 20, 1943, *EP*, #831.

39. Interview of General Jacob by Hamilton, cited in Hamilton, *Monty*, vol. 2: 139.

40. Eisenhower, *Crusade in Europe*, 135; Howe, *Northwest Africa*, 383.

41. Bradley accompanied Smith on this trip. Bradley and Blair, *General's Life*, 135.

42. Butcher, *Three Years with Eisenhower*, 273.

43. Butcher, *Three Years with Eisenhower*, 266.

44. Eisenhower wrote a long defense of American effectiveness to Marshall and discussed it in his book. Eisenhower to Marshall, April 15, 1943, *EP*, #945; Eisenhower, *Crusade in Europe*, 152-54.

45. Tedder, *With Prejudice*, 410-11.

46. Butcher, *Three Years with Eisenhower*, 281.

47. Eisenhower Memorandum, July 1, 1943, *EP*, #1091.

48. Eisenhower, *Crusade in Europe*, 161-64; Montgomery, *Memoirs*, 153-65; Garland and Smyth, *Sicily*, 53-65.

49. Tedder, *With Prejudice*, 233-34.

50. Eisenhower to CCS, April 10, 1943, *EP*, #941.

51. Eisenhower, *Crusade in Europe*, 162-63; Tedder, *With Prejudice*, 429-30.

52. Brian Horrocks, *A Full Life* (London, 1971), 159.

53. Montgomery to Brooke, April 30, 1943, Montgomery Papers, in Hamilton, *Monty*, vol. 2: 259-60.

54. For accounts of the famous "lavatory conference," see Montgomery, *Memoirs*, 153-165; Hamilton, *Monty*, vol. 2: 261.

55. Montgomery, *Memoirs*, 160.

56. Sidney Matthews interview with Smith, no date given, USAMHI.

57. Eisenhower to CCS and BCOS, May 4, 1943, *EP*, #969.

58. Tedder, *With Prejudice*, 425-35; Eisenhower, *Crusade in Europe*, 164, 178-79; Garland and Smyth, *Sicily*, 57-63.

59. Montgomery Diary, July 9, 1943, Montgomery Papers, cited in Hamilton, *Monty*, vol. 2: 271-72.

60. Montgomery Diary, May 6, 1943, Montgomery Papers, cited in Hamilton, *Monty*, vol. 2: 261.

61. Montgomery to Brooke, May 6, 1943, Montgomery Papers, cited in Hamilton, *Monty*, vol. 2: 269.

62. Montgomery to Alexander, May 5, 1943, Montgomery Papers, cited in Hamilton, *Monty*, vol. 2: 265.

63. Patton Diary, May 7, 1943, *Patton Papers, 1940-45*, Martin Blumenson, ed., 641.

64. Montgomery Diary, May 7, 1943, Montgomery Papers, cited in Hamilton, *Monty*, vol. 2: 268.

65. Marshall to Eisenhower, April 27, 1943, Pre-Presidential Papers.

66. Butcher, *Three Years with Eisenhower*, 301.

67. Brooke Diary, May 18, 1943, in Bryant, *Turn of the Tide*, 507-8.

68. Matloff, *Strategic Planning for Coalition Warfare,1943- 44*, 126-45; Morton, *Strategy and Command*, 454-60; Garland and Smyth, *Sicily*, 20-24.

69. Smith to Eisenhower, May 14, 1943, Smith Papers.

70. Butcher, *Three Years with Eisenhower*, 313.

71. Smith to Eisenhower, May 15, 1943, Smith Papers.

72. Butcher, *Three Years with Eisenhower*, 314.

73. Smith to Eisenhower, May 14, 1943, Smith Papers.

74. Butcher, *Three Years with Eisenhower*, 313-14.

75. Churchill, *Hinge of Fate*, 811.

76. See, "Minutes of Meetings, 31 May-3 June, 1943," Smith Papers. See also Ismay, *Memoirs*, 300-303; Garland and Smyth, *Sicily*, 12-25.

77. The best account of AMGOT is contained in Coles and Weinberg, *Civil Affairs*. See also C. R. S. Harris, *Allied Military Administration in Italy, 1943-45* (London, 1957), 1-4. For statements of policy, see Smith to Alexander, June 26, 1943, *EP*, #1078; Eisenhower to CCS and BCOS, July 19, 1943, *EP*, #1123.

78. *EP*, #1050, n. 3; Churchill, *Closing the Ring*, 173-76.

79. Butcher, *Three Years with Eisenhower*, 335; Charles de Gaulle, *The War Memoirs of Charles de Gaulle*, vol. II, *Unity, 1942-1944*, 126-27.

80. Smith to Marshall, June 17, 1943 and Eisenhower (written by Smith) to BCOS, June 22, 1943, Smith Papers; Macmillan, *Blast of War*, 440-45.

81. Churchill to Eisenhower, June 28, 1943, Smith Papers.

82. Eisenhower to Alexander Surles, May 17, 1943, *EP*, #1001.

83. Macmillan, *Blast of War*, 364.

84. Michael Balfour, "The Origins of the Formula: 'Unconditional Surrender' in World War II," *Armed Forces in Society*, 5 (1979): 281-301.

85. The policy was outlined in "Psychological Warfare Plan for HUSKY," April 16, 1943, Smith Papers. The Eisenhower-signed communication from Strong to the CCS, May 17, 1943, is also contained in the Smith Papers.

86. Eisenhower to Smith, May 30, 1943, *EP*, #1029.

87. Smyth interview of Smith, May 13, 1947, USAMHI.

88. BCOS to AFHQ, June 17, 1943, Smith Papers.

89. Howe, *Northwest Africa*, 84.

90. Butcher, *Three Years with Eisenhower*, 345-47.

91. Eisenhower expressed his concern over communications in the theater in Eisenhower to Marshall, July 9, 1943, *EP*, #1105.

92. Smith's views on the nature of an integrated staff were outlined in a presentation he made to the Royal United Service Institution shortly after the war. See "Problems of an Integrated Headquarters."

CHAPTER 10

1. Eisenhower to CCS and BCOS, July 19, 1943, *EP*, #1127.

2. Butcher Diary, July 27, 1943; Macmillan, *Blast of War*, 307. The best summary of the fall of Mussolini and its impact on Allied decision making is Feis, *Churchill-Roosevelt-Stalin*, chap. 17.

3. Churchill, *Closing the Ring*, 55-56.

4. Marshall to Eisenhower, July 29, 1943, Smith Papers.

5. Butcher, *Three Years with Eisenhower*, 372.

6. Macmillan, *Blast of War*, 308-9.

7. AMGOT (written by Smith) to Marshall, May 14, 1943, *EP*, #1012, n. 3.

8. CCS to Eisenhower, July 27, 1943, Smith Papers. See also Coles and Weinberg, *Civil Affairs*, 98; Bruno Arcidiacono, "La Grande-Bretagne et les États-Unis Face au Problème de l'Armistice avec L'Italie et du Contrôle du Territoire Italien Libéré," *Relations Internationale* 10 (October 1977): 143-61.

9. Butcher, *Three Years with Eisenhower*, 372-384.

10. Garland and Smyth, *Sicily*, 348-67.

11. Eisenhower to CCS and BCOS, July 28, 1943, *EP*, #1145; Eisenhower to Marshall, July 30, 1943, *EP*, #1154; Eisenhower to Marshall, August 3, 1943, *EP*, #1161.

12. Tedder, *With Prejudice*, 456-63.

13. Eisenhower to Alexander, August 4, 1943, Smith Papers.

14. Eisenhower (written by Smith) to Marshall, August 3, 1943, Smith Papers.

15. Butcher, *Three Years with Eisenhower*, 378-79.

16. *EP*, #1160. n. 2; Eisenhower (written by Smith) to Marshall, August 4, 1943, *EP*, #1162.

17. Churchill to Eisenhower, July 29, 1943, *EP*, #1148, n. 2.

18. Craven and Cate, *TORCH to POINTBLANK*, 474.

19. Marshall paraphrased Churchill's letter to Hopkins, Marshall to Eisenhower, August 3, 1943, *EP*, #1164, n. 3.

20. Churchill to Eisenhower, August 16, 1943, *EP*, #1188, n. 1.

21. Butcher, *Three Years with Eisenhower*, 381-82.

22. Eisenhower to Marshall, August 4, 1943, *EP*, #1166.

23. Hughes Diary, June 22, 1943.

24. Hughes Diary, August 6, 1943

25. AFHQ Secretariat, Historical Section, "AVALANCHE," Smith Papers.

26. Matloff, *Strategic Planning*, 211-13.

27. Eisenhower (written my Smith) to Marshall, August 12, 1943, *EP*, #1181.

28. Hughes Diary, August 17, 1943.

29. Smith, "Problems of an Integrated Headquarters."

30. Feis, *Churchill-Roosevelt-Stalin*, 150; Matloff, *Strategic Planning*, 227-29.

31. For a discussion of the negotiations leading up to the Italian surrender and Smith's role in them, see Kenneth Strong, *Intelligence at the Top: The Recollections of a British Intelligence Officer* (Garden City, N.Y., 1968), 137-59; see also Garland and Smyth, *Sicily*, 440-68; Macmillan, *Blast of War*, 296-337.

32. Reprinted in Garland and Smyth, *Sicily*, 558-64.

33. CCS to Eisenhower, August 16, 1943, Pre-Presidential Papers.

34. Smith to Anderson, August 30, 1943, Smith Papers.

35. Smyth interview of Smith, May 13, 1947.

36. Eisenhower to CCS, July 27, 1943, *EP*, #1139.

37. Eisenhower to CCS, August 17, 1943, *EP*, #1189.

38. Macmillan, *Blast of War*, 380-81.

39. Strong, *Intelligence at the Top*, 145.

40. Cited in ibid., 148.

41. For Smith's views of Castellano and the negotiations see Smyth interview of Smith, May 13, 1947.

42. Strong, *Intelligence at the Top*, 148-52. See also Garland and Smyth, *Sicily*, 455-61; David Brown, "The Inside Story of Italy's Surrender," *Saturday Evening Post*, September 9, 1944.

43. Strong, *Intelligence at the Top*, 147.

44. Eisenhower (written by Smith) to CCS and BCOS, August 20, 1943, *EP*, #1200.

45. Smyth interview of Smith.

46. Garland and Smyth, *Sicily*, 448-68.

47. Eisenhower (written by Smith) to CCS and BCOS, August 28, 1943, *EP*, #1213.

48. Giuseppi Castellano, *Come firmai l'armistizio di Cassibile* (Milan, 1945).

49. General Taylor, for one, believed that Smith used "psychological arm-twisting" to pressure Castellano. Hamilton interview of Taylor, October 17, 1981, cited in Hamilton, *Monty*, vol. 2: 400.

50. Murphy, *Diplomat Among Warriors*, 193.

51. Smith to Eisenhower, September 1, 1943, outlined in Eisenhower to CCS and BCOS, September 1, 1943, *EP*, #1221. See also, Garland and Smyth, *Sicily*, 474-79.

52. Smyth interview of Smith.

53. Garland and Smyth, *Sicily*, 476-80.

54. Butcher, *Three Years with Eisenhower*, 405.

55. Murphy, *Diplomat Among Warriors*, 190.

56. Butcher, *Three Years with Eisenhower*, 406.

57. Eisenhower to Smith, September 2, 1943, *EP*, #1228; Eisenhower to CCS, September 3, 1943, *EP*, #1229.

58. Accounts of the negotiations are in, Strong, *Intelligence at the Top*, 156-59; Murphy, *Diplomat among Warriors*, 193-94. See also Butcher, *Three Years with Eisenhower*, 405-06; Garland and Smyth, *Sicily*, 480-84.

59. Smyth interview of Smith.

60. Garland and Smyth, *Sicily*, 484.

61. Smyth interview of Lemnitzer, March 3, 1947, USAMHI.

62. Smyth interview of Smith.

63. Ibid.

64. Hamilton interview of Taylor; Smyth interview of Lemnitzer; Murphy, *Diplomat Among Warriors*, 195.

65. Garland and Smyth, *Sicily*, 498-505.

66. *EP*, #1244, n. 1.

67. Eisenhower to Badoglio, September 8, 1943, *EP*, #1244; Eisenhower to CCS, September 8, 1943, *EP*, #1248.

68. Garland and Smyth, *Sicily*, 508-9.

69. Smyth interview of Smith.

70. Smyth interview of Strong, October 29, 1947, USAMHI.

71. Smyth interview of Smith.

72. *EP*, #1243, n. 4.

73. Reprinted in Garland and Smyth, *Sicily*, 508-9.

74. Ibid., 512-13.

75. Montgomery Diary, September 5, 1943, cited in Hamilton, *Monty*, vol. 2: 404.

76. Butcher, *Three Years with Eisenhower*, 419-20.

77. Montgomery Diary, September 13, 1943, in Hamilton, *Monty*, vol. 2: 412.

78. 8th Army Headquarters, War Diary, "Minutes of Planning Conference," August 19, 1943, in Hamilton, *Monty*, vol. 2: 387.

79. Montgomery to Frank Simpson, September 20, 1943, in Hamilton, *Monty*, vol. 2: 412.

80. Eisenhower to Marshall, September 13, 1943, *EP*, #1249.

81. Eisenhower to McNarney, September 11, 1943, *EP*, #1262.

82. Eisenhower (written by Smith) to Marshall, September 10, 1943, Pre-Presidential Papers.

83. Garland and Smyth, *Sicily*, 535.

84. Eisenhower to CCS and BCOS, September 15, 1943, *EP*, #1257; Devers to Eisenhower, September 16, 1943, Eisenhower to Devers, September 18, 1943, Smith Papers.

85. Eisenhower to Marshall, September 20, 1943, *EP*, #1271; Marshall to Eisenhower, September 24, 1943, *EP*, #1286, n. 2.

86. Butcher, *Three Years with Eisenhower*, 424.

87. Murphy, *Diplomat Among Warriors*, 178-82; Macmillan, *Blast of War*, 242.

88. Eisenhower (written by Smith) to CCS, September 18, 1943, *EP*, #1264.

89. Eisenhower to Smith, September 19, 1943, *EP*, #1266; Butcher Diary, September 21, 1943.

90. Smyth interview of Smith.

91. Press conference, September 30, 1943; transcript in Smith Papers.

92. Smyth interview of Smith.

93. Garland and Smyth, *Sicily*, 548-49.

94. Eisenhower to Dill, September 30, 1943, *EP*, #1301.

95. Eisenhower (written by Smith) to Badoglio, September 29, 1943, *EP*, #1298.

96. Eisenhower to CCS and BCOS, September 30, 1943, *EP*, #1299.

97. Smith to Ismay, September 12, 1943, Smith Papers.

98. Smith to Theodore Roosevelt, Jr., December 30, 1943; Smith to Earle, October 3, 1943, Smith Papers.

99. Smith to Ismay, September 12, 1943, Smith Papers.

100. Wedemeyer to Eisenhower, September 2, 1943, *EP*, #1248, n. 3.

101. Eisenhower to Marshall, October 13, 1943, *EP*, #1335.

102. Eisenhower to Marshall, October 4, 1943, *EP*, #1316; Eisenhower to Marshall, October 13, 1943, *EP*, #1335.

103. Eisenhower, "Notes for Chief of Staff," October 2, 1943, *EP*, #1310.

104. Eisenhower to Marshall, October 4, 1943, *EP*, #1316.

105. Eisenhower to Smith, October 2, 1943, *EP*, #1311.

106. Butcher, *Three Years with Eisenhower*, 421.

107. Ibid., 427-28.

108. Eisenhower to Marshall, October 4, 1943, *EP*, #1316.

109. Smith, "Chief of Staff, Notes, Washington Trip, October 1943," Smith Papers; Butcher Diary, October 28, 1943.

110. Eisenhower to Marshall, October 25, 1943, *EP*, #1428.

111. Hughes Diary, March 11-12, 1943.

112. Hughes Diary, March 28, 1943.

113. Hughes Diary, March 12, 28; April 26; June 10; June 25, 1943.

114. Hughes Diary, May 5, 1943.

115. Hughes Diary, June 2, 19, 27, 1943.

116. Hughes Diary, October 27, 29; November 3, 1943.

117. Ambrose, *Supreme Commander*, 296-97.

118. Eisenhower to McNarney, September 16, 1943, *EP*, #1262.

119. Butcher, *Three Years with Eisenhower*, 464,

120. Ibid., 442.

121. Eisenhower, "Memorandum," December 6, 1943, *EP*, #1408; Eisenhower, *Crusade in Europe*, 194.

122. Joint Chiefs of Staff, "Minutes of Meeting Between the President and the Chiefs of Staff," November 15, 1943, RG-218, Records of JCS; Pogue, *Supreme Command*,

30-32, *George C. Marshall: Organizer of Victory* (New York, 1973), 311; Leahy, *I Was There*, 209-09.

123. Eisenhower to Marshall, October 4, 1943, *EP*, #1316.

124. Butcher, *Three Years with Eisenhower*, 426-29.

125. Smith to Paul Stone, November 21, 1943, Smith Papers.

126. Smith to Ivan Cobbold, July 15, 1943, Smith Papers.

127. Smith to Ed Merkle, February 14, 1944, Smith Papers.

128. Interview with Burgess.

129. Kay Summersby, *Past Forgiving: My Love Affair with Dwight D. Eisenhower* (London, 1986), 88-89.

130. Hughes Diary, February 13, 1943; January 15, 1944.

131. Interview with Burgess.

132. Eisenhower to Alexander Surles, December 15, 1943, *EP*, #1417; Eisenhower to Walter Campbell Sweeney, December 28, 1943, *EP*, #1448.

133. Hughes Diary, November 26, 1943.

134. Eisenhower to Marshall, November 23, 1943, *EP*, #1396, n. 1; Eisenhower to Marshall, November 24, 1943, *EP*, #1396.

135. Butcher, *Three Years with Eisenhower*, 454.

136. Ibid., 456, 458.

137. Smith to Truscott, December 15, 1943, Smith Papers.

138. Ambrose interview of Eisenhower, October 11, 1967, cited in *Supreme Commander*, 317-18; Interview with Burgess.

139. Eisenhower to Roosevelt, December 22, 1943, *EP*, #1425.

140. *EP*, #1425, n. 4.

141. Eisenhower to Smith, December 30, 1943, Smith Papers.

142. Eisenhower to Marshall, December 31, 1943, *EP*, #1466; de Gaulle, *Unity*, 291; Viorst, *Hostile Allies*, 186-87.

143. Montgomery Diary, August 17-22, 1943, in Hamilton, *Monty*, vol. 2: 375-81.

144. Wedemeyer, "Commanders and Others Contacted," n.d., Smith Papers; Eisenhower to Wedemeyer, September 13, 1943, *EP*, #1248.

145. Eisenhower to Handy, January 28, 1943, *EP*, 796.

146. Eisenhower, "Commander-in-Chief's Dispatch, North African Campaign, 1942-43," n.d., Smith Papers.

147. Eisenhower to Marshall, October 24, 1943, *EP*, #1359.

148. Hughes Diary, September 20, 1943.

149. Eisenhower to Ethel Wyman, October 16, 1943, *EP*, #1341.

150. Eisenhower to Marshall, October 24, 1943, *EP*, #1359.

151. Eisenhower to Wyman, *EP*, #1341.

CHAPTER 11

1. Eisenhower to Smith, December 30, 1943, Smith Papers.

2. Marshall to Eisenhower, December 23, 1943, Pre-Presidential Papers.

3. Eisenhower to Marshall, December 25, 1943, *EP*, #1428.

4. Morgan, *Overture to Overlord*, 256.

5. COSSAC, "Digest of Operation 'OVERLORD'," July 30, 1943, Smith Papers; Morgan, "Operation OVERLORD-Command and Control," September 11, 1943, Morgan to Devers, September 16 and 24, 1943, RG-319, Records of the Army Staff, National Archives; Pogue interview of Morgan, February 8, 1947, USAMHI.

6. Pogue interview of Smith, May 9, 1947.

7. On October 27, 1943, General Chambers met with Eisenhower. *EP*, "Chronology," 5: 134.

8. Pogue interview of Smith, May 9, 1947.

9. Eisenhower to Ismay, December 3, 1960, Pre-Presidential Papers.

10. Pogue interview of Smith, May 9, 1947.

11. Ibid.

12. Smith to Eisenhower, January 5, 1944, Smith Papers. Montgomery added his voice, arguing gainst ANVIL. Montgomery to Eisenhower, January 10, 1944, Pre-Presidential Papers.

13. Eisenhower to Marshall, December 25, 1943, *EP*, #1428. See also, Eisenhower to Montgomery, January 13, Pre-Presidential Papers.

14. Eisenhower to Smith, January 5-6, 1944, *EP*, #1473.

15. Smith to Eisenhower, January 8, 1944, Smith Papers.

16. Smith to Joint Chiefs, May 21, 1943, Marshall Papers; Pogue interview of Smith, May 9, 1947.

17. Smith to Eisenhower, December 30, 1943 and January 1, 1944, Smith Papers; Tedder, *With Prejudice*, 505.

18. Eisenhower, along with Smith, thought Tedder slow to take charge. Pogue interview of Smith, May 9, 1947; Butcher Diary, January 23, 1944.

Smith sent two cables to Eisenhower, December 30, 1943, both dealing with the command setup, particularly that for air. See also Smith to Eisenhower, January 1, 1944, Smith Papers.

19. Eisenhower to Marshall, December 31, 1943, *EP*, #1470.

20. Pogue interview of Smith, May 9, 1947.

21. Smith to Eisenhower, December 30, 1943, Smith Papers.

22. Eisenhower to Smith, December 31, 1943, *EP*, #1469.

23. Bryant, *Triumph in the West*, 74.

24. Pogue interview of Smith, May 9, 1947.

25. Ibid.

26. Butcher, *Three Years with Eisenhower*, 772-74.

27. Smith reproached Devers as narrow minded and called him a "light-weight." Butcher Diary, January 20, 1944. See also, Ambrose, *Supreme Commander*, 340-41.

28. Smith to Eisenhower, January 9, 1944, Smith Papers.

29. Pogue interview of Smith, May 9, 1947.

30. Hughes Diary, January 18, 1944; Interview with Burgess.

31. Eisenhower, "Memo," March 22, 1944, *EP*, #1602.

32. Pogue, *Ordeal and Hope*, 424.

33. Butcher, *Three Years with Eisenhower*, 498; Eisenhower, *Crusade in Europe*, 221-22.

34. Eisenhower to Tedder, February 29, 1944, *EP*, #1575; Eisenhower to Marshall, March 3, 1944, *EP*, #1577; Portal to Eisenhower, March 7, 1944, Pre-Presidential Papers; Eisenhower to Tedder, March 9, 1944, *EP*, #1584; Eisenhower to Marshall, March 21, 1944, *EP*, #1599; Eisenhower, "Memo," March 22, 1944; Churchill to Eisenhower, April 3, 1944 and Portal to Spaatz, April 15, 1944, Pre-Presidential Papers.

35. For a discussion of the issue, see Craven and Cates, eds., *Europe: Argument to V-E Day* (Chicago, 1958), 67-83.

36. Pogue interview of Smith, May 9, 1947.

37. "Extracts from Minutes of Meeting Between the President and Joint Chiefs of Staff in the White House," February 21, 1944, Leahy Papers. See also, Leahy to Eisenhower, February 21, 1944, Pre-Presidential Papers; Joint Chiefs of Staff Meeting, "OVERLORD vs ANVIL," February 21, 1944, RG-319, Records of the Army Staff.

38. Smith to Eisenhower, January 5, 1944, Smith Papers; Montgomery to Eisenhower, January 10, 1944, SHAEF Secretary/General Staff File [hereafter SHAEF S/GS], Modern Military Records Division, National Archives; Frederick de Guingand, *Operation Victory* (London, 1947), 340-44. For the debate, see Pogue, *Supreme Command*, U.S. Army in World War II. (Washington, D.C., 1954), 108-17; Gordon Harrison, *Cross-Channel Attack*, U.S. Army in World War II. (Washington, D.C., 1951), 168-70.

39. For the British view see BCOS to Joint Staff Mission, February 19, 1944, RG-319, Records of the Army Staff; Montgomery to Eisenhower, February 21, 1944, Pre-Presidential Papers. "Minutes of White House Meeting," February 21, 1944, Leahy Papers; Eisenhower to Marshall, February 6, 1944, *EP*, #1531; Marshall to Eisenhower, February 7, 1944, Pre-Presidential Papers; Eisenhower, "Memo," February 7, 1944, *EP*, #1536; Eisenhower to Marshall, February 8, 1944, *EP*, #1538.

40. Eisenhower to Montgomery, January 13, 1944, *EP*, #1475; Eisenhower to Smith, January 13, 1944, *EP*, #1476; Butcher Diary, February 7, 1944.

41. Eisenhower to War Department, February 8, 1944, RG-218, Records of JCS.

42. Marshall to Eisenhower, February 10, 1944, Pre-Presidential Papers; Eisenhower to Marshall, February 19, 1944, *EP*, #1575; Smith and Handy, February 20, 1944, telephone conference, Admiral Kirk Papers, United States Navy Classified Archives, Washington, D.C.

43. Even a simultaneously staged ANVIL, in Smith's opinion, could not materially affect OVERLORD for the first fifteen to thirty days. Smith and Handy, February 20, 1944, Kirk Papers.

44. "Minutes of Supreme Allied Commander's Conference," February 26, 1944, SHAEF S/GS, RG-319, Records of the Army Staff.

45. Butcher, *Three Years with Eisenhower*, 474,

46. Pogue interview of Smith, May 8-9, 1947.

47. Smith and Handy, March 17, 1944, telephone conference, War Plans Division-- Operations Division Message Center File, Modern Military Records Division. See also

Maurice Matloff, *Strategic Planning for Coalition Warfare, 1943-44*, U.S. Army in World War II. (Washington, D.C., 1959), 422.

48. Butcher, *Three Years with Eisenhower*, 494.

49. Smith and Handy, March 17, 1944, telephone communication, WPD-OPD Message Center.

50. Marshall to Eisenhower, March 17, 1944, Pre-Presidential Papers.

51. Pogue interview of C. A. West, February 19, 1947, USAMHI.

52. Hamilton, *Monty*, vol. 2: 485-507.

53. "Minutes of SAC Conference," January 21, 1944, SHAEF S/GS.

54. Butcher, *Three Years with Eisenhower*, 478.

55. Hamilton, *Monty*, vol. 2: 516.

56. Betts, Oral History.

57. Butcher, *Three Years with Eisenhower*, 478.

58. The best description of the nature and organization of SHAEF is in Pogue, *Supreme Command*, especially chaps. 3-4.

59. Gilmer to Burgess, January 14, 1944, Smith Papers.

60. Smith to Eisenhower, January 21, 1944, Smith Papers.

61. Smith to Eisenhower, December 30, 1943, Smith Papers; Pogue interview of Smith, May 9, 1947; Pogue interview of N. C. D. Brownjohn, March 28, 1947, USAMHI.

62. These impressions of SHAEF and the differences between the American and British staff systems are derived from the oral histories of two American officers Smith brought with him from Algiers, Arthur Nevins, Oral History; Betts, Oral History.

63. Smith to Joint Chiefs of Staff, May 21, 1943, Marshall Papers; Nevins and Betts, Oral Histories; See also, Pogue, *Supreme Command*, chap. 3.

64. David Irving interview of General Mark Clark, January 4, 1970, in Irving, *Papers relating to the Allied High Command, 1943-45* [materials collected for Irving, *War Between the Generals*, in the author's possession].

65. Betts, Oral History.

66. Smith to Joint Chiefs, May 21, 1943, Marshall Papers.

67. Thomas J. Davis to H. V. Roberts, February 12, 1944, Thomas J. Davis Papers, Eisenhower Library.

68. Smith to Eisenhower, January 21, 1944, Smith Papers; Pogue interview of Smith, May 9, 1947; Betts, Oral History.

69. Smith to Eisenhower, January 21, 1944, Smith Papers; Pogue interview of Smith, May 9, 1947.

70. Betts, Oral History.

71. Smith to Brooke, January 9, 1944, Smith Papers.

72. Pogue interview of Gale, January 27, 1947, USAMHI; Betts, Oral History.

73. Pogue interview of Smith, May 8, 1947.

74. Smith to Eisenhower, January 21, 1944, Smith Papers.

75. Ray Barker, Oral History.

76. Pogue interview of Smith, May 13, 1947.

77. Pogue interview of Robb, February 3, 1947, USAMHI.

78. Interview with Burgess.

79. Pogue interview of Smith, May 9, 1947; Pogue, *Supreme Command*, 62-63; Ambrose, *Supreme Commander*, 591.

80. Pogue, *Supreme Command*, 68-71.

81. Betts, Oral History.

82. Ibid.

83. Morgan, "Operation OVERLORD--Command and Control," September 11, 1943.

84. Roland G. Ruppenthal interview of Smith, September 14, 1945, USAMHI.

85. Morgan to Smith, May 6, 1944; Morgan to BCOS, May 21, 1944, SHAEF Diary. Copies in Smith Papers. See also Morgan to Basil Liddell Hart, July 5, 1959, Liddell Hart Papers, King's College. University of London.

86. Ruppenthal interview of Smith.

87. Eisenhower to Pogue, March 10, 1947, Pre-Presidential Papers.

88. Betts, Oral History; Pogue, *Supreme Command*, 71-73.

89. Smith to Strong, July 4, 1944, Smith Papers.

90. Pogue, *Supreme Command*, 73-74.

91. Eisenhower to Marshall, January 17, 1944, *EP*, #1483.

92. The best description of the organization and command of the European Theater of Operations is Ruppenthal, *Logistical Support of the Armies, May 1941 - September 1944*, U.S. Army in World War II. (Washington, D.C., 1953).

93. Eisenhower, "Memo," March 22, 1944, *EP*, #1602.

94. Morgan, *Overture to Overlord*, 227-228.

95. Smith to Joint Chiefs, May 21, 1943, Marshall Papers.

96. Hilldring to Smith, January 22, 1944, Eyes Only Cables, Smith Papers.

97. Smith's views are summed up in Smith to Hilldring, January 7 and 12, 1944, Eyes Only Cables, Smith Papers; Frank McSherry to Lumley, January 30, 1944, SHAEF Selected Records, Modern Military Records Division. See also Coles and Weinberg, *Civil Affairs*, 674-75. For an examination of the creation of the Civil Affair Division see Earl Ziemke, *The U.S. Army in Occupation of Germany*, U.S. Army in World War II. (Washington, D.C., 1975), chap. 4.

98. In November 1943 the War Department had assigned two generals and ninety officers to the COSSAC Civil Affairs Division, but only fifteen officers had arrived by the end of the month. The situation did not much improve after Smith's arrival in London. COSSAC, "Civil Affairs War Diary," in SHAEF G-5, SHAEF Selected Records, Modern Military Records Division.

99. Smith to Lumley, February 8, 1944, SHAEF War Diary, SHAEF Selected Records [hereafter, SHAEF War Diary].

100. Smith to Lumley, February 7, 1944, Smith to SHAEF Division Heads, February 11, 1944, SHAEF War Diary.

101. SHAEF Staff Memo, February 15, 1944, SHAEF War Diary.

102. Hilldring to Smith, January 23, 1944, Smith Papers.

103. Ibid.

104. Smith told the Assistant G-5, Colonel Julius Holmes, that the Civil Affairs Division could not be overhauled owing to "substantial political reasons." Pogue, *Supreme Command*, 82, n. 20.

105. SHAEF Staff Memo, February 15, 1944, SHAEF War Diary.

106. Smith-authored SHAEF Staff Memo, March 14, April 8, April 9, 1944, SHAEF War Diary.

107. Smith-authored SHAEF Staff Memo, March 30, 1944, SHAEF War Diary.

108. Ziemke, *Occupation*, 50-51.

109. For a discussion of the G-6 Division see Pogue, *Supreme Command*, 84-91.

110. Pogue interview of Smith, May 9, 1947.

111. McClure to Smith, April 5, April 10, 1944, SHAEF Selected Records.

112. SHAEF Staff Memo, April 13, 1944, SHAEF War Diary; Pogue interview of Smith, May 13, 1947.

113. Pogue, "U.S. General Staff," USAMHI.

114. Murphy, *Diplomat Among Warriors*, 200.

115. Pogue, "U.S. General Staff."

116. Wertenbaker, "The Invasion Plan."

117. T. J. Davis Diary, April 24, 1944, Davis Papers.

118. Pogue, *Supreme Command*, 89-90.

119. Smith to Strong, February 7, 1944, Smith Papers.

120. Smith to Frank McCarthy, April 15, 1944, McCarthy Collection, Marshall Library.

121. Davis to Roberts, February 12, 1944, Davis Papers.

122. Eisenhower, "Memo," May 22, 1944, *EP*, #1701.

123. Marshall to Leahy and King, February 8, 1944, Leahy Papers.

124. Pogue interview of Smith, May 9, 1947.

125. Eisenhower to Marshall, February 19, 1944, *EP*, #1558, n. 1.

126. Churchill to Eisenhower, April 3, 1944, Eyes Only Cable, Smith Papers.

127. For a discussion of the Transportation Plan, see Craven and Cates, *Arguments to V-E Day*, chap. 3; Pogue, *Supreme Command*, 123-37.

128. Churchill discusses the exchange with Roosevelt, Churchill, *Closing the Ring*, 529-30.

129. Smith to Marshall, May 17, 1944, Smith Papers; Tedder, *With Prejudice*, 528-30.

130. Churchill to Roosevelt, May 7, 1944, in *Roosevelt and Churchill: Their Secret Wartime Correspondence*, Francis Loewenheim et al., eds. (New York, 1975), 493.

131. Eisenhower, *Crusade in Europe*, 247-48.

132. Eisenhower to CCS, January 4, 1944, *EP*, #1489, n. 1.

133. Smith to Hilldring, January 7, 1944, Smith Papers; Eisenhower to Marshall, January 19, 1944, *EP*, #1489.

134. SHAEF War Diary, March 8, 1944.

135. Coles and Weinberg, *Civil Affairs*, 667-68; *EP*, #1602, n. 5.

136. SHAEF to War Department, March 20, 1944, Leahy Papers; Eisenhower to Marshall, April 26, 1944, *EP*, #1653, n. 2.

137. SHAEF War Diary, March 25, 1944.

138. SHAEF to War Department, April 20, 1944, Leahy Papers; Butcher, *Three Years with Eisenhower*, 523.

139. Pogue, *Supreme Command*, 146-47.

140. Butcher Diary, April 14, 1944.

141. Eisenhower to CCS, May 11, 1944, *EP*, #1681.

142. Roosevelt to Eisenhower, May 13, 1944, Eyes Only Cables, Smith Papers.

143. Eisenhower, "Memo," May 22, *EP*, #1701; "Memo," May 23, 1944, *EP*, #1708. See also Eisenhower, *Crusade in Europe*, 247-48; Churchill, *Tightening the Ring*, 629-30; de Gaulle, *Unity*, 253; Pogue, *Supreme Command*, 142-50; Ambrose, *Supreme Commander*, 383- 84.

144. Eisenhower to Marshall, February 15, 1944, *EP*, #1549; Eisenhower to Smith, May 20, 1944 *EP*, #1696.

145. SHAEF War Diary, May 3, 1944.

146. Smith to CCS, May 17, 1944, SHAEF War Diary.

147. Smith to CCS, May 21, 1944, SHAEF War Diary.

148. Eisenhower to Marshall, May 21, 1944 and Roosevelt to Acting Secretary of State, February 22, 1944, RG-218, Records of JCS; Feis, *Churchill-Roosevelt-Stalin*, 358-73.

149. Eisenhower to Smith, May 20, 1944, *EP*, #1696; Eisenhower, *Crusade in Europe*, 431.

150. Stettinius to Hull, April 14, 1944, copies in Butcher Diary. The diary entry for April 14, 1944, differs markedly from the published version; Butcher, *Three Years with Eisenhower*, 518.

151. Eisenhower to Marshall, February 15, 1944, *EP*, #1549; Pogue, *Supreme Command*, 347-51; Feis, *Churchill-Roosevelt-Stalin*, 355.

152. Cited in Pogue, *Supreme Command*, 140.

153. Eisenhower to Montgomery, May 26, 1944, *EP*, #1716.

154. See text of answers and questions, Smith, "Problems of an Integrated Headquarters," *JRUSI*, copy in Smith Papers.

155. Butcher Diary, January 20, 1944.

156. Pogue interview of Smith, May 9, 1947.

157. Churchill to Roosevelt, June 20, 1944, *Secret Wartime Correspondence*, 537-38.

158. Description of Bushey Park in Butcher, *Three Years with Eisenhower*, 499- 500; Merrill Mueller, "Inside Invasion Headquarters," *Look*, July 11, 1944, 74; Wertenbaker, "The Invasion Plan."

159. Wertenbaker, "The Invasion Plan."

160. Butcher, *Three Years with Eisenhower*, 494.

161. Donovan to Smith, February 8, 1944, Smith Papers.

162. Smith to Hughes, February 9, 1944, Smith Papers.

163. Smith to Eisenhower, January 21, 1944, Smith Papers.

164. Eisenhower had pushed for Smith's promotion since September 1943. "I feel particularly keenly about Smith [for promotion to permanent brigadier general]," he told McNarney. Eisenhower to McNarney, September 16, 1943, *EP*, #1262.

165. Marshall to Eisenhower, April 26, 1944, Pre-Presidential Papers; Butcher, *Three Years with Eisenhower*, 531.

166. Farago, *Patton*, 416-23.

167. Butcher, *Three Years with Eisenhower*, 531. See also "Operation TIGER," United States Navy Classified Archives; Eisenhower to Marshall, April 29, 1944, Eyes Only Cables, Smith Papers; Bull to Plans and Operations Section, April 29, 1944, Bull Papers, Eisenhower Library.

168. Butcher, *Three Years with Eisenhower*, 538.

169. SHAEF had been alerted to German beach defenses since early in March through intercepts of Japanese coded messages. "MAGIC Summary," March 11, 1944, RG-319, Records of the Army Staff.

170. "MAGIC Summary," March 8 and 11, 1944; and War cabinet Joint Intelligence Sub-Committee, "German Appreciation of Allied Intentions Regarding OVERLORD," May 29, 1944, RG-331, Records of Allied Operational and Occupational Headquarters, World War II, National Archives.

171. Butcher, *Three Years with Eisenhower*, 538.

172. Hughes Diary, May 6, 14, 16, 17, and June 6, 28, 1944.

173. Pogue interview of Ford Trimble, December 17, 1946, USAMHI.

174. Hughes makes several references to the faulty command structure in his diary. See also, Ambrose, *Supreme Commander*, 346.

175. Cited in Butcher, *Three Years with Eisenhower*, 811.

176. Henry Aurand, "SHAEF-ETOUS-COM Z: A Lesson in Organization for National Defense," unpublished manuscript, Aurand Papers, Eisenhower Library.

177. SHAEF War Diary, February 8, 1944.

178. Butcher, *Three Years with Eisenhower*, 539-40; Eisenhower, *Crusade in Europe*, 245.

179. For a description of the working of the headquarters see James Robb, "Higher Direction of War," unpublished manuscript, Robb Papers, Eisenhower Library.

180. For the size and national composition of SHAEF see Pogue, "SHAEF Personnel," *Supreme Command*, 529-35.

181. Eisenhower, "Memo," May 22, 1944, *EP*, #1701.

182. Pogue interview of Smith, May 9, 1947.

183. Pogue interview of Trimble.

CHAPTER 12

1. In addition to Eisenhower, Tedder, Smith, Montgomery, Ramsay, and Leigh-Mallory, the participants were Robb, Wigglesworth, Bull, de Guingand, Gale, and Creasy (Allied Naval Expeditionary Force). Pogue, *Supreme Command*, 169.

2. Tedder, *With Prejudice*, 545-46.

3. Smith, "Memo for Chief, Historical Section," February 22, 1945, Smith Papers; W. B. Smith, *Eisenhower's Six Great Decisions* (New York, 1956), 55.

4. The description of the June 4-5 meetings is derived from, Smith, *Eisenhower's Decisions*, 53-55; Pogue, *Supreme Command*, 166-70; Ambrose, *Supreme Commander*, 415-17; Frederick de Guingand, *Operation Victory* (London, 1947), 372-74; J. M. Stagg, *Forecast for Overlord* (London, 1971), 113-15; and Robb, "Memo," June 5, 1944, Robb Papers.

5. Butcher, *Three Years with Eisenhower*, 574-75.

6. Interview with Burgess. The situation reports are in Supreme Headquarters, Allied Expeditionary Force, Selected Records, 1943-45, Eisenhower Library [hereafter, SHAEF, "Daily Intelligence Summary," date.].

7. Montgomery, "Notes on High Command--Stage Management of War," in Papers of Sir James Grigg, Correspondence with Montgomery, Churchill Archives, Churchill College, Cambridge University [hereafter, Grigg Papers].

8. Montgomery, M-501, June 13, 1944. Copies in the Montgomery File, Pre-Presidential Papers, Eisenhower Library. The entire collection of the Montgomery Papers is now available at the Imperial War Museum, London [hereafter Montgomery, M-number, date].

9. Montgomery, M-502, June 18, 1944; Montgomery to Grigg, "Notes for Minister of Defense," July 22, 1944, Grigg Papers.

10. War Cabinet, Joint Intelligence Committee, "German Appreciation of Allied Intentions in the West," July 10, 1944, RG-331, Records of the Allied Operational and Occupational Headquarters, National Archives, Washington.

11. Montgomery, M-505, June 30, 1944. See also Chester Wilmot, *The Struggle in Europe* (London, 1957), 372; Grigg, *Prejudice and Judgment* (London, 1948), 48. For German view, postwar interview with General Walter Warlimont, Deputy Chief of Wehrmachtsführungsstab, Smith Papers.

12. Smith, "Memo for Chief, Historical Section," February 22, 1945, Smith Papers.

13. Butcher Diary, August, n.d., 1944.

14. Montgomery, M-505, June 30, 1944. In the margin of his copy of Montgomery's M-505, Smith scribbled a check mark and the note: "first mention."

15. Smith, "Memo," February 22, 1944; Pogue interview with Smith, May 7, 1947; Smith, *Eisenhower's Decisions*, 73. Montgomery's position is supported by Grigg. "The bloody Yanks are beginning to crab Montgomery because they say he is making them do all the fighting," he wrote his father. "It is an absolute outrage because I know for a fact that the plan is working out as he designed it from the beginning, that we were all along the hinge and the Americans the door." Grigg to F. A. Grigg, June, n.d., 1944, Grigg Papers.

16. Wilmot, *Struggle in Europe*, 338-41; Tedder, *With Prejudice*, 557, 566.

17. Smith, *Eisenhower's Decisions*, 73.

18. Smith, "Memo," February 22, 1945.

19. Pogue interview with Smith, May 8, 1947.

20. Ibid.

21. Montgomery, M-505, June 30, 1944.

22. Montgomery, M-510, July 10, 1944.

23. Smith, "Memo," February 22, 1945.

24. Butcher, *Three Years with Eisenhower*, 617.

25. Tedder, *With Prejudice*, 557.

26. Eisenhower to Montgomery, July 7, 1944, *EP*, #1807.

27. Butcher, *Three Years with Eisenhower*, 601-30.

28. Tedder, *With Prejudice*, 557.

29. Ambrose, *Supreme Commander*, chap. 7.

30. Butcher Diary, July 19-21, 1944.

31. Brooke to Montgomery, July 28, 1944, in Bryant, *Triumph in the West*, 181-82.

32. Recollections of General Sir Frank Simpson, cited in Hamilton, *Monty*, vol. 2: 766.

33. Montgomery, M-510, July 10, 1944; Montgomery, M-46, July 10, 1944; Bradley and Blair, *General's Life*, 272-73; Russell Weigley, *Eisenhower's Lieutenants*, 137-38.

34. Montgomery, M-511, July 14, 1944.

35. For a brief analysis of what is meant by "breakout" and "breakthrough," see Martin Blumenson, *Breakout and Pursuit*, U.S. Army in World War II. (Washington, D.C., 1961), 350-51.

36. For views from the "other side of the hill," see interviews with Warlimont and Generaloberst Alfred Jodl, Smith Papers.

37. Montgomery, M-512, July 21, 1944; M-515, July 27, 1944.

38. Bradley, *Soldier's Life* (New York, 1951), 367.

39. U.S. Forces, European Theater, 1942-46, "Strike No. 1," n.d., Modern Military Division, National Archives.

40. Blumenson, *Breakout and Pursuit*, 457-75, 492-97; Bradley and Blair, *General's Life*, 191-94.

41. Farago, *Patton*, 514-42; Blumenson, *Breakout and Pursuit*, 506-58; Bradley and Blair, *General's Life*, 294-96; Carlo D'Este, *Decision in Normandy* (London, 1984), chaps. 24-26.

42. Smith to Eisenhower, April 1, 1948, Smith Papers.

43. SHAEF, "Post-NEPTUNE Courses of Action After the Capture of Lodgment Area," Records of 21 Army Group, War Office, 219/2506, Public Records Office, London [hereafter, PRO]. See also, Eisenhower (written by Smith) to Marshall, February 11, 1944, *EP*, #1543.

44. For a critical analysis of the American "direct approach" see, Weigley, *Eisenhower's Lieutenants*, chap. 1, "To the Crossing of the Rhine: American Strategic Thought to World War II."

45. For statements of American doctrine see *FM 100-5, Field Service Regulations,* "Operations," 91 (para. 112-13, 115, 132, 154). See also Martin van Creveld, *Fighting Power*, chap. 5.

46. Eisenhower to Montgomery, January 13, 1944, Pre-Presidential Papers; Eisenhower, "Memorandum to Dr. Pogue," March 10, 1947. See also Eisenhower, *Crusade in Europe*, 225-29, 255-59.

47. Eisenhower to Herbert Brees, February 28, 1944, *EP*, #1573.

48. Smith, *Eisenhower's Decisions*, 211.

49. Eisenhower, *Crusade in Europe*, 229.

50. For the most complete statement of Eisenhower's strategic views see Eisenhower to Montgomery, October 13, 1944, *EP*, #2038. See also *Crusade in Europe*, 284-85.

51. Butcher, *Three Years with Eisenhower*, 647-49; Pogue, *Supreme Command*, 263-64.

52. Marshall to Eisenhower, August 17, 1944, Pre-Presidential Papers.

53. Eisenhower to Montgomery, August 19, 1944, *EP*, #1901; Eisenhower to CCS, August 22, 1944, *EP*, #1907; Betts, Oral History.

54. Montgomery, *Memoirs*, 238-57, 266.

55. Brooke Diary, in Bryant, *Triumph in the West*, 181, 195-96. See also de Guingand, *Operation Victory*, 411-12.

56. Montgomery to Brooke, August 9, 1944, cited in Hamilton, *Monty*, vol. 2: 781.

57. Montgomery, *Memoirs*, 266-69.

58. Smith to Montgomery, August 22, 1944, Records of 21 Army Group, War Office 219/259, PRO.

59. Eisenhower to Montgomery, August 24, 1944, *EP*, #1909; Eisenhower to Marshall, August 24, 1944, *EP*, #1910; Butcher Diary, September 5, 1944; Montgomery, *Memoirs*, 240-42; Bradley, *Soldier's Story*, 398-401, 410-12. For a good description of the August 23 meeting, see L. F. Ellis, *Victory in the West*, vol. 1, *The Battle of Normandy*. History of the Second World War, J. R. M. Butler, ed. (London, 1962), 461-64. See also Blumenson, *Breakout and Pursuit*, 657-60, 684-88.

60. Eisenhower, "Memorandum," September 5, 1944, *EP*, #1936.

61. Brooke to Montgomery, July 27, 1944, in Bryant, *Triumph in the West*, 181-82.

62. Eisenhower, *Crusade in Europe*, 335.

63. Bradley claimed that Montgomery was "deceitful" for saying that he supported the narrow-front approach. Bradley, *Soldier's Story*, 312-13.

64. Strong, *Intelligence at the Top*, 199-200; Pogue interview with Smith, May 9, 1947. Montgomery believed that SHAEF placed too much emphasis upon logistics at the expense of operational boldness. "Administration in battle must ride in a Ford Utility," he commented, "not in a Rolls Royce de Luxe." Montgomery, "Notes on High Command," October 10, 1944, in Grigg Papers.

65. Eisenhower to Commanders, August 29, 1944, *EP*, #1920.

66. Montgomery, *Memoirs*, 282-90.

67. Pogue interview with Smith, May 9, 1947.

68. 2d (British) Army to SHAEF G-4, August 30, 1944, Records of 21 Army Group, WO 219/259, PRO; 21st Army Group, *Administrative History* (London, n.d.), 47.

69. Model to Rundstedt, September 27, 1944, reprinted in War Office, ed., *German Army Documents Dealing with the War in the Western Front from June to October 1944*, Records of 21st Army Group, PRO; Smith, "Memo: Advance to the Siegfried Line," September 1, 1944, Smith Papers (also Records of 21 Army Group, WO 219/260, PRO); Eisenhower to Commanders, September 4, 1944, *EP*, #1933.

70. Pogue interview of C. H. Bonesteel, June 18, 1945, USAMHI.

71. Eisenhower Office Diary, in Kay Summersby, *Eisenhower Was My Boss*y (New York, 1948), 170.

72. The arguments over Arnhem are summed up in Charles MacDonald, "The Decision to Launch Operation Market Garden," *Command Decisions*, K. R. Greenfield, ed. (Washington, D.C., 1960), 429-42. For a discussion of the operation see MacDonald, *The Siegfried Line Campaign* (Washington, D.C., 1963), 119-39.

73. Office Memo, September 5, 1944, *EP*, #1936.

74. Eisenhower to Montgomery, September 15, 1944, *EP*, #1957.

75. Montgomery to Eisenhower, September 18, 1944, Pre-Presidential Papers.

76. Eisenhower to Marshall, September 18, 1944, *EP*, #1968.

77. Eisenhower to Montgomery, September 20, 1944, *EP*, #1975.

78. Montgomery to Eisenhower, September 21, 1944, Pre-Presidential Papers.

79. Montgomery, *Memoirs*, 253; Wilmot, *Struggle in Europe*, 533-34.

80. Eugene Wason interview of F. Simpson, no date given, cited in Hamilton, *Monty: Final Years of the Field Marshal, 1944-1976* (New York, 1987), 79-81 [hereafter, Hamilton, *Monty*, vol. 3: page number].

81. Eisenhower to Montgomery, September 22, 1944, *EP*, #1979; Bradley, *Soldier's Story*, 422-23; Pogue, *Supreme Command*, 294. .

82. de Guingand to Montgomery, September 22, 1944, Smith Papers.

83. Patton, *War as I Knew It* (Boston, 1947), 125, 133; Grigg to Montgomery, September 25, 1944, Grigg Papers..

84. Eisenhower to Montgomery, drafted by Smith, October 9, 1944, *EP*, #2031; de Guingand, *Generals At War* (London, 1964), 202; Ambrose interview with Morgan, July 17, 1965, cited in *Supreme Commander*, 525.

85. Montgomery to Smith, October 10, 1944, Smith Papers; Montgomery, "Notes on Command in Western Europe," October 10, 1944, copy in Smith Papers; Montgomery, *Memoirs*, 283.

86. Eisenhower to Montgomery, drafted by Smith, October 9, 1944, *EP*, #2031.

87. Eisenhower to Montgomery, October 13, 1944, *EP*, #2038.

88. Montgomery to Eisenhower, M-281, October 16, 1944.

89. Eisenhower to Commanders, October 28, 1944, *EP*, #2074; November 2, 1944, *EP*, #2093.

90. Brooke Diary, November 26, 1944, in Bryant, *Triumph in the West*, 256.

91. Montgomery to Brooke, November 17, 1944, in Bryant, *Triumph in the West*, 252.

92. Brooke Diary, November 2, 29, 1944, in Bryant, *Triumph in the West*, 259, 264.

93. Montgomery to Eisenhower, November 30, 1944, Pre-Presidential Papers. The letter is reprinted in Bryant, 260-61.

94. Eisenhower to Montgomery, December 1, 1944, *EP*, #2145.

95. "Notes of Meeting at Maastrict on 7 December 1944," RG-331, Records of Allied Operational and Occupational Headquarters; Montgomery, *Memoirs*, 270-74; Tedder, *With Prejudice*, 620-23; Byrant, *Triumph in the West*, 264-65; Pogue, *Supreme Command*, 316-17; Ambrose, *Supreme Commander*, 549-551.

96. Eisenhower to Marshall, December 13, 1944, *EP*, #2163; Eisenhower, "Memo," December 23, 1944, *EP*, #2198.

97. Eisenhower to Montgomery, August 14, 1944, *EP*, #1901.

98. Earlier, during the Normandy fighting, Montgomery asked Eisenhower why public opinion should prompt him to make unsound military decisions. Montgomery to Archibald Nye, August 26, 1944, cited in Hamilton, *Monty*, 2: 816. As Montgomery related to Grigg, "I fear political and national considerations are influencing Eisenhower to take a course of action which is militarily unsound." Montgomery to Grigg, August 26, 1944, Grigg Papers. See also Ronald Lewin, "World War II: A Tangled Web." Lecture given at the Royal United Services Institute for defense Studies, *RUSI Journal* (December 1982): 18.

99. Eisenhower, *Crusade in Europe*, 185.

100. The best summary of the command and staff structure is in, Pogue, *Supreme Command*, 261-78.

101. Betts, Oral History; D'Este, *Decision in Normandy*, 466.

. 102. Betts, Oral History; Smith to Hilldring, November 6, 1944, Pre-Presidential Papers.

103. Hughes Diary, September 5, 1944.

104. Pogue, *Supreme Command*, 22-34, 277; Bradley, *Soldier's Story*, 405-6.

105. Eisenhower to Arnold, September 27, 1944, *EP*, #2004; Eisenhower to Admiral Harold Stark, September 28, 1944, *EP* #2007.

106. Smith to Eisenhower, April 1, 1948, Smith Papers.

107. Pogue interview with Smith, May 8, 1947.

108. Bradley, *General's Life*, 322.

109. Pogue interview with Smith, May 8, 9, 1947.

110. Montgomery to Eisenhower, September 9, 1944, Pre-Presidential Papers.

111. SHAEF grounded three American divisions in order to furnish supplies to Montgomery. Only about one-half of the promised materials arrived.

112. Pogue interview with Smith, May 8, 1947. See also Bradley, *General's Life*, 330-31; MacDonald, *Siegfried Line Campaign*, 122.

113. Montgomery, *Memoirs*, 247.

114. The best discussions of the logistical breakdown are Martin van Creveld, "War of the accountants," *Supplying War* (Cambridge, 1977), 202-30; Roland Ruppenthal, "Logistics and the Broad Front Strategy," *Command Decisions*, Kent Roberts Greenfield, ed. (Washington, D.C., 1960), 419-28; Pogue, *Supreme Command*, 259-60.

115. Hughes Diary, June 20, July 14, 1944.

116. Hughes Diary, July 17, 19-20, 1944.

117. Pogue, *Supreme Command*, 267.

118. Pogue interview with Smith, May 13, 1947.

119. Pogue interview with Smith, May 9, 1947.

120. Pogue interview with Smith, May 13, 1947.

121. Ibid.

122. Eisenhower to Smith, "Memo," July 18, 1944, *EP*, #1842; July 21, 1944, *EP*, #1845. See also Pogue, *Supreme Command*, 167-68.

123. Aurand, "SHAEF-ETOUSA-COM Z," Aurand Papers; Hughes Diary, February 2, 19, 1945.

124. Pogue interview with Smith, May 13, 1947.

125. Aurand Diary, November 18-21, 1944, Aurand Papers.

126. Leroy Lutes, Oral History, Eisenhower Library. Related letters and diary of the tour of inspection are contained in the Lutes Papers (photocopies and microfilm), Eisenhower Library.

127. Smith's first choice was Lucius Clay. Smith to Hilldring, November 6, 1944, Smith Papers; Pogue interview with Smith, May 13, 1947.

128. Hughes Diary, January 23, 1945.

129. "Lear says he never saw so much politics as in ETO." Hughes Diary, April 3, 1945.

130. Pogue interview with Smith, May 13, 1947.

131. Hughes Diary, January 12, 1945.

132. Smith to Marshall, September 6, 1944, Marshall Papers, Smith to McCarthy, September 9, 1944, Smith Papers.

133. Interview with Burgess.

134. SHAEF Forward to SHAEF Main, September 23, 1944, SHAEF S/GS; Vittrup Interview.

135. Eisenhower to CCS, September 5, 1944, *EP*, #1937.

136. Butcher Diary, June 6, 1944.

137. McClure, Journal Extract, June 6, 1944, in Pogue interview with McClure, USAMHI.

138. Combined Chiefs to Eisenhower, June 14, 1944, Eyes Only Cables, Smith Papers.

139. Smith to Hilldring, July 4, 1944, Smith Papers.

140. Smith to AFHQ Liaison, August 17, 1944, Smith Papers.

141. de Gaulle to Eisenhower, August 21, 1944, *EP*, #1908. n. 1.

142. SHAEF Secretary/General Staff, "Zone of Interior, France," September 13-15, 1944; "Civil Affairs Directive for France," Vols. 1-2. Both in Office of the Secretary/General Staff (France). See also SHAEF G-5, "Directive/France," Foreign Relations. All of the above sources are in Modern Military Records Division, National Archives.

143. U.S. Department of State, Foreign Relations of the United States, 1944. vol. 3: 733-36.

144. Pogue, *Supreme Command*, 319-20.

145. Joint Chiefs to SHAEF, October 17, 1944, in SHAEF SGS, Foreign Relations, vol. 3, SHAEF Diary; Caffrey to Hull, October, 23, 1944, Department of State, Foreign Relations, 1944. vol. 3: 742-43.

146. McCloy to Smith, October 2, 1944; Smith to McCloy, November 7, 1944; Smith to Hilldring, November 6, 8, 1944, Smith Papers.

147. Eisenhower to Montgomery, September 24, 1944, Pre-Presidential Papers.

148. Churchill, *Triumph and Tragedy*, 442-43; John Ehrman, *History of the Second World War*, vol. 6, *Grand Strategy* (London, 1956), 150-51.

CHAPTER 13

1. SHAEF, Office of Assistant Chief of Staff, G-2, "Weekly Intelligence Summary, #38," Week ending December 10, 1944, Eyes Only Cables, Smith Papers.

2. Eisenhower, *Crusade in Europe*, 337.

3. Clausewitz, *On War*, Michael Howard and Peter Paret, trs. and eds. (Princeton, N.J., 1976), 238.

4. MacDonald, *Siegfried Line Campaign*, 377-80, 390-578; Farago, *Patton*, 664-68; Brooke Diary, November 2, 1944, in Bryant, *Triumph in the West*, 241.

5. Brooke Diary, November 9, 1944, in ibid., 244.

6. Brooke Diary, November 28, 1944, in ibid., 257.

7. British Chiefs of Staff to Churchill, November 18, 1944, in ibid., 267.

8. SHAEF to Montgomery, December 1, 1944, Pre-Presidential Papers.

9. Brooke Diary, November 24, 1944, in Bryant, *Triumph in the West*, 256. Montgomery took up the same theme in a letter to Eisenhower, November 30, 1944, Pre-Presidential Papers.

10. Marshall to Smith, November 29, 1944, Marshall Papers.

11. Smith to Marshall, December 3, 1944, Marshall Papers.

12. Pogue interview with Smith, May 8, 1947; Smith, *Eisenhower's Decisions*, 90-91.

13. ULTRA intercepts did detect the flow of meteorological information from German U-Boats in the North Atlantic back to German headquarters. Strong, *Intelligence at the Top*, 204-11; Pogue interview with Smith, May 8, 1947.

14. Eisenhower, "Memo," December 23, 1944, EP, #2198; Pogue interview with Smith, May 8, 1947; Smith, *Eisenhower's Decisions*, 90.

15. Strong, *Intelligence at the Top*, 210-212; Strong also recounted this meeting with Bradley in an August 31, 1951 letter to Pogue. Pogue, *Supreme Command*, 361-65.

16. The official history is Hugh Cole, *The Ardennes: Battle of the Bulge*. U.S. Army in World War II. (Washington, D.C., 1965).

17. Jodl, "Interviews with Senior German Commanders," Smith Papers.

18. Strong, *Intelligence at the Top*, 213.

19. Bradley, *A Soldier's Story*, 449-50.

20. Butcher, *Three Years with Eisenhower*, 723.

21. Hughes Diary, December 17, 1944.

22. Pogue interview with Smith, May 8, 1947.

23. Eisenhower to Somervell, December 17, 1944, EP, #2177; Pogue, *Supreme Command*, 374.

24. Bryant, *Triumph in the West*, 274.

25. Eisenhower, "Memo," December 23, 1944.

26. Smith, *Eisenhower's Decisions*, 91-92; Eisenhower, *Crusade in Europe*, 348-49; Pogue, *Supreme Command*, 372.

27. Pogue interview with Smith, May 8, 1947.

28. Ibid.

29. For a complete account of the Bastogne fighting, see S. L. A. Marshall, *Bastogne: The First Eight Days* (Washington, D.C., 1946).

30. Eisenhower to Bradley and Devers, December 18, 1944, EP, #2178.

31. For accounts of the Verdun meeting, see Eisenhower, *Crusade in Europe*, 350-53; Bradley, *A Soldier's Story*, 469-73; Farago, *Patton*, 705-9; Tedder, *With Prejudice*, 625; Strong, *Intelligence at the Top*, 219-22.

32. Pogue interview with Smith, May 8, 1947.

33. Betts, Oral History.

34. Strong, *Intelligence at the Top*, 224-25.

35. Eisenhower (written by Smith) to Montgomery, December 20, 1944, EP, #2184; Montgomery to Eisenhower, December 20, 1944, Pre-Presidential Papers.

36. Pogue interview with Smith, May 8, 1947; Cole, *The Ardennes*, 423-24.

37. Bradley, *Soldier's Story*, 476-77.

38. Strong, *Intelligence at the Top*, 226.

39. Eisenhower to CCS, December 20, 1944, EP, #2182; Eisenhower, "Memo," December 23, 1944, EP, #2198; Ambrose, *Supreme Commander*, 563-64.

40. Strong, *Intelligence at the Top*, 226.

41. The best discussion of Montgomery's conduct of the Bulge is in Hamilton, *Monty*, vol. 3: 179-357.

42. Pogue interview with Smith, May 8, 1947; Bryant, *Triumph in the West*, 272-73.

43. Butcher, *Three Years with Eisenhower*, 728.

44. Pogue, *Organizer of Victory*, 497.

45. Eisenhower to Lee [draft], January 4, 1945, EP, #2218.

46. Ulysses Lee, *The Employment of Negro Troops*. U.S. Army in World War II. (Washington, D.C., 1961), 688-98.

47. Weigley, *Eisenhower's Lieutenants*, 568.

48. Pogue interview with Smith, May 13, 1947.

49. Robb, "Notes," December 27, 1944, Robb Papers; Eisenhower to Churchill, December 23, 1944, EP, #2191.

50. Pogue interview with Smith, May 8, 1947.

51. Murphy, *Diplomat Among Warriors*, 239. as Butcher reported, the assassination scare produced considerable "trigger-happy shooting." Butcher, *Three Years with Eisenhower*, 727-28.

52. Robb, "Notes," December 21, 1944.

53. Pogue interview with Smith, May 8, 1947.

54. Montgomery, *Memoirs*, 282-85.

55. Robb, "Notes," December 18, 1944.

56. Montgomery, *Memoirs*, 284-85; Bryant, *Triumph in the West*, 278-79.

57. For a full account of de Guingand's trip to Versailles, see de Guingand, *Generals at War* (London, 1964), 108-11.

58. Smith to Caffrey, November 24, 1944, Smith Papers; McCarthy to Marshall, November 24, 1944, McCarthy Papers.

59. de Guingand, *Generals at War*, 111.

60. de Guingand, *Operation Victory*, 348; Thames Television Interview with de Guingand, "World at War, 1939-1945," Imperial War Museum, London; Montgomery, *Memoirs*, 286-89.

61. Robb, "Notes," January 1 and January 3, 1945, Eisenhower Manuscripts, Eisenhower Library.

62. Eisenhower to de Gaulle, January 2, 1945, EP, #2216.

63. Vigneras, *Rearming the French*, 329-34.

64. Robb, "Notes," January 3, 1945.

65. Brooke Diary, January 3, 1945, in Bryant, *Triumph in the West*, 283.

66. de Gaulle, *Salvation*, 169.

67. Eisenhower to Marshall, January 6, 1945, EP, #2224; Eisenhower to de Gaulle, January 5, 1945, EP, #2221.

68. Smith to Handy, January 12, 1945, Smith Papers. Copy also in the Thomas Handy Papers, Marshall Library.

69. de Guingand, *Operation Victory*, 434. Text of press conference in Montgomery, *Memoirs*, 279.

70. Robb Diary, January 28, 1944, Robb Papers, PRO. The Robb Diary and records of supreme commander and chief of staff conferences are not among the Robb Papers in the Eisenhower Library.

71. Bradley, *Soldier's General*, 484-88.

72. Smith to Handy, January 12, 1945, Smith Papers.

73. Michael Powell and Emeric Pressburger, *Life and Death of Colonel Blimp* (London, David Low), motion picture.

74. Pogue interview with Kenneth Strong, December 12, 1946, USAMHI.

75. Smith to Maxwell Taylor, September 1, 1946, Smith Papers.

76. Ibid.

77. Pogue interview of Robert Crawford, May 5, 1948, USAMHI.

78. W. Averell Harriman and Elie Abel, *Special Envoy to Churchill and Stalin* (New York, 1975), 737-74.

79. Smith to Taylor, September 1, 1946.

80. Pogue interview of T. P. Gleave, January 9, 1947, USAMHI.

81. Richard Nixon, *Memoirs* (New York, 1978), 198.

82. Pogue interview with Ford Trimble, December 17, 1946, USAMHI.

83. Ibid.

84. Montgomery, *Memoirs*, 235.

85. Pogue interview of Smith, May 8, 1947.

86. This view was endorsed by Brooke; see Brooke Diary, November 24, 1944, in Bryant, *Triumph in the West*, 255.

87. Betts, Oral History.

88. Pogue interview with James Gault, February 13, 1947, USAMHI.

89. Interview of Vittrup.

90. Pogue interview with Leslie Scarman, February 25, 1947, USAMHI.

91. Ibid.

92. Ambrose interview with Jacob, July 21, 1965, cited in *Supreme Commander*, 82.

93. Interview with Albert Jodl, August 3, 1945, Smith Papers.

CHAPTER 14

1. Cited in Charles V. P. Luttichau, "The German Counteroffensive in the Ardennes (1944)," in *Command Decisions*, 356.

2. Eisenhower to Montgomery, January 17, 1945, EP, #2247.

3. Eisenhower to Marshall, January 10, 1945, EP, #2233.

4. Eisenhower to Marshall, January 15, 1945, EP, #2245

5. Robb, "Meeting in Supreme Commander's Office," January 12, 1945; "Meeting in Chief of Staff's Office," January 16, 1945, Robb Papers, PRO.

6. Robb, "Meeting in Chief of Staff Office," January 16, 1945.

7. Robb, "Higher Direction of War," unpublished article in Robb Papers, Eisenhower Library.

8. Eisenhower to CCS, January 20, 1945, EP, #2253.

9. Marshall to Eisenhower, January 9, 1945, Pre-Presidential Papers.

10. Brooke Diary, December 13, 1945, in Bryant, *Triumph in the West*, 287.

11. Bryant, *Triumph in the West*, 277-83. See also Correlli Barnett, *The Collapse of British Power* (London, 1972), 587-88.

12. Marshall to Eisenhower, January 9, 1945, Pre-Presidential Papers.

13. Marshall to Eisenhower, December 30, 1944, Eyes Only Cables, Smith Papers.

14. Brooke Diary, January 3, 1945, in Bryant, *Triumph in the West*, 284.

15. Pogue interview with Smith, May 8, 1947.

16. Pogue interview with Smith, May 8, 1947; Eisenhower to Marshall, January 10, 1945, EP, #2233.

17. Eisenhower to Marshall, January 10, 1945, *EP*, #2232-2233; Marshall to Eisenhower, January 11, 1945, Pre-Presidential Papers; Eisenhower to Marshall, January 12, 1945, #2235.

18. Eisenhower, "Notes on Conference with Marshall," January 28, 1945, EP, #2264; Pogue, *Organizer of Victory*, 516-17.

19. Combined Chiefs of Staff, "Minutes of Meeting," January 30, 1945, RG-319, Records of the Army Staff; Brooke Diary, January 30, 1945, in Bryant, *Triumph in the West*, 297.

20. Joint Chiefs of Staff, "Minutes of Meeting," January 30, 1945, RG-319, Records of the Army Staff.

21. Smith to Eisenhower, January 30, 1945, Smith Papers.

22. Eisenhower to Smith, January 31, 1945, *EP*, #2268.

23. For accounts of the meetings, see Pogue interview with Smith, May 8, 1947; Brooke Diary, January 31, 1945, in Bryant, *Triumph in the West*, 301; Summersby, *Eisenhower Was My Boss*, 218-19, and Kay Summersby Desk Diary, January 31, 1945, Eisenhower Library.

24. Bryant, *Triumph in the West*, 301; Pogue interview with Smith, May 8, 1947.

25. Smith to Eisenhower, February 2, 1945, Smith Papers.

26. Cited in Ehrman, *Grand Strategy*, vol. 6: 93.

27. Cited in Byrant, *Triumph in the West*, 302-3.

28. Patton Diary, February 23, 1945. The diary contains material not in Blumenson's published version. Diary in author's possession.

29. Farago, *Last Days of Patton* (New York, 1981), 211, 275, 277-80, 305.

30. Patton Diary, February 16, 1945.

31. Patton Diary, February 27, March 1, 19, 1945.

32. Patton Diary, March 9, 1945.

33. Patton Diary, March 16, 1945.

34. Bradley, *Soldier's Story*, 510-11; Eisenhower to BCOS, March 8, 1945, EP, #2319; Interviews with Albert Kesselring, March 12, 1945, and Hermann Göring, July 21, 1945, in Smith Papers.

35. Eisenhower to CCS, March 24, 1945, EP, #2351.

36. Eisenhower to Montgomery, March 31, 1945, EP, #2378.

37. Hughes Diary, March 3, 1945.

38. Hughes Diary, March 4, 1945.

39. Hughes Diary, "Memorandum, 1945," March 4, 1945.

40. Hughes Diary, March 5, 1945.

41. Eisenhower to Marshall, April 15, 1945, *EP*, #2416.

42. Bradley, *Soldier's Story*, 535-36.

43. Smith, *Eisenhower's Decisions*, 147.

44. Marshall to Eisenhower, March 27, 1945, Pre-Presidential Papers.

45. Eisenhower to CCS, March 24, 1945, *EP*, #2351; Eisenhower to Bradley and Devers, March 25, 1945, *EP*, #2353; Eisenhower to Commanders, March 26, 1945, *EP*, #2354.

46. Eisenhower to Major General John Deane, March 28, 1945, *EP*, #2363.

47. For the exchange of views see Churchill to Eisenhower, March 31 and April 2, 1945, Pre-Presidential Papers; Eisenhower to Montgomery, March 31, 1945, *EP*, #2378.

48. Eisenhower to Churchill, April 3, 1945, *EP*, #2387. Smith made the same point at an April 21, 1945, press conference. "The most interesting [fact] of all is that of all the campaigns I have known of or studied, [the campaign in northwest Europe] has followed most exactly the pattern of the commander who planned it." Transcript in Butcher, *Three Years with Eisenhower*, 806-815.

49. Eisenhower to Marshall, March 30, 1945, *EP*, #2373; Eisenhower to Marshall, March 30, 1945, *EP*, #2374.

50. Churchill, *Triumph and Tragedy*, 463-65, 515; Ehrman, *Grand Strategy*, 6: 131-51; Ellis, *Victory in the West*, 295-304.

51. Churchill to Eisenhower, April 2, 1945, Pre-Presidential Papers; BCOS to JCS, April 11, 1945, in SHAEF G-3, "Correspondence and Communication with the Russians," Smith Papers.

52. Leahy, *I Was There*, 303.

53. Karl von Clausewitz, *On War*, 607.

54. Eisenhower to Marshall, April 23, 1945, *EP*, #2440.

55. Cited in Butcher, *Three Years with Eisenhower*, 814.

56. Smith to Handy, February 9, 1945, Smith Papers.

57. Summersby, Eisenhower Office Diary, March 28, 1945, Pre-Presidential Papers.

58. Pogue interview with Smith, May 9, 1947; Smith's April 21, 1945, press conference, Butcher, *Three Years with Eisenhower*, 809-15; Smith, *Eisenhower's Decisions*, 226. Discussions of the decision to stop at the Elbe are in Ambrose, *Eisenhower and Berlin* (New York, 1967); Pogue, "the Decision to Halt," in Greenfield, ed., *Command Decisions*, 479-82.

59. Strong, *Intelligence at the Top*, 298.

60. Pogue interview with Smith, May 9, 1947.

61. Simpson, Oral History.

62. Eisenhower to Deane, April 21, 1945, *EP*, #2432.

63. SHAEF, Office of Assistant Chief of Staff, G-2, "Weekly Intelligence Summary, #38," December 10, 1944, Eyes Only Cable, Smith Papers; SHAEF, Joint Intelligence Committee, "Intelligence Report," April 10, 1945, RG-218, Records of the JCS. Copy also in the Leahy Papers.

64. Smith, *Eisenhower's Decisions*, 177.

65. Smith's press conference, Butcher, *Three Years with Eisenhower*, 809-15. See also Rodney Minott, *The Fortress That Never Was* (New York, 1964); Weigley, *Eisenhower's Lieutenants*, 700-16.

66. Hughes Diary, April 22, 1945.

67. SHAEF Diary, December 6, 1944.

68. Gerbrandy to Eisenhower, December 16, 1945, in Walter Maass, *The Netherlands at War; 1940-45* (London, 1970), 206.

69. Cited in ibid.

70. SHAEF Diary, December 14, 20, 1944.

71. Prince Bernhard to Smith, April 14, 1945, Eyes Only Cable, Smith Papers; Churchill to Eden, copy sent to Joint Chiefs of Staff, April 18, 1945, RG-218, Leahy Papers.

72. Churchill to Eden, April 18, 1945; Churchill to Eisenhower, April 19, 1945, Pre-Presidential Papers; Churchill to Eisenhower, April 20, 1945, Eyes Only Cables, Smith Papers.

73. Eisenhower to Marshall, April 19, 1945, Pre-Presidential Papers; Eisenhower to Marshall, April 20, 1945.

74. Combined Chiefs of Staff to Eisenhower, April 24, 1945, SHAEF to 21st Army Group, April 25, 1945, Eisenhower to Seyss-Inquart, April 25, 1945, Eyes Only Cables, Smith Papers; Eisenhower to Marshall, April 27, 1945, Pre-Presidential Papers; Eisenhower to Combined Chiefs of Staff, April 29, 1945, Eyes Only Cables, Smith Papers; de Guingand, *Operation Victory*, 445-49; Pogue, *Supreme Command*, 457-59.

75. Pogue interview with E. T. Williams, May 30-31, 1947, USAMHI.

76. Smith, *Eisenhower's Decisions*, 197-99. For the results of the Acheterveld meeting, see Eisenhower to CCS, May 1, 1945, *EP*, #2467; de Guingand, *Operation Victory*, 450-51; Maass, *Netherlands at War*, 240.

77. Smith to Commanders, May 2, 1945, Smith Papers.

78. Eisenhower to CCS and BCOS, May 3, 1945, *EP*, #2474.

79. Smith, *Eisenhower's Decisions*, 200.

80. Montgomery, *Memoirs*, 299-305; Pogue, *Supreme Command*, 474-81.

81. Karl Dönitz, *Memoirs: Ten Years and Twenty Days* (Cleveland, 1959), chap. 22.

82. Strong, *Intelligence at the Top*, 269-71; Pogue interview with Smith, May 9, 1947; Murphy, *Diplomat Among Warriors*, 240-41; Pogue, *Supreme Command*, 484-85.

83. SHAEF to Military Mission in Moscow, May 4, 1945, Eyes Only Cables, Smith Papers; Eisenhower to Combined Chiefs, May 4, 1945, *EP*, #2485; SHAEF to Military Mission in Moscow, May 5, 1945, Eyes Only Cables, Smith Papers.

84. I am drawing upon Smith's account of the negotiations in Smith, *Eisenhower's Decisions*. A full description of the events is contained in Butcher, *Three Years with Eisenhower*, 821-34, and Strong, *Intelligence at the Top*, 268-82.

85. Pogue interview with Smith, May 9, 1947.

86. Butcher, *Three Years with Eisenhower*, 826.

87. Friedeburg to Dönitz, May 5, 1945, SHAEF to War Department, May 5, 1945, in Eyes Only Cables, Smith Papers; Eisenhower to Combined Chiefs, May 5, 1945, *EP*, #2494.

88. Butcher, *Three Years with Eisenhower*, 827.

89. Military Mission in Moscow to SHAEF, May 5, 1945, Eyes Only Cables, Smith Papers; Eisenhower to Military Mission in Moscow, May 6, 1945, *EP*, #2495; Strong, *Intelligence at the Top*, 276.

90. Butcher, *Three Years with Eisenhower*, 828-30.

91. Strong, *Intelligence at the Top*, 277-78; Smith, *Eisenhower's Decisions*, 206.

92. Eisenhower to Combined Chiefs, May 6, 1945, *EP*, #2498.

93. Strong, *Intelligence at the Top*, 280-82.

94. Smith, *Eisenhower's Decisions*, 210.

95. Strong, *Intelligence at the Top*, 282.

96. Smith, *Eisenhower's Decisions*, 229.

97. Eisenhower to Combined Chiefs, May 7, 1945, *EP*, #2499.

EPILOGUE

1. For a description of the ceremonies in Paris and Washington, see Butcher, *Three Years with Eisenhower*, 868-70. For Smith's reception in Indianapolis, see articles in *Indianapolis Star*, June 21, 24, 1945, Smith File, ISL. For a short outline of Smith's career see *Current Biography 1953*.

2. His list of honors included: American--Distinguished Service Medal with two Bronze Oak Leaf Clusters; Distinguished Service Medal (Navy); Legion of Merit; Bronze Star. Foreign--Knight Grand Cross, Order of the British Empire; Knight Commander, Order of the Bath (British); Lion of the Netherlands; Crown of Belgium; Croix de

Guerre (Belgium); Legion of Merit (France); Croix de Guerre (France); Cavalier of the Order of Kutuzov, First Class (Soviet Union); and White Lion (Czechoslovakia).

Smith also received several honorary degrees after the war: LLD from Duquesne University, Butler University, University of New Hampshire, and the University of South Carolina; the D.Sc. Military from Pennsylvania Military College; and the D.C.L. from Colgate University.

3. Eisenhower to Marshall, August 22, 1945, Pre-Presidential Papers.

4. Smith to Eisenhower, November 28, 1945, Smith Papers.

5. Eisenhower to Smith, December 4, 1945, Smith Papers.

6. W. H. Lawrence, "Beetle Is Back on the Eisenhower Team," *New York Times Magazine*, March 1, 1953, 11.

7. Lawrence, "Tough Man For a Tough Job," *New York Times Magazine*, March 13, 1946, 15.

8. Smith's memorandum is in Walter Millis, *The Forrestal Diaries* (New York, 1951), 409.

9. Smith, My Three Years in Moscow (New York, 1950).

10. Smith's medical file is contained in his 201-File, Smith Papers.

11. "Newsmakers," CBS Radio program, first aired on January 8, 1950. Transcript in Smith Papers.

12. Smith to Eisenhower, September 7, 1950, Smith Papers.

13. Smith to John D. Hickerson, Assistant Secretary of State, August 23, 1950, Smith Papers.

14. Hinton, "Soldier, Diplomat, Intelligence Chief," *New York Times Magazine*, August 27, 1950, 30.

15. The text of the October 2, 1950, memorandum is in U.S. Department of State, *Foreign Affairs, 1950-Korea*, vol. 7: 933-34.

16. "Beedle Smith: Of Spies and Counterspies...An Accidental Glimpse into a Supersecret Agency," *U.S. News and World Report*, October 10, 1952, 47.

17. Townshend Hoopes, *The Devil and John Foster Dulles* (New York, 1973), 145.

18. *U.S. News and World Report*, October 10, 1952, 47.

19. John Hanes, cited in Leonard Mosley, *Dulles* (New York, 1978), 379.

20. *U.S. News and World Report*, October 10, 1952, 47-49.

21. *New York Times Magazine*, March 1, 1953, 44.

22. Hoopes, *Devil and Dulles*, 144.

23. Ibid., 145.

24. *New York Times Magazine*, March 1, 1953, 11; "Beedle Smith: On Way Up as the Top Aide for Ike," *U.S. News and World Report*, July 31, 1953, 47.

25. Hoopes, *Devil and Dulles*, 138.

26. For a discussion of Dulles's thinking behind the Smith appointment, see ibid., 145.

27. *New York Times Magazine*, March 1, 1953, 11.

28. Ibid.

29. Anthony Laviero discusses the creation of the Operations Coordinating Board in *New York Times*, September 4, 1953, 37.

30. Hoopes, *Devil and Dulles*, 219-20.

31. Louis Gerson, *John Foster Dulles*. The American Secretaries of State and Their Diplomacy Series, vol. 17 (New York, 1967), 173-74.

32. The Smith-Molotov conversation is recorded in, Gerson, *Dulles*, 176-77.

33. Hoopes, *Devil and Dulles*, 279.

34. My discussion of Smith's role in the Guatemalan coup is derived from Richard Immerman, *The CIA in Guatemala: The Foreign Policy of Intervention* (Austin, Texas, 1982).

35. Immerman, *The CIA in Guatemala*, 120-21.

36. Ibid., 18.

37. Ibid., 140.

38. Ibid., 152.

39. Hanes, cited in Mosley, *Dulles*, 379.

40. Immerman, *CIA in Guatemala*, 134-35.

41. U.S. District Court of the District of Columbia, September 7, 1961, cited in *Indiana Biography Series*, vol. 59. ISL.

42. See the postwar correspondence with Carter Burgess, Cornelius Wickersham, Ruth Briggs, Strong, Morgan, and de Guingand, Smith Papers.

43. For an example, see Smith to Tedder, July 27, 1945, Smith Papers.

44. Pogue, "Marshall and the War Department," USAMHI.

45. Nixon, *Memoirs*, 198.

46. See obituaries, *New York Times*, August 10, 1961; *Times* (of London), August 11, 1961; *Indiana Biography*, 24.

Bibliography

ESSAY ON PRIMARY SOURCES

The most fruitful official records for this study of General Walter Bedell Smith proved to be those of his immediate superior, General D. D. Eisenhower. Of secondary importance were Smith's own collection of documents and papers. Both are contained in the holdings of the Eisenhower Presidential Library, Abilene, Kansas.

What follows is not an exhaustive examination of all the sources used in this project but rather a survey of those primary materials most significant to the study of Smith's wartime career as Eisenhower's chief of staff.

Over one-third of Eisenhower's Pre-Presidential Papers deal with the period from Pearl Harbor to May 1945. Although the extensive collection is divided into two major files (Principal and Secondary) and subdivided further into eleven series, the most profitable set of papers are found in the series entitled, "Correspondence with Individuals and Organizations" (Principal File/Series One). It was from this source the preponderance of entries for the four volume *The Papers of Dwight David Eisenhower: The War Years* were extracted. The second series, the "Subject File," includes cables, diaries, correspondence, reports, publications and other papers. Among the most valuable source in the Subject File are the official diaries of Harry Butcher and Kay Summersby. While both Butcher and Summersby wrote books based upon these sources, the contents contained in the diaries differ significantly from the published versions. The Subject File also contains incoming and outgoing cables from the Combined Chiefs of Staff and a large file of communications with General Marshall.

Together, the "Correspondence" and "Subject File" Series serve as the central source for the book. When taken from the published source, citations are noted as "Eisenhower Papers." Otherwise, they are cited as "Pre-Presidential Papers."

Rivalling the Eisenhower papers in value are those of Smith himself. Smith initially deposited his papers and printed materials in the War Department Library. After examining the collection, he removed two cubic feet of personal letters. As a result, historians are left only with the official record.

The documents contained in the Papers of Walter Bedell Smith ("W. B. Smith Collection") provide ample materials for the reconstruction of the "official" Smith. They are ordered by the title of the organization responsible for the dissemination of the document. The final three sections—approximately one half of the total collection—include documents relating to the Combined Chiefs of Staff, the Allied Force Headquarters, and to Supreme Headquarters, Allied Expeditionary Force. Within the latter two series there are two large and important files. The first file, the "Cable Log," contains extracts and complete copies of incoming and outgoing messages. The second file, "Eyes Only Cables," houses communications exchanged at the highest levels: from Marshall and the other members of the Joint Chiefs of Staff and from Churchill and the British Chiefs of Staff to Eisenhower and Smith. Frequently copies found in the "Eyes Only" file are not in the Eisenhower papers or the records of AFHQ or SHAEF. Together, these two files, along with the "SHAEF Diary," provide an extremely valuable record of the daily correspondence both within the headquarters and between them and London and Washington.

The third category of primary sources constitute those records found in the Modern Military Records Division of the National Archives. These include the records of the Office of the Chief of Staff of the Army, of AFHQ, and those of SHAEF.

The records of the Office of the Chief of Staff of the Army are organized in two distinct segments. For the period 1941-1942, see "COS Numerical File, 1921-1942"; for 1942, see "COS Decimal File, 1942-1943." These sources were critical for examining Smith's role as Marshall's secretary of the General Staff.

The microfilm copies of the AFHQ Collection is in the custody of the Archives Branch of the Washington National Records Center in Suitland, Maryland. Without question, the best materials are those contained in the collection of Colonel E. Dwight Salmon, a historian assigned to the Historical Section of the AFHQ Secretariat. The Salmon Collection, a multivolume history of the headquarters, house the various documents of the general and special staff divisions. Of less importance is the extensive "AFHQ Message Center File."

The records of SHAEF are also in the possession, on microfilm, of the National Records Center. The best organized and most useful file in the SHAEF collection is that of the "Office of the Secretary of the General Staff, SHAEF." Included in this file are all those documents that were brought to the attention of Eisenhower and Smith for action. Therefore, this material offers an excellent insight into the day-to-day functioning of the headquarters. Like all U.S. Army records, the documents are organized by general and special staff division and for the SHAEF missions to foreign governments. Also of value are the records of "European Theater of Operations, U.S. Army" and those of the "Office of G-3 Records, 1943-46, SHAEF."

What follows is a listing of other primary materials employed in this study.

A. Dwight David Eisenhower Presidential Library, Abilene, Kansas

Aurand, Henry   Commanding Officer, Normandy Base Section, 1944-1945.
  Papers.
  Oral History.

Barker, Ray   Assistant Chief of Staff, SHAEF G-1, 1944-1945.
  Papers.
  Oral History.

Betts, Thomas   Deputy G-2, SHAEF, 1944-1945.
  Oral History.

Bolté, Charles   Staff Officer, War Department, 1942-45.
  Oral History.

Bull, Harold   Assistant Chief of Staff, SHAEF G-3, 1944-45.
  Papers.

Butcher, Harry   Eisenhower's personal aide.
  Papers.
  Unedited Diary, 1942-1945.

Burgess, Carter   Secretary to the General Staff, SHAEF.
  Oral History.

Clark, Mark   Commander, U.S. Fifth Army, 1944-1945.
  Oral History.

Combined Chiefs of Staff.   Conference Proceedings, 1941-1945.

Davis, Thomas   Adjutant General, SHAEF, 1944-1945
  Papers.

Dever, Jacob   Commander, 6th Army Group
  Oral History

Eisenhower, Dwight David   Supreme Commander of AFHQ and SHAEF, 1942-1945
  Diary, 1942.
  Pre-Presidential Papers

Hodges, Courtney   Commander, U.S. First Army
  Papers
  First Army Diary
Holmes, Julius   Assistant Chief of Staff, SHAEF G-5.
  Papers.
Gilmer, Dan   Secretary/General Staff, SHAEF
  Oral History
Lutes, Leroy   Director of Operations, Army Service Forces,
  War Department, 1942-1945.
    Oral History.
Nevins, Arthur   Deputy G-3, 1944-1945.
  Oral History.
Robb, Sir James   Deputy Chief of Staff for Air, SHAEF, 1944-1945.
  Papers.
  Narrative, "Higher Direction of War."
Simpson, William   Commander, Ninth U.S. Army, 1944-1945.
  Oral History.
SHAEF, Selected Records, 1943-1945
SHAEF Daily and Weekly Intelligence Reports
Smith, Walter Bedell   Chief of Staff, AFHQ and SHAEF
    Walter Bedell Smith, personal papers, 1942-1944
    "History of COSSAC." Prepared by the Historical Subsection,
      Office of Secretary, General Staff, SHAEF.
    "Interrogations of German Senior Officers." Conducted by the
      ETO staff.
    SHAEF Diary.
    War Room Daily Summaries.
    Checklist for W. B. Smith Collection in Pre-Presidential Papers
      (Box 184)
Summersby, Kay   Eisenhower's Secretary
    Desk Diary, June 1, 1944 to March 10, 1945
Supreme Commander's Conferences.
    Minutes, January-June, 1944

B. Library of Congress, Manuscripts Division, Washington, D.C.
  Hughes, Everett   Military associate of Eisenhower, 1942-1945.
    Diary.
  Leahy, William   Chief of Joint Chiefs of Staff, 1942-1945.
    Papers.
    Diary.

C. National Archives, Washington, D. C.
    Records of the State Department (RG-59)
    Records of Headquarters, Army Service Forces, Trips (RG-160)
    Records of American-British Conferences (RG-165)
    Records of General Lutes (RG-200)
      Notes on ETO, December 1944-January 1945
    Official Files of Admiral William D. Leahy (RG-218)
    Records of U.S. Joint Chiefs of Staff (RG-218)
      Minutes of Combined Chiefs of Staff Conferences, January 23, 1942-
        February 17, 1945
      Minutes of Joint Chiefs of Staff Meetings, February 9, 1942-July 2,
        1945
      Plans for OVERLORD and ANVIL, January 11, 1944
      Deception Plans for OVERLORD, June 25, 1943
      Long Terms - Italian Surrender, October 6, 1943
    Records of the Army Staff (RG-319)
    Records of Allied Operational and Occupation Headquarters, World
      War II (RG-331)
    Secretary/General Staff - AFHQ and SHAEF
    War Cabinet Correspondence - including Joint Intelligence Committee
    estimates Supreme Commander Conferences

D. United States Navy, Classified Operations Archives, Navy Yard,
    Washington, D.C.
    Kirk, Alan   Task Force O Commander, D-Day
      Papers
    Leahy, William Chairman, Joint Chiefs of Staff
      Records

E. United States Army Military History Institute, Carlisle Barracks,
    Pennsylvania
    Audio-Visual Archive
      Edward Coffman, "Social History of the Old Army."
      Jay Luvaas, "Military Legacy of the American Civil War."
      Forrest Pogue, "Marshall and the Army," and "United States
        General Staff."
    United States Army Military History Research Collection
      Historical Section/Joint Secretariat of the Joint Chiefs of Staff,
      "History of the Joint Chiefs in World War II."

Interviews

"Conferences with General W. B. Smith," September 14, 1945.
Sidney Matthews,
    interview of Smith, n.d.
Howard Symth,
    interview with Smith, May 13, 1947.
    interview with Major General Lyman Lemnitzer, United
        States Army Air Corps, Mediterranean, March 3,
        1947.
    interview with Major General Kenneth Strong, SHAEF
        Chief of Intelligence, October 29, 1947.
Roland Ruppenthal,
    interview with Smith, September 14, 1945.
Pogue,
    interview with Field Marshal Lord Alanbrooke, Chief
        of the Imperial General Staff, n.d.
    interview with Brigadier David Belchem (Director of
        Plan, later Operations, 21 Army Group), February,
        2, 1947.
    interview with Major General N. C. D. Brownjohn,
        Deputy Chief of Staff under Morgan, March 28, 1947.
    interview with Air Chief Marshal Sir Arthur
        Coningham, Commander, 2nd Tactical Air Force,
        Northwest Europe, February 14, 1947.
    interview with Major General Robert W. Crawford,
        SHAEF Chief of Administration, May 5, 1948.
    interview with Admiral of the Fleet Lord Cunningham,
        Commander-in-Chief(Navy), Mediterranean, and
        British Chiefs of Staff, February 12, 1947.
    interview with Lieutenant General Sir Humphrey Gale,
        Chief Administration Officer (AFHQ), Deputy Chief
        of Staff (SHAEF), January 27, 1947.
    interview with Colonel James Gault, Eisenhower's Aide,
        February 13, 1947.
    interview with Group Captain T. P. Gleave, Chief of
        Air Mission/France, January 9, 1947.
    interview with General Sir Hastings Ismay, chief of
        staff to Churchill, December 20, 1947.

interview with Général Alphonse-Pierre Juin, Chief of
Staff, Ministry of National Defense, December 6,
1947.

interview with Alan Moorehead, author, January 21,
1947.

interview with Lieutenant General Sir Frederick Morgan,
Deputy Chief of Staff, SHAEF, February 3, 1947.

interview with Viscount Portal of Hurtfort, Chief of the
Air Staff, February 7, 1947.

interview with Air Chief Marshal Sir James M. Robb,
February 3, 1947.

interview with Wing Commander Leslie Scarman,
Tedder Aide, February 25, 1947.

interview with Air Chief Marshal Sir Arthur Tedder,
Commander-in-Chief (Air), Mediterranean;
Deputy Supreme Commander (SHAEF), February 14,
1947.

interview with Colonel Ford Trimble, Secretary/General
Staff (SHAEF), December 17, 1946.

interview with Brigadier E. T. Williams, Operations,
21st Army Group, May 30-31, 1947.

interview with Major General J. F. M. Whiteley,
Deputy Chief of Staff (AFHQ);
Deputy Chief of Operations (SHAEF), December 18,
1947.

interview with Major General Charles A. West,
COSSAC and briefly SHAEF G-3, February 19, 1947.

interview with Major General C. H. H. Vulliamy, Chief
of Signal Division (SHAEF), January 22, 1947.

Pogue and G. A. Harrison,
interview with Colonel C. H. Bonesteel, SHAEF, June
18, 1945.

F.   George C. Marshall Library, Lexington, Virginia.
Handy, Thomas T. Assistant to Chief of Staff/Operations Division.
Papers
Marshall, George C.   Army Chief of Staff.
Papers
MacCarthy, Frank   Aide to Marshall
Papers

MacDonald-Buchanan, Reginald   British Mission to CCS
   Papers
Pogue, interview with Smith, July 25, 1958.

G. British Archives, Public Records Office, London.
    Records of 21 Army Group
    Robb, J. M.
        Diary
        Papers

H. Center for Military Archives, King's College, University of London.
    Alanbrooke, Lord. Chief of the Imperial General Staff
        Diary.
        Papers.
    Ismay, Hastings L. Chief of Staff to the Minister of Defense
        Papers

I. Imperial War Museum, London.
    de Guingand, Frederick
        Interview, "World At War, 1939-1945," Thames Television.
    Montgomery, B. L. Commander: 8th Army and 21st Army Group
        Papers.

J. Churchill Archives, Churchill College, Cambridge University.
    Grigg, Sir James. Secretary of State for War.
        Papers.

K. The Collection of the Columbia University Oral History Research
    Office, New York.
    Burgess, Carter
    Clark, Mark
    Nevins, Arthur

L. Interviews by author
    Lieutenant General Russell Vittrup. Infantry School and Joint Chiefs
        staff, Alexandria, Virginia, November 15, 1988
    Colonel Carter Burgess.   Secretary/General Staff
        Roanoke, Virginia, November 18, 1988

M. Materials in author's possession.
    Diary of General George S. Patton, transcript.
    Diary of Lieutenant General Everett Hughes, transcript.

Index

Aachen, 275, 280, 315
Acheson, Dean, 337
Act of Military Surrender, 323, 326
Adcock, Clarence, 58
Air Corps, 65, 73, 75: autonomy for, 49;
   roles and missions, 57, 58
Air Forces:
—Allied: Air Support Command, 163;
   Expeditionary, 214; Northwest
   African, 222; Strategic, 211, 212, 265
—British: Bomber Command, 193; Eastern
   Air Command, 124, 143
—U.S.: 8th, 143; 12th, 124, 143; 15th, 196
Airborne armies: First, 258
Alexander, Harold: and Montgomery, 164,
   165-66, 203, 309; and Smith, 162, 179,
   240, 267, 308; as commander of FORCE
   141, 159; cooperation with U.S., 157, 163,
   240, 267, 308; conference in Algiers, 164-
   65; failure to submit sitreps to AFHQ, 179;
   HUSKY planning, 171, 178; in Med.
   command (deputy SAC, ground force
   commander, commander of 18th Army
   Group), 156-58, 162, 164-65, 215, 217;
   Italian campaign, 195, 196, 215; Italian
   surrender, role in, 186, 187-88, 195;
   military governor of Sicily, 178; preference
   for AVALANCHE, 191; proposed for
   commander of Allied ground forces in
   Northwest Europe, 307-8, 310, 311; Rome
   airborne operation, 187, 189
Algiers, 133, 136, 142, 144, 145, 146, 149,
   156, 162, 171, 177, 180, 183, 185, 190,
   193, 195, 196, 199, 200, 202, 209,
   219,221, 222, 299, 237; AFHQ, plans for
   establishing in, 132, 143; American Joint
   Chiefs in, 157, 158; Brooke in, 158, 161;
   Churchill in, 158, 159, 168; conferences in,
   164-65, 166, 168-69, 210, 214, 231;
   operations around, 129; Smith's arrival in,
   135, 137, 138, 147; target area for
   TORCH, 114-16, 129
Allied Force Headquarters (AFHQ), 113,
   114, 116, 118, 120, 124-26, 132, 134-37,
   143, 149, 156-57, 160, 162, 165, 166, 168,
   173-75 177, 180-82, 185-88, 190, 191,
   193-198, 200-2, 204, 205, 211-14, 217,
   219-23, 225-28, 234, 238, 239, 269, 288
—Command. *See* Eisenhower, Dwight
—Chief of Staff. *See* Smith, Walter Bedell;
   Deputy Chiefs of Staff, 140-41
—Administrative Level: Chief
   Administrative Officer (CAO), 140-41. *See
   also* Gale, Humphrey; Secretariat, 139-40,
   142, 150, 158
—General Staff Divisions:
   G-1 (Personnel) Division, 140, 142
   G-2 (Intelligence) Division, 121, 141,
      170-71, 183. *See also* Mocker-Ferryman,
      E.E.; Strong, Kenneth
   G-3 (Operations) Division, 121, 141, 147,
      159, 178, 183. *See also* Whiteley, J.F.M.;
   G-4 (Supply) Division, 140, 142, 170
—Special Staff Sections: Joint Rearmament
   Committee, 170; Military Government
   Section, 142. *See also* Allied Military
   Government of Occupied Territories;
   Political and Civil Affairs Section, 119,
   142, 144, 150, 169, 223. *See also* Mack,
   W.H.B.; Macmillan, Harold; Murphy,
   Robert; Liaison Section, 123, 170;
   Political Section, 119, 123; Psychological
   Warfare Section, 123, 147, 150, 170-71,
   179; Propaganda Operations subsection,
   146
Alam Halfa, 287

Smith—Continued

staff organization, 123-24, 140, 173

Home and family: ancestry, 3-4; boyhood in Indianapolis, 4-7; civilian education, 5,7; fascination with military, 4-5; relationship with wife, 6, 9, 10, 12, 42, 50, 63, 92, 135, 198, 200, 329, 339; relationship with mother, 4,5, 63

Personal Qualities: health problems of, 63, 98, 121-22, 131-32, 135, 139, 237, 281, 288, 291, 305, 307, 318, 332, 334, 338, 340; love of outdoors, 5, 6, 28, 37, 42, 50-51, 63, 199-200, 237; narrow-mindedness of, 91, 96, 185, 288, 300-1; personality, 6, 7, 42, 62-63, 92, 97-98, 110, 119, 127, 138-39, 142, 147, 150, 181, 188, 221, 230, 234-35, 292, 299-300, 312, 315, 334, 339; political views of, 40, 333, 335; professionalism of, 36, 40-43, 51-52, 65, 72, 110, 116, 135, 168, 331; relationship with Ethel Westerman, 200

Early Military Career: at Camp Dodge, 28-29; in 95th Division, 27-28; in Military Intelligence Division, WDGS, 22, 26-27; in Indiana National Guard, 6-8; in 4th Division (AEF), 10-17; Mexican crisis, 8, 22; wounded in France, 17, 20-21;

Interwar Army: aide to Moseley, 40; attends War College, 63, 65, 72, 76; Bureau of the Budget, Washington, 40-41; class standing, 58, 61; Fort Sheridan, 37, 40; instructor, Infantry School, 51; student, Infantry School, 46, 50, 51; student, Command and General Staff School, 52, 57-58, 60-61, 72; the Philippines, 41-42

Washington

—War Department General Staff: "jeep" decision, 80-81; liaison to White House, 78-79, 81, 84, 117; Secretariat, WDGS, 7, 78, 82-84, 85, 89, 90-91, 95, 103

—Joint Chiefs of Staff: and Pearl Harbor intercepts, 95; as secretary, 85, 89, 90-91, 95, 113-14; role in organizing staff committees, 95-96

—Combined Chiefs of Staff: as secretary, 85-86, 88, 91, 93, 94, 103, 105; London conference, 101-4; partnership with Dykes, 88, 91-93, 101-4, 113-14; role in organizing CCS, 94, 95; supports North African operation, 102-3

Mediterranean Theater:

—AFHQ: as chief of staff, AFHQ, 110, 116-17, 118, 125, 127, 131, 134-35, 138-39,141-43, 149-50, 158, 162, 171-74, 177, 195, 197-98; as chief of staff, NATOUSA, 142; censorship, 124; command structure in NATOUSA, 197-98; expansion of operations in Mediterranean,

196; missions to North Africa, 120-21; move AFHQ to Naples, 199; political and civil affairs, AFHQ, 119, 223-24, 144, 159-60, 168, 177-78, 193-94; proposed as deputy SAC in, by Churchill, 199, 202, 205, 209; retention of landing craft in, 193; role in organization of AFHQ, 116, 123, 139-41, 147, 159; TRIDENT conference, 167-68, 169

—North Africa: air command, North Africa, 142-43; and Giraud, 170; arrival in Algiers, 138; Darlan Deal, 133-35; fears German intervention through Spain, 118; predictions for TORCH, 117; the relief of Fredendall, 162

—Italian campaign: abortive Rome airborne operation, 187, 189-90; air operations in, 179, 196; alternative plans for, after HUSKY, 155, 166-69, 175, 178-81, 182, 185, 188; confers with Badoglio, 194-95; estimate of Badoglio, 195, 204; HUSKY, plans for, 164-65; military government in Italy, 159, 177-78; post-HUSKY plans, 171, 180

—Italian armistice: announcement of, 190-91; cobelligerent status for Italy, 193, 194; conditions governing, 182, 183, 184, 185, 188; conferences with Italian representatives, 183-86, 187-88, 194; directives to, regarding, 183-84, 186, 188, 195; execution of terms, 191; insistence on acceptance by the time of Salerno, 187-88; Malta surrender ceremony, 195; political factors concerned with, 182-83; postponement of, 187-88, 189-90; rejection of postponement, 190-91; surrender signed by, ceremony, 188

Northwest Europe:

—SHAEF: and Soviets, 233, 274; appointed chief of staff, SHAEF, 198; as chief of staff, 211-13, 215, 220, 224, 226, 228, 230, 233, 234, 238-39, 266-67, 270, 296-301, 322, 330; logistical command structure, 212-13, 224-25, 238-39; moves SHAEF, 234, 254, 266; organizes SHAEF, 211-14, 219-30; political and civil affairs, 225-27, 272-75; proposed by E. for command of, 330

—OVERLORD: air command for, 211-12, 214; invasion announcement, 236; landing craft shortage, 211, 236; need to preserve ANVIL, 216-17; opposes ANVIL, 211, 215; post-Normandy planning, 223; reaction to COSSAC plan, 209-11; support Montgomery's revised plan for, 218; supports Transportation Plan, 231

—Northwest Europe, Normandy and the advance through France: Arnhem, estimate of, 267-68; broad vs narrow front, 247-48,

About the Author

D.K.R. CROSSWELL is Lecturer in the Department of History at the National University of Singapore. He has previously published articles on Generals Eisenhower and Smith in *Valley Forge Journal* and in the *Indiana Journal of Military History*. Dr. Crosswell has also taught at Kansas State University. He is currently conducting research for a book on the General Staff of the U.S. Army.